Survey of LABOR ECONOMICS

Survey of
LABOR ECONOMICS

FLORENCE PETERSON
PROFESSOR OF SOCIAL ECONOMY
BRYN MAWR COLLEGE

NEW YORK LONDON
HARPER & BROTHERS PUBLISHERS

SURVEY OF LABOR ECONOMICS

Copyright, 1947, by Harper & Brothers

Printed in the United States of America

K-X

11291

To the
Workers and Managers
of
Industry

CONTENTS

vii

PART TWO—WAGES AND HOURS

Contents

PART FOUR—SOCIAL SECURITY

FIGURES

TABLES

PAGE

PREFACE

FEW INDEED ARE THE COLLEGE MEN AND WOMEN WHO WILL NOT some time be called upon to make some important decisions involving employer-labor relations and the status of wage earners in our economic and political life. Many will enter business as managers, industrial engineers, or labor relations officers and thus be directly involved in all phases of labor problems. Some will enter the labor movement as economic advisers; others will go into some branch of the government service where they will be called upon to administer labor laws and to assist in the adjustment of employer-labor disputes. Those who become lawyers, educators, and clergymen will find themselves called upon to counsel with employers and workers' representatives and to render decisions on specific labor issues. Even though never directly engaged in labor matters, as voters and participants in public affairs all citizens are called upon to make decisions which vitally affect the well-being of millions of workers as well as the economic and political destiny of the nation.

Persons who are directly and indirectly concerned with labor matters must have not only a background knowledge of the general principles and underlying forces, but also an intimate awareness of the specific problems ensuing from the application of these principles and the impact of these forces. This text is designed to provide the basic factual data, which are the tools for action and thought, as well as a knowledge of the major theories which seek to explain the causes and results of economic phenomena relating to labor. Because one cannot understand the present, or plan for the future, without a knowledge of past thinking and action, some emphasis is given to the historical development of current theories, practices, and institutional arrangements.

"Labor" has many facets and a study of labor economics must therefore have a number of different approaches. Labor can be

considered as a "natural" resource, in which case one is interested
in population problems and the amount and kinds of labor available in the labor market. Labor can be considered as a commodity
or service to be bought and sold, in which case wages or the
amount of money paid and received for labor is of paramount
interest. Labor can be treated as a productive machine with discussion centered around the conditions which promote its maximum efficiency and productivity. But "labor" is all these and
much more. The most fundamental fact about labor is that it is
inseparable from the laborer himself. Labor is not an amorphous
flow of energy or an abstract economic element; workers are consumers as well as producers, and as human beings they are subject to the same desires and motivations as other mortals. A study
of labor economics, therefore, must give consideration to personal
reactions and group relationships as well as the conditions which
affect the well-being of workers.

Although this volume deals with the same general subjects commonly included in texts on labor problems, the present approach
is not of labor as *a* problem or as an aggregation of problems, but
rather as one special field of economics. The economics of labor
is no more or no less a "problem" than is taxation, money and
banking, marketing, or any other subject included in the family
of economic sciences. True, there are many problems peculiar to
labor and labor relations, but it appears to the present author
that they can be best understood within a framework of economic
analysis rather than approached as pathological phenomena. To
illustrate, the present volume includes a separate chapter on productivity in which modern technological developments are treated
as assets to the general well-being, in contrast to the more usual
treatment in labor problems texts which deal with them solely as
causes of unemployment, although, of course, the impact of improved technology is considered in the discussion of unemployment.

This text is intended for a survey course; it is equally adaptable
for use by smaller colleges which offer a limited number of specialized courses, and by larger institutions as a foundation for further
advanced study in the field of labor economics and labor relations.
While it is assumed that most students will have had a general
principles course before taking a course in labor economics, so

closely interrelated are all economic elements that a study of one branch, such as the economics of labor, could well be used as a cornerstone for the study of general economic principles. A discussion of wages, for example, necessarily involves a consideration of all other prices and could, therefore, be used as a point of departure for a general discussion of the concepts of value, principles of distribution, and theories of marginal productivity. Members of adult education classes, in particular, might become more interested in a study of the general principles of economics via the approach of wages and unemployment about which they have personal and intimate knowledge.

This volume was written while the author was on leave of absence from her official duties with the Bureau of Labor Statistics, U. S. Department of Labor, and the contents are entirely her responsibility. However, she wishes to express her appreciation to several of her associates for their criticisms and suggestions on particular chapters. Among these are Witt Bowden, Dorothy Brady, and John H. G. Pierson of the Bureau of Labor Statistics, Bernard Cushman of the Solicitor's Office, Elizabeth S. Johnson of the Division of Labor Standards, Collis Stocking of the U. S. Employment Service, and W. S. Woytinsky and Wilbur Cohen of the Federal Social Security Administration. The latter contributed most of the material in Part IV. Mary Eleanor Spear prepared the illustrations.

FLORENCE PETERSON

January, 1947

PART ONE

EMPLOYMENT
AND UNEMPLOYMENT

1

POPULATION

HUMAN BEINGS ARE THE SOURCE AND END OF ALL ECONOMIC AC-
tivity. It is the wants and needs of people which create the demand
for goods and services, and the supply of those goods and services
is possible only through the mental and physical efforts of people.
If people are at once the producers and the consumers of economic
products, why, at certain times, is there an insufficiency of persons
to do the work at hand or, as more frequently happens, why does
there seem to be a greater number of people than are needed to
supply the demands for goods?

This is the basic and major problem of labor economics. It is
directly and indirectly related to all other problems affecting
workers and their relations with their employers. The way it is
resolved determines not only the comparative well-being of workers, but the very type of political government which entire nations
live by.

The crux of the problem lies in the fact that, while the labor of
human beings is a primary factor, it is not the sole factor involved
in the productive process. The production of physical goods is the
result of the joint action and interaction of natural resources,
capital goods which are actually the result of past labor, and
business risk and enterprise, as well as direct labor. Although it is
true that the employment of human beings determines what shall
be produced and how much, the converse is also true; the kinds and
amounts of commodities produced determine the number of persons who are employed.

The problem then is one of adjustment, and many theories have
been offered to explain the many and frequent maladjustments
which are always in evidence between the demand for labor and the
supply of labor. Basically it is a question of population and its

3

relation to the other factors involved in the production and consumption of economic goods.

THEORIES OF POPULATION

The theory on the cause and effect of population changes which has aroused the most discussion during the last 150 years is that of Thomas R. Malthus, who published his first essay on population in 1798. Malthus lived at a time when the population of England was rapidly expanding, and general living conditions were improving for most people as a result of the passing of feudalism and the beginning of modern industrial development resulting from such inventions as the spinning mule (1779), the steam engine (1785), and the power loom (1784–1787). Along with the general improvement, however, the conditions of large masses of the people were becoming worse. In contrast to the comparative security which they had had under the manorial system of agriculture, the introduction of machinery and factories had caused unemployment and pauperism.

Malthusian Theory

Malthus contended that the primary cause of this misery was an excessive growth in population; that population is necessarily limited by the means of subsistence; and that, if unchecked, it always outruns the food supply. This he explained by saying that population tends to increase in geometrical ratio (1, 2, 4, 8, 16, 32, 64, etc.), whereas subsistence and food supply can at best increase only in arithmetical ratio (1, 2, 3, 4, 5, 6, 7, etc.). If these ratios endured, any given population would increase to 64 times its original size in about 150 years, but its subsistence would increase only 7 times.

Obviously, such a ratio could not persist, and Malthus concluded that vice and misery operated as checks on population growth. While voluntary reduction in the birth rate[1] might serve as a preventive check to population growth, Malthus believed population would always tend to increase beyond the means of

---

[1] Malthus spoke in terms of "moral restraint" and postponement of marriage, rather than in terms of the modern birth control methods, which are sometimes referred to as neo-Malthusian.

subsistence, and consequently vice and misery were inevitable. War, disease, famine, bad housing, and other conditions causing a high death rate were necessary to offset a naturally high birth rate. Thus, the belief that population tends to grow more rapidly than available food supplies developed the "natural" theory of poverty.

During most of the 19th century, Malthus' pessimistic conclusions on the conflict between the biological urge of man and the relative niggardliness of nature were commonly accepted, not only as a valid theory of population growth, but as an explanation and justification for child labor, low wages, and the miserable living and working conditions existing at the time. His theory was used as an argument against all economic and social reforms, as a scientifically proved "natural" law against which it was futile to strive, no matter how laudable the motive might be.

More recent scientific developments, as well as changes in social attitudes, seem to indicate that many of Malthus' assumptions may not be entirely true, and this has caused his doctrine of the natural law of population to be questioned. Agricultural technology, soil conservation and enrichment, physiochemical research in the use of synthetics have resulted in an enormous actual and potential increase in food supplies. Improved means of transportation enable each region to specialize in those crops for which its soil and climate are best suited, and also reduce the hazards of famine. Except for the very important effect of war,[2] the death rate in most countries has declined as a result of improved sanitation and medicine.

Of greatest significance, so far as Malthus' theory is concerned, has been the decline in the birth rates in most modern industrial countries. The implied assumption of Malthus' theory that workers' families would become larger as the means of subsistence increased (which in turn would cause the downward spiral as a result of population pressure) has not been substantiated by experience. The reverse seems to be true, namely, when people are able to rise above the subsistence level of living, they have smaller families. Ambition is substituted for resignation, and parents de-

___

[2] While outside the scope of this brief discussion, any comprehensive treatment of theories of population would be clearly deficient if it ignored the relationship between war and pressure of population on means of subsistence.

cide to have fewer children in order to give them the opportunity to advance still further.[3] Experience indicates that: "The initial stage of the Industrial Revolution, wherever its impact has been felt, has been characterized by a period of rapid population growth which has resulted from the joint effects of the persistence of the high fertility pattern of an agricultural society and the rapidly declining mortality rate which has accompanied the introduction of modern sanitation and medicine. The later stages of industrialization, characterized by the presence of predominantly city populations and urban patterns of life, have inevitably been accompanied by rapidly declining fertility and the retardation of rates of population."[4]

Optimum Theory

The fact that there has been a declining birth rate in industrialized countries when the means of subsistence have markedly improved would seem to refute any theory of the "natural" law of population. It raises the question whether the growth of population is affected more by social than by biological forces. If the former is true—that is, if it is the social will and desire of the people which primarily determine population growth—then the population of any country would tend to be the size which secures the highest per capita production of the goods and services that the population wants and needs.

According to this optimum theory of population, the highest possible level of living is attained with a certain population size. If the population increases beyond this number the means of subsistence are spread too thin; if there are too few people there is insufficient specialization or division of labor to bring about maximum production. The two forces of potential production and pop-

---

[3] Also Malthus, born in the 18th century, could not foresee the change in the economic condition and mental attitude of women which has caused them to marry later in life, as well as to have fewer children after marriage. One authority on Malthus tritely comments: "One can read the essay from cover to cover without encountering a passage which indicates that Malthus even thought women have anything to do with population." (A. B. Wolfe in *Population Problems*, edited by Louis Dublin.)

[4] G. C. Hauser and Conrad Taeuber, "The Changing Population of the United States," *Annals of the American Academy of Political and Social Science*, January, 1945.

ulation tend to balance, however, for mankind is always striving toward that "number which—taking into consideration the nature of the environment, the degree of skill employed, the habits and customs of the people concerned, and all other relevant facts —gives the highest average return per head."[5]

This is a comforting theory and as acceptable as any other theory which seeks to explain the causes of the present obvious maladjustments as forces *tending* toward that ever future but never attained state of equilibrium. As a matter of abstract reasoning, there is no doubt that there is an optimum density of population for any given area at any given time. Moreover, the theory has the virtue of assuming that the function of the economic process is to serve individual people; that growth of population is determined by the economic desires of the people of a nation rather than by the military and political designs of those who happen to be in control of a nation.

However, as a guide or principle for social planning or action, the optimum theory has little practical value. Population is fixed not by anything happening at the moment, but by the habits and actions of millions of disconnected households a generation back. No one is able to say what the optimum population really is under a given set of circumstances—much less foretell what circumstances will prevail a generation hence!

Theories of population may be laid aside, then, but the factor of population remains a fundamental force in every phase of economic development. The number of workers available for productive enterprise at any given time or place, as well as their capacities for producing, is ultimately dependent upon the size and composition of the general population. The trend of population in any region or country is a major influence on the trend of business activity. An expanding population automatically creates additional markets which in turn increase the demand for labor; a stationary or declining population provides no automatic extension of markets and requires an entirely different complement of economic adjustments.

---

[5] Alexander M. Carr-Saunders, *The Population Problem,* Clarendon Press, Oxford, 1922, p. 476.

POPULATION GROWTH

During the century preceding the First World War the population of Europe doubled and that of the United States increased twelvefold—from 8 million to 100 million. The increase in European population took place while more than 40 million[6] persons emigrated to the Americas and elsewhere. Population expansion in this country was a result of both natural increase and immigration. During that century the population of the United States was augmented by 30 million immigrants. The estimated natural rate of increase was 30 per 1000 per year at the beginning of the 19th century, declining gradually to 15 per 1000 per year at the turn of the 20th century.

In both Europe and the United States there was a decreasing rate of population growth between the two World Wars, although the actual population increased in most countries.[7] In France there was a decrease not only in rate but in actual numbers. In Europe the lessening in the rate of growth was due to a decreasing birth rate; in this country to both a decline in the birth rate and a drastic curtailment of immigration.

IMMIGRATION

Migrations of people from one area to another have been an almost constant phenomenon of human history. Throughout the ages discontented and oppressed peoples have journeyed to far

---

[6] It is estimated that 60 million persons actually emigrated, but that one-third or one-fourth of these returned home. (W. S. Thompson, *Population Problems,* McGraw-Hill Book Company, Inc., New York, p. 376.)

[7] According to the League of Nations *Statistical Year Book 1939–1940,* the estimated world population in 1940 was:

World	2,175,600,000	Africa	155,500,000
Europe	540,000,000	Asia	1,193,600,000
Americas	275,700,000	Oceania	10,600,000

According to calculations made by the Swedish Statistiska Centralbyrain, the numbers of persons per square mile of arable land living in various countries in 1937–1939 were:

Canada	121	Sweden	442	Greece	796	Switzerland	2153
Australia	137	France	524	Italy	883	Netherlands	2210
U. S.	259	New Zealand	537	Germany	927	Great Britain	2421
Spain	427	British India	780	Belgium	2126	Japan	3131

lands in search of opportunities to improve their conditions of living. Since the dawn of history, however, there has never been such an extensive and prolonged voluntary[8] migration as the movement of Europeans to the United States during the hundred years between 1825 and 1925.

Although immigration was the genesis of our national life, the number of persons migrating to our shores averaged no more than a few thousand each year during the 180 years of colonial history and the first few decades after the Republic was founded.[9] Beginning in 1832 the stream of immigration increased, an average of 77,500 persons entering the country each year during the following fifteen years, and an annual average of more than 266,-000 thereafter until the outbreak of the War Between the States; immigration increased after this war except for brief periods of business depressions. The all-time peak was between 1903 and 1914. During these eleven years there was an average entry of almost a million people a year. Following the close of the First World War the flow of immigration was resumed, over 800,000 persons entering in 1921 and over 700,000 in 1924. Immigration was drastically curtailed thereafter because of restrictive legislation in this country as well as in many European countries.[10] The average annual immigration during the decade before World War II was only about 50,000, and during the war about 30,000.

National Origins of Immigrants

Where did these immigrants come from? During the first 250 years of settlement of what is now the United States, almost all

---

[8] We are here referring to voluntary and permanent movements of people. The forced migrations of Europeans, estimated to have involved 30 million persons, during the recent war is undoubtedly without precedent so far as numbers are concerned.

[9] The first census was taken in 1790 and showed a population slightly under 4 million. Assuming a normal natural increase in population during the long years of colonial history, a large majority of the 4 million persons living in this country in 1790 must have been native-born. The first five immigration reports available indicate an annual entry rate of 6000 to 10,000 persons between 1820–1825.

[10] Although Great Britain and the Scandinavian countries encouraged overseas settlement after World War I, most of the other countries discouraged or prohibited their citizens from emigrating. The Soviet Union, for example, made emigration practically impossible, as did also Italy and Germany after the rise of Fascism.

the settlers came from northern and western Europe except for the slaves imported from Africa.[11] It was not until after 1880 that any considerable number of persons from southern and eastern Europe came to this country; but by the middle of the 1890's over half, and after the turn of the century about three-fourths, of the immigrants arriving from Europe came from the southern and eastern countries, mostly Italy, Austria-Hungary, Poland, and Russia.

In 1854 the Chinese began to arrive, although the net immigration from China never amounted to more than a few thousand a year. In 1900 a Japanese wave of immigration started; it numbered from 10,000 to 30,000 a year for several years when it dropped sharply.[12] Mexicans began crossing the border in considerable numbers in 1908–1909; by 1944 more than 750,000 had legally entered the country, and additional numbers had crossed the border without benefit of legal approval.

Not all the immigrants who arrived became permanent settlers. Between 1908 (the earliest date for which emigration records are available) and 1923, almost 3½ million persons left the country. This was equal to about one-third the number who entered the country during these years. During the depression of 1929–1933 the emigrants who departed numbered 100,000 more than those who entered the country. Although most of the persons who came from northern and western Europe remained, over one-half of those from southern and eastern Europe returned home after a few years in this country. The Italians, especially those from southern Italy, were most prone to return after a few years' stay. Slightly more than 2 million immigrated to this country between 1908 and 1923, but more than 1 million went back to their native land.

Change in Attitude Toward Immigration

Why did these millions of people leave their homes to settle in this country? Some came to escape religious and political persecu-

---

[11] Nobody knows how many slaves were imported into this country during the 180 years prior to 1800 when importation practically ceased. The 1790 census showed 727,208 Negroes in the United States; they constituted almost 20 per cent of the total population.

[12] The 1940 census showed 127,000 residents of the Japanese race, of whom 47,300 were foreign-born and 79,700 were born in this country. The same census indicated 77,500 Chinese residents, of whom 37,200 were foreign-born and 40,300 native-born.

tion, but most of them came to find jobs, and during most of those
years an expanding America seemed to have jobs for all of them.
A growing country was able to absorb an augmented population
and to use a greatly increased labor force.

This fact is true, however: In almost every year when these immigrants were arriving there were hundreds of thousands of idle
workers walking the streets of our cities.[13] The newly arrived immigrants were able to find jobs because they were willing to work
for less wages and under conditions which native-born workers
were unable or unwilling to accept. Employers encouraged immigration and, until forbidden by law, colluded with the steamship
companies—who found transporting these steerage passengers to
be a profitable business—in advertising and sending agents to
Europe to contract for laborers.

Immigration was profitable to the employers in several respects.
It furnished them with an abundant supply of cheap and docile
labor; the presence of mixed nationality and language groups
made it difficult for unions to organize the immigrants but easy for
the employers to play one group against another and all the
"foreigners" against the native Americans;[14] the available immi-
grant labor supply could be used as a threat by the employers to
discourage strikes; and if strikes occurred, immigrants could be
used as strikebreakers.

Organized labor, as might be expected, vigorously opposed un-
restricted immigration and every American Federation of Labor

---

[13] See chap. 5, on unemployment.

[14] One well-known authority on labor problems gives the following report on
a visit he made to a large Chicago packing company in 1904: "I saw seated
around the benches of the company's employment office a sturdy group of
Nordics. I asked the employment agent, How comes it you are employing only
Swedes? He answered, Well you see, it is only for this week. Last week we
employed Slovaks. We change about among the different nationalities and
languages. It prevents them from getting together. We have the thing systematized. We have a luncheon each week of the employment managers of the large
firms of the Chicago district. There we discuss our problems and exchange information. We have a number of men in the field who keep us informed. . . .
If agitators are coming or expected and there is considerable unrest among
the labor population, we raise the wages all round. . . . It is wonderful to
watch the effect. The unrest stops and the agitators leave. Then when things
quiet down we reduce the wages to where they were." (John R. Commons in
D. D. Lescohier and Elizabeth Brandeis, *History of Labor in the U. S.*, The
Macmillan Company, 1935, vol. iii, p. xxv.)

convention passed resolutions demanding legislative action. Comprehensive legislation did not come, however, until the general public was aroused during the First World War by the dangers of divisive groups within the population; "hyphenated Americans" became a popular slogan. When the threat of communism spread throughout Europe following that war, most employers also favored restriction because of their fear that immigrants might bring "foreign" ideologies into this country.

Restriction of Immigration

Although there had been previous legislation establishing health and character requirements for admission into the country, the first attempt at government restriction of immigration in order to protect American labor was directed against the Chinese coolies. In 1862 a law was enacted forbidding American vessels to transport coolies, and in 1882 the Exclusion Act was passed which altogether debarred Chinese coolies from entering the country. During the 1880's several laws were passed which prohibited the immigration of contract laborers (foreign laborers under agreement to work for particular employers), and in 1891 the steamship companies were forbidden to encourage immigration through advertisements in foreign countries. In 1903 the Immigration Service was transferred to the Department of Commerce and Labor as an official recognition that immigration was largely a labor problem.[15] In 1907 a "gentlemen's agreement" was made with Japan whereby that country agreed not to issue passports to her citizens who sought to immigrate to this country.

The first comprehensive attempt to control immigration was made in 1917 when an act was passed which required all adult immigrants to demonstrate their ability to read some language— English or any other. While this was called a measure to improve the quality of immigration, it actually was meant to be restrictive, and was directed primarily against Italians and eastern Europeans.[16] Over 20 per cent of the immigrants who arrived in

---

[15] The Immigration and Naturalization Service was transferred from the Department of Labor to the Department of Justice in 1940 because of war conditions and the responsibilities incident to the Alien Registration Act.

[16] A literacy test law was passed by Congress in 1897 but was vetoed by President Cleveland; President Taft vetoed another in 1913 as did President

1914 were illiterates, including over 100,000 southern Italians.[17]

Drastic restrictive measures were taken after World War I when the general public, alarmed about the problem of assimilation, joined with organized labor to obtain legislation which would limit the flow of immigrants into the country. A law passed in 1921 retained the literacy test and restricted the number of immigrants from any country to 3 per cent of the number of persons of such nationality who were residents of the United States in 1910. Three years later (1924) further restrictions were imposed when the 2 per cent quota law was enacted and the base year upon which the quotas were fixed was shifted to 1890, a period before the great influx of southern and eastern Europeans. The 1924 law excluded the Japanese by denying admission to all aliens, except for temporary purposes, who are ineligible for citizenship.

The 1924 law also included a "national origins" provision which was put into effect in 1929 and is the basis for current determinations for admittance into the country. A total of approximately 154,000 immigrants are now allowed from the quota area each year, the quota for each country depending upon its relative contribution to the population as determined by the census of 1920. The quota allotments for countries with quotas of 300 or more persons are as follows:

Asia[a]	1,649	Hungary	869
Belgium	1,304	Italy	5,802
Czechoslovakia	2,874	Lithuania	386
Denmark	1,181	Netherlands	3,153
Eire	17,853	Norway	2,377

[a] Quotas for colonies and dependencies are included with allotments for the European country to which they belong.

Wilson in 1915, but the latter law was enacted over Wilson's veto in 1917. In his first veto message President Wilson said: "The new tests here embodied are not tests of quality or of character or personal fitness, but tests of opportunity. Those who come seeking opportunity are not to be admitted unless they have already had one of the chief opportunities they seek, the opportunity of education."

[17] At the outbreak of World War I there were approximately 13½ million foreign-born residents (almost 15 per cent of the entire population), almost one-fourth of whom could not speak English. In 1940, there were 11½ million foreign-born residents in the country, representing almost 9 per cent of the total population.

Finland	569	Poland	6,524
France	3,086	Portugal	440
Germany and Austria	27,370	Rumania	377
Great Britain and		Soviet Union	2,712
Northern Ireland	65,721	Sweden	3,314
Greece	307	Switzerland	1,707
		Yugoslavia	845

In 1943 the Chinese Exclusion Act was repealed and Chinese immigrants are now eligible for citizenship; China's quota is 105 immigrants a year. None of the quota laws apply to the western hemisphere, although immigrants from these countries are subject to the other laws pertaining to contract labor, literacy, and health and character requirements. During the recent war emergency, special arrangements were made for the admission of alien agricultural workers from other American countries; these arrangements provided exemptions from the contract labor and literacy laws but included the requirement that these immigrants were to leave the country 30 days after the close of the war.

INTERNAL MIGRATION

Immigration into this country has been an important factor in the nation's rapid development, but equally important has been the mobility of the domestic population. While there have been a few spectacular cross-continent movements, such as the California gold rush of 1848–1849, most of the Middle West and Far West has been developed through a process of constant and numerous short migrations of peoples, the settlers from the Atlantic seaboard moving across the Appalachians, some of their children moving into the Northwest Territory and the southern Mississippi valley, and some of their children in turn moving to the Far West, Southwest, and Northwest.

Reasons for Migration

As new areas develop and old ones become stationary or decline, people move elsewhere in order to develop new resources and relieve the older communities of surplus population. Migration is a normal process of adjustment to changes in economic opportunities. It may take place in response to known advantages in distant areas, or simply as a means of escaping onerous conditions at home but with no assurance of better conditions elsewhere.

The better opportunities in the new areas, as well as the worsening of conditions in already settled communities, may be due to natural or man-made causes, or both. The pioneer settlements were made in response to the natural opportunities offered by a new country having fertile soil and physical resources for industrial development. Subsequent migrations have been the result of major changes in industrialization and agriculture, prolonged droughts and business depressions, or the exhaustion of natural resources within particular areas.

The gradual migration from rural to urban communities, which has been particularly noticeable during the past fifty years, has been due both to increasing mechanization on the farms and to expanding industrialization in the cities. In normal peacetime, movements from one industrial center to another may be caused by the general decline of an entire industry or the bankruptcy or transfer of large individual plants. In wartime the shifts in

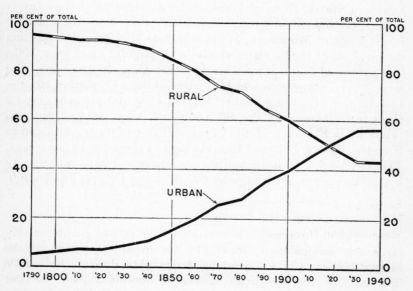

FIG. 1. *Trend of Urban and Rural Population, 1790–1940. (Based on census data.)*

population are the result of loss of job opportunities in non-war plants, and also of the pull of better jobs in war plants elsewhere.

Migrations During the 1920's

Between 1920 and 1930 approximately 4½ million persons moved across state lines, and in the five-year period 1935–1940, almost 6½ million. Over 4½ million persons born east of the Mississippi River were living west of the river in 1940, and 2 million born west of the river were living in the east. These figures do not include the third and more moves made by some persons, or the number who moved one or more times within their original state.

The dominant migratory trend during the relatively prosperous 1920's was the movement from farms to cities. In 1920 about 51 per cent of the country's population was urban; in 1930, more than 56 per cent. During this decade there was a net movement of almost 6⅓ million persons from farms to cities. A majority of them came from farms in the New England, Atlantic, and Southern States, although considerable numbers came from farms in the North Central States and others were from the cut-over forest lands of Minnesota, Wisconsin, and Michigan. During this decade, half of the 93 cities which had a population of over 100,-000 increased their population by more than 20 per cent. The largest percentage increases took place in three California cities— Los Angeles 115, Long Beach 156, San Diego 99 per cent; in two cities in Oklahoma—Tulsa 96, Oklahoma City 103 per cent; in two cities in Florida—Miami 274, and Tampa 96 per cent; and in Houston, Texas, 111, and Chattanooga, Tennessee, 107 per cent. The New York City metropolitan area increased its population by 1⅓ million persons, Chicago by 675,000, and Detroit by 575,000.

Migrations During the 1930's

Since 1930 three major occurrences have caused comparatively large and sudden migrations: (1) the great depression of the early 'thirties, (2) the prolonged droughts during the middle 'thirties, (3) the necessities of war production during the first half of the 'forties. In some instances the population movements occasioned by these events were a reversal of normal trends, but in most cases the shifts represented accelerations of movements already in process.

During the severe depression of 1930–1933, when the total pay roll of the country dropped to less than half its previous amount, the trend of migration to the cities was reversed when people began to move back to rural communities. In these three years there was a net movement of more than 764,000 persons from cities to farms. These people moved, not because the farms to which they returned offered economic opportunities, but in order to escape distress in cities where there were no jobs and little or no public relief. Those who were anxious to have the cities relieved of caring for these jobless families referred to this as a "back-to-the-land" movement. However, most of those who left the cities were forced to return to depleted areas which provided only the barest subsistence.[18] With the first sign of business recovery and adequate relief in the cities, the farm-to-city migration was resumed and continued at an increasing rate. During the war period there was a reduction of almost 3 million persons in the farm-area population.

Another kind of migration was caused by the combined effects of the business depression, the innovation of the mechanical cultivation of cotton lands, and the prolonged droughts and subsequent dust storms in the Great Plains region during 1933–1936. This was a westward migration to the Pacific coast, mostly to California. This flight of poverty-stricken families, in old automobiles piled high with poor household belongings, aroused nation-wide interest[19] because of the numbers involved and because the direction in which they migrated was concentrated. It was essentially a movement of dislocated agricultural people who sought resettlement on other agricultural lands. Even though these refugees re-

---

[18] In 1929 approximately 7,700,000 men, women, and children lived on 1,700,-000 farms which provided a gross income of less than $600 a year, based on value of used, traded, and sold products. A study made after the depression revealed the fact that 1 in every 4 rural families in the U. S. received public relief sometime during the depression and that more than 1 million farm families moved from one farm to another each year in a constant effort to find greater economic opportunities. According to this report, "The land of more than 500,000 of the nation's farms is so poor that it means actual starvation for the families dwelling on them." (Farm Security Administration of the Department of Agriculture, *Social Research Report VIII,* 1938.)

[19] As indicated by the popularity of the book and moving picture, *Grapes of Wrath,* by John Steinbeck.

ceived a cold, if not hostile, reception in the areas to which they fled, their exodus from their former places of residence was an economic necessity. The many who migrated from the Great Plains moved away from a soil that was unsuited to the type of farming which had been begun in that area a few years previously.

The effect of this migration, together with the normal westward movement, was reflected in the 1940 census, which indicated that 57 per cent of the persons then resident in California, and approximately 54 per cent of those resident in Washington and Oregon, were born in other states. With the subsequent development and expansion of war industries on the Pacific coast, migration was again accelerated.

Effect of War Shifts

In 1945 more than 15 million civilians (12 per cent of the civilian population) were living in counties different from their counties of residence before Pearl Harbor, and several million men in the military forces indicated that they did not intend to return to their former places of residence. Never before in the history of our country had there been so great a shuffling and redistribution of population in so short a time as had taken place between 1941 and 1945.

The flow of population was largely to metropolitan centers in the Far West and South, although a few northern cities, especially Detroit, also gained in population. During the war there was a net gain of 1,750,000 in the civilian population of the three Pacific coast states; almost a half million persons moved into Los Angeles and more than one-third million into the San Francisco Bay area. At the close of the war 30 per cent of the residents of Portland, Oregon, and 20 per cent of those residing in the Puget Sound area were migrants. The civilian population of Charleston, S. C., increased 38 per cent and that of Mobile, Alabama, 65 per cent.

Seven states in addition to those on the Pacific coast experienced abnormal growth as a result of war production: Michigan and Ohio, and five states on the Atlantic coast—Connecticut, New Jersey, Maryland, Virginia, and Florida. In contrast, thirty states suffered a loss in population. Several million persons migrated from the states between the Rocky Mountains and the

Mississippi River and those south of the Ohio, and the population of New York and Pennsylvania declined by one-third million.

Although many people moved away from the war centers during the winter of 1945–1946, the indications were that thousands would remain in their new places of residence. This was especially true with respect to those on the Pacific coast.

Migration of Negroes

One of the most extensive and significant population movements in this country has been the migration of large numbers of Negroes from the south to the north and west. For a time after the War Between the States the southern Negroes moved in two diverging directions: Those from the northern rim of southern states moved farther north, and those from the lower east Atlantic section moved southward and westward to Florida, Louisiana, Oklahoma, and especially Texas.[20]

Job opportunities during the First World War reversed this southwest movement to the north and east. The 1920 census indicated that over 780,000 southern-born Negroes were residents of northern states and that the Negro population of the North had increased about 50 per cent during the preceding decade. By contrast, the proportion of Negroes in the south had declined from one-third to one-fourth of its total population. The trend northward continued after the war; during 1923 almost one-half million Negroes went north, 60 per cent of whom moved into Ohio and Pennsylvania.

The movement of Negroes represents not only a shift in geographical distribution but also a change from rural to urban settlement. In the south, a large majority of the Negroes are farm laborers or tenants; when they move north they go to the cities, especially the larger cities. In 1930, the latest year for which such

---

[20] The apparent growing concentration of Negroes in the Southwest during these years led one well-known observer of American life to consider the possibility that the Negroes would become an ever smaller proportion of the northern population and the center of Negro population would more and more shift southward; that "the African is leaving the colder, higher, and drier lands for regions more resembling his ancient seats in the Old World." (James Bryce, *American Commonwealth,* The Macmillan Company, New York, 1895, vol. ii, p. 492.)

data are available, 81 per cent of the Negro population of Chicago were southern-born; 84 per cent of those residing in Detroit, 77 per cent of those in Cleveland, almost 70 per cent of those in Philadelphia, and 54 per cent of those in New York City had migrated from states to the south. (More than one-fifth of the Negro residents in New York City in 1930 were born in the West Indies and outlying islands.) Today, at least half the Negroes in the country live in urban communities, in contrast to fewer than one-fifth fifty years ago.

According to the 1940 census, there was a net gain during the preceding decade of almost 1½ million Negroes in the north due to migration from the south. However, 77 per cent of the total 12,866,000 Negroes in the country were still living in the south; less than 22 per cent were in the north and only 1 per cent on the Pacific coast. During World War II the migration of Negroes was greatly accelerated, many moving to the Pacific coast to accept employment in war plants.

The urge and the opportunity for better jobs elsewhere have been the dominant reasons for Negro migration during past years. Another reason looms: Within the next decade it is expected that 5 to 8 million Southerners, of whom the majority are Negroes, will be driven off the land by the mechanical picker and the geographical shift of cotton farming. The prospects are that several million southern Negroes will move to northern and Pacific coast cities during the next few years, regardless of business conditions and whether or not urban jobs are available for them.

OUR FUTURE POPULATION

Labor conditions in the future, as in the past, will continue to be influenced by the rate of growth and change in composition of the country's population. Because almost all labor problems stem from maladjustments of labor supply and labor demand, the future trend of population must be taken into consideration as an important factor in most of the labor problems which will arise. The economics of a rapidly expanding country is drastically different from that of one having a stationary or slow-growing population, and the very process of slowing up results in shifts in age groups and other changes in its general make-up, as well as in its economic behavior.

Economic Effects of Changes in Population

A rapidly expanding population means not only an increase in the supply of available labor but also an increase in the number of consumers or purchasers for the goods produced. Millions of additional homes must be built and furnished, thousands of schools, churches, and other community facilities constructed, roads and transportation vehicles provided to take care of an expanding population—in addition, of course, to the constantly increasing volume of food, clothing, and other consumers' goods which are required. A certain amount of business expansion is automatic with an increase in population and number of consumers; this is especially true with respect to those businesses which provide the necessities for living, for no matter how poor the expanded population may be it will consume a minimum amount of food and clothing.

In a country with a slow-growing or stationary population, all other things remaining the same, there will be little or no demand for net additions in building construction or volume of consumers' goods; the only demand will be for replacements. Business expansion, excluding the factor of foreign trade, becomes entirely dependent upon increasing the individual purchasing power of the existing population. Since there is no increase in the number of purchasers, there must be an increase in the amount of individual purchasing. Furthermore, accompanying a change in the level of individual consumption there will be a change in the character of purchases, for after the basic necessities have been obtained, more and more of the purchasing will be for goods and services which provide the comforts and luxuries of living.

It is obvious, then, that changes in a country's population not only affect the nature and volume of the country's business activity but also create many problems of economic adjustment. Later chapters will deal with the impact of population changes upon labor supply and job opportunities, as well as the effect of a lifting or lowering of individual purchasing power on business enterprise, work, and living conditions. Here we are concerned only with the question of what changes in our population are likely to take place in the near future.

Size of Population

Until the First World War the population of this country grew very rapidly, with increases from 20 to 35 per cent every decade. During that war and the following years the rate of increase dropped to around 15 per cent, and the census of 1940 indicated a rise of only 7.2 per cent in population between 1930 and 1940. The rate increased somewhat during the early years of World War II, because of economic prosperity and the hastening of marriages in expectation of departure for military service. However, the rate started to decline again in 1944, as a result both of a decrease in the birth rate and of an increase in mortality in our military forces.

Judging from these trends it is apparent that significant changes have already taken place in our population growth and that we have passed from an era of rapid expansion to a period of very slow increase and perhaps stationary or declining numbers. As already mentioned, the population of any country is augmented through one or both of the following means: through immigration from other countries and through an excess of births over deaths, that is, by natural increase. According to the laws now on our statute books, the maximum possible increase through immigration, except from other countries in the western hemisphere, is about 150,000 persons per year. Any greater expansion, therefore, is dependent upon the rate of natural increase of the native population.

A decline in the death rate, of course, tends to increase a nation's population. In this country, as in most of the civilized countries, there has been a gradual but significant decline in the trend of the death rate during the past 100 years. Better sanitation, medical discoveries, public health measures, and improved living conditions have resulted in a marked decrease in the number of deaths caused by epidemic germ diseases and individual physical ailments. A child born soon after the Revolutionary War had an average life expectancy of 35 years; in 1940 he might reasonably expect to live 60 years. Most of this increase in life expectancy has been brought about by the saving of lives of newborn babies and infants. In the 18th century fewer than half the babies lived to be six years of age. At the beginning of the 20th century, 10 out of every 100 infants born alive each year died during their first year; currently fewer than 4 out of 100 babies born alive in this country fail to survive their first year.[21]

The fact that the decline in the death rate has been chiefly a result of a decrease in infant mortality rather than of a prolongation in the span of life (that is, the extreme age to which people are apt to live) would seem to indicate that a decline in the death rate cannot continue indefinitely. In fact, there has been little change in the death rate in this country during the past twenty years. The civilian death rate of about 12 per 1000 in the early 'twenties has gradually declined to about 10.5 per 1000, exclusive of deaths in the military forces.

Far offsetting any influence of the declining death rate on an increase in our country's population has been the drastic decrease in the birth rate. The slowing down in this country, although it probably began somewhat later, has followed the trend which has been present throughout most of the western world since the middle of the 19th century. In 1800 the birth rate in this country was about 3½ times as great as in 1930; in 1880 it was twice as high.[22] Since the First World War it has declined from 23 per 1000 population a year to 17 per 1000 (in 1940). There is no scientific evidence to prove how much, if any, of this decline in births is due to involuntary causes, that is, to biological inability of men and women to have as many children as their ancestors had. There is ample evidence to indicate that the birth rate has been affected by voluntary birth control as well as by social practices, such as later marriages, which tend to reduce the number of births.[23]

---

[21] Warren S. Thompson, *Population Problems,* p. 243. The life expectancy is the number of years that persons at a given age can, on the average, expect to live. It is arrived at by dividing the sum of all the years lived by persons born during a certain period by the number born during that period. Early data are for European countries since no death rate records were kept in this country prior to 1918.

[22] National Resources Committee, *Problems of a Changing Population.* These estimates are based on the ratio of children to women because there were no birth statistics for the U. S. as a whole before 1933.

[23] It might be pertinent to note that deliberate control of population is not confined to modern society. Comments one authority: "The adjustment of his numbers to his environment so that he could live as seemed good to him has

A discussion of the numerous factors, social and psychological, which have caused this reduction in the birth rate lies outside the

TABLE 1.   Future Population of the United States According to Certain Assumed Trends[24]

Year	A Medium Fertility and Mortality and No Net Immigration	B Same as A, with Annual Net Immigration of 100,000	C Low Fertility, High Mortality, No Net Immigration	D Low Fertility, Medium Mortality, No Net Immigration	E High Fertility, Low Mortality, Net Annual Immigration of 200,000	F Same as E, But No Net Immigration
	Future Population (Thousands)					
1945	137,096	137,607	134,172	135,163	139,938	138,916
1950	141,213	142,301	136,725	137,636	146,829	144,627
1955	144,732	146,458	137,688	139,244	153,605	150,082
1960	147,612	150,010	137,570	139,947	160,246	155,297
1965	149,957	153,054	136,478	139,832	166,923	160,469
1970	151,783	155,601	134,473	138,889	173,657	165,608
1975	153,043	157,610	131,621	137,091	180,325	170,575
1980	153,628	158,967	127,947	134,381	186,713	175,151
	Per Cent Increase or Decrease					
1940–50	6.5	7.3	3.8	4.3	10.2	8.5
1950–60	4.5	5.4	0.6	1.7	9.1	7.4
1960–70	2.8	3.7	−2.3	−0.8	8.4	6.6
1970–80	1.2	2.2	−4.9	−3.2	7.5	5.8

scope of this volume, but it is pertinent to consider what the future population trend is likely to be. Before World War II, most population authorities predicted that the forces making for a decline

always been one of man's major problems . . . even the so-called primitive peoples have frequently developed population policies which have aimed at controlling their growth in numbers." Among these, he lists infanticide and abortion, sexual taboos such as segregation of women for frequent and long periods of time, prohibition of remarriage of widows, and killing of aged people. (Thompson, *Population Problems,* chap. 1.)

[24] Estimates made by Warren S. Thompson and P. K. Whelpton of the Scripps Foundation for the National Resources Committee. See *Population Statistics, National Data,* Government Printing Office, 1937, p. 282.

in the birth rate would continue for some years, if not indefinitely. However, the social and economic changes wrought by the war caused a sharp rise in the birth rate, with the result that, in spite of the war casualties, our population was higher in 1946 than had been anticipated a decade previously.

At the beginning of 1946 the population of the United States had passed the 140 million mark. How far this exceeds some estimates prepared ten years previously is indicated in Table 1. However, it is probable that there will be a slowing down in the birth rate during the next few years. If so, the estimates for 1980 based on "medium fertility" may be fairly accurate.

Composition of Population

One of the effects of a slowing down in population growth is a change in the proportion of young people to old. In 1920 more

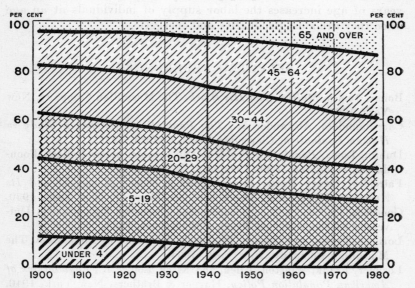

Fig. 2. *Distribution of U. S. Population by Age, 1900–1980.* (*Based on the census and column B of Table 1.*)

than 44 per cent of our population was composed of persons under 20 years of age; in 1940 only 34 per cent and by 1980 it is estimated, only 26 per cent of the population will be in this age group. There will be little change in the proportion of middle-aged persons during the next few decades. About 59 per cent of the population in 1940 was between 20 and 64 years of age, and this proportion will continue until 1980, although with some decreases in those under 45 years of age, according to the estimates shown in Fig. 2.

The economic effects of these shifts in age groups are apparent. There will be a reduction in the number of children attending grade schools and, unless other forces begin to operate, there will be a sharp decline in businesses catering to children's needs. The proportion of persons over 65 years of age will more than double in the near future, and this means an increase in the number of people who have retired from active work and are living on their own savings, old age pensions, or public and private assistance. The increase of several millions of persons between 20 and 45 years of age increases the labor supply of individuals at an age when they are most productive and energetic.

SELECTED REFERENCES

Bonar, James, *Malthus and His Work,* The Macmillan Company, New York, 1924.

Carr-Saunders, Alexander M., *The Population Problem; a Study in Human Evaluation,* Clarendon Press, Oxford, 1922.

Dublin, Louis, *Population Problems,* Symposium under Pollack Foundation, Houghton Mifflin Company, Boston, 1926.

Fairchild, Henry Pratt, *Immigration; a World Movement and Its American Significance,* The Macmillan Company, New York, 1930.

Goodrich, Carter, *et al., Migration and Economic Opportunity,* University of Pennsylvania Press, Philadelphia, 1935.

Lorimer, Frank, and Osborn, Frederick, *Dynamics of Population,* The Macmillan Company, New York, 1934.

Lorimer, Frank, Winston, Ellen, and Kiser, Louise K., *Foundations of American Population Policy,* Harper & Brothers, New York, 1940.

Malthus, Thomas R., *An Essay on Population,* E. P. Dutton & Co., Inc., New York.

Myrdal, Gunnar, *Population: A Problem for Democracy,* Harvard University Press, Cambridge, 1940.

National Bureau of Economic Research, *International Migrations,* National Bureau of Economic Research, New York, 1929–1931, 2 vols.

National Resources Committee, *The Problem of a Changing Population,* Government Printing Office, Washington, 1938.

Taft, Donald R., *Human Migration,* The Ronald Press Company, New York, 1936.

Thompson, Warren S., and Whelpton, P. K., *Population Trends in the U. S.,* McGraw-Hill Book Company, Inc., New York, 1933.

Thompson, Warren S., *Population Problems,* McGraw-Hill Book Company, Inc., New York, 1942.

Woytinsky, W. S., *Labor in the United States,* Social Science Research Council, Washington, 1938.

2

THE LABOR FORCE
AND EMPLOYMENT

ALL MEMBERS OF A POPULATION ARE CONSUMERS OF ECONOMIC goods and services, but only about 40 per cent of the residents of this country in 1940 were active or potentially active in occupations which are considered as "gainful" employment. About 30 per cent of the population were too young to work or were attending schools and colleges preparatory to employment. At least 6 per cent were retired or physically, mentally, or otherwise disqualified for productive work; over a million of these were temporary or permanent inmates of institutions.

Approximately 29 million women, including 22 per cent of the population, were housewives who were not working for wages and are therefore not included in the labor force. Invaluable as their services are to the national and family well-being, they are not classified as economic producers. They do, however, perform a major function in the economy of any community because they are the purchasers of a large proportion of all consumers' goods and thus influence the kinds and quantities of such goods which are produced.

The labor force, as defined by the census, includes all persons who have jobs or who are actively seeking jobs, thus including the unemployed who are actively seeking work as well as those who are actually employed. Employment is defined as work in an occupation in which money or the equivalent of money is earned or which results in the production of marketable goods or services. Unpaid family work which is not directed toward producing something for sale, or involved in the selling process itself, is excluded. However, members of a family—for instance, on a farm or in a family grocery store—who perform work which otherwise would require hired labor are included in the definition of labor force.[1]

TRENDS IN THE LABOR FORCE

The proportion of the population within the labor force is not static. For various reasons, gradual shifts and changes take place over a period of years and abnormal conditions sometimes arise which cause sudden and temporary expansions or retractions in the number of persons working for wages and salaries. During the past half century there have been significant changes in the size of the labor force in relation to the total population, as well as in its general composition. Some of these changes are the result of legislative action, some of economic developments, and others of changes in social attitudes and customs.

State and federal laws have been enacted which prohibit or restrict children under certain ages from entering gainful employment. At the same time, educational facilities have been expanded and young people have been encouraged to continue in school longer than their parents and grandparents were privileged to do. The movement toward increased school attendance was especially noticeable during the period between the two World Wars. In 1920 only 32 per cent of the young people in this country between 14 and 17 years of age, inclusive, were enrolled in secondary schools, compared to 80 per cent in 1940. School attendance declined considerably during the next few years when young people entered

---

[1] In the censuses previous to 1940 the terms "gainful workers" and "gainfully occupied" were used instead of "labor force." Although the change in definition does not seriously affect the comparability of the 1940 data with those of earlier censuses because of several offsetting factors, there are some major differences. The 1940 census, which was taken the last week in March, 1940, excludes seasonal workers not working or seeking work at the time of the census; unlike earlier censuses it includes new workers such as those who had just left school and had had no previous work experience. The 1940 census excludes all retired persons, some of whom were previously included, and also all inmates of institutions; previously those who performed regular work in institutions were included.

As with all technical classifications, the lines of distinction between those in and those not in the labor force become vague, if not anomalous, in certain situations. For example, if a widower employs a housekeeper to maintain his household, she is a member of the labor force; but if he marries her, she is no longer a member of the labor force.

the war industries, but by 1946 it had returned to the pre-war level. College enrollment also climbed during the period between the wars; in 1940 almost 1½ million persons were attending collegiate institutions and this number has been increased since the war, largely because of the veterans' program. All these students,

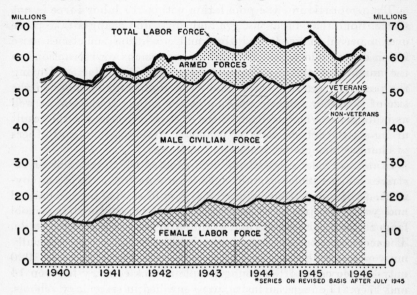

FIG. 3.   *Total Labor Force, March, 1940, to August, 1946.* (*Source: Bureau of the Census.*)

however, are not entirely removed from the labor force since many of them pursue part-time employment while attending school.

At the other end of the life span, the old age insurance provided by the social security laws passed during recent years has made it possible for some people to withdraw from the labor market who otherwise would have had to continue to work until total disability or death. The delay in the intake of young persons and the accelerated withdrawals of the old both tend to reduce the size of the labor force. While this is taking place there is another trend which causes expansion, namely, the movement of more women into the labor market. The tendency toward an increase in the proportion of women who have entered gainful employment during the past fifty years has been due chiefly to industrial and economic developments, although social attitudes have played a part.

Industry has gradually taken over much of the preparation of foods, the making of clothes, laundering, and other services formerly performed in the home, and women have followed these activities and thus become wage earners. Although their work is much more specialized, considered as a whole the commodities and services produced by these women in factories, laundries, etc., are not essentially different from those produced by their grandmothers at home. Because of industrialization, the results of their labor have become commercial goods and services, and many wives and daughters who previously were engaged in unpaid family work are now members of the labor force.

However, the transfer of activities from the home to the factory does not entirely account for the increase in the proportion of women wage earners. Changes in manufacturing processes and methods of doing business have resulted in the increased employment of women in industries and occupations altogether remote from the activities formerly carried on in the home. The invention of automatic and semi-automatic machines which require a minimum of physical strain and time to learn to operate has resulted in the employment of women in industries which formerly employed only men. The increase in "paper work" in industry and the use of the telephone have caused the employment of thousands of clerks, stenographers, and telephone operators. The expansion of merchandising, especially department and apparel stores, has resulted in an increase in the employment of women. Much of this expansion in merchandising, in turn, is an indirect result of the transfer of former home activities to mill and factories, for clothing and other goods made in factories must be sold through stores.

Later chapters will discuss in more detail the causes and results of the changes in the employment of young people, old people, and women; here we are concerned with the quantitative impact upon the labor force of the changes in their employment. Old age insurance is of too recent origin for us to know accurately about its effect upon the employment of older people. Census figures reveal the changes which have taken place in the employment of women and young people. Fifty years ago more than 18 per cent of the children between the ages of 10 and 15 years were gainfully employed, in contrast to less than 6 per cent in 1940. In 1890 less than 19 per cent of the women 16 years of age and over were working for wages and salaries; fifty years later almost 27 per cent were employed outside their homes.

Elasticity of the Labor Force

There are not only long-time, more or less permanent changes in the relative size of the labor force, but also sudden temporary shifts in response to unusual conditions or seasonal demands for additional labor. Seasonal peaks of employment may indicate that a portion of the normal labor force is unemployed during the slack seasons. Some of the seasonal expansion, however, is effected through the employment of persons outside the normal labor force, such as students who work during the summer months and women who do not seek regular jobs.

Strange as it may seem, subnormal economic conditions may be the cause of an expansion in the labor force. During a serious business depression when the chief wage earners of families are thrown out of employment or have only two or three days' work a week, the wives or others in the household who normally do not work for wages will obtain or seek jobs. Thus, while there is a drastic decline in the available man-days of work, there may be an actual increase in the number of persons in the labor market. This, obviously, is an artificial expansion and is one of the factors which create confusion in the taking of an unemployment census.

The elasticity of the labor force is dramatically revealed during periods of extraordinary demands for additional labor, such as wartime. During the recent war the peak labor force, including those in military service, exceeded by almost 7½ million persons the normal increase which would have taken place had peacetime trends continued. Where did these millions come from? Almost 3 million of these extra workers were teen-age boys and girls, two-thirds of them under 18 years of age, who accepted jobs outside of school hours or left school to take civilian jobs or enter the armed forces.[2] About 2 million adult men were employed who in peacetime are not usually at work. Some of them would have been in college;

---

[2] This is in excess of the number who would normally have completed or left school to go to work. See *Monthly Labor Review,* January and August, 1945.

some were past retirement age; others came from the "fringes" of
the labor market, that is, because of physical or other reasons they
were on the borderline of employability. More than 2½ million
women entered the labor market who would not normally have accepted industrial employment. Many of these women were young
wives of servicemen, but the majority were women over 35 years of

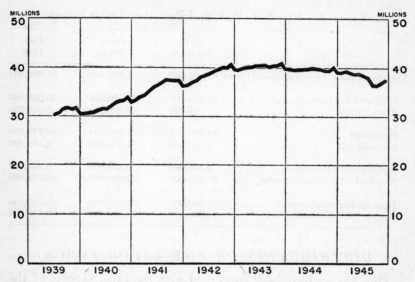

FIG. 4. *Wartime Trend of Employees in Non-Agricultural Establishments. (Source: U. S. Bureau of Labor Statistics.)*

age who had previously stayed at home. For most of these women,
employment in war industries represented responsibilities in addition to their normal household duties, and when the war was over
they dropped out of the labor market. By April, 1946, almost
1⅓ million women had left factory employment, and the proportion of total factory workers who were women was almost the same
as before the war.

The change which took place in the labor force during the war
period is indicated in Table 2, which shows that the total civilian
labor force actually declined during the war by more than a
million persons. However, more than 6 million people who were
unemployed or on emergency relief work in 1940 obtained employ-

ment during the following years, and they were equivalent to one-half of the increase in the armed forces. Ten months after V-J Day, the civilian labor force included 5 million more persons than before the war, and the number employed was almost 10 million higher. Almost all the increase in employment occurred in non-agricultural pursuits.

TABLE 2.   Pre-War, War, and Post-War Labor Force[3]

	1940 Average	June, 1945	June, 1946
Total labor force, including armed forces	54,592,000	65,370,000	62,300,000
Civilian labor force................	54,230,000	53,070,000	59,300,000
Armed forces.....................	362,000	12,300,000	3,000,000
Employed........................	46,930,000	51,990,000	56,740,000
Unemployed.....................	7,300,000	1,080,000	2,560,000
Agricultural employment...........	9,500,000	9,090,000	9,980,000
Non-agricultural employment.......	37,430,000	42,900,000	46,760,000
Male civilian employment..........	35,600,000	33,770,000	40,030,000
Female civilian employment........	11,330,000	18,220,000	16,710,000

DISTRIBUTION OF THE LABOR FORCE

Thus far we have been concerned with the total aspects of the labor market, but as a basis for a study of the manifold problems of labor economics it is necessary to know how the labor force is distributed throughout the national economy. For this purpose it is advisable to consider the situation as it existed during a period of approximately normal circumstances rather than that existing under wartime or immediate post-war conditions. Fortunately, the 1940 census was taken before our entry into war and during a time of relatively normal business activity. Even at such a time, however, more than 7½ million persons were either unemployed or working on federal emergency relief projects. This raises the problem, discussed elsewhere, of the extent of unemployment during periods when business is considered to be "normal."

According to the 1940 census, there was a total labor force of

---

[3] *Monthly Labor Review,* August, 1945 and 1946.

almost 52.8 million persons during March of that year, approximately 800,000 of whom were new workers, mostly young people just out of school who had had no occupational experience. Of the experienced labor force, over 9 million were proprietors and managers of industrial establishments or farm owners or farm tenant operators—persons with whom this discussion is not immediately concerned. The distribution of the entire labor force by major occupations is shown in Table 3, which indicates that the

TABLE 3. Labor Force Distributed by Major Occupational Groups, 1940[4]

(In thousands)

	Total	Male	Female	Total	Male	Female
Total labor force....................	52,789	39,944	12,845			
New, inexperienced workers..........	767	462	305			
Experienced labor force.............	52,022	39,482	12,540	100%	100%	100%
Professional and semi-professional......	3,549	2,006	1,543	6.8	5.1	12.3
Proprietors, managers and officials [a].....	9,027	8,443	584	17.4	21.4	4.7
Clerical, sales, and kindred.............	8,307	4,809	3,497	16.0	12.2	27.9
Craftsmen, foremen, and kindred.......	5,877	5,752	125	11.3	14.6	1.0
Operatives and kindred...............	9,416	7,011	2,406	18.1	17.8	19.2
Protective service[b]....................	742	734	8	1.4	1.9	0.1
Personal and domestic service[c]........	5,517	1,900	3,618	10.6	4.8	28.8
Laborers, including farm..............	8,605	8,139	465	16.5	20.6	3.7
Occupation not reported..............	982	688	294	1.9	1.6	2.3

[a] Includes farm owners and tenants, postmasters and other government officials, in addition to officials and managers in private industry.
[b] Includes policemen, firemen, guards, sheriffs, as well as all federal military forces except commissioned officers.
[c] Includes charwomen, porters and elevator operators, cooks and waiters, barbers, beauticians, etc., as well as domestic servants.

number of laborers was about the same as those engaged in clerical, sales, and kindred occupations, and that the number employed in personal and domestic service was slightly more than one-third the number of craftsmen, factory, mining, and other operatives.

Table 4 reveals the shifts which have taken place in employment among the various groups of industries during the thirty years

[4] *Population*, vol. iii, *The Labor Force*, part i, p. 10. These figures are for March, 1940, which is a low month so far as seasonality is concerned, as is revealed by the 10-month average (March-December) in Table 2.

TABLE 4. Per Cent Distribution of Employed Persons, 1910–1940,
by Major Industry Groups[5]

	1940	1930	1910
Total	100.0	100.0	100.0
Agriculture, forestry, and fishing	17.6	21.2	31.4
Mining	2.3	2.5	3.0
Construction	7.6	6.6	6.3
Manufacturing	23.6	22.9	20.4
Transportation, communication, and other public utilities	6.8	8.6	8.6
Wholesale and retail trade	16.4	14.3	11.0
Finance, insurance, and real estate	3.1	3.1	1.5
Business and repair services	2.0	2.1	0.9
Personal services	8.9	8.9	10.4
Amusement, recreation, and related services	1.0	0.7	0.4
Professional and related services	7.0	6.2	4.2
Government[a]	3.7	2.8	1.8

[a] Includes military, postal service, and all federal, state, and local government workers in "activitie-that are peculiarly government functions"; does not include public construction workers or publics school teachers.

between 1910 and 1940. In these years there was a marked decline in the proportion of employed workers who were engaged in agriculture, and an increase in manufacturing, trade, professional, and other "white-collar" occupations.

Within these various industries there were also significant changes in types of employment, as is indicated in Fig. 5, which shows a rising trend in the proportion of clerical, professional, and semi-skilled groups and a decline in the proportion of unskilled workers, the proportion of skilled workers remaining about the same during these years.

MAJOR TYPES OF EMPLOYMENT

The term "labor force" carries with it the connotation of labor in the abstract, a lump sum of labor which can be measured somewhat as energy is measured in thermal or horsepower units. Labor, however, is the work of human beings, and the employment of human beings cannot be dissociated from the persons who perform the labor. Likewise, that portion of the labor force which is un-

[5] From the Bureau of Census. Data for 1930 and 1910 are based on the 1940 census industrial classifications.

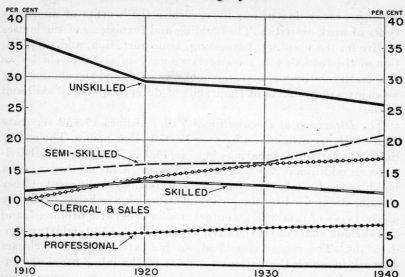

PER CENT

FIG. 5.   *Trends in Major Types of Employment, 1910–1940. (Based on census data.)*

employed represents human beings, most of them being people who are deprived of the opportunity of working for wages in spite of their own needs and desires.

The size of the labor force and the proportion of it which is employed and unemployed at any time are important criteria of a country's economic development and potential productive capacity. But they signify much more than statistical measurements because of the fundamental fact that it is people who are employed and unemployed and not units of energy or matter. Therein lies the difference between physical science and social science, of which labor economics is an important branch. The unemployed portion of the labor force will be discussed in Chapter 5. The present chapter and the following deal with those who are employed, the various characteristics of some of the major occupations, and the results of work efforts in terms of output or productivity.

Variety of Occupations

It is almost impossible to visualize the multitudes of different kinds of work which exist in a modern industrial society, although all of us, every day of our lives, receive the benefits of numerous types of work activities. The building and furnishing of the houses we live in, the planting, harvesting, transportation, and preparation of the food we eat, the streets we walk on and the vehicles we ride in, the clothes we wear, the books we read, and the amusements we enjoy are products of thousands of different persons' skill and labor.

The *Directory of Occupational Titles*[6] defines 17,452 separate jobs which are also known by over 12,000 other names. The census lists 221 distinct occupations but includes in its industry subdivisions an additional 230 titles—for example, a farm laborer and a building-trades laborer whose work is obviously different. Other classifications used by the government, which are based primarily on the types of products manufactured or otherwise produced, and the various kinds of services rendered, include 1530 industry subdivisions.[7] The census classifications indicate the general classes of work in which the various members of the labor force are engaged, and cover broader categories than do the occupational titles defined in the *Directory*. The latter is concerned with detailed job descriptions and minute differences in job performance.

So far as the individual worker is concerned, the particular occupation in which he is employed determines not only the kind of activity in which he is engaged during his workday but also, to a large extent, the manner of life he and his family enjoy or endure. The amount and regularity of his income, his exposure to physical hazards and nervous fatigue, his place of residence and his ability to maintain prolonged residence in a particular community, his social acquaintances and cultural opportunities are all affected by his type of employment. A migrant agricultural worker and his family live an entirely different kind of life from a factory worker and his family; a sailor on the high seas lives and works under entirely different conditions from a miner in the bowels of the earth.

Although there are basic economic problems which are common to all wage earners, conditions of employment vary greatly among

---

[6] Prepared by the U. S. Department of Labor, Government Printing Office, Washington, 1939.

[7] *Standard Industrial Classification Manual*, Division of Statistical Standards, Bureau of the Budget, Government Printing Office, Washington.

the different occupations and industries. Some of these are indicated in the following brief descriptions of the more important types of employment.

AGRICULTURAL LABOR

The two major classifications of activities which are universally used are agricultural and non-agricultural employment. There are, of course, other reasons for maintaining these two distinct categories in practically all economic analyses than the differences in employment conditions, but the latter is our concern in the present discussion.

One of the outstanding differences between farm and industrial employment is the much greater dispersement of farm workers throughout all regions and most of the counties in this country. A second is the extreme seasonality of the work and the consequent mobility of labor from one area to another, and from agricultural to other types of employment and back again with the change of seasons. Another difference is the predominance on farms of what are called family workers as distinguished from hired workers, and closely allied to this is the greater prevalence, as compared to industry, of direct owner operation.

All these factors have contributed toward the treatment of farm laborers as a special category of workers who are excluded from many of the legal protections and benefits enjoyed by other workers. Agricultural workers are not at present covered by federal social security and minimum wage and hour laws, and most of them are excluded from state workmen's compensation laws.

Aside from the farm owners and their families, with whom this volume is not concerned, there are three general types[8] of agricultural labor, namely, the hired "hands" who are employed on a year-round or fairly regular basis; the sharecropper tenants who receive no fixed money wage; and the migratory or casual

---

[8] The census maintains only two classifications of agricultural employment, namely, family workers and hired workers. Family workers include owner operators and members of their families when working on farms without wages. Tenants of all types, including sharecroppers, are classed as farm operators and family workers. Because of their direct dependence upon their landlords, sharecroppers are here treated as employed labor.

workers who are employed for only a few days or weeks at a time for the planting or harvesting of particular crops.

Regular Hired Laborers

Approximately 60 per cent of the 1½ million laborers[9] who are hired on a year-round or fairly regular basis, work on farms which have only one or two hired hands. Many of them live in the homes or on the premises of the farm owners; they are helpers or assistants and their relationship with their employers is quite unlike that of other farm and most industrial workers. The same situation does not obtain for the 600,000 laborers who work on large farms which employ numbers of persons who are under the supervision of farm managers and foremen. Most of these large farms which employ numerous laborers on a more or less regular basis are in the Range and the Delta cotton areas, and in Florida and California. Of the more than 6½ million farms in the country, fewer than 50,000 are operated by paid managers, although a considerably greater number are operated by tenants on either a cash rental or a share basis.

Sharecroppers

In 1940 there were more than one-half million sharecropper families living and working on southern cotton plantations; about two-thirds were white and one-third were Negroes. The distinguishing feature of sharecropping is that money wages are not paid for work performed. The sharecropper supplies all the labor in the production and harvesting of crops and receives a portion, usually one-half, of the product of the 15 or 20 acres assigned him. The owner of the plantation supplies the equipment, the stock and their feed, and the seed for planting. Such costs as fertilizer and the ginning and bagging of the cotton are usually shared. Certain perquisites such as a cabin in which to live, and sometimes a gar-

---

[9] According to a special study of the Bureau of the Census, there were 1,645,-602 hired farm laborers employed in January, 1935. Since January is the lowest employment month of the year it can be assumed that most of these workers were hired on a regular or yearly basis. The number, however, has probably declined since this 1935 census. (See Julius T. Wendzel, "Distribution of Hired Farm Laborers in the U. S.," *Monthly Labor Review,* September, 1937.)

den plot and fuel from the plantation wood lot, are furnished by the owner. Sharecroppers customarily depend upon credit advances from their landlords for their share of crop expenses, and usually for a large part of their living expenses between harvest seasons. Many of them are perpetually in debt to their landlords, with local police authorities making it virtually impossible for sharecropper debtors to move or change their place of employment so long as their landlords want them to stay.

The cash income of sharecroppers is subject to a greater number of variable factors than that of most wage earners. Unlike the latter, whose wages are based on the number of hours worked or units produced, the income of sharecroppers is contingent upon the amount of cotton actually sold as well as the market price. Some years the sharecroppers earn more than they would if paid by the day; other years much less. Offsetting the great uncertainty and small amount of cash income received, the sharecropper has housing and subsistence, poor as they usually are.

From the point of view of labor utilization, the sharecropping system is not an efficient method of getting work done, for each plantation must maintain throughout the year a sufficient number of sharecropper families to take care of peak needs. As a result, sharecroppers are underemployed much of the time and this idle time is extended as one machine after another is invented to displace hand processes. Years ago machines were introduced which transformed cotton planting and ginning; the recent mechanization of chopping and cotton picking practically eliminates the early summer and fall peak seasons. The number of sharecroppers is already less than a decade ago and will undoubtedly decline further with the expanding mechanization of cotton production.

Migratory Farm Laborers

In addition to the regularly hired and tenant laborers attached to particular farms, there are the hundreds of thousands of migratory farm workers who follow the crops and seasons. Before the introduction, in the 1920's, of the combine harvester which enables five men to do the work of 350, several hundred thousand men were annually on the move from wheat fields in Texas in early June to fields in North Dakota in late August, following the ripening

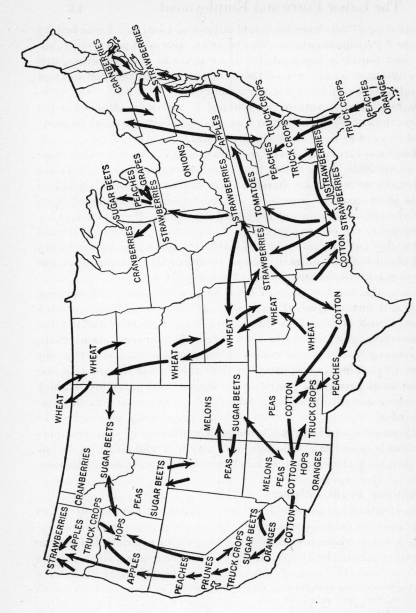

Fig. 6. *Flow of Seasonal Migratory Farm Labor.* (*From Pictorial Statistics, Inc.*)

wheat crop. These harvest hands were men who traveled in freight trains.[10] Present-day migratory workers are predominantly families who travel in automobiles, and the kinds of crops for which they are used makes it possible to utilize the women and children as well as the men.

Annual fluctuations in the volume of migratory labor are extreme, depending upon both crop conditions and general business conditions. The number of migrants may increase, not because additional migratory labor is needed, but because workers have been displaced from their regular jobs in the factories or on farms and "take to the road." Sharecroppers no longer needed, drought-ridden farm owners or tenants, and unemployed city workers may join the ranks of the migrants in lieu of any better way of making a living.

So long as considerable hand work is required for the planting and harvesting of crops, the labor of migratory workers is essential to the production of our food. In the eastern part of the country, seasonal labor is needed in the apple orchards of the Shenandoah valley and upper New York, on the citrus fruit farms in Florida, and in the grape and orchard areas around Lake Erie. Many thousands of workers follow the strawberry harvest from Florida to Michigan; others move each year from surrounding areas to pick the strawberries grown in Arkansas. Harvesting of tomatoes begins in the Southeast in March, and reaches a peak in May and June in Mississippi and Texas and as late as July in Tennessee.

Although mechanization is becoming more general, tens of thousands of migratory workers are still used in Oklahoma and Texas for chopping and picking cotton. Many of them follow the season from the Gulf northward into the Texas Panhandle and Oklahoma, a distance of almost 1000 miles. Unlike many other migratory workers who keep on the move as crops need harvesting, sugar-beet workers move only twice a year—to the beet fields in the spring, where they remain to cultivate and harvest the crop, usually on a contract basis, and back to their winter quarters in the

---

[10] There are many colorful stories of these "hobos" and their radical "wobbly" agitation. For more details on the characteristics of migratory harvest labor, see D. D. Lescohier, *Harvest Labor Problems in the Wheat Belt,* Department of Agriculture, Government Printing Office, Washington, 1922.

fall. In former years, many of the sugar-beet workers came from great distances, some from as far as central Mexico; more recently the industry has endeavored to use workers from surrounding areas and thus reduce the necessity for long migrations.

The greatest seasonal migrations of farm labor in the entire country take place on the Pacific coast, especially California, where migrants move in great surges, shifting from ranch to ranch to finish each crop. Seeking to dovetail brief seasons of employment, they move from the Imperial Valley on the Mexican border northward to the San Joaquin and Sacramento valleys, with some going as far north as the Hood River valley in Oregon and Yakima valley in Washington.

Migratory families labor and live under some peculiar hardships. They necessarily spend a considerable part of their time in moving from job to job and thus, even when employment is plentiful, they are seldom able to work more than half the time. Most of them are compelled to live in huts or tents and their nomad existence makes it impossible for the children to attend school regularly or for the adults to participate in normal community life. Like other agricultural workers they are not protected by social security legislation and, because of their frequent moves, many of them have no legal residence which would entitle them to community relief when in need.[11]

COAL MINING

For the past 200 years coal has been an indispensable source of energy and without it our modern industrial system would never have developed. Coal made possible the industrial use of steam power because it provided a cheap and convenient fuel; coal is

---

[11] One student of the migratory labor situation has summed up the problem thus: "Migratory farm labor is a focus of poverty, bad health and evil housing conditions. Its availability in large numbers at low wages aids large-scale agriculture in its competition with the family farm. Migratory laborers are victims of all the prejudices of settled folk against outlanders and nomads, without the advantages of an organized group life of their own. They are discriminated against by arbitrary and illegal blockades. They cannot participate in democracy. The education of their children is seriously impaired if not completely neglected. Race prejudices are heightened and labor conflicts intensified. Migrants and public welfare suffer alike." (Paul Taylor, "Migratory Farm Labor in the U. S.," *Monthly Labor Review,* March, 1937, p. 548.)

also a necessary ingredient in the production of iron and steel and thereby made possible steel machinery, railroad equipment, and many other products produced and used by modern industry. The struggle for coal resources has been an underlying cause of many international disputes, and in time of war coal is necessary for national survival.

The United States is fortunate in having a generous supply of coal resources within her borders; bituminous coal is mined in 32 states, and one state, Pennsylvania, also produces anthracite. Without this coal supply, this country probably would have remained a loose federation of rural communities, or perhaps several separate nations, for there would have been no railroads to connect the West and the East and no industrial development to encourage political unity.

In spite of its paramount importance to our national life, the coal industry has suffered some loss during recent decades because of the competition of petroleum. Currently, petroleum is furnishing more than 28 per cent of all the energy used in this country. With the recent construction of mammoth dams, the use of water power is also increasing.[12] And there is now some expectation that the future may witness the substitution of atomic energy for much of these present sources of power.

Mining Employment

During the twenty years before the outbreak of World War II, employment in coal mining was reduced by one-half, and miners worked, on the average, not more than 180 days per year. In the early 1920's over 9300 bituminous coal mines were in operation; in 1940 only 5700 mines were operating and there was common agreement among employers, workers, and the government that the industry was overdeveloped. The situation was reversed during

---

[12] According to the 1944 *Minerals Year Book,* the relative contribution in B.t.u. equivalents of the several mineral fuels and water power was as follows (water power is counted at a constant fuel equivalent of approximately 4 pounds per kilowatt-hour):

Anthracite	4.9 per cent
Bituminous coal	45.5 " "
Petroleum	28.2 " "
Natural gas	10.2 " "
Water power	11.2 " "

the war period when the problem became one of mining a sufficient amount of coal to keep the war plants in operation; more than a thousand new mines were opened or old ones reopened. Tonnage increased almost 50 per cent over pre-war levels, but there was little change in the number of miners employed. However, there was a considerable increase in the number of hours per day and days per week each man worked. Largely because of mechanization, the average production per miner increased from less than 4 tons per day during the First World War to more than 5 tons during World War II.

Of the 400,000 currently employed coal miners, about 80,000 are employed in anthracite mining and about 320,000 in bituminous coal mines. Anthracite mining is highly concentrated, almost all the mines being located in ten counties in Pennsylvania. Most of these mines are owned, or at least largely controlled, by the railroad companies which carry the coal to the consuming centers. Anthracite is largely used for household fuel, less than one-fifth of the production being used for industrial purposes.

Unlike the situation in anthracite mining, the location and ownership of bituminous coal mines are widely scattered and 80 per cent of the production is used for industrial purposes—to run railroads, factories, and public utilities and to make steel. Although bituminous coal is mined in 32 states, 90 per cent of the miners are employed in 9 states. More than 25 per cent are employed in Pennsylvania bituminous mines and almost an equal number in West Virginia. Southern coal mines have expanded during recent years and at present almost 10 per cent of all the miners are employed in the two states of Tennessee and Alabama, and another 13 per cent in Kentucky. Mining in Virginia is also expanding, whereas coal production in the central states (Ohio, Indiana and Illinois) as well as in the western and southwestern states is declining or at least not increasing.

Employment Conditions

Coal is found in more or less horizontal seams at different depths of the earth's surface. When close to the surface, it can be dug out by hand or steam shovel. This type of mining, called strip or surface mining, lends itself to mechanization with power loading machines following directly behind the stripping shovels. Surface mining has increased during recent years, although only about 12 per cent of all the bituminous coal is strip mined at the present time. Most coal lies deep underneath the earth's surface and requires the sinking of shafts with entrances which may be several miles from the working faces.[13] Underground mining is becoming more and more mechanized. Electric cutters and power drills have largely replaced the pick; mechanized loaders are taking the place of the shovel; motor-driven cars or conveyers are being substituted for the mule.[14] More than 90 per cent of the coal now being mined underground is cut by machine and almost half is mechanically loaded.

The underground work of coal mining is divided between two main groups of workers: the miners proper, or "tonnage men," who dig the coal at the work place, and the "day men," who carry on the auxiliary tasks of hauling, ventilation, pumping, power supply, timbering, and maintenance. As in other types of employment, the use of machinery has brought factory methods into coal mining, for the whole productive process must be synchronized in order to obtain the maximum use of expensive machine installations. Work must be concentrated and the work place must be mined out quickly to save the cost of timbering and at the same time prevent the falling of the roof. In mechanized mining there is no place for the single miner working in a room, perhaps with an assistant, isolated from the remaining force, setting his own pace and leaving the mine when his stint is finished, regardless of the time of day.

While power-driven machines have eased some of the physical labor connected with the mining of coal, and the workers through their unions have been able to obtain substantial improvements in their working and living conditions, the lot of the miners and their families continues to be one of the least desirable of any group of

---

[13] The distance between the mine entrance and the place of work is indicated in a report of a committee appointed by the President in 1944 during a coal dispute over the issue of portal-to-portal pay. The committee found that underground miners, on the average, spend approximately one hour traveling from the entrance of the mine to the place of operations and back again. The time varied greatly, however, some mines which were close to the surface requiring only five minutes and others requiring over three hours' daily travel time.

[14] The pony is generally used in British mines. In the early days of mining in Europe women and children were sometimes used to haul coal to the surface.

American workers. Except during wartime most miners are chronically underemployed.[15] Mining is predominantly an underground activity, with all the unpleasantness and risks to health which constant working in the bowels of the earth entails. It is a dirty and extremely hazardous occupation; hundreds of miners are killed and thousands seriously injured each year.

By necessity miners and their families are a segregated group with little opportunity to associate with people of other callings and background. The location of mines requires most of them to live in isolated rural areas, without the conveniences and amenities of urban living but with few of the compensations which agricultural families enjoy. Thousands of miners' families must live in houses provided by the company, buy their food and clothing in company-owned stores,[16] and rely upon company doctors for medical services.[17] The situation of the women is especially unhappy, living, as many of them must, in drab homes covered with coal soot, having the grimy work clothes of their men to wash without running water, and having few if any recreational facilities for themselves or their children. For the miners' daughters there are

---

[15] The average miner during normal years works less than 200 days a year. Because work is always less than full-time, a prolonged strike in the industry can take place without interfering with the full annual output, although it delays delivery to customers. This, of course, is not true during wartime when an extraordinary output is required.

[16] As indicated in chap. 14, a number of states, including the coal mining state of Pennsylvania, have laws prohibiting company stores and the use of scrip, but these laws have not always been enforced. A study made by a committee appointed by the National Recovery Administration in 1935 indicated that food prices in company stores were 4 to 10½ per cent higher than in independent stores; that over half the coal companies having stores paid in scrip, and that the employees had to discount scrip for cash at a loss of from 15 to 25 per cent to pay for goods and services not furnished by the company stores. While compulsion to trade at company stores was not as common as in former years, the survey indicated that indirect pressure was not uncommon and that numbers of workers were in a chronic state of indebtedness to the stores which, of course, had first claim upon their wages.

The study also indicated that there was little doubt that the stores were run for profit and in competition with independent stores. More than one-third of the total pay rolls of the coal companies operating stores was in turn expended in the company stores. During the serious depression of 1930–1933, when independent stores suffered serious losses because of their customers' inability to pay their bills, the stores operated by coal companies had an average loss of only 1 per cent. (*Monthly Labor Review*, July, 1935, pp. 45–53.)

[17] In 1946 the United Mine Workers union negotiated a contract which calls for union-administered medical services. (See chap. 13.)

scarcely any work opportunities close at hand and most of them are compelled to leave home in order to obtain employment.

CONSTRUCTION EMPLOYMENT

The largest single group of workers outside agriculture are employed in the building and construction industry. In normal years an average of 2½ million workers are employed at the site of construction projects during the building season and an additional

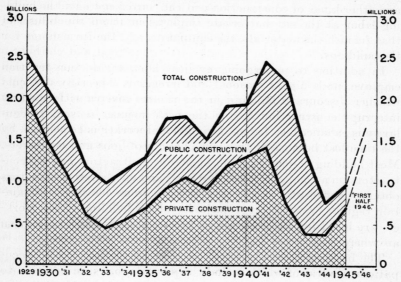

FIG. 7.   Construction Employment, 1929 to July, 1946. (Source: U. S. Bureau of Labor Statistics.)

2 or 3 million are engaged in the manufacture and distribution of materials used in construction.

The amount of employment in construction is greatly affected by both general business conditions and government policy. Private construction, both industrial and residential, is one of the first industries to feel the effects of an impending business depression and one of the last to resume full employment upon business recovery. Neither business nor private householders are inclined to embark upon building projects if economic conditions are not promising and steady income is not assured; likewise, both will carry on with existing facilities and housing until depression losses are recouped and business recovery is absolutely certain.

As indicated in Chapter 7, declines in private construction may be, and frequently are, offset by public construction programs. Within recent years it has been the policy of government, especially the federal government, to use public construction as a balance wheel to stabilize general employment. Construction is a particularly effective device for this purpose because new buildings and other kinds of construction projects utilize not only the building labor at the site but create employment in all the industries that furnish the materials, the equipment, and the furnishings for the buildings.

In addition to undergoing cyclical fluctuations, construction employment is highly seasonal and irregular. The rigors of cold weather discourage building in the winter, and rains frequently interrupt construction during the peak summer season. Irregularity is enhanced, so far as the individual worker is concerned, by the time lost because of frequent changes of jobs and employers. Most building is done through numerous contractors and subcontractors on a competitive bidding basis and only a few contractors obtain a sufficiently steady flow of work to enable them to maintain regular crews. A large majority of the building-trades workers are hired for the duration of each contract, which may mean anywhere from a few days' to several months' employment.

The building trades comprise at least 26 distinct skilled occupations, several of which include helper categories, in addition to laborers, truck drivers, and miscellaneous workers. Not all construction projects require the services of all the trades, although at least a dozen different classes of workers are usually needed for building even a comparatively modest home. Carpenters are by far the most numerous group among the skilled trades (almost half the total skilled workers), for even in non-wood construction carpenters are used to build concrete forms and install interior woodwork and hardware. All the skilled trades require prolonged apprentice training and there is little interchange of jobs between classes of workers.

Handicraft methods still prevail in the building industry, although structural steel and concrete have brought in mechanical methods, especially for large building projects. More and more wooden and metal parts—windows, stairs, cupboards, bathroom units, etc.—are being prepared and fabricated in the mill, thus reducing the amount of labor at the site. During recent years there has been some experimentation in factories with mass production of prefabricated houses which are delivered in sections and set upon foundations at the site. General adoption of prefabricated methods would, of course, cause radical changes in the volume of labor and the skill required in the building trades.

RAILROAD EMPLOYMENT

Railroads continue to be the backbone of our transportation system, although carloadings and passenger mileage have declined more than half since the First World War. In 1920 over 2 million persons were employed in the railroad industry; in 1940 slightly more than 1 million. The railroads were heavily burdened during the recent war period, but the maximum number of workers never reached 1½ million. Although the freight ton-mileage was double and the passenger mileage four times greater in 1944 compared to 1940, the increase in the number of employees was less than 40 per cent. Greater production per employee was largely due to more effective utilization of railroad track and equipment facilities, although postponed repair work and long working hours of those employed partially accounted for the relatively low employment in relation to the traffic handled during the war.[18]

Although technological improvements have been the cause of considerable labor displacement, the major cause of the downward trend in railroad employment has been the decline in the business itself. The competition of motor trucks and buses, automobiles and airplanes has considerably reduced railroad haulage. Also railroads are required to haul less coal, their largest single commodity, because of the development of hydroelectric power, the use of pipe lines for petroleum and natural gas, and the improved efficiency in the use of coal which reduces the amount needed by industry.

Railroad employment, like building employment, is predomi-

---

[18] *Monthly Labor Review,* May, 1946, p. 753.

nantly on a craft basis, with sharp lines of distinction between each category of workers. There are between 25 and 30 major types of occupations ranging from laborers to highly skilled engineers. The various occupations are classified in a number of ways, the basic distinction being the operating versus the non-operating personnel, or the train and engine service versus the maintenance-of-way, railroad shop crafts, and miscellaneous groups. The proportions of workers employed in the seven main categories are approximately as follows: train and engine service, 22 per cent; maintenance of way, 20 per cent; railroad shops, 28 per cent; professional and clerical, 16 per cent; others, 14 per cent.

There is considerable fluctuation in railroad employment aside from the long-time trends mentioned above. Haulage is directly affected by general economic conditions and employment therefore fluctuates with business cycles. There are seasonal variations also, resulting from heavier freight and passenger movements from different sections of the country at different times of the year. The permanent reduction in business has caused consolidations of railroad lines and the transfer or closing down of numerous railroad shop and terminals. The latter has meant not only loss of jobs, but sometimes serious loss of workers' savings invested in homes and other real estate, because these terminals are frequently located in isolated communities having no other businesses to absorb the shock. Employees who are dismissed because of railroad consolidation are now provided indemnities under provisions of a so-called "Washington Agreement" negotiated in 1936 between the railroad employers and unions.

MARITIME EMPLOYMENT

Although numerically not a major occupation, maritime employment is of unique importance because of the strategic position of shipping in relation to the national defense in time of war and to foreign trade in time of peace. The peculiar risks inherent in water transportation make it necessary to surround maritime employment with rules and regulations not required in other types of employment. Like seamen throughout the world, for hundreds of years seamen in this country were held by the courts to be wards of the state; it was not until 1915 that Congress extended to seamen the rights against involuntary servitude which are guaranteed by the Thirteenth Amendment. Although the severe physical discipline on vessels in former years has been abolished, seamen today are subject to rules and discipline which are peculiar to their employment. As a precaution against disloyalty, all officers and pilots and most of the crew of United States ships are required by law to be citizens of the United States. To protect passengers and property, the government has established rules regarding certification of seamen, manning scales, and investment of ships' officers with special authority and power to discipline employees.[19]

Maritime workers fall into two main categories: those who work aboard ship and those who work on the shore, that is, seafaring personnel and longshoremen. In the United States they are also divided geographically on the basis of their home port or place of work, namely, inland waterways, Atlantic coast, Pacific coast, Gulf, and Great Lakes. Deep-sea maritime workers are further classified according to the routes of their ships: those engaged in foreign trade; those in coastwise trade, up and down the Atlantic or Pacific coast; and those in intercoastal shipping between ports on the Atlantic and Pacific coasts.

Because of the irregular and casual nature of maritime work there are no accurate employment figures. It is estimated that in 1938, before the war, there were approximately 250,000 men engaged in maritime occupations, about half of whom were seamen and half longshoremen. Of those on board vessels, about 70,000 were engaged in deep-sea shipping, probably about 10,000 on inland river boats, chiefly the Ohio-Mississippi Rivers and their

---

[19] The Merchant Marine Act, as amended in 1936, provided government subsidies to cover differentials in the cost of operating U. S. merchant vessels on routes where they competed with foreign flag vessels. According to the Act, all the crew on subsidized cargo vessels, at least 90 per cent of the crew on subsidized passenger vessels, and at least 75 per cent of the crew on non-subsidized vessels must be United States citizens.

Every seaman by signing the ship's articles as a condition of employment binds himself in the following terms: ". . . the said crew agree to conduct themselves in an orderly, faithful, honest, and sober manner, and to be at all times diligent in their respective duties, and to be obedient to the lawful commands of the said master, or of any person who shall lawfully succeed him, and of their superior officers in everything relating to the vessel, and the stores and cargo thereof, whether on board, in boats, or on shore; . . ." (U. S. Department of Commerce, *Navigation Laws of the United States,* 1935, p. 74.)

tributaries, and the balance on Great Lakes vessels. Because of the freezing of the Great Lakes, few of the latter are employed during the winter.

During the war there was a great expansion in employment when the merchant marine was engaged in carrying war materials and military forces across both oceans. At the peak of wartime activities, approximately 200,000 seamen were employed on ocean-going vessels. The size of the merchant marine largely depends upon government policy with respect to ship subsidies, as well as upon tariffs and trade treaties which influence the amount and kinds of shipping which is carried on United States bottoms at any time and place. The United States came out of the recent war with 55½ million dead-weight tons of merchant shipping (about 6000 ships), which was far more than that for the rest of the world combined.

Seamen

Workers aboard ships are divided into two classes: licensed and unlicensed personnel. In the first group are the masters, mates, pilots, engineers, radio operators, and others who have special training for their work and hold government licenses. The unlicensed seamen include the stewards and cooks, the firemen and oilers in the engine room, and the able and ordinary seamen on deck. The government maintains training centers for both officers and unlicensed seamen. On a deep-sea vessel approximately 20 to 25 per cent of the crew is composed of licensed personnel. Altogether, about 60 different occupations are represented in the crew on a passenger vessel, almost as many on a freighter, and less than half as many on a tanker.

According to custom, seamen are employed for a single round-trip voyage only, although some workers are attached to one ship for several months or even years. Considerable periods of idleness may occur between jobs; this may be due to inability to find employment on another ship but it may also be due to the seamen's desire to stay ashore for a time following a protracted sea voyage. Of necessity, seamen must live on their ship and hence are away from home practically all the time they are employed. From the moment he reports for duty until the voyage ends, the seaman is "in the service of the vessel." On board ship, he lives in the quarters assigned to him; he eats the food served to him; he is on duty 8 hours per day—4 hours "on watch" at a time, with 8 hours "off watch." He cannot leave the vessel at any port without the master's permission and on duty he must obey the master no matter how hazardous the mission to which he is assigned.

Although living conditions are good on modern ships, many of the older ships offer only the barest of comforts. Frequently no medical attention is available, in which case injured or ill seamen are treated by one of the officers and put ashore at the nearest port if conditions require it. At most of the major United States and foreign ports, hotels and clubs are maintained for the convenience of seamen by the United Seamen's Service, a non-profit private service organization.

Longshoremen

Longshoring, sometimes called stevedoring, includes the work of loading and unloading ships and allied water-front occupations.[20] The longshoreman does not work alone, as an individual. In order to transfer the ship's cargo to the pier and vice versa, the workers are arranged into gangs and definite functions are allocated to the separate groups which make up the gang—one group works on the pier, the second on the deck, and the third in the hold of the ship. Although booms and winches, cranes, belt conveyers, tractors, and other mechanical appliances have considerably reduced the amount of physical hand labor necessary to load and unload a ship, the longshoremen are still required to handle, and often also to lift, individual pieces of cargo.

Longshoring is an outstanding example of casual employment, for longshoremen can get work only for the period the ships remain in port, and a varying number of ships may arrive and leave the port every day and at any hour of the day or night. A storm at sea may delay an expected arrival; certain seasons of the year bring more shipping than others. Moreover, unlike most other casual employment, longshoremen are employed not on a full day basis but by the hour and only where and when actually needed. The casual nature of the work, combined with the fact that much

---

[20] The longshoremen's unions include many warehousemen in their membership, especially those employed in warehouses located close to the docks and handling goods going from or to vessels.

of it requires little skill or experience, tends to create a situation in which any man out of work can go to the waterfront and compete with the men who regularly follow longshoring. Furthermore, the traditional method whereby individual employers hire at each pier through the "shape-up" results in a reservoir of labor sufficient to take care of each employer's maximum needs, thus increasing the total supply of workers to a number far in excess of the demands of the entire port. To an increasing extent, however, the practice of hiring through a central office at each port is replacing the traditional "shape-up" system of hiring by individual employers; through central hiring and control on the Pacific coast, longshoring has been greatly decasualized.

WHITE-COLLAR EMPLOYMENT

White-collar employment has no precise meaning but is commonly used to include those persons who receive salaries or commissions for clerical and other office duties, selling, and professional and technical work. It includes office workers in private industry and in government service, salesmen and saleswomen, teachers, nurses, actors, musicians, technicians, engineers, and members of other professions. In its broadest meaning it includes the self-employed, such as most doctors, dentists, lawyers, etc., as well as proprietors and managers; but these are excluded from the present discussion.

According to this loose definition, in 1940 about one in every four employed persons was a white-collar worker. Of the $11\frac{1}{3}$ million white-collar employees, almost 3 million were in wholesale and retail trade; 2.7 million were engaged in professional activities, including over 1 million teachers; more than 2 million were in manufacturing, business and repair services, mining, and agricultural industries; almost 1 million were employed by financial, insurance, and real estate companies; about a million were in amusement, recreation, and other miscellaneous activities. Approximately 800,000 white-collar workers were employed by transportation, telephone and telegraph, and other public utility companies, and an equal number were employees of federal, state, and local governments, excluding elected officials.

Although white-collar work is predominantly urban, a considerable number of technicians, clerks, and sales persons live and work in rural and mining communities. Those engaged in teaching, in government, cultural, and amusement activities, and in selling and finance are employed in vocations which are almost exclusively composed of persons of similar employment status. Most other white-collar workers are attached to industries in which they are in a minority and their work is incidental to the production of physical goods. Although indispensable to these business enterprises, in bookkeeping terms they are considered "overhead" or "non-productive employees."

Diverse and heterogeneous as are the activities of white-collar workers, there are some similarities in their employment conditions as compared to those in other classes of work. In general, their income is not as fluctuating or their employment as insecure as that of other workers. In a period of rising prices their salaries seldom increase as rapidly or as much, proportionately, as the wages of production workers. On the other hand, their employment is usually more stable and their income is not as drastically reduced during periods of falling prices and depressions. Many a household has had to rely upon the salary received by the schoolteacher or stenographer member of the family when the head of the family was laid off because of a factory shutdown.

White-collar employment tends to expand as industrial progress takes place. The generally higher standard of living resulting from industrial development creates a demand for more professional and semi-professional services such as teaching, medical and personal services, amusements, etc. At the same time large numbers of the population are released from hand labor and are afforded an opportunity to prepare for and pursue professional vocations.

Most significant, perhaps, is the increase in clerical, selling, and allied work caused by the complexities and ramifications of modern industry. (In 1940 over 17 per cent of the total labor force was engaged in clerical and sales activities, in contrast to only 10 per cent thirty years previously.) "Scientifically" run businesses require technicians and a great deal of paper work; many establishments now maintain scientific laboratories; and all the larger plants, at least, must have careful planning and routing of work, complicated cost accounting systems, and pay-roll records. Commercial activities expand with industrial development, causing large numbers of persons to be employed in advertising, sales, financial, and similar lines of work. Some white-collar work directly displaces hand or foot work—it is difficult to imagine how many messengers would be needed if there were no telephone or telegraph services!

Although there has been a net gain in the proportion of white-collar work during the past generation and this trend will probably continue into the future, the number of white-collar workers in some occupations will decrease. Technology does not stop at the factory door but enters the office also. Typewriters, bookkeeping machines, automatic telephones, teletypes, and many other mechanical improvements and scientific discoveries enable fewer white-collar people to do some types of work which formerly required large numbers of employees.

SELECTED REFERENCES

AGRICULTURAL LABOR

Jamieson, Stuart, *Labor Unionism in American Agriculture,* Bureau of Labor Statistics, Bulletin No. 836, Government Printing Office, Washington, 1945.

Kester, Howard, *Revolt Among the Share Croppers,* Covici-Friede, New York, 1936.

Lange, D., and Taylor, Paul S., *An American Exodus: A Record of Human Erosion,* Reynal & Hitchcock, 1939.

McWilliams, Carey, *Ill Fares the Land; Migrants and Migratory Labor in the U. S.,* Little, Brown and Company, Boston, 1942.

Parker, Carleton, *The Casual Laborer,* Harcourt, Brace & Company, Inc., New York, 1920.

Steinbeck, John, *The Grapes of Wrath,* The Viking Press, Inc., New York, 1939.

Taylor, Paul S., "Migratory Farm Labor in the U. S.," *Monthly Labor Review,* March, 1937.

COAL MINING

Berquist, F. E. *et al., Economic Survey of the Bituminous Coal Industry Under Free Competition and Code Regulation,* N.R.A., Washington, 1936.

Coleman, McAlister, *Men and Coal,* Farrar & Rinehart, Inc., New York, 1943.

Fisher, Waldo, *How Collective Bargaining Works,* Twentieth Century Fund, Inc., New York, 1942, chaps. 5, 6.

Parker, Glen L., *The Coal Industry,* American Council on Public Affairs, Washington, 1940.

Perry, Josephine, *The Coal Industry,* Longmans, Green & Company, Inc., New York, 1944.

Report of the Anthracite Coal Strike Commission, 1903, Department of Labor, Bulletin No. 46.

Tryon, F. G., *The Trend of Coal Demand,* Ohio State University Press, Columbus, 1929.

U. S. Bureau of Mines, *Mineral Resources of the U. S.,* Government Printing Office, Washington, 1917.

CONSTRUCTION

Haber, William, *Industrial Relations in the Building Industry,* Harvard University Press, Cambridge, 1930.

Hearings Before the Temporary National Economic Committee, Government Printing Office, Washington, 1940, Part II.

Schumm, George A., *The Construction Industry in the U. S.,* Bureau of Labor Statistics, Bulletin No. 786, Government Printing Office, Washington, 1944.

TRANSPORTATION

Academy of Political Science, *Transportation Development in the U. S.,* Columbia University Press, New York, 1937.

Association of American Railroads, *Quiz on Railroads and Railroading,* Washington, 1940.

Bogen, Jules I., *The Anthracite Railroads,* The Ronald Press Company, New York, 1927.

Healy, Kent T., *The Economics of Transportation in America,* The Ronald Press Company, New York, 1940.

Hinshaw, David, *Stop, Look and Listen,* Doubleday & Co., Garden City, 1932.

Hohman, Elmo P., "Maritime Labor in the U. S.," *International Labour Review,* August and September, 1938.

Miller, Sidney L., *Inland Transportation; Principles and Policies,* McGraw-Hill Book Company, Inc., New York, 1933.

Moulton, Harold G., *et al., The American Transportation Problem,* Brookings Institution, Washington, 1933.

Parmalee, Julius H., *The Modern Railway,* Longmans, Green & Company, Inc., New York, 1940.

Stern, Boris, *Cargo Handling and Longshore Labor Conditions,* Bureau of Labor Statistics, Bulletin No. 550, Government Printing Office, Washington, 1932.

U. S. Maritime Commission, *Economic Survey of the American Merchant Marine,* Government Printing Office, Washington, 1937.

3

MANUFACTURING EMPLOYMENT

MANUFACTURING IS THE PROCESSING AND FABRICATION OF THE RAW materials which are procured from nature; it includes the occupations involved in the mechanical or chemical transformation of inorganic or organic substances into new forms. The final product of a manufacturing establishment may be "finished" in the sense that it is ready for utilization or consumption, or it may be "semi-finished" to become a raw material for an establishment engaged in further processing. A manufacturing establishment is described variously as a plant, factory, shop, or mill, and characteristically uses power-driven machines.

GENERAL CHARACTERISTICS

Manufacturing industries are commonly classified into two groups: those which produce durable goods and those which produce non-durable goods. As the titles imply, the first pertains to goods which last indefinitely or for a number of years before they disappear or become obsolescent, and the second refers to perishable products or those which wear out or are quickly consumed. The line of distinction is somewhat arbitrary, and in some situations misleading. For example, glass containers and tin cans are listed under "durable" goods although most of them are soon out of use. Goods for war purposes are peculiarly "expendable"; nevertheless plants which manufactured aircraft and bombs were classified among the "durable" goods industries. In addition to the two general divisions, government and other statistical agencies

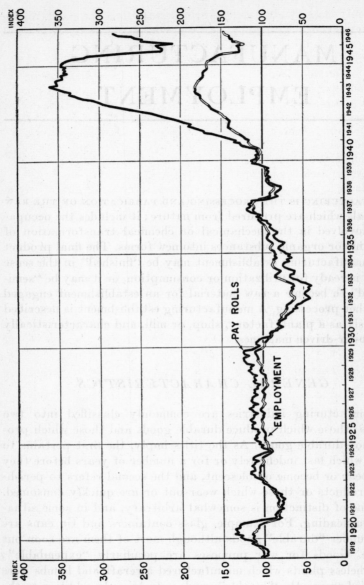

Fig. 8 *Employment and Payrolls, All Manufacturing Industries, 1919 to October, 1946. (Source: U. S. Bureau of Labor Statistics.)*

commonly classify all manufacturing establishments under twenty industry groups according to products manufactured, as follows:

Durable Goods	Non-Durable Goods
Iron and steel and their products	Textile mill products
Electrical machinery	Apparel and other finished textile
Machinery, except electrical	products
Transportation equipment, except automobiles	Leather and leather products
	Food
Automobiles and parts	Tobacco manufactures
Non-ferrous metals and their products	Paper and allied products
	Printing and publishing
Lumber and timber basic products	Chemicals and allied products
Furniture and finished lumber products	Products of petroleum and coal
	Rubber products
Stone, clay, and glass products	Miscellaneous products

In this country more persons are employed in manufacturing than in any other one activity. This has been true only within comparatively recent times. As late as 1910 more people were employed in agriculture than in manufacturing. During 1945 an average of 14 million persons in this country were employed in

TABLE 5.   Distribution of Manufacturing Wage Earners According to Size of Establishments, 1939[1]

Size of Group				Per Cent of Total Establishments	Per Cent of Total Wage Earners
Total				100.0%	100.0%
No	wage earners			4.5	
1–5	"	"		41.2	2.6
6–20	"	"		26.6	6.9
21–50	"	"		12.8	9.7
51–100	"	"		6.5	10.7
101–250	"	"		5.2	18.6
251–500	"	"		2.0	16.1
501–1000	"	"		0.8	13.0
1001–2500	"	"		0.3	11.9
2501 and over	"	"		0.1	10.5

[1] 1940 Census of Manufactures, vol. i, pp. 119, 120.

manufacturing industries, of whom more than 12 million were production workers and almost 2 million were managers, supervisors,
office, and other white-collar workers. Of the production workers,
about 7 million were employed in durable goods and 5 million in
non-durable goods industries.

The 1939 census indicated that 97 per cent of all manufacturing establishments had fewer than 250 wage earners on their pay
rolls, but that the total number of workers employed in these
relatively small plants included less than half of all manufacturing workers. Approximately 52 per cent of the total workers in

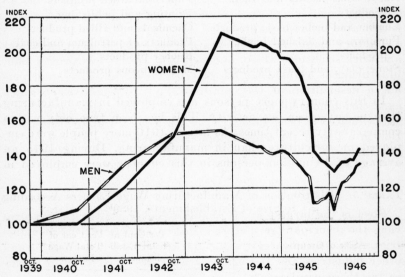

Fig. 9. *Manufacturing Wage Earners, by Sex, October, 1939, to
September, 1946. October, 1939 = 100. (Source: U. S. Bureau of
Labor Statistics.)*

manufacturing were employed in the 3 per cent of the establishments which had more than 250 workers on their pay rolls, and
over 10 per cent of all factory workers were employed in establishments which had 2500 or more employees. This trend toward
concentration of employment in large plants was accelerated during the war. In 1946 it was estimated that more than 60 per cent

of all factory workers were employed in 2 per cent of the total manufacturing plants in the country.

Many small as well as large plants are not independently owned and operated but are branch plants of a centrally administered corporation. Considerably more than half of all factory wage earners in the country are employed by plural-unit organizations, that is, in branch plants of large corporations. During the decade preceding World War II the proportion of manufacturing workers employed in single-unit or independent plants declined approximately 23 per cent. This trend toward centrally administered, multiple-plant operations is of the utmost significance in collective bargaining procedures and employer-labor relations, as is indicated in later chapters.

Factory employment includes a great variety of occupations and work situations which no general statements concerning manufacturing as a whole can adequately reveal. Space does not permit a description of the manifold types of employment which exist throughout all manufacturing; hence the following is necessarily limited to brief summaries of the general employment situation in a few of the more important or especially significant industries.

STEEL

Steel is the largest of the manufacturing industries and provides the principal raw material used in a great variety of industries. As a consequence, it has a far-reaching influence upon many other industries and is commonly used as a barometer for indicating the general economic condition throughout the country.

The term "steel industry" includes both the making of steel and the manufacture of steel products. Steel production plants, which are commonly referred to as the "basic" or "heavy" iron and steel industry, differ with respect to their degree of integration. The fully integrated plants have blast furnaces for manufacturing pig iron, steel-making furnaces, and rolling mills. Non-integrated plants buy the pig iron or the raw steel and operate rolling mills. Most of the fully integrated companies also operate their own iron and coal mines—so-called "captive" mines.

As a result of the great investment required in plants and machinery as well as the economies of large-scale mass production, a very few large companies dominate the basic or heavy branch of the industry. Ten companies[2] have almost 80 per cent of the steel-making capacity in the country; the U. S. Steel Corporation alone has more than 30 per cent of the total. The industry has tended to concentrate in Pennsylvania, West Virginia, and Ohio where coal and iron are easily accessible; but within recent years large plants have been opened in Birmingham, Alabama, and in the Chicago-Gary area, and during the war several steel plants were established in the Far West. The manufacture and fabrication of steel products are more widely scattered geographically than is steelmaking, and ownership is not confined to a few large companies.

Employment Conditions

The entire steel industry, including the making of steel and steel products,[3] normally employs slightly more than 1 million persons, although during World War II the capacity of the industry was increased about 30 per cent and employment rose to 1.7 million.[4] Just prior to the outbreak of the war the automatic continuous sheet rolling mill was widely introduced and is leading to drastic changes throughout the industry. Older plants are being closed and new mills with the improved technology are being opened in other communities, causing considerable labor dislocation. In addition to permanent labor displacement due to technological developments, steelworkers suffer irregularity of employment as a result of drastic fluctuations in business. Like other durable goods manufacturing, the steel business is dependent upon orders received from other businesses and it is therefore very sensitive to the ups and downs of general prosperity and depressions.

---

[2] In addition to U. S. Steel, they are Jones and Laughlin, Wheeling, Crucible, Bethlehem, Republic, Youngstown Sheet & Tube, Inland, National, and the American Rolling Mill Companies.

[3] The census includes under "steel products" heating equipment and boiler shop products, tinware and wire, hand tools, cutlery, and general hardware. It does not include machinery, automobiles, and other transportation equipment.

[4] In 1944 steel production reached an all-time high of 89½ million tons, compared with the peacetime record year of slightly less than 67 million tons in 1940. (Automotive Council for War Production, August, 1945.)

The types of occupations involved in the making of steel range from the highly skilled rollers and melters to common laborers. The semi-skilled and unskilled jobs are in the majority; fewer than one-fourth of the occupations are now rated as skilled work and technical changes are tending toward further reduction of the more skilled jobs. On the other hand, technical improvements such as lifting and conveying machines in the furnace operations have replaced much heavy physical labor. In the steel products branch of the industry much of the work involves the use of delicate precision tools. In the smaller plants all-round skilled machinists are used for this work, but in the larger plants the work tends to be subdivided into numerous semi-skilled occupations.

Although work in steel plants is not as monotonous as assembly-line work, much of the labor is dirty and hot and is performed in drafty rooms filled with noxious gases, smoke, and dust. In plants having the continuous sheet mill process, the work is less arduous and the working environment much cleaner. Because of the noise and the great mass and weight of much of the materials and equipment which are handled, employment in steel mills involves hazards, although accidents have been greatly reduced through safety programs. Steelmaking is a round-the-clock process and furnaces are seldom banked so long as there is steel to be produced. Until recent years blast furnace workers were employed on a 7-day-week schedule, some working on a 2-shift, 12-hour-day basis; others on a 3-shift, 8-hour-day basis. At present the 8-hour-day, 5-day-week shifts prevail, with individual workers rotating shifts, one week on the day shift, the next week on the afternoon shift, and the third week on the midnight shift.

The large size of mills required for the making of steel, together with the advantage of having them near railroad facilities and coal and iron supplies, has caused many steel plants to be located in outlying communities where company towns have been established similar to company towns in coal mining regions. In some instances the steel companies have owned or controlled entire towns; in most instances the company's influence is less direct but nevertheless dominant because the steel mill is the only place of employment in the community.

AUTOMOBILES

Motor vehicle manufacturing, a giant industry developed during the 20th century, has become a popular symbol of the assembly-line technique of mass production. It is the largest single consumer of steel products[5] and, like steel manufacturing, automobile assembly plants require large capital investments and thus tend to be concentrated among a few large companies. However, motor vehicle manufacturing is the final link in a chain of industrial processes which involves the assembling of thousands of parts,[6] and a large proportion of these parts are produced by small scattered concerns on a contract basis for the large automobile companies. The Ford Motor Company, which is unique in its high degree of self-sufficiency, depends upon outside sources for at least half its materials and parts, even though it operates its own lumber, steel and glass plants, ore fields and rubber plants, and even a railroad.

Although fewer than a dozen corporations[7] produce most of the automobiles that are now being manufactured, a majority of the companies operate numerous plants located in different areas. Michigan, more particularly Detroit, has always been the center of the industry. At least 60 per cent of all automobile workers are employed in Michigan plants, with another 15 per cent in Ohio and Indiana plants.

Approximately one-half million persons are employed in the automobile and parts industry. During the war automobile plants

[5] According to the 1939 census, the motor vehicle industry had a capital investment of 1.3 billion dollars and produced 5 billion dollars' worth of products. The industry consumed 18 per cent of the steel industry's annual capacity, 80 per cent of the total weight of passenger cars and commercial vehicles being represented by various kinds of steel. (Automotive Council for War Production, August, 1945.)

[6] One authority describes a car as "an assembly of more than 15,000 parts held together by a variety of devices, including nuts, bolts, cotter pins, screws, nails, tacks, rivets, welding, brazing, soldering, adhesives, clamps and air pressure (in tires)." Other authorities, however, say there are about 7000 parts in a modern passenger car. The difference in figures is due to difference in definition of a "part," the larger number listing every different type and size of a screw, for example, as one part. (Automobile Facts, January, 1946.)

[7] In 1940 the Ford Motor Company produced about 20 per cent of the total passenger cars; General Motors, which includes a consolidation of a half dozen companies, produced 40 per cent; Chrysler, 25 per cent.

were converted to the manufacture of many other products—aircraft engines and parts, cannon and ammunition, bombs, tanks, containers, and a host of other ordnance equipment—and employment reached a peak of 750,000. Employment in the industry is seasonal, with plants closing down several weeks or months each year while they get ready to manufacture new models of cars.

Because of the minute subdivision of work in assembly plants, the labor is highly specialized and most of it is semi-skilled or unskilled. A majority of the workers are machine tenders and assemblers who perform specified tasks as material flows by them on a conveyer line. Even in the tool and die room the work has been subdivided, largely as a result of war production, so that relatively fewer all-round tool and die craftsmen are needed than before the war. The conveyer system lends itself to the speed-up which has been a controversial issue between employers and workers for many years. Speed-up on an assembly line can be easily accomplished either by mechanically adjusting the lines to move faster or by reducing the number of men working on the line so that each one will have to do more work.

RUBBER

Prior to World War II, the rubber industry was correctly termed the rubber *products* industry since it was largely confined to the processing of raw rubber into manufactured goods. When the war with Japan shut off the supply of rubber from the East Indies, the industry was forced into the making of synthetic rubber. Like the steel industry, the rubber industry now includes the making of rubber as well as the manufacture of rubber products. Although rubber products embrace a wide variety of goods, two-thirds of the entire value of the rubber output goes into tires and tubes; and employment therefore is dependent to a great extent upon the automobile industry.

The rubber industry is largely dominated by four companies[8] which produce at least three-fourths of the tires and tubes manufactured in the entire country. Since the beginning of the rubber industry in the 1870's, Akron, Ohio, has been the world's tire-

[8] Goodyear, U. S. Rubber, Firestone, and Goodrich. In addition to other tire companies, several chemical and petroleum companies make synthetic rubber.

making capital.[9] Until a few years ago more than half the rubber workers in this country were employed in plants located in Akron, but during the war a number of new plants were established, chiefly in the South and West, and employment is now more widely scattered.

Important as the rubber industry is, the volume of employment is comparatively low because of extreme mechanization. During the ten-year period 1921–1931 technological changes doubled the number of tires produced per man-hour, despite the improvements in size and weight of tires. If the 1921 methods had continued, 43,000 additional tire workers would have been required to make the number of tires produced in 1931.[10] Currently, slightly more than 200,000 production workers are employed in the entire rubber industry, including tires and other rubber products.

The processing of both crude and synthetic rubber involves a considerable amount of skilled labor, but the manufacture of rubber products is now so highly mechanized that semi-skilled and unskilled workers perform most of the tasks. Considerable skill is required of the tire builder when the various parts of the tire are assembled or put together by hand on a drum, but some factories use the assembly-line method of building tires in which each member of a crew of workers has a specialized task which he can learn to do in a few days. Formerly, the curing or vulcanizing of tires (heating under pressure so that the tires will withstand changes in temperature and humidity) required a great deal of strength and endurance, with the men working in "pits"; however, mechanization has eliminated most of the physical discomforts in this process, although physical strength is still required in the handling of heavy tires.

GLASS

Although not one of the major industries in volume of employment, modern glass manufacturing is of interest because it exem-

---

[9] Originally there was no natural reason for Akron to become the rubber center. In 1870 Benjamin F. Goodrich was persuaded by Akron businessmen to move his small rubber factory from Hastings-on-Hudson, N. Y. The success of his venture persuaded others to follow suit. With the great automobile boom in nearby cities, Akron proved to be in a favorable location to meet the demand for tires.

[10] *Monthly Labor Review*, December, 1932, p. 1258.

plifies the transition of an ancient handicraft into mass machine production. The making of glass is one of the oldest of occupations and in ancient and medieval times glassworkers were held in high esteem, second only to painters and sculptors, for their artistic abilities. For thousands of years[11] there was very little change in the method of glassmaking, although improvements were made in the furnaces and coal was substituted for wood; later gas replaced coal as a fuel. During a quarter of a century (1900–1925) glassmaking changed from an almost 100 per cent hand process to a completely mechanized industry. Simultaneously there was a vast expansion as a result of the increased needs for glass from the electrical (light bulbs), automobile (window glass), and food (container) industries.

The glass industry has three major divisions: flat glass, which includes ordinary window glass and plate glass, most of the latter being used in automobiles; pressed and blown (flint) glass, used for tableware; and containers or glass bottles. Most of the glass now being manufactured is produced in Pennsylvania, West Virginia, Ohio, Indiana, and Illinois, in localities which are close to fuel supplies and to the markets for the finished goods. Concentration in ownership has accompanied mechanization and a large proportion of all the glass now manufactured is produced by a half dozen companies.[12]

Prior to mechanization, glass blowing was a highly skilled occupation. For bottle making, the expert reached into the furnace with his pipe, got a gob of the sticky molten glass, pulled it out, dropped it into a mold, and then shaped the bottle by using his lung power and the manipulative skill of his fingers to twirl the

---

[11] The manufacture of glass probably originated in Egypt and from there spread throughout the ancient world. After the downfall of Rome the secret of glassmaking was lost for almost a thousand years until Venetian glassmakers rediscovered the art. In 1900 the process of blowing bottles and other glassware was essentially the same as that used in Egypt 3500 years previously.

[12] About 90 per cent of the flat glass is produced by the Libby-Owens-Ford, Pittsburgh Plate Glass, and American Window Glass companies; about a dozen companies, including Corning Glass Works, produce the bulk of the pressed and blown ware; 40 per cent of the containers are manufactured in plants operated by the Owens-Illinois Company, and most of the other companies producing glass bottles are licensed by the Hartford-Empire Company which controls the patent rights to the equipment used.

pipe. Window glass was made by blowing huge cylinders which were then split and flattened into sheet form.

The blower's job required great skill and lung power and he was exposed to the intense heat and gases from the furnaces as well as to the danger of silicosis. Present-day methods of production have removed much of this unpleasantness and danger. It has also left few skilled workers in the industry but has eliminated the use of child labor—the young boy helpers who made up almost half the work force in hand shops. The mechanical revolution in glassmaking has naturally resulted in a greatly increased output per worker. Expansion of business, however, has enabled the industry to employ more workers than in the days of hand methods. In 1900 about 53,000 wage earners were employed in the glass industry; currently almost 100,000 production workers are employed.

MACHINERY

Machinery is the basis of all modern industry. The transition from hand tools to power-driven machines marked the beginning of the Industrial Revolution and the factory system of production. The making of machinery is a fabricating process, but machines, in turn, are used to make the metals and parts of which they themselves are made. So far as their ultimate use is concerned, machines fall into three general categories:[13] those which are used in the making of other machines; those which are used in the manufacture of other commodities; and those which are used by consumers—office, farm, and household machines and appliances, including radios.

Machines which are used to make other machines are commonly called machine tools and primarily have to do with forming and cutting metal; they are the lathes, drills, grinders, planers, milling machines, etc. Machines used in the manufacture of other goods may be general-purpose machines such as engines and turbines, pumps, air and gas compressors, power transmission equipment, etc. An increasing number of machines, however, are single-pur-

---

[13] This is a somewhat different basis of classification than that used by the census; it incorporates both the machinery and the electrical machinery industry groups which the census uses.

pose machines—for example, textile machinery, shoe machinery, printing machines, mining and construction machinery, and numerous other machines made especially for particular industries.

Machines, of course, are of all sizes, from tiny bench tools and appliances which can be lifted with one hand, to large milling machines and immense water turbines. The types of employment vary as much as the kinds of machinery manufactured. In spite of much subdivision or dilution of jobs, machine shops and fabricating plants employ many all-round machinists, tool and die makers, pattern makers, metal polishers, molders and foundrymen, and other craftsmen who have spent years in learning their jobs. On the other hand, there are many semi-skilled and unskilled occupations, especially in the electrical equipment industries where there are mass-production and assembly-line operations and where many women are employed to do minute, specialized tasks.

During normal times approximately 1¼ million workers are employed in the various machinery industries; during World War II there was a great expansion in production and employment reached a peak of 2 million. Employment is widely dispersed, for almost every community has at least one machine shop for repairs and the making of small parts. The bulk of the industry, however, is in the Great Lakes region, especially in Illinois and Wisconsin where some of the largest machinery manufacturing plants in the world are located. Most of the shoe and textile machinery is manufactured in New England and the Atlantic seaboard states, and plants producing other electrical machinery of various kinds are located in New York, Pennsylvania, and elsewhere in the East and Middle West.

TEXTILES

Spinning and weaving are among the oldest of human occupations, but for thousands of years there were no essential changes in the methods used. The primitive instruments for spinning were a pole or distaff on which the raw fiber was fastened, and a slender shaft of wood known as the spindle upon which the fibers were twirled. For weaving, warp threads were tied to two horizontal poles attached to trees or upright posts and the woof (weft) was inserted by means of a pointed stick. The spinning wheel, intro-

duced in Europe in the 6th century from India, was the first mechanical device; later came the hand loom which was used for
hundreds of years throughout Europe and in the American colonies.

The Industrial Revolution had its beginnings in Great Britain
in the textile industry. The first use of power machines was in the
making of textiles and this industry was the first to substitute the
factory system for household manufacturing.[14] During a fifty-
year period in the middle of the 18th century one machine after
another was invented which revolutionized the process of textile
making. Some were designed to substitute mechanical for manual
power, others to improve and speed up the spinning and weaving
operations.[15] For a hundred years after these 18th-century inventions there were no fundamental changes in the process of textile
manufacturing. During the past fifty years, following the introduction of the battery loom[16] in 1895, there have been many new
developments to provide greater automaticity and speed of operations as well as better quality of products. Probably the most important are the inventions for automatically stopping the loom
when a warp breaks, for they make it possible to increase greatly
the number of looms a weaver can tend. At the present time one
weaver sometimes operates more than 100 looms.

According to the type of fiber used, there are three major
branches in the textile industry: cotton, which provides almost 80
per cent of the total fiber consumption; wool, which provides about
10 per cent; and rayon and silk, the former of which now includes
almost 10 per cent, and the latter less than 1 per cent, of the
total fiber used in the American textile industry. Almost 40 per

---

[14] In these early factories about half the textile workers were children. The
deplorable child labor conditions existing at that time is indicated by the British factory laws enacted in the early 1800's which sought to improve conditions.
The first act, for example, forbade binding out children under 9 years of age to
employers, restricted labor to 12 hours a day, and prohibited night work for
minors.

[15] The more outstanding of these numerous British inventions were the Kay
flying shuttle and "drop box," which permitted the use of several shuttles with
different colored yarns, the Hargreaves spinning jenny, the Arkwright water
frame, the Crompton mule, the Cartwright power loom.

[16] The battery loom automatically ejects the empty bobbin from the shuttle
and inserts a fresh bobbin during the fraction of a second in which the shuttle
is at rest between trips across the loom.

cent of all textiles goes into non-clothing items such as twine, tires, awnings, carpets, etc.

A comparatively few textile plants are fully integrated; that is, they perform all the processes from the preparation of the raw fiber through the final finishing of the textile fabrics. Half the cotton textile mills do only spinning or only weaving, and even plants which do both operations rely very largely upon converting plants for the dyeing and finishing processes. The manufacture of rayon and nylon[17] is entirely separate from the production of rayon or nylon goods.

There is specialization also in the kinds of processing done. There are hosiery plants and mills producing knitted products of various kinds, woolen goods mills, and mills producing worsted goods. Worsted goods are tightly spun and closely woven materials produced from long fibers combed from virgin wools, and woolen goods are loosely woven with a rough surface and are made from short fibers and reworked or "shoddy" wool. Preparatory to spinning, the individual fibers which comprise the woolen yarn are crossed and intermixed in one major process. The manufacture of worsted yarn for either knitting or weaving is somewhat more complicated, inasmuch as the wool fibers must lie parallel to each other, be of relatively even lengths, and be stretched or drawn prior to spinning. This involves three major processes—carding, combing, and drawing. These added processes, of course, require the use of additional labor and machinery not necessary in the manufacture of woolens.

Textile manufacturing is highly decentralized. Although there are several comparatively large companies, a few concerns do not dominate the industry as is the case in the so-called "heavy" industries. There are more than 1000 cotton mills and at least 700 woolen plants, in addition to the several hundred plants devoted exclusively to printing, dyeing, and finishing. A few large companies make most of the rayon and nylon,[18] but there are over a thousand silk and rayon throwing (yarn and thread) and weaving mills.

---

[17] The census classifies the making of rayon and nylon filament under chemical industries.

[18] In 1941 the American Viscose Corporation produced 46 per cent of all synthetic yarns, duPont 10 per cent, and Industrial Rayon 8 per cent. Nylon is a duPont product introduced in 1939.

Textile Employment

From colonial times until the latter part of the 19th century most cotton mills were concentrated in New England where there were abundant water power and shipping facilities for the receipt of raw cotton from the South. New England was also the center of woolen manufacturing, although many woolen plants were also located in New York, Pennsylvania, and New Jersey. Paterson, N. J., became known as the "silk city," but many throwing mills have been established in the mining and other rural communities of Pennsylvania and Maryland, where there were plentiful supplies of female labor.

Sixty years ago cotton textile manufacturing began to move South; by 1925 the South's cotton textile capacity equaled that of New England and at present there are three times as many spindles in southern mills as in New England mills. There are various reasons for this great southern expansion. In addition to the economies involved in bringing cotton mills to the cotton fields, there were also economies resulting from the lower taxes and wages in the southern states. Also companies found it easier to install the latest and most efficient machinery in entirely new localities where there was no labor resistance to innovations which reduced the number of jobs.

In many industries the labor displacement caused by technological advancement has been compensated by expansion of the industry. This has not been true in the textile industry where the long-time trend in volume of production has remained about stationary and mechanical improvements, therefore, have caused a reduction in the total amount of employment. In 1939 employment in all branches of textile manufacturing was 8 per cent less than during the early 1920's, and during the busy months of 1945 it was 10 per cent less than in 1939. In spite of the tendency toward reduction in the labor force, however, the textile industry furnishes a large amount of employment. Over 1 million wage earners are normally employed in the various branches of the industry.

Because textile manufacturing is highly mechanized, many of the occupations require only a few days or weeks to learn, although a considerable degree of skill and experience is required to operate the spinning and weaving machines. Most textile mill employment involves dexterity of hands and arms, good vision, coordination of movement, and work at high speeds. In general, although the rooms are well lighted, they are kept humid and lint is usually prevalent in the air, particularly in the wool carding room. The weavers generally work under rather unpleasant conditions because of the noise and vibration of the looms; in the dye house there is usually some odor from the dyestuffs and the floors are generally wet. In nearly all the jobs, workers are required to stand and some jobs require a considerable amount of walking.

CLOTHING

Garments

Ready-to-wear garments are produced in a dozen or more different industries all of which, however, have a common technology which also designates the predominant type of employment, namely, "needle trades." Until about fifty years ago most men's, women's, and children's clothing was made in the home or in the corner tailor shop where the only tools were a pair of scissors, a needle, a foot-power sewing machine, and a pressing iron. In the modern clothing factory there are high-speed electrically driven cutting devices which cut through thick layers of materials, hundreds of specialized forms of power sewing machines, some of which make as many as four or five thousand stitches a minute, and special pressing machines for each part of a garment. The work is highly subdivided. There are 50 or 60 separate operations in making a coat, for instance, and as many as 200 different workers participate in the making of a single suit.

Most of the manufacture of coats, suits, and dresses is concentrated in a few areas. Over one-fourth of those employed in the making of men's clothing and almost two-thirds of those making women's clothing are located in the New York City area. Chicago, Philadelphia, and St. Louis are also centers for the manufacture of both men's and women's clothing and a considerable amount of men's clothing is made in Baltimore, Rochester, N. Y., Cleveland, Boston, and Cincinnati. Cotton dresses and work clothes are also made in numerous small towns scattered throughout the country, especially in the South.

Although highly concentrated geographically, the clothing industries are notable for their wide diffusion in ownership and management. There are eight or ten comparatively large companies in the men's clothing branch, but they employ only about 10 per cent of the total workers. Practically all women's garments and most of the clothing for men are made in thousands of small shops employing from a dozen to several hundred workers. Aside from a few of the large integrated plants, mostly in men's clothing, garment manufacturing is predominantly under the jobber-contractor system, a situation which creates unique problems in labor relations and wage setting.

Under the contract system the patterns are designed and the materials are cut in the factory or "loft" of the jobber-manufacturer and the pieces are then sent out to numerous contract shops for completion, the finished parts being returned to the jobber who handles the selling. Each of these small contract shops is highly specialized, making a single part of a garment—for instance, a coat or a vest—and some of them specialize in particular operations such as buttonholes, trimmings of particular types, etc.

Numerically, the contractors are by far the most important employing group, but they in turn receive their orders from the jobbers; the latter, therefore, actually control wages and working conditions. Because of the severe competitive bidding among the numerous contractors, the jobber is able to play one against the other, thus frequently forcing the contractors to reduce wages to stay in business. A few years ago "contract shops" were almost synonymous with "sweatshops." This condition has been greatly improved since labor unions have grown sufficiently strong to negotiate uniform agreements and methods for price settlement, as well as regulations pertaining to jobber-contractor relationships which alleviate the cutthroat competition among the contractors.

Normally, about 800,000 workers are employed in the ready-to-wear garment industry, although employment fluctuates with the seasons as well as with the general purchasing ability of consumers. For those employed in the making of women's clothing, there is additional irregularity of employment caused by frequent changes in styles and consequent shifts in kinds of operations and processing required, as well as by turnover in plant management and the moving of shops to other locations. Although clothing manufacture is highly mechanized, employment involves much more than the mere tending of automatically run machines, for in spite of all the gadgets to minimize the need for human judgment and skill, there is still need for close attention and dexterity on the part of the machine operator.

Shoes

Clothing, of course, includes many other items in addition to garments made from cloth—hosiery and other knit goods, fur coats, hats made of various materials, rubber raincoats and boots, and, most important, leather shoes. Each of these industries has its own peculiar employment conditions and problems, but here we limit ourselves to a few comments about shoe manufacturing.

For thousands of years, until the middle of the 19th century, shoes were made in the home by itinerent cobblers[19] or in little shops where a master shoemaker and his apprentices worked with hand tools consisting of knife, curved awl, needle, pincers, hammer, lapstone, a tub of water to wet-up the leather, and shoe lasts of various sizes and shapes. In 1835 a leather rolling machine was invented which eliminated the lapstone and hammer. During the 1850's the sewing machine was adapted to leather sewing for stitching the uppers of shoes. A revolutionary change came a few years later when the McKay and Goodyear machines were invented to stitch together the upper and bottom parts of the shoes.[20] Following these basic innovations there have been many inventions to speed up the process and improve the quality of shoemaking. In a modern shoe factory there are hundreds of different kinds of machines; not all of them are used on every pair of shoes, however, for different machines are used for the various grades and styles. Nevertheless, every pair of shoes passes through no less than a hundred different hands in the process of manufacture.

A unique feature of the shoe industry, and one which has far-reaching effects upon its economy, is the machinery leasing system. Unlike most other manufacturers who buy their machines, shoe manufacturers rent theirs, mostly on a royalty basis, from two or three shoe machinery manufacturing companies who hold

---

[19] In England the term "cordwainer" was used instead of shoemaker. This was because the leather came from Cordoba, Spain. "Cobeler," derived also from this name, later came to mean repairer (cobbler) of shoes.

[20] The McKay machine reduced the cost of stitching from 75 cents to 3 cents a pair and thus made possible the stitching of the cheapest shoes which formerly had been pegged.

patent rights on practically all the machinery required in shoe-making. The renting of machines materially reduces the amount of capital needed to operate a shoe plant and encourages many persons to enter the business who are soon compelled to close. With little to lose, enterprising individuals establish new plants more on hope than on sound business needs, and to attract initial orders they sell their products below the cost of production. This, of course, causes unemployment in the older established firms and after a season or two the workers in the new plants are thrown out of employment when these collapse.[21]

Shoemaking, like other clothing manufacturing, tends to be concentrated in certain geographical regions. Shoemaking started during early colonial times in Massachusetts, and for many years Brockton, Lynn, and Haverhill were the chief centers, although a number of plants were established in New York and Philadelphia early in the 19th century. During the past fifty years shoe manufacturing has migrated and expanded in two directions: from large urban centers to surrounding small communities, and from the eastern seaboard states to the Middle West. Almost 90 per cent of the 200,000 normally employed shoemakers are located in nine states: Massachusetts 22 per cent, Maine and New Hampshire 15 per cent, New York and Pennsylvania 20 per cent, and the Middle West states of Ohio, Illinois, Wisconsin, and Missouri 33 per cent. Of the remaining, most are employed in recently established plants in Tennessee, Kentucky, and California.

Shoe plants tend to be comparatively small in size. Almost 10 per cent of all shoe workers are employed in plants which have fewer than 100 employees, and 60 per cent are in plants which have 100 to 500 employees. While a majority of these plants are independently owned, several large shoe corporations own and operate many branch plants.[22] In spite of all the machinery used

---

[21] The average life of all shoe firms that did business in the thirty-year period ending in 1935 was only six years. Since many companies operated continuously, the turnover of the unstable plants was much greater. (H. B. Davis, *Harvard Business Review,* vol. xvii, No. 3, p. 332.)

[22] The International Shoe Corporation of St. Louis, the largest shoe manufacturer in the world, operates no less than 45 branch plants in different towns in Missouri and Illinois, besides several in New Hampshire and Kentucky. The Brown Shoe Company, with headquarters also in St. Louis, the Endicott-Johnson Co. in New York State, and the General Shoe Corporation in Tennessee, are among other large companies with a number of branch plants.

in the industry, many of the jobs require considerable skill and most of them require great precision and some degree of judgment. The cutter not only must know how to use a hand knife or operate a cutting machine, but must also use judgment in placing the patterns on the skins of leather; the topstitcher and vamper must not only operate stitching machines with speed and precision but simultaneously fit different parts of the shoe together.

SELECTED REFERENCES[23]

GENERAL

Alderfer, E. B., and Michl, H. E., *Economics of American Industry,* McGraw-Hill Book Company, Inc., New York, 1942.

Bliss, C. A., *The Structure of Manufacturing Production,* National Bureau of Economic Research, New York, 1939.

Bogart, E. L., and Landon, C. E., *Modern Industry,* Longmans, Green & Company, Inc., New York, 1927.

Bowden, Witt, *The Industrial History of the United States,* Adelphi Co., New York, 1930.

Clark, V. S., *History of Manufactures in the U. S.,* McGraw-Hill Book Company, Inc., New York, 1929.

Glover, J. G., Cornell, W. B., et al., *The Development of American Industries,* Prentice-Hall, Inc., New York, 1941.

Keir, M., *Manufacturing Industries in America,* The Ronald Press Company, New York, 1928.

Millis, Harry A., et al., *How Collective Bargaining Works,* Twentieth Century Fund, Inc., New York, 1942.

Shannon, F. A., *America's Economic Growth,* The Macmillan Company, New York, 1940.

Ware, C. F., and Means, G. C., *The Modern Economy in Action,* Harcourt, Brace & Company, Inc., New York, 1936.

AUTOMOBILE

Dunn, Robert W., *Labor and Automobiles,* International Publishers Co., Inc., New York, 1929.

Epstein, Ralph C., *The Automobile Industry; Its Economic and Commercial Development,* A. W. Shaw Co., Chicago, 1928.

[23] The literature for each of the industries is too voluminous to cite here. For additional references on particular industries, the student is referred to his library card catalogue. The periodicals and special reports of the Departments of Labor and Commerce, as well as those of the trade associations and labor unions, provide current information.

Kennedy, Edward D., *The Automobile Industry,* Reynal & Hitchcock, New York, 1941.

McPherson, William H., *Labor Relations in the Automobile Industry,* Brookings Institution, Washington, 1940.

CLOTHING

Crawford, M. C., *Ways of Fashion,* G. P. Putnam's Sons, New York, 1941.

Davis, H. B., *Shoes: The Workers and the Industry,* International Publishers Co., Inc., New York, 1940.

Norton, T. S., *Trade Union Policies in the Massachusetts Shoe Industry, 1919–1929,* Columbia University Press, New York, 1932.

Seidman, Joel, *The Needle Trades,* Farrar & Rinehart, New York, 1942.

Teper, Lazare, *The Women's Garment Industry,* International Ladies' Garment Workers' Union, New York, 1937.

U. S. Shoe Machinery Corporation, *How Modern Shoes Are Made,* Boston, 1936.

Zaretz, C. E., *The Amalgamated Clothing Workers of America,* Ancon Publishing Co., New York, 1934.

RUBBER

Firestone, H. S., and Crowther, Samuel, *Men and Rubber,* Doubleday, Doran & Company, Inc., New York, 1926.

Holt, E. G., and Barker, P. W., *Rubber Industry of the U. S., 1839–1939,* U. S. Department of Commerce, Trade Promotion Series No. 197, Washington, 1939.

McKenney, Ruth, *Industrial Valley,* Harcourt, Brace & Company, Inc., New York, 1939.

Perry, Josephine, *The Rubber Industry,* Longmans, Green & Company, Inc., New York, 1941.

Roberts, Harold S., *The Rubber Workers,* Harper & Brothers, New York, 1944.

Ufford, Charles W., *Occupations in Rubber,* Science Research Associates, Chicago, 1942.

STEEL

Camp, J. M., and Francis, C. B., *The Making, Shaping and Treating of Steel,* Carnegie-Illinois Steel Corp., Pittsburgh, 1940.

Daugherty, Carroll R., de Chazeau, M. G., and Stratton, S. S., *The Economics of the Iron and Steel Industry,* McGraw-Hill Book Company, Inc., New York, 1937.

Leyson, B. W., *Careers in the Steel Industry*, E. P. Dutton & Co., Inc., New York, 1945.

Parker, Clark M., *Steel in Action*, Jaques Cattell Press, Lancaster, 1943.

Perry, Josephine, *The Steel Industry*, Longmans, Green & Company, Inc., New York, 1943.

TEXTILES

Avram, M. H., *The Rayon Industry*, D. Van Nostrand Company, Inc., New York, 1929.

Cole, A. H., *The American Wool Manufacture*, Harvard University Press, Cambridge, 1926.

Lahne, Herbert J., *The Cotton Mill Worker*, Farrar & Rinehart, New York, 1944.

Lemert, B. F., *The Cotton Textile Industry of the Southern Appalachian Piedmont*, University of North Carolina Press, Chapel Hill, 1933.

Michl, H. E., *The Textile Industries*, The Textile Foundation, Washington, 1938.

4

LABOR PRODUCTIVITY

FOR THOUSANDS OF YEARS THE FOOD, CLOTHING, AND A LIMITED number of other necessities and luxuries used by man were produced by human labor with the aid of simple hand tools and domestic animals. Transportation and communication, the life line of modern industry, were practically the same at the turn of the 19th century as they were at the dawn of history. On land, people and goods were hauled by man or beast, and on water by the wind or oarsmen. So far as the long history of mankind is concerned, the substitution of mechanical energy for animate labor is relatively recent—a development of the past 150 years.

The impact of this change upon the whole environment of human life has caused immeasurable adjustments in the economic and political balances of nations and the cultural patterns of peoples. It can safely be said that the greater part of all the social and political changes which have already occurred and are now taking place have been precipitated by the introduction of mechanical power and subsequent mechanical inventions and chemical discoveries. The effects of these technological developments upon all aspects of our individual lives and group relationships are challenging subjects, but many of them lie within the realm of the other social sciences. The present discussion is confined to the impact of recent technological developments upon volume of production and employment.

GENERAL EFFECTS OF IMPROVED PRODUCTIVITY

In the preceding chapters only a few of the many types of work activities were described, but they serve to suggest some of the outstanding characteristics of employment in modern times. Some,

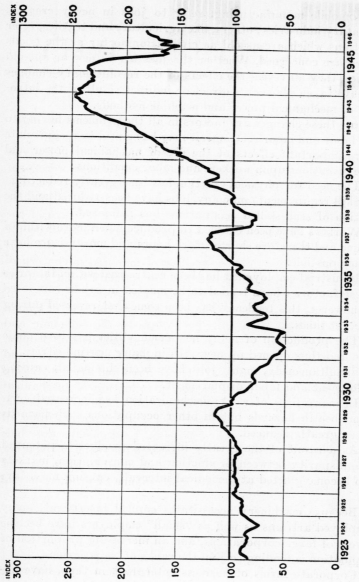

FIG. 10. Physical Volume of Industrial Production, 1923 to October, 1946. Adjusted for seasonal variation, 1935–1939 = 100. (Based on Federal Reserve Board data.)

like automobile manufacturing, refer to jobs in newly created, 20th-century industries; others, like agriculture and textiles, refer to vocations which are as old as civilization so far as the goods produced are concerned. Whether the jobs are in new or age-old industries, they all reveal the effects of the revolutionary changes which have taken place as a direct or indirect result of the introduction of mechanical power and machine methods.

Because these changes are factors in all the problems having to do with labor and labor relations, it may be helpful to recapitulate the more important effects of the use of mechanical power and machine inventions upon workers and labor conditions:

1. The need for physical exertion has been greatly reduced.

2. Skill requirements on many jobs have been reduced and the proportion of semi-skilled occupations has increased.

3. Workers have been enabled to produce much more within a given time and therefore shorter work hours and more leisure have been made possible.

4. Industrial employment has been centralized within factories and these factories have tended to be located in urban congested areas; however, this tendency has been somewhat reversed during more recent times.

5. The production of many new commodities has been made possible and thus opened up new jobs in many new industries.

6. Simultaneously, many jobs have been eliminated, causing unemployment and labor displacement.

7. In many lines of work, mechanization has increased accident and health hazards but in other occupations such hazards have been greatly reduced.

8. As a result of the greatly increased productive potential and the disparity between production and consumption, markets tend to become glutted at periodical intervals, causing mass lay-offs.

9. Because machinery necessitates capital investment, many self-employed artisans as well as "small" employers have become employees of large corporations, and an increasing proportion of the population is tending to join the ranks of wage earners.

10. Corporate forms of business enterprise, in turn, have impersonalized ownership (shareholders with hired managers, in contrast to owner operation) and created complex hierarchies of

management control which have given rise to unique problems in management-labor relationships.

MEANING OF LABOR PRODUCTIVITY

When considering the wealth of a nation or the status of any particular industry, one of the most important elements is total production or total productive capacity. The volume of production of any country or industry is a measure of the accomplishment of its total resources, natural and human, but it does not necessarily reveal the efficiency of its productive processes or indicate the amount of goods and services which are available for individual consumption. To illustrate: The volume of production of two countries may be equal, although one has twice the area and population of the other. Likewise, the total production of any industry may be the same at two different periods, even though the number of persons employed in the industry has increased or decreased. For certain purposes, comparisons of total volume of production are necessary and useful. It is obvious, however, that total volume must be related to the number of persons who produce and are supported by that production if a measure of the economic well-being, or potential well-being, of these persons is sought.

This ratio of the quantity of production to the number of workers employed (or man-hours worked) is termed labor productivity. Productivity is essentially a measure of the efficiency of the productive enterprise expressed in terms of output per worker or per man-hour or other unit of time. It is not a measure of human energy expended, for the volume of productivity under any given circumstances is contingent upon how human labor is implemented and utilized, as well as upon the efforts put forth by the workers themselves.

Measuring output in terms of the employed worker, or the man-hours or man-years worked, is merely a matter of convenience. In agriculture, productivity is frequently stated in terms of acres of soil, although, of course, the yield from any acre of ground depends not only upon the fertility of the soil but also upon how the farmer works the soil—the selection of crops best suited to the particular soil, the effectiveness of pest control, the use of machinery in planting and harvesting, and the labor of the farmer himself. In industry, productivity can also be measured in terms of dollar investment or unit of mechanical energy or plant equipment used. Because of the impact of changes in productivity upon employment and the entire economy of an industry and upon the welfare of the nation, its measurement as a ratio of labor utilized or expended has wider application and more general significance than its measurement in terms of any other factors involved in the productive process.

Productivity is a relative matter, and can be measured only by comparing the amount produced by any given number of workers with the output of the same number of workers at another time or under other circumstances. In its broadest aspects, productivity signifies the difference between existing standards of living in contrast to a bare subsistence living obtained by continuous work from dawn to dark, for it is only through improvement in productivity that the mass of people have been able to obtain the comforts and luxuries of living and the leisure time with which to enjoy them. Even before the invention of machinery, the use of hand tools, as well as specialization and division of labor and the interchange of products and services, had lessened the burdens of work and provided a greater variety of commodities than had existed in more primitive times. Modern methods of production, communication, and transportation have resulted in great increases in productivity; and it is this volume of increase, the methods by which it has been achieved, and, more especially, its effect upon labor conditions, with which this discussion is primarily concerned.

FACTORS INVOLVED IN INCREASED PRODUCTIVITY

The technological developments which characterize modern industry have many facets. The most important, at least in the past, have been the mechanical inventions which have provided substitutes of numerous kinds of machinery for human and animal labor. More recent are the chemical discoveries and developments in metallurgy which have brought forth new materials and improved machines and tools. Accompanying these physical innovations has been the progress in education, both formal and informal, which has provided the psychological atmosphere and the knowledge and skill of management and workers with which to adapt these technical inventions and discoveries to productive purposes, and to utilize them with increasing efficiency.

Mechanical Power

The foundation of all technical and mechanical advancement is mechanical power. It was the invention of the steam engine which ushered in the Industrial Revolution[1] and it is mechanical power which underlies our whole mass-production system of today. All modern industrial activity—mining, transportation, communication, manufacturing, and agriculture—is dependent upon mechanical power, and expansions in production have been due primarily to machines driven by natural energy.

The principal sources of mechanical power production are fuels and waterfalls. Steam generators and turbines, gas and gasoline engines, and water turbines convert the dormant power potentials of nature into energy, and electricity transmits this generated power to the machines where it is used. At the present time there are probably no less than $1\frac{1}{2}$ billion horsepower of mechanical energy available each year in the United States. Translated into human power, this is equivalent to the physical labor of 15 billion men.[2] For manufacturing purposes alone, an average of more than 5 horsepower of power-driven machinery is used for each worker employed.

The result of the use of mechanical power on productivity is obvious: A worker can accomplish more with less physical effort on his part to the extent that he is aided by mechanical energy. Or, to state it in another way, the number of workers needed to do a given amount of work tends to be in inverse ratio to the amount of mechanical power utilized. Mechanical power, moreover, not

---

[1] In 1769 James Watt invented an engine for pumping water out of coal mines which embodied nearly all the principles that were afterward perfected in the modern steam engine.

[2] This refers to horsepower available for all purposes—illumination, transportation, communication, agriculture, etc., as well as for industrial production. Since the summer of 1945 we have heard much about the possibility of atomic energy. Judging from past experience with most major discoveries and inventions, it will be twenty-five years at least before means for developing atomic energy for industrial purposes will be perfected and put into wide use.

only is a substitute for human and animal energy but also performs work which could never be done by men or animals. No conceivable number of men or horses could take the place of a modern freight locomotive or of some of the huge cranes which haul materials over deep canyons; the flying of airplanes, of course, would be impossible except for mechanical power. Without such means of transportation, production could not have expanded to the extent that it has; thus, the contribution made by mechanical power goes far beyond the output of the mechanically driven machines directly engaged in the manufacture of a product.

TABLE 6. Index of Supply of Energy from Mineral Fuels and Water Power in the United States, 1889–1944[3]

Year	Index (1918 = 100)
1889	20
1899	34
1904	48
1909	65
1913	82
1918	100
1919	86
Average:	
1920–24	97
1925–29	113
1930–34	93
1935–39	110
1940–44	145

This country, with its rich deposits of coal and oil as well as water resources, has always had an ample supply of natural energy. The amount actually used has varied with the fluctuations of industrial needs rather than because of any limitation in the volume of the natural energy available. During business depressions the amount consumed declines; in contrast, during the recent war the average annual consumption was 30 per cent more than the annual consumption during the preceding five years.

[3] Measured in B.t.u. with water power at constant fuel equivalent. Adapted from annual data presented in *Minerals Yearbook* for 1937 (p. 809) and 1944 (p. 14).

Machinery

Expansion in power resources provides the basis for improved productivity, but goods are actually produced by the use of power-driven machines and tools. Various tools and devices were used by man long before the invention of the steam engine; but the development of power facilities greatly stimulated inventions, and it is the power-driven machine which is the distinctive characteristic of modern production methods. Although the increase in the power supply has multiplied labor's capacity to produce, the invention of new kinds of machinery and equipment enhances the efficiency in the use of power as well as human labor, and both tend to raise the general level of productivity. As examples of the former: During the past twenty-five years technological improvements on steam railroads have resulted in a 33 per cent reduction in their coal consumption per mile of freight tonnage; improvements in coke manufacturing have resulted in coal savings of at least 20 per cent; electric power plants consume 60 per cent less coal per kilowatt-hour than they did twenty-five years ago. Such advances in the efficiency of using coal, although they do not affect labor productivity at the coal mines, nevertheless greatly influence general productivity because fewer miners are needed to keep the machines of industry running.

Even more remarkable than the improvements in the production and effective utilization of mechanical power is the continuous stream of new inventions of power-driven machines. In these few pages it is impossible and indeed unnecessary to discuss any particular inventions, even the more spectacular. Many of them are well known to everybody and one has only to glance at the advertisements in current periodicals to learn of the latest achievements in mechanical progress. Because of their effect upon labor productivity, it is pertinent for the present discussion to consider the inherent nature and the varied functions of power-driven machines and tools in general.

Essentially, machines and mechanical devices duplicate man's power to feel form, size, weight, temperature, and pressure. The recently developed photoelectric cell, radar, and televox not only are substitutes for the human eye and ear but they also produce action in response to what they see and hear. But machines and electrical devices do more than duplicate human (or animal) motion; they are able to make these motions at much greater speed and accuracy, and to perform them under circumstances and conditions in which they are impossible for man. No human eye has the range or the ability to see through fog and great distances as does radar.

Machines perform various functions. Many of them process and fabricate; some lift, haul, and otherwise move materials; others perform inspection, assembling, and packaging tasks. Some machines—for example, some of the machines used in the making of garments and shoes—are by no means automatic but require careful human manipulation. In contrast, the machines used for textile spinning and weaving, cigar and cigarette making, the making of glass bottles and blown ware, and brick manufacturing are highly automatic and perform practically the entire production process, relegating human labor to tenders, feeders, and inspectors. Automatic control machines and devices used in continuous-process industries go still further by preparing the materials for processing and by packaging the finished product, in addition to the processing itself.

Chemical Developments

Advances in machinery and methods of manufacturing are dependent in large part upon new discoveries and new developments in chemistry and metallurgy. These sciences, which have to do with changes in the composition of matter, have produced improvements in the metals used in the machines themselves as well as new raw materials and semi-finished materials used in the final processing of consumers' goods. Few raw materials can be utilized in their natural form, and in most cases a chemical change must take place before they are suitable for use. Chemical discoveries are constantly revealing new combinations of matter which make it possible to increase the speed and precision of machines and tools, and to eliminate or shorten processing operations.

Metallurgy has developed thousands of alloys for industrial use. Some have greater corrosive resistance than the natural metals, thus lessening replacements; this not only eliminates the labor directly required in the making of the replacements but also affects the amount of labor needed in metal mining. Some alloys improve the strength and reliability of machines, enabling them to withstand greater stresses and shocks with fewer interruptions for repairs and adjustments. Some have the advantage of being lighter in weight, thereby increasing the working capacity of the machine, conveyer, or tool. A major discovery was that of high-speed tool steels which have greatly increased the usable cutting speeds of tools, with resulting efficiencies in all industries.

Metallurgical progress has made possible the elimination of many steps in the processing of metals. Power metallurgy, centrifugal casting, and continuous casting are methods for producing finished or nearly finished products from metal without the necessity for many intermediate steps. Continuous processes for making iron castings and brass sheets from the molten metals, and steel sheets from the ingots, eliminate many reheating processes and handling operations. Improved induction heating reduces the time required for hardening metals from ten or more hours to a few moments. The substitution of electric welding for riveting is one of the most striking illustrations of a change in process; it affects many important industries such as aircraft manufacture, shipbuilding, machinery production, and structural steel fabrication of all kinds.

Outside of the metals, chemistry has developed a number of new products which have had marked effects on productivity. Various plastics furnish a new structural material which comes from the mold in the shape and color desired, thus eliminating the necessity for finishing cuts, polishing and grinding, lacquering or painting. The development of high octane gasoline, among other advantages, makes possible higher engine-power output, and improved lubricating oils facilitate machine operations. The chemical treatment of railroad ties has more than doubled their length of life and thereby reduced the labor connected with the laying of ties and the maintenance of roadbeds. Well known to everyone are such synthetic materials as rayon and nylon which have resulted in spectacular developments in productivity in the manufacture of fabrics and fabric products.

Specialization

When comparing the output per worker employed in industry today with that of earlier periods, one naturally thinks first of the great improvements and expanded use of machinery. As important as mechanization has been, there are also many non-mechanical factors which have contributed to increased productivity. Some of these are of a general nature, having to do with the economic or industrial situation as a whole; others concern operations within individual plants. Some are the result of management's effort and direction; others have resulted from the quality and type of effort expended by the workers.

Although closely related to machine utilization, the division and specialization of labor, in the absence of machinery, have a tendency to increase productivity, as was recognized by Adam Smith, the 18th-century economist, before power machinery had come into general use. Division of labor is achieved at two different levels: first, from industrial specialization within a country or geographical area, and second, as a result of dividing a complicated process in a plant into numerous operations, each of which is assigned to a different worker or group of workers.

The total per capita production of a nation or geographical area tends to increase when all or most of the productive processes are directed into those channels which allow the maximum utilization of the country's peculiar natural and human resources. For example, our New England States greatly expanded their per capita production when agriculture assumed a minor role as a means of employment, and industries were developed which took advantage of the waterfalls and seaport facilities. The resulting increase in production was due not only to the direct contributions of the natural resources, but also to the development of special skills in workers and management as a consequence of industrial specialization.

Within a given industry or plant, the potentials of work specialization are advanced further as all-round jobs are subdivided into numerous operations, because greater speed is possible and much waste motion is eliminated when operations are simplified and routinized. Also, since the simplified operations require a shorter time to learn, there is a reduction in the time lost as a result of labor turnover and the training of new workers. While the invention of new machines usually is the initiating force for the division of labor, the reverse is also true, namely, the breaking down of complex skilled jobs into numerous simple operations facilitates and encourages the substitution of machines for hand labor.

Standardization and Substitutions

Standardization of parts and finished products has been an important factor in advancing the per capita volume of production, chiefly because standardization makes possible mass production and mechanized methods. To cite a few of the numerous examples: In consumers' goods one has only to compare the productive possibilities of ready-to-wear clothing factories with custom-made tailor shops, or the labor saving involved in the making of standardized windows, bath and kitchen units in mill shops in contrast to individual construction at the building site. Standardization in producers' goods, such as machine parts and the size and content of materials, has contributed to greater productivity, not only because it permits mass production of these parts and materials, but also because it makes possible mass production in their further processing. A further advantage of standardized machine parts is their interchangeability which facilitates repairs and thus reduces lost time due to machine breakdowns.

Substitution of one process or product for another, and the combination of processes, have greatly enhanced output in relation to the number of workers required. Pipe lines for transporting petroleum require less labor than do tankers and trucks; the integration of the blast furnace and steelmaking plants virtually eliminates the casting process; the fabrication of paper products at the site of pulp and paper mills, and of wood products at sawmills, eliminates much handling and transportation. One reason for the greater productivity in the aluminum and steel industries during the recent war was the relative increase in the production of aluminum sheets, heavy steel plates, and other products which require fewer man-hours per pound of aluminum or ton of steel than is required for making smaller miscellaneous products. Agriculture provides many illustrations of improved production as the result of using superior plant varieties which have greater resistance to disease, cover crops, and crop rotation—changes which do not necessarily involve the use of different or better machinery.

Plant Utilization and Improvement

Productivity is also affected by the volume of production or ratio of output to plant capacity. A decline in production tends to increase the overhead and in other ways to add to the amount of

labor required per unit of output, whereas the maximum use of
facilities, by spreading maintenance and other overhead labor over
a larger output, tends to increase per capita production. A study
of the steel industry several years ago revealed a change in man-
hours ranging from 34 hours per ton of steel at 55 to 60 per cent
of the total capacity, to 47 hours per ton at 20 to 25 per cent of
capacity. The 13 per cent increase in man-hour output in the
generation of electrical energy between 1939 and 1942 was largely
due to more complete utilization of power-plant capacity because
little or no additional labor is required when the load increases.
The 40 per cent increase in revenue traffic per man-hour on steam
railroads during the same war years was largely the result of the
fuller loading of freight and passenger cars and the more continuous operation of trains.[4]

So far as an entire industry is concerned, a rise in productivity
may be achieved through the elimination of less inefficient plants
even without any improvement in the productivity of the remaining plants. As an example, in leather manufacturing there have
been no major changes in the machinery used during the last two
decades, but productivity has increased at least one-third. Much
of this is attributable to the closing down of many small plants
and the concentration of production in fewer, larger plants where
greater economies in the use of men and equipment are possible. In
a competitive industry this process of closing down the less efficient plants is continually taking place, but it is greatly accentuated during periods of business depression when maximum efficiency is necessary if a firm is to remain in business. Census figures
indicate that in spite of the great expansion in manufacturing
there has been a steady decline in the total number of establishments in this country during the past twenty-five years. Thus, in
1919 there were 214,383 manufacturing establishments producing
goods valued at more than $5000; in 1939 there were 30,000 fewer
establishments.

Closely allied to the shift toward larger, newer plants are the
improvements in factory construction, the newer buildings being
especially designed to accommodate the most modern machines
and methods of production. The better lighting, heating, ventila-

---

[4] For more details concerning productivity in these three industries, see
Monthly Labor Review, May, 1935, September, 1943, and January, 1944.

tion, and sanitation, the reduction of noise, and the scientifically adjusted seats, work benches, and tool arrangements provided in the newer plants have had an immeasurable influence upon productivity. Not only do they improve worker morale and thus indirectly lead to greater output, but they are also direct aids to efficiency because they tend to reduce fatigue and absenteeism, as well as damages to materials and machinery.

Management and Worker Efficiency

All the above-mentioned mechanical and non-mechanical improvements and changes have been brought about by human effort and imagination. But they also involve physical and natural resources and represent man's better control and use of material equipment. To a considerable degree improvement in productivity is also the result of the exercise of human ingenuity and effort in ways which involve few if any physical aids. Such improvements in management and worker efficiency are especially significant because they represent net gains; unlike physical innovations they involve no large capital or money outlay.

During the past two or three decades there have been notable changes in management methods throughout most of American industry. The so-called "rationalization" of industry has made the function of management a distinct profession, as is attested by the recognition given it by engineering and business administration schools in our leading universities, and by the growth of numerous management consulting and industrial engineering firms whose function is to provide employers with technical advice and assistance for the improvement of their management policies and procedures.

The development of industrial management lagged behind other technological innovations. As one observer has commented about the management methods fifty years ago:

American industrial management had not awakened in the 19th century to the possible benefits which might accrue to it from radically improved shop methods. Large plants were still using the same methods of management within the shop as had obtained in earlier decades. Internal management had not improved *pari passu* with the growth of the industrial unit. Business executives were absorbed in problems of markets and prices rather than of internal management. As a class they were not alert to discover new ways of handling materials, laying out plants, using scientific research, and increasing labor efficiency. . . . Management was not adequately systematized. Decentralized purchasing and storage with frequent overstock or understock of raw materials, accounting systems which were little more than a statement of profits and loss at the close of the year, and an absence of definite written instructions to executives and workmen, were the practices of the day. Establishments had grown larger, machinery more complex and intricate, jobs subdivided and often delicately interrelated, but the type of internal organization remained the same. Each foreman and executive was the supreme authority over all the processes and men within his jurisdiction. It remained for an entirely different group of men to find the causes and remedies for the wastefulness and inefficiency within industrial establishments. Engineers discovered the almost unlimited possibilities of improving internal shop management.[5]

Management covers a wide range of techniques having to do with all aspects of running a business, including the financing, buying of raw materials, and selling of finished products, as well as the internal handling of materials and personnel, plant layout, and job methods. Each of these activities vitally affects the productive potential of the business. Present-day changes in management methods and policies have occurred in response to the problems and complexities of mass production. Essentially, they serve to retain or reestablish within large enterprises some of the inherent merits of owner-operated small business and at the same time to obtain the maximum advantages from large-scale production.

Without going into the broad purposes or the detailed techniques of industrial management, it is sufficient here merely to mention a few of the ways in which management efficiencies have affected labor productivity. Among these are synchronization in the purchasing and flow of materials to be used, which has re-

---

[5] D. D. Lescohier, *History of Labor in the U. S.*, The Macmillan Company, New York, 1935, vol. iii, p. 303. According to this same volume, the New York Public Library had no American titles on management prior to 1881 and in the following twenty years they had only 27. Between 1900 and 1910, however, they had 240, with a rapid increase thereafter. Although there were several engineering schools in this country before the Civil War, schools interested in management came later. The Wharton School of Finance was established in 1881; the Harvard School of Business, in 1908.

duced congestions and delays; the timing of sales and advertising programs, and other means for regularizing work and reducing seasonal fluctuations which result in increased per capita annual production; improved layout of machines, and careful planning and routing of work through the plant to reduce delays and wasted time; personnel procedures, which see that the right person is placed in the right job and given adequate training for the job, thereby improving individual efficiency.

A spectacular achievement of industrial engineering has been the assembly line. While this depends upon mechanical conveyers and belts, it is essentially a management device rather than a scientific invention. Systems of continuous flow of production were introduced in the automobile and meat-packing industries in the 1920's and are now in extensive use throughout many industries. Instead of having materials and parts carried or hauled to the various machines and work benches, workers are stationed alongside of belts or conveyer lines and each man performs a specialized task as the work passes by him. There is thus a steady flow of work, with great savings in time and labor previously consumed in crisscross delivery of materials and parts to individual operators. In some industries, the efficiencies resulting from the introduction of conveyer assembly lines have equaled or exceeded those of any other recent improvement.

One of the cornerstones of scientific management, namely, the establishment of job standards and incentive wages based on time and motion study, has resulted in increases in productivity ranging from 20 per cent in some plants to over 100 per cent in others.[6] Not so apparent, but nevertheless important, are the effects on output of other conditions of employment such as hour schedules sufficiently short to avoid fatigue, rest periods and hot-lunch facilities, safety and health programs, and harmonious management-labor relations—matters which will be discussed in detail in later chapters.

Many of the improvements installed by management have resulted from the suggestions and creative thinking of the workers. Whether initiated by management or workers, their successful operation depends upon the intelligent cooperation of the men and women who perform the tasks. New management arrange-

[6] See chap. 12.

ments and devices are useless if the workers are reluctant or incompetent to make the necessary adjustments or meet the new standards of workmanship. No small part of the progress made by business in America has been due to the fact that workers generally have benefited from public-school education. Few of the recent innovations could have been imposed upon an illiterate work force, and many of them require the special skills and aptitudes acquired in vocational and high schools.

CHANGES IN PRODUCTIVITY

As indicated earlier, there are various ways in which productivity can be measured. For any particular time and industry, productivity can be indicated in terms of volume produced per unit of labor, e.g., four pairs of shoes per man-day employment. What is usually wanted, however, is a comparison of one year's productivity with that of another period. For this purpose, productivity can best be measured by means of index numbers which show the relative increase or decrease with reference to some base period.

The index numbers can refer to output either per worker employed or per unit of work time. The most precise method for measuring changes in efficiency is to use a brief unit of time, such as man-hours, because this excludes such variable factors as increases or decreases in working hours. Thus longer hours and steadier work might cause a rise in a productivity index based on the number of persons employed, even though there was no improvement in efficiency; likewise, shorter hours or irregular employment might lower an index based on man-years, even though the man-hour output had improved. In some situations, as in agriculture, it is necessary to measure productivity in terms of workers rather than time worked, because there are no records of the actual hours worked by farmers and farm laborers.

General Trend in Productivity

According to the best authorities, there has been an average annual rate of increase of approximately 3 per cent in manufacturing productivity since the beginning of the 20th century. During the thirty years before the recent war, output in manufactur-

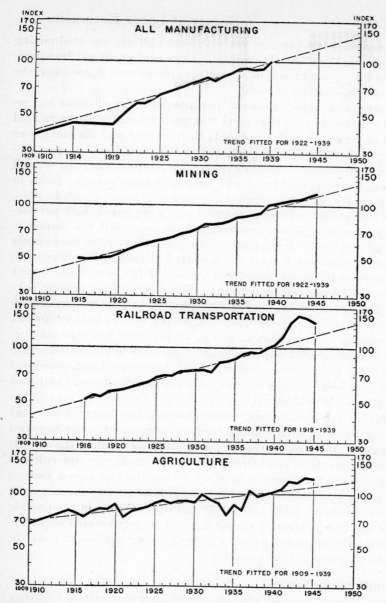

FIG. 11. Trends in Productivity, 1910–1945. Output per man-hour in manufacturing, mining, and railroad transportation; output per worker in agriculture. 1939 = 100. (Based on U. S. Bureau of Labor Statistics data.)

ing increased 164 per cent per man-hour; bituminous coal mining 103 per cent; anthracite mining 111 per cent; railroad transportation 98 per cent; and in agriculture the output per worker employed increased 50 per cent.

There is no index of output per man-hour for all manufacturing industries during the recent war period because of the radical shift in types of goods produced; shell loading and the making of superbombers cannot be evaluated in the same terms as the production of refrigerators or passenger automobiles. It is well known, however, that most war industries made striking gains in productivity as mass-production methods were adopted. Also, most industries producing non-war goods improved their productivity even though wartime restrictions precluded the introduction of new kinds of machinery—an indication of the importance of non-mechanical factors in improved efficiency. To illustrate: During the six years from 1939 through 1945, man-hour output increased 10 per cent in shoe manufacturing, 26 per cent in baking, 21 per cent in canning and preserving, at least 21 per cent in the manufacture of glass products, 38 per cent in hosiery and 51 per cent in rayon manufacturing, 33 per cent in cigar making, 11 per cent in meat packing, and 18 per cent in the manufacture of woolen goods. Some industries, on the other hand, increased their man-hour output only slightly during these years and in a few productivity declined.[7]

Output per agricultural worker increased at least 25 per cent during the war, even though farmers were greatly handicapped because of the lack of tractors and other mechanical equipment. However, weather conditions, a primary factor in agricultural productivity, were unusually good during the war years. Output (in tons) per man-hour in bituminous coal mining increased 29 per cent between 1938 and 1945, and productivity in the electric light and power industry almost doubled, largely because of power-pooling arrangements whereby all generating equipment could be operated nearer its full capacity.

Variations in Trends

The introduction of machinery and improvements in efficiency is a never-ending process which at times is accelerated by favor-

---

[7] Bureau of Labor Statistics mimeographed report issued in May, 1946.

able conditions and at other times retarded, but is always progressing at innumerable points throughout industry. One major invention may revolutionize manufacturing methods and double the productivity of an industry within a very few years, but subsequent to the general introduction of this machine there may be only slight changes in productivity for a considerable period of time. Comparative differences in productivity among the several industries during any short period of time, therefore, do not necessarily indicate the long-time comparative trend.

This is revealed in Tables 7 and 8, which show the percentage

TABLE 7.   Trend in Labor Productivity, 1909–1939[8]

	Indexes (1923–1925 = 100)						Per Cent Increases	
	1909	1919	1923	1929	1932	1939	1919–1929	1929–1939
Manufacturing........	62.3	71.9	94.1	124.1	129.6	164.2	72.6	32.3
Bituminous coal mining.	69.5	85.1	99.2	107.2	115.0	141.0	26.0	31.5
Anthracite mining......	84.8	100.0	103.5	99.8	119.0	178.6	0.0	79.0
Steam railroads........	75.4	85.4	96.4	113.9	111.9	149.3	33.4	31.1
Agriculture............	78.3	96.1	96.6	108.0	110.2	118.1	12.4	9.4

increases in productivity during a period of two decades for a number of industries. In all the major lines of activity except coal mining there were greater advances in productivity during the 1920's than during the 1930's. The lesser rate of progress during the latter period was largely due to depressed business conditions, many new discoveries and replacements of old equipment being held in abeyance. However, in spite of general business conditions, output per man-hour increased about one-third in manufacturing and on steam railroads, and output on farms increased almost one-tenth per person employed. The great improvement in mining productivity was due not only to increased mechanization but also to the closing of many "marginal" mines, especially in the anthracite fields.

Among the various manufacturing industries the differences in rates of increase in productivity during various periods are very

[8] Based on data appearing in *Monthly Labor Review*, September, 1940, p. 520, and March, 1944, p. 515.

TABLE 8.   Increases in Man-Hour Output, 1919–1939, in Various Manufacturing Industries[9]

	Per Cent Increase	
	1919–1929	1929–1939
Agricultural implements	75.4	53.2
Automobiles and parts	134.2	18.8
Canning and preserving	27.6	45.6
Cotton goods	17.6	46.1
Flour and other grain milling	55.5	15.0
Furniture	37.6	6.3
Glass—flat and blown	68.6	81.7
Paper and pulp	65.6	34.3
Petroleum refining	102.4	93.4
Rubber tires and tubes	115.1	98.1
Slaughtering and meat packing	34.6	26.4
Woolen and worsted goods	12.5	41.3
Cigars	22.9	81.0
Cigarettes	223.6	26.9
Iron and steel	96.1	36.9
Printing and publishing	76.7	29.3

marked. In automobile manufacturing, productivity increased 134 per cent during the 1920's, in contrast to less than 19 per cent during the 1930's. Petroleum refining and tire manufacturing, on the other hand, made almost as great advances during the 1930's as in the preceding decade, and the rate of progress in cotton and woolen goods manufacturing and in canning and preserving was greater during the later period. A striking contrast is seen in cigar and cigarette manufacturing. Fully integrated machines for the manufacture of cigarettes were introduced throughout the industry during the 1920's; the result was a 224 per cent increase in man-hour output. Machine-made cigars, on the other hand, did not become general until the 1930's, when productivity advanced 81 per cent.

A more recent example of a phenomenal rise in productivity is seen in airframe manufacturing, where technological improvements, which would normally be spread over ten or twenty years, were telescoped into a little over one year. During the three years after Pearl Harbor the output per man-hour in airframe plants

[9] Based on Bureau of Labor Statistics, *Productivity and Unit Labor Costs in Selected Manufacturing Industries*, February, 1942, multilithed report.

more than tripled, and most of this increase took place in 1943. Inasmuch as this increase was achieved when most of the workers were completely inexperienced, the phenomenal gain was due almost entirely to efficiencies resulting from the large-scale mass production of standard products, line production methods, highly specialized machinery and tools, and minute division of labor—a sum total of factors which represent the epitome of modern technology and illustrate the potential possibilities of an industry faced with a large assured market for standard products and unlimited capital to invest in new plant equipment.

PRODUCTIVITY AND EMPLOYMENT

Inventions and other technological advances have brought munificent benefits to mankind and made possible a high standard of living for all peoples. Luxuries previously limited to a few are now enjoyed by many; goods and services unknown fifty or a hundred years ago to either rich or poor have come into general use. A host of commodities which we eat and wear, conveniences in the home, methods of travel and communication, and various forms of entertainment would be non-existent for all, or at least most people, were it not for mechanical inventions and scientific discoveries.

Granted that technological advances and other improvements in production have brought advantages to the general public and thus to workers who make up the large portion of the general public, what effect have they had upon the employment of the men and women who are directly engaged in the production processes? Any such revolutionary changes as have taken place and are currently taking place with accelerating speed in industry are bound to have manifold repercussions, good and bad, with advantages accruing to some groups and misfortune to others.

New Employment Opportunities

Inventions have resulted in the creation of many new industries and many more new kinds of jobs. Some of our major industries which now employ millions of workers were unknown a generation or two ago. The automobile, aircraft, electrical products, rayon and nylon, motion-picture, telephone, plastics, rubber tire, and

radio manufacturing industries are distinctly 20th-century industries. The machine-producing and power-generating industries are
synchronous developments of the inventive progress made in other
industries, new and old, as are also most of the steel and non-ferrous metal industries which supply the materials and parts for
the machines and power generators.

More than half the workers employed in manufacturing today
are employed in these relatively new industries which are the direct offspring of modern technology. These industries, in turn,
have created other lines of activities which engage additional hundreds of thousands of workers. Automobile mechanics, radio and
other electrical repairmen and salesmen, filling-station attendants,
truck drivers and pilots, telephone operators, radio technicians
and entertainers occcupy new types of employment which are out-
growths of inventions for the manufacture of new products. The
indirect effects of inventions in the producing of new products go
still further. Much of the highway and bridge construction undertaken in recent years has been in direct response to the general use
of automobiles; airports are a concomitant phase of aircraft
manufacture; many new factories have been built to house new or
expanded industries created by improvements in manufacturing
methods.

Simultaneous with the creation of new industries and employment opportunities, inventions and their accompanying technological developments have caused drastic changes in the general
character of jobs and job environments in both old and new industries. As already mentioned, power-driven machines have relieved men (and women) of much of the heavy work which formerly had to be done by hard physical labor. Concurrently with
the elimination of a great deal of monotonous drudgery, however,
technology has also caused the disappearance of many skilled
handicrafts and the division of numbers of all-round manual jobs
into numerous routine, repetitive operations.

The psychological effect on workers of the dilution of skilled
jobs and the centralization of work in large factories and mills
has been pungently described by one observer: "The modern machine tender is an unhappy creature. He does not feel himself a
whole man. His daily, monotonous, repetitive motions have broken
down his skills. He cannot make an entire shoe nor a suit of

clothes. He is caught in the vise of mass production, division of labor, atomization of skill. He is a human cog, tied to a machine he does not own and which he can only operate when somebody else gives him permission."[10]

Although the above aptly describes the condition of millions of workers now employed in large mechanized plants, there are some offsetting factors in the dominant trend toward diminution of skilled manual jobs formerly performed by self-employed artisans or in small owner-operated shops. The highly complicated machines themselves must be designed and built; improvements and attachments must be constantly made to adapt them to particular purposes; after being installed, intricate machinery requires maintenance and frequent repairs; large establishments demand the scientific layout of equipment; the routing of work and the direction of the work of men and machines require special types of supervision.

Mechanical engineers and draftsmen, maintenance workers, industrial engineers, clerks, laboratory technicians, and numerous other persons with special skills and aptitudes are necessary adjuncts to mass production and make up an increasing proportion of our total industrial employment. These types of work offer substitute means of employment for many persons who otherwise would be performing manual labor. Many parents who work on routine jobs in factories have been able to send their children to engineering or vocational schools to prepare themselves for the technical and other white-collar jobs required by modern methods of production.

Labor Displacement

Technological advances must also be considered in connection with their effect upon employment. The labor-saving possibilities of a new machine are one of the first considerations of a business manager, who naturally weighs the cost of the machine against estimated pay-roll savings before making the purchase. The workers who are immediately affected by the installation of a new machine naturally blame the machine for the loss of their jobs.

Directly and indirectly, technological advances are the cause of the disappearance of many occupations and the displacement

---

[10] Louis Stark, New York *Times Magazine,* September 30, 1945.

of many individuals and groups of workers. So far as these particular persons are concerned, technology has resulted in loss of jobs and more or less extended periods of unemployment. New methods not only may mean the displacement of a particular group of workers in a particular locality, but they may result in the employment of an entirely different type of person. When machines were introduced in the manufacture of cigars, not only was there a shift in the location of many plants and a decrease in the total number employed in the industry, but an entirely different type of work force was used—men skilled in rolling cigars by hand were displaced by new, unskilled workers, predominantly women. Similar displacements have taken place in many other industries and occupations, although in some—for example, the printing industry —the unions have been sufficiently strong in a majority of plants to insist upon the retention of their journeymen members and their transfer to machines as these were introduced.

Inventions have also resulted in expanded markets, increased volume of production, and the creation of new industries and occupations. Do technological improvements, therefore, merely cause job shifts and temporary dislocations of particular individuals? Or do machines and other substitutes for manual labor cause permanent reductions in the total number of available jobs and a lowering of the general level of employment?

This is the major problem facing all modern industrial societies, and to solve it many theories and explanations have been offered. They involve a complex of factors having to do with wages, hours, prices, and many other aspects of the economy—subjects which are discussed in the following chapters.

SELECTED REFERENCES

Anderson, H. D., and Blair, J. M., *Technology and Economic Balance,* Temporary National Economic Committee, Monograph No. 22, Washington, 1941.

Barnett, G. E., *Chapters on Machinery and Labor,* Harvard University Press, Cambridge, 1926.

Burns, Alfred C., *Production Trends in the U. S. Since 1870,* National Bureau of Economic Research, Inc., New York, 1934.

Chase, Stuart, *Men and Machines,* The Macmillan Company, New York, 1929.

Fabricant, Solomon, *The Output of Manufacturing Industries, 1899–1937*, National Bureau of Economic Research, Inc., New York, 1940.

Federated American Engineering Societies, *Waste in Industry*, McGraw-Hill Book Company, Inc., New York, 1921.

Gilfillan, S. C., *The Sociology of Invention*, Follet Publishing Co., Chicago, 1935.

Jerome, Harry, *Mechanization in Industry*, National Bureau of Economic Research, Inc., New York, 1934.

Mumford, Lewis, *Technics and Civilization*, Harcourt, Brace & Company, Inc., New York, 1934.

National Resources Committee, *Technological Trends and National Policy*, Government Printing Office, Washington, 1937.

National Research Project, *Production Employment and Productivity in 59 Manufacturing Industries, 1919–1936*, Works Progress Administration, Philadelphia, 1939.

Riegel, John W., *Management, Labor, and Technological Changes*, University of Michigan Press, Ann Arbor, 1945.

Senate Committee on Military Affairs, *Wartime Technological Developments*, Monograph No. 2, 79th Congress, Government Printing Office, Washington, 1944.

Smith, Elliott Dunlop, *Technology and Labor; a Study of Human Problems of Labor Saving*, Yale University Press, New Haven, 1939.

Usher, A. P., *History of Mechanical Invention*, McGraw-Hill Book Company, Inc., New York, 1929.

Williamson, Harold F., *et al.*, *The Growth of the American Economy*, Prentice-Hall, Inc., New York, 1944.

5

UNEMPLOYMENT

IN A SOCIETY WHERE FOOD, CLOTHING, AND SHELTER CAN BE HAD only for money, one might well say, as Shakespeare said 350 years ago, "You take my house when you do take the prop that doth sustain my house; you take my life when you do take the means whereby I live."[1]

Insecurity of job tenure is the lot of most American workers. Few indeed are the families of wage earners whose memories do not include the specter of serious privations caused by one or more prolonged periods of unemployment, and the inconveniences of many more shorter periods of loss of income because of temporary layoffs. Physical privations are not the sole effects of forced idleness.

Unsteady employment attacks the worker's efficiency, undermines his physique, deadens his mind, weakens his ambition, destroys his capacity for continuous, sustained endeavor; induces a liking for idleness and self-indulgence; saps self-respect and the sense of responsibility; impairs technical skill; weakens nerve and will power; creates a tendency to blame others for his failures; saps his courage; prevents thrift and hope of family advancement; destroys a workman's feeling that he is taking good care of his family. . . . Irregularity of income prevents intelligent expenditure of the income, encourages improvidence and prevents planning of purchasing. It leads almost inevitably to extravagance when earnings are good and debts when work is slack. . . . The nervous reactions to such demoralizing influences are so powerful as to transform many strong-willed, well-intentioned workmen into the irregular material that overfills the army of casual labor or even into the will-less, hopeless, indifferent objects called the unemployable.[2]

---

[1] *Merchant of Venice,* Act IV, Scene 1.
[2] D. D. Lescohier, *The Labor Market,* The Macmillan Company, New York, 1919, pp. 106–108.

The above describes the psychological effects of unemployment upon the mature workman with a family. As we shall see later, during a period of serious unemployment it is the young people just out of school who frequently find it most difficult to get jobs. Only the young person who has gone through the experience can appreciate what it means to have left school filled with high hopes

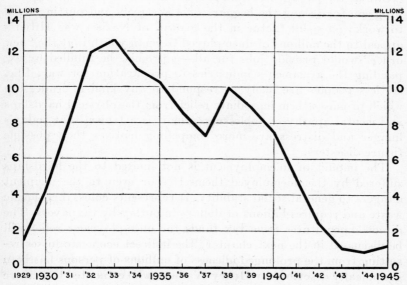

FIG. 12.   *Average Annual Unemployment, 1929–1945. (Based on U. S. Bureau of Labor Statistics estimates.)*

and ambitions to make a place in the world, only to discover that he is not needed or wanted. Many of the young men who left school during the recent war were not particularly enthusiastic about having their normal careers interrupted by several years' military service, but they had the deep satisfaction of knowing that their country needed them. Thousands of their older brothers who left school a decade previously belonged to the "lost generation" who spent months and years tramping the streets and highways vainly searching for opportunities to be of service to themselves and their country.

The vicious effects of irregular employment and fear of unemployment upon workers, their wives and children, have long been appreciated by social workers, public-school teachers, and others who have intimate contact with workingmen's families, as well as by the workers themselves. The dangers to social and political stability of mass unemployment with millions of jobless citizens have become apparent to all who have lived through the world-shaking events of the past generation. Mussolini won support through his program for taking the beggars off the streets and putting them to work; no small factor in the growth of Nazism was Hitler's appeal to the millions of unemployed German youth that the "new order" would provide jobs for all—a promise he fulfilled by expanding the armaments industries in preparation for war. Idle, restless peoples are likely to respond to any kind of leadership which promises them immediate relief from the physical hardships and mental apathy of joblessness, for it is a truism that today's hunger and distress are more compelling motives than possible future disasters.

The impact of unemployment is not limited to the hardships suffered by the unemployed themselves or even to the incipient dangers to general social stability. It represents colossal economic waste and requires billions of dollars in outlay by taxpayers. The direct expenditures from tax funds for unemployment relief will be discussed in the next chapter; the indirect economic losses resulting from the prolonged idleness of millions of persons has been graphically described by Henry Wallace, who estimated that there was a loss of 88 million man-years of work because of the depression unemployment during the eleven years between 1929 and 1940; this represented a loss of around 350 billions of dollars— a sum more than equal to the entire federal debt at the end of the recent war. This huge loss, Mr. Wallace says, was enough to pay in full for 70 million homes at $5000 each, which is more than three times as many homes as would be necessary to eliminate all the slums in the United States, both urban and rural. It was more than double the capital stock of all the private corporations in this country, and was enough to build 350 river-valley authorities of the size of the T.V.A.[3]

3 Henry A. Wallace, *Sixty Million Jobs,* Simon & Schuster, New York, 1945. Part I, Sec. III. The 88 million man-years does not include idleness due to sickness, turnover, and other so-called "normal" unemployment.

NATURE OF UNEMPLOYMENT

If unemployment is recognized as the outstanding curse of our economic and social life, why is it allowed to continue? As with most evils, its destructive and costly effects are recognized more easily than its causes can be eliminated. Unemployment is a result of many complex factors, and any one individual's joblessness may represent the concurrence of many different causes. Some may be due to the individual's personal characteristics, but most are the result of pathological economic and social conditions. Fundamentally, unemployment represents a maladjustment of labor supply and labor demand. The potential supply of labor, at least in the mass, changes only with the steady, slow change in population. The demand for labor, on the other hand, fluctuates from year to year, from season to season, and even from day to day. Because these fluctuations do not take place simultaneously throughout all industry, there is always a residual labor supply, even in the most prosperous years and boom seasons. When general business conditions become depressed, these pools of surplus labor increase in number and size until mass unemployment emerges. In good times as well as bad, however, there is considerable unemployment and there is some evidence that the amount has risen steadily despite temporary reductions during prosperous years.

Unemployed versus Unemployable

Unemployment may be voluntary as well as involuntary. Even though involuntary, it may result from personal deficiencies rather than from the absence of job opportunities. There are people who do not want to work steadily and who welcome periods of unemployment between jobs. There are others who want regular employment but because of lack of training or physical or mental handicaps are "marginal" workers whom employers are willing to hire only when they cannot obtain better-qualified workers. Sickness is a direct and indirect cause of a considerable amount of unemployment.

Idleness for all these reasons can be classified as non-industrial, the persons involved being unemployable rather than unemployed. However, the line of demarcation is not rigid, and to a considerable degree it varies with the demand for labor and the kinds of job opportunities available. A casual worker or floater may settle down to steady work if he finds a job which interests him and which pays what he considers is a good wage. An employer with many vacancies will hire handicapped persons whom he would not usually employ, and many times these people prove to be satisfactory employees after given a trial. Furthermore, as already indicated, mental and physical deficiencies, loss of desire for steady work, and lack of education and training may be due to the demoralization and lack of opportunity resulting from previous periods of unemployment. Many unemployables are casualties of unemployment rather than predestined shirkers or incompetents.

By legal implication and common parlance, involuntary or industrial unemployment includes those persons who are able and willing to work but are unable to find suitable employment.[4] In any given case, of course, there may be differences of opinion as to what constitutes "suitable" employment; some would eliminate the factor of suitability entirely, including in their definition of involuntary unemployment only those who could not get a job at any occupation, at any wage, anywhere. Theoretically, as discussed later, there may be some point to this concept of unemployment but in actual practice it is both infeasible and shortsighted. A jobless watch repairer with a home and family in New York City is for all practical purposes unemployed if the only available openings are for lumbermen on the west coast. Any adult wage earner must be considered unemployed even though he can pick up odd jobs at 20 or 25 cents an hour. Employment is a means of gaining a livelihood; and work which does not provide even the barest subsistence, or which destroys a person's skill or capacity for the future pursuit of his usual trade, cannot be considered economic employment, although it has sometimes been used as a test for unemployment relief.

TYPES OF UNEMPLOYMENT

Statistics on the total volume of unemployment are an important indicator of general economic conditions, but they do not

---

[4] See chap. 25 for an interpretation of "suitability" under the unemployment compensation laws.

show the full incidence of unemployment because many more workers suffer from unemployment than is revealed by the total annual figure, which is an average of monthly estimates. Although charts with fluctuating lines are a convenient means of portraying the changing number of employed and unemployed workers, the actual

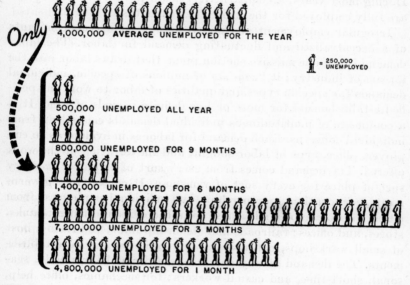

FIG. 13.   *Average Annual Employment versus Total Number Affected by Part-Time Employment.*

The illustration shows that if unemployment averages only 4,000,000 over the entire year, this could mean that more than 14,000,000 persons experienced unemployment. While 500,000 workers might be unemployed for an entire year, a much greater number might be out of work for shorter periods. For example, the 1,400,000 persons who were out of work for six months would add only 700,000 to the annual average of 4,000,000.

fluctuations in the employment status of individual workers are much more erratic, for the total number affected is not limited to the portion falling between the upper and lower extremities of the unemployment "curve." During any twelve-month period, regardless of whether business conditions are good or bad, some workers lose jobs which they have had for a long time, and are out of work for varying periods before finding new jobs; some persons are employed on numerous short-time jobs, with days or weeks of unemployment between each job; many workers continue at their same work places but experience irregular or part-time employment; others are employed on jobs which last for only a season. During most years, a comparatively small proportion of workers are fully employed for the entire twelve months.

Irregular employment and underemployment are concomitants of a decentralized and fluctuating demand for labor. The labor demand is not one massive suction pump that draws labor into the stream of industry; it "consists of millions of specific, individual demands for specific types and qualities of labor to work in specified establishments for more or less definite periods of time. It is a composite of multitudinous individual demands emanating from individual concerns. Each demand for labor is individual as to employer, place, type of labor sought, and the duration of the work offered. The demand comes from every sort of employer in every sort of place for every sort of workman. It comes from governments, corporations, partnerships, and individual employers; from cities, towns, camps, and farms; from factories and mines; banks, stores, and offices; railroads and steamship lines; and from a host of small workshops, contractors, and personal service establishments. The demand at any one time is a demand for steady, seasonal, short-time, and casual workers; for mechanics, office help, skilled operatives, semi-skilled, slightly skilled, and unskilled laborers."[5]

The unemployment resulting from such normal diversities of demand is not, however, the full measure of unemployment. Indeed, it represents the minimum which is present only when business is prosperous. When business conditions are only "fair," larger numbers of workers experience longer and more frequent intervals of unemployment, and some remain totally unemployed. When business conditions are severely depressed, millions of persons remain totally unemployed and a large majority of the others work only part time. It is this type of unemployment that is most disturbing, both to those who are directly affected and to those who are concerned with the national well-being. Its acuteness is due not only to the fact of its large volume, but also to the fact that its causes

[5] D. D. Lescohier, *The Labor Market*, p. 21.

lie deep at the roots of our economic system and represent disequilibriums which are difficult to diagnose and far more difficult to correct. But let us first consider the nature and causes of the unemployment that is not primarily due to general economic disturbances.

"Normal" Unemployment

So-called "normal" unemployment refers to the idleness which arises from the inherent irregular nature of some jobs and industries, or is the result of the voluntary turnover of workers, or is caused by shifts and changes in industrial operations which are unavoidable and in the long run may be desirable. It is the aggregate of a multitude of short periods of idleness resulting from numerous particular causes, each of which is peculiar to the individual situation in which it occurs. It is sometimes referred to as "frictional" or "structural," because in its totality it is considered a necessary force for the progressive development of industry and a natural result of free decisions and actions of individual employers and workers.

"Normal" unemployment is supposed to represent the *minimum* idleness that is required to keep a dynamic industrial system in operation. What the minimum is or should be is a matter of opinion and conjecture. During the peak of war production, unemployment amounted to about 1 per cent of the total employable workers. However, a considerable number of persons beyond the age of retirement—as well as women, children, and others who normally do not want to work for wages—were employed during the war. Some economists are of the opinion that "normal" unemployment is equal to about 2 per cent of the total work force; others maintain that it is necessary and inevitable that 5 or 6 per cent, or even more, of the workers shall be idle at all times. The difference between the lower and higher estimates is equivalent to two or three millions of wage earners—a disparity which is of the utmost importance to the wage earners and families concerned, as well as to the social costs involved.

Employers are naturally inclined to think in terms of a relatively high figure for "normal" unemployment. They prefer a buyers' labor market which allows them wide latitude for the selection of new employees and serves as an indirect warning to their present employees that replacements can easily be made. "The American employer has been able to assume as a matter of course that there would be idle men at his gate this morning, tomorrow morning, every morning. He has accepted orders upon the security of that expectation. If the reserve at his place of business or in the immediate locality disappeared, he complained of a labor shortage. In his mind, consciously or unconsciously, was an idea that *he was entitled to have available at all times enough labor to man his plant* to maximum capacity, even though he did not run at maximum capacity thirty days in the year. He expected that those who did his hiring for him would be able to *select* from an assembled group the man best suited to do his work, and that laborers would compete with each other for the jobs he offered. . . ."[6]

Whatever the optimum volume of unemployment may be, there is little doubt that much could be done to improve some of the conditions that create idleness which some persons now consider unavoidable. This will become apparent as we discuss further the various types of unemployment and the means for its alleviation, the question of labor turnover, and the machinery for labor placement.

Unemployment Due to Changes in Business Organization

Regardless of fluctuations in general business conditions, changes are always taking place within and among individual plants and companies which cause varying periods of unemployment to numbers of persons. Each year thousands of companies go bankrupt or for other reasons close their doors; other companies transfer some or all of their business from one plant to another in a different locality. Reorganizations and mergers are continually being made, most of which result in the layoff of sizable groups of workers.

To the workers who lose their jobs because of plant shutdowns, their unemployment is the antithesis of "normal," for many of them probably spent long years in these plants. Also, even though there may be openings in other plants, these workers may not be hired because of their age or lack of required skills. To them, the

---

[6] *Ibid.*, p. 14.

closing of the plant may mean prolonged and possibly permanent unemployment. By and large, however, much of the dislocation resulting from changes in business organization represents a healthy state of dynamic business operation; some of it is inevitable under a business system which is carried on by millions of different enterprises whose continued existence is affected not only by their ability to survive under competition and changes in consumer demands, but also by the death or retirement of their owners.

What, in terms of unemployment, is the irreducible price to pay for the risks and possible ultimate benefits of new business ventures, consolidations, and reorganizations, can be determined only by thorough knowledge of all the facts in each case.

Seasonal Unemployment

The term "normal" is likely to be misleading because it seems to imply a healthy condition, or at least one which it is impossible to improve. This is certainly not true with respect to all seasonal unemployment. In its strictest interpretation, seasonal unemployment is that which results from a change of seasons—spring, summer, fall, and winter. Some industries, however, operate on a seasonal basis because of long habit and inertia or as a result of artificially created seasonal changes in styles, and not because the inherent nature of the industry requires seasonal operation. As we shall see later, it is frequently possible to reduce, if not altogether eliminate, seasonal unemployment through changes in methods of production and marketing.

Weather or natural factors affect employment in four ways: (1) Most important, it determines the time for the growing and supplying of many raw products. Cotton and most food crops are raised in the summer; each crop has its own peculiar time for harvesting, and therefore for canning or otherwise processing. The season for fishing varies with the catch, but most fishing ceases with the freezing of the waters; the cutting of wool, slaughtering, and meat packing depend upon cattle and sheep raising. (2) The weather affects employment in most outdoor work. Lumbering in the north is best done in the winter before the spring rains and thaws; Great Lakes shipping ceases during the winter when the lakes are frozen. Building and road construction are greatly affected by the seasons and weather. (3) Changes in seasons affect consumers' demands. Different clothing is worn in the different seasons. Coal is needed for heating in the winter, whereas the demand for electric fans, screens, cold drinks, and vacation services increases in the summer. (4) Seasonality in the growing and procuring of raw materials, in construction and other outdoor work, and in what people wear and use, affects the employment which is necessary for the transportation and packaging of these products. Railroad carloadings fluctuate with the needs for the hauling of wheat, cattle, and coal; the manufacture of tin cans and bottles is influenced by the seasonal operations of the canneries; building materials must be delivered at the time and place of construction.

Almost every industry is directly or indirectly affected by the exigencies of the seasons and weather, but the fluctuations they cause in employment vary in degree and in the months they take place. The seasons of maximum activity in some industries and occupations duplicate each other, in some they overlap, and in some they dovetail, either naturally or by conscious effort. Although the patterns of fluctuation vary, industrial employment in the total tends to be higher in the spring and fall, with some slump in the summer and a severer slump during the winter. For manufacturing as a whole, the seasonal variation in the number who are employed averages about 10 per cent; for building construction at least 30 per cent; for wholesale and retail trade somewhat less than 10 per cent; for transportation and public utilities about 15 per cent.

Irregular and Casual Employment

Not all irregular or under-employment is due to seasonal fluctuations. Throughout industry irregular employment occurs within the busy as well as the dull seasons. In an industry or plant where the number employed varies only 5 or 10 per cent from season to season, the pay roll may fluctuate as much as 40 or 50 per cent from day to day or week to week. Although the plant force is made up of *regular* employees, the income or take-home wages of these employees is very *irregular* because of part-time work.

In some occupations irregularity of employment shades off into casual work. Examples are longshoring, which is dependent upon the arrival and departure of ships, the services of the extra waiters and musicians hired for banquets, and much of the common labor hired by building contractors, farmers, and other employers to meet special needs and emergencies. Casual workers suffer the added inconvenience of frequent changes in employers and are thus deprived of the psychological benefits which come from the feeling of belonging to a job and a particular group of fellow workers.

The irregular employment of "regular" employees stems from the practice of paying workers by the hour, day, or piece. Unlike office and supervisory personnel, production workers are usually dismissed whenever there is no work for them, in order to keep down labor costs. Lack of work may be the result of internal situations such as machine breakdowns, insufficient materials on hand, or uneven flow in the processing of the work. Frequently it is due to the practice of working up orders as they are received from customers, without any sales program to promote continuity of orders, and with no provision for manufacturing for stock when there is a lull in orders. This condition is prevalent among small shoe plants and garment shops whose owners have limited cash reserves and pay rolls must be met with current receipts from sales.

Irregularity in daily and weekly employment in many instances is due to the existence of pools of surplus labor and the practice of sharing the work among a larger force than is actually needed. This situation may develop as an aftermath of a declining industry or business, especially in one-industry communities such as New England textile mill towns and coal mining areas, where there is little opportunity to obtain other kinds of employment as the work tapers off in the declining industry. Under such circumstances, it is a matter of dividing the available work until death or retirement removes the labor no longer needed.

Surplus labor reserves may also be the result of company policy or mismanagement. For reasons of "discipline" a company may plan to have more workers on its pay roll than it can keep busy. More frequently, perhaps, the surplus labor is the consequence of departmental or non-centralized hiring practices which result in the various foremen retaining the maximum number of workers needed for the peak loads in each department. Instead of employees being transferred from one department to another as fluctuations occur in the flow of work, each department maintains a full crew with division of work and temporary layoffs during its slack periods. Such pools of labor reserves have been traditional in the steel industry, for example. During the comparatively stable production period in the 1920's, an average of 30,000 to 70,000 steelworkers were idle each month; this represented 7 to 15 per cent of the total number attached to the industry.[7] And these monthly figures do not reveal the unknown daily and weekly irregularities in employment.

Cyclical Unemployment

Irregular, seasonal, and occasional unemployment, which in the aggregate is called "normal" or "frictional," affects different groups of workers at different times and places. It occurs in normally prosperous years; and although the interruptions of income cause hardships to the particular workers and communities concerned, they create no widespread economic destruction. In some instances other workers and communities may even benefit from the losses suffered elsewhere, as for example, in the dislocations resulting from one business having captured the market from a competing business, or a new industry or product having supplanted another.

The unemployment that results from a cyclical business depression is an entirely different phenomenon in its far-reaching effects upon every class of persons throughout the nation. During a major depression like that of the 1930's the "farmers learned that it meant reduced markets, lower prices, and a multitude of sons and daughters coming home from the cities to be supported, often bringing families with them. The taxpayers found that it meant millions and then billions for relief. The sales of merchants and manufacturers dwindled until tens of thousands went into bankruptcy. Even larger numbers cashed their investments at ruinous figures and surrendered their life insurance trying to save their businesses. A multitude of concerns closed their doors. Landlords

[7] Carroll R. Daugherty, M. G. deChazeau, and S. S. Stratton, *The Economics of the Iron and Steel Industry,* McGraw-Hill Book Company, Inc., New York, 1937, p. 1125.

found business property, homes and apartments vacated as tenants crowded into small quarters or left the community. Cities and counties by thousands reached the verge of bankruptcy, as both relief burdens and tax delinquencies rose. Debts which had not caused concern became an incubus. Wage earners by millions consumed their savings, lost their homes, reduced their standards of living, endured both physical and psychical misery. Thousands of farmers, professional people and business men found themselves in the same plight. Unemployment relief became the major non-military public expenditure. The nation learned that unemployment, itself an effect of other causes, can crush a nation."[8]

Cyclical depressions, moreover, are not confined to a single nation but have an international sweep. Although their effects are most severe in highly industrialized countries, the majority of whose citizens live by making and spending money incomes, major business depressions reach every corner of the globe to a greater or lesser extent.[9] During the fifty-year period 1890–1940 there have been five periods of general and severe business depression, and additional years when unemployment has been less severe but of considerable volume. Unemployment was acute throughout most of the 1890's and for a briefer period in 1907–1908. A severe and what would probably have been a prolonged period of unemployment began in 1913 but was terminated by a sudden pickup in business in response to war needs, first for Europe and then for this country. The post-war depression of 1920–1921 resulted in the idleness of more than one-fifth of all manufacturing and transportation employees and one-fourth of the building-trades workers.

So far as the number of persons and the duration of idleness are concerned, the most severe period of unemployment which this country has yet experienced began with the stock market crash in the fall of 1929. For more than three years the volume of un-

---

[8] D. D. Lescohier, *History of Labor*, The Macmillan Company, New York, 1935, p. 114.

[9] W. C. Mitchell, *Business Cycles*, National Bureau of Economic Research, Inc., New York, 1927, pp. 424–450. The conspectus of business fluctuations in various countries between 1790 and 1925 given in Professor Mitchell's study shows the international impact of the depressions in 1815, 1825, 1837, the crisis of 1847 and the panic of 1857, the big depressions in the 1870's and 1890's, the panic in 1907, the depression in 1912–1913, and the post-war depression in 1920–1921.

employment grew steadily until, by the spring of 1933, it reached a peak of 12 to 14 millions. Following unprecedented action by the federal government, as explained in the next chapter, the amount of unemployment gradually declined to slightly less than 7 million. In the latter part of 1937, however, it again started to rise, reaching almost 10 million by the summer of 1939 before the outbreak of war in Europe caused an upturn in business activity in this country.

Should the unemployment during this entire ten-year period be classified as cyclical unemployment? If so, how long would it have been prolonged if there had been no war? Was half the maximum total—that is, the amount in excess of the low point in 1937 when business had seemingly recovered—due to other factors? Several million unemployed could be attributed to the effects of seasonal irregularities and to layoffs due to other specific reasons. What of the remaining 4 or 5 million? Does this represent a continuing pool of unemployment, a growing residue of persons displaced by technological improvements?

Technological Unemployment

During the early years of the Industrial Revolution the workers who were displaced or were threatened with displacement by machinery frequently engaged in machine-breaking riots in a futile attempt to save their jobs.[10] When cotton textile machines threatened to destroy their wool market, English sheep growers were instrumental in getting laws enacted to curb the manufacture of cotton goods. In more recent times there has been little display of violent opposition to the introduction of machinery, although improved technology has been the indirect cause of some of the strikes which have occurred recently. There is also no disposition at present to discourage technological progress by legal restrictions. Nevertheless, there is real concern over the effect of technology upon various kinds of employment opportunities and a great deal of discussion about whether or not it results in a permanent net reduction in the ratio of jobs to available workers.

---

[10] See J. L. and B. Hammond, *The Age of the Chartists, 1832–54; The Skilled Laborer, 1760–1832; The Town Laborer,* all published by Longmans, Green & Co., London, in 1930, 1919, and 1917 respectively; also, G. D. H. Cole, *Chartist Portraits,* Macmillan & Co., Ltd., London, 1941.

These facts are true: (1) Machine production makes possible a higher standard of living for a larger national population than a handicraft and agricultural economy. (2) Technological changes which displace some workers and make some jobs obsolescent also create new kinds of jobs and employment opportunities. (3) Some inventions, e.g., radio and motion pictures, are more labor producing than labor saving since they create many new kinds of jobs and cause few displacements.

When considering the apparent paradoxes of the effect of technology upon employment, the following basic characteristics of technological progress must be borne in mind: (1) Until recently at least, technical improvements have involved ever-increasing amounts of capital investment per worker employed.[11] (2) The increase in fixed capital investment tends to enlarge the size of individual enterprises and to increase the concentration of production. (3) The stages in industrial processing tend to be multiplied and to become more complex. This roundaboutness of production introduces time lags, multiplies the effect of an interruption of work at any one stage, and enhances the potential areas of friction in employment.

The impact of technology upon the number of jobs or volume of employment is not obvious and direct since, in actual practice, summary mass layoffs at the time new machines are installed are not frequent. Most technological improvements are introduced in small doses, scattered among hundreds and thousands of different plants, their immediate effects being absorbed in the dynamics of

---

[11] The amount of capital requirements per worker varies greatly among the various industries. A study by the Chamber of Commerce in 1945 showed that an average investment of $7000 per worker was required in the city of Gastonia, N. C., ranging from $1500 for such enterprises as filling stations and cleaning and eating establishments, to more than $44,000 for wholesale cotton merchants. The Pullman-Standard Company estimates an average investment in their company of $9000 per employee. The average for all industries has been estimated to be from $5000 to $7000 per worker.

Some economists contend that there is no evidence of a marked increase in capital investment *per unit of output* during the past twenty years, and that the efficiency of some machines has been improved without increases in capital investment. This does not necessarily mean that there is not an increase in investment *per worker employed,* however. According to a recent survey, more than 90 per cent of all investments in business plant and equipment during the decade 1931–1940 was for replacement purposes only. (Announcement of the Twentieth Century Fund, February, 1946.)

industrial expansion and normal labor turnover or, in reverse, obscured in the ground swell of a general economic depression.

During a business depression following a prolonged shutdown, a concern may install new machinery and equipment in readiness for the resumption of business. When the plant is reopened, fewer workers are taken on than were previously employed, although the volume of business may exceed the former output. But no one has actually been displaced at the time the machines were installed, the layoffs having already been made at the beginning of the depression. Likewise, if a concern installs labor-saving machines when its business is expanding, it does not need to lay off any employees and may even take on additional workers. Even though the business is not expanding, displacements are frequently absorbed through the process of normal labor turnover, the displaced persons being transferred to the jobs vacated by employees who quit for personal reasons. During the conversion from the manual to the dial operation of telephones, practically no telephone operators lost their jobs. The change-over was made gradually in each city and the decreased demand for switchboard operators was absorbed by the naturally high turnover among young women operators. Nevertheless, complete conversion to the dial system means the loss of about two-thirds of the employment opportunities afforded by manual operation.[12]

The impact upon employment is even less direct when the technological changes are introduced in newly established plants. A company may branch out into an entirely different locality and construct a new building with the most modern equipment. Because of the reduced manufacturing costs, more and more of its business will be done at the new plant, with a gradual decline in employment in the old plant. Industry is replete with illustrations

---

[12] A study made by the Bureau of Labor Statistics in 1930, when one-third of the Bell companies' telephones had been converted to the dial system, indicated that if the output of calls per operator had remained the same in 1930 as in 1921 (when less than 3 per cent of the telephones were dial), the number of operators necessary for handling the calls made in 1930 would have required almost 70,000 additional operators. (*Monthly Labor Review,* February, 1932, p. 235.)

The census shows that between 1930 and 1940 there was a 16 per cent decrease in the number of telephone operators, even though many more telephones were in use than ever before.

of this kind. New England textile companies constructing new mills in the southern states, Akron rubber companies opening branch plants in numerous scattered communities, steel companies building new continuous strip mills in different localities from their old mills, are only a few of the outstanding examples. The transfer of business to more efficient plants may not be due to the planned, overt action of individual companies, but may be the result of a company's losing business because of competition from other concerns which have more efficient machines and methods of production. Whether the new plants are owned by the same or different companies, employees in the old plants gradually lose their jobs and fewer persons *per unit of output* are employed in the more modern plants located elsewhere.

Problem of Measuring Technological Unemployment

If the effects of technological improvements upon employment are obscure so far as individual instances are concerned, can their total impact be measured or known? What formula should be used? Let us use a hypothetical case[13] which is analogous to the telephone experience discussed above. Suppose that in one year 100 men were employed in a given industry to produce 100 units of output and that in the next year the use of labor-saving techniques made possible the manufacture of 110 units with only 90 men. Since employment declined by 10 men despite the increase in output, one might conclude that the technological displacement amounted to 10 men. One might also point out that if the new techniques had not been used and production had increased 10 units, 110 men would have been employed instead of the 90 actually at work. On this basis it is possible to state that the increased productivity affected 20 men—the 10 who actually lost jobs they had held the previous year and the 10 who would have been employed but for the increase in productivity. On the other hand, it is equally valid to maintain that if the improved techniques had been put into operation while production amounted to 100 units, only 82 men would have been required, indicating a displacement of

---

[13] As cited by David Weintraub, "Unemployment and Increasing Productivity," in National Resources Committee, *Technological Trends and National Policy,* Government Printing Office, Washington, 1937, chap. 5, p. 80.

18 workers which, however, was offset in part by the actual increase in output requiring the services of 8 more men. Thus, it is possible to draw three different conclusions as to the displacement effected by improved efficiency within a single industry.

However, a gain in output per man-year in any particular industry adopting a new method or machine does not always mean a decline in the total amount of labor required for the final product, for the new method may involve increases in labor requirements in the production of the materials or capital investment needed in the earlier or later stages of the processing. In the illustration above, some men were employed in the making of the new machines and others were constantly needed to keep the machines in repair and running order. Also, as indicated in Chapter 4, the demand for the product may increase as a result of the decreased prices made possible by improved efficiency, and the expanded volume of production may require as many workers as were employed prior to the introduction of the new method, or even more men.

Although the impact upon employment of technological changes within a particular industry or trade cannot be conclusively measured, reasonably accurate estimates can be made of the interindustry or over-all effects of such changes by comparing total output to total employment from year to year. If these comparisons are based upon "normal" years of business activity when extraneous influences such as depressions or booms are absent, it can be assumed that any reduced ratio of employment to output is a result of technology. Two such years are 1923 and 1939 (or 1940), which cover the period following the post-World War I depression and the period before the World War II boom started.

What happened to production and employment during these seventeen years? Agricultural production was almost 18 per cent higher in 1940 than in 1923, but agricultural employment was 7 per cent less. Although 18 per cent fewer tons of bituminous coal were mined in 1940 than in 1923, the number of miners had declined almost 38 per cent. During this same period there was a decrease of 50 per cent in the number of railroad workers, although the decrease in revenue traffic units was less than 23 per cent. Several thousand fewer wage earners were employed in all manufacturing industries in 1939 than in 1923, but the volume of production was over 33 per cent greater.[14] Moreover, the persons employed in 1940 worked fewer hours than they did in the earlier period. In manufacturing, for example, workers were actually employed 10 hours less per week, on the average, in 1940 than in 1923. If there had been no reduction in hours, it can be reasonably assumed that the decline in employment would have been considerably greater.

INCIDENCE OF UNEMPLOYMENT

Who are the first to be laid off during a recession in employment, and what workers find it most difficult to find new jobs? Even in the most serious periods of unemployment some workers retain their regular jobs, or, if laid off, find other employment. There have been several studies of persons who lost their jobs because of plant shutdowns or technological changes, and a number of surveys were made during the depression of the 1930's for the purpose of discovering what classes of workers were laid off first and found it most difficult to obtain reemployment. Although these experiences may not be exactly duplicated in the future, the studies reveal what is likely to happen during any period of mass layoffs or declining employment.

Occupation and Skill

During a business depression, the people attached to the construction and durable goods industries are most severely affected, especially those engaged in manufacturing machine tools and other capital equipment. Not only the mechanics and laborers, but also the professional and semi-professional workers in these industries feel the impact to a greater extent than do most other professional people. During the four year period 1930–1934, more than one-third of all the engineers in this country had had some period of unemployment and half of these had been out of work for more than a year.[15] Although similar statistical data are not available for architects and draftsmen, it is known that relatively

---

[14] These figures are derived from data in the *Monthly Labor Review*, September, 1940, p. 520, and from revised employment data in later issues of the *Review*.

[15] *Ibid.*, January, 1937, p. 37.

few of them were employed in their normal vocations during the worst years of the depression.

Throughout industry as a whole, all indications point to the fact that during a depression the hardships of unemployment fall more heavily upon the unskilled and inexperienced than upon the skilled and versatile workers.[16] This does not necessarily mean that unskilled jobs disappear to a greater extent than skilled jobs; indeed, the reverse is probably true because of the relatively greater proportion of skilled mechanics in the construction and metal industries, the industries most affected by business depressions. So far as individuals are concerned, however, a greater proportion of the unskilled tend to be laid off because the more skilled workers are substituted for the less skilled through the downgrading and "bumping" process which takes place during a retraction of employment.

The impact of unemployment is quite different in the case of isolated plant shutdowns due to other than general business depressions, or to layoffs of particular groups of workers as a result of the introduction of a new machine. In such instances there is little or no sifting of those laid off or retained; and the incidence of the initial unemployment, at least, is solely a matter of who happens to be employed in the closed plant or on the jobs affected by the change in technology. Following such layoffs, the skilled and specialized workers frequently find it more difficult to find other jobs than do the less skilled, and thus experience longer periods of unemployment. If the skilled workers are beyond middle age, as many of them are, they are handicapped in obtaining employment in other plants, because the higher skilled jobs in most plants are filled by promotions from within. Also, if the skilled, experienced worker has a home and family it is not as easy for him to move elsewhere to find employment as it is for a younger, unattached individual. The resulting effect of this geographical and occupational immobility is aggravated when the change in the employment situation takes place in isolated, one-industry communities. It is almost impossible for a coal miner who has spent

---

[16] The 1937 federal unemployment registration indicated that 42 per cent of the male unemployed, excluding those on emergency work programs, were unskilled, whereas only 27 per cent of all males were classified as unskilled in the 1930 census. (*Ibid.,* August 1938, p. 322.`

long years in the mines "to pull up stakes" and reestablish himself and his family elsewhere. When machines were introduced in the glass industry, it resulted in permanent joblessness for many of the older craftsmen, one reason being that the hand factories had been located in small, isolated communities in the natural gas areas.

Most of the hand cutters who were laid off between 1919 and 1926, when machines were introduced in the men's clothing industry in Chicago, experienced considerable unemployment despite the fact that business conditions were relatively good. Less than one-fourth of these cutters found other jobs immediately after their layoffs; 7 per cent had found no work as late as 1928, and those who were reemployed had lost an average of 5½ months.[17] The skilled rubber workers laid off in Hartford, Connecticut, in 1929 because of a plant shutdown fared worse during the subsequent depression years than the unskilled rubber workers who lost their jobs in the same plant shutdown. Said one who investigated this situation: "Apparently the qualities which helped men to rise to skilled jobs and high wages while at work are of limited use in helping men to readjust satisfactorily when the job goes."[18]

Race

During a mass layoff, Negroes are usually the first to be laid off and they find it most difficult to obtain reemployment. Relative skill and seniority are no doubt important factors in the initial layoffs, but when jobs are scarce Negroes frequently find themselves at a competitive disadvantage when seeking new jobs, regardless of skill. According to the 1937 federal registration of the unemployed, the proportion of unemployed skilled male Negroes was twice as great as the proportion of skilled white workers, whereas the proportion of total male Negroes who were unemployed was only one-third higher than that of male white workers.

---

[17] R. J. Myers, "Occupational Readjustments of Displaced Skilled Workers," *Journal of Political Economy*, August, 1929, pp. 473–489. See also Isador Lubin, *The Absorption of the Unemployed by American Industry*, Brookings Institution, Washington, 1929.

[18] Ewan Clague, W. J. Couper, and E. W. Bakke, *The Readjustment of Industrial Workers Displaced by Two Plant Shutdowns*, Yale University Press, New Haven, 1934.

Surveys in a number of cities in 1931 showed that the percentages of unemployed Negroes, skilled and unskilled, were two to four times greater than their percentage of the total population.[19] In 19 cities the unemployment of native white women ranged from 10 to 22 per cent, in contrast to a range of from 20 to 75 per cent for Negro women.[20] In 1934, less than one-fifth of all employable whites in Massachusetts were unemployed, although one-third of the colored were without jobs; and in Cincinnati 21 per cent of the employable whites were unemployed, compared with 53 per cent of the Negroes. In 1938, during the business recession following partial recovery from the worst of the depression, 51 per cent of the employable Negroes in Philadelphia were without jobs, as against 30 per cent of the native white and 24 per cent of the foreign-born white workers. In Cincinnati that same year 53 per cent of the employable colored, in contrast to 16 per cent of the white workers, were unemployed.[21] The 1940 census for the entire country showed a 20 per cent higher ratio of unemployment among Negro than white workers. All these figures refer to total unemployment. If partial unemployment or part-time work were included, the differences would be much larger because of the greater prevalence of casual employment among Negroes.

Sex and Age

During the early years of the 'thirties depression a greater proportion of men than women were unemployed. In Massachusetts in 1934 more than 26 per cent of the employable men and 21 per cent of the employable women were unemployed; in Michigan in 1935 almost 20 per cent of the men, in contrast to 14.5 per cent of the women, were unemployed.[22] As the depression continued, however, the proportion of unemployed women tended to increase, but this probably resulted from the fact that additional women entered the labor market because their husbands or fathers were without jobs.[23] The smaller incidence of unemployment among women who

---

[19] *Monthly Labor Review*, June, 1931, p. 60; May, 1932, p. 1038.

[20] *Ibid.*, April, 1934, p. 794.

[21] *Ibid.*, December, 1934, p. 1333; October, 1939, pp. 840, 837.

[22] *Ibid.*, December, 1934, p. 1334; November, 1936, p. 1160.

[23] A study of urban unemployment in Pennsylvania in 1934 showed 30 per cent of the women and 27 per cent of the men unemployed. However, 35 per cent of the jobless women were new workers, in contrast to 17 per cent of the men. (*Ibid.*, September, 1935, p. 618.)

normally work is chiefly due to their type of employment. In general, during a depression employment does not decline as much in the retail, clerical, and service occupations, where women predominate, as in manufacturing, construction, and mining. It is also true that women are sometimes placed on jobs formerly held by men, at a lower rate of pay, during a depression.

A severe depression is especially hard on very young workers and those above middle age. Young people leaving school with no previous work experience find it extremely difficult to compete for jobs when there is an abundance of experienced applicants. Older persons who have regular jobs are usually retained as long as possible; but after they once lose their jobs they find it difficult, and sometimes impossible, to obtain new ones.

Engineers are an example of this. Half the engineers in this country who attempted to enter the profession after the depression began in 1930 were idle at one time or other during the subsequent four years, compared with one-fourth of the older engineers. However, the younger engineers experienced less unemployment, on the average, than those who were beyond middle age. Thus the median period of unemployment for those graduating from school during 1925–1929 was about one year, in contrast to almost two years for those graduating prior to 1905.[24]

Although young people probably have less difficulty in finding jobs than persons beyond middle age, the proportion of youth who are unemployed is greater during prolonged depressions than that of older persons, because additional young people are continually leaving school and seeking employment.[25] A study of all the unemployed in Philadelphia in the spring of 1931 indicated the largest percentage of unemployment in the 16–25 age group and the smallest in the 36–45 group.[26] In New York City in 1935, approximately one-third of the young persons 16–24 years of age who were out of school and wanted work were without jobs. About 10 per cent had less than eighth-grade education, slightly under 24 per cent had completed eight grades, 40 per cent had from one to three years of high school, 20 per cent were high-

---

[24] *Ibid.*, January, 1937, p. 38.
[25] This is true in foreign countries as well as in the United States. See *International Labour Review,* May, 1935, September, 1935, May, 1940.
[26] *Monthly Labor Review,* May, 1932, p. 1038.

school graduates, and 6 per cent had anywhere from one to seven years of college.[27]

Two state-wide and one national census vividly reveal the relatively greater impact of unemployment upon young persons. These surveys, it will be noted, were made at different times—the Massachusetts census, about four years after the beginning of the great depression; the Michigan census five years, and the federal census a decade after it began. Each survey revealed that unemployment among the 15–19 age group was about twice as great as the total for all ages, and the unemployment of persons between 20 and 24 years of age was from one-fourth to one-third greater.

TABLE 9.   Percentage Unemployed, by Age Group, 1934 and 1940

	Massachusetts[a] January, 1934	Michigan[a] January, 1935	Federal Census March, 1940
All Ages	24.9	18.8	14.9
15–19 years	50.5	34.3	32.7
20–24	29.9	24.0	18.4
25–29	21.0	15.1	11.6
30–34	19.0	13.0	
35–39	19.5	13.2	11.2
40–44	20.0	14.2	
45–49	22.0	16.8	12.7
50–54	23.3	19.7	
55–59	25.6	23.0	14.6
60–64	27.2	27.3	
65 years and over	28.0	24.5	10.2

[a] *Ibid.*, December, 1934, p. 1334, and November, 1936, p. 1160. To obtain comparability in age classification, slight adjustments were made in the Massachusetts data.

STATISTICS OF UNEMPLOYMENT

Despite all the concern over the effects of unemployment and the discussions about its causes, it is only within very recent years that data have been collected which make it possible to estimate how much unemployment actually exists from time to time. This is not too surprising when one realizes the complexities and difficulties involved in taking a census of unemployment. In addition to the vast machinery necessary for collecting and tabulating informa-

[27] *Ibid.*, February, 1937, p. 267.

tion, there is the perplexing problem of whom to consider unemployed. Is a person unemployed who has a job but is temporarily laid off? Is one who is sick or otherwise incapacitated unemployed? Should a woman whose primary responsibility is managing her home but who customarily works for wages part of her time be counted as unemployed if she loses her part-time job? What of the man who has lost his job but who wants to loaf a while before going to work again? Are young men and women unemployed who are helping their families on the farm after being laid off from their city jobs? Should jobless old people be included if they indicate they would like to work provided they could find jobs which were suitable for their advanced years? Are students unemployed if they cannot find after-school jobs which they need and want?

In terms of lost income and production, idleness resulting from these conditions is tantamount to unemployment. In terms of the number of persons who need and are able to work in relation to the number of job opportunities available, not all of this idleness can be considered unemployment. It is obvious that the census taker must exercise considerable discrimination in the collection and assembling of unemployment data, and the user of census material must bear these different concepts in mind when citing unemployment figures.

Available Statistics

There have been five federal censuses of unemployment and one nation-wide voluntary registration. In addition, numerous area surveys have been conducted by federal, state, and local governments and other agencies. These various censuses, together with population and employment data, furnish the basis for all the available estimates on unemployment in this country.

A federal census of unemployment was taken as early as 1890, when gainfully occupied persons[28] were asked if they had been out of work the preceding year, and if so, for what length of time. Similar censuses were taken in 1900 and 1910, but the returns from the latter were never tabulated. In 1915 the U. S. Bureau of Labor Statistics made several surveys of unemployment on a sampling basis in New York City and in 28 other cities scattered

---

[28] See p. 29, footnote 1, in which the meaning of "gainfully occupied" is explained.

throughout the country.[29] During the next fifteen years nothing
further was done by the federal government, although other
agencies made surveys in a number of cities and various persons
compiled nation-wide estimates.[30]

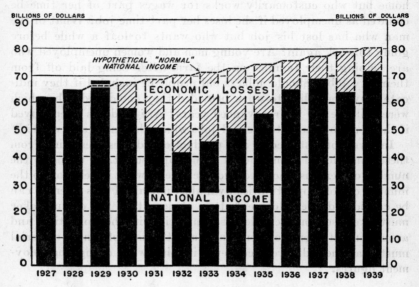

Fig. 14. *Losses in National Income During the Depression of the
1930's, at Average Prices in 1935–1939.* (*Source: Federal Security
Agency,* Social Security Bulletin, *vol. viii, no. 12.*)

When unemployment became acute following the business crash
late in 1929, there was considerable demand for comprehensive

[29] Bulletin Nos. 172 and 195; *Monthly Labor Review,* January, 1916, p. 14.
[30] Using the indexes of employment compiled by the Bureau of Labor Statistics and other federal agencies, the figures of the Bureau of the Census on
gainful workers, and data from the various censuses and surveys of unemployment which had been made up to that time, Professor Paul Douglas compiled
estimates of unemployment in the manufacturing, transportation, building
trades, and mining industries from 1897 through 1926. (P. H. Douglas and
A. Director, *The Problem of Unemployment,* The Macmillan Company, New
York, 1931, chap. 2.)
In 1940 the National Industrial Conference Board published a series of figures on total unemployment from 1900 to 1940 which were derived by subtract-
ing estimated employment from the total number of gainful workers. (*Economic Record,* vol. ii, no. 8, 1940.)

figures on the volume of existing unemployment, and the Bureau
of the Census was authorized to include questions on unemployment in the 1930 census. In this canvass, instead of people being
asked how much time they had lost from work during the preceding year as in the 1890–1910 censuses,[31] they were simply asked
whether they had been at work the last preceding workday, and if
not, what was the cause of their idleness. Persons who reported
that they were unemployed were divided into several categories.
Class A included those out of a job, able to work, and looking for
a job; Class B included those who considered they had jobs but
who had been laid off without pay because of slack work; Classes
C-G included those who had and those who did not have jobs but
who were sick or voluntarily idle. No one was very satisfied with
the returns from this census, which showed approximately 2½
million persons in Class A and ¾ million in Class B; this, combined, was equivalent to 6.6 per cent of the total gainful workers.[32]

One of the ironic aspects of the 1930's depression was the numerous registrations of the unemployed whenever clamor for additional relief became especially acute. The only dependable surveys
were those conducted by a few state and local relief agencies
which made house-to-house canvasses of their areas and carefully
interviewed each family. None of the voluntary registrations, including the one conducted by the federal government in 1937, provides reliable data either on the total number or the characteristics of the unemployed.[33] Nevertheless, in lieu of more accurate

---

[31] Census authorities had concluded that there was a considerable margin of
error in the earlier censuses because people did not remember how much time
they had lost from work the entire preceding year. This was one reason the
1910 material was never tabulated.

[32] It was generally felt that the enumerators failed to obtain reports from
many unemployed persons since they were paid only 2 cents for each schedule
filled out and probably did not make return calls if people were not at home at
their first or second visits.

[33] In the federal registration, which cost over $2,000,000, cards were distrib-
uted to each home throughout the country by postmen. As a check on the reliability of these voluntary returns, a house-to-house canvass was made in a
few selected areas. These test censuses revealed that only 72 per cent of the
totally unemployed and only 57 per cent of the partly employed were included in the registration—a difference of 3 million in the totally unemployed
figure. With such a wide margin of error in the total figure, the report's conclusions on the characteristics of the unemployed cannot be accepted as entirely accurate. Their undependability is further enhanced by the fact that
persons filling out the cards obviously interpreted the questions differently.

data, the returns from this registration as well as the 1930 census were used by various employer, union, and other organizations and individuals for estimating unemployment for the decade 1930–1940. With each making such adjustments in the available data as was deemed necessary, it is not surprising that there were considerable differences among the various estimates. For example, the estimates for 1933, when unemployment was highest, ranged from less than 12 million to more than 16 million.[34]

Current Statistics

The comprehensive survey of unemployment which was made in March, 1940, in connection with the decennial census, removed the arguments and controversies which had previously existed about the exact volume of unemployment. In this census all persons in the labor force were classified into three major categories: (1) The employed, which included those who were at work at the time of the census and those who had a job but were not actually at work because of vacation, illness, or layoff of less than four weeks, but who had definite instructions to return to their jobs at a specified time. (Although the latter would appear to be comparable to Class B in the 1930 census, actually there is a good deal of difference because of the stricter definition in 1940.) (2) Those who were engaged on federal, state, or local unemployment relief projects. Because these persons were on relief as a result of their inability to get other work, they were considered unemployed. (3) Persons who were able to work and were actively seeking it but had no job of any sort at the time of the census.

According to the 1940 census, 3,042,000 persons were on emergency work-relief projects and 4,919,000 others were seeking work. These 7,961,000 individuals represented 14.9 per cent of the total labor force who were "unemployed" during the last week in March 1940. Over 767,000 of the unemployed were "new workers," that is, persons who had not previously worked for as much as one month.

---

[34] The A. F. of L. estimate was 13,271,000. Most of the others were between 12 and 13 million, except that of the Cleveland Trust, which reported 14,098,000; the Alexander Hamilton Institute, which estimated 14,394,000; the National Research League, which gave 14,722,000; and the Labor Research Association, which reported 16,138,000.

Since the taking of the 1940 census, the Bureau of the Census has issued monthly estimates of unemployment based on monthly enumerations of a sample of households within a carefully selected number of counties throughout the United States.[35] Thus, since 1940 there have been official monthly data on the volume of employment and unemployment in this country, classified on the basis of such major categories as agricultural and non-agricultural workers, sex, age, and certain other characteristics.

Using these census data, various indexes of employment, and other source material, the Bureau of Labor Statistics has made estimates of unemployment for the period 1929–1940. These estimates and annual averages computed from the monthly figures currently issued by the Census Bureau are shown in Table 10.

TABLE 10. Trend of Unemployment, 1929–1946[a]

Year	Number	Percentage of Civilian Labor Force
1929	1,499,000	3.1
1930	4,248,000	8.8
1931	7,911,000	16.1
1932	11,901,000	24.0
1933	12,634,000	25.2
1934	10,968,000	21.6
1935	10,208,000	19.9
1936	8,598,000	16.5
1937	7,273,000	13.8
1938	9,910,000	18.7
1939	8,842,000	16.5
1940	7,476,000	13.9
1941	5,010,000	9.3
1942	2,380,000	4.4
1943	1,070,000	2.0
1944	840,000	1.6
1945	1,050,000	2.0
1946	2,270,000	3.9

[a] Figures for 1929–1940 are estimates of the Bureau of Labor Statistics; those for 1941–1946 are based on the Bureau of Census monthly reports.

It should be noted that those engaged on work-relief projects are counted as unemployed. As indicated in Chapter 7, a considerable number of those classified as "unemployed" during 1933–1940 were earning some income from government work-relief programs.

[35] Students interested in sampling techniques are referred to the article describing the theory underlying the sample design in *Annals of Mathematical Statistics*, vol. xiv, 1943, pp. 333–362.

It should be borne in mind that these are average annual figures and that there was a much greater monthly fluctuation than is indicated by this table. For instance, the number of persons who were unemployed in March, 1933, at the depth of the depression, included at least 30 per cent of the labor force. Moreover, it should be remembered that urban unemployment was much greater than the average for the entire country. Surveys of all employable workers in Philadelphia, for example, showed 42 per cent unemployed in 1932 and 46 per cent in 1933, with an additional 20 per cent having part-time employment.[36]

SELECTED REFERENCES

Bakke, E. Wight, *The Unemployed Worker,* Yale University Press, New Haven, 1940.

Beard, Charles A. (ed.), *America Faces the Future,* Houghton Mifflin, Boston, 1931.

Douglas, Paul H., and Director, Aaron, *The Problem of Unemployment,* The Macmillan Company, New York, 1931.

Ezekiel, Mordecai, *Jobs for All,* Alfred A. Knopf, New York, 1939.

Hammond, J. L. and Barbara, *The Rise of Modern Industry,* Harcourt, Brace & Company, Inc., New York, 1937.

Lescohier, D. D., *The Labor Market,* The Macmillan Company, New York, 1919.

Mitchell, Wesley C., *Business Cycles,* National Bureau of Economic Research, Inc., New York, 1927.

National Industrial Conference Board, *Lay Off and Its Prevention,* New York, 1930.

National Industrial Conference Board, "Employment and Unemployment of the Labor Force, 1900–40," *Economic Record,* vol. ii, no. 8, 1940.

Smith, Edwin S., *Reducing Seasonal Unemployment,* McGraw-Hill Book Company, Inc., New York, 1931.

Stead, William H., *Democracy Against Unemployment,* Harper & Brothers, New York, 1942.

U. S. Senate Committee on Education and Labor, *Unemployment in the U. S.,* 70th Congress, 2nd Session, Government Printing Office, Washington, 1929.

---

[36] *Monthly Labor Review,* October, 1939, p. 838.

6

THEORIES OF UNEMPLOYMENT

THE FOLLOWING FACTS ARE APPARENT FROM THE PRECEDING DIS-cussion: (1) Since the beginning of the wage system there has always been some unemployment and, except during war periods, the amount has been greater than could reasonably be assigned to the inability or unwillingness of certain individuals to accept and retain jobs. (2) At recurring periods, the volume of unemployment sharply increases as a result of what has come to be called cyclical business depressions. (3) Although business resumed and exceeded former levels of production following the depression after the First World War, there was a substantial amount of unemployment all during the "prosperity" period of the 1920's. (4) The volume of unemployment was unprecedented in both its severity and its duration during the depression of the 1930's, and there was little evidence of a "natural" recovery such as had taken place after earlier depressions. In spite of extraordinary government measures of "pump priming" (discussed in the next chapter), almost 10 million persons were unemployed ten years after the beginning of this depression; the subsequent disappearance of mass unemployment was due to the exigencies of war production.

COMPLEX NATURE OF THE PROBLEM

It has already been indicated that the effects of labor-saving innovations are seldom direct and visible because large groups of workers are usually not laid off at the exact time and place a new machine is introduced. The repercussions are therefore remote and, so far as the general introduction of a new invention throughout all industry is concerned, they extend over a considerable length of time. During this time other factors appear such as cyclical depressions, wars, the development of entirely new industries, and social and political changes which affect export trade, currency and credit, etc. Because technological progress takes place in a changing and complex world, it is impossible to isolate its impact from other influences. It is not even possible to prove, statistically, whether cyclical and technological unemployment are two distinct phenomena or whether they stem from the same complex of causes. There is not even agreement as to whether the peak, or the low, or the average level of employment within a cycle represents "normal" employment for that particular period.

Because causal relationships are obscure, one must delve into the realm of theory in search of an answer. In its positive aspect, the question to be answered is: Under what conditions, if any, can full employment be attained in a progressively advancing technological economy?

In a capitalistic economy where the goods produced are offered for sale, the solution to full employment necessarily hinges on two elements, namely, a sufficient market for the product of labor, and a sufficient volume of capital for the employment of labor. Inseparable from these are the factors of market prices and the returns to labor in the form of wages, and to capital investment in the form of interest, dividends, and profits. All theories[1] on unemployment must necessarily revolve around the relationships of these factors and attempt to answer such questions as these:

If savings are a requisite to capital investment, do they not at the same time imply a curtailment of consumption and therefore a diminished demand for labor's output? Is expansion in production, sufficient to provide full employment, initially and primarily dependent upon increases in capital investment, or is it contingent upon a growth of consumers' demands? If the former, what conditions must exist to produce more savings and encourage their investment in labor-using enterprises? If the latter, how can sufficient purchasing power be obtained? Is inadequacy of total pur-

---

[1] The author is indebted in the following discussion on 19th-century theories to *Survey of Economic Theory on Technological Change and Employment* prepared by Alexander Gourvitch and published in multilithed form as a National Research Project by the Work Projects Administration in May, 1940.

chasing power due to the oversaving and underspending of the higher-income groups, or to the low level of income received by the masses who make up the bulk of the purchasers? Is cyclical unemployment a component part of technological development, or is it the result of entirely different factors? Does a gradual increase in unemployment and the consequent curtailment or threat of curtailment in purchasing power bring on a depression, or are depressions caused initially by the exhaustion of savings and the consequent curtailment in investment that provides the means for employment?

Let us review briefly some of the more commonly accepted theories which seek to explain why unemployment exists, under what conditions it is minimized or increased, and whether it is a permanent and inevitable phase of our existing type of economy or whether it is subject to substantial reduction and control.

EARLY THEORIES

Concern over unemployment is not of recent origin. It existed before there were power-driven machines and whenever changes and improvements were taking place in either agriculture or manufacturing. In 1623 the Privy Council of England ordered a needle machine to be broken up, and in France the statesman Colbert described the inventor of labor-saving machines as an enemy of labor.[2] Gradually, however, machines came to be accepted as beneficial to the nation, especially when they promoted export trade, although it was recognized that innovations caused temporary displacements of labor. It is the statesmen's task, said a political economist in 1767, not to discourage change but "to prevent the vicissitudes of manners and innovations from hurting any interest within the commonwealth."[2] The mercantilists of that age believed that it was the duty of the government to promote a nation's industry, if necessary by subsidies and government orders, and to encourage export trade which would absorb the increased output and also provide money for the additional expansion of production and employment.[3]

[2] Sir James Stewart, *An Inquiry into the Principles of Political Economy* London, 1767, vol. i, p. 120.

[3] The mercantile system was developed in Europe at the close of the Middle

Adam Smith, pioneer of the English classical economists, was opposed to any government stimulation of the flow of capital into industry. He and his successors considered capital as a wages fund, that is, a stock of commodities available for the maintenance of laborers during the production period, and argued that employment is solely dependent upon the amount of available capital and that nothing else could alter its total volume. Capital is synonymous with a wages fund, and capital accumulation, he maintained, involves no curtailment of consumption because what is saved annually is consumed as regularly as what is spent annually. The only difference is that what is saved is consumed by a different group of people, namely, by productive workers instead of by the idle rich and their servants. Smith recognized that all capital was not directly used for wages but that some went into the purchasing of materials, plants, and equipment which, however, he considered an indirect form of wage payment because to him all costs ultimately resolved themselves into labor costs.

The Industrial Revolution had hardly got under way at the time of Adam Smith. As machines and the factory system developed, an increasing proportion of capital was invested in the means of production and a diminishing proportion in the payment of wages. With this change, was it not possible for too much capital to be invested in machines, leaving too little for wages? Obviously, the distinction between fixed capital used for investment in plant and equipment and circulating capital used for wages became more important and raised the question, among others, whether savings invested in capital equipment did not represent a withdrawal from consumption (contrary to Smith's theory) and, at the same time, serve to displace labor.

NINETEENTH-CENTURY THEORIES

Most economists of the 19th century answered in the negative by maintaining that there is an automatic reabsorption of dis-

---

Ages. The doctrine, stated in its extreme form, held that wealth and money were identical and therefore each nation should attract to itself the largest possible share of the precious metals by increasing its exports and keeping its imports to a minimum, receiving the difference in value in gold and silver.

placed workers through the operation of the Law of Markets as first enunciated by J. B. Say in 1814. Every product which is produced according to this "law," offers instantaneously, to the full extent of its value, a market for other products. This is so because this value is equivalent to the sum of the income of the several agents—the owners of natural resources, the capitalists, and the workers—who cooperated in creating the product. No general overproduction is therefore possible. What appears as overproduction reflects only a disproportion between production and prices; the existence of overproduction in some industry or industries means that there has been underproduction in others. Such disproportions, however, will not be maintained unless there is unnatural interference; otherwise the equilibrium will be reestablished, for the movement of prices will cause a shift of capital and labor from the overexpanded to the lagging industries.

Although the introduction of machinery, according to Say's law, will cause a temporary displacement of workers, it will at the same time set in motion forces working toward their reemployment. It may do so directly as a result of lowered prices calling forth an increased demand for the product whose production methods have been improved, or indirectly as the savings to consumers resulting from the lower prices make it possible for consumers to increase their demands for other commodities. Since the aggregate revenues and purchasing power in the community remain unimpaired, increasing cheapness anywhere means increasing demand and expanding production all around.

Some economists of the 19th century were not as optimistic about the automatic reemployment of workers displaced by machinery as Say was. Sismondi in 1827 maintained that technological improvements may be a benefit or a calamity, depending upon the relation of consumers' demands to productive power. He argued that the introduction of new machines, unless called for by a preexisting demand for goods, will become a factor of general overproduction and of crises; that a technological improvement will not necessarily be reflected through reduced costs and prices in an expanding demand sufficient to enable all displaced workers to be reemployed; and that prices are never reduced in proportion to savings in labor, and hence the augmented demand for that particular product, or the expansion in the demand for other products, is never sufficient to offset the lost demand for the displaced workers.

Ricardo at first accepted the theory of the automatic reabsorption of displaced labor, but later he became skeptical and argued that the introduction of machinery reduces the labor force since the use of the machines implies conversion into fixed capital of a portion of the circulating capital which had previously served to pay wages. His explanation indicated that during the year when the machine is under construction, the same labor force is employed in the aggregate as in previous years, and it is maintained with the aid of the circulating capital already produced. In the following year, however, when the machine is to be put into operation, the supply of circulating capital available in the shape of goods for the maintenance of labor will have diminished in proportion to the labor diverted to the construction of the machine, and a portion of the labor previously employed will then become superfluous. "Machinery and labour are in constant competition . . . with every augmentation of capital, a greater proportion of it is employed on machinery. The demand for labour will continue to increase with an increase of capital, but not in proportion to its increase; the ratio will necessarily be a diminishing ratio."[4] As we shall see in a later chapter, however, Ricardo also argued that the introduction of machinery will be retarded when wages decline, thus reducing the possibilities of unemployment.

Karl Marx, who thought in terms of long-time historical trends, stressed the cyclical nature of the effects of technological changes upon employment. Contrary to other opinions of his day, he contended that the introduction of a machine did not release capital which might afford employment to the displaced workers, but that it involved a conversion of variable into constant capital, with a relatively decreasing share serving for the payment of labor. He maintained that capital is not a subsistence fund for labor, as classical economists had held, and the existence of goods susceptible of use for the maintenance of workers does not constitute a demand for labor. In other words, there may be unemployment

---

[4] David Ricardo, *Principles of Political Economy and Taxation*, 3rd ed., 1821, p. 241.

in the face of an abundance of consumption goods, and the introduction of machinery displaces workers who thereupon cease to be purchasers of goods.

Thus, according to Marx, the whole movement of modern industry tends toward a continuous transformation of part of the working population into what he termed "a surplus working-class population," an "industrial reserve army." Portions of this "reserve army," he maintained, are drawn back into employment from time to time because technical improvements proceed sporadically owing to fluctuations in the profit rate. As capital accumulation progresses, profit rates decline to the point where investments slow down, with a consequent redundance of capital. This overaccumulation is reflected in a crisis—falling prices, curtailment of production, unemployment, and destruction and depreciation of capital values. Eventually, the crisis is overcome through the advancement of the profit rate as a result of wage reductions, the marking down of capital values, and, finally, new technical improvements in production. A new expansion period sets in, and the demand for labor increases as capital investment is resumed, only to be followed by a repetition of the same cycle of changes of falling profit rates, overaccumulation, crisis, and unemployment.[5]

THEORY OF EQUILIBRIUM

The main threads of the 19th-century classical theories[6] may be summarized thus: At the beginning of the Industrial Revolution it was generally believed that all capital represented a wage fund for the maintenance of laborers while they were engaged in producing additional goods; since accumulated savings in the form of capital investment in machines continued to be a wage fund, it could not cause permanent unemployment and the only limit to ever-increasing employment was the physical factor of food supply. Later there were expressions of misgiving in regard to the effects of technological change, with the recognition that an increasing share of capital investments represented outlays other

---

[5] Karl Marx, *Das Kapital,* as summarized by Gourvitch, in *Survey of Economic Theory,* pp. 73–79.

[6] There were, of course, many variants of these major theses, and some which differed radically from the more generally accepted views.

than for the payment of wages, and that therefore an increase in the demand for labor was contingent upon the growth of capital investment at an ever faster pace. However, the incentives to investment, and hence the demand for labor, tended to diminish because of a tendency for the profit rate to fall.

Such misgivings seemed to have little foundation during the decades preceding the First World War when there appeared to be inexhaustible opportunities for investments in railroads and in the general industrial development of the United States, and for the extension of colonial trade by European countries. The prevailing optimism of this period was reflected in the so-called "equilibrium" theory of the neo-classical economists, based on Say's Law of Markets.

The earlier theories admitted that there were two potential obstacles to a continued growth of production sufficient to offset the increasing productivity of labor—inability of the market to absorb the increased output, and non-availability of sufficient capital as a source of a demand for labor. According to the equilibrium theory, adjustments of these factors are brought about through the operation of the several price mechanisms. The mechanism of commodity prices precludes the possibility of general overproduction; for as commodities become more plentiful, prices will decline and thus discourage too much production, and vice versa. Likewise, the price mechanisms of the factors of production—wage rates and interest rates—will automatically tend toward equilibrium, the point of equilibrium being determined by the marginal productivity of each factor.

Thus when labor costs (wages) tend to become too high, labor-saving machines will be introduced; the resulting unemployment will thereupon cause a lowering of the wage level and competition for capital will cause a rise in the interest rate. These concurrent developments will check the substitution of capital investments (machines), and equilibrium will be restored, with full employment of labor and capital producing the exact quantity of goods at prices which insure their purchase. This happy condition of perfect equilibrium seldom if ever actually exists, for there are always frictions and lags in the various price mechanisms which result in fluctuations in employment. Nevertheless, the long-time trend is always toward equilibrium, and any existing unemployment is a temporary phenomenon which will automatically disappear when the proper adjustments in prices, wages, and interest have taken place. Disequilibriums caused by the process of adjustments are elements in the business cycle, but there is no problem of a permanent displacement of labor because the several price mechanisms (commodity prices, interest, and wages) are self-regulating in such a way as to assure the parallel growth of savings and of a demand for commodities adequate to prevent any labor displacement other than temporary and localized dislocations.

The logical conclusion to be drawn from such a theory is that there should be no "artificial tampering" with any of the price mechanisms. The *laissez-faire* doctrine of the orthodox economists, therefore, opposes any governmental or other concerted action which would directly or indirectly alter the "natural" levels of prices, interest, and wage rates.

Shortcomings of Equilibrium Theory

There was little or no questioning of this doctrine and its accompanying course of action, or lack of action, before the First World War. The leading British authority on unemployment, Sir William Beveridge, optimistically held that ". . . there is no general failure of adjustment between the growth of the demand for labor and the growth of the supply of labor. . . . With every pair of hands God sends a mouth."[7] This belief was shaken after the First World War, when the presence of unemployment appeared to be persistent even when business activity seemed normal. Some economists then began to question both the fact of the automatic adjustment of the various price factors and the assumption that it necessarily results in full employment. At the same time, persons concerned with the human problem of unemployment suggested courses of action which implied a disbelief in the equilibrium theory and the wisdom of a *laissez-faire* policy.

The Secretary of Labor, for example, stated in 1925: "The greatest source of unemployment in this country is the over-development of industry. The fact is that our productive machinery and equipment cannot run 300 days in the year without

---

[7] William H. Beveridge, *Full Employment in a Free Society*, W. W. Norton & Company, New York, 1945, p. 91.

producing a stock so large that it cannot be sold in this country, nor in any and all other countries."[8] He suggested, as a remedy, a law to compel the closing down of excess plants similar to the merging of railroads under the auspices of the Interstate Commerce Commission. While such action would remove the surplus pools of labor attached to particular industries, the Secretary's suggestion included no remedy for finding employment elsewhere for these displaced persons.

Viewing the unemployment problem in its entirety, present-day economists differ in their interpretation of its causes as well as its remedies. Some accept the theory of equilibrium but maintain that the self-adjusting processes are not taking place for various reasons, and therefore overt action is required periodically to restore equilibrium. Others are inclined to believe that equilibrium does not necessarily imply full employment, that it is possible to reach a state of economic maturity with a fully developed regime of technology, and that in such a stationary economy investment opportunities are restricted, causing chronic unemployment. This persistent unemployment, these individuals believe, can be alleviated only through extraneous developments outside the price mechanism.

Relation of Wage Rates to Equilibrium

Those who maintain that unemployment is a result of rigidities in the cost-price structure do not agree as to which factor plays the chief causal role nor as to how equilibrium to bring about full employment can be effected. Some economists and many businessmen believe that "excessive" wages cause unemployment, that the very existence of mass unemployment indicates that the price of labor is too high for the conditions of the market, and that unemployment will disappear if wages are reduced to the point where employers find it profitable to use all the available labor.

The theory that excessive wages was the factor causing disequilibrium and therefore unemployment, lost many of its adherents after the business collapse of 1929, when conditions prior to the depression were analyzed. During the period of comparative prosperity between 1923 and 1929, consumers' prices and wage

---

[8] J. J. Davis, in *Monthly Labor Review*, October, 1925, p. 10.

rates remained relatively stable and manufacturing productivity increased at least one-third. According to the automatic equilibrium theory, prices should have gone down with the decreased costs resulting from improved technology, and as the increased volume of goods competed for the consumers' dollars. The reduced prices would have resulted in increased purchasing power which, in turn, would have stimulated further production and thereby absorbed the workers displaced as a result of the increase in productivity. Or, since the major portion of the purchasers of consumers' goods is composed of wage and low-salaried workers, almost the same state of equilibrium would have been achieved if wages and salaries had advanced parallel to productivity.

The fact is that total wage payments were substantially less in 1929 than in 1923 and consumer price levels were not lowered. The outstanding characteristic of this period, according to a government report, was a "decline of income payments in manufacturing, minerals and railroads. Total wages fell from 63.6 per cent of all income payments in 1923 to 57.1 per cent in 1929. The benefits of the rising productivity of labor were not in general transferred through price reductions to consumers, for the index of the cost of living was higher during most of the period than in 1923."[9]

THEORY OF OVERSAVING AND UNDERSPENDING

Of the three factors involved in maintaining equilibrium (interest and profits, wages, and consumer prices), many persons stress the role of rigid prices as the major cause of disequilibrium. They maintain that monopolistic and other forms of collectivism in private business operations cause "imperfect competition" which keeps prices above their "natural" or competitive level. The growth of monopolistic trends and other conditions which lead to price rigidity lie outside the scope of this volume. It is pertinent to the present discussion, however, to mention one approach to the problem of full employment which is currently receiving considerable attention. This is the theory that the root cause of mass unemployment is oversaving and underspending.

[9] Witt Bowden, in *ibid.*, September, 1940, p. 522.

According to this theory, oversaving and underspending are the dominant trends in our modern industrial economy and this condition is caused by a maldistribution of incomes. The great mass of people receive incomes that are too low to enable them to buy the goods and services which technological production brings to the market; at the same time oversaving takes place among the relatively few who receive high incomes because they can spend only to the point at which their consumer wants are satiated and this is much below their available incomes. This is in complete contradiction of all the classical theories of both savings and wages. It maintains that "in contemporary conditions the growth of wealth, so far from being dependent on the abstinence of the rich as is commonly supposed, is more likely to be impeded by it. One of the chief social justifications of great inequality of wealth is therefore removed."[10]

Also, according to the underspending theory, a reduction in wage rates to reduce costs will not restore equilibrium and bring about full employment, and, conversely, generally high wages are not the cause of business stagnation and mass unemployment.[11] The underspending theory is not new. It lies at the roots of Karl Marx's doctrines enunciated in the middle of the 19th century, and early in the present century John A. Hobson, who was not a socialist, claimed that the existing distribution of incomes results in a large portion of wealth going to a small class and that, for the community as a whole, this results in a deficiency of spending. This is true, he said, because the purchases of the higher-income group do not prevent an oversupply of goods, and their savings are invested in capital goods which cause a continual further increase in the supply of consumers' goods. Oversaving and underspending therefore culminate in overproduction and a glutting of the market.[12]

Approaching the problem of oversavings from another angle than its effect on employment, but implicitly recognizing it as a

---

[10] J. M. Keynes, *The General Theory of Employment, Interest and Money,* Macmillan and Co., Ltd., London, 1936, p. 64.

[11] This does not mean that excessively high wages in a particular industry or plant may not cause a decline and hence unemployment in that industry or plant. See chap. 9.

[12] John A. Hobson, *The Industrial System,* Longmans, Green & Company, Inc.. New York. 1909.

cause of cyclical business depressions, Foster and Catchings made these prophetic statements before the 1929 collapse:

Progress toward greater total production is retarded because consumer buying does not keep pace with production. Consumer buying lags behind for two reasons: First, because industry does not disburse to consumers enough money to buy the goods produced; second, because consumers, under the necessity of saving, cannot spend even as much money as they receive. There is not an even flow of money from producer to consumer, and from consumer back to producer. The expansion of the volume of money does not fully make up the deficit, for money is expanded mainly to facilitate the production of goods, and the goods must be sold to consumers for more money than the expansion has provided. Furthermore, the savings of corporations and individuals are not used to purchase the goods already in the markets, but to bring about the production of more goods.

Under the established system, therefore, we make progress only while we are filling the shelves with goods which must either remain on the shelves as stock in trade or be sold at a loss, and while we are building more industrial equipment than we can use. Inadequacy of consumer income is, therefore, the main reason why we do not long continue to produce the wealth which natural resources, capital facilities, improvements in the arts, and the self-interest of employers and employees would otherwise enable us to produce. Chiefly because of shortage of consumer demand, both capital and labor restrict output, and nations engage in those struggles for outside markets and spheres of commercial influence which are the chief causes of war.[13]

Keynesian Theory

The theory that oversavings and underconsumption are the fundamental causes of mass unemployment gained added impetus when promulgated by J. M. Keynes, the noted British economist, who repudiated most of the traditional theories of full employment through automatic adjustments within the price mechanism. According to his analysis, employment depends upon spending. Spending is of two kinds—for consumption and for investment. What people spend on consumption gives employment, but what they save gives employment only if it is invested in adding to capital equipment such as machines, factories, etc. (In this sense,

---

[13] William T. Foster and Waddill Catchings, *Profits*, Houghton Mifflin Company, Boston, 1925, p. 409.

the buying of land and buildings, and bonds and stocks on the exchange, is not investment but a transfer of property already in existence).[14] In our present unplanned market economy there is nothing that automatically keeps spending and investment at the point of full employment, and therefore an adequate total demand for labor cannot be taken for granted.

Keynes differentiated between the tendency to save and the inducement to invest, and attacked the theory of a harmony between savings and investment attained through the rate of interest which, according to the older theories, kept the free capitalistic system in a prosperous equilibrium in which the demand for labor was constantly being adjusted to the supply of labor. He recommended a controlled rate of interest kept consistently below the anticipated marginal yield on capital in order to induce savings to enter into investments. Many economists, at least in the United States, place less importance upon the interest rate as a major consideration in investment, or the lack thereof; they believe that businessmen are influenced by the prospective volume of business and the labor-saving possibilities of new machines more than they are by the cost of capital.

Influence of Income Distribution on Investment

Adherents of the oversaving and underspending theory maintain that oversaving has become accentuated during the past generation because of the current practice of corporations of withholding large portions of their annual profits to "plow back" into the business, thus adding corporation savings to individual savings. It has been estimated that American corporations, on the average, do not disburse as dividends much over half of their profits, and there is evidence that since 1920 business has been largely financ-

---

[14] One authority on unemployment, in explaining the causal relationship between speculation and business depressions, says: "In August, 1929, stockholders held approximately $52 billion in fictitious values, gains from stock speculation in 2½ years. . . . The prosperity of the 1920's was a tower built on the sands of progressive inflation. The fact that there was no price rise at that time does not change the basic character of that era. It was inflationary and doomed to collapse because, at that time, not only further expansion of production but also maintenance of the existing level depended on the continuous expansion of credit and accumulation of fictitious gains from security speculation." (W. S. Woytinsky, *Postwar Economic Perspectives,* Social Security Bulletin, December, 1945, p. 23.)

ing itself rather than depending on borrowings from banks as in former years.[15]

To an individual company, maintenance of a reserve fund for future contingencies and development seems to be a prudent and "businesslike" practice. For the economy at large, the holding back of large portions of the profits of production interferes with the free play of the forces of equilibrium because profits held at the source are not subject to the free decisions of the "market place"—they are not distributed among vast numbers of people, either stockholders or wage earners, each of whom would decide how much to save and how much to spend.

The crux of the oversaving thesis is that the amount of savings within any community or nation is governed primarily not by opportunities for investment but by the total income and its pattern of distribution. In general, the more unevenly income is distributed, the greater the total savings because persons with large incomes are able to save, whereas those with low incomes must spend most or all of their earnings on daily living needs. What little the people with low and medium incomes can save is primarily for their own security—to tide them over periods of sickness, unemployment, and other adversities. Such savings represent postponed consumption and cause little or no net accumulation over a period of time, because, while some are saving, others are forced to use their "nest egg." Oversaving results from the savings of the high-income groups and is the residual of their income that is neither spent for consumers' goods nor invested in new capital equipment.

Savings will not go into investment, of course, unless there is a market to consume the products of the increased investment. In a technically progressive society such as ours, where productivity is advancing at a rate of 2 or 3 per cent per year, it is axiomatic that general consumption must increase at the same rate in order to provide continuing channels for investment. "Increased productivity per head mathematically involves either increased con-

---

[15] According to Treasury Department and Security and Exchange Commission reports, manufacturing, wholesale, and retail corporations during 1941–1945 retained over 21 billion dollars of their net earnings after taxes and dividends were paid. In 1945 the total reserve of all corporations, excluding banks and insurance companies, amounted to 48 billion dollars, in contrast to 24½ billion in 1939. This indicates that a substantial proportion of the war profits were not paid out in either dividends or wages. (Figures cited in *United States News*, December 7, 1945, p. 20.)

sumption per head, or idleness, which must be taken in the form either of leisure or of unemployment. In other words, the fundamental problem of a progressive society is to distribute the results of the progress among its citizens, either by shortening hours or by increasing the purchasing power of the citizens so that they can consume more."[16]

SUGGESTED REMEDIES

Although the theory that oversaving and underspending are the root causes of mass unemployment has become increasingly popular, it is by no means universally accepted. Neither is there common agreement that the problem of unemployment is sufficiently serious and persistent to require concerted action of any kind. Many persons take the optimistic view that unemployment is not becoming more acute in the long run, and that periodic increases which occur at particular times will disappear because of the automatic self-adjusting processes within the business community.

Many believe that a continuing pool of several million unemployed is salutary because it provides a buyers' market for labor which gives the employer an opportunity to select and reject, and furnishes workers the necessary stimulant for good workmanship. Mass unemployment such as occurred during the 1930's is a passing phenomenon, an outcome of the usual recurrent cyclical operation of business, which will gradually disappear if economic forces are allowed to adjust themselves without interference. Unemployment, whether in a large volume as a result of business depressions or in smaller amounts at other times, is an inevitable by-product of a free society, and the rules of that society should not be tampered with in an attempt to eliminate one of its natural characteristics.

However, an increasing number of people are of the opinion that the business collapse of 1929 marked a turning point in our economic development which must be accompanied by a change in our thinking and social policy. They are convinced that the general trend of unemployment is rising, despite its occasional downswings during war and post-war booms, and that automatic self-adjustment processes cannot be depended on to absorb this surplus labor.

[16] William H. Beveridge, *Full Employment in a Free Society*, p. 101.

But there are differences of opinion as to particular remedies as well as the goals to strive for. Some set their sights at "full" employment, others at a "high level" of employment. All rely on some governmental action but in varying degrees and in varying avenues of approach.

Full Versus a High Level of Employment

The distinction between "full" employment and a "high level" of employment is a matter of both mathematics and principle. Mathematically, in this country with its present population, it signifies the difference between one or two million and four or five million, the low figure representing the irreducible frictional unemployment occasioned by the lag between a person losing one job and finding another, and the higher figure representing the number which presumably could be idle even though business activity was good.

In principle, the distinction between "full" and a "high level" of employment symbolizes the difference between a buyers' and a sellers' market for labor. Full employment is assumed to indicate a state of affairs in which vacancies approximate the number of available unemployed persons,[17] which means that the employers, or the buyers of labor, must compete for the services of the average and better-than-average worker and also make use of marginal

---

[17] The British authority on unemployment, Sir William Beveridge, goes further by saying that full employment means having *more* vacant jobs than unemployed individuals. He reasons thus: Society exists for the individual, and difficulty in selling labor has consequences of greater harmfulness than the difficulties associated with the buying of labor. A person who has difficulty in buying the labor that he wants suffers inconvenience or reduction of profits. A person who cannot sell his labor is in effect told that he is of no use. The first difficulty causes annoyance or loss. The other is a personal catastrophe. The difference remains even if most people are unemployed for only relatively short periods. As long as there is any long-term unemployment not obviously due to personal deficiency, anyone who loses his job fears that he may be one of the unlucky ones who will not get another job quickly. The short-term unemployed do not know that they are short-term unemployed until their unemployment is over.

The human difference between failing to buy and failing to sell labor is the decisive reason for aiming to make the labor market a sellers' rather than a buyers' market. There are other reasons, only slightly less important. One reason is that only if there is work for all is it fair to expect workmen individually, and collectively in trade unions, to cooperate in making the most of all the productive resources, including labor, and to forego restrictionist practices. (*Ibid.*, p. 19.)

workers. A "high level" of employment, on the other hand, allows for a pool of idle labor; this gives the employer considerable latitude in selection so that only during his extreme peak needs will he be required to employ marginal or below-average workers.

The implications of full employment are far reaching and go beyond the simple fact that everyone has a job who wants and is able to work. A condition of full employment would have an influence on the level of wages since it automatically increases the bargaining strength of the sellers of labor, the wage earners. The impact of this will be discussed in a later chapter. So far as employer-employee relations are concerned, it implies a change from the situation in which the employer can say, "If you don't like conditions here, there are plenty of others to take your job," to one in which the employee can say, "If you don't like the way I'm doing, there are plenty of other jobs to go to." Some would argue that this kind of situation tends to destroy industrial discipline and efficiency, that the fear of losing one's job is a needed incentive for doing good work. Others would contend that there are other motives for good workmanship than fear of losing one's job —the possibility of promotion, for example. Moreover, full employment does not mean that a poor worker has to be kept on in his present job; the natural aversion to changing jobs, and perhaps going to an entirely new location, may be sufficient inducement for satisfactory work performance.

To most people who are concerned with the immediate problem of alleviating unemployment, the distinction between "full" and a "high level" of employment is more abstract than real. They are of the opinion that maintaining a high level of employment at all times will require unprecedented action and that until this is accomplished no one need be unduly concerned about the impact of "full" employment upon employer-employee relations and shop management. The important question is whether a "standard" should be established in advance, and a program set in motion for achieving it.

Proposals for Government Action

Those who accept the validity of the oversaving and underspending theory believe that the problem of unemployment cannot be solved without government action. The moot questions are:

what kind of action, and will such action tend to destroy our present system of free competitive enterprise and in the long run lower our general standard of living? No one questions the theoretical assumption that a totalitarian government can provide all its citizens with jobs. Such a government has complete control over what shall be produced and the price at which everything will be sold. It has absolute authority to tell its citizens where they shall work and at what wages, and power to penalize them for disobedience. This is the antithesis of an economy in which prices are determined in a competitive market and wages are established by voluntary negotiations between employers and employees.

Can the essentials of a competitive economy be preserved with a government policy directed toward the maintenance of full employment? Many believe this is possible, for they envisage only a minimum of government regulation of wages and prices and no direct control over the particular kinds of goods which are produced. Government action pertaining to prices would be limited to seeing that prices are in fact competitive and not monopolistic. Government policy with respect to wages would be limited, except for government-financed employment, to establishing a floor upon which the general rate structure would be determined by the employers and workers directly concerned.

The essence of government action for attaining full employment lies in fiscal and monetary controls based on a new kind of national budget. It assumes that the taxing power of the government should be used to serve a twofold purpose in addition to its traditional role of providing revenue: First, taxes should be used as a lever for regulating the flow of capital investment and consumer purchasing, and second, they should be used as a means for diverting surplus savings into channels which would increase consumption and employment. The first would be accomplished through policies of tax levying, and the second through the government spending of funds attained through taxation or borrowing or, as some suggest, through the creation of new money. There is not common agreement upon the specific program which should be adopted, but the general outline is as follows:

The federal government should prepare each year a national budget based on the optimum total expenditures for the coming year, assuming that all available manpower is employed. The government would thereupon assume the responsibility for seeing that the aggregate expenditures during the ensuing year are equivalent to the budget estimate. If inflationary forces are at work, the tax and other policies would be directed toward keeping private expenditures within the budget limits; for example, taxes would be raised and stock market and credit controls would be tightened. If there are indications that private expenditures will not meet the budget estimate, the tax and other policies would be adjusted in order to stimulate private consumption and investment. The government would absorb any balance through a public works program such as the building of roads, schools, hospitals, etc., which has the advantage of providing employment without creating additional capital equipment whose output must be sold. Some of the taxes levied on high incomes to prevent oversaving would be used for the continuing expansion of public services, such as educational, health, and recreational facilities, which serve the twofold purpose of raising the general standard of living and providing additional employment opportunities.

SELECTED REFERENCES

Beveridge, William H., *Full Employment in a Free Society,* W. W. Norton & Company, New York, 1945.

Committee for Economic Development, *Jobs and Markets,* McGraw-Hill Book Company, Inc., New York, 1946.

Copland, Douglas B., *The Road to High Employment,* Harvard University Press, Cambridge, 1945.

Fitch, Lyle C., and Taylor, Horace, *et al., Planning for Jobs,* The Blakiston Company, Philadelphia, 1946.

Gourvitch, Alexander, *Theory of Technological Change and Employment,* Works Progress Administration, Philadelphia, 1940.

Groves, Harold M., *Production, Jobs and Taxes,* McGraw-Hill Book Company, Inc., New York, 1944.

Hansen, Alvin H., *Fiscal Policy and Business Cycles,* W. W. Norton & Company, Inc., New York, 1941.

Hayes, H. Gordon, *Spending, Saving and Employment,* Alfred A. Knopf, New York, 1945.

Hobson, J. A., *Economics of Unemployment,* The Macmillan Company, New York, 1931.

Keynes, John Maynard, *The General Theory of Employment, Interest and Money,* Macmillan and Co., Ltd., London, 1936.

Mills, Frederick C., *Economic Tendencies in the U. S.,* National Bureau of Economic Research, Inc., New York, 1932.

Pierson, John H. G., *Full Employment,* Yale University Press, New Haven, 1941.

Pigou, A. C., *The Theory of Unemployment,* Macmillan and Co., Ltd., London, 1933.

Wallace, Henry A., *Sixty Million Jobs,* Simon & Shuster, Inc., New York, 1945.

Wernette, John P., *Financing Full Employment,* Harvard University Press, Cambridge, 1945.

7

UNEMPLOYMENT RELIEF
AND ALLEVIATION

IT IS DIFFICULT NOWADAYS TO APPRECIATE THE PLIGHT OF PERSONS unfortunate enough to have lost their jobs in the days before the federal government assumed any active responsibility for the relief or mitigation of unemployment. Unemployment insurance was practically non-existent in this country before 1935,[1] and there were no state or federal programs of unemployment relief before 1930. The traditional concept was that the care of the poor was entirely the responsibility of the local community; that aid could best be given through private philanthropy, although in unusual situations the city or county should extend some assistance. There was no legal distinction between paupers or confirmed ne'er-do-wells and people temporarily in need because of enforced joblessness, and there was little difference in their treatment by either private charity or public officials.

GRADUAL ACCEPTANCE OF PUBLIC RESPONSIBILITY FOR RELIEF

Prior to the depression of the 1890's there was little thought of a need for mass relief. Although there had been periods of severe depression before that time, the country was predominantly agricultural, and many of the unemployed were able to return to their families and relatives on farms when they lost their city jobs. In 1893–1896 the unemployed experienced for the first time the services of organized charity, but the sporadic activities of hastily organized temporary agencies were the predominant means of pro-

---

[1] See chap. 25.

viding relief. Whether these were special committees appointed by mayors and using city funds, or self-appointed groups that raised their own money, their chief idea seemed to be that relief giving should be visible and audible. Every city had its soup lines and mass distribution of groceries—the system practiced by the Caesars two thousand years before. The newspapers eagerly devoted pages to describing the distress and suffering, but, unfortunately with the same zeal, they also rushed into indiscriminate charitable activities that drew crowds to their doors for handouts and sent "wagons blazoned with their names into crowded tenement streets calling aloud the names of those for whom they had charity packages."[2]

Similar methods prevailed during subsequent periods of mass unemployment, although there was a tendency away from the spectacular, demoralizing handouts of groceries and work tickets by hastily improvised civic organizations. There was a greater use of the existing relief agencies, both public and private, and they expanded their programs to care for the greater numbers needing assistance. Some cities provided funds for direct relief and for public works, but frequently such funds were not divorced from political patronage; hence jobs were given not to those who needed them most but to those who controlled the most votes.[3]

In a majority of the states the county was the responsible government unit for the care and financing of the needy. Unemployed

---

[2] Charles D. Kellogg, "Relief of Unemployed in United States During Winter of 1893–94," *Journal of the American Social Science Association*, No. 32, 1894.

[3] In April, 1931, New York City appropriated 10 million dollars for a work relief program. Jobs were supposed to be distributed through the offices of the Department of Public Welfare to legal residents and voters of at least two years who were heads of families with dependents. Investigation revealed that the Tammany district leaders practically lived at the borough halls where the workers were selected, and that in one district alone 90.9 per cent of those given jobs were Democrats, 8.7 per cent Republicans, and 0.4 of one per cent were Socialists. The ratio of enrolled Democrats to Republicans in that district was 4 to 1. Letters sent out to voters in another district read:

"It is the purpose, aim, and object of the Yucatan Democratic Club to strive to foster the welfare of its members, with special emphasis on the relief of those who are unemployed and special efforts toward securing them positions in city government; the appropriation recently made by the Board of Estimate in which $20 million was made available for the unemployed, is positive proof that the City Government under Tammany Hall administration, is determined that no deserving member of the Party shall suffer acute want." (W. B. and J. B. Northrup, *The Insolence of Office*, G. P. Putnam's Sons, New York, 1932.)

persons who wanted assistance were usually compelled to plead their case before commissioners of the poor, and the names of those who received relief were listed in the published minutes of the county boards and sometimes given pitiless publicity in the local papers—a measure designed to discourage requests for aid. In a considerable number of states the township (or incorporated city or village) was the financial and administrative unit for relief. Thus, Illinois had 1500 taxing and administrative poor relief units, Ohio over 1500, Wisconsin 1200. The small taxing area limited the spread of the financial burden so that towns which had the greatest relief costs often had the smallest tax income. This was particularly true of townships contiguous to industrial cities; they often included a large number of wage earners who had moved away from the city to escape high rents.

A considerable portion of unemployment relief, especially in the cities, was administered by private charitable organizations. An outgrowth of the individualistic philanthropy of churches and lodges, the private social agency had developed into a highly efficient mechanism staffed by trained social workers whose professional ethics and practices were the result of scientific study and experimentation. These private agencies were supported by voluntary gifts, and members of the policy-making boards were naturally drawn from among the larger contributors. While the technique of family service was apparently non-partisan, the basic policies and attitudes were colored by the ideology of the wealthy contributors; the recipients and their sympathizers had little or no representation

Poor Laws

State laws for the care of those unable to support themselves were essentially the same as had existed under Queen Elizabeth in England over 300 years ago.[4] Their general character is revealed by their nomenclature: "pauper laws," "support of the poor," "poor relief," "care of the indigent." Almost without exception, persons in need were assumed to be mental, physical, or moral defectives for whom the almshouse was the logical retreat, but for

---

[4] Many of the laws referred to in this section still remain on the statute books. See American Public Welfare Association, *Poor Relief Laws, a Digest,* Public Administration Services No. 37.

whom in some instances home relief might be given to the amount of $8 or $10 a month. A typical state law stated: "The overseers of the poor shall have the care and oversight of such persons in their town or precinct as are unable to earn a livelihood in consequence of any bodily infirmity, idiocy, lunacy or other unavoidable cause and are not supported by their relatives or at the county poorhouse, subject to such restrictions and regulations as may be prescribed by the county board or by the town." In some states the courts and police handled cases of dependency with funds provided from fines and forfeitures of bonds in criminal cases. In several states overseers of the poor were legally privileged to bind out to labor every person who needed public support. Many of the unemployed were disfranchised by laws in some states which deprived persons receiving public relief of the right to vote. Because of the heterogeneous types of settlement laws[5] in the various states, people often found themselves stranded, with no one legally responsible for their care. They were citizens of the United States but not of any state. A family might have moved from a state whose laws specified that legal residence was lost upon 30 days' absence, into a state in which legal settlement was not attained until after a year or more of continuous residence.

Relief Situation, 1930–1932

When business collapsed in 1929 and mass unemployment swept over the nation, these antiquated poor laws and private charitable organizations were practically the only available resources for the millions of jobless workers and their families. Toward the beginning of the depression, during the fall and winter of 1930, the prevailing attitude was "do nothing." Enterprising advertising and business concerns dotted the highways with posters which proclaimed "America *Is* Prosperous," and government spokesmen confidently said, "Prosperity is just around the corner." Leaders in local communities typically deemed it unnecessary and unwise to give too much recognition to the needs of the unemployed. Private charitable organizations expanded their programs as best they

---

[5] The legal term "settlement" as respects pauper laws indicates a person's right to support from the government in case of need. For residence requirements as of September, 1939, see Harry M. Hirsch, *Compilation of Settlement Laws*, American Public Welfare Association, Chicago.

could, retrenching on all their other services in order to buy more milk and bread for the hungry. Even so, they frankly admitted that they were unable to cope with the situation, that they were turning hundreds away with nothing, and reducing the budgets of those they were helping. Unemployed men, women, and children, not getting any relief at home, took to the road. Flophouses and jails were opened in small villages as well as large cities; here the migrants were given a meal and a night's lodging and then told to move on.

Before the winter was over, practically every county, city, and village in the country was forced to undertake special public works programs, some by bonding themselves to the legal limit, others by raising their tax rates. New York was the first state to provide substantial funds to help local communities meet their relief needs, the first relief law in 1931 being financed through a 50 per cent increase in the state income tax. Wisconsin's first relief act increased the state income tax approximately 100 per cent. A number of states inaugurated sales taxes to finance relief; others diverted gasoline taxes from their road funds; several borrowed from their teachers' pension and annuity funds, and many raised money through bond issues. Frequently there were constitutional limitations, not only on the incurring of state debts, but on income or sales taxes or raising money in any way for relief. A number of state courts stretched the police powers of the state and sanctioned relief appropriations as a means for the self-preservation and protection of the state. For example, the Washington State Supreme Court held an act for unemployment relief to be constitutional under the power of the state to suppress insurrection—an indication of the seriousness of the unemployment situation.

In spite of the tremendous increase in total costs, relief to individual families was becoming more meager and in some cases was cut off entirely. Most of the relief agencies were working pretty close to the starvation standard; few of the larger agencies gave as much as $1.00 per person per week, and in some cities the amount fell as low as 50 cents a week. The Illinois Emergency Relief Commission in its manual for local relief administrators said: "The commission . . . has defined its aim as the maintenance of a standard of living which will prevent suffering. . . . Clothing has a place in the relief program only as a preventive of physical suffering. Comfort, appearance, decency or even school attendance are not primary aims of the commission. . . . Rents, hospital care, school supplies, have been specifically denied by the commission."[6]

In many communities kerosene lamps displaced electricity for lighting, and wood was substituted for coal and gas for cooking and heating. It was an exceptional case when rents were paid for families on relief; in most instances the family had to be threatened with eviction before the relief agencies even started to dicker with the landlords. In many communities evictions were permitted and families were kept constantly on the move. City commissaries became increasingly popular because of their cheapness. Some mayors proudly boasted that their cities were able to feed their unemployed at an average of eight to ten cents per day per person.

As is usually the case, certain groups suffered more than others. Single men everywhere were discriminated against. In some cases they were sent to county almshouses to live with the derelicts typically inhabiting such places; usually they were simply ignored and had to resort "to the road." In the southern states the Negroes and Mexicans suffered neglect, as did the coal miners in West Virginia and Illinois.

The third winter of the depression came to a close with the almost complete exhaustion of private contributions, with local public funds diminishing to an alarming degree, and state governments struggling to assume some of the responsibility. A minority group in Washington was battling for federal action, although President Hoover had said in his message to Congress in December, 1931, "I am opposed to any direct or indirect government dole."[7] In an

---

[6] Illinois Emergency Relief Commission, *Relief Guidance and Control*, Chicago, 1932.

[7] There was a good deal of confusion as to just what the term "dole" meant. In England unemployment insurance was sometimes popularly referred to as a "dole." In this country, because of the prevailing opposition to such insurance (an opposition which is difficult to understand at this time), the word "dole" became a term of opprobrium which might refer to any kind of relief assistance the speaker happened to oppose. President Hoover confined the term "dole" to federal assistance and not to relief by local governments or private agencies. Some referred to cash relief as a "dole," in contrast to food allowances. Social workers were inclined to use the term "dole" in a situation where relief was given promiscuously without careful investigation of the actual need. Many of

attempt to allay further agitation for federal aid and also to dispose of some surplus agricultural commodities which farmers were unable to sell in the existing depressed markets, Congress directed that millions of bushels of wheat and bales of cotton which the Farm Board had on hand be distributed to the needy. This saved many persons from starvation, particularly in areas where there was no organized relief.

Agitation for more substantial federal relief was dramatized during the summer of 1932 by the tragic march on Washington of some 20,000 idle and ragged veterans of World War I who camped in and around the capital city for several months before they were dispersed with tear gas by federal troops. During this same year there were a number of "hunger marches" by other groups of unemployed which aroused both the sympathy and the fears of the public.[8] In the ensuing presidential campaign the fight over federal relief bills became part of the political tug of war. Opponents of federal aid for the unemployed congratulated Hoover's stand "for national solvency"; those in favor of federal aid, recalling how the government was helping the banks and railroads, proclaimed that their fight was for "Main Street versus Wall Street."

A conference of all factions resulted in the passing in July, 1932, of the Emergency Relief and Construction Act, which provided 300 million dollars for loans to states and cities for unemployment relief purposes and for self-liquidating public works.[9] The loans made for relief purposes, which actually proved to be gifts, were of material assistance to the local relief agencies, but these funds were virtually exhausted by the time President Roosevelt took office in March, 1933; at that time it was estimated that 4,250,000 families, or nearly 19 million persons, were receiving public assistance.[10]

---

the unemployed contemptuously referred to "dole" as meaning inadequate and meager relief.

[8] There had been similar occurrences during the depression of the 1890's; the best known was the march led by Jacob Coxey, an Ohio businessman and farmer; these marchers were later referred to as "Coxey's Army."

[9] H. R. 9642, Public. No. 302, 72nd Congress. An Act "to relieve destitution, to broaden the lending powers of the Reconstruction Finance Corporation, and to create employment by providing for and expediting a public-works program."

[10] *Monthly Report of the Federal Emergency Relief Administration,* December, 1933, p. 1.

RELIEF UNDER THE NEW DEAL

The Roosevelt administration, breaking sharply with the traditional philosophy that relief was a responsibility of local communities and private philanthropy, proclaimed it a national duty and immediately launched a colossal program for the relief of the unemployed industrial and agricultural workers. In May, 1933, the Federal Emergency Relief Administration[11] was created, with funds to augment the depleted resources of the state and local relief agencies.

From the outset the F.E.R.A. sought to do more than subsidize the existing state and local programs by establishing more adequate relief standards as well as improving the methods of administration. It encouraged the substitution of cash relief for the humiliating grocery orders and commissary systems, and urged the local agencies to provide clothing, medical care, and rent payments where necessary. As a result, the average amount of relief per family increased for the country as a whole from $15 per month in 1933 to $30 in 1935. Nevertheless, the fact that 70 per cent of the relief dollar went for food indicated that relief was still pretty much a bread and butter matter. In order to effect a closer union between industrial and agricultural relief the Federal Surplus Relief Corporation was organized for the purpose of purchasing surplus agricultural products and distributing them to persons on the relief rolls. This two-way transaction helped farmers by removing price-depressing surplus commodities from the open market, and it also provided a means for augmenting the food allowance in the family relief budgets.

A temporary but ambitious federal work relief program was put in effect for several months during the winter of 1933-1934. Under the Civil Works Administration, an agent of the F.E.R.A., more than 4 million persons were employed on hastily established public works projects requiring little or no machinery or materi-

---

[11] The original fund established under this Act was 500 million dollars, of which half was to be granted to the several states on the basis of one-third of their relief expenses. The second half was to help states without adequate resources, to aid needy persons who had no legal settlements, and to assist cooperative and self-help associations for the barter of goods and services.

als. The C.W.A. was the first large-scale federally sponsored experiment in public employment of the jobless; it was designed as a temporary measure to put the largest possible number of persons to work, regardless of costs.

The W.P.A. Program

After two years of federal grants to the states for the relief of their unemployed, there was a drastic change in federal policy. In 1935 the F.E.R.A. program was gradually liquidated and replaced by a work relief program under centralized federal control. The Works Progress Administration, which a few years later was renamed the Works Projects Administration, provided employment on numerous types of public activities to unemployed workers who were certified by their local relief agencies to be eligible for relief. Some of these projects were federal but most were sponsored by local governmental authorities.

During its almost six years of operation, the W.P.A. expended approximately 9 billion dollars. At its peak, during the winter of 1938–1939, it employed an average of more than 3 million persons a month; almost 7,800,000 different individuals were furnished jobs during the entire course of the program. The employment of a worker on a W.P.A. project for a month cost the federal government an average of $61.50. Out of this amount, the worker received an average of $54.25 in wages, $5 was spent for materials and other non-labor items, and $2.25 for administration. The physical accomplishments of the W.P.A. program included the construction or improvement of more than 100,000 public buildings and 565,000 miles of roads, 100,000 bridges and viaducts, 36,000 schools and libraries, and 7000 parks and playgrounds.

Relief for Youth

The federal relief program included two major activities designed especially for young people—the Civilian Conservation Corps and the National Youth Administration. Under the former, several thousand camps were established throughout the country for young men who were employed on conservation work such as forest protection and improvement, reforestation, recreational developments, range rehabilitation, aid to wildlife, flood control, soil conservation, and emergency rescue work. Each camp maintained

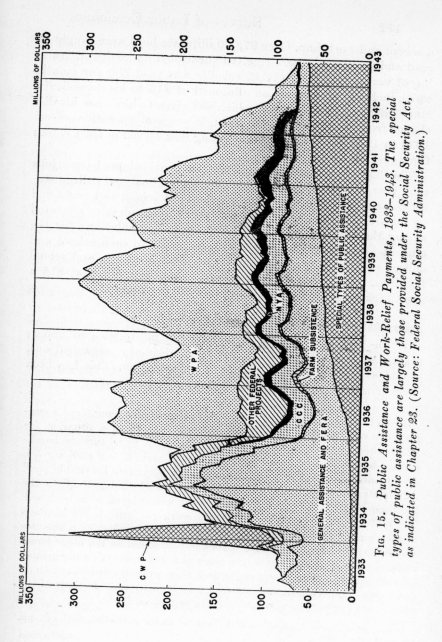

Fig. 15. *Public Assistance and Work-Relief Payments, 1933–1943. The special types of public assistance are largely those provided under the Social Security Act, as indicated in Chapter 23.* (Source: *Federal Social Security Administration.*)

a school and workshop. Over 87,000 illiterate boys were taught to read and write and others received vocational and cultural training of various kinds. A C.C.C. enrollee was paid $30 per month, which included $8 in cash, an allotment of $15 to his dependents, and $7 deposited to his credit which was given to him upon his discharge from the camp. During its eight years of operation—from 1933 to 1941—some 2½ million young men served in the Civilian Conservation Corps.

The National Youth Administration provided part-time jobs each year for approximately 500,000 high-school and college students, as well as young persons who had left school and could find no jobs. Funds for the out-of-school work program were allocated among the states on the basis of the youth population; for the student-work program allotments were made to each school and college on the basis of enrollment, needs of students, and school facilities. The young persons earned an average of about $15 a month for an average of 53 hours of work per month.[12]

Appraisal of New Deal Relief Measures

It was inevitable that a mammoth and unprecedented undertaking such as the W.P.A., and its subsidiary organizations, should arouse criticism as well as commendation. This has been summarized by one historian as follows:

From the first the government's relief efforts had encountered a running fire of criticism. Those in charge not only faced a situation for which there was no prior experience, but they were further handicapped by the lack of an adequate, well-paid and efficient civil service. As a result, politics, waste and incompetence played an inevitable part. Administration foes quickly applied the term "boondoggling" to the inconsequential tasks to which some of the unemployed were assigned. But quite apart from the value of the work performed, the business classes tended to favor the dole rather than work relief as a cheaper way of caring for the destitute. Labor's spokesmen, on the other hand, criticized the relatively low wages allowed relief workers on the ground that the government's course might encourage private employers to hold down pay. The Washington authorities made many modifications of the wage scale without, however, satisfying organized labor.

[12] Bureau of Labor Statistics, *Handbook of Labor Statistics,* 1941 ed., pp. 900 ff., 1000 ff., 1006 ff.

On the credit side of the ledger the gains were indubitably great. Work relief not only kept people from starvation, but at the same time fostered their self-respect and enabled them to retain their occupational skills. Moreover, as hastily prepared projects gave way to more maturely conceived ones, public improvements of lasting value resulted in every part of the land. It should also be noted that the work program, initiated primarily for manual and clerical laborers, was expanded until it included many thousands of unemployed writers, artists, teachers, architects, musicians and actors as well as research experts in the natural and social sciences. . . . Every part of the United States shared in these far-reaching public undertakings, and the people witnessed a physical transformation of the nation such as they had never before known. Among the white-collar projects, countless historical records were ferreted out of forgotten places and arrangements made for their preservation; the compilation of a series of comprehensive guidebooks was undertaken for the various states and local communities; and free concerts and inexpensive plays afforded entertainment and inner enrichment for vast numbers unaccustomed to such opportunities.[13]

PUBLIC WORKS

Government-financed public works were advocated by some 18th-century political economists and statesmen as a palliative for the unemployment resulting from changes in industry and agriculture which were taking place at that time. However, the policy of public works programs as a device for providing employment for those laid off by private industry[14] was not widely accepted during the century preceding the First World War, although some cities and towns hastily provided make-work as a relief measure during the more serious business depressions.

Subsequent to the First World War the principle of a planned public works program as a means for "smoothing the business cycle curve" by "priming the pump of industry" gained acceptance

---

[13] Arthur Meier Schlesinger, *The New Deal in Action, 1933–1939,* The Macmillan Company, New York, 1940, pp. 8–9.

[14] Public works construction, of course, is as old as government itself, and in this country the local communities have always been zealous in their efforts to get their share of federally financed river and harbor improvements, roads, post offices, etc. However, these were considered in terms of the projects themselves, rather than as planned programs for relieving unemployment.

by economists and public officials, although few of the proposals were put into effect. Anticipating widespread unemployment after the armistice in 1918, the War Labor Policies Board recommended a public works construction program, but these plans were abandoned with the sudden dissolution of the Board following cessation of hostilities. In 1921 President Harding's Conference on Unemployment urged the national government to adopt the policy of expanding its public works during periods of depression and reducing such expenditures when private business was active. Congress did nothing about these proposals, although during the following year a number of bills were introduced—but not passed—for the purpose of establishing a federal public works agency which would anticipate declines in private employment, and have plans and funds ready for public works construction.

Soon after the 1929 business crash a law was enacted creating a Federal Employment Stabilization Board which was to report to the President whenever a state of depression existed, or was likely to arise within six months; the President thereupon was to submit this report to Congress with an estimate of the appropriations needed to undertake public works. The Administration at that time was reluctant to admit that any sustained period of unemployment was imminent and the program came to nought because Congress failed to appropriate funds. In response to the rapidly worsening unemployment situation, the Reconstruction Finance Corporation was created in 1932 in an endeavor to stimulate business through federal loans to private business.

The Emergency Relief and Construction Act, enacted later that same year, provided money for public works. Because of delays in undertaking specific projects, however, only a small portion of these funds were actually expended under the provisions of this Act. The amount which was spent by the federal government, moreover, did not compensate for the decrease in construction undertaken by state and local governments which were obliged drastically to curtail their public construction because of depleted treasuries. The total volume of contracts for new construction in the first six months of 1933 was only 14 per cent as large as for the corresponding period in 1929.[15]

---

[15] U. S. Department of Labor, *P.W.A. and Industry,* Bulletin 658, 1938.

Public Works Administration

Public works as a means of providing employment and stimulating business recovery gained new impetus with the change in administration in 1933. Title II of the National Industrial Recovery Act authorized the creation of a Public Works Administration and a "comprehensive program of public works." Originally established for two years, the P.W.A. was continued until the approach of World War II, when unemployment virtually disappeared.

Unlike those on W.P.A. projects, the persons employed on Public Works Administration projects were not selected from relief rolls, although consideration was given to qualified individuals in greatest need. Also unlike the W.P.A., which employed people directly, most of the P.W.A. projects were let on a competitive basis to private contractors who selected their own crews and paid prevailing wages for a standard 40-hour week.[16]

The Public Works Program was undertaken in three major divisions: projects to be conducted directly by agencies of the federal government; projects to be undertaken by state and local authorities or other non-federal bodies; and loans to industry on a commercial basis for such purposes as the development and improvement of railroads or other private construction activities.

State and local authorities which operated under the program provided most of the funds for their projects, but the P.W.A. was authorized initially to make direct grants from the federal Treasury amounting to 30 per cent of the cost of labor and materials to be used on the projects. Later the maximum grant was raised to 45 per cent of the total cost, with the state or local agency financing the remaining 55 per cent. In some cases, the P.W.A. provided necessary funds for local projects in the form of loans. All public works projects, in order to be approved, were required to have specific social value and to be conducted in such a way as to relieve unemployment in areas where the local employment situation had become serious.

Many different kinds of public works were undertaken under the

[16] Originally, the P.W.A. itself fixed minimum rates for skilled and unskilled labor on a three-zone basis, but later wages were predetermined, before contracts were let, in accordance with going rates in the local community. The state director of the P.W.A. was given the power to disapprove any rate, other than those fixed by statute, which was lower than the prevailing union rate if the type of work affected had normally been done under union conditions.

program. The most popular type was public buildings constructed by state and local authorities. They built schoolhouses, court-houses, city halls, hospitals, and many other needed public build-ings valued at more than $1,200,000,000. Road work undertaken by the federal Bureau of Public Roads and other federal agencies cost nearly $700,000,000, and water and sewerage systems for local use over $450,000,000. Federal army engineers and other federal agencies spent $360,000,000 on flood control along the Mississippi, Missouri, Ohio, and other rivers, and in deepening river channels and harbors. In addition to vast federal highway, power, and low-cost housing projects which were financed entirely by the P.W.A., local governments were assisted in the construc-tion of several thousand educational buildings, more than 300 hospitals, several thousand sewer and water systems, and numer-ous flood control, reclamation, and other community improve-ments.

More than $1,600,000,000 was spent in wages to persons di-rectly employed on P.W.A. construction projects. The total em-ployment amounted to over 2 billion man-hours of work; this is the equivalent of more than 1 million men for one year, assuming that 2000 hours represents a normal year of full employment. During the peak months in 1934 and 1935 an average of 500,000 to 600,000 men was employed each week. Furthermore, in terms of amount of employment, it is estimated that the indirect employ-ment, the "behind-the-lines employment," amounted to at least $2\frac{1}{2}$ times the employment at the site of construction; in other words, to the latter is added the employment in industries supplying and transporting the materials used in construction. If the secondary employment in industries supplying the living needs of the workers directly and indirectly engaged on these projects were also taken into account, the total amount of employment created by the P.W.A. would be at least five times the amount actually engaged at the site of construction.

EMPLOYMENT ACT OF 1946

Production for war absorbed the public works as well as all the public relief programs, and mass unemployment disappeared as the demands for military and civilian employment expanded after

Pearl Harbor. With the depression after the First World War and the long depression of the 1930's in mind, many persons and organizations actively supported the "Full Employment Bill" which was introduced in Congress soon after V-J Day. This bill declared that all persons able and willing to work have "the right to useful, remunerative, regular and full-time employment and it is the policy of the United States to assure the existence at all times of sufficient employment opportunities to enable all . . . freely to exercise this right."

Specifically, the bill provided that the President should submit to Congress at the beginning of each session a National Production and Employment Budget which would include estimates of the number of jobs needed for full employment, the volume of goods and services which could be produced at full employment, and the amount of investments and expenditures which would be needed to purchase this volume. If the budget report showed a deficiency— that is, spending ability insufficient to maintain full employment— the President was to recommend a program "with respect to, but not limited to, taxation; banking, credit and currency; monopoly and monopolistic practices; wages, hours and working conditions; foreign trade and investment; agriculture; education; housing; social security; natural resources; public works; and other revenue, investment, expenditure, service or regulatory activities of the Federal Government."

This bill was not enacted. In its stead an act was passed which declared that it was the government's policy ". . . to coordinate and utilize all its plans, functions and resources for the purpose of creating and maintaining, in a manner calculated to foster and promote free competitive enterprise and the general welfare, conditions under which there will be afforded useful employment opportunities, . . . and to promote maximum employment, production and purchasing power." Under the act as passed, a Council of Economic Advisers makes annual reports, beginning in 1947, on the "current and foreseeable trends in the levels of employment, production, and purchasing power," together with recommendations for a program which will create conditions affording job opportunities for all who are able and willing to work, and seeking employment.

This 1946 Employment Act says nothing about a guarantee of

jobs, nor does it call for a planned federal budget with implied commitments to stimulate flagging business activity and take up any employment slack, which were the two basic features of the original proposal. Sponsors of the Act maintained that the program for fact-finding and recommendations by a council of non-partisan economists would serve to stimulate action by government and business which, in the words of President Truman when he appointed the members of the Council, would provide the country with an "economy free from the evils of both inflation and deflation" and one which "can go forward to greater heights of prosperity and full employment than have yet been achieved."

EMPLOYER EFFORTS FOR THE ALLEVIATION OF UNEMPLOYMENT

Government programs in the form of direct cash assistance and jobs on public works represent two lines of attack for the relief of unemployment. Is government action the sole means for alleviating unemployment or is it possible for business, the provider of jobs, to take any action which would tend to reduce unemployment? From earlier discussions it is apparent that no single industry can solve the problem of mass unemployment resulting from general economic disequilibriums. However, there is ample evidence that individual industries and business firms can do much to prevent or at least mitigate, some type of unemployment. As already indicated, substantial amounts of unemployment are the result of seasonal and other irregularities in business operation, or of layoffs due to special causes unrelated to general economic conditions. The amelioration of such insecurity of jobs and income lies within the realm of individual employer action to a large degree, as is evidenced by measures which have been taken by some employers.

In general, the efforts of employers toward stabilizing employment and wages have included one or more of the following: (1) readjustments in plant operation in order to regularize the flow of work; (2) plans for guaranteed annual employment and wages; (3) dismissal pay, in case of unavoidable layoffs, to provide income until new jobs are found; (4) centralized and improved methods of hiring, training, and transfer. The latter will be discussed in the next chapter; here we shall deal with the various means used for obtaining greater stability in production, as well as with instances of guaranteed employment plans and payment of dismissal wages to workers laid off through no fault of their own.

Stabilization

Stabilization of production is an ideal which no one seriously questions because it benefits everyone concerned in a business enterprise—the owners, the employees, and indirectly the customers. An even flow of work through the plant twelve months a year not only provides steady jobs but makes possible the maximum utilization of plant facilities, thereby reducing waste and costs and enhancing profits. Conceding the desirability of regularization is one thing, however, and attaining it is quite another, for it hinges on every aspect of business operation as well as the desires and habits of customers. It involves questions of business financing, methods of sales and distribution, the intricacies of routing hundreds of different parts to numerous workers at different machines, and constant vigilance to avoid machine breakdowns and other interruptions in the flow of work all along the production line. Its attainment requires management foresight and imagination, a desire and will to break long-rooted habits both within and without the plant, a high degree of efficiency throughout the hierarchy of management, and the cooperation of all the workers.

In view of the difficulties involved, it becomes apparent that production stabilization can never be perfectly achieved throughout all industry. Nevertheless, some companies have made notable progress in stabilizing production within their plants, and their experiences provide illustrations of the various factors which must be taken into consideration in any plan for steadying work.

Although it is impossible to eliminate seasonal demands for some kinds of goods and services, there are various ways in which seasonal irregularities in employment can be reduced. One is through diversification of product or the development of side lines to fill in the seasonal gaps. The coal and ice business is the classical example of a combination of seasonal industries. Canning companies have gone into making jellies, soups, and other prepared foods which fill in the dull periods between harvest seasons; some manufacturers of toys that are largely confined to the Christmas trade have introduced gadgets which have year-round sales. In lieu of or supplementary to product diversification is a program for widening the sales market to include areas of divergent seasonal demands. Thus summer clothes can be manufactured for winter sale in Florida and southern California, and markets in the southern hemisphere make possible a dovetailing of seasonal production for all commodities whose sales are affected by climate and weather.

There are, of course, difficulties in the introduction of new products in any business. New markets and sales programs must be developed; the products must be carefully chosen to make sure that they will even out production and not accentuate existing seasonal fluctuations; their manufacture may require new techniques and skills on the part of both management and workers; and if new machinery is required, there is additional capital investment.

Some seasonal and other irregularities in production are due to habit and custom more than to real necessity; they are the result of marketing and distribution methods rather than the actual needs of ultimate consumers. At one time, for example, the manufacture of soap was a highly fluctuating business, although there is little variation in the daily use of soap. The irregularity was due to the fact that the manufactured products were distributed through speculative jobbers who stocked up heavily when they sensed a rise in prices, and ceased purchasing when it appeared that prices would fall. A prominent soap company was able to regularize its production when it largely eliminated the jobbers and began selling direct to retail dealers.[17] Some manufacturers of shoes and other clothing have gone further in controlling the disposal of their products by establishing their own retail outlets.

The automobile industry, notorious for its extreme fluctuations in employment, greatly reduced the impact of its seasonal operations by shifting the annual date for bringing out new models from January to early fall. The twofold aim of this change was to stimulate consumer demand for cars in the winter time through the appeal of new models, and to get dealers to stock new cars well in advance of the peak spring demand. Although this change in the introduction of new models has by no means eliminated irregularity in employment, the seasonal layoffs have been shifted from

---

[17] Herbert Feis, *Labor Relations, a Study Made in the Procter and Gamble Co.*, Adelphi Company, New York, 1928.

winter to late summer when workers are better able to find other employment on farms, in canneries, resort hotels, and so forth.

Some employers consider regularization sufficiently important to make price reductions on goods purchased during slack seasons, and others stimulate purchases by giving their salesmen increased commissions on orders taken for dull-season delivery. A not unusual practice is for manufacturers to give their customers discounts graduated according to the delivery date, thus discouraging spot deliveries which reduce opportunities for factory planning. One of the most effective means for regularizing the flow of work is to manufacture for stock during dull seasons. This, of course, entails the "freezing" of capital which has been expended on the materials and labor used in the manufacture of the stock items and also involves some risks. If there is a style factor, the stock goods may become obsolete before sold; and if there is a decline in market prices, they may have to be sold at a loss. For large items there is also the problem and cost of storage space, and for many products there is the possibility of deterioration.

Frequent change in styles, not only in clothing but in many other consumer goods, is a major cause of production irregularities, although business defends and encourages style changes and multiplicity in types and kinds of products on the ground that they stimulate and increase total purchases. It is doubtful if much can be done to discourage the trend toward ever-increasing changes in styles and fashions in consumers' goods, but progress has been made toward standardizing some products and parts and this has greatly facilitated regularization. For example, automobile parts have become standardized to a large degree, even though there has been diversification in colors and models. (The Ford Motor Company at one time produced only black cars in two or three models.) While an increasing variety of electrical appliances is being manufactured, there is continued standardization of size and design of parts which permits interchangeability.

Aside from the resulting convenience to customers,[18] standardi-

---

[18] Americans who travel in Europe, where there is no standardization in size and voltage, are constantly reminded of the inconvenience of not being able to plug any kind of electrical appliance into any socket. For a discussion of the significance of standardization in terms of business efficiency and regularity of employment, see the report of the Federated American Engineering Societies, *Waste in Industry,* McGraw-Hill Book Company, Inc., New York, 1921.

zation of tools and parts tends to stabilize employment because it reduces the delays incident to securing replacements during the process of manufacture, broadens the possible market for the finished products, and, as already mentioned, encourages manufacturers to produce for stock during slack seasons.

Guaranteed Employment Plans

Although a number of employers have made efforts toward regularizing employment within their plants, only a few have gone so far as to guarantee annual wages or employment to all or substantial groups of their employees. The explanation of the infrequency of annual-wage and guaranteed-employment plans in American industry today lies in the very problem that such plans are designed to correct. As a rule, the only companies which feel they can guarantee full-time employment or annual wages are those that have substantially solved the problem of regularizing employment. Some guarantee plans, after being in operation for a year or two, have been abandoned when the companies found themselves unable to finance them during a prolonged decline in production.

Limited as are the existing employment-guarantee plans in industry today, they represent a partial fulfillment of the workers' quest for job security; they may also indicate the beginning of a more general adoption of plans which will provide some measure of security to an increasing number of workers. As indicated in Chapter 16, the government has given its official blessing to guaranteed-employment plans by exempting employees who work under specified types of guarantees from certain provisions of the Fair Labor Standards Act.

Existing guarantee plans are of two general types, namely, those guaranteeing employment and those guaranteeing annual wages. The employment-guarantee plans specify the number of weeks or hours of work to be provided employees each year, without specifying the amount of earnings to be received. In other words, what is guaranteed is a year's job (or in some cases, a fraction of a year), with the total annual earnings left a variable. Under annual-wage plans, the employee is guaranteed a weekly income throughout the year, regardless of daily or seasonal fluctuations in employment. Actually, the distinction between guaranteed-employment and annual-wage plans is one of emphasis only, for if the employer cannot furnish sufficient work to fulfill the contract, he must pay wages for the remainder of the time guaranteed. The significant differences among the several plans have to do with the relative completeness of the guarantee, that is, with how closely the guarantee, whether expressed in wages or in work, comes to providing the equivalent of full employment at normal wages.

Existing guarantee plans represent various arrangements and degrees of regularizing employment or income. In some instances the regular weekly wage is assured for a given number of weeks and a proportion of the wages (half pay) is guaranteed during all or a specified number of the remaining weeks. Certain plans guarantee a specified number of hours' or weeks' work a year. Under the hour guarantee, weekly earnings fluctuate according to the actual hours worked in any week; under either plan, if less than 52 weeks or 2080 hours are guaranteed, the worker has no assurance of a full year's employment or earnings.

Under some plans, full pay during weeks of less than full employment is compensated to the employer by extra work during peak seasons with no increase in the weekly pay during these overtime weeks; under others, the guaranteed wage represents a minimum to which overtime is added when worked. Somewhat similar to a guaranteed-wage plan is the wage-advance arrangement whereby an employer makes a cash loan to eligible workers in "short" weeks to bring their wages up to specified amounts, these advances being subsequently repaid by automatic deductions from wages earned during full-time or overtime weeks. One well-known plan guarantees each eligible employee 52 pay checks per year regardless of business conditions or regularity of employment, but the total annual wage fluctuates because the fund from which the pay checks are drawn is a specified percentage of the company's gross income.

The plans differ not only with respect to the proportion of a year's normal income or work which is guaranteed, but also as to the inclusiveness of the labor force that benefits from the guarantees and the conditions, if any, which relieve the employer of fulfilling the guarantee obligations. For example, if the guarantee applies to only a small number of key employees, the plan may involve no major effort toward plant-wide stabilization but represent merely a contractual arrangement for employees who would in any case be fairly regularly employed.

Three well-known examples of guaranteed-employment or annual-wage plans justify brief description because they illustrate different types.

The *George A. Hormel & Co. annual-wage plan* amounts to advances on wages during periods of unemployment, and repayment of such advances by working extra hours during peak periods, up to 53 hours. The hours of work fluctuate, but the weekly payment remains unchanged.

Under the Hormel "straight-time" plan each worker is employed on an annual basis and is assigned a regular weekly rate which is determined by budgeting over a 52-week period the estimated annual labor cost of the department. The total annual labor expenses for a department are estimated and one fifty-second part of this cost is allocated as a weekly wage cost; this is divided into equal weekly payments, graduated according to occupation, among the workers estimated as necessary to do the work, regardless of the number of hours worked in any particular week. In return, the employees regularly attached to a department work, without extra pay, as many hours as are required to turn out the scheduled production, up to a maximum of 53 hours during peak periods; however, when they are required to work more than 10 hours in any one day, they receive overtime for the hours over 48 worked in that week.

The yearly wage is calculated on the basis of a 40-hour week in most departments, with an allowance for vacation and sick leave. In other departments, in which the budget is insufficient to guarantee 40 hours' pay or for which it is difficult to forecast yearly production accurately, the yearly wage is based on 38 or 36 hours' pay as a safety margin. If at the end of the year the employees in these departments have worked more than the hours paid for, they receive a year-end check for the extra hours actually worked.

Bonuses are paid to all plant employees (except a small group of engineers, maintenance men, and elevator operators) if actual production exceeds the estimated volume. In general, the scheduled annual total of unit production divided by 2000 constitutes one production-hour for a department. Each department is reimbursed for the excess of production-hours over total man-hours actually worked, and this money is allocated to the individual workers on the basis of their "hourly" rates. When members of a gang are absent, their wages are credited to the gang and are divided among the employees in that gang at the end of the year.

The *Nunn-Bush Shoe Co. plan* guarantees 52 pay checks a year to practically all employees with at least two years' service. A specified percentage of the wholesale value of the shoes sold, representing the ratio of labor costs to the wholesale value of shoes as determined from past experience, is put into a Share Production Fund from which all wage payments except those for overtime are made.

Individual weekly drawing accounts are established for each eligible employee from this fund on the basis of one fifty-second of his "yearly differential rate," obtained by multiplying his present average hourly drawing by 2080 (40 hours $\times$ 52). Individual "differential rates" vary according to occupation. A reserve fund of $12\frac{1}{2}$ per cent of the yearly differential rate is maintained to insure regularity of income. Full weekly drawings (one fifty-second of the employee's yearly differential rate) are issued unless the individual employee's reserve falls below 5 per cent of the annual estimated income, in which case the weekly drawing may be reduced. When an individual's reserve account exceeds $12\frac{1}{2}$ per cent of the annual estimated income, the excess is paid as a monthly (or adjusted compensation) check.[19]

The *Procter & Gamble plan* covers all employees paid by the hour who have been in the company's service for a period of two years. Eligible employees are guaranteed work for 48 weeks per year, less time lost for holiday closings, disability because of sickness or accident, voluntary absence, and certain emergencies such as floods, fires, and strikes.

The plan has certain protective clauses which permit the company to transfer employees to other work (even to that paid at a lower rate), to change the number of hours constituting the established work week to which the guarantee applies, and to reduce the hours of guaranteed work to 75 per cent of the standard work week in effect at each plant.

[19] A verbatim statement of the Nunn-Bush plan is given in Bureau of Labor Statistics Bulletin No. 828, Government Printing Office, Washington, 1945.

Dismissal Pay

Dismissal compensation has not been common in American industry. When adopted, it has most frequently been applied to layoffs caused by technological improvements or to retrenchments involved in consolidations, and not to general layoffs resulting from slack work. Although dismissal compensation is designed to ease the burden resulting from unemployment, it is basically different from unemployment compensation or unemployment insurance. The latter may or may not be financed from a joint fund, whereas dismissal compensation is financed solely by the employer. Unemployment compensation provides weekly (or biweekly or monthly) payments for the duration of unemployment or for the maximum number of weeks specified in the particular plan. Dismissal compensation, on the other hand, is usually a lump-sum payment which is based on the employee's length of service, and it takes no account of the actual time lost before a new job is found.

Dismissal compensation is an indemnity to the employee for the final loss of his job; it represents a payment made for breaking a valuable relationship rather than reimbursement to cover a period of unemployment, and it is intended to compensate him for the loss of certain rights acquired on the job, such as seniority, vacation, pension, or retirement benefits.

The amount of dismissal pay is in almost all instances based on the employee's length of service with the company and his rate of pay during his employment. A week's wages or a month's salary is usually the unit for determining compensation, but most plans establish a limit on the amount payable in terms of either a number of weeks' or months' pay or a specified sum.

One of the first dismissal plans was established in a Chicago men's clothing company in 1926 to encourage a reduction in the surplus of cutters resulting from changes in manufacturing processes. Under this plan every cutter who relinquished his job was paid a dismissal wage of $500. About one-fifth of the cost incurred was borne by the union, and the rest by the firm. More recently, dismissal-pay plans have been adopted when large numbers of workers were to be laid off because of business consolidations or retrenchments. Outstanding examples of such plans are those provided for railroad, telegraph, and newspaper office workers, although scattered groups of employees in other industries also benefit from them.

Railroad Workers. Because of the fear of railroad workers that possible consolidation among the railroads under the Emergency Railroad Transportation Act would result in widespread layoffs, a nation-wide agreement was negotiated between the railroad unions and the carriers which established a plan for compensating employees laid off as a result of "coordination." Displaced employees are entitled to receive monthly payments for periods ranging from 6 months after 1 year of service to 60 months after 15 years' service or more. The monthly payment is equivalent to 60 per cent of the employee's average monthly pay for the 12-month period preceding dismissal. Employees with less than 1 year of service receive a lump-sum payment equivalent to 60 days' pay at the straight-time daily rate for the last position held prior to loss of employment.

Telegraph Workers. Early in 1943, Congress amended the Communications Act of 1934 to permit the consolidation and merger of domestic telegraph carriers and made provision for dismissal pay to workers whose jobs were terminated as a result of the merger and for the continued employment of other workers. The amendment provided that employees of any merged company, who began work before a specified date, were to be assured employment for at least 4 years after the merger without reduction in compensation, and that any employee whose employment began after the specified date and who was discharged as a result of the merger would at any time within 4 years after the merger be entitled to severance pay of one month's wages for each year worked.

Newspaper Guild. Almost all the agreements negotiated by the American Newspaper Guild covering employees (except those in mechanical trades) working for newspapers, wire services, news weeklies and magazines, radio stations, and allied fields, provide for severance pay. Under most of the agreements, dismissal pay is allowed for all dismissals except those for gross misconduct and neglect of duty, although under some there are no exceptions and payment is made regardless of the reason for dismissal. All the Guild agreements contain graduated plans in which the dismissal payment is based on earnings and length of service, most commonly one week's pay for every six months' or one year's service.

SELECTED REFERENCES

Relief and Public Works

Abbott, Grace, *From Relief to Social Security*, University of Chicago Press, Chicago, 1941.

Brown, Josephine C., *Public Relief 1929–1939*, Henry Holt & Company, Inc., New York, 1940.

Calkins, Clinch, *Some Folks Won't Work*, Harcourt, Brace & Company, Inc., New York, 1931.

Colcord, Joanna, Koplovitz, William C., and Kurtz, Russell H., *Emergency Work Relief*, Russell Sage Foundation, New York, 1932.

Feder, L. H., *Unemployment Relief in Periods of Depression*, Russell Sage Foundation, New York, 1936.

Gayer, Arthur D., *Public Works in Prosperity and Depression*, National Bureau of Economic Research, Inc., New York, 1935.

Gill, Corrington, *Wasted Manpower: The Challenge of Unemployment*, W. W. Norton & Company, Inc., New York, 1939.

Howard, Donald S., *The WPA and Federal Relief Policy*, Russell Sage Foundation, New York, 1943.

Ickes, Harold L., *Back to Work, the Story of PWA*, The Macmillan Company, New York, 1935.

Lescohier, D. D., *History of Labor in the U. S.*, The Macmillan Company, New York, 1935, chaps. 7–12.

McMahon, A. W., Millett, John D., and Ogden, Gladys, *The Administration of Federal Relief*, Public Administration Service, Chicago, 1941.

Millis Harry, and Montgomery, Royal, *Labor's Risks and Social Insurance*, McGraw-Hill Book Company, Inc., New York, 1938.

W.P.A., *Inventory: An Appraisal of Results of the Works Projects Administration*, Government Printing Office, Washington, 1938.

Employer Programs

American Legion, *To Make Jobs More Steady and To Make More Steady Jobs*, Webb Book Publishing Co., St. Paul, 1938.

American Management Association, *Annual Wages and Employment Stabilization Techniques*, Research Report No. 8, New York, 1946.

Balderston, C. Canby, *Executive Guidance in Industrial Relations*, University of Pennsylvania Press, Philadelphia, 1935.

Chernick, Jack, and Hallickson, George C., *Guaranteed Annual Wages*, University of Minnesota Press, Minneapolis, 1945.

Feldman, Herman, *Stabilizing Jobs and Wages*, Harper & Brothers, New York, 1940.

Hawkins, Everett D., *Dismissal Compensation,* Princeton University Press, Princeton, 1940.

Koepke, Charles A., *Plant Production Control,* John Wiley & Sons, Inc., New York, 1942.

U. S. Bureau of Labor Statistics, *Dismissal Pay Provisions in Union Agreements,* Bulletin 808, Government Printing Office, Washington, 1945.

U. S. Bureau of Labor Statistics, *Guaranteed Employment and Annual Wage Provisions in Union Agreements,* Bulletin 828, Government Printing Office, Washington, 1945.

8

LABOR PLACEMENT,
TRAINING,
AND TURNOVER

WHEN CONSIDERING THE CAUSES AND CURES OF UNEMPLOYMENT, one usually thinks in terms of labor en masse, or the total number of jobs available in relation to the entire labor force. Within the broad boundaries of the total labor market, however, are numerous specialized labor markets differentiated by types of jobs and geographical location. Total business activity is comprised of hundreds of thousands of enterprises, and the total labor force includes millions of individual persons. Enterprises are located all over the country and their employment requirements call for varied aptitudes and skills. Likewise the composition of the labor force includes all kinds of persons with different abilities, ambitions, and training, who may or may not be living where the jobs they need or want happen to be located.

While the crucial problem of the general economy is to maintain an equilibrium between the total supply of and the total demand for labor, a mere balance in numbers does not of itself assure maximum labor utilization, or the social stability and personal satisfaction ensuing from having people working at jobs for which they are best fitted. Many persons may be doing jobs for which they are not suited and do not like; a job misfit not only means indifferent and poor workmanship, but represents incipient labor turnover which usually results in a greater or lesser period of unemployment.

Irrespective of the over-all employment situation, there is always the problem of individual job placement. At any given time, thousands of men and women are seeking new jobs, and employers simultaneously are seeking replacements and additional workers. Some employers and workers have ready access to each other; others must depend upon an intermediary. A method for bringing jobs and workers together promptly, with selective discrimination and in an orderly manner, is a basic requirement in any program to achieve maximum employment. Of equal importance are facilities for training young persons and retraining older persons for the jobs at hand.

JOB PLACEMENT

There are four avenues by which workers and jobs can be brought together: (1) direct application to the employer, (2) union hiring halls, (3) private employment agencies, and (4) public employment offices.

Direct Application to Employers

Regardless of whether applicants are referred to an employer by an intermediary agent or apply directly, the final selection is of course made by the employer. An employer's method of selection and his method of recruitment vitally affect the general employment situation, as well as the stability and efficiency of his own work force. Recruitment of labor by an individual employer tends to be wasteful for both himself and the applicants for jobs. Whether applicants are attracted by advertising in newspapers or apply without solicitation, the employer must usually spend time interviewing many more persons than he intends to hire. Likewise, applicants lose a great deal of time going from one plant to another on the chance of finding work.

So far as the general labor market is concerned, every group of applicants for jobs represents a pool of unemployment, and the number of such pools tends to increase in direct ratio to the number of recruitment centers. The situation was much worse a generation ago, when it was common practice to have each foreman in the plant do his own hiring.[1] In most companies today, the re-

---

[1] During the First World War when there were no government controls on transfers and hiring, many companies paid their foremen a fee of one or two dollars for each new employee they recruited. In some cases foremen in the

cruiting and initial selecting of employees take place in the plant's centralized employment or personnel office, the foremen or department heads having the right to accept or reject the applicants thus referred to them.

The employment manager is expected to be acquainted with all possible sources of needed types of labor and to know the best procedures for using each source. The employment office usually has at hand job specification charts showing the normal line of progression from job to job, individual employee records, and applications of desirable applicants. The department heads are responsible for making intra-department upgradings before placing requisitions for new employees. Transfers and promotions involving changes from one department to another are handled through the company employment office in consultation with the supervisors affected. If seniority rules are involved, the employment office maintains an up-to-date seniority roster.

In selecting new employees, chief reliance is placed upon personal interviews, but many companies supplement their interviewers' judgment with trade and aptitude tests. Trade tests attempt to measure what a person can do or has already learned about a job, while aptitude tests assist in determining the applicant's "learnability" for an occupation in which he has had no previous experience. The latter may include hand and foot dexterity tests, as well as general intelligence and temperament tests. Detailed job specifications, in which the elements of each job are ranked according to their importance, are used as the basis for such tests, each test being worked out especially for the particular job for which the applicant is being selected.

Physical examinations are also a recognized part of the employment process in many companies. Like the other types of tests, the physical examination is designed to eliminate the expense and waste involved in employing persons who are incapable of performing the work efficiently, as well as to prevent new workers from being assigned to tasks that are beyond their physical capacities. For some workers—for example, transportation employees and food handlers—physical examinations are also necessary

same company entered into collusive arrangements whereby they would discharge employees at frequent intervals and send them to other foremen in the plant who collected recruitment fees.

for public safety and health. In addition to general physical check-ups, some occupations involve special physical requirements, or at least the absence of the slightest impairment of certain particular faculties. Thus, a person who must match colors and shades must not be color-blind and must have good vision; telephone operators must have good hearing; streetcar operators must have wide peripheral vision.

Although aptitude and general intelligence tests are useful in the selection of people for particular jobs, they are not the final measurement of potential effectiveness, because they cannot definitively indicate an applicant's ability and willingness to acquire the necessary skills after being placed on the job. For putting the right person in the right job there is no mechanical substitute for careful interviewing by an intelligent, trained interviewer who knows the requirements of the job and has penetrating insight and sound judgment of human capabilities and temperament.

Union Hiring Halls

In some industries and localities employers rely upon unions for the referral of applicants. This is especially true in certain skilled trades, such as the building construction industry, where the unions have assumed much of the responsibility for providing employers with required labor. Also in a number of the clothing centers as well as for maritime workers much of the job referral is done through union hiring halls. The hiring of longshoremen and seamen through the unions was one of the first reforms which the newly organized unions insisted upon in the 1930's. Previously, hiring had been the sole prerogative of the ships' officers and long-shore contractors, and had frequently been attended by graft and favoritism.

The assumption by the unions of the function of job assignment has developed because of certain peculiar characteristics of the industry or the local labor market. Although hiring through the union is synonymous to a closed shop, as explained in Chapter 19, this practice is not solely or always followed because of the unions' desire to assure one hundred per cent union membership in the industry or trade. There are other reasons which seemingly benefit employers as well as the unions.

This is illustrated by the situation in the building construction industry where a dozen or more distinct job skills are required for short and irregular periods of time. Many construction projects are located miles away from the source of the labor supply; even though the required workmen may be close at hand, the project may be in charge of an out-of-town contractor who is unfamiliar with the local labor market or the proficiencies of job applicants. Under such circumstances the local building-trades unions are in a peculiarly advantageous position to supply the necessary labor, for not only do they know who among the local membership is qualified for the various kinds of jobs, but if the local supply is insufficient they can get in touch with neighboring unions and have them send over some of their members. On many of the large construction projects undertaken during the recent war, many of which were located in isolated communities, skilled craftsmen were brought in from all sections of the country by the national offices of the unions.

Where a union supplies workmen for the employer, the union assumes responsibility for the competence of its members, although the employer has the privilege of refusing to accept a workman if he considers him unqualified. For the union members, the union hiring-hall system makes possible an even rotation of jobs, which is a major consideration in industries where there is intermittent employment and frequent change of employers. The longshore hiring halls on the Pacific coast maintain detailed records of the work-hours of each member, and these are used as the basis of job assignment to see that all longshoremen receive approximately the same number of hours of work each month. In the maritime and building trades, the men register at the union offices upon the completion of each job and are referred to new jobs in the order in which their names appear on the roster.

Private Employment Agencies

Private or commercial employment agencies antedate public employment offices and have continued in operation despite the establishment of a nation-wide system of employment exchanges administered by the government. Private employment offices are operated for profit and their income usually comes from fees and other collections levied upon applicants for jobs; very rarely are employers charged reciprocal fees. Hence when an applicant goes to a private employment agency, he has to pay for its services in finding him a job.

Although some private employment agencies perform a useful function at minimum cost to persons seeking jobs, the social value and desirability of these agencies is open to question. Aside from the matter of fees, which in itself imposes a hardship upon the applicant,[2] private employment agencies sometimes indulge in practices which are detrimental to workers, to say the least. To quote a government report: "While the majority of agencies are honestly and efficiently operated, some are not. This type of business may be started on a shoestring, and offers opportunity for abuse by the unscrupulous agent anxious for a quick return on his investment. . . . One of the most serious abuses is to give false or sketchy information about the job. Without knowing what lies ahead, the worker takes the job and pays his fee to the agent, only to find that the wages offered, the hours of work required, or the living or other conditions are totally different from those described to him by the agent, and are such that he cannot accept or continue the work. . . ."[3]

The most serious abuses take place among migratory and seasonal workers recruited by "labor contractors" who operate across state lines and thereby escape the controls of state laws. During the period of heavy Italian immigration before the First World War it was common practice for highway and railroad construction companies to get their unskilled labor through padrones, who not only recruited the workers but frequently served as gang bosses and had the privilege of charging the non-English-speaking immigrants for interpreters' fees, commissions for getting them jobs and keeping them from being discharged, and collecting other petty graft.[4]

The labor contracting system has continued to operate, espe-

[2] In California during one year (1942) job seekers paid $1,637,400 to private employment agencies in that state. This does not include theatrical and motion-picture employment offices, or agricultural contractors supplying workers for farm operation. (M. I. Gershenson, *Fees Charged by Private Employment Agencies in California*, Department of Industrial Relations, San Francisco, 1943.)

[3] United States Department of Labor, Division of Labor Standards, *Private Employment Agencies*, Bulletin No. 57, Washington, 1943, p. 3.

[4] See Don D. Lescohier, *History of Labor*, The Macmillan Company, New York, 1935, vol. iii, pp. xi and 186 ff.

cially among migratory agricultural workers. Again quoting a government report:

Labor contractors may recruit workers in one part of the country for employment in some far-distant State. They have frequently misled workers on wages, hours, living and transportation costs and conditions, the length of the job, and on other vital matters. When workers find that they cannot keep the job, they are unable to secure a refund on the fee that they paid either because they have signed away their rights or they have no written agreement. They may travel some distance only to be discharged at the end of the week or month when their fee is paid out of their wages. That occurs over and over again because of fee splitting between the agency and the employer involved. . . .

The system encourages agreements between employer and contractor that result in hardship to the worker. For example, the employer has nothing to lose if the contractor operates camps, stores, and transportation facilities with a high charge for poor service to the worker. Until the employer provides the money for the pay roll, workers may be forced to accept from the contractor checks, counters, scrip, tickets, and other promises-to-pay, redeemable only at his store or camp. When pay day finally comes, these workers often find all their wages eaten up by such credit. The contractor may disappear with the pay roll, leaving stranded workers in his wake. These abuses often leave workers and their families high and dry, far from home, without funds to help them to a new start. They suffer lack of proper food and housing and become public charges, burdening relief funds and hospital facilities.[5]

Ever since the 1880's there have been attempts to correct these abuses by state legislation, but for many years such efforts were handicapped by the courts. In 1941 the United States Supreme Court reversed a previous decision and declared that the states had the right to exercise their police powers to regulate fee-charging employment agencies.[6] By 1943 all but eight states had

---

[5] U. S. Department of Labor, *Private Employment Agencies*, pp. 16–17.

[6] *Olsen* v. *Nebraska*, 313 U. S. 236 (1941), which overruled *Ribnik* v. *McBride*, 277 U. S. 350 (1928). This is one of many illustrations of the change in thinking on labor and social problems which took place in the Supreme Court during the late 1930's. In the 1928 decision the Court had ruled that a state law fixing the maximum compensation which a private employment agency might collect from an applicant was unconstitutional under the due process clause of the Fourteenth Amendment. In the 1941 decision the Court said: "The statutory provisions in question do not violate the due process clause of the Fourteenth Amendment. The drift away from *Ribnik* v. *McBride*, supra, has been so great that it can no longer be deemed a controlling authority."

private employment agency laws[7] on their statute books, but some are quite limited in their effectiveness. Agencies which operate across state lines can be adequately regulated only by federal legislation; this has not as yet been enacted, although bills have been introduced into Congress from time to time.

Public Employment Service

The shortcomings of private employment agencies, as well as the growing sense of public responsibility for unemployment, led to an active movement for the establishment of a nation-wide system of public employment offices. The movement, which started early in the century, has had a checkered career. During the periods of acute unemployment, or when labor was extremely scarce as during the two world wars, public employment offices have received a great deal of publicity and support; but when the emergency has disappeared, popular interest has tended to decline and the public employment system has shrunk to mediocre proportions. There is evidence, however, that the system of public employment services has now reached maturity and, having survived the vicissitudes of indifference and numerous unsuccessful experiments, has become a permanent institution, with increasing responsibilities for the recruitment and placement of workers.

The first public employment offices in this country were city-administered; as early as 1890 five cities in Ohio were operating public employment offices which were partially supported by the state. Within twenty years nine additional states (Illinois, Missouri, Connecticut, Wisconsin, Michigan, Massachusetts, Colorado, Oklahoma, and Indiana) established state systems and several others instituted a "mail-order" type of labor exchange within the office of the state bureaus of labor. "But while the theory of placement work as a State function was thus gaining ground

---

[7] Laws to protect workers from abuses of private employment agencies should be differentiated from the Emigrant Agent Acts, now on the statute books of at least ten southern states, which are designed to protect local employers against loss of their labor supply. These laws, most of which have been enacted since 1930, discourage migration of workers by requiring any person who recruits labor to pay annually to the state, *and to each county* from which labor is recruited, license fees ranging anywhere from $500 to $5000. The laws are very detailed and carry heavy penalties. For the texts of these laws, see U. S. Department of Labor, *Private Employment Agencies,* pp. 465 ff.

steadily, the system in practical operation could not be credited
with conspicuous success. Some individual offices were efficiently
operated and gained reputation and standing; in others the superintendent made no effort to do more than the minimum amount of
routine which a political sinecure involved. The whole system was
chaotic and planless, handicapped by political considerations,
public indifference, and more important, wholly inadequate salaries and appropriations."[8]

The federal government made its initial entry into employment
service activities in 1907 for the specific purpose of diverting im-
migrant labor from the port of entry into less congested areas
where employment opportunities were greater. The Bureau of Immigration at first confined its placement activities to encouraging
immigrants to go on farms; in 1915 the country-wide organization of immigration offices began to be used as general placement
centers. Two years earlier, the Bureau of Immigration had become
a unit of the newly created Department of Labor, one of whose
statutory duties was to advance the opportunities of workers for
profitable employment. Also that same year, various state and federal labor officials, and other interested persons in the United
States and Canada, formed an International Association of Public Employment Services[9] which spearheaded the movement for the
extension and improvement of public employment offices, and for
cooperation and closer connection between the offices within each
state and in the various states.

In response to war needs, the United States Employment Service was established in January, 1918, as a distinct unit in the
United States Department of Labor, with sufficient appropriations for a greatly expanded program. Within ten months over
800 offices were established throughout the country. This was a
mushroom growth, however. A year after the armistice, federal
appropriations were almost entirely discontinued, largely because
of pressure from private employment agencies and the National
Association of Manufacturers, which claimed that the service was
manned by union men or sympathizers and discriminated against
non-union labor, a charge the Secretary of Labor denied. Nevertheless, a system of cooperation with the state and city offices was

[8] *Monthly Labor Review,* January, 1931, p. 13.
[9] Originally called The American Association of Public Employment Offices.

maintained, the head of each state employment service acting as a federal director of the United States Employment Service as a dollar-a-year employee, with franking privileges and clerical services to facilitate the uniform collection of reports from the various local offices. Meanwhile, a number of states and cities had expanded their public employment services; in 1930 there were 148 offices in 23 states. In addition, the United States Employment Service maintained ten permanent field offices for recruiting and distributing harvest labor.

Throughout the decade 1920–1930 efforts were made to induce Congress to enact a law creating an adequate federal-state employment system, and a bill to that effect was introduced every year until 1931, when it passed Congress but was vetoed by the President.[10] One of the early actions of the New Deal administration was the passage of the Wagner-Peyser Act in June, 1933, establishing the present federal-state employment service.

The Wagner-Peyser Act charges the United States Employment Service with the duty of promoting and developing a national system of employment offices, of maintaining a veterans' bureau and a farm placement service, and of assisting "in coordinating the public employment offices throughout the country and in increasing their usefulness by developing and prescribing minimum standards of efficiency, assisting them in meeting problems peculiar to their localities, promoting uniformity in their administrative and statistical procedure, furnishing and publishing information as to opportunities for employment and other information of value in the operation of the system, and maintaining a system for clearing labor between the several States."

No employment service, however, efficiently administered, can

---

[10] Immediately after President Hoover's veto a federal system was established which in most areas duplicated existing state systems. This system survived little more than a year. Said a disinterested observer, after a thorough canvass of these offices, "No unbiased observer could fail to be dismayed by the lack of performance, the waste of public money, the inefficiency, even the bad faith, to be found in these offices at a time when there is special need for the kind of service the public was led to believe would be supplied. . . . On the whole it seems certain that politics and the spoils system have had much to do not only with the determination of cities in which offices were to be located but also in the selection and appointment of staff. . . ." (Ruth M. Kellogg, *The United States Employment Service*, University of Chicago Press, Chicago, 1933, pp. 96–103.

create jobs and thus eliminate unemployment. But a nation-wide, adequate employment service can contribute to employment stability and to the maintenance of a high level of employment. The United States Employment Service, as it is presently operating, seeks to achieve this by performing six major functions:

1. *Placement Service.* The fundamental task of a public employment system is to bring workers and jobs together, although the need for public employment exchanges varies between communities and employers. Such exchanges are especially useful to small employers with limited facilities for recruiting workers and evaluating their qualifications. They are likewise useful to large employers whose extensive labor demands require continuous access to the widest possible supply of labor, to employers engaged in seasonal or intermittent production who at the beginning of each work season are faced with the necessity of recruiting their entire work force, and to employers who need workers not available within normal or convenient recruiting distances of their establishments.

In small communities where there are few industries, and in large compact communities having a single industry or a small number of industrial plants engaged in similar types of production, only limited types of public employment service are needed. In a highly industrialized, heavily populated community, however, the labor market is usually so complex that an effective public employment exchange is essential, regardless of other organized methods for bringing jobs and workers together.

2. *Labor Market Analysis.* The United States Employment Service endeavors to collect and analyze for use in the local community all the labor market information, such as general employment trends and opportunities in various fields; shrinking and expanding industrial activities; the number and types of workers actually or potentially needed; the number and types of unemployed workers; community practices regarding the employment of women, youth, and veterans; local wage rates; opportunities for advancement in the principal industries; training needs for employment; and community facilities for accommodating or attracting additional workers. This information is useful to workers in providing them with a knowledge of where particular job opportunities exist, to those responsible for vocational guidance and

counseling, and to employers for timing their expansion and contraction so as best to utilize the labor resources available.

3. *Employment Counseling.* The Employment Service tries to provide in every community an employment counseling service for individual workers and potential workers and to assist in strengthening the counseling services of schools, places of business, and other private organizations. The objective is to assist the individual in making a practical and satisfactory occupational choice and in finding employment in his chosen field.

4. *Personnel Management Services to Employers.* The Service assists personnel and employment managers in private industry to evaluate the jobs in their plants and the skills and aptitudes of applicants, and to solve problems growing out of the working environment which cause labor turnover and instability.

5. *Services to Special Groups.* An important function of the public employment service, which it is peculiarly qualified to perform, is service to special groups such as veterans, handicapped workers, and young persons seeking their first jobs after leaving school. The Veterans Employment Service, a unit of the United States Employment Service, devotes its full attention to job counseling and the placement of veterans. By careful study of job requirements and of the qualifications of disabled veterans, as well as of those who have been injured in civilian employment, the Employment Service is able to place partially disabled people in jobs which they are able to perform despite their handicaps. Many of the local employment offices maintain junior placement programs under which specially trained counselors help young persons to understand their interests and abilities and guide them to occupations for which they are fitted, as well as interesting employers in utilizing young workers.

6. *Cooperation with Community and Other Government Agencies.* The Social Security Act and all state unemployment compensation laws require that persons claiming unemployment benefits must first register for work at a public employment office. The employment office, as indicated in Chapter 25, must not only apply the work test to benefit claimants, but also be familiar with the standards relating to suitable work and the procedures involved in taking claims. An aggressive placement activity by the Employment Office is very important in shortening the duration of

unemployment of individual workers and thereby reducing the social and monetary costs of joblessness. The Employment Service also assists federal, state, and municipal government agencies concerned with the development of public works; its labor market information indicates the location, volume, and characteristics of the surplus labor supply as well as prospective employment opportunities in all the important labor market areas. Government programs designed to alleviate unemployment or to avoid depressed labor market conditions are most effective when the location and timing of the proposed projects take into account available occupational skills and the extent to which private enterprise can utilize the available labor supply. When there is severe and continuing unemployment, the Employment Service assumes the responsibility of registering workers and certifying them for employment on public projects.

JOB TRAINING

The recruitment and selection of persons for particular jobs is only one phase of the employing process. Power machine industries as well as hand tool occupations require people with varied skills which need to be learned. Every year thousands of inexperienced young persons enter industry, and every year, too, thousands of older ones shift to new jobs which require skills different from those previously learned. Methods and adequacy of job training have an important bearing on workers' earnings, the rate of industrial progress, and the maintenance of stable employment.

Adequate job training promotes job efficiency and reduces labor turnover; it results in reduced fatigue through the elimination of unnecessary motions, in a reduction in spoilage and waste of materials and damage to machines and tools, as well as a reduction in accidents. To the individual worker, job training means a possibility of increased earnings and the personal satisfaction and self-confidence derived from the ability to do a job well; a knowledge of several jobs is a protection against unemployment. Industrial training can be provided within and by industry, or outside of industry through educational institutions, or by a combination of both.

Vocational Education

The American public-school system has played a vital role in the development of our industrial society, for modern industry is dependent upon an abundance of people with education sufficient to enable them to become highly skilled and semi-skilled workers. While public schools are primarily concerned with general education rather than specific occupational training, vocational education has spread rapidly during the past generation, especially since the passage of the Smith-Hughes Act of 1917, which provides federal financial aid to states for the maintenance of vocational schools.[11]

Vocational education, as construed by the Vocational Division of the United States Office of Education which administers the Smith-Hughes Act, means education given to boys and girls who, having selected a vocation, desire preparation for entering it as trained wage earners; to boys and girls and older wage earners who, having already taken up wage-earning employment, seek greater efficiency in it; and to wage earners who wish through increased efficiency and wage-earning capacity to advance to positions of responsibility.

Currently more than one-half million persons are enrolled in the trade and industrial education classes of vocational schools throughout the country.[12] To meet the varied needs of these persons several types of schools, classes, and programs offering instruction of less than college grade are provided. In general these are evening trade extension, part-time day, and all-day trade preparatory. The all-day schools provide instruction in manipulative skills and technical subjects to youth from 14 to 18 years of age who have left school but are too young to enter employment. Part-time classes are of several types. The part-time trade extension program is for young persons who have entered occupations as apprentices and who need to supplement their on-the-job train-

---

[11] The Smith-Hughes Act provided that federal money must be matched dollar for dollar by the states. Under the George-Deen Act of 1936 the states are required to match only 50 per cent of the federal funds allotted to them.

[12] Another million and a half persons are enrolled for other kinds of instruction such as vocational agriculture, business, trade, and home economics. (U. S. Office of Education, *Vocational Education in the Years Ahead,* Washington, 1945.)

ing with classroom instruction. The part-time trade preparatory program is for young persons who have left full-time school and entered employment, but who wish preparatory instruction in a different trade than that in which they are employed. For this type of youth there is also the general continuation school which provides instruction similar to that obtainable in the public schools. Evening industrial schools, also called trade extension schools, are for employed adult workers who wish instruction supplemental to their regular employment.

Learning on the Job

Vocational education at its best can never take the place of training on the job. Vocational schools enable young persons to discover and try out their aptitudes, to learn to use some of the basic tools of their chosen trade, and to acquire the fundamental disciplines of work—carefulness, precision, and thoroughness. Individuals with such general preparation, as well as the many more who never attend vocational schools, must learn the details of their particular jobs in the plant itself, and for this the employer assumes the responsibility.

Job training is essentially "learning by doing," and in most plants newly hired persons are taken to their machines or work benches immediately upon being hired. At their jobs they learn by observing others and from instructions given by their foremen. An increasing number of employers consider that this "pickup" method of job learning has certain deficiencies. The learning period is unduly prolonged, too many new workers become discouraged and quit or are discharged by impatient foremen, and wrong methods are acquired which are a permanent handicap to efficient production.

The alternative to "breaking in" on the job is short, intensive instruction by trained instructors away from the production line, the so-called vestibule training. Some of the advantages ascribed[13] to vestibule training are:

(1) It eliminates productive time lost by skilled workers and by foremen when employees are trained on the job. (2) A larger number of trainees can be efficiently handled. (3) The conditions

---

[13] American Management Association, *How to Train Workers for War Industries,* Harper & Brothers, New York, 1942, pp. 65–66.

created within the training room make for quicker and more complete training. (4) The disturbances created in the plant when employees are trained on the job are eliminated. (5) The method of instruction is standardized. The one best method of performing an operation is taught and perpetuated. (6) Trainees are permitted to form working habits during the period of training. (7) Trainees are familiarized with the daily routine of the plant and with company rules and regulations before being placed on production. (8) Trainees' nervousness is eliminated or minimized, and accidents thus prevented. (9) The cost of hiring misfits is decreased because deficiencies are discovered early. (10) Breakage and waste of material and damage to machinery are minimized through constant supervision.

Teaching methods in vestibule schools vary, depending upon particular job requirements as well as company policy. In some plants the training is very informal; it is conducted in a corner of the work room, with the trainees following the same routine as the other workers except that they receive close personal attention from their instructors. In other plants vestibule training is given in a separate room and instructions on the details of the jobs are supplemented by orientation lectures to inform new employees about the general affairs of the plant and industry, company policies, and so forth. Motion pictures are frequently used to illustrate right and wrong methods of job performance.

Apprenticeship Training

Apprenticeship is the training of beginners in the all-round skilled trades, that is, trades which take at least two years to learn. An apprentice is differentiated from a "learner," the latter applying to persons in repetitive occupations which require a relatively short time to learn. Apprenticeship is in its very essence a deliberate and organized system of training on the job—sometimes supplemented with classroom instruction—to which fixed rules are applied such as ratio of apprentices to journeymen, length of apprenticeship, and graduated wage rates during the period of apprenticeship.

Most of the skilled craft unions in the metal, printing, and building trades have assumed a major responsibility in the training of apprentices. There are several reasons why these unions have been willing to assume this responsibility instead of relying upon employers to train new workers. The unions' ability to guarantee employers a sufficient supply of competent, skilled workers has helped them in their collective bargaining; by establishing fixed training rules and procedures, the unions are able to maintain the skill and job standards which they consider of prime importance; moreover, formal apprenticeship provides a means of regulating the intake of workers into the trades.[14]

While apprentice training programs rely chiefly upon learning on the job, they frequently include supplementary classroom or other off-the-job instruction. In former years a number of the unions undertook classroom instruction for their apprentices, but this was seldom satisfactory because of lack of equipment and able instructors. With the development of vocational schools as part of the public-school system, the classroom and laboratory training of apprentices has been largely taken over by the vocational schools which work in close cooperation with the local unions and employers. The usual plan is for an indentured apprentice to spend at least one day a week at school; by the end of his apprenticeship he not only has learned a skilled trade on the job but has received sufficient vocational and general education to secure a high-school diploma. In many communities the principal of the vocational school is in effect the director of apprentice training, under the plans and procedures sponsored by joint committees of unions and employers concerned with the particular trades taught.

To stimulate and promote apprenticeship under acceptable standards and under the safeguards and protections of formal indenture agreements, the Federal Committee on Apprentice Training was established in the Department of Labor in 1934; it is composed of union, employer, and government representatives, with a full-time staff financed by federal funds. The Committee has formulated a definition of the term "apprentice" and has recom-

---

[14] During periods of expanding employment it has sometimes been charged that the scarcity of skilled workers was due to union restrictions and rules for admittance to journeyman status. An impartial study indicated, however, that the employers' reluctance to undertake the expense and responsibility of apprentice training has been the chief factor. Also actual shortages of skilled workers in any trade have always been confined to short-time employment periods in particular areas. (See *Monthly Labor Review,* June, 1928, pp. 21 ff.)

mended certain basic standards as essential to the all-round development of an apprentice. An apprentice is defined as "a person at least 16 years of age who is covered by a written agreement registered with a State apprenticeship council, providing for not less than 4000 hours of reasonably continuous employment, and for his participation in an approved schedule of work experience through employment, which should be supplemented by 144 hours per year of related classroom instruction." The agreement must also specify a progressively increasing scale of wages for the apprentice, averaging over the entire apprenticeship period approximately half the journeyman's rate.

The written agreement includes a statement of the trade or craft being learned, the length of the apprenticeship, and the length of the period of probation—usually from three to six months—during which the apprenticeship may be terminated by either employer or apprentice. It holds the employer, the foreman, the journeyman, and the apprentice to the purpose of apprenticeship. More than any other device, it is an aid to the completion of the training period within the length of time specified.

Owing to ever-changing processes and improvements in machinery and materials, completion of the best kind of apprentice training is no guarantee of continued competence, and those unions which have assumed the responsibility of providing skilled workmen for employers have had to face the problem of keeping the skills of their journeymen members up to date. Most commonly this has been accomplished by arrangements with individual employers whereby journeymen versed in old methods are given an opportunity to learn to operate the new machines after they are installed in the plant. In some instances, unions provide fellowships or otherwise assist their members to take classroom instruction to improve their job skills.[15]

---

[15] An example is the program recently undertaken by the Brotherhood of Electrical Workers for training members in the operation and maintenance of electronic equipment, by arrangement with the Engineering College of Marquette University in Milwaukee. The Brotherhood is financing six-weeks' resident courses for about 700 members who in turn will become instructors in night classes conducted by their locals for other members needing and desiring to learn the new technology. Tuition, averaging about $30,000 a year, is furnished by the International; the local unions pay the transportation and lodging expenses of the members they select to attend. (*Journal of Electrical Workers and Operators,* August, 1944.)

The printing unions provide the outstanding examples of continuing programs for advanced training and technical research, as well as courses for apprentices. Not only do colleges and vocational schools use the texts and materials prepared by the educational bureau of the International Typographical Union, but the bureau also conducts correspondence courses for its enrolled apprentices which number between two and three thousand a year. The Printing Pressmen's Union owns and operates what is probably the largest technical trade school for printing in the world. This school not only conducts correspondence courses for apprentices, but provides facilities for journeymen members who wish to qualify for better positions by learning the most modern letterpress and offset processes.

LABOR TURNOVER

Labor turnover is the change in personnel in the labor force of a plant or company. It is usually indicated in terms of the number of workers hired and separated in relation to the average number on the payroll. Labor turnover is most commonly considered as a problem of labor instability and therefore something to be minimized, although a certain amount of labor mobility is unavoidable and, under some circumstances, desirable for everyone concerned.

When considered in its broadest sense, labor turnover could be used as a title for a general treatise on labor economics, since the volume and causes of the movement of workers into and out of industrial establishments involve practically every problem relating to employment and labor conditions. For example, a major cause of labor turnover is irregularity of work resulting in involuntary layoffs, and many of the voluntary separations are the result of the workers' dissatisfaction with job conditions. These basic causes of labor turnover are discussed in detail in other chapters of this book; here we shall deal more with the volume, trend, and meaning of labor turnover.

Significance of Labor Turnover

Commented some early students of labor turnover:

Labor instability is regarded by all those who have given any serious consideration to the problem as one of the maladjustments of our industrial life, wasteful and destructive of the potential man power of the Nation and a serious obstacle to the complete utilization of the country's productive forces. In tackling this problem it should be recognized at the outset that within certain limits labor mobility is a normal and necessary thing. A certain amount of shifting from shop to shop and city to city is quite normal and even desirable; part of this necessary movement of labor is an entirely natural ebb and flow resulting from the normal expansion and contraction of industrial activity. Interest in the question of labor mobility is centered, therefore, not only upon its general extent but more specifically upon whatever part of it may be considered abnormal and unnecessary. When it is considered from this standpoint it is essential to know (1) the nature and extent of labor instability, (2) the various factors which are likely to increase or diminish its volume, and (3) whether any employment methods have been or can be devised which will make it possible to reduce labor instability to such an extent that maximum production may be attained at minimum cost and to the mutual advantage of employer and employee. . . .

In its relation to employer and employee this problem of labor instability becomes a more or less personal one and presents itself essentially in two aspects, depending upon whether it is the employee or employer who is concerned: (1) To the individual workman, job changing may mean either gain or loss. In prosperous times, when there are more numerous and attractive job opportunities, the change of jobs may represent an actual gain to the worker. . . . (2) The individual employer, however, is chiefly interested in the maintenance of a stable working force and regards excessively numerous terminations of employment, and especially voluntary or more or less avoidable separations, as a serious obstacle to efficient and continuous operation.[16]

Employers think of labor turnover strictly with reference to the shift and replacement of workers necessary for the maintenance of the labor force. Costs of labor turnover to the employer are both direct and indirect. There are the bookkeeping costs involved in taking persons on and off the pay roll, an item which has increased with the extra records and reporting entailed in the government social security programs. The greatest expense is that incurred in the interviewing, selection, and breaking in of new workers. For skilled jobs prolonged periods of training with spe-

---

[16] Paul F. Brissenden and Emil Frankel, "Mobility of Labor in American Industry," *Monthly Labor Review,* June, 1920, pp. 36–37.

cial instructors may be necessary, but even for unskilled work the costs of replacement are not insignificant.[17] During this period of training and breaking in, the new employee's output is naturally low, causing an increase in unit labor costs. In former years much of this cost was at the worker's expense, for it was common practice in many piece-work industries for learners to receive pay only for their actual output, and in time-work industries for learners to receive only a few cents per hour. Under existing state and federal minimum wage laws, more of this cost of learning is borne by the employer.

In addition to the direct costs of hiring and training are the hazards of greater spoilage of materials and wear and tear on machines, possible delays in deliveries, increase in accidents, and the expenses incident to under-utilization of plant equipment, tools, and machinery, and increased supervision. Industrial engineers have computed that the replacement of an unskilled worker costs the employer anywhere from $25 to $100 and of a skilled worker from $100 up to $1000 or more.

Trend in Turnover

Since the beginning of the scientific management movement, which aroused employers to a consciousness of the costs involved in the hiring and training of new workers, the causes and extent of labor turnover have been a major concern of management. This was especially true, for reasons discussed later, during the years before and following the First World War. Studies made before that war indicate that a machine shop in Pittsburgh hired 21,000 persons in a single year in order to maintain a force of 10,000;

[17] Professor Slichter, after a firsthand study of labor turnover in 1913–1916, commented: "It is not true that common laborers do not go through a breaking-in process. A common shoveler, a ditch digger, a trucker, accomplishes much less at the beginning than after several days on the job. Moreover, where the work has been studied, it is possible to increase greatly the output of this class of labor by definite training. There is also a great difference in men. A gang of carefully selected permanent yard laborers is much more valuable than a gang picked up on short notice from those readily available. The temporary character of work which makes impractical the maintenance of picked gangs of trained laborers is a real cost because it increases the expense of doing the work." (Sumner H. Slichter, *The Turnover of Factory Labor*, D. Appleton & Company, Inc., New York, 1919, p. 5.)

that the coal mining industry hired 2000 men a year for every 1000 permanent positions;[18] that twelve metal-working establishments during the year 1912 employed $6\frac{1}{3}$ times as many people as constituted the permanent increase in the force at the end of the year;[19] that the average annual rate of turnover in 90 New York garment shops was more than 230 per cent; and that the annual rate of terminations among 105 other industrial establishments was 100 per cent, varying from 348 per cent down to 8 per cent.[20]

Labor turnover mounted yet higher in the tight labor market of the First World War when there were no government controls on the movement of workers such as existed in World War II. In a study of 260 establishments it was found that, on the average, there were more than four labor changes for each full-year worker. This was as if during the year all the employees in these establishments had left their jobs, an entirely new set had come in to fill their places, and afterward all the employees in this second set had left their jobs and had in turn been fully replaced by a third set of workers.[21] The costs, in terms of dollars and loss in production resulting from such excessive wasteful turnover during critical war years, can only be left to the imagination. It is not surprising that, as described earlier in this chapter, the government took forceful measures when a similar situation threatened in the Second World War.

During the decade following the First World War, many employers took definite action to reduce their turnover. It was a major subject of discussion at most of the industrial managers' conferences held during the 1920's, and improved personnel practices, badges and bonuses as rewards for long service, and recreational and benefit programs were advocated and justified as measures for reducing the high cost of labor replacement. The money cost of a high labor turnover stood second only to the fear of unionization as a motive for installing welfare programs to win employee loyalty and continued service.

[18] John R. Commons, *Wage Earners of Pittsburgh,* Charities and Commons, The Charity Organization Society, New York, 1909, vol. xxi, p. 1054.
[19] Bureau of Labor Statistics, Bulletin No. 227, Government Printing Office, Washington, 1917, p. 16.
[20] Slichter, *The Turnover of Factory Labor,* pp. 19–21.
[21] Brissenden and Frankel, "Mobility of Labor in American Industry," p. 42.

Decline in Quit and Discharge Rates

The rate of labor turnover includes all separations of employment, regardless of cause. The number of layoffs during any year depends very largely upon economic conditions and the seasonal nature of the work, subjects which have been discussed in earlier chapters. Separation rates also include workers who voluntarily quit their jobs and those who are discharged for other causes than lack of work. Some so-called "voluntary" quits are for personal reasons—marriage, family responsibilities, health, and so on. Many are due to other reasons, and these, together with discharges, are primarily problems of labor relations. The proportion of workers who quit for personal reasons does not vary greatly from year to year,[22] so any considerable change in the rate of all voluntary quits and discharges can be assumed to be in response to changes in labor relations and working conditions.

Of major significance is the fact that during recent years there has been a marked decline in the rate of voluntary quits and discharges. Ignoring abnormal war and depression periods for comparison, available statistics indicate that before the First World War the voluntary separations constituted 75 per cent and discharges about 17 per cent of the total separations;[23] during the relatively normal period, 1928–1929, voluntary separations included almost 70 per cent and discharges about 12 per cent of the total separations. In contrast, during 1938–1939, only 20 per cent of the total separations were voluntary quits and less than 3 per cent were the result of discharges. (See Table 11.) From all present indications this decline represents a permanent trend.

What has brought about this drastic reduction in voluntary quit and discharge rates? The answer seems to be the recent extension in the unionization of workers. Through collective bargaining and by indirect influence, unions have succeeded in obtaining changes in working conditions and management practices which tend drastically to reduce both discharges and the individual quit-

[22] Unfortunately, there are no adequate statistics by specific cause of voluntary quits. Even if figures were available, they would not be conclusive. For example, a worker may cite health as his reason for quitting his job but accept another kind of job, or even the same type of work in another plant where he considers conditions more advantageous to his physical well-being. Such a quit might just as well be attributed to working conditions as to health.

[23] Brissenden and Frankel, "Mobility of Labor in American Industry," p. 41.

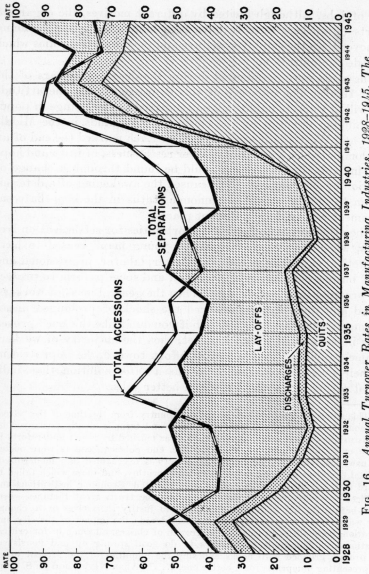

FIG. 16. Annual Turnover Rates in Manufacturing Industries, 1928–1945. The quit rate after 1940 includes departures for military service. (Source: U. S. Bureau of Labor Statistics.)

ting of jobs. Although incited by different motives, the organized efforts of workers seem to have been more effective in reducing turnover than the employer welfare and personnel programs which preceded unionization.

The seeds were germinated during the depression years of the early 1930's. The influence of this depression upon the attitude and will of workers might well be compared to the change in popular thinking wrought by the closing of free lands in the Middle West and West a half century earlier. Each marked the end of an era dominated by a spirit of pioneer restlessness, of faith and hope that individual advancement could be found through a change of location or environment. Both caused the awakening of a determination to obtain improved economic status in the immediate environment rather than in distant places.

When there were no further opportunities for settlement on free lands, when the slogan "Go West, young man" ceased to have a practical significance, then the farmer, laborer, professional and small businessman turned to political and social reform to protect and promote their well-being.[24] When the general mass of workers, skilled and unskilled, experienced the shock of prolonged unemployment, when "Get a better job if you don't like this one" proved to be illusory more often than not, then the majority of workers became convinced that a united effort toward the improvement of their present job conditions was a safer solution than individual roving in search of new and better jobs.

---

[24] This spirit of reform which swept the country from the time of the "Great Commoner" Bryan to President Wilson's second term is vividly portrayed by the historians Nevins and Commager: "It was marked by revolt and reform in almost every department of American life. Old political leaders were ousted and new ones enlisted; political machinery was overhauled and modernized; political practices were subjected to critical scrutiny, and those which failed to square with the ideals of democracy were rejected. Economic institutions and practices—private property, the corporation, the trust, great fortunes—were called before the bar of reason and asked to justify themselves or to change their ways. Social relationships were reconsidered—the impact of the city, immigration, inequalities in wealth, the growth of classes, all came in for critical attention. . . . Hundreds of societies to do good sprang up and flourished. The presses groaned with books exposing the iniquities of the present order and presenting blueprints for a better one. . . ." (Allan Nevins and H. S. Commager, America: The Story of a Free People, Little, Brown & Company, Boston, 1942, chap. 17.)

Influence of Unionization on Quit and Discharge Rates

Specifically, these efforts have been directed toward three major objectives: (1) contractual rights to jobs based on relative seniority; (2) machinery for redress of individual grievances and injustices; (3) improvements in general working conditions through collective pressure and influence. How labor unions seek to accomplish these objectives and their measure of success will be taken up later, but it is pertinent to the present discussion to indicate how these objectives have affected labor turnover.

The right to jobs is expressed in the seniority rules which are now prevalent in union-employer agreements. The aim of these rules is to afford the maximum job security and reward to those who have rendered the longest service to their employer. In respect to employment tenure, the rules specify that the oldest employees shall be the last to be laid off and the first to be reemployed. In respect to promotion opportunities, choice of work assignments, and other privileges, they specify that relative length of service shall be the sole or at least a major consideration in the selection of the employees to be benefited.

Strict seniority rules result in some disadvantages to both workers and management, as is discussed in Chapter 22. But the application of such formalized and objective rules eliminates the possibility and fear of favoritism and discrimination in the various phases of the employment relation, and thus tends to reduce discontent. An employee who is assured of his progress up the promotion ladder so long as he continues to give satisfactory service is not likely to turn elsewhere for a better job. Seniority rules have a two-way impact: A worker not only hesitates to lose his accumulated seniority by transferring elsewhere, but he finds it harder to secure employment in another plant because the present employees of that plant also have established seniority rights which tend to minimize the number of available openings.

Formerly the only recourse for a worker who had a real or fancied grievance against his employer or working conditions was to quit his job. Likewise, if his employer held a real or fancied grievance against him, he had no recourse against summary discharge. As indicated in a later chapter, practically all union-employer agreements now provide formal machinery, with final referral to outside arbitration if necessary, for the appeal of discharges and the adjustment of employee grievances. Redress of grievances *on* the job has greatly reduced the need and desire for *changing* jobs, and this has been a major factor in the recent reduction in the voluntary quit and discharge rates.

Improvements which have already been made in conditions of work, together with the employees' conviction that they should stick together and hold on to their jobs while pressing for further improvements, have materially contributed to a lessening in turnover. (The latter, of course, tends to substitute strike action for individual quits, but usually involves no permanent separations from jobs.) One of the important changes in working conditions which has had an influence on turnover has been the shortening in hours of work. The accumulated fatigue and boredom of the 9- or 10-hour day and the 6- or even 7-day week which were prevalent throughout industry in years past, caused many workers to quit their jobs at frequent intervals in order to get a few weeks' rest and a change of environment in a new job. Improved safety and health conditions have also had their influence, both physical and psychological, for labor turnover tends to be greatest on unattractive, dangerous, and onerous jobs.

Labor Turnover Statistics

The term "labor turnover" is generally used to refer to the whole phenomenon of the movement of labor into and out of industrial establishments, although sometimes it is used in a more restricted sense to indicate the rate of necessary replacement, that is, the number of positions vacated and filled per 100 employees. According to this restricted meaning, if a plant is reducing its force, the net turnover would be equivalent to the rate of hirings or accessions; if the plant is increasing its force, the net turnover rate would be the same as the separation rate because all these vacancies have to be filled. Such a concept of turnover is based on the principle that only the costs to the employer involved in immediate replacements are pertinent; it ignores the incidence of turnover upon workers and the public, as well as the future costs to the employer of having to fill vacancies when production picks up.

The monthly reports currently issued by the Bureau of Labor

Statistics[25] present labor turnover rates under two major classifications, *separations* and *accessions*. Under *separations* there are four classifications: voluntary quits, involuntary layoffs, discharges, and miscellaneous. As used by the Bureau, a *separation* is the termination of employment of any of the following types: A

TABLE 11. Annual Turnover Rates in Manufacturing Industries, 1928–1945[26]

Year	Total Separation	Voluntary Quit	Layoff	Discharge	Military and Miscellaneous[a]	Accession Rate
1928	37.1	25.8	6.5	4.8		44.5
1929	45.2	32.6	7.2	5.4		52.3
1930	59.7	18.7	35.9	5.1		37.1
1931	48.4	11.4	34.3	2.7		36.6
1932	52.0	8.3	41.7	2.0		39.8
1933	45.4	10.7	32.2	2.5		65.2
1934	49.2	10.7	36.3	2.2		56.9
1935	42.7	10.4	30.0	2.3		50.0
1936	40.3	13.0	24.7	2.6		52.2
1937	53.1	15.0	35.8	2.4		42.6
1938	49.2	7.5	40.5	1.3		46.2
1939	37.7	9.5	26.7	1.5		48.9
1940	40.3	10.9	25.9	1.8	1.6	52.7
1941	46.7	23.6	15.9	3.0	4.2	64.5
1942	77.9	45.2	13.0	4.7	15.0	91.7
1943	87.2	62.3	7.0	7.1	10.8	89.6
1944	81.8	61.0	7.2	7.7	5.9	73.2
1945	99.7	61.0	27.7	7.3	3.7	75.8

[a] Prior to 1940 included under Quits.

quit is a termination initiated by the employee, regardless of his reason which may be dissatisfaction with hours, wages, working conditions, the obtaining of a better job, or any other reason.

[25] As indicated earlier, the first of a number of special studies on labor turnover was made as early as 1906. In response to the growing interest in turnover, the Metropolitan Life Insurance Company in 1926 began issuing regular reports on a national basis. In 1929 the Bureau of Labor Statistics took over the task of collecting monthly turnover data, gradually enlarging the number of reporting concerns and industry coverage. At present, the Bureau's turnover reports are based on information received from approximately 8000 establishments employing about 4 million workers.

[26] From Bureau of Labor Statistics reports in *Monthly Labor Review*, various issues.

A *discharge* is a termination initiated by the employer, with prejudice to the worker, for such reasons as incompetence, violation of rules, etc. A *layoff* is a termination initiated by the employer, but without prejudice to the worker. A short furlough during which the name of the worker is retained on the pay roll is not regarded as a layoff, nor are suspensions of operations during inventory and vacation periods. All other separations, whether caused by lack of orders or materials, breakdown of machinery, release of temporary help, introduction of labor-saving machinery, etc., are considered layoffs. (It is noted that this definition of layoff may lead to some distortion in the general layoff rate because, under certain conditions, some companies may furlough an employee but keep him on the pay roll while other companies under the same conditions may remove him from the pay roll.) The *miscellaneous* group of separations includes those due to death, permanent disability, retirements on pensions, and separations for military service.

The turnover rates reported by the Bureau are computed by dividing the number of separations (and accessions) by the number working during the period covered, and multiplying by 100 to get the rate per 100 employees. In compiling the over-all rates or the rates for a particular industry, the actual numbers for the several establishments are added and the general rates computed from the grand total. Thus, each establishment has an influence or "weight" in the general rate in proportion to its size. The Bureau of Labor Statistics' data do not reveal some of the significant aspects of turnover such as comparative quit rates by size of plant, types of jobs, and different groups of workers involved, and the proportion of the accession rate represented by new hirings compared to the rehiring of former employees. There is no information available showing the relative turnover rates of large versus small plants; the proportion of the turnover among new employees, for instance, those of less than a year's service; young persons compared to mature workers, skilled workers to unskilled. For a comprehensive picture of the stability of a labor force, one should know what workers have *not* changed as well as the number of changes which have taken place. A turnover rate of 100 per cent may indicate a complete turnover of the entire force or a change of one-tenth of the force ten times during the year. This, of course, is important in a consideration of the costs involved or of the means of reducing turnover.

SELECTED REFERENCES

Employment Services

Commons, John R., and Andrews, John B., *Principles of Labor Legislation,* Harper & Brothers, New York, 1936.

Harrison, Shelby, and associates, *Public Employment Offices,* Russell Sage Foundation, New York, 1924.

Lescohier, D. D., *History of Labor,* The Macmillan Company, New York, 1935, vol. iii, chaps. 10, 14.

National Industrial Conference Board, Inc., *Employment Procedures and Personnel Records,* Bulletin No. 38, New York, 1942.

Princeton University Industrial Relations Section, *The Employment Division,* Bulletin II, and *Selection Procedures,* Bulletin X, Princeton, 1941.

Stead, William H., and associates, *Occupational Counseling Techniques,* American Book Company, New York, 1940.

Stewart, Bryce M., *Planning and Administration of Unemployment Compensation in United States,* Industrial Relations Counselors, New York, 1938.

United States Department of Labor, Division of Labor Standards, *Private Employment Agencies,* Bulletin No. 57, Washington, 1943.

Training

American Management Association, *How to Train Workers for War Industries,* Harper & Brothers, New York, 1942.

Cooper, Alfred M., *Employee Training,* McGraw-Hill Book Company, Inc., New York, 1942.

Patterson, William F., and Hedges, M. H., *Educating for Industry,* Prentice-Hall, Inc., New York, 1946.

Peffer, Nathaniel, *Educational Experiments in Industry,* The Macmillan Company, New York, 1932.

Reitell, Charles, *Training Workers and Supervisors,* The Ronald Press, New York, 1941.

Schaefer, Vernon G., *Job Instruction,* McGraw-Hill Book Company, Inc., New York, 1943.

Scrimshaw, Stewart, *Apprenticeship: Principles, Relationships, Procedures,* McGraw-Hill Book Company, Inc., New York, 1932.

Struck, F. T., *Vocational Education for a Changing World,* John Wiley & Sons, Inc., New York, 1945.

United States Office of Education, *Vocational Education in the Years Ahead,* Washington, 1945.

TURNOVER

Brissenden, P. F., and Frankel, Emil, *Labor Turnover in Industry: A Statistical Analysis,* The Macmillan Company, New York, 1922.

Federated American Engineering Societies, *Waste in Industry,* McGraw-Hill Book Company, Inc., New York, 1921.

Myers, C. A., and Maclaurin, W. R., *The Movement of Factory Workers,* John Wiley & Sons, Inc., New York, 1943.

Slichter, Sumner H., *Turnover of Factory Labor,* D. Appleton & Company, Inc., New York, 1919.

PART TWO

WAGES AND HOURS

9

THEORY OF WAGES

IT IS FREQUENTLY SAID THAT WE LIVE IN A WAGE ECONOMY, WHICH means that a majority of the people at the present time live under a system whereby fixed amounts of money are paid and received for work performed. In the past, and to some extent today, the means for living and for procuring the services of others was not primarily through a system of wage payment. People *can* live and work *can* be performed without the process of a money transaction. Each individual (or family or clan) may procure all his food, clothing, and shelter from natural resources directly at hand; or he may produce a surplus of certain goods and barter or trade these for items he does not or is not able to produce for himself. Under a slave or serf system, a minimum subsistence in kind is provided the slaves and serfs by the masters or lords who enjoy the fruits of their labor. In a simple handicraft system, the independent artisan or craftsman markets the products which he himself has made with his own tools.

Under none of these modes of living are wages, as we conceive them, paid or received for work performed or commodities produced. What are the distinctive features of a wage economy and how did our present wage system come about?

PRECURSORS OF THE WAGE SYSTEM

Obviously, it is only under the most primitive pastoral or agricultural conditions that an individual or family can be entirely self-contained, and under such conditions the kind and amount of food, clothing, and shelter depend almost entirely upon the immediate natural environment. There is no division of labor except as among members within the family, no tools except those the individual himself is able to devise and make, no specialization in the use of land and other resources beyond the narrow confines in each family's possession.

A limited degree of specialization, and hence a broadening of the kinds of goods made available to each person, is afforded when there is bartering of commodities between individual producers. The variety of goods which can be exchanged, however, is almost entirely limited to the things which can be produced within a single market area, for with no medium of exchange (money) any interexchange of goods among several markets is all but impossible. There are also other limitations, aside from the factor of market area; the two parties must each have goods which the other wants and in amounts which the traders consider of equivalent value.

Under the self-contained family or household economy and simple barter system there is no wage problem, for no one works for another or hires another to work for him. Each family or local community lives on what it itself produces and its economic well-being is dependent entirely upon what use it makes of the bounties and scarcities of its immediate natural environment. While remnants of these primitive forms of living remain in the world today and tend to revive during periods of social breakdown, such as extreme inflation occasioned by wars, from the earliest recorded times there has existed some form of economic interdependence between communities, and some specialization of tasks among individuals.

Slavery

One of the earliest divisions of activities was between the warriors who fought for the land and those who tilled the land. This division of "labor" projected itself throughout the entire social, legal, and economic pattern of living until the beginning of the commercial and industrial age, for the warriors not only assumed ownership of the land but also became the masters and owners of those who worked the land.

Slavery as a system of labor has existed to a greater or lesser extent throughout the period of recorded history. Most of the slaves were captives of war and their descendants; some were persons who were kidnaped by piracy; others were in bondage because

of unpaid debts and criminal offenses.[1] While slaves in medieval
Europe and the United States were used mostly, although not
entirely, for agricultural labor, in ancient Greece and Rome they
were used in the skilled trades and even the professions; many
Roman lords were taught to read and write by their Greek slaves.

The slave was a form of capital for his owner, who used him
directly or lent him for a price to a third person. The owner fed
the slave as much as he considered necessary to keep him working
efficiently. When the supply of new slaves was plentiful and cheap
the master could afford to feed his slaves little and work them
quickly to exhaustion; when conquests slowed down and slaves became scarce, they were better cared for—perhaps even to the point
where they were able to rear families and provide their masters
with additional slaves.

All the time of the slave was at his owner's disposal. The
master's income was dependent upon the number of slaves he
owned and the extent to which the sale of the goods they produced,
or the fee obtained when they were hired out to others, exceeded
the outlay for their subsistence. The slave himself was a person
with no legal or social rights;[2] his very existence and subsistence
depended upon whether his owner considered him sufficiently valuable to keep alive; the amenities and comforts of life could not be

---

[1] Most of the Greek and Roman slaves were captives of war. There was considerable acquisition of slaves by conquest during the Crusades. The Celts and
other natives of Britain were enslaved by the Anglo-Saxon invaders. Capture
of slaves by piracy reached its peak in the Barbary States in the 17th century,
when many Europeans were sold into Mohammedan captivity. The enslavement
of African Negroes in this country is well known; not so well remembered is
the prevalence of white servitude during our colonial and early national history. This involved the indentured servants who came or were brought to the
New World under contract for a stipulated period of time, commonly seven
years, in return for their keep and in payment of their transportation. During
the 17th century shipowners openly kidnaped English children and adults; it is
claimed that in 1627 over 1400 children, mostly from almshouses, were brought
into Virginia alone; between 1717 and 1775 at least 50,000 political and criminal
prisoners were sent from British jails. Unlike other forms of slavery, however,
these indentured servants were freed after their stipulated period of service,
and to help them get established their masters gave them "freedom dues" of a
few dollars, plus a suit of clothes and a few tools.

[2] As in any human relationship, however, certain customs and usages developed, especially in ancient Greece and Rome, which mitigated somewhat the
harshness of legalistic mandates.

secured as a reward for labor but were contingent entirely upon the disposition of his master.

Serfdom

Serfdom, a milder form of slavery, was an integral part of the manorial or feudal system which prevailed in western Europe during the Middle Ages and in parts of eastern Europe late into the 19th century.[3] The manorial system served a twofold purpose: It provided a military organization for defense and conquest and it also provided a means for the cultivation of the soil. Each manor or estate, which averaged perhaps 5000 acres, was largely a self-sustaining economic unit except for trinkets, salt, and spices bartered at the annual fairs. Most of the work of tilling the soil was performed by serfs who were not personal or chattel property like slaves, but were legally attached to the estates on which they were born. A serf could be transferred along with the property to other owners, but he could not leave the place in which he was born, or change his accustomed work, without the consent of the lord of the manor. Although he did not own the allotment of land which he cultivated, he was entitled to it by usage and could appeal to the manorial court for redress if necessary.

The ordinary allotment to a serf was about 30 acres, usually assigned in half-acre or acre strips from different parts of the estate in order that each should receive a share of both good and poor land. Allotments were paid for by labor, the amount being fixed by immemorial custom. For two or three days a week throughout the year each serf worked on the portion of the land which the lord retained for himself; in addition there was "boon day" work—one or two weeks of continuous work during the plowing and harvesting seasons—as well as the special presents and services required at stated seasons and occasions.

The serf, generation after generation, was doomed to a life of subservience and to hard and monotonous work. With no exchange of goods and no stimulus to competition, he produced and consumed the same products year after year, used the same tools and the same methods which his father and his father's father had used. In recompense, the serf had security; no employer could discharge

---

[3] The German states abolished serfdom in 1806–1812; the Russian decree for the emancipation of the serfs was passed in 1861.

him or landlord evict him. Although half his time was spent working for his lord, what he produced on his own allotment was his own and there was no intermediary between the products of his labor and the commodities he consumed.

The manorial serf system had its roots in an agricultural economy at a time when transportation facilities were poor and travel was dangerous, when there was a scarcity of money and other forms of wealth that could be saved or easily transported, and when there was no strong central government to afford military protection from invaders. In theory, the lord of the manor furnished the military protection in return for the labor of his serfs.

Transition to the Wage System

Contemporaneous with the serfs in the country were the artisans or craftsmen in the towns which grew up during the latter part of the Middle Ages.[4] These urban centers facilitated trade and thus encouraged specialization in the use of skills and work time. Although manufacturing was in the handicraft state, being performed with simple hand tools, each worker or family could specialize in one product because the towns afforded opportunities for trade and the exchange of surpluses. With the wider use of money as a medium of exchange,[5] it was not necessary to barter surpluses; each artisan could sell his product at a fixed price. The artisan's income represented the difference between what he paid for materials and the price he obtained for the products he sold. The work done by these craftsmen was not paid for in wages, for they worked in their own shops with their own tools. The apprentices who assisted them in return for instruction in the "mysteries" of the trade were provided their keep in their masters' homes, and when their apprenticeship periods were completed their masters helped them set up their own shops and frequently provided them with kits of tools.

The artisan-apprenticeship system of production and market-

---

[4] Many of these towns originally were parts of the manors upon which they were located, but later won or purchased their freedom. Some gained their freedom through alliance with rising kings who were seeking dominance over other lords.

[5] Money came into general use as gold and silver mines were discovered, and as centralized governments were established which could determine monetary units of value and regulate the coinage of money.

ing continued as long as simple tools were used and market areas were limited to the surrounding countryside and neighboring towns. As tools were improved and became more costly, when markets expanded and required more money and time for the buying of raw materials and the selling of finished products,[6] another type of specialization became necessary which added to the complexity of economic transactions and greatly extended the wage system.

The artisan represented a division of labor by the type of goods produced (shoemaker, weaver, etc.), but he performed all the functions involved in making the particular product and getting it into the hands of the consumers. There was no intermediary between production and the sale of his product, and the selling price did not have to include the cost and upkeep of expensive machinery. When improvements in methods required capital investment in machinery and larger shops, separated from the home, to work in, the artisans who had the money became master craftsmen who employed journeymen for fixed wages. As markets expanded, the master craftsmen began to depend upon traveling traders to furnish them with their raw materials and to market their finished products. In time, some of these traders expanded their functions and became managers of production enterprises as well as merchants of materials and finished products. Some established shops where a number of workmen were employed under a single roof. More frequently, before the advent of power machinery, the merchant-employer distributed his raw materials to numbers of masters who produced the finished products on a contract basis. The masters, in turn, employed others to help them, either in their own homes or in the master's home or nearby small shop.

Under this so-called "cottage" system of production, there was one middleman, and frequently two, between those who actually made the product and the purchasers of the product—between the "price" paid for the labor and the price paid by the consumer. The master was no longer an independent artisan making and selling the goods he produced, but a journeyman or journeyman-foreman working for a merchant capitalist. He was, however, in a somewhat different position from the modern wage earner. Since the work was performed in his own home or work place he was not

---

[6] The discovery and settlement of America provided a powerful impetus to the development of new markets and the extension of trade routes.

subject to fixed hours or work rules, other than those affecting quality of performance, and he was paid on a contract basis which allowed him a "margin" which he could appropriate if he was able to get the work done at less than the contract price. However, those whom he employed, whether on a piece or a time basis, were wage earners, even though they did their work in their own homes and used their own hand tools.

Effect of the Industrial Revolution

Although the wage system preceded the Industrial Revolution, it was the introduction of power machinery and the factory system of production which created a large class of workers who were entirely dependent upon wages for their living. When work was done with tools in the home or in a master's nearby shop, money wages could be supplemented with food from the workers' gardens or small farms. Independent hand craftsmen, no longer able to compete with cheap machine-made products, were forced to join the ranks of the wage earners. These ranks were further augmented by hordes of children as soon as employers found that they could be used on machines which required no skills.

The basic and fundamental economic change was the shift in the importance of labor relative to capital investment in the manufacturing process, and the complete separation of the worker from the ownership of the instruments of production and the disposal of the product. This brought forth the unresolved question between workers and the owners of capital as to the amount each contributes to the joint product, and how each shall share in the proceeds.

MEANING OF WAGE THEORY

"Theory" is defined by Webster as being "a general principle, formula, or ideal construction, offered to explain phenomena and rendered more or less plausible by evidence in the facts or by the exactness and relevancy of the reasoning." Early economists were inclined to consider their ideas and beliefs as ultimate truths, and to label their explanations as "natural" or "iron" laws. By "natural" they implied something God-given, something morally right and not to be tampered with by man except at the risk of great peril and final devastation. They did not think of "natural" economic laws in the way we consider physical phenomena, that is, as something existing but not necessarily to be left in their natural state of operation. For example, the natural law of gravity is accepted as a working basis for engineering developments; although water naturally flows downward we do not hesitate to pump it upward.

Present-day economists who have seen many of the presumed "natural" laws of economics refuted or drastically modified by further evidence and developments are inclined to speak in terms of *theories*, and to recognize the possibility that a theory which may seem valid at one stage of economic development may be inapplicable under a different set of circumstances. Theories, therefore, must be treated as tentative assumptions in the quest for truth. Their usefulness and validity rest upon whether or not they have taken into account *all* the existing realities and factors, and given each one its proper weight.

Inherent Weaknesses of Economic Theories

Economic truths are difficult to discover because of the inherent problem of having to segregate and properly evaluate the primary long-time factors from what appears to be true during the period studied, the "period" being an entire economic or industrial era which may extend over several generations. Economic theory, in other words, must recognize and dissociate the basic phenomena from the institutional setting in which they happen to be operating, and account for the interaction of both. The test of any theory is whether or not it has accurately balanced the variable factors against those which are constant. If a theory is postulated on an assumption that some factor is fixed or constant, when in fact it is transient and a result of temporary influences, obviously the theory lacks validity and is merely a description of transitory conditions.

The difficulty in economics, as well as in other social sciences, is to segregate the variable from the constant. The social sciences deal with the attitudes and behavior of people who are influenced not only by their own physical, psychological, and environmental situations, but by the customs and beliefs of preceding generations. A factor or condition may be assumed to be constant because it has existed throughout an historical period; but a revolutionary change in the economic environment, whether gradual or sudden, violent or peaceful, may prove that what was considered fundamental and everlasting was a condition peculiar to a given set of circumstances. What are proclaimed as immutable principles may be only partial truths at best, and applicable only to particular periods of human history.

In spite of their pitfalls, theories have their place in an attempt to understand economic phenomena and business behavior. Although no one theory provides a complete explanation, a chain of successive theories carefully worked out over a long period of time, each an outgrowth and further development of the preceding, is likely to contain elements of lasting truth.

Wage Theories and General Theories of Distribution

Theories of wages, with which we are here concerned, deal with the payment of labor employed in competitive enterprises. Wage theories in a non-competitive economy, such as state capitalism or communal socialism, would of course be based upon entirely different concepts. In a "free" capitalistic economy, wages represent the payment of one of the factors involved in production. Since the problem turns on the question of the sharing or distribution of the total income derived from productive enterprises, theories of wages cannot be dissociated from the other factors of production.

As indicated previously, it is the *indirectness* of modern business activity that gives rise to the perplexing problems concerning the sharing of the goods produced or, practically speaking, their money equivalent. Direct labor, land sites and use of the soil, machinery and equipment, managerial planning and direction—all contribute to the joint output and there is no way concretely to separate the contribution of each. Moreover, the capital investments—the buildings, machinery, and equipment—were themselves made with labor, and in this roundaboutness there is no way statistically to distinguish the product of labor from that of the other factors in the productive process.

Wage theories, therefore, are inextricably interwoven in general theories of distribution since they deal with the problem of how the total income from a business enterprise is distributed or apportioned among all the so-called agents or factors which contribute toward producing that income. Theories of wages must necessarily deal with the interrelationships of the prices paid for or the value placed upon land (rent), capital (interest), and capital risk (profits), as well as the wages of labor.

Wages, as discussed in this chapter, have to do with the "general" wage rates for all workers as a group rather than specific rates for particular occupations or individuals; the latter are discussed in later chapters: The theories pertaining to wages concern the price or value of labor en masse, and the general wage levels of workers as homogeneous groups.

CLASSICAL WAGE THEORIES

As England and western Europe emerged from rural serfdom and the urban gild system, many theories were developed to explain why owners of land and business enterprises received the income they did, and why laborers on the farm and in the shops received the amount of wages which were paid to them. The most obvious fact during the early phases of the Industrial Revolution was the prevailing poverty of the workers. As means were developed to increase the wealth of nations, the lot of the mass of laborers was not improved; in many respects it grew worse because, in addition to low wages, they suffered insecurity of employment. Not unlike some of the theories of a later day, the wage theories of the 18th and 19th centuries sought not only to explain, but to justify, the existing low level of wages. Instead of being offered as explanations of conditions existing at a particular time, these theories were esteemed to be based upon an irrevocable "iron law" of wages.

Subsistence Theory

The early 19th-century theories of wages, now referred to as the "classical" theories, were based upon the fundamental premise that labor is a commodity whose price is controlled by the same market conditions as other commodities. According to the classical "iron law" of wages, the price of labor is determined by the mechanical forces of supply and demand, and like the price of any other commodity its value is ultimately based on its cost of production. "The natural price of labour is that price which is necessary to enable the labourers to subsist and to perpetuate their race without either increase or diminution," said David Ricardo. Wages, in other words, are the exact equivalent of the cost of subsistence; they are forever constant and will never rise or fall except for short periods as a result of unusual circumstances.

Ricardo and the later classical economists were influenced by Malthus' theory of population, discussed in Chapter 1, which was based on a belief in the niggardliness of nature and the "law of diminishing fertility of the soil." According to Malthus, the production of food cannot keep pace with the *potential* rate of increase of the population, and the size of the population at any given time therefore tends to equal the number which are just able to subsist. Converted to the realm of wages, this theory of population holds that wages cannot fall below subsistence else the supply of labor will be reduced, causing competitive bidding among the employers which will raise wages. A rise in wages above the cost of subsistence, on the other hand, will encourage population growth to the point where there will be an excess of workers, which, in turn, will lead to a decline in wages.

Labor, according to such a theory of population, has its natural and its market price. The natural price is the equivalent of the cost of subsistence and perpetuation of the race; the market price is the amount that results from the operation of the law of supply and demand. The latter, however, is secondary and always tends to conform to the first. As stated in Ricardo's own words:

The market price of labour is the price which is really paid for it, from the natural operation of the proportion of the supply to the demand; labour is dear when it is scarce, and cheap when it is plentiful. However much the market price of labour may deviate from its natural price, it has, like commodities, a tendency to conform to it. . . .

It is when the market price of labour exceeds its natural price, that the condition of the labourer is flourishing and happy, that he has it in his power to command a greater proportion of the necessaries and enjoyments of life, and therefore to rear a healthy and numerous family. When, however, by the encouragement which high wages give to the increase of population, the number of labourers is increased, wages again fall to their natural price, and indeed from a reaction sometimes fall below it.

When the market price of labour is below its natural price, the condition of the labourers is most wretched: Then poverty deprives them of those comforts which custom renders absolute necessaries. It is only after their privations have reduced their number, or the demand for labour has increased, that the market price of labour will rise to its natural price, and that the labourer will have the moderate comforts which the natural rate of wages will afford.[7]

The subsistence theory provided one loophole for improvement in wages, namely, that habit and custom were factors in the subsistence level and that natural wages could therefore include a modicum of comforts as well as the bare essentials for survival. If during a temporary period of relative prosperity workers grow accustomed to certain small comforts, these become conventional necessities and the workers thereafter delay marriage rather than sacrifice their newly acquired standard of living. Thus the population may be checked somewhat above the point where labor must subsist at the lowest possible level of poverty and distress. The early classical economists, however, were not optimistic about the possibility of any long-time improvement in the wages and living conditions of workers, although they observed that English laborers, in contrast to the Irish, would not accept wages which would give them no other food than potatoes and no better habitation than a mud cabin!

Wages Fund Theory

The notion that wages were not rigidly and always fixed at bare subsistence levels opened the way for the later classical economists to emphasize rather than minimize the influence of supply and demand and to develop further the concept of demand. The demand for labor, said John Stuart Mill and his followers, is determined by the amount of capital or other funds devoted to the purchase of labor. At any given time employers have available a certain amount of capital which is the accumulation of profits and savings from previous years' operations. Employers first use this capital to purchase raw materials and equipment, and what is left becomes a wages fund which represents the demand for labor. To quote Mill:

Wages, then, depend mainly upon the demand and supply of labour; or as it is often expressed, on the proportion between population and

---

[7] David Ricardo, *Principles of Political Economy and Taxation,* 1821, in J. R. McCulloch (ed.), *The Works of David Ricardo,* John Murray, London, 1876, pp. 50–51.

capital. By population is here meant the number only of the labouring class, or rather of those who work for hire; and by capital, only circulating capital, and not even the whole of that, but the part which is expended in the direct purchase of labour. . . . Wages not only depend upon the relative amount of capital and population, but cannot, under the rule of competition, be affected by anything else. Wages (meaning, of course, the general rate) cannot rise, but by an increase of the aggregate funds employed in hiring labourers, or a diminution in the number of the competitors for hire; nor fall, except either by a diminution of the funds devoted to paying labour, or by an increase in the number of labourers to be paid.[8]

The wages fund theory, like the subsistence theory, was based on the Malthusian theory of population and the law of diminishing returns. While the wages fund determines the market rate of wages at any particular time, wages in the long run are always determined by the ratio of population to the supply of food, and the only way to improve wages is to check population growth. If one group of workers, through legislation or trade union pressure, secures an advance in their wages, they absorb an unduly large part of the wages fund, and this leaves less for other workers. Likewise, if employers are taxed to provide for the poor, this reduces the amount of capital available for wages, and the level of wages is consequently lowered. Wages can be increased only at the expense of profits, but a reduction in profits causes a decline in savings and hence in the capital from which the wages fund is derived. Said Malthus: "It may naturally appear hard to the labouring class that, of the vast mass of productions obtained from the land, the capital, and the labour of the country, so small a quantity should fall to the share of each individual. But the quantity is at present determined, and must always in future be determined, by the inevitable law of supply and demand."[9]

Discussing the feasibility of statutory minimum wages, J. S. Mill came to some doleful conclusions:

Such an obligation acknowledged and acted upon, would suspend all checks, both positive and preventive; there would be nothing to hinder population from starting forward at its rapidest rate; and as the nat-

---

[8] J. S. Mill, *Principles of Political Economy,* D. Appleton & Company, New York, 1883, vol. i, pp. 420–421.

[9] Thomas R. Malthus, *Principles of Political Economy,* William Pickering, London, 1836, 2nd ed., p. 279.

ural increase of capital would, at the best, not be more rapid than before, taxation, to make up the growing deficiency, must advance with the same gigantic strides. . . . Let them work ever so efficiently, the increasing population could not, as we have so often shown, increase the produce proportionately: The surplus, after all were fed, would bear a less and less proportion to the whole produce and to the population; and the increase of people going on in a constant ratio, while the increase of produce went on in a diminishing ratio, the surplus would in time be wholly absorbed; taxation for the support of the poor would engross the whole income of the country; the payers and the receivers would be melted down into one mass. The check to population either by death or prudence could not then be staved off any longer, but must come into operation suddenly and at once; everything which places mankind above a nest of ants or a colony of beavers, having perished in the interval.[10]

As late as 1874 a well-known Irish economist, J. E. Cairnes, in criticizing a contemporary who took exception to Malthus by maintaining that "subsistence tended to increase faster than population," expressed his views regarding the prospects of workers as follows: "The margin for the possible improvement of their lot is confined within narrow barriers which cannot be passed, and the problem of their elevation is hopeless. As a body they will not rise at all. A few, more energetic or more fortunate than the rest, will from time to time escape, as they do now, from the ranks of their fellows to the higher walks of industrial life, but the great majority will remain substantially where they are. The remuneration of labour as such, skilled or unskilled, can never rise above its present level."[11]

Is it any wonder that 19th-century economics was called "the dismal science"?

Surplus Value Theory

Parallel in time, but deviating in ideology from the orthodox classical economists, was Karl Marx the socialist. Marx accepted

---

[10] Mill, *Principles of Political Economy,* pp. 445–446. In spite of his firm belief in the orthodox theories of wages, Mill was a reformist who believed that the salutary influence of education would result in controls in population growth and improvements in the existing economic system.

[11] J. E. Cairnes, *Political Economy,* Harper & Brothers, New York, 1875, Lecture VII.

the basic premises of the theories which held that market wages tend to equal the cost of physical subsistence, although he stressed the influence which habit and custom had in the establishment of subsistence levels of living. He maintained that "the value of labour . . . is formed by two elements—the one merely physical, the other historical or social. Its *ultimate limit* is determined by the *physical* element: That is to say, to maintain and produce itself, to perpetuate its physical existence, the working class must receive the necessaries absolutely indispensable for living and multiplying. . . . Besides this mere physical element, the value of labour is in every country determined by a *traditional standard of life*."

Thus Marx explained the considerable differences of wages between countries and between different periods of time, but he also recognized wage differences between different workers at the same time and place. Wages are higher for skilled work, he maintained, because of the greater time and cost involved in educating skilled workers than unskilled laborers. Marx also accepted the wages fund doctrine that the demand for labor depends upon the amount of capital which is or can be devoted to that purpose, and that the amount of the wages fund is predetermined in the sense that it is dependent upon how much and what has been produced in the past. "Wages . . . are not a share of the worker in the commodities produced by himself. Wages are that part of already existing commodities with which the capitalist buys a certain amount of productive labour-power."[12]

Marx's theory concerning wages, it is seen, was not unlike that of his contemporaries. His unique contribution was his conception of the relation of wages to the value of the product which labor produced, and the social and political implications he attached to his theory. The fundamental thesis of Marx's economic and political philosophy was that labor creates *all* value; that "the value of a commodity is determined by the quantity of labor expended during its production." Raw materials have value only to the extent that labor was employed in producing and getting them to the market, and capital equipment is a conversion of raw materials and labor. It is labor, then, which produces all wealth, but

---

[12] Karl Marx, *Wage-Labor and Capital,* New York Labor News Co., New York, 1902.

labor is actually paid only its cost of subsistence—the difference or surplus value is retained by the employers.

Basically, Marx's theory of surplus value followed the thinking of Adam Smith, the founder of classical economics, for Smith also held that it was labor which created economic value and that rent and profits were "deductions" from the "product of labor." In his advocacy of higher wages Smith stated that it was but equity "that they who feed, clothe, and lodge the whole body of the people should have such a share in the produce of their own labour as to be themselves tolerably well fed, clothed, and lodged."[13] Marx, however, disagreed with Smith that workers are entitled merely to be "tolerably" well fed. According to the Marxian philosophy, wages should amount to the *total* value of the product; and if workers had control of industry, which Marx believed in and advocated, there would be no employing class to appropriate the surplus value which belonged to labor. (Marx did not think in terms of individual laborers receiving the total value of their production but in terms of the surplus value going to the state which would be controlled by the workers.)

The "orthodox" economists of Marx's time and later took exception to Marx's claim that the value of a thing consists exclusively of the labor that has been spent in making it and that therefore interest on capital is robbery of labor. Alfred Marshall, the noted British economist, expressed the views of many when he said that capital represents postponement of gratifications—that is, present spending—and thus "a sacrifice on the part of him who postpones, just as additional effort does on the part of him who labours; and if it be true that this postponement enables man to use roundabout methods of production by which the aggregate volume of human enjoyments is increased, as certainly as it would be by an increase of labour, then it cannot be true that the value of a thing depends simply on the amount of labour spent on it."[14]

MARGINAL PRODUCTIVITY THEORY

It was not until late in the 19th century that the Malthusian theory of population and diminishing returns from the land (food

---

[13] Adam Smith, *Wealth of Nations,* E. P. Dutton & Co., New York, Everyman's Library, 1911, Vol. I, p. 70.

[14] Alfred Marshall, *Principles of Economics,* Macmillan & Co., Ltd., London, 1890, p. 619.

supply) was questioned. Then it was observed that the rate of population increase tends to be lower, instead of higher, with improvements in the standard of living. If this was true, a rise in wages might reduce rather than increase a nation's supply of labor, excluding of course the factor of immigration. Also it was observed that "high" wages had another effect—they increased the efficiency of labor. This latter was recognized by Adam Smith a century earlier but his immediate successors had given little attention to his statement: "The wages of labour are the encouragement of industry, which, like every other human quality, improves in proportion to the encouragement it receives. A plentiful subsistence increases the bodily strength of the labourer and the comfortable hope of bettering his condition, and of ending his days perhaps in ease and plenty, animates him to exert that strength to the utmost. Where wages are high, accordingly, we shall always find the workers more active, diligent, and expeditious than where they are low. . . ."[15]

During the latter half of the 19th century a number of the classical economists, even those who were regarded as upholders of employer interests, conceded that low wages are by no means equivalent to low costs. Senior, who invented the term "wages of abstinence" to explain and justify interest on capital, observed that in spite of the fact that wages in England were three times as high as in Ireland, the cost of production in England was no greater. "It may be supposed, indeed, that the price of labour is everywhere, and at all times, the same."[16]

Recognition of the factor of labor efficiency was a radical departure from the concept of labor as mere numbers or a rigid "lump of work," because it differentiated between the nominal cost of labor, represented by the wages which workers receive, and the real cost of labor, which depends upon the relation of wages to the volume and value of the goods produced. From this it was concluded that if higher wages resulted in higher productivity, this affected not only the supply of but also the demand for labor. The supply was augmented because more man-hours were available as a result of the increased intensity and skill of labor; the demand tended to expand because persons with money at their disposal,

---

[15] *Wealth of Nations*, p. 73.

[16] N. W. Senior, *Political Economy*, Charles Griffin & Co., London, 1863, 5th ed., p. 151.

attracted by the prospects of the larger profits resulting from
lower labor costs, would be encouraged to invest larger portions
of their funds instead of spending their money for present enjoyment. Instead of a rigid wages fund which could be augmented
only slowly with the growth of the surplus product of industry,
investment funds for the employment of labor came to be thought
of as flexible circulating capital which expanded or contracted according to the confidence investors had in their ability to make
profits.

This new attention to labor productivity or efficiency as a
factor in the value or price of labor not only discredited the absolutism of the wages fund doctrine but pointed the way to a new
theory—that of marginal productivity, which deals in terms of
increments, the small additions and subtractions of labor at the
"margin."

Meaning of Marginal Productivity

The marginal productivity theory is one aspect of a general
theory of value, and is premised on the fact that the amount of
goods and services produced is dependent upon the willingness
and ability of consumers to purchase. Basic to economic value are
two conditions, utility and scarcity, which in the market place
are manifested as demand and supply. To illustrate: Air has
utility for all living beings, but because of its abundance it has
no economic value except in crowded cities where "plenty of air"
may be an item in the rent paid for an apartment. In contrast,
work horses may be scarce but nevertheless may be a drug on the
market if farmers are able to obtain all the tractors they need.

The value of any commodity or service depends upon its marginal utility to those to whom it is or could be made available. In
other words, the money value or price depends upon what existing
or potential buyers are willing to pay for the last or marginal
unit which is produced and offered for sale. The utility of that
marginal unit is determined by the "law of diminishing returns,"
which holds that the utility of, and hence the value placed upon,
any unit diminishes as the number of units increases, because its
net contribution falls off as additional units are made available and
used.

Four factors contribute to production, namely, land, capital, business enterprise, and labor. The problem is, what determines the relative share or value of each? With respect to labor's share or value, the theory holds that wages tend to be fixed at the point that represents the employer's estimate of the contribution of the last unit of labor employed, which becomes the marginal unit. The number of units of labor which he will employ will be determined by what he must pay for the marginal unit of labor in comparison to the cost of the marginal units of land (rent) and capital (interest), and by what he thinks his own marginal risks should yield in the way of profits. In other words, the supply of labor in relation to the supply of land, capital, and business enterprise determines its marginal productivity or value, and the level of wages paid will equal the exact value of the marginal unit.

The theory can be more simply explained by considering only two factors which are of prime importance in manufacturing— labor and capital. To paraphrase the illustration used by John Bates Clark, the economist who has been most influential in this country in expounding this theory: If 100 workers are employed in an enterprise having $1,000,000 worth of capital, their per capita productivity will be great because their work will be aided by $10,000 worth of machines and other equipment per man. If another 100 workers are employed without increasing the capital investment, the output per man will be much smaller, because this second increment of workers has at its disposal capital amounting to only $5000 per man, and this they have taken from the men who were formerly using it. Therefore, "The product that can be attributed to this second increment of labor is, of course, not all that it creates by the aid of the capital that the earlier division of workers has surrendered to it; it is only what its presence adds to the product previously created." With 100 workers using the whole capital, the product has X units of value; with 200 workers it has X plus, and "the plus quantity, whatever it is, measures the product that is attributable to the second increment of labor only."[17]

When it is said that marginal productivity determines the rate of wages existing at any given time or place, does this have any practical meaning? Basically, as has been indicated in Chapter 4,

[17] J. B. Clark, *The Distribution of Wealth*, The Macmillan Company, New York, 1902, pp. 174–176.

the productivity of any unit of labor depends as much or more upon mechanical and chemical inventions, the efficiency of organization, and available natural resources, as upon the workers' own skill and effort. Let us assume, for the sake of simplicity, that these other factors, referred to as the "state of the arts," are constant, and also that all the workers' skill and effort are similar so that their price or wage rate is uniform. If all these factors are constant, the theory then turns on the relationship of the demand for labor to the supply of labor.

Demand for Labor

Fundamentally, the demand for labor is a demand for the *products* of labor, and the demand at any time is dependent upon general economic conditions and the needs and desires of consumers. The total volume of production, therefore, ultimately determines the receipts of all factors involved in production. But the theory of marginal productivity as applied to wage determination is concerned with the *ratio* of the receipts going to capital and labor or, more specifically, the value assigned to labor by the owners and managers of capital. In this sense, the demand for labor is represented by the amount of capital made available by employers for investment in wages.

The marginal productivity theory differs from the wages fund theory in that the amount of capital available for employing labor is not regarded as a fixed proportion of the total income from industry. It is a fund which may be added to or reduced by the action of investors in accordance with the relative attractiveness of investment as against present enjoyment—investing in stocks or bonds or spending for personal comforts and luxuries. The fund, however, remains elastic only within certain limits, and these limits are determined by the preference which investors have for spending their money immediately or putting it by to bring in future income. This preference for present pleasure or spending, referred to as "time preference" or "discounting the future," acts as a resistant against the flow of capital into industry and measures the cost price of capital.

The price necessary to overcome the "time preference" of investors, and thus to attract different amounts of capital into industry, tends to vary. With bright prospects for profits the amount will expand and with poor prospects it will contract. While it depends upon past accumulations of capital, it fluctuates with the willingness of investors to add to existing capital by new investments. The limits of the varying amounts of capital which are available for wages represent the demand curve for labor, shown as *DD* in the accompanying diagram.

Supply of Labor

The supply of labor is also elastic within certain limits, and these limits determine the cost price of labor. Fundamentally, as was brought out in the early chapters of this book, the supply of

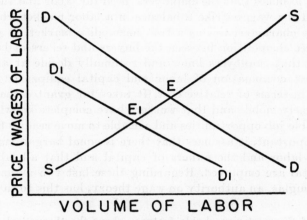

Fig. 17. *Equilibrium and Wage Determination.*

labor is contingent upon the total population, but population is relatively inelastic. The elasticity of supply, at least within short periods of time and for particular demands, depends upon such factors and conditions as the proportion of the population available for work (for example, not needed in the military forces), the acquired skills and intensity of work of those in the labor force, and the willingness of workers to accept jobs at a given price.

There is thus a supply curve for labor as well as a demand curve. The supply curve is indicated by *SS* in the diagram; and the point of intersection of the two curves, *E*, is the point of equilibrium which determines the level of wages. According to the marginal productivity theory, this is true because if any employer sought to pay less, workers would leave him and go elsewhere since there are unfilled demands; likewise if workers insisted upon more than the equilibrium wage, they would not be employed because there are enough available workers to supply the demand at this figure. However, should the demand for labor be reduced, as shown by D_1D_1, and the supply remain the same, the wage level would drop to a new point of equilibrium, E_1.

Assumptions of Marginal Productivity Theory

This theory obviously is based upon many hypothetical assumptions. It assumes that the employers' need for labor and the workers' need for wages strike a balance in a labor market which has the same characteristics as a free commodity market. It presupposes free competition between the buyers and sellers of labor. It assumes that employers know and rationally decide at all times just what combination of labor and capital equipment is most efficient in terms of relative cost. It takes for granted that labor is extremely mobile and that workers have complete knowledge of all possible job opportunities and are able to move readily to them. Most important, it assumes that there is equal bargaining power between labor and the owners of capital and that all labor and all capital are employed. Regarding these last two assumptions, Paul Douglas, an authority on wage theory, has this to say:

One of the most remarkable features about the theoretical work of both the classical and neo-classical schools has been their failure to recognize the possibility of unemployment. In their desire to disprove the "heresy" of overproduction, they have tended to ignore the fact which the advocates of overproduction have sought to explain, namely, that of unemployment. Intent upon demonstrating that the production of goods constitutes the demand for goods (which under a barter economy is the case) they have tended to satisfy themselves by showing that it is, therefore, impossible for widespread unemployment to exist. Until the last decade, the business cycle has been viewed by the "orthodox" economists as an excrescence upon business activity rather than as a tendency which is organically a part of it.

The productivity theorists and the neo-classical school have treated unemployment as resulting solely from the attempt of labor to secure a higher wage than their product at the margin, and as only operating as the mechanism by which the workers' demands were forced down to the point where the employers would be justified in hiring them. The possibility that it might lead to the workers offering their services for less than their marginal product was seldom considered.

Whatever, therefore, may be the condition in the real world of affairs, the productivity theory is based upon the assumption that there is work for all, and that all who really want work and are able to perform it and who are willing to work for the marginal wage are employed. Thus the marginal productivity of labor is made identical with the marginal productivity of employed labor. There is no idle fringe of labor whose productivity is nil. . . .

In orthodox theory there is no more room for unemployed capital than for unemployed labor. All capital is actively at work in production, save that which has been discarded or lost and has consequently ceased to be capital, or that which is temporarily out of use because of the attempt to secure a higher rate of interest than its marginal unit adds. There is indeed in the classical theory no realistic explanation as to why capital instruments which are in good repair should be employed at one time and should be idle at another. The fact that many industries are so overequipped with fixed capital that a large proportion lies idle even in periods of prosperity has been similarly ignored by the main theorists of the orthodox tradition. In consequence of all this the main stream of the marginal productivity theory has made the marginal productivity of capital virtually synonymous with the marginal productivity of employed capital.[18]

BARGAINING THEORY

The marginal productivity theory rests upon the assumption of equal bargaining power between the buyers and the sellers of labor in a perfectly "free" labor market; otherwise, there will be interferences in the competitive forces of supply and demand which will cause an "unnatural" equilibrium or wage level. It is a theory which holds that the mechanistic operation of unconscious forces will bring about normal or "natural" rates of wages which, because they are "natural," are therefore right and best for all concerned.

If the theory has any practical use, even as a tendency, it must be assumed that it is possible to have or to attain approximately

---

[18] Paul H. Douglas, *The Theory of Wages,* The Macmillan Company, New York, 1934, pp. 70–71.

the conditions upon which its validity is premised. Accordingly, it is imperative to know and to recognize the actualities of existing conditions, for if they do not conform to the hypothetical conditions upon which the theory is posited, it must be accepted that existing wages are not the equilibrium wages which the theory talks about. The practical question is, then, what constitutes a free labor market and when is there equal bargaining power between capital and labor? Correlatively, is it possible to have a free labor market and equality of bargaining in a complex and dynamic industrial system such as ours?

Let us consider some of the relevant characteristics of capital and labor which affect their bargaining relationship. Some of them, it will be seen, are inherent in any wage economy and will continue to exist, to a greater or lesser extent, so long as there are employers and employees engaged in private enterprise. Others, however, are not so much an intrinsic part of the nature of the capital-labor relationship as the result of customs, laws, and other institutional influences.

Inherent Factors in the Bargaining Relationship

It is the managers of capital who decide each quarter or each year how much of the business income shall be used for managers' salaries and distributed in dividends, how much shall be laid aside for future capital investment, and, in effect, how much shall be allocated for wages. The very nature of their position, therefore, gives the managers of capital an advantage in wage bargaining, because the income from business flows through their hands. No matter how strong their union may be, the employees of a business enterprise have no voice in this initial distribution of gross income, and usually they have no way of even learning about their company's financial condition.[19]

Another inherent advantage of capital lies in the fact that labor is inseparable from the worker himself. It is this inseparability of

---

[19] An interesting feature of our corporate form of business enterprise is the almost equal limitation placed upon the providers of capital (stockholders). Most large corporations have clauses in their certificates of incorporation similar to that of the General Motors Corporation, which says: ". . . No stockholder shall have any right to inspect any account or book or document of the Corporation, except as conferred by statute or authorized by the Board of Directors or by a resolution of the stockholders. . . ."

labor from the laborer which produces a number of fundamental distinctions between the capital and the labor market and their relative bargaining power. To begin with, the supply of labor, at least in the mass, is comparatively inflexible. Since the size of the population changes slowly, the size of the labor market is more or less fixed for long periods of time.[20] Unlike capital, labor must be delivered "in person," and persons (with their families) cannot always transport themselves to new jobs offering a better income. The labor of people cannot be as versatile as is capital. Investment-seeking capital can enter any kind of business, but persons seeking jobs are limited by their job skills and must also consider the physical and other conditions surrounding the jobs.

Of prime importance is the fact that labor will not keep; it must bring in an income immediately and continually because the daily work of a wage earner usually represents the day-to-day subsistence of himself and his family. The "withholding" power of labor, in other words, is much weaker than that of the owners of capital, for the latter enjoy one or all of the following benefits: Owners of capital are usually in the higher-income groups and thus have greater reserves and credit to tide them over a period of reduced or no income. Their capital investments usually are widely dispersed so that a cessation of dividend receipts from one source (e.g., from a company closed down because of a bargaining dispute) is not tantamount to complete stoppage of income. It is the usual practice of business concerns to carry reserves so that dividend payments can be continued long after workers are laid off because of depression or cease work because of a wage dispute.

Almost two hundred years ago, during the early days of the modern wage system, the French statesman, Necker, made the following pungent comment on the inherent differences in the bargaining relationship between those who derive their income from property or capital and those who work for wages:

Whence is the misery of all times and in all lands and what is its eternal source?

---

[20] An important exception in this country, mentioned in chap. 1, was the period of large-scale immigration prior to World War I which, incidentally, was encouraged by employers for the purpose of increasing the labor supply and keeping down wages. As indicated in chap. 2, the labor force is capable of considerable expansion during war periods when women, retired men, and youths are encouraged to accept employment.

This source is the power which the owning classes possess, the power to give in exchange for labor which they need, the lowest possible wage, that is, a wage which is determined by absolute minimum necessity. . . .

Such a power in the hands of the owning classes is based on the insignificance of their number as compared with the number of people who are deprived of property. It is, also, based on the intense competition between the propertyless among themselves, and, particularly, upon the terrible inequality between the two groups of people, those who, on the one hand, sell their labor in order to be able to meet the needs of the day, and, on the other hand, those who buy this labor in order to obtain greater comforts and luxury. The first are always under the pressure of immediate need; the others are altogether not affected by it. . . .

The power of the owner over the man who is deprived of property, must be attributed to this difference in the situation. . . . [Furthermore] as the society becomes altered, there takes place an accumulation of great quantities of products. . . . This accumulation of riches which daily grows is hidden, and unnoticeably competes with the labor of new workers. . . .[21]

Institutional Factors in the Bargaining Relationship

In addition to the distinctions which are inherent in the very nature of capital and labor, their relative bargaining strength is also vitally affected by laws, customs, social arrangements, and practices which are referred to as "institutional." In contrast to the characteristics which, basically, cannot be changed except by changing the structure of which they are a part, institutional factors are variable and are constantly subject to change. Some of these changes take place unconsciously and are by-products of a developing industrial society so far as their impact upon wage bargaining is concerned. Many of the changes—for example, legislation or the organized activities of employers or workers— are the result of a deliberate and conscious effort to alter existing bargaining relationships. Sometimes they are for the purpose of enhancing existing inequalities, or at least they have had that effect; others are designed to compensate for "natural" inequalities in order to effect a more equal balance in bargaining strength.

Before the advent of power machinery and the factory system as

---

[21] Jacques Necker, Paris, 1775. Quoted in M. T. Wermel, *The Evolution of the Classical Wage Theory*, Columbia University Press, New York, 1939, pp. 77, 80.

we know factories today, and prior to many of our modern business practices and institutions, the inequalities due to inherited privileges, group behavior, and existing legal institutions were recognized. Said Adam Smith in 1776:

> What are the common wages of labour, depends everywhere upon the contract usually made between those two parties, whose interests are by no means the same. The workmen desire to get as much, the masters to give as little as possible. . . . It is not, however, difficult to foresee which of the two parties must, upon all ordinary occasions, have the advantage in the dispute, and force the other into a compliance with their terms. . . . The masters, being fewer in number, can combine much more easily. . . .
> We rarely hear, it has been said, of the combinations of masters, though frequently of those of workmen. But whoever imagines upon this account that masters rarely combine, is as ignorant of the world as of the subject. Masters are always and everywhere in a sort of tacit, but constant and uniform combination, not to raise the wages of labour above their actual rates. To violate this combination is everywhere a most unpopular action and a sort of reproach to a master among his neighbors and equals. . . . Masters, too, sometimes enter into particular combinations to sink the wages of labour even below this rate. These are always conducted with the utmost secrecy, till the moment of execution and when the workmen yield, as they sometimes do, without resistance, though severely felt by them, they are never heard of by other people.[22]

The introduction of the corporate form of business enterprise greatly enhanced the inequalities referred to by Smith. Corporations, which are "creatures" of the state and an outstanding example of an institutional arrangement for conducting business, represent amalgamations of large amounts of capital under control of a single company or legal entity. One can appreciate the great change in the balance of competition in the labor market which corporations have brought about only if one can imagine a situation in which no business organization had control of more capital than that owned by a single individual or even a partnership. Even then there would not be parity between individual workers and employers because capital, unlike labor, can accumulate. But capital accumulation is also an institutional phenomenon

[22] *Wealth of Nations*, pp. 58–59.

since it is affected by man-made laws in the form of taxes and governmental controls, as well as benefits. For example, portions of the capital in the hands of many employers represent inherited funds, and inheritances are made possible through legal arrangements and social protections.[23]

If the mere fact of corporate control of aggregations of capital funds automatically causes a change in the character of the labor market, the forces of equilibrium are further distorted, of course, when corporations combine into trade associations or less formal arrangements for purposes of controlling production, prices, and wages. In this volume we cannot go into the theoretical or the actual implications of monopolistic and quasi-monopolistic practices, although all of them directly or indirectly affect wages in some way. Suffice it to say that they are the antithesis of free competition and, to the extent that they exist, they destroy the basis of any wage theory founded upon the principle of equilibrium resulting from the competitive forces of supply and demand.

Combinations, however, are not limited to the capital side of wage bargaining. Union organizations represent combinations of labor and their *raison d'être* is to achieve approximate parity between employers and workers. Labor organizations are also an institutional phenomenon, their existence and effectiveness being promoted or hindered by social attitudes and, most of all, by legal controls or protections. What these are and how they have developed will be discussed in later chapters.

As conditions are today, labor unions cannot be ignored or relegated to a minor role in any realistic consideration of wage determination. Labor unions are designed to supplant individual worker bargaining with collective bargaining. Their presence not only alters the method of wage negotiation but also causes a readjustment in the balance of forces. In theory at least, they establish a "balance" which does not exist in their absence, because of the inherent and institutional advantages on the employers' side. Through their unions workers can and do exercise control over the supply of labor. Their most effective weapon is their ability to withhold labor, and many wage determinations are the result of strikes or threats of strikes.

---

[23] The annulment of the laws of primogeniture, for example, vitally affected the distribution and accumulation of inheritances.

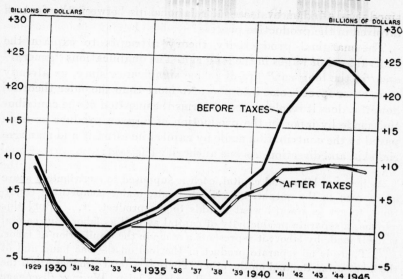

BILLIONS OF DOLLARS

BEFORE TAXES→

AFTER TAXES

FIG. 18. *Corporate Profits Before and After Federal and State Income and Excess Profits Taxes, 1929–1945.* (*Source*: Current Business, April, 1946.)

Bargaining Versus the Marginal Productivity Theory

Does the presence of such man-made institutional factors as employer-union bargaining (as well as wage legislation, discussed later) entirely invalidate the theory of a natural rate of wages established at a point of equilibrium of marginal productivity? Do the conscious and deliberate controls of the labor market by combinations of capital and labor utterly negate the law of supply and demand? Is it possible to say that certain independent conditions of supply and demand create a certain equilibrium to which the wage level will inevitably tend, or are these very conditions the result of previous bargaining? In other words, does the point of equilibrium continually change as the result of successive bargains, each of which was influenced by the superior bargaining strength which one party or the other happened to possess at the time?

In brief, is there a general "law" of wages, a "natural" rate of wages, or even a theory which can serve as a guide to long-time

trends and fundamental causal relationships between the factors
involved in the productive process?

The marginal productivity theory attempts to explain the
general level of wages in the long run. The qualifications "general"
and "in the long run" are of prime significance since, as already
seen, other forces come into play. No more than the older theories,
however, does it resolve in exact terms the question of the contribution made by labor in the production of a given product as compared to the contribution made by capital investment and managerial skill and direction. As one authority has said:

> As between labor and capital, each is supposed to contribute a share
> of its own to the output. . . . Each tends, under competitive condi-
> tions, to get as reward what it adds to the product. . . . [But] this
> assumes a separate productivity of capital as well as labor. But capital
> is itself made by labor; it represents a stage in the application of labor.
> . . . There is no separate product of the tool on the one hand and of
> the labor using the tool on the other. There is a joint product of all the
> labor applied—earlier labor as well as later labor. We may disengage
> the causes determining why and how the laborers who use and make the
> tools get wages, from the causes determining why and how the owners
> of the tools get interest; but we can disengage no concretely separable
> product of labor and capital.[24]

The fact of this inseparability constitutes the core of the
modern wage problem, for if it could be known with accuracy what
each of the agents of production actually contributed, the allocation of the gross income would be merely a matter of administration and enforcement. But there is no way, under modern industrial and social conditions, to establish a continual process
which would allocate an even-handed justice to all the elements
concerned in the production of goods or economic values.

The only thing which is certain is that, through the joint efforts of all the factors, surplus value is produced, and this is
available for either higher profits or higher wages.[25] (The surplus
can also be distributed through the lowering of prices which in

---

[24] F. W. Taussig, *Principles of Economics,* The Macmillan Company, New
York, 1921, vol. ii, pp. 213–214.

[25] This does not mean, of course, that *every* business enterprise produces a
surplus every year, but that the value of the goods and services produced by
the entire economy is greater than the costs involved in their production.

effect is equivalent to higher "real" wages, as is explained in the next chapter.)

. . . Though our general conclusion may be that no rigid theory of wages is possible, we are not left entirely in the dark. We know what are some of the important relations and connections between factors—how the variations of different things are connected together. Moreover, there are still limits within which the indeterminateness is contained.

The general wage-level is unlikely to fall for long below a bare physical subsistence standard—a standard which will not, of course, be a fixed level, since the amount of subsistence will depend on how arduous or intensive is the work; although, if plentiful new supplies of labour from outside (e.g., by immigration from rural districts or other countries) are available, this minimum standard may be very low, sufficient only for the worker's physical needs of the present, and not for a long life or for rearing a family, just as slaves could be undernourished and worked out quickly if plentiful new supplies of slaves were forthcoming. . . . On the other hand, the wage-level could not rise (at least, for any length of time) so as to absorb more than that part of the surplus produce that is at present *spent*: If it absorbed more than this, it would inevitably eat into the capital-supply. Wages under the most favourable conditions could not absorb more than the gross produce *minus* the necessary capital accumulation. . . .

In practice, however, it seems almost certain that, given the continuance of the present wage-system, the actual limit to the upward movement of wages stands considerably lower than this. Indeed, it seems probable that economists have been right in concluding that the upward limit to wages, whatever its precise character, is more rigid and definite than the lower limit to wages. . . . During prosperous periods when the gross produce of industry is expanding, wage-earners, if strongly organised, are probably in a good position for raising their wages, both in the aggregate and relatively to their own effort and to the share which goes to property-owners; and the extent to which they can do this depends mainly on their bargaining strength. But at less prosperous times, when the gross produce of industry is stationary, the power of trade unions, however strongly organised, seems in practice to be much more limited. While they may raise the price of labour, and even raise wages relatively as a share of the total produce, their efforts to do so are likely to result in a shrinkage of the demand for labour, so that their power to increase aggregate earnings (other than by increased intensity of work) under these circumstances, and short of more sweeping institutional change in the wage-system itself, is probably fairly small.[26]

To summarize: Combinations of capital and labor cause shifts in bargaining power but they do not fundamentally change the mechanism of the market. Aggregate wages cannot exceed the productive efficiency of the industrial process. Marginal subsistence determines the level of minimum wages, else workers could not survive; marginal productivity establishes maximum levels because marginal employers cannot pay more in a competitive system. In a progressive society the difference between subsistence and productivity levels tends to widen, and the extent to which actual wages rise above subsistence depends largely upon the supply of labor relative to the demand for labor.

Returns to capital could probably be reduced within limits without impairing the supply or the incentive to invest and manage business enterprises. The concept of "normal" returns to capital is not something fixed. During recent years the general interest rate has been reduced at least one-half[27] without any apparent diminution in the flow of "safe" investment money. Likewise "risk" capital and managerial effort would probably be forthcoming even though there was some gradual and general reduction in profit levels. But in a free enterprise system there are limits beyond which capital returns cannot be reduced. Within these limits, however, wages are affected by the relative bargaining power of employers and workers, aided or restrained by legal sanctions and public opinion.

SELECTED REFERENCES

Brentano, L., *Hours and Wages in Relation to Production,* Charles Scribner's Sons, New York, 1894.

---

[26] Maurice Dobb, *Wages,* Nisbet and Co., Ltd., London, 1928, pp. 105–108.
[27] Declines in interest rates as cited by the *U. S. News* (March 1, 1946) were:

	1920	Today
Federal government bonds	5.3%	1.5%
City government bonds	5.0	1.6
Corporation bonds	7.0	2.8
Home mortgages	7.0	4.5
Bank loans	6.6	2.0
Savings accounts	3.0	1.0
Common stock	6.2 (1941)	3.5

Carey, H. C., *Essay on the Rate of Wages,* Carey, Lea and Blanchard, Philadelphia, 1835.

Clark, J. B., *The Distribution of Wealth, a Theory of Wages, Interest and Profits,* The Macmillan Company, New York, 1902.

Commons, J. R., *Institutional Economics,* The Macmillan Company, New York, 1934.

Davidson, John, *The Bargain Theory of Wages,* G. P. Putnam's Sons, New York, 1898.

Dobb, Maurice, *Wages,* Nisbet & Co., Ltd., London, 1928.

Douglas, Paul H., *The Theory of Wages,* The Macmillan Company, New York, 1934.

Hamilton, Walton, and May, Stacy, *The Control of Wages,* The Macmillan Company, New York, 1942.

Hicks, J. R., *The Theory of Wages,* Macmillan & Co., Ltd., London, 1932.

Hutt, W. H., *The Theory of Collective Bargaining,* P. S. King & Sons, Ltd., London, 1930.

Marshall, Alfred, *Principles of Economics,* The Macmillan Company, New York, 1910.

Mill, J. S., *Principles of Political Economy,* D. Appleton & Co., Inc., New York, 1883.

Ricardo, David, *The Principles of Political Economy and Taxation,* E. P. Dutton & Co., Inc., New York, Everyman's Edition, 1912.

Valk, Willem L., *The Principles of Wages,* P. S. King & Sons, Ltd., London, 1928.

Wermel, Michael T., *The Evolution of the Classical Wage Theory,* Columbia University Press, New York, 1939.

10

THE NATURE OF WAGES

WAGES MEAN DIFFERENT THINGS TO DIFFERENT PERSONS AND TO the same persons in their several capacities. For the wage earner, the wages he receives are his primary, and most frequently his sole, means of livelihood for himself and his family. As a purchaser of goods and services, however, he is a payer of wages to others— directly in the case of many services and indirectly in the case of manufactured commodities. To the individual employer, the wages he pays his employees represent labor costs which comprise an important portion of the total cost of operating his business. But to employers in general, and to the national economy, wages represent the bulk of the total consumer purchasing power, the means by which most of the goods and services which are produced are taken off the market.

Wages therefore can be considered in the abstract as a mechanism by which goods and services are transferred from those who want to dispose of them to those who wish and need them for consumption. As such, the total money wages paid at any time or place become a measure of business activity, but not necessarily an indicator of the prosperity of those who offer the goods for sale, or of the wage earners who purchase them. There are other important factors which influence the income of any particular business or the degree of prosperity of all business. Likewise the purchasing ability of wage earners, individually and collectively, is affected by other factors than the amount of dollars and cents received in the pay envelope.

As a basis for the discussion of these factors and their interrelationships, it is necessary first to get a clear understanding of the meaning and significance of the various terms that are used in connection with the payment to workers for services performed and the money they have with which to make their purchases.

REMUNERATION OF WORKERS

The remuneration of workers is expressed variously as income, earnings, wages, and wage rates. Each term has its special significance and is used to describe particular forms of financial remuneration or their money equivalents. None of these terms, however, conveys what the remuneration is actually worth, that is, what it can procure in goods and services. Remuneration expressed in terms of what it will buy is called "real" wages or "real" income.

Workers' Income

Individual or family income is most commonly used to denote the total net money income from all sources as well as the money equivalent of living items not paid for in cash. Money income includes not only wages but non-earned income such as interest and dividends, rent from real estate other than the home, pensions and annuities and money gifts. Non-money income includes the rental value of homes owned by the families who occupy them, the money equivalent of lodging and perquisites received as part compensation (as when agricultural and domestic workers are furnished with living quarters), and the value of home-grown foods and other products used by farm families.

Income is a broader term than wages and earnings. It is a more accurate measurement of economic well-being than wages (or salaries) alone, for it represents the total potential ability for purchasing and savings. However, only a small proportion of industrial workers have other sources of income than their daily or weekly wages. For the most part, wage payments represent the total income of wage earners and their sole means of livelihood.[1]

Income is usually considered in relation to annual receipts and thus takes into account loss of wages due to unemployment and other absences from work during the year. Annual income, therefore, should not be confused with the currently popular term

---

[1] In a study made in 1934–1936 it was found that less than 2 per cent of the total income of families in the $1500–$2100 income bracket represented non-earned income. This percentage has probably increased slightly as a result of the expanded unemployment compensation program. (*Money Disbursements of Wage Earners and Clerical Workers,* Bureau of Labor Statistics Bulletin No. 628, Government Printing Office, Washington, 1941, p. 22.)

"annual wages" which, as explained in Chapter 7, is frequently used to connote guaranteed wages on an annual basis.

Employer Pay Rolls

A *pay roll* represents the amount of money paid by an employer to all his employees as remuneration for services to him. It denotes gross wage payments, for it includes not only wages and salaries[2] for work performed during the normal work week but also overtime and other premium payments, commissions, pay for vacations and holidays not worked (when such periods are actually paid for), and any other payments which directly or indirectly are considered as compensation for work performance. To the employer, his pay roll represents his labor costs; unit labor costs are computed by dividing the total volume of business or output by the total pay roll.

In the aggregate, employer pay rolls are equivalent to total employees' earnings. Fluctuations in total pay rolls reflect the increases and decreases in the number employed, the number of hours they work during the pay-roll period, premiums and bonuses, and the shifts which take place from lower- to higher-paid occupations and industries, or vice versa.[3]

Earnings, Wages, and Wage Rates

Wages and earnings are sometimes used interchangeably to designate the amount of money paid to a worker for a specified period of time, that is, hour, day, week, etc. *Earnings* could more accurately be used to refer to the total remuneration for services

---

[2] In practice, most employers maintain two pay rolls, one for their production workers or wage earners, and one for their "overhead"—clerical, supervisory, and sales personnel. The pay-roll indexes published by the Bureau of Labor Statistics refer to the former; the pay-roll data compiled by the Department of Commerce include both, that is, salaries and wages. This difference should be kept in mind when comparing average payments per employee, for obviously the per capita average is higher when the salaries of supervisors and corporation officials are included.

[3] An example of the effect upon total pay rolls of shifts of workers between lower-paid and higher-paid industries is illustrated in the pay rolls for the years 1942 and 1943. Approximately 11 per cent of the increase in total pay rolls in these years was attributable to the shift in employment from the relatively low-paid textile and other consumers' goods and service industries to the higher-paid metal and other war industries. (*Survey of Current Business,* April, 1944, p. 9.)

rendered or time worked, including overtime premiums, bonuses, commissions, and other extra rewards. *Wages*, on the other hand, are usually understood to cover regular pay for work performed under normal conditions, exclusive of overtime and holiday premium pay. Under piece or other incentive systems of payment, wages include total earnings during normal hours, that is, the guaranteed amount referred to as the base rate, plus the amount earned for output above the established standard. Briefly, then, *earnings* are total or gross wages, in contrast to regular or straight-time *wages*.

A *wage rate* represents the amount of pay for a specified unit of time, most commonly an hour. The distinction between *wages* and *wage rates* springs from the fact that customarily wage earners are paid only for the actual time worked, regardless of how their wage payments are expressed. In this respect wages differ from most salary payments, for white-collar employees usually receive a given amount each week or month irrespective of slight fluctuations in the hours they actually work. A weekly wage of $40, however, is no assurance that that amount will be received because wage earners are usually docked for lateness, for time lost due to absence, or when sent home early because of slack work or machine breakdown. For all practical purposes, a $40 weekly wage (for a normal 40-hour week) is a wage rate of $1 an hour and this is usually the way it would be expressed.

The above distinctions are much more than academic, for a confusion in the use of these terms may result in conclusions which are misleading and perhaps entirely inaccurate. For example, data may be presented which show that the average earnings of all workers, or a particular group of workers, have greatly increased, and the conclusion may be drawn that wage rates have taken an upward turn, when in fact they have remained stationary or even declined. The increase in earnings may be due entirely to overtime payments and premium pay for night and holiday work. Differences between gross earnings and straight-time wages, of course, are most pronounced during abnormal production periods. For example, during the recent war, the average gross weekly earnings of factory workers went up 77 per cent, but only one-fifth of this increase resulted from basic rate increases. One-third resulted from increased hours and extra pay for overtime, and one-third came from the wartime upgrading of workers from unskilled to semi-skilled and skilled jobs, from increased output under incentive or bonus schemes and the shift of workers from low-wage to high-wage industries. In October, 1945, a few months after the close of the war, gross weekly earnings had declined almost 13 per cent, although hourly wage rates had increased 1 per cent during those few months.

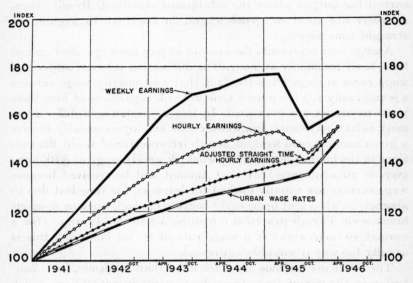

Fig. 19.   *Trend of Earnings and Wage Rates in Manufacturing, 1941 to April, 1946. January, 1941 = 100. (Source: U. S. Bureau of Labor Statistics.)*

The difference between earnings, wages, and wage rates, it is evident, turns on the vital factor of hours and time of day worked and, in some instances, on the amount of individual output. Although all three represent remuneration for work performance, each has a different connotation and unique usefulness for purposes of measurment and comparison.

Wage rates provide the basis for comparing and determining the relative value of different types of jobs and for comparing wage levels at different periods. Pay rolls or gross wage payments provide a measure for computing labor costs to total cost of production; when in the hands of the recipient these wage payments become earnings for the given pay period. They are gross earnings, however, and usually represent more than "take-home" wages or spendable income. From these gross earnings there are fixed deductions such as social security and income taxes and perhaps union dues. For example, income taxes for most wage earners during the war amounted to 4 per cent or more of their earnings,[4] and therefore must be taken into consideration when comparing earnings during World War II with earnings before or after it. Likewise a change in the social security tax rate or other fixed deductions must be taken into account in measuring "take-home" wages or net spendable earnings.

"Real" Wages

Earnings or take-home wages provide the means for livelihood, but the kind or standard of living which can be obtained from a given amount of wages depends equally as much upon what can be bought with those earnings. The purchasing power of a dollar of wages—that is, money wages in relation to costs of commodities and services which workers need and want—is expressed as "real" wages. "Real" wages increase if prices fall and wages remain the same, or if wages increase and prices remain the same, or if both rise, but wages to a greater degree. Likewise, "real" wages decline if prices rise even though wages remain the same, or if both wages and prices rise, but prices increase relatively more than wages.

"Real" wages can be computed either on the basis of gross weekly or annual earnings or on the basis of hourly wage rates, depending upon the purpose in mind. If one is considering the available purchasing power or the material well-being of workers irrespective of the number of hours they have worked for their income, the valid comparison is between cost of living and gross earnings. If, however, one is considering the comparative trends of wage rates and consumer prices, then "real" wages should be

[4] The tax rate for most wage earners amounted to 5 per cent—later raised to 6 per cent—of their taxable income, that is, after specified deductions and exemptions. The tax on a weekly wage of $44.86 was $1.73 for a man with a wife and two children. For a single person earning the same wage the tax was $7.17, or approximately 16 per cent of the total wages. (N. Arnold Tolles, "Spendable Earnings of Factory Workers, 1941–43," *Monthly Labor Review,* March, 1944, p. 484.)

expressed in terms of the relationship between cost of living and average hourly wage rates.

WAGES AS COST OF PRODUCTION

As indicated above, total wages largely determine the volume and kinds of goods and services which are purchased at any given time. As sellers of these goods and services, employers as a group benefit from high wages and suffer when total and per capita wages are low. As a producer of these goods and services, however, the individual employer is concerned with wages as an item in his cost of production. He is concerned not only with the wages he himself pays his own employees, but also with the wages paid by those employers from whom he buys the materials and equipment he uses, for these wages affect his costs, though indirectly.

Similarly, workers as buyers and consumers benefit from high wages when these wages enable them to increase their volume of purchases and thus raise their standard of living. If, however, the costs of consumers' goods are also high, "real" wages and workers' purchases are not increased. The standard of living is advanced only when wages increase *more* than the cost of living.

Wages as a cost factor become a problem of wage and price relationships. Pertinent to this problem are such questions as: Does an increase in wage rates necessarily and automatically entail an increase in prices? If so, must the two advances be exactly parallel or can wages be increased more than prices? Under what conditions is it most or least difficult to raise wages without increasing prices? Finally, what actually has taken place in the relationship between wages and prices in various industries during recent years?

Inextricably involved in these questions are two facts: (1) Although wages are a factor in the cost of production they are by no means the *sole* factor. (2) Increases in wage rates or individual earnings do not necessarily mean comparable increases in wage costs for the same amount of production. Consequently, the extent to which factors and influences other than wages enter into costs of production is the measure of the resilience between wage rates and prices.

Among these other factors are profits, which represent the difference between total costs and sales value; in manufacturing the latter is synonymous with wholesale prices. The preceding chapter outlined some of the principal theories which seek to explain the relative rewards of labor and capital, and we shall not here discuss profits versus wages as competing elements, although profits added to total costs determine ultimate prices. Our concern here is with wages in relation to total costs of production. Some of the more important cost items other than wages are salaries of officials of corporations, interest, rent, taxes, depreciation, insurance, research and advertising expenditures, fuel and power, and, above all, materials and supplies. The relative proportion of total cost expended for each of these items varies greatly among the several industries, among different companies within the same industry, and in the same company at different periods.

Relation of Labor Costs to Total Costs

For an individual employer, the proportion of his total costs which is expended for labor is of vital significance when considering the impact of changes in wage rates. For example, in an industry where wages represent only 5 per cent of the total costs of production, a 20 per cent increase in wages would result in only a 1 per cent increase in total costs. In contrast, in a plant where wages represent 50 per cent of the total cost, a 20 per cent wage advance would cause a 10 per cent increase in total costs, provided, of course, there were no offsetting savings.

Except in the case of industries engaged in the processing of such relatively cheap raw materials as clay, stone, and sand, labor costs tend to be less in proportion to total costs in industries engaged in the primary processing of raw materials, and more in the fabrication industries. As illustration: In sugar refining more than 75 per cent of the total 1939 value of products was expended for raw materials, in petroleum refining almost 80 per cent, copper smelting and refining over 90 per cent, meat slaughtering and packing 84 per cent, flour milling about 78 per cent, pig iron production 85 per cent, and cigarette manufacturing 78 per cent. In none of these industries did total wages (in 1939) represent more than 6 per cent of the total value of the products manufactured. In contrast, the cost of raw materials represented less than half the total value of products produced in the machine tool, hosiery, shipbuilding, and bread baking industries, while wages included anywhere from 22 to 37 per cent of the total value.

In the service industries, labor costs represent a major portion of all costs, because the materials used are a minor item. For retail trade as a whole, wages and salaries account for about one-half of the total operating costs, although this varies greatly among individual establishments according to location (rent paid) and type of store.

The above represent averages for entire industries. For particular products in any industry, there are considerable differences in the proportion of wage cost to total costs. For certain kinds of garments, for example, wages may represent 70 per cent of the total cost of manufacturing, although for the clothing industry as a whole wages include approximately 25 per cent of the total value.[5] Also, within a given industry, the various companies' labor costs in proportion to total costs are greatly affected by whether they engage in the entire processing from raw materials to the completed product, or whether outside contractors do some of the hand operations. The labor costs of an automobile concern which assembles parts purchased from contractors tend to be less per automobile than for a company which makes most of its parts as well as assembles them into finished cars. Wages include 75 per cent of the total value of clothing produced in contract shops, in contrast to only 15 to 20 per cent in regular "inside" factories.

Fundamentally, these differences in relative labor costs are merely a matter of bookkeeping by individual companies, for they have no significance so far as the relation of total wages to total value of product throughout the entire industry is concerned. However, they may have a major influence upon the wages paid by a particular employer. For example, before unions were sufficiently strong to negotiate industry-wide wage standards, the wages paid in automobile assembly plants and "inside" clothing factories were higher than those paid by automobile parts' producers and in clothing contract shops. The general manufacturers, being in a stronger competitive position, were able to bid one con-

---

[5] The above percentages are based on the 1939 census. "Value" of product represents selling value at the factory, which covers cost of production *and* profits. There are no data available for costs alone. However, for a comparison of labor versus other costs in the various industries, the use of "value" of completed product offers a feasible basis for measurement.

tractor against another; and, since wages represented the contractors' chief item of expense, the bidding was at the expense of the wages paid by the contractors. This was true to such an extent in the clothing industry that contracting shops came to be called "sweatshops."

The cost of labor relative to total cost of production is affected not only by the type of industry and the structural arrangements for processing within it, but also by the methods used in production. In general, the ratio of labor costs to total costs varies inversely with the degree of mechanization. Where machines play a major role in the productive process, relatively more is expended for machine replacements, repair, and upkeep, and for fuel and power, although further improvements in machinery may reduce fuel and power costs. Because mechanization and enlargement in size of enterprise usually go hand in hand, the amount spent in "overhead" also tends to increase. (The proportion spent for rent, however, may be less if the use of machines results in decreased floor space. Although property taxes may be greater, social security taxes will tend to be less, proportionately, because fewer workers will be employed.) In some industries mechanization has made possible the use of cheaper materials, whereas in others the substitution of machine for hand labor has required the use of more costly materials.

By and large throughout industry, with very few exceptions, the gross cost of items other than labor tends to increase *proportionately* more than gross labor costs as operations are transferred from human hands to power machines. To the extent that this takes place, changes in wage rates become of less importance in the total cost of production.

Table 12 shows the proportion of wage payments to the total value of products for the major industries in 1939. Because there have been many changes in methods of production since 1939, some of these percentages do not accurately reveal the present situation. For example, the introduction of mass production of airplanes during the war more than tripled the man-hour output, thereby greatly reducing proportionate labor costs. Similarly, the recent extension in the use of welding and other new processes in shipbuilding and other metal fabrication industries has greatly affected labor costs in those industries.

TABLE 12.   Wages as a Percentage of Value of Product in Selected
Industries[6]

	Per Cent
All manufacturing	16.0

Low Labor Cost Industries

Cigarettes	2.5
Non-ferrous primary smelting and refining	4.0
Sugar refining (cane)	4.2
Flour and other grain mills	4.4
Blast furnace products	5.1
Petroleum refining	5.2
Meat slaughtering and packing	6.1
Soap	6.2

Medium Labor Cost Industries

Canned fruits and vegetables	11.1
Crude petroleum	11.3
Malt liquors	11.8
Aluminum	15.0
Paper and pulp mills	15.1
Rubber tires and tubes	15.5
Automobiles and other motor vehicles	16.0
Leather tanning—contract and regular factories	16.4
Cement	16.4
Electrical appliances	17.4
Iron ore mining	18.0
Newspaper printing and publishing	18.3
Rayon goods (broad woven)	19.6
Woolen and worsted—contract and regular factories	20.0
Agricultural machinery	21.0
Steel works and rolling mills	21.0
Book printing and publishing	21.3
Cigars	21.3
Women's dresses—contract and regular factories	21.4
Carpets and rugs (wool)	21.5
Glass containers	21.6
Bread bakeries	22.0
Men's and boys' suits and coats—contract and regular factories	23.4
Furniture (household)	24.9

High Labor Cost Industries

Shoes (except rubber)	25.0
Commercial job printing	25.8
Cotton goods	26.0
Aircraft and parts	27.7
Machine tools	28.6
Sawmills	31.0
Building construction	31.0

[6] Based on 1939 census. Includes all manufacturing, railroad, mining, and construction industries which had a total value of product or service of 500 million dollars or over, in addition to some others of smaller value.

TABLE 12.   Wages as a Percentage of Value of Product in Selected
Industries—(*Continued*)

	Per Cent
Shipbuilding and repairing.	31.9
Stone quarrying.	32.1
Brick and tile.	33.7
Hosiery (full fashioned).	36.4
Railroads.	41.0
Bituminous coal mining.	61.9

Unit Labor Costs

Employers are willing to increase their expenditures for machinery because it greatly reduces their total cost per unit of output; the increased productivity resulting from mechanization and other improved plant equipment much more than offsets the cost of the new machinery and its upkeep. In other words, machine production not only lessens the ratio of labor cost to total costs but also tends to reduce the actual amount paid in wages for each unit produced.

Unit labor costs are affected by two factors: the output achieved per hour of labor, and the wages paid per hour of labor. Unit labor costs thus vary directly with average hourly wages and inversely with productivity. If increases in hourly wages are matched by increases in output per man-hour, the cost to the employer per unit of output remains the same.

During the period between the two world wars when average wages in manufacturing changed very little, whereas productivity was advancing, average unit labor costs were reduced by about one-third.[7] Productivity continued to advance in many industries during World War II, as was indicated in Chapter 4. However, there was a greater proportionate increase in wage rates in many industries, with the result that in these industries the unit labor costs were higher in 1945 than in 1939. (The selling prices of manufactured products also advanced materially during this period, but price relationships lie outside the scope of this discussion.) Changes in unit labor costs in a few industries are indicated in Table 13.

---

[7] Wages fluctuated during this period, especially during the 1930–1933 depression; but from the limited information available it is estimated that average hourly wages in manufacturing were at about the same level in 1920 as in 1939. Wholesale prices during these years declined 50 per cent

TABLE 13.   Changes in Unit Labor Costs in Ten Industries,
1919–1945[8]

	Per Cent	
	1919–1939	1939–1945
Bituminous coal........................	[a]	+32
Cane sugar refining.....................	−29	+47
Cotton goods...........................	−34	+74
Flour.................................	−25	+60
Petroleum refining......................	−57	+44
Paper and pulp.........................	−38	+53
Lumber and timber products............	−25	+75
Railroads (revenue traffic)..............	[a]	−5
Shoes.................................	−37	+51
Non-ferrous smelting and refining........	−30	+56

[a] No information available.

WAGES AS A MEANS OF LIVELIHOOD

To the employer, wage payments represent cost expenditures; to employees, wages represent the means by which they and their families live. How well they live depends upon how much they receive in wages and how much they must pay for the things they buy, namely, their "real" wages. The level of living thus depends upon the amount of money which the worker takes home in his pay envelope as well as the prices which he must pay for the goods and services he needs and wants. So far as an entire family is concerned, their level of living is also contingent upon the number of wage earners in the family in relation to the number of persons dependent upon their wages.

From a larger point of view, the standard of living is also vitally influenced by the services and facilities provided by the government from general revenues. Free education and health and recreational facilities contribute greatly toward raising the general standard of living as do also improved highways and government-sponsored housing. To illustrate: In many countries "free schooling" virtually stops with elementary education. One can only speculate upon the effects on the standard of living of the average American wage or even salaried worker if he had to spend $500 a

---

[8] *Monthly Labor Review,* July, 1940, p. 34, and December, 1946, p. 916.

year or more for each child he wished to send to high school. On
the other hand, some countries have gone much further than the
United States in programs of medical care and child allowances.[9]

Since the subject of the present discussion is *wages* as a means
of livelihood, government supplements or indirect contributions to
the standard of living will not be mentioned further, except to say
that such public services should be taken into account when comparing wages and standards of living between different countries,
or even between communities within this country.

Meaning of Standard of Living

What, in concrete terms, do we mean by the standard of living
and, more especially, what do we mean by the oft-repeated expression the "American standard of living"? Does it mean that no one
in this country shall starve? In a world where even in peacetime
there is seldom a year in which thousands of people do not die because of lack of food, is it a matter of pride and satisfaction that
we have no mass starvation? As evidence that the fear of starvation is not entirely non-existent even in this country, we have only
to recall the promise "No one shall starve" that was used as a
political slogan in several presidential campaigns during the 'thirties.

Assuming that the American standard of living implies that no
one shall starve, does it mean merely that everyone shall have sufficient "bread" in the literal sense, or does it mean that everyone
shall be able to procure the quantity and variety of food necessary to insure maximum health and vigor? (The most costly foods
for urban industrial workers are not the grain products but milk,
meat, fruit, and vegetables.) Does adequate clothing according to
the American standard of living mean the minimum number of
garments required to clothe the body and protect it from cold, or
does adequate clothing imply psychological satisfactions as well as

---

[9] An example is Australia which, during recent years, has emphasized social
services rather more than wage increases. At present Australia provides old
age and invalid pensions, maternity allowances, unemployment insurance, child
endowments providing graduated weekly grants to families with two or more
children, widows' pensions, funeral benefits, and pharmaceutical benefits.
(Article by P. S. Clarey, President of the Australian Council of Trade Unions,
in *Personnel Journal,* December, 1945.)
See chap. 13 for a discussion of family allowances.

bare physical needs?[10] Does housing mean a "roof over one's head"
even though it is the roof of one of the alley shacks within view of
the nation's Capitol? Does the American standard of living assume
that all our citizens shall have some recreational facilities and access to medical care beyond that provided through charity?

The concept of standard of living means many different things
to different people at different times and places. Even a minimum
standard is not static or uniform for all persons at the same income level. An automobile a generation ago was a luxury for everyone; today it is a necessity for many workers in some parts of the
country, although still a luxury in urban centers like New York
City where public transportation is reasonably adequate for necessary traveling. Theater attendance at one time could have been
considered a luxury, but motion pictures are now considered a
form of entertainment to which everybody is entitled. The dynamic
nature of the concept of the standard of living is aptly described
by an eminent sociologist as follows:

As it develops, the standard of living is not describable in simple and
unqualified terms. Presently comes an idealization of the actual and
customary notion of well-living, an enhancement toward which men
reach out. There is a sort of inkling of what might be, and this is
gradually attached to the standard, or thrust under it, so that it lifts
somewhat. It easily springs up to the limit of what is possible, and is
prone to range beyond. At each stage of societal existence new wants
arise, and the visualized satisfaction of them enters into the standard.
What is seen is a set of prospective adjustments to life-conditions,
called for by needs that have sprung out of present adjustment and
whose entrance has made of the latter, insofar, a maladjustment. What
is wanted is something a little farther ahead on the present road. The
standard becomes thus a moving, a non-static conception; yet at recurrent intervals of comfortable living, and sometimes for long ones, it

---

[10] The author is reminded of a "case" brought before a public relief agency
which was caring for a family while the father was unemployed. It was before
the bare-leg and bobby sox era, when it was customary for all girls on arriving at their teens to wear silk hose. The daughter in this family was "ashamed"
of the cotton hose provided by the agency and refused to attend high school
because she would appear "different" from all her companions. The male
directors of the agency were incensed—"she should be thankful for the cotton
hose"—but the woman social worker, recognizing that silk hose were a psychological necessity for this girl as a social being in her immediate environment,
made arrangements for her to obtain stockings "like all the other girls wore"
from earnings from after-school employment.

appears as what is, rather than as what may be. . . . It is really a sort
of indicator as to the character and destiny of a society. If the standard of living remains steady and traditional, sensitiveness to life-conditions and consequent adaptability are shown to be weak, whereas an
ever more ambitious standard, implying discontent with what is in comparison with what may be, indicates responsiveness to environment
together with some qualities of imagination and foresight. Variability
and adaptability can then be counted upon.[11]

Evaluating Levels of Living

Although ever striving to improve their standard of living, most
wage earners never attain the standard which they seek and want;
their actual level of living represents an adaptation of aspirations
to economic necessity. An individual's or a group of individuals'
"plane" or "level" of living refers to the goods and services which
can be bought with the money earned, rather than the standard of
living actually desired. The level of living, of course, approaches
the standard of living as income permits buying more and more of
the things needed and desired.

The dual implications of "standard" and "level" of living present some difficulties when one wishes to estimate the cost of living
for any particular group of wage earners, for in order to determine costs it is first necessary to know what goods and services
are included in the standard budget. The concrete determination
of the budgetary content at various levels of living can be made in
either of two ways: (1) Hypothetical budgets can be established
to include the goods and services which are believed to meet the
various standards of adequacy. (2) The actual expenditures of
families within different income levels can be described to represent various levels of living. Obviously the latter represents the
existing "content" of living to a greater extent than the former,
which is influenced by what is desirable as well as what is attainable.

A number of attempts have been made to define various levels of
living and in some instances these definitions have been translated
into concrete budgets or itemized bills of goods and services. Some
deal only with budgets which hover around mere subsistence levels

---

[11] W. G. Sumner and A. G. Keller, in Thomas D. Eliot (ed.), *American
Standards and Planes of Living,* Ginn Company, Boston, 1931, pp. 43–44.

of living; others describe budgets which include many comforts and some luxuries. Only a few of these budgets have been priced to estimate total costs.

One of the earliest classifications defined two levels of "decent livelihood"; the lower provided "an unvarying standard that is applicable to all conditions of human existence," and the upper provided the "conventional standard of the community." The former "takes no account of needs based on custom or on any subjective appreciation of the requisites of welfare, nor does it make any allowance for the possibilities of progress. It is measured solely by man's essential and universal needs, and describes in general terms the requisites of normal and reasonable human life. The latter is somewhat more liberal."[12]

Another classification lists four different levels, all applicable to wage earners but covering the better-paid as well as the lowest-income group: (1) The poverty level, which requires supplemental charity to maintain even the barest existence; (2) the minimum of subsistence, which provides for the barest physical existence without outside aid but provides for no social needs; (3) minimum health and decency, which includes meager provision for education, amusement, and insurance; and (4) minimum of comfort standard.[13]

None of the above was ever translated into concrete lists of itemized goods and services, the costs of which could be determined from time to time on the basis of current prices. The first comprehensive attempts at estimating the cost of maintaining an adequate family living were made during and immediately after World War I for the settlement of wage controversies. In 1918 the National War Labor Board prepared and priced two family budgets —a "minimum of subsistence" budget for a family of five costing $1386, and a "minimum comfort" budget costing $1760. A few years later the Bureau of Labor Statistics prepared a list of items providing a "minimum quantity budget necessary to maintain a worker's family of five in health and decency," for which the average cost for ten large cities in 1922 was $2282. This budget in-

---

[12] J. A. Ryan, *A Living Wage* (1906), summarized in Eliot, *American Standards and Planes of Living,* p. 60.

[13] Paul H. Douglas, *Wages and the Family,* University of Chicago Press, Chicago, 1925, pp. 41–43.

cluded no automobile, radio, or beauty-parlor services which were
rare luxuries at that time.

The Heller Committee[14] has prepared standard budgets based
on actual expenditures of families living in San Francisco. The
one most frequently cited, which is priced at frequent intervals, is
the "comfort" budget adapted from the average expenditures of
five-person families of skilled wage earners. This budget provides
for "adequate food at low cost," a five-room home or apartment
in a "working-class neighborhood," the maintenance of a radio
and a secondhand automobile, and a small life insurance policy.

The Works Progress Administration formulated and priced
two standards of living—the "maintenance budget," which in 1935
for a four-person manual worker's family cost $1261, and the
"emergency budget," which cost about 72 per cent as much. The
maintenance level is described as representing "normal or average
minimum requirements with some consideration to psychological
values. It is not so liberal as that for a health and decency level
which the skilled worker may hope to obtain but it affords more
than a minimum of subsistence living. The emergency level provides for material wants almost exclusively, allows for cheaper
kinds of foods and less desirable housing than the maintenance
budget, and might be questioned on the grounds of health hazards
if the family had to live at this level for a considerable period of
time."[15]

For a number of years the Bureau of Labor Statistics used the
W.P.A. maintenance budget to price intercity differences in cost
of living, but this was discontinued in 1943 because it was felt that
the budget no longer reflected the buying habits of wage earners.
At present there is no official "standard budget" and consequently
no estimates by any federal agency[16] on the actual cost of living
for any group of wage earners. However, the Bureau of Labor
Statistics has in preparation (1946) a list of items and quantities
making up a budget for a city worker's family composed of four

---

[14] Heller Committee for Research in Social Economics, *Cost of Living
Studies,* University of California Press, Berkeley.

[15] Works Progress Administration, *Intercity Difference in Cost of Living in
March, 1935, 59 Cities,* Research Monograph XII, p. xiii.

[16] Certain state and local governments make estimates of the cost of living
for women workers from time to time in order to determine rates under their
minimum wage laws. See chap. 14.

members—an employed father, a mother not employed, a son in high school, and a daughter in grade school. This budget is not a "luxury" or a "subsistence" budget but is designed to represent the goods and services required to maintain this size of family at a minimum level of "adequate" living. It is intended that similar budgets will be developed for families of other sizes and composition. These city worker families' budgets will be priced at regular intervals in order to find out the trends in cost of living as well as relative differences in living costs between cities.

The point at which income is sufficient to cover expenditures, on the average, provides one useful measure of the income required for living essentials. In 1944 the Bureau of Labor Statistics made a survey of family incomes and expenditures in a cross section of all city consumers and found that (at 1944 prices) it took an annual income of $2070 for the typical city family to "break even." Such families, averaging three persons in size, lived very modestly, spending an average of barely 22 cents per meal per person and $30 per month for housing, fuel, light, and refrigeration. Clothing expenditures for the entire family amounted to $250 during the year, and medical care took $105. It paid $119 during the year in income, poll, and personal property taxes. With this income of $2070 a family was able to make small gifts and contributions amounting to $73 during the year, but nothing was left for life insurance premiums or savings.[17]

The National Consumers' Price Index

The Bureau of Labor Statistics' consumers' price index (more commonly referred to as the cost of living index) shows the trend of prices of the goods and services purchased by city families of moderate income. It indicates how much more or less it costs in any year (or month) compared to any other year (or month) to buy a bill of goods and services typically purchased by a family which in 1934–1936 had an income of about $30 a week. It is a *national* average, combining city indexes for 34 large cities for all goods and services, and food prices for additional cities.

[17] The average family with an income of $2070 did pay social security taxes and many paid on life insurance and bought war bonds; to do so, however, debts were incurred or previous savings were drawn upon. See Dorothy S. Brady, "Expenditures and Savings of City Families in 1944," *Monthly Labor Review,* January, 1946, p. 1.

TABLE 14. Trend in Consumers' Prices, 1913–1946[18]
(Index Numbers 1935–1939 = 100)

1913	70.7	1929	122.5	1944	125.5
1914	71.8	1930	119.4	1945	128.4
1915	72.5	1931	108.7	1946	
1916	77.9	1932	97.6	Jan. 15	129.9
1917	91.6	1933	92.4	Feb. "	129.6
1918	107.5	1934	95.7	Mar. "	130.2
1919	123.8	1935	98.1	Apr. "	131.1
1920	143.3	1936	99.1	May "	131.7
1921	127.7	1937	102.7	June "	133.3
1922	119.7	1938	100.8	July "	141.2
1923	121.9	1939	99.4	Aug. "	144.1
1924	122.2	1940	100.2	Sept. "	145.9
1925	125.4	1941	105.2	Oct. "	148.4
1926	126.4	1942	116.5	Nov. "	152.2
1927	124.0	1943	123.6	Dec. "	153.3
1928	122.6				

The index covers prices for all important essentials in the family budget—food, clothing, house furnishings, rent, utilities, fuel, and a variety of miscellaneous goods and principal services, such as medical care, laundry, and shoe repair. The selection of articles to be priced was made on the basis of an extensive study of the actual expenditures of over 14,000 wage-earners' and clerical workers' families conducted by the Bureau in 1934–1936. Since it obviously is impossible to price everything consumers buy, a representative list was selected which includes all essentials commonly bought by city workers' families. The list of goods now priced for the index includes approximately 200 articles and essential services which they use. For many goods a number of different grades and qualities are priced.

Because there are constant changes in the nature and quality of the goods available in the market, these changes frequently necessitate the substitution of one article for another in the list of goods which are priced for the index. This is particularly important in the case of clothing. The Bureau follows the practice of carrying a particular article on its list as long as it is commonly sold. When a change occurs in consumption habits and this article is no longer

[18] Official Index of Bureau of Labor Statistics. Prices are for moderate-income families in large cities. The index only partially shows the wartime effects of changes in quality, availability of consumer goods, etc.

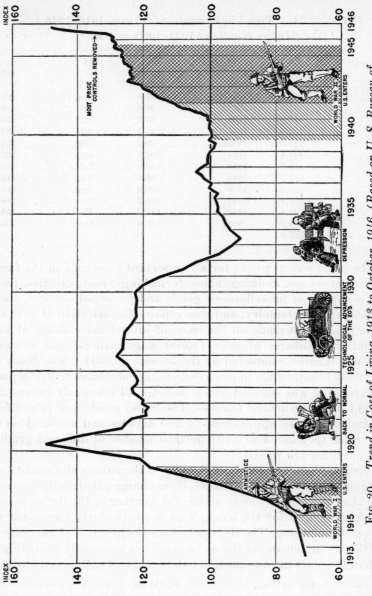

FIG. 20. *Trend in Cost of Living, 1913 to October, 1946. (Based on U. S. Bureau of Labor Statistics consumers' price index for moderate-income families in large cities.)*

representative of current wage-earner purchases, another article is substituted, of approximately the same grade, that serves the same purpose. When new models of automobiles, radios, refrigerators, vacuum cleaners, and washing machines are introduced, the practice is to use the price of the largest selling lines of the current model. Taxes paid by wage earners on their incomes have not been taken into account, and social security taxes are treated as savings and omitted from the index. Retail sales taxes, however, and automobile and other consumption taxes are specifically included, and property taxes are implicitly included in rental costs.

In order to give a true picture of price changes as they affect the cost of living, account must be taken of the relative importance of each item in the total family budget. In making its index, the Bureau determined the importance of each article priced city by city on the basis of actual reports collected in the 1934–1936 survey of expenditures. Because of differences from one city to another in climate, in the economic level of wage earners, in prices and consumer preferences, the manner in which families apportion their expenditures among different items differs considerably.

The differences in the proportions spent for food are largely due to differences in income. For example, New Orleans families with a low average income in 1934–1936 made almost 40 per cent of their total expenditures for food, whereas families in Washington, D. C., with a comparatively high level of income, spent less than 30 per cent. In New York, however, where the average money income is relatively high, food prices were high enough to bring the proportion of the total spent for food to slightly more than 36 per cent. In cities in which rental costs are high relative to the cost of other items, and in which a large proportion of the rents include heat as well as shelter, rent tends to claim a higher-than-average portion of the total expenditure. Thus in Washington, D. C., New York, Boston, and Chicago, rental costs comprised about 20 per cent of total expenditures, in contrast to 13 and 14 per cent in cities like Manchester (New Hampshire), Portland (Oregon), Mobile (Alabama), and Indianapolis.

In warm climates the reduction in fuel requirements more than balances the increased need for refrigeration. Thus, higher percentages of total expenditures went for fuel and electricity in Manchester (New Hampshire) and Portland (Maine) where win-ters are long and cold, than in Los Angeles where the climate eliminates any necessity of central heating. Fuel expenditures are also affected by the number of apartment houses in which fuel is included in the rent. Apartment dwelling also affects the proportion of the total expenditures which is spent for household furnishings. The apartment, with its restricted living space, offers little opportunity for the acquisition of items like washing machines, and frequently eliminates the necessity of purchasing such items as refrigerators and stoves. Expenditures for the purchase and operation of automobiles are influenced by the general community situation as well as by the amount of income. In large eastern cities, especially New York, where automobile ownership is more expensive and more easily dispensed with, a lower proportion of total wage-earner expenditures is used for cars than in cities in the Middle West or on the Pacific coast.

The relative importance of the various groups of items used in computing the national consumers' price index in the base period is shown in the accompanying tabulation.

Average Per Cent Expenditures
1935–1939

Food	35.4
Clothing	11.0
Rent	18.8
Fuel, electricity, and ice	6.7
House furnishings	4.4
Miscellaneous	23.7
All goods and services	100.0

City Consumers' Price Indexes

In addition to the national index, the Bureau issues separate consumers' price indexes for the 34 large cities[19] included in the national index, which covers 72 per cent of the population of American cities. These indexes are not constructed to show intercity differences at a given time, but rather the measure of changes which occur within a specified city from one time to another. The index of 100 in the base period, therefore, represents a different total in each city; the fact that an index for one city is higher than that of another does not mean that the total spent for living

---

[19] The cities are those listed in Table 15, with the addition of Mobile, Alabama.

is greater in this city than in the other but rather that prices since 1935–39 have gone up more.

Intercity Indexes

In 1945 the Bureau of Labor Statistics began to issue an intercity index which measures the average differences in retail prices of the same items in 33 large cities at a given period of time. This intercity index, in contrast to the consumers' price index referred

TABLE 15. Relative Differences in the Cost of Equivalent Goods, Rents, and Services in 33 Large Cities, March, 1945[20]

Washington, D. C., = 100

Atlanta	93	Milwaukee	97
Baltimore	93	Minneapolis	94
Birmingham	92	New Orleans	91
Boston	96	New York	102
Buffalo	92	Norfolk	93
Chicago	98	Philadelphia	94
Cincinnati	93	Pittsburgh	97
Cleveland	95	Portland, Me.	97
Denver	93	Portland, Ore.	97
Detroit	97	Richmond	95
Houston	88	St. Louis	95
Indianapolis	92	San Francisco	100
Jacksonville	93	Savannah	92
Kansas City	91	Scranton	90
Los Angeles	94	Seattle	103
Manchester	93	Washington, D. C.	100
Memphis	93		

to above, is designed to show how much more or less would be required in one city than in another to purchase the consumption items included in a typical budget for a city family. It measures the effect of two factors of variation in costs among cities: first and more important, the level of prices and rents; second, variations in requirements imposed by differences in climate. For instance, the importance of fuel in the index varies from city to city in relation to the length and severity of the cold season. The relative importance of heavy clothing is determined on a similar basis.

[20] Mimeographed release, Bureau of Labor Statistics, June 1, 1946.

The intercity indexes relate to differences in the cost of one given level of living. In March, 1945, as indicated in Table 15, the differences between the cities covered in this intercity index ranged from 88 to 103 per cent, Washington, D. C., being taken as 100. Thus, between the highest-priced and the lowest-priced cities, the range of differences in living costs due to price differences and the influence of climate on clothing and housing requirements amounted to about 15 per cent.

WAGES AS PURCHASING POWER[21]

Wage earners and their families form a large and important segment of the market for consumer goods and services. Wages therefore provide the ultimate means by which most of the goods produced are taken off the market. It is not only the amount of the aggregate wages which affects purchasing power, but also the general levels of wages received by the various groups of workers. With the same total national pay roll, the pattern of purchasing would be radically different if half the workers were employed at relatively high wages while the other half were only partially employed or were earning extremely low wages. Thus, the volume and kinds of goods and services purchased are affected by both the numbers and the proportions of families at various levels of income.

Changing Pattern of Purchases by Workers' Families

In a consideration of wages as purchasing power, it is necessary to know how families of various incomes spend their money and how general purchases would be affected by changes in levels of wages. Families with an income of $4000 have about twice the purchasing power of families with an income of $2000 living in the same community at the same time. Families with an income of

---

[21] The author is indebted to Dorothy S. Brady, Chief of the Bureau of Labor Statistics' Cost of Living Division, for most of the data in this section. The source materials used for the various periods are: *Cost of Living and Retail Prices of Food,* Eighteenth Annual Report of the Commissioner of Labor, 1903; Bureau of Labor Statistics, *Cost of Living in the U. S.* (Bulletin No. 357), *Money Disbursements of Wage Earners and Clerical Workers, 1934–36* (Bulletin No. 638, summary volume), and *Expenditures and Savings of City Families in 1944,* Serial No. R. 1818.

$4000 actually do spend nearly twice as much for goods and serv-ices as families with an income of $2000. They purchase more goods and services of better quality; nearly twice as many auto-mobiles, vacuum cleaners, and oranges; 50 to 70 per cent more meat, more men's suits, and more women's coats and dresses; 40 per cent more butter, and 30 per cent more washing machines.

The best-known generalization about family expenditures is called Engels' Law, and was enunciated by an engineer, Friedrich Engels, on the basis of studies of Belgian workingmen's families in the 1890's. The theory states that "the proportion of outgo used for food, other things being equal, is the best measure of the level of living of the population," and further that "the poorer an indi-vidual, a family or a people, the greater must be the percentage of the income necessary for the maintenance of physical sustenance, and again of this a greater portion must be allowed for food." Studies of workers' expenditures in our own and other countries confirm Engels' Law, that the percentage of income spent on food tends to vary inversely with the level of income, although the actual food expenditures of higher-income families are more than those of low-income families.

This generalization on the proportion of income spent for food has been extended by other investigators to the kinds of foods purchased. The diets of poorer families include a larger propor-tion of cereal foods and vegetables and proportionately less meat, dairy products, and fruits than the diets of the well-to-do. An estimate of the effect of four levels of diets on the annual per capita purchases of various foods is indicated in Table 16.

Studies made in 1917–1919 and 1934–1936, and again in 1944, reveal some interesting information on the changing character of purchases by wage-earners' families in this country. Prices were about 5 per cent lower in the second than in the first period sur-veyed, and the average income of $1524 for city workers' families was slightly higher.

In 1934–1936 families were spending considerably more for food than would have been required to buy the foods purchased twenty years previously; their diet was much nearer nutritional stand-ards, with a considerably greater consumption of milk, oranges, lettuce, and other vegetables. The worker's family spent less on clothing in 1934–1936 than would have been required to buy the

TABLE 16.   Approximate per Capita Yearly Quantities of Various Foods for Four Diet Levels[22]

Item		Restricted Diet for Emergency Use	Adequate Diet at Minimum Cost	Adequate Diet at Moderate Cost	Liberal Diet
Flour, cereals................	pounds	240	224	160	100
Milk or its equivalent..........	quarts	155	260	305	305
Potatoes, sweet potatoes........	pounds	165	165	165	155
Dried beans, peas, nuts.........	do	30	30	20	7
Tomatoes, citrus fruit..........	do	50	50	90	110
Leafy, green, and yellow vegetables.....................	do	40	80	100	135
Dried fruits...................	do	10	20	25	20
Other vegetables, fruits.........	do	40	85	210	325
Fats (including butter, oils, bacon, salt pork).............	do	45	49	52	52
Sugars.......................	do	50	43	60	60
Lean meat, poultry, fish........	do	30	60	100	165
Eggs........................	dozen	8	15	15	30

equivalent of that purchased in 1917–1919. This was probably due to the introduction of centrally heated dwellings, which reduced the necessity for warm clothing, as well as to the desire to have automobiles and radios rather than new clothes. Relatively few families had automobiles in 1917–1919, whereas 50 per cent of the families had them in 1934–1936. Radios were unknown in the earlier period, but more than three-fourths of the employed wage-earners' families in 1934–1936 owned radios. Nine-tenths of the families who rented houses had bathrooms in 1934–1936, compared with slightly over one-half in 1917–1919. More movies, permanent waves, silk stockings, and many other items had been added to the family spending during this twenty-year period.

---

[22] The figures in this table are computed from diets adapted to the needs of individuals in different age, sex, and activity groups and from the number of persons in each group as shown by the 1930 census of population. The quantities are those which should be delivered to the family kitchen. To convert them into production figures, suitable margins must be added to the different food groups to cover the unavoidable losses in harvesting, grading, storage, manufacture, and distribution. (Hazel K. Stiebeling and Medora M. Ward, *Diets at Four Levels of Nutritive Content and Cost*, U. S. Department of Agriculture, Circular No. 296, Washington, 1933.)

In 1944 the average income (after taxes) of families of wage earners and clerical workers in large cities was $3113. The average size of these families was 3.46 persons, compared to 3.6 in 1934–1936. Although their incomes were considerably higher during the war period, it was not possible for workers' families to buy automobiles and other durable consumer goods. There was, however, an expansion of consumption of both food and clothing, as is indicated in Table 17. On the basis of the same price levels, families in 1944 spent almost 85 per cent more for clothing and 36 per cent more for food than they did ten years previously. Their miscellaneous expenditures, which included recreation among other items, were 53 per cent greater. Significantly, the average wage-earner family in 1944 was able to lay aside more than $400 for gifts, contributions, and savings (not shown as an expenditure in the table), whereas in 1934–1936 the net difference between expenditures and income was only $12 a year.

TABLE 17.   Wage-Earner Family Expenditures in 1944 Compared to 1934–1936[23]

	Expenditures in 1934–1936	Expenditures in 1944		
		Actual	At 1934–1936 Prices	Per Cent More at 1934–1936 Prices
Food.......................	$508	$966	$689	35.6
Housing, fuel, and light........	367	434	384	4.6
Clothing....................	160	425	295	84.4
Furnishings.................	60	81	56	−6.6
Miscellaneous...............	410	779	629	53.4

Purchases at Different Income Levels

The above indicate some of the changes in the expenditures of wage-earners' families as their average level of income has changed over a period of years. Purchasing potentialities are also indicated by the spending patterns, at any given time, of families with different incomes.

In 1944, families consisting of four persons who had an average

[23] Based on unpublished material of the Bureau of Labor Statistics.

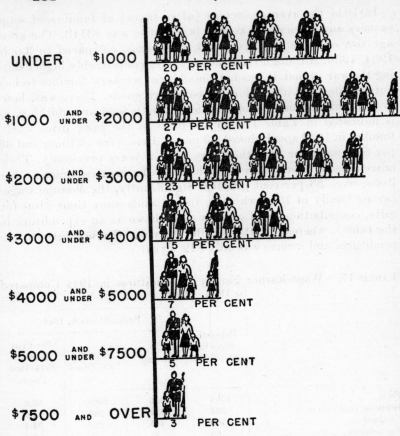

UNDER $1000   20 PER CENT

$1000 AND UNDER $2000   27 PER CENT

$2000 AND UNDER $3000   23 PER CENT

$3000 AND UNDER $4000   15 PER CENT

$4000 AND UNDER $5000   7 PER CENT

$5000 AND UNDER $7500   5 PER CENT

$7500 AND OVER   3 PER CENT

FIG. 21. *Distribution of Families According to 1945 Family Income Before Taxes.* (*Source*: Federal Reserve Bulletin, *July, 1946.*)

annual income of approximately $5000 spent almost 50 per cent more for food, twice as much for clothing, almost three times as much for recreation, and about 70 per cent more for housing, than families of equal size with an average income of $1800. However, the food budget of the $5000-income families amounted to only 22 per cent of their total expenditures, in contrast to 40 per cent for the lower-income families. These are comparisons of expenditures of families of the same size. In Table 18 are shown the average expenditures, by income level, for all city families consisting of two or more persons.

TABLE 18. Expenditures of City Families of Two or More Persons at Different Income Levels in 1944[24]

Money income	$1275	$1865	$2069	$2439	$3027	$3882	$4967
Food[a]	555	701	733	797	913	1043	1150
Clothing	163	234	250	283	364	462	623
Housing[b]	403	473	499	546	628	723	845
Automobile and transportation	55	86	98	119	156	182	261
Medical care	94	105	105	104	123	149	190
Miscellaneous[c]	137	189	192	202	226	279	370
Personal taxes[d]	32	86	119	180	270	402	559
Gifts and contributions	47	66	73	86	119	119	203
Net savings[e] or deficits	−211	−75	0	122	228	523	766
Average number of persons	2.78	3.03	3.05	3.10	3.13	3.69	4.01
Average number of earners	1.15	1.22	1.24	1.27	1.31	1.57	1.97

[a] Includes alcoholic beverages.
[b] Includes rents, or current operation expenses of home owners (principal payment on mortgages excluded), fuel, light, refrigeration, household operation, furnishings, and equipment.
[c] Includes personal care, recreation, tobacco, reading and formal education, and other expenses.
[d] Includes income, poll, and personal property taxes.
[e] Includes life and annuity insurance premiums, and social security taxes.

To the extent that incomes increase more than prices, workers' families achieve a better plane of living. Likewise, total purchasing power expands as increased numbers of families receive larger incomes; purchases of many kinds of commodities and services are dependent upon the incomes that are above the amount necessary to purchase the bare necessities for living. The purchases made on the $5000 annual income cited above do not refer to the mass of wage-earners' families, as few of them have incomes of that amount. In 1944, when family incomes had reached their highest level in history, fewer than one-fourth of all the families in the country received incomes of $5000 or more, and over one-fifth received less than $2000 during the year.

In 1945, according to a survey of the nation's potential buying

[24] Adapted from *Monthly Labor Review,* January, 1946, p. 4. Based on Bureau of Labor Statistics survey of a cross section of all city families of two or more persons. Lowest and highest income levels not shown in above.

power,[25] the 20 per cent of the families in the higher brackets received almost one-half of the total income for that year and held over three-fourths of the total liquid assets. In contrast, 22 per cent of the total income was spread among one-half of the families who had practically no liquid assets for future spending. During this year of war "prosperity," 17 per cent of the families in the country went into debt, 13 per cent met their current expenses but saved nothing, and 20 per cent saved small amounts which, in the aggregate, amounted to 3 per cent of all personal savings during the year.

Family Income and Individual Earnings

The above discussion of wages and purchasing power is concerned with family incomes rather than individual earnings. The amount of the family income is affected not only by the earnings of the principal wage earner, but also by the number of earners in the family. Many families are able to have automobiles and other comforts and luxuries because of the presence of more than one earner in the household. In 1944, when the great demand for war production made jobs easy to find, it was common for several members of a family to work; and this accounts, in part, for the fact that the average wage-earner family income was higher that year than in previous years. There were two or more earners in 28 per cent of the families with incomes of $2500–3000, in half of the families with incomes of $3000–4000, and in two-thirds of those with incomes of $4000 or more for the year.

This raises the question whether or not, in a consideration of wage rates and the cost of living, it should be assumed that an adult's wages should be sufficient to cover all the family's expenses. If family purchases of bare necessities, as well as luxuries, are contingent upon a second or third earner in the family, this obviously has general economic as well as social implications.

---

[25] Federal Reserve Bulletin, *A National Survey of Liquid Assets*, Federal Reserve System, Washington, June, 1946. The "family" or "spending unit" used in this survey is defined as "all persons living in the same dwelling and belonging to the same family who *pool their income* to meet their major expenses."

SELECTED REFERENCES

WAGES AS COST OF PRODUCTION

Alderfer, E. B., and Michl, H. E., *Economics of American Industry,* McGraw-Hill Book Company, New York, 1942.

Bell, Spurgeon, *Productivity, Wages and National Income,* Brookings Institution, 1940.

National Industrial Conference Board, *Costs and Profits in American Industry 1914–33,* New York, 1935.

Temporary National Economic Committee, *Industrial Wage Rates, Labor Costs and Price Policies,* Monograph No. 5, Washington, 1940.

WAGES AND CONSUMPTION

Douglas, Paul H., *Wages and the Family,* University of Chicago Press, Chicago, 1925.

Eliot, Thomas D. (ed.), *American Standards and Planes of Living,* Ginn & Company, Boston, 1931.

Heller Committee for Research in Social Economics, *Cost of Living Studies,* University of California Press, Berkeley.

McMahon, Theresa S., *Social and Economic Standards of Living,* D. C. Heath & Company, Boston, 1925.

National Resources Committee, *Consumer Expenditures in the U. S.,* Government Printing Office, Washington, 1939.

Office of Economic Stabilization, *Report of the President's Committee on the Cost of Living,* Government Printing Office, Washington, 1945.

Stecker, Margaret L., *Intercity Differences in Cost of Living,* Works Progress Administration, Washington, 1937.

Stiebeling, Hazel K., and Ward, Medora M., *Diets at Four Levels of Nutritive Content and Cost,* U. S. Department of Agriculture, Circular No. 296, Washington, 1933.

U. S. Bureau of Labor Statistics, *Studies of Consumer Purchases in 1935–6,* Bulletin No. 638, Government Printing Office, Washington, 1941.

Williams, Faith, and Zimmerman, Carle C., *Studies of Family Living in the U. S. and Other Countries,* U. S. Department of Agriculture, Miscellaneous Publication No. 223, Washington, 1935.

11

WAGE STRUCTURE

GENERAL PRINCIPLES AND THEORIES REGARDING THE BASIS FOR wage determination seem very remote to the student who is dickering for a part-time job at the corner drugstore to help pay his college expenses, to the worker who depends upon his union to bargain the highest wage it can for him, to the woman who is pondering whether or not to employ a maid so that she may return to the job she had before her marriage, to the employer who is figuring his labor costs and his next weekly pay roll. Yet, remote as it may seem, the amount of wages received or paid by each of these persons represents the confluence of many interrelated impersonal factors, as well as the deliberate decisions of individuals and organized groups of people.

The wage rates prevailing at any given time or place are the result of a complex of forces stemming from past as well as current influences. Fundamentally, the general economic situation and the competitive position of the individual industry and employer concerned are the ultimate determinants of the upper limits of wage levels; but custom and social policy, organized and individual bargaining strength, and other factors all affect the wages which are paid under any given circumstances. Although there are dominant factors which influence the general movement of wages over a period of time, there is no one logical explanation to account for any of the different rates paid in the myriad of jobs throughout industry. Indeed, the most outstanding characteristic of the existing wage rate structure is the absence of any consistent pattern which can be explained on any logical basis or within the scope of any one general principle.

Preceding chapters have discussed the various theories which attempt to explain what proportion of the total income of business goes to labor in the form of wages, and what proportion goes to the other factors involved in production; also what any given amount of wages means in terms of cost of production and standard of living. They discussed wages as lump sums of money, the total amounts paid to and received by labor. This chapter will deal with specific wage rates, what factors determine the rates received by particular groups of workers and how these various rates compare with one another.

FACTORS AFFECTING SPECIFIC RATES

The existing wage structure throughout all industry represents a composite of thousands of job rates, some of which have been established through formal collective bargaining, some by arbitration and legislation, some by "scientific" job evaluation, and many through informal agreement between individual employers and workers. When each of these rates was established, whether through formal procedure or otherwise, a number of factors entered into its determination, although not all were discussed or given conscious consideration by the parties making the determination. Consciously or unconsciously, new rates are established on a basis of comparison with other rates already in existence, and seldom are all the factors which influenced the existing rates considered or even known when new rates are being determined.

Every rate has its roots in past experience, although changes are constantly being made in response to new conditions and influences. Productivity and social policy are fundamental factors which underlie the *general* wage structure at any time, and these are discussed in detail in other chapters. Some of the more important criteria which enter into *specific* rate determinations are:

Internal Job Factors
1. Training and skill requirements of the job.
2. Custom.
3. Responsibility and authority attached to the job.
4. Opportunities for advancement.
5. Regularity of employment.
6. Unpleasant or hazardous nature of the job.
7. Perquisites.

External Factors
   8. Employer's financial condition.
   9. Prevailing wage for similar work.
   10. Cost of living.
   11. The labor market.
   12. Potential substitutes for labor.
   13. Elasticity or inelasticity of the demand for the product.
   14. Strength of union organization.

Half of the above, it will be noticed, have to do with influences and situations not inherently a part of the job itself, while the others are related to the characteristics and conditions of the job. Although no one criterion stands alone as the sole determinant of any rate, not all of them are taken into consideration in every wage settlement, and the emphasis and weight attached to each varies according to circumstances. This is necessarily true because wages, by their very nature, represent expedient agreements between the buyers and sellers of labor, each of whom is thinking in terms of his own interests and his present and future welfare. There can be no definitive answer regarding the emphasis which should or can be assigned the various criteria that enter into day-to-day wage determinations; we can merely discuss some of the aspects and problems connected with each, and some of the arguments of the parties who are most directly concerned.

Training and Skill Required

Occupational rate differences may stem from the relative scarcity or abundance of qualified workers to perform specific tasks. The reasons and justification for such differences, however, go much further than the numerical relationship of men to jobs. The higher rates paid for skilled work represent both a reward and an incentive. They are a reward for the time and effort spent in learning the trade and an inducement to perform the more difficult tasks.

Regardless of differences of opinion between the payers and the receivers of wages with respect to minimum wage levels, employers themselves realize the importance of wage differentials as incentives to make persons willing to learn and to perform skilled operations. The initial policy of communist Russia was based on the idealistic principle "From each according to his ability, to each according to his need"; but the Soviet government, as an employer, soon learned that it was necessary to relate wages to skill and performance—that *above* minimum wages must be paid to obtain an *above* minimum work effort.

To accept the principle of wage differentials according to training and skill requirements does not provide the answer as to how much these differences shall be in a given wage dispute; neither does it preclude the possibility that some of the existing differences between occupational rates are due, in part at least, to other factors such as the bargaining strength of the particular group of workers concerned, or merely to custom. During recent years the policy of some of the industrial unions has tended to reduce the spread between the rates of skilled and unskilled workers. Minimum wage legislation and the dilution of skilled handicrafts as a result of mechanization have also caused a narrowing in occupational rate differences.

Custom

At first glance, customary and prevailing wages may appear to be synonymous, but there is a distinction. "Prevailing" applies to what predominantly obtains, regardless of its origins or causes, whereas "custom" refers more to the state of mind or habitual attitude which determines what *shall* prevail. Prevailing wages are the result of overt action as well as custom or tradition. For example, the prevailing wages of women are in general lower than those of men, largely because it has been customary to think that they should be. Some but not all of this difference would disappear if the principle of equal pay for equal work were actually put into effect. This does not mean that the *average* wages of women would necessarily equal those of men, because a larger proportion of women may be doing unskilled work. But there is no doubt that the prevailing wages on many so-called "women's jobs" would be higher if they were based solely on skill and other objective factors. Another illustration of the influence of "custom" is the relatively lower wages which are paid in the southern sections of our country. Many of the North-South differences are not justified on the basis of productivity, cost of living, or any other objective factors, as is indicated later, but represent holdover attitudes and practices of a rural, slave economy.

Responsibility and Authority Attached to the Job

Closely akin, but somewhat distinct from skill requirements, is the factor of responsibility attached to the particular job. A "responsible" job may be so rated because of the costs involved if mistakes or errors in judgment are made, or because it involves the supervision or checking of the work of others. Higher wages may be paid on a job which entails the possibility of damaging very expensive machines or materials, even though it requires no greater skill than other jobs where the cost risks are not as great. Higher wages for supervisory jobs are justified for both pecuniary and psychological reasons. They give prestige to the job and offer an inducement to persons who are willing and able to undertake the onerous task of being responsible for the work of others.

Opportunities for Advancement

Wages for particular jobs may be relatively low because these jobs are stepping stones to higher jobs and the time spent on them is considered in the nature of an apprenticeship. Thus, bank messenger jobs may pay less than custodial work although they require considerably more intelligence and a greater sense of responsibility; the messengers, however, do not expect to stay on these jobs indefinitely and hence accept them because they offer opportunities for advancement. Similarly, the wages of helpers and apprentices to journeymen craftsmen may be less than those of common laborers although the skill requirements of the former are much higher.

Regularity of Employment

With some important exceptions, the hourly wage rates for casual and seasonal jobs tend to be higher than those paid for comparable jobs which provide regular employment. An outstanding example is the building-trades rates for outside construction workers compared to those paid inside maintenance workers employed on a year-round basis. A portion of the hourly wages received by carpenters, plumbers, and so forth, engaged in home and other building construction is in the nature of unemployment pay, representing partial compensation for the time lost between jobs and because of inclement weather. Important exceptions to this tendency are the wages of migratory agricultural workers where a surplus of unorganized labor has made it impossible for them to command higher wages, and those paid on seasonal jobs where women are employed who do not want year-round employment— for example, in retail trade where housewives are employed during the Christmas and other busy seasons.

Unpleasant or Hazardous Nature of the Job

Jobs which are especially hazardous or unpleasant, or require unusual strength and endurance, commonly but not always pay higher rates than work of comparable skill under more favorable working conditions. Comparatively high wages are paid sand hogs who work under air pressure sinking caissons for under-water tunnels; "penalty" rates are paid longshoremen for handling explosives and acids which give off unpleasant or dangerous fumes; the rates of steeple-jack painters and those who operate spray guns are usually higher than those paid ordinary brush painters. Here again, other factors may have more influence than that of job hazard. One of the most hazardous types of employment, according to statistical evidence, is coal mining, and to many persons such underground work would seem one of the most unpleasant types of employment. But the wages of coal miners have been relatively low except during those periods when the union has been sufficiently strong to raise the general wage level.

Perquisites

In some types of employment the presence or absence of perquisites is an important factor in wage determination. The privilege of retail clerks to buy goods at a discount, or railroad men and their families to travel free or at a discount, is a factor which both employers and workers take into consideration. In many service trades, the question of whether or not uniforms are to be furnished and laundered by the employer is frequently an issue. When meals and lodging are furnished, this is usually taken into account in determining the monetary wage rate, although there is always a question of how much to allow for lodging when the nature of the work—for example, that of seamen—requires absence from home and, presumably, the maintenance of the worker's family on shore.

Employer's Financial Condition

A company's ability to pay any proposed amount of wages is a fundamental issue in most wage negotiations. In the long run, a company's ability to pay represents the outside limit beyond which wages cannot go; if an employer's wage bill is higher than he can afford he will eventually go bankrupt or close his business. In any given case of wage negotiations, however, there may be wide differences of opinion as to the company's ability to meet specific wage demands, for the issue is much more than a matter of bookkeeping.

The question of an employer's ability to meet a given wage demand involves the basic principle of how the company's total income should be distributed between those who furnish capital and take business risks and those who furnish labor. It raises the question of how much, if any, of the year's income should be withheld from distribution altogether, and laid aside for future contingencies and expansion. It also raises the question whether economies could be effected in the present operation of the business which would offset the costs of proposed wage increases, namely, the possibilities of improvement in productivity. In actual practice, numbers of wage increases have been agreed upon on the assumption that certain changes in methods of management and production would be introduced which would compensate for the additional wage costs. Involved in a company's ability to pay a specified wage is the relative importance of wage costs to total costs, discussed elsewhere.

In some industries the wage rates are geared to the grade or price of the product manufactured or the services rendered, thus indirectly reflecting the ability of the employer to pay higher or lower scales of wages. In clothing and shoe manufacturing, for example, rates tend to be higher in plants producing more expensive garments and footwear; in hotels and restaurants earnings tend to differ according to the grade of the establishment; in metal mining, in times past, it was common practice to have a sliding scale of wages which fluctuated with the price of copper, lead, silver, or other metal mined. This latter practice has been largely discontinued where unions have grown sufficiently strong to demand a change in policy. Most workers object to the principle of sliding scales for the same reason that they oppose automatic adjustments of wages to cost of living indexes, for when profits increase without price changes the workers do not share in the benefits. Gearing wages to the selling price of the product has the additional disadvantage that the price of any one commodity may be advanced or reduced without reference to the general prosperity, so that a sliding scale of wages in a particular industry may take an opposite direction to wages generally, or to the cost of living.

The question of a company's ability to pay impinges upon other considerations which concern the general public as well as those directly involved in the paying or receiving of wages. Suppose a particular company cannot afford to pay the prevailing wage or even a bare minimum living wage. Should the union jeopardize the general wage level for that industry by allowing this employer to pay less than the prevailing wage? Should the community indirectly subsidize the employer by supplementing his low wages with private charity or public relief for the families of his employees? Suppose these low wages enable this employer to lower his prices and thus give him a competitive advantage over other companies, thereby forcing the latter, in turn, to lower their wages. These are very real problems which many communities, workers, unions, and employers have had to face, especially in declining industries and in small, one-industry towns which offer few or no alternative employment opportunities.

Let us consider the reverse situation. Suppose a particular company is much more prosperous than its competitors because of natural advantages or some other reason, such as having exclusive patent rights to a new process. Should this company pay substantially more than the prevailing wages, thus attracting all the best workers and thereby accentuating the difficulties of the other companies in surviving? If this company happens to be a large corporation approaching quasi-monopoly proportions, is it sound social policy to encourage or allow a disparity of wage rates which would work to the disadvantage of smaller concerns? Or is it better for all concerned, employers and employees, to have more or less uniform wages throughout an industry, which would mean, of course, that the wages of the more prosperous companies were not proportionate to their ability to pay?[1]

Prevailing Wages for Similar Work

One of the most prevalent criteria for determining new wage rates and measuring existing rates is the scale of wages paid for similar kinds of work in other industries and by competitors. During a wage dispute, employers and unions are anxious to prove or disprove the contention that existing wages compare favorably with those paid elsewhere, and the payment of prevailing wages is commonly associated with the concept of "fair" wages. An abritrator is prone to make a favorable award to any group of workers who are seeking to have their wages increased to prevailing levels, although compromises are sometimes made to allow marginal firms who cannot pay these rates to remain in business.

In any particular wage dispute, however, there may be wide differences of opinion whether to use, as a basis for comparison, the wages prevailing within the community or within the industry concerned. This question involves fundamental principles and has important repercussions. If plant A happens to be located in a low-wage area and wages are based on prevailing wages in the community, employer A obviously has an advantage over his competitors located elsewhere and the latter are encouraged to move into low-wage areas. If, on the other hand, wages in plant A are based on those prevailing throughout that particular industry, they will be "out of line" with other wages in the community and will work to the disadvantage of other local employers. If the cost of living is also lower in this community (it does not necessarily follow that the cost of living is lower in communities where wages are comparatively low), the workers in plant A will receive higher "real" wages than other workers in the same industry who are employed in plants located elsewhere.[2]

---

[1] A good illustration of this problem is seen in coal mining, where the condition of the natural resources at the various mines largely determines the relative costs of production. Although many coal companies operate at a profit, the industry as a whole operated at a net loss almost continuously during the 1920's and 1930's. At the same time, operators of low-cost mines pay wages on the basis of what the high-cost mines have to pay.

[2] The National War Labor Board was constantly faced with the problem of community wage levels versus prevailing wages in the industry. The cornerstone of the war stabilization program was the adjustment of all rates

Irrespective of the basis used for determining prevailing wages, it is obvious that if wage adjustments were solely contingent upon their measuring up to prevailing rates, there would never be any rise in existing levels. If there is to be any advancement in the trend of wages in line with industrial and social progress, there must be a breakthrough somewhere; some employers or group of employers must increase wages beyond the prevailing rates. It is at this point that other factors, such as the financial condition of the employer or of the entire industry, are taken into consideration, on the basis of the principle that those who can afford to pay higher rates than those currently in effect should serve as the vanguard of a general rise in wage levels.

Cost of Living

Theoretically, as was discussed in Chapter 9, general wage levels over an extended period of time cannot fall below the cost of family subsistence unless the government adopts the policy of subsidizing low-wage earners through public relief measures. But this does not preclude the theory, or the possibility, that many individual rates cannot fall below the cost of subsistence for either a short period of time or indefinitely. Actually, many "going" minimum rates are below what could reasonably be considered sufficient to provide subsistence living for an average-sized workingman's family. This is true in certain areas and occupations in normal times; it is even more true during business depressions, such as the early 1930's when many rates fell as low as 15 and 20 cents an hour.

The principle that the cost of subsistence should be the basis for determining all minimum rates is not accepted by all employers or by others, such as legislators, who have to do with wage setting. There are also differences of opinion as to what constitutes the basis for measuring subsistence living. Should minimum wages be

---

in accordance with what the Board called the "going rates" or "sound and tested" rates in the community. However, the Board stated that its policy "may cease to be appropriate when labor is transferred to the peacetime production of goods whose prices will be again subject to competitive conditions, usually in a national market. Under such circumstances wage rate relationships between competitors within an industry may be even more important than wage rates paid in other industries in the local labor market." (National War Labor Board letter to the President, February, 1945.)

determined on the cost of maintaining a family or only the wage earner? This is a moot question, especially with respect to legal and other wage determinations for women workers discussed in a later chapter. Should a subsistence wage include provision for minimum day-to-day living and assume that private charity or public assistance will provide for medical care and other irregular but inevitable contingencies? Should it be assumed that the cost of living is to be the basis for determining minimum wages for able-bodied workers of at least average intelligence, and that less than subsistence wages are appropriate for submarginal workers who should look to charity or the government to supplement their earnings?

The above pose some of the problems with respect to *minimum* wages, but there is also the question of the relationship of the general level of wages to *changes* in the cost of living. Should all wage rates, minimum and above minimum, be raised when there is a rise in consumer prices and be lowered when prices decline? Although organized labor during periods of rising prices has stressed the importance of the cost of living in negotiating wage changes, workers and their unions have always opposed the principle of gearing the level of wages to the cost of living alone. The reason is obvious, for any automatic plan of tying wages to price changes would have the effect of depriving workers of what they consider their share of the benefits of expanding business and increased labor productivity. It would freeze standards of living at present levels, regardless of their adequacy or of what an employer can afford to pay.

That a mere adjustment of wage rates to a cost of living index would have the effect of maintaining but never increasing "real" wages is true, of course, to the extent that the content of the budget upon which the index is based is not changed to take rising standards of living into account. If the budget upon which the index is based were adjusted from time to time, a stationary level of "real" wages would actually reflect changes in living standards. As explained in the preceding chapter, there have been some changes in the budget used by the Bureau of Labor Statistics for pricing. During recent years, for example, it has included the maintenance of a small radio and an automobile. Such changes in the budget, however, are a posteriori; they are made after con-

sumer purchasing habits reveal that such items are commonly used
—an indication, obviously, that the income of workers has permitted such purchases.

The Labor Market

In a completely *laissez-faire* economy the condition of the labor
market in relation to the need for labor would be the ultimate determinant of all wage rates because the cash value of everything
would be determined solely by its utility and scarcity. In our present-day society there are forces and controls which mitigate some
of the automatic operation of the law of supply and demand as it
affects wages. Laws and union pressure intervene to alleviate some
of the effects of a redundancy of labor and act as a brake on the
downward swing of wages. Seldom, however, do such forces intervene in the upward movement of wages, especially in a situation in
which the higher wages result from a scarcity of particular skills.[3]
"Union" rates, for example, are usually base rates for the job;
they do not preclude an employer paying higher than union rates
if the scarcity of qualified workers compels him to do so. Even in
the establishment of minimum or base rates, union and legal controls are influenced, and sometimes become inoperative, when there
are abnormal surpluses in the labor market. During the mass unemployment of the 1930's many of the union rates specified in the
building-trades agreements became mere "paper" rates as union
members competed for the few jobs that were available.

Regardless of any other factor, the circumstances of a scarcity
or abundance of qualified workers at the time and place needed
have a major influence on the amount of wages paid. Common
laborers in an extremely isolated community may receive wages as
high as those paid skilled workers in other communities; the wages
of skilled workers in a pioneer, rapidly expanding country are
likely to be higher than the rates for similar work in an older community. This was illustrated by the condition existing in early
colonial times. In 1633 Governor Winthrop of the Massachusetts
Bay Colony noted that the "scarcity of workers caused them to

---

[3] The outstanding exception was the government wage stabilization program
during the recent war and post-war reconversion period. Government experiences with setting ceilings as well as floors for wages are discussed in the
next chapter.

raise their wages to an excessive rate"; a quarter of a century later the colonial governor of North Carolina complained that "the Price of Labor is very high . . . the artificers and labourers being scarce . . ."; in 1698 an historian of Pennsylvania asserted that "Poor People of all kinds can here get three times the wages for their Labour they can in England or Wales."[4]

Potential Substitutes for Labor

Wages at any given time or place are influenced not only by the existing but also by the potential possibilities within the labor market, that is, by the presence or absence of competitive kinds of labor or substitutes for human labor. The fear of being replaced by immigrants or by women willing to accept lower wages has frequently served as a restraining influence upon demands for higher wages. Likewise workers who are aware of the imminent substitution of a newly invented machine for their hand labor are not likely to press for a wage increase; they may, in fact, accept a wage decrease.[5] The influence of potential substitutes may be indirect and may not involve immediate changes in the particular jobs in which wages are under discussion. In order to obtain "cooperation" from his employees, the employer may need only to suggest that he will transfer these operations elsewhere, or contract this portion of the work to another employer who will utilize the cheaper labor or more economical machines.

Elasticity or Inelasticity of the Demand for the Product

Closely akin to an employer's ability to pay is the relative elasticity of the demand for a given product or service. During a business depression the wages of persons attached to luxury industries tend to decline more than the wages of people who are providing necessities; the earnings of caterers, for example, may drop proportionately more than those of waiters in moderate-priced and cheap restaurants. Even in normal times there is a great deal of competition for the consumer's dollar; and, to the extent that

---

[4] Bureau of Labor Statistics, *History of Wages in the U. S. from Colonial Times to 1928,* Bulletin No. 604, p. 7.

[5] In 1908 the Glass Bottle Blowers took a reduction of 20 per cent on beer bottles to "protect the manufacturer who was unable to secure one of those machines . . . and to protect ourselves." (*Union Convention Proceedings,* 1929, p. 213.)

wages affect prices, wages are more or less influenced by the consumer's willingness to buy or not buy certain products or kinds of services. The average family spends more for automobiles and radios than it did twenty-five years ago, and this is reflected in the wages in these industries. The wages of beauty parlor operators are more susceptible to elasticity of demand than those of barbers since women can "do their own hair," or at least are more willing to, if the cost of professional service seems too high. The elasticity of demand may not be a measure of what many would consider sound social values but nevertheless it represents a measure of the willingness to pay. Thus during the recent war, many communities were willing to lose their schoolteachers rather than increase their pay.

Strength of Union Organization

The general theory and philosophy of collective bargaining per se are discussed elsewhere; in this chapter we are concerned with the impact of collective bargaining upon specific wage rates and the influence of various union policies upon the wage structure within particular industries and trades.

The dominant concern of organized workers, and indeed all workers, is to improve and protect their wage standards. "Fair" wages usually connotes "more" wages in the minds of those who work for wages, since wage earners, like business and professional persons, are never content with what they have but are constantly seeking to improve their economic and social status. To this end, unions strive to take advantage of every opportunity to obtain wage increases and to remove the competitive menace of low wages. Although these two courses lead to the same goal, they may conflict in a particular situation, in which case the union must decide where to lay greater emphasis, that is, whether to strive to bring up the rear before advancing further, or to drive forward at strategic times and places regardless of how wages lag behind elsewhere.

Union Versus Non-Union Wages. In general, wages in organized plants are anywhere from 10 to 30 per cent higher than in unorganized plants engaged in similar lines of work. It is almost impossible to make any accurate comparisons, however, because of the difficulty of isolating the influence of unionization from the other factors which affect wage levels. Within any industry, union-ization may be confined to the larger plants or it may be much more extensive in northern than in southern regions. If this is the case, the higher wages prevailing in unionized plants may be due as much to the size and location of the plants as to the fact of unionization, although it might be argued that the wages paid in the smaller plants, or those located in the South, would be higher if they were under collective bargaining agreements.

In some industries wages may be higher in the smaller-sized plants than in the larger plants, regardless of unionization, be-cause jobs are less mechanized and therefore require a higher and more varied degree of manual skill. This is not always the case, as is indicated by the differences in wages in union and non-union plants of various sizes in the rubber industry in 1942.

TABLE 19.   Average Hourly Earnings in Primary
Mechanical Rubber Goods Plants, by Size
of Plant and Unionization, 1942[6]

Size of Plant	Union	Non-Union
100 workers and under............	$0.775	$0.707
101 to 250 workers...............	0.839	0.751
251 to 500 workers...............	0.816	0.684
501 workers and over.............	0.844	0.765
All plants.....................	$0.839	$0.740

At a given time, union rates may actually reflect non-union con-ditions because of the recency of union organization. An illustra-tion is the union bakeries in the South, where collective bargaining is comparatively new and wage rates in 1944 averaged 23 per cent less than those in northern cities of the same size. In contrast, in the printing trades which have been fairly well organized for many years in southern as well as northern cities, the North-South dif-ference is only 10 per cent. In areas or industries which are in the process of being unionized, the non-union plants may pay higher

---

[6] *Monthly Labor Review*, March, 1943, p. 557. Premium overtime pay and shift differential premiums are included in these averages. If these had been eliminated it is probable that the average hourly earnings in the plants em-ploying 251 to 500 workers would have exceeded those in the smaller plants.

wages than are paid in union jobs in an effort to forestall unionization. Many of the wage increases "voluntarily" granted by employers during the active union campaign in 1936–1937 were for the purpose of discouraging organization in their plants.

Another element affecting wage levels is the presence or absence

TABLE 20. Comparison of Earnings in Union and Non-Union Plants for Selected Occupations in Machinery Manufacturing Industries, 1942[7]

	Time Payment			Incentive Payment		
	Av. Hourly Earnings		Per Cent Union Excess	Av. Hourly Earnings		Per Cent Union Excess
	Union	Non-Union		Union	Non-Union	
Bench assemblers, Class A.	$1.098	$0.840	31.0%	$1.090	$0.977	11.6%
Bench assemblers, Class B.	0.884	0.717	23.3	1.005	0.867	15.9
Bench assemblers, Class C.	0.724	0.579	25.0	0.827	0.757	9.2
Drill press operators, Class A....................	1.018	0.760	33.9	1.100	0.961	14.5
Drill press operators, Class B....................	0.835	0.709	17.8	0.971	0.801	21.2
Lathe (turret) operators, Class A..............	1.101	0.857	28.5	1.126	1.095	2.8
Milling machine operators, Class A..............	1.129	0.820	37.7	1.147	1.092	5.0
Milling machine operators, Class B..............	0.817	0.677	20.7	0.978	0.896	9.2
Packers.................	0.753	0.622	21.1	1.010	0.731	38.2
Welders, hand, Class A....	1.068	0.954	11.9	1.242	1.175	5.7
Welders, machine........	0.793	0.669	18.5	1.023	0.923	10.8

of incentive methods of wage payment. As indicated in the next chapter, average hourly earnings (but not base rates) tend to be higher under incentive systems than under time-work methods of wage payment. Some unions, but by no means all, have opposed incentive systems, and the absence or smaller proportion of incentive wage plans in union shops would thus minimize the earnings differences between union and non-union employees within the industry. Even where unions have accepted incentive systems, however, earnings are usually higher than in non-union shops under similar systems of wage payments. This is illustrated in Table 20,

[7] *Ibid.*, May, 1943, p. 852.

which shows significant differences in earnings between union and non-union workers under incentive systems in the machinery manufacturing industries, although the differences under time-payment plans are two or three times greater for most occupations.

Government action may, and frequently does, result in lessening the differences between union and non-union rates. The lowest rates that are automatically lifted by minimum wage legislation are predominantly non-union rates. While such a lifting of the wage "floor" tends to advance all wages, some time may elapse before the unions are able to obtain advances sufficient to restore the differentials which existed prior to the minimum wage legislation. The wage stabilization program during World War II affected union wages in two ways: First, it established a fixed ceiling on rates beyond which unions could not bargain; and second, most of the wage increase awards of the Board were extended to all workers in the industry or area, non-union as well as union. Thus, unions were not permitted to advance their wages beyond an established level and, at the same time, the lower non-union rates were lifted to union levels.[8] As a result, non-union employees benefited from the efforts of unions to improve the wages of their members.

The indirect influence of unionization in raising wages generally is not limited to abnormal situations such as existed under the War Stabilization Program. Although it is impossible to measure statistically the degree to which unions are responsible for general rises in wage levels, it is known that unions act as spearheads and that non-union wages move along with union rates, although at lower levels.

The influence of union pressure was displayed dramatically during the winter of 1945–1946, immediately after the close of the war. While the war was in progress, many persons had expected that there would be drastic cuts in wage rates as soon as industry returned to competitive peacetime production, and members of the War Labor Board speculated whether or not they would be called

_____

[8] The effect of this wartime policy was similar to that of the wage policy which was adopted by several of the Canadian provinces before the war. The "Collective Labor Agreements Extension Act" of Quebec provides for the extension, to all employers and employees of an industry, of the wages and hours agreed upon under collective bargaining by the majority in that industry. The Ontario and Alberta "Industrial Standards Acts" have practically the same provision.

upon to exercise their authority to disallow "decreases in wage rates"—an all but forgotten provision of the Wage Stabilization Act. Such hopes—or fears, depending upon one's outlook—quickly vanished before the onslaught of strikes for higher wages which took place following V-J Day. As a consequence of these vigorous union campaigns, wage rates in many industries were advanced from 15 to 20 per cent.[9] It is probable that there would have been practically no wage increases, and possibly many decreases, at that time if there had been no effective union organizations.

UNION WAGE POLICIES

While the major purpose of labor unions is constantly and persistently to improve the wages of their members, there is no inflexible or standardized procedure among the various unions or even in the same union at all times and places. Collective bargaining implies a policy of "give and take," a willingness to recognize the immediate circumstances at hand and to accept expedient compromises. A particular employer's condition, whether of weakness or strength, may require the union temporarily to deviate from some of its basic policies. Union wage strategy is further complicated by the fact that in a given case the issue may not be entirely a matter of an employer versus *all* of his employees; there may be differences between various membership groups or crafts. Although such differences usually are settled amicably within the union (or among the various unions where the craft situation exists) before the bargaining with the employer gets under way, some intra-union conflicts over wage policies have resulted in permanent schisms which have had significant effects upon the wage structure within an industry or plant.

The determination of wage rates through collective bargaining does not remove the presence of the other factors described earlier in this chapter, although union policy and strength may tend to minimize the influence of some of these factors and magnify the emphasis given to others. No union, however strong, can ignore the financial condition of employers and their prospects for sell-

---

[9] These rate increases, however, did not result in comparable increases in weekly earnings because of the elimination of overtime and shift premiums which had prevailed under war production.

ing their goods or services in a competitive market; the very strength of the union is affected by the abundance or scarcity of workers in relation to employer needs; specific wage rates are never negotiated in a vacuum but within the framework of prevailing wages and conceptions regarding wage differentials pertaining to different kinds of jobs.

If union response to any wage situation is strongly influenced by the immediate circumstances surrounding each case, is it possible to say that organized labor has any wage policy other than that of getting wages increased or keeping them from being decreased wherever and whenever possible? The answer is yes; in spite of expedient compromises and hedging, organized labor has developed some guiding principles of wage policy and has been able to put them into effect in many wage determinations.

The present wage structure of American industry follows no orderly plan; the inconsistencies, if so they may be called, are a result more of the absence than the presence of effective collective bargaining. As unionization becomes more extensive throughout an industry, the wage structure tends to follow a more uniform pattern because wage determinations tend to cover larger units, and unions realize that wide differences in rates for comparable work are a constant threat to the maintenance of the higher rates. Collective bargaining, in other words, tends to remove purely fortuitous factors as well as the divergencies caused by competitive pressures of numerous employers. In doing this, it is the purpose or desire of the unions not to eliminate competition between employers, but to have competition take place within the realm of efficient management, sales policies, and use of technological improvements, rather than in the wages of workers.

Principle of Equal Pay for Equal Work

A cardinal wage policy of most unions is "equal pay for equal work." While this appears to be an equitable basis for wage determination, its application entails drastic alterations in existing wage structures. It also runs counter to some other important considerations, such as the competitive and financial conditions of the industry or individual employer concerned, differences in the cost of living, and "customary" wage differentials. The establishment of equal pay for equal work throughout American industry would eliminate regional differences, plant differences, differences between larger and smaller communities, and differences based on the race or sex of workers.

The ability of a union to reduce or eliminate differences in wage rates for comparable work is contingent, of course, upon whether or not it has effective collective bargaining throughout all sections of the industry or occupation in which it functions. The degree of wage standardization is also greatly affected by the bargaining procedures within the union, that is, whether bargaining is pursued on an industry-wide basis through the union's central office or by each local on a more or less independent basis. As indicated in a later chapter, the practice varies widely in the different unions, although the tendency is toward more centralized, industry-wide bargaining.

A major issue between employers and unions in many industries during recent years has been the differences in wage levels in different localities. The Rubber Workers have sought to reduce the spread between Akron wages and those in rubber plants located elsewhere; the Mine Workers have successfully narrowed the gap in wages between the southern and northern mines; the Railroad Brotherhoods have obtained standardization of many of the rates throughout the railroad industry; the Automobile Workers seek company-wide bargaining with uniform rates throughout all plants of each corporation.

The above-mentioned industries all serve national (and international) markets where there is least justification for wage differences so far as labor costs are concerned. In industries producing goods and services for local markets, intercity wage differences are likely to be accentuated, regardless of union desires and policies. Also, in these industries, local union autonomy is more prevalent than in the mass-production industries. Union rates in the building construction and newspaper printing industries and for city streetcar and bus drivers are 50 per cent higher in the largest than in the smallest cities. Wages in union bakery shops in large cities average more than twice as much as in small cities. The service trades would probably show similar differences, but few of them are unionized in the smaller communities.

Skill Differentials

Unions as well as employers accept the logic and necessity of maintaining wage differentials between skilled and unskilled occupations. The newer industrial unions, a majority of whose membership are semi-skilled and unskilled workers, are inclined to reduce some of the spread between the lowest and the highest rates, whereas the craft unions, whose membership consists mostly of skilled workers, are more concerned with maintaining traditional differentials. In some of the industrial unions, the highly skilled members have shown signs of discontent and are insisting that their unions give them more latitude in wage bargaining so that they can obtain what they consider justifiable differentials above the rates for less skilled jobs.

Wages Versus Job Security

In theory, unions hold that security of income is as important as the question of wage rates, and in a few instances they have accepted reduced hourly rates, or at least not pressed for higher rates, when furnished with a guarantee of steady employment. This question has come to the fore on numerous occasions in the construction industry, as one government agency after another has sought to reduce the costs of home building. Plans have been suggested to stabilize employment and reduce hourly rates, or to have a graduated scale of rates in accordance with annual employment guarantees. The unions have viewed such plans with a great deal of skepticism, fearing that their wage standards would suffer a permanent setback and that the meritorious stabilization plans would be abandoned after a year or two of experiment.[10]

However, unions have upon occasion accepted wage reductions when faced with the alternative of the loss of jobs. In the long history of the shoe and glass industries, for example, the unions have several times accepted rate reductions for hand operations in order to discourage the introduction of new machines or to protect employers who were forced to compete with companies which had

---

[10] The above refers to annual guaranteed employment as an alternative to higher wage rates. A number of unions at the present time are actively seeking the adoption of annual wage plans, and, as indicated in chap. 7, several companies have established guaranteed employment or annual wage programs in their plants.

already installed machine methods. Such concessions, at best, have only postponed the inevitable layoffs; they have never resulted in permanent solutions for unemployment. For this reason the acceptance of general wage reductions is not endorsed as "good" trade union policy.

WAGE STRUCTURE CHARACTERISTICS

The existing wage structure throughout American industry includes a medley of rates which are the result of a commingling of all the factors and influences discussed above. No particular rate in any industry, plant, or area can be explained on the basis of any one factor alone, and seldom is it possible to evaluate the relative degrees of influence of the several factors. The best that can be done is to portray some of the outstanding characteristics of the general wage structure, and to suggest some of the considerations which may have had an effect in causing the various wage scales to be what they are.

It must always be borne in mind that wages are in a constant state of flux; that a factor which may have become dominant in certain sections of an industry or area may not yet have been felt but soon may be evident throughout the entire industry or area. Wages may be comparatively low in one branch of an industry because it has not yet been affected by unionization, but this condition may change within a very short time. There may be wide differences in the wage structure of an industry even though all sections of it are under union agreements, simply because these differences existed prior to unionization and collective bargaining is of too recent origin in some sections to have become effective in bringing up the lower rates. Likewise, wage differences due primarily to shortages or abundance of the labor supply may disappear at any time as workers migrate in search of new job opportunities.

Because wages are a dynamic phenomenon, many of the facts and conclusions herein cited may not be true a decade hence. Nevertheless, some wage characteristics have existed for many years to a greater or lesser degree, and can therefore be said to represent "normal" tendencies. Although the degree of the relative differences may change, certain distinguishing features will probably continue indefinitely.

Regional Differences

Although there are some exceptions, wages in general are higher in the northern and Pacific coast states than in the southern states, and higher in larger cities than in smaller cities. Since there are many more large cities in the North and on the Pacific coast than in the South,[11] any North-South comparisons must take this into account.

In general, average industrial wages in the South are approximately 20 per cent lower than in the same-sized communities in the North, although the differences in some industries, particularly in agriculture and some of the local service trades, are considerably greater. In 1943 farm wages, without board, ranged from an average of $2.02 to $2.74 per day in the South, compared to a range of $4.04 to $6.57 in the North, depending upon types of farming. During the same year the wages of women in retail stores in medium-sized southern cities averaged less than 30 cents an hour, compared to 38 cents in northern cities of the same size.[12]

North-South differences prevail in unionized as well as unorganized trades. Average union rates in the journeymen building and printing trades in medium-sized cities are approximately 10 per cent higher in the North than in the South, and those of unionized laborers and helpers are almost 50 per cent higher. Average wages in organized ship repair yards on the Great Lakes in 1943 were 20 per cent and on the Pacific coast 30 per cent higher than those in the Gulf Coast region which were also under union agreements.

Prior to federal minimum wage legislation, North-South differences tended to be greater in the lower-paid than in the higher-paid industries and occupations. This has changed somewhat because the establishment of nation-wide minimum levels has thus far resulted in a proportionately greater lifting of rates which were below the legal minimum (more prevalent in the South than in

---

[11] According to the 1940 census, the South had no cities with as much as one-half million population, whereas there were 14 cities in the North and on the Pacific coast which had populations of over one-half million, and 5 with populations of over one million. There were 13 cities in the North with populations between one-fourth and one-half million, compared to 8 in the South.

[12] Except where otherwise noted, wage data in the remainder of this chapter are based on Bureau of Labor Statistics reports which have appeared in various issues of the *Monthly Labor Review* since January, 1941.

the North) than of rates which were above the minimum levels. In 1933 the average wages of cotton textile workers were 42 per cent higher in the North than in the South, but ten years later the difference was reduced to 21 per cent. This reduction was due primarily to the greater-than-average lifting of southern wages in the lowest-paid occupations. For example, in 1933 the average wages of northern female spinners were 49 per cent higher than in the southern mills, where spinners averaged 16 cents an hour, but in 1943 the difference was 21 per cent. On the other hand, the North-South difference in the average wages of male loom fixers, the highest-paid occupation in the textile goods industry, was 43 per cent in 1933 and had declined to only 31 per cent ten years later.

When the 30-cent minimum wage went into effect in 1939, more than half the southern loggers were earning below this amount. Similarly, the wages of about 23 per cent of the employees in southern household furniture factories had to be raised, but only 3 per cent of those in the northern plants. Unskilled furniture workers in the North averaged 55 per cent more than those in the South prior to the passage of the Fair Labor Standards Act; four years later this difference was reduced to 36 per cent, although the North-South differences for the skilled workers remained about the same, approximately 44 per cent. In 1944 when the National War Labor Board permitted a 50-cent minimum hourly rate, almost 40 per cent of the workers in the southern lumber industry were earning less than this amount, compared to 4 per cent in the North and less than 1 per cent in the West.

In the higher-paid industries, however, regional differences tend to be greater among the less skilled than among the skilled workers, primarily because of the relative scarcity of skilled workers in the South. As already indicated, the North-South difference for building trades laborers is much greater than for journeymen. The average common labor entrance rate in southern manufacturing industries is less than 75 per cent of that in northern industries. In the machinery industry in 1945, tool and die makers' wages were only 10 per cent greater in the North than in the Southeast, and in the Southwest average wages were higher than in the North; sand mixers, on the other hand, averaged 60 per cent more in the North than in the South.

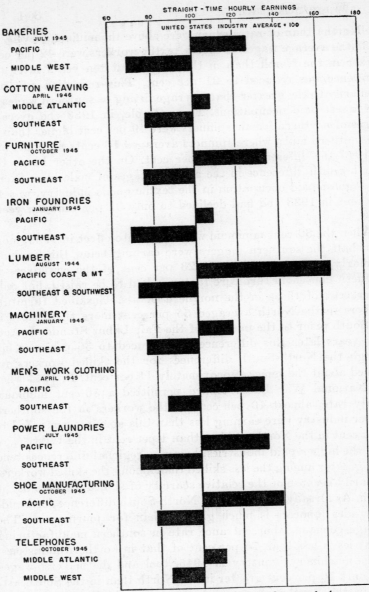

FIG. 22. *Highest and Lowest Regional Indexes of Average Hourly Earnings in Ten Selected Industries.* (*Source: Monthly Labor Review, October, 1946.*)

Regional variations in wages are not confined to North-South differences. In many instances the differences between Southeast and Southwest, and between the Northeast, Central, and Pacific coast regions, are greater than the North-South differences. This is illustrated in Table 21, which shows average wages in 1945 for a few of the skilled and unskilled occupations in the machinery plants.

TABLE 21. Average Hourly Wages for Selected Occupations in Machinery Establishments, by Region, January, 1945[13]

	New Eng- land	Mid- dle At- lantic	South- east	Great Lakes	Mid- dle west	South- west	Pa- cific
Skilled, Male							
Grinding machine operators, Class A	$1.12	$1.24	$0.97	$1.21	$1.06	$1.14	$1.27
Inspectors, Class A	1.05	1.16	1.06	1.16	1.07	1.23	1.26
Machinists, production	1.02	1.18	1.04	1.20	1.10	1.18	1.32
Milling machine operators, Class A	1.08	1.18	0.98	1.17	1.06	1.15	1.27
Tool and die makers	1.24	1.28	1.17	1.29	1.19	1.36	1.45
Pattern makers, wood	1.21	1.26	1.10	1.25	1.07	1.07	1.49
Unskilled, Male							
Janitors	0.74	0.73	0.51	0.76	0.68	0.60	0.86
Sand mixers	0.79	0.81	0.54	0.86	0.76	0.56	0.98
Female							
Assemblers, Class C	0.72	0.77	0.55	0.87	0.72	0.84	0.83
Grinding machine operators, Class B	1.00	0.96	...	1.12	...	...	1.06
Welders, machine, Class B	0.91	0.85	...	0.98	0.74	1.13	1.17

Many reasons have been given for the existing wide differences in North-South wages. Absence of state labor legislation, lack of or recency of labor unionism, racial discrimination, lower labor efficiency, cheaper living costs, higher freight rates and greater distances from markets, poorer machinery and capital equipment,

[13] Bureau of Labor Statistics Mimeographed Report, *Wage Structure, Machinery*, 1945, Series #2, No. 1, Table 4. (Border and Mountain State areas are omitted.)

have all been cited as reasons and justifications. However, one authority states:

Investigation reveals that the claims regarding a number of these factors are of doubtful validity. It is questionable, for example, whether living costs for the same standard of living are much lower in the South than in the North. Many products have uniform national prices; others increase in price with the distance from producing or marketing centers. Consequently, various cost of living studies have shown that, on a comparable basis, living costs in the South have averaged no more than 3 to 5 per cent below such costs in the North and that it costs more to live in some Southern cities than in some Northern cities of comparable size.

Capital equipment in the South is not generally poorer in quality or quantity. On the contrary, in many industries such as paper and pulp, textiles, furniture and rubber, the newest and best equipped plants are in the South. As another indication of relative mechanization, census data show that the electric energy used per man-hour in Southern manufacturing has generally averaged well above the average for manufacturing in the Northeast.

A number of studies have been made of the comparative effectiveness of factory labor in the North and South. Two detailed studies of three textile firms with plants in both regions indicated that Southern labor was fully as efficient as Northern labor. In response to a comprehensive questionnaire, 23 out of 41 interregional concerns reported the efficiency of factory labor in their Southern plants equal to or (in four instances) above that of labor in their Northern plants, yet a majority of those 23 concerns were paying wage rates in the South averaging from 10 to 25 per cent lower than in the North.

Also, eight out of twelve replies from industrial engineering firms doing consulting work in both regions stated that labor productivity in the South was as great as or greater than in the North under comparable conditions. Such data contain little support for the contention that regional wage differentials are largely due to sectional differences in labor productivity. . . . There can be little doubt that the economic bases for a South-North wage differential in most Southern industries have been weakened during the past decade. The most important factor explaining the continued existence of differentials in wage levels appears to be the high rate of population growth that causes a rapid expansion in the Southern labor supply.[14]

[14] Richard A. Lester, "Must Wages Differ North and South?" *Virginia Quarterly Review,* Winter, 1946, pp. 24 ff.

Intercity Differences

A consideration of wage differences in various cities can be approached in two ways: by comparing the average per capita wages of all employed residents, or by comparing the wages paid in the various cities for identical or closely similar jobs. The former is useful for comparing the economic well-being and purchasing power of the people in various cities, but it does not take into account the effect on wage levels resulting from the types of industries which happen to be located in the different cities. Per capita wages in a city may be relatively high, not because the rates are above the average paid for similar work elsewhere, but because "high-wage" industries are located in that city. Industry wage differences are discussed later; here we will deal with intercity differences in wages paid for comparable kinds of work.

Although wages for similar jobs tend to be higher in larger than in smaller cities, there is no consistent pattern of graduation according to size of city. In a particular city the wages paid by some industries may be high in comparison to those in the same kinds of plants located elsewhere, but the wages paid by other of that city's industries may be comparatively low. Other factors, such as the extent of unionization, the prosperity and efficiency of management, the productivity of labor, labor market conditions, traditional regional differences, and fortuitous circumstances, may have more influence than mere size of city. Moreover, the location as well as the size of the city is an important factor. Wages in a small community which is contiguous to a metropolitan center reflect the wage and living standards prevailing in that area and for that reason alone may be higher than the wages in a larger city located in a predominantly rural area.

Insufficient wage data are available to make possible any comparisons between the smallest towns or villages and the larger cities. That the range in wages paid for similar work in cities having populations of more than 40,000 is very marked is indicated by the following, based on 1943 wage levels:[15] The average union wages of building-trades journeymen were 67 per cent greater in Newark (New Jersey) than in York (Pennsylvania), and those of

[15] Although wage rates have changed since 1943, the comparative levels between cities have probably remained about the same.

building laborers 140 per cent greater than in Charleston (South Carolina) ; the rates of union book and job printers in New York City averaged 65 per cent more than in Portland (Maine), and those of newspaper printers 50 per cent more than in Mobile (Alabama) ; the average rate in unionized bakeries was 136 per cent higher in Seattle than in Nashville (Tennessee) ; the beginning rate for one-man streetcars and busses was 70 per cent higher in Chicago than in Little Rock (Arkansas) ; truck-drivers' rates averaged 100 per cent more in Seattle than in San Antonio (Texas) ; the average wages in metal-working industries were 87 per cent higher in Detroit than in Atlanta (Georgia).

Although there is a fairly consistent spread in wages between the largest and smallest cities for similar work, there is a great deal of variation among the several occupations in the various cities. This is shown in Table 22, in which the 35 largest cities in the country are ranked in accordance with their 1943 average wage rates in six different types of work. The first two columns pertain to wages in factories producing goods which enter into competitive national markets; the other four columns relate to wages paid in industries which primarily serve local markets. Although the rank indicates how one city compares with another, it does not reveal the *extent* of wage differences between the cities; for example, St. Paul has a rank of 14.5 and Minneapolis a rank of 24 for the printing trades, but the actual difference in their average rates was less than 4 cents an hour. Where there is relative uniformity in rates throughout the country, as in the printing trades, a point difference in rank amounts to only a fraction of a cent in hourly wages, whereas in other occupations it may amount to several cents per hour.

The ranks for the various occupations in the southern cities are more consistent than those in the northern cities, the greatest deviation for any of the southern cities being 7 points, except for Houston which has a comparatively high rank for the bakery trades. Detroit ranks high in the factory occupations but comparatively low in the building and bakery trades. Chicago ranks low for a city its size in the factory occupations but comparatively high in the building and printing trades, while the four Pacific coast cities stand relatively low in these latter trades. As would be expected, New York ranks first in newspaper printing;

TABLE 22.   Ranks of 35 Largest Cities According to 1943 Wage Levels in Various Occupations[16]

	Metal Manufacturing[a]	Mfg. Common Labor[b]	Women Switchboard Operators	Journeymen Building Trades	Newspaper Printing Trades	Bakeries (Machine)
1 Million and Over						
Chicago	10.5	14	9	4	2	14
Detroit	1	2	1	9.5	5	15
Los Angeles	9	7	13	24	20	6
New York	*	21	*	2	1	10
Philadelphia	8	10	8	8	19	17
500,000 and Under 1 Million						
Baltimore	20.5	17	24	20	18	32
Boston	24	22.5	10	17	4	29
Buffalo	15	13	2	6	21	12.5
Cleveland	6	8	11	7	7	22
Kansas City	17	9	12	15	28	7
Milwaukee	10.5	16	20	27.5	13	19
Minneapolis	12.5	11.5	15.5	29	24	27
Newark	*	18	*	1	3	11
Pittsburgh	7	6	4	3	22	18
St. Louis	23	27	23	16	17	8
San Francisco	4	3	5	14	10	3
Washington, D. C.	*	*	17	5	6	2
250,000 and Under 500,000						
Atlanta	26	32	*	32	32	33
Birmingham	27	31	*	26	34	34
Cincinnati	18	30	14	12.5	9	12.5
Columbus	16	22.5	21.5	21	12	20
Dallas	25	26	21.5	31	29	30
Denver	*	24	26	19	27	5
Houston	20.5	25	25	23	26	9
Indianapolis	14	20	18.5	18	14.5	25
Louisville	19	29	28	22	31	23
Memphis	*	33	27	33	25	31
New Orleans	*	28	29	34	35	28
Portland, Oregon	3	1	6	27.5	23	4
Providence	22	19	18.5	30	11	21
Rochester, N. Y.	*	15	*	11	30	16
St. Paul	12.5	11.5	15.5	25	14.5	26
San Antonio	*	34	30	35	33	*
Seattle	5	4	3	12.5	16	1
Toledo	2	5	7	9.5	8	24

[a] Weighted average hourly wages in 1943 of major metal-working occupations, also some janitors and truckers.

[b] Entrance rates of male common laborers in manufacturing.

[16] Data from Bureau of Labor Statistics Bulletins Nos. 793, 767, 781, 778. An asterisk indicates that no information is available. When comparing a city's various rankings, consideration must be given to the fact that some of

however, its rank for entrance rates for common labor in manufacturing plants is low, as is also its rank for the machine bakery
trades. (Rates in New York for special kinds of hand baking are
relatively high, but these are not included in this table.) In relation to its size, Philadelphia does not rank high in any of the occupations shown; it has a low ranking for the printing and bakery
trades. Baltimore's rank is also low for a city its size, as is that
of Boston, except for the printing trades. Cleveland's ranks are
fairly consistent for its size except in the bakery trades, as are
Pittsburgh's except for the printing and bakery trades, which
are relatively low. St. Louis, Kansas City, Denver, and Houston,
on the other hand, have comparatively high ranks for the bakery
trades.

Industry Differences

There are wide differences in average earnings[17] among the various industries. In May, 1946, average factory earnings ranged
from 63 cents an hour in the cottonseed oil and work-shirt industries to $1.45 an hour in the rubber tire and locomotive manufac-
turing industries. (These are averages for all occupations and
plants within the industries; the spread between the lowest- and
highest-paid workers was much greater.) Although the average
hourly earnings in several manufacturing industries were relatively high, the hourly earnings of all manufacturing workers
averaged less than those of coal mining, building-trades, railroad,
and some other non-manufacturing employees.

The wide differences in average earnings in the several industries
are a reflection of the relative importance of all the factors which
determine specific rates, that is, the occupational skills existing in

---

the series are incomplete; e.g., a relatively high rank in the first column may
be due in part to the fact that the lowest rank in this column is 27 and not
35. In cases where two or more cities have the same rank, the rank given
represents the average of the rank in which they fall; i.e., 10.5 is the average
of 10 and 11, etc.

[17] A comparison of average wage rates instead of hourly earnings would
be more significant because, as previously explained, rates do not reflect
overtime premiums and other bonuses. No comprehensive data on wage rates
for all industries are available, however. Since little overtime was worked in
the two periods used in this discussion (May, 1939, and May, 1946) the comparisons of "earnings" probably give an accurate reflection of comparative
wages.

TABLE 23.   Pre-War and Post-War Average Hourly Earnings in
Selected Industries[18]

	May, 1939 (Cents)	May, 1946 (Cents)	Per Cent Increase
All manufacturing	64.9	107.1	65.0
All durable goods manufacturing	72.4	114.8	58.6
All non-durable goods manufacturing	58.4	99.6	70.5
Selected Durable Goods			
Agricultural machinery	78.7	117.5	49.3
Aircraft	73.7	126.2	71.2
Aluminum manufactures	68.1	116.0	70.3
Automobiles	93.1	131.8	41.6
Blast furnaces, steel works, and rolling mills	83.6	129.8	55.3
Bricks, tile, and terra cotta	53.4	95.4	78.7
Electrical equipment	74.4	117.0	57.3
Engines and turbines	78.7	128.2	62.9
Foundries and machine-shop products	71.0	118.7	67.2
Furniture	53.0	94.2	77.7
Glass and glassware	71.0	108.1	52.2
Hardware	65.1	102.1	56.8
Machine tools	74.9	125.1	67.0
Radios and phonographs	58.9	102.7	74.4
Sawmills and logging camps	55.2	86.0	55.8
Shipbuilding	82.1	140.1	70.6
Tin cans and other tinware	61.6	104.6	69.8
Selected Non-Durable Goods			
Baking	62.0	93.0	50.0
Canning and preserving	50.0	89.3	78.6
Clothing, men's	57.4	99.7	73.7
Clothing, women's	50.1	121.1	141.7
Cotton goods	38.6	80.3	108.0
Dyeing and finishing textiles	53.4	94.3	76.6
Hosiery	52.4	88.8	69.4
Paper and pulp	61.6	102.4	66.2
Petroleum refining	97.0	141.7	46.1
Printing: book and job	80.2	118.6	47.9
Printing: newspapers and periodicals	100.1	143.5	43.4
Rubber tires and tubes	94.4	145.2	53.8

[18] *Monthly Labor Review,* August, 1939, and August, 1946. There are some
slight differences in industry titles in the two tables from which the above
data were obtained, but only in the first two industries was the classification
sufficiently changed to affect the comparability of the figures: The 1946 earnings figure for agricultural machinery excludes tractor manufacturing, and
the 1946 figure for aircraft excludes the manufacture of aircraft engines. If
these were included (as they are in the 1939 figures), the 1946 earnings averages
would be slightly higher than appear in the table.

Table 23.   Pre-War and Post-War Average Hourly Earnings in Selected Industries—(*Continued*)₁

	May, 1939 (Cents)	May, 1946 (Cents)	Per Cent Increase
Shoes	49.4	92.1	86.4
Slaughtering and meat packing	68.9	108.1	56.9
Soap	75.1	112.8	50.2
Tobacco manufactures	47.2	84.8	79.7
Woolen goods	52.6	101.4	92.8
Non-Manufacturing			
Building construction	94.1	143.8	52.8
Coal, bituminous	86.0	131.4	52.8
Crude petroleum producing	86.1	129.0	49.9
Electric light and power	85.2	123.6	45.1
Laundries	42.4	70.3	65.8
Railroads	70.4	107.3	52.4
Trade, wholesale	71.1	113.5	59.6
Trade, retail	55.0	86.1	56.5

the industry, the location of plants, the prosperity of the industry, the strength of unionization, and the other influences previously discussed. Space does not permit an analysis of the reasons for the relatively high or low earnings in each industry, although such information is necessary for an understanding of the existing wage structure. For instance, the higher average earnings in durable goods manufacturing are due to several factors, although all are by no means dominant in each industry. Durable goods last a long time and this fact tends to minimize the importance of wage costs in the sales price; workers in these industries are predominantly men; a majority of the plants are located in the northern sections of the country; mass-production techniques prevail more generally than in the non-durable goods industries, although there are important exceptions in both groups.

Table 23 shows the average hourly earnings in some of the major manufacturing and non-manufacturing industries for a pre-war and a post-war period. The latter, May, 1946, represents a pay period following the initial round of wage increases which took place immediately after the close of the war. When considering the rise in average earnings during these years, it must be remembered that the cost of living advanced at least 32 per cent during this same period, and rose rapidly during the ensuing months.

SELECTED REFERENCES[19]

Bell, Spurgeon, *Productivity, Wages and National Income*, Brookings Institution, Washington, 1940.

Bureau of Labor Statistics, *Handbook of Labor Statistics*, 1941 ed., Vol. II, Bulletin No. 694, Government Printing Office, Washington.

Bureau of Labor Statistics, *History of Wages in the U. S. from Colonial Times to 1928*, Bulletin No. 604, Government Printing Office, Washington, 1934.

Cox, Jacob D., *The Economic Basis of Fair Wages*, The Ronald Press Company, New York, 1926.

Dickinson, Z. Clark, *Collective Wage Determination*, The Ronald Press Company, New York, 1941.

Douglas, Paul H., *Real Wages in the U. S., 1890–1926*, Houghton Mifflin Company, Boston, 1930.

Dunlop, John T., *Wage Determination Under Trade Unions*, The Macmillan Company, New York, 1944.

Hamilton, Walton, and May, Stacy, *The Control of Wages*, The Macmillan Company, New York, 1942.

Lester, R. A., and Robie, E. A., *Wages Under National and Regional Collective Bargaining*, Princeton University Press, Princeton, 1946.

Millis, Harry, and Montgomery, Royal, *Labor's Progress and Problems*, McGraw-Hill Book Company, Inc., New York, 1938.

Riegel, John W., *Wage Determination*, University of Michigan Press, Ann Arbor, 1937.

Slichter, Sumner H., *Union Policies and Industrial Management*, Brookings Institution, Washington, 1941.

---

[19] The student is also referred to current publications of the U. S. Bureau of Labor Statistics, the National Industrial Conference Board, and the American Economic Association.

12

"SCIENTIFIC" WAGE DETERMINATION

A NEW INFLUENCE IN THE DETERMINING OF WAGE RATES AROSE toward the close of the 19th century when engineers began to interest employers in what came to be known as scientific management. Although this new movement was concerned with all phases of internal shop management,[1] the question of wages in relation to production was one of its earliest and major interests. The problem as viewed by the industrial engineers hinged on two basic questions, namely, what is the best method of doing a job, and how can workers be induced to achieve maximum performance?

Their answer to the first was to make an accurate time study of each individual job with the aid of a stop watch, for the purpose of determining the one best way of performing each motion made by the operator, as well as the best physical conditions, machines, tools, and working arrangements. The answer to the second ques-

[1] Frederick W. Taylor, referred to as the father of scientific management, is best known for his time and motion study and incentive wage system, but his primary interest was broader and covered the whole field of shop management. The essentials of many of his ideas have been widely adopted, although in different forms from his original suggestions. Taylor was a proponent of functionalized management. Because of the "difficulty in obtaining in one man the variety and special information and the different mental and moral qualities necessary to perform all the duties demanded," he divided the job of foremen as it existed in his day into eight functions. Three were transferred to the office—the preparation of written job instructions, the routing of jobs, and cost and time keeping. In the factory was the teacher of special skills, the inspector to look after quality, the gang boss to direct the work, the speed boss, the repair boss to see that machinery was in order, and the "disciplinarian" to serve as employment supervisor and handle cases of discipline. (*The Principles of Scientific Management,* Harper & Brothers, New York, 1911, pp. 124 ff.)

tion was the fixing of definite time standards on the basis of stop-watch time and motion studies, and the payment of premiums, or extra wages, for performance above the specified task or standard. Thus was laid the foundation for the many types of premium wage systems which have been devised during the past fifty years, the more important of which are described in later pages.

JOB EVALUATION

Premium wage systems in themselves do not establish wage levels or occupational wage rates, for as a base they accept the going rates and upon these superimpose the formula for premium payments. It was a number of years after premium pay systems were initiated before industrial engineers turned their attention to "scientific" methods for establishing base rates for various jobs. This came to be known as job evaluation, which, essentially, is the process of determining job relationships according to skill and other requirements, and fixing wage differentials.

Job evaluation is a distinctly different phase of wage determination from the establishment of job standards and incentive rates through time and motion study, although both depend upon the application of scientific or engineering techniques. The one deals with the qualitative characteristics of jobs; the other, with the quantitative measure of the output. While both processes are used in many plants, they are not inseparable. Many companies have adopted methods of job evaluation without changing their pay systems; other companies have installed time and motion study and premium wage systems without using systematic methods for determining differences in the base rates for various jobs.

Most important to bear in mind is that neither job evaluation nor premium pay systems have as their purpose the establishing of general wage levels. They are means for determining compensation for particular occupations and for a specified output, and are not inherently concerned with whether general wages are "high" or "low." So far as the application of these processes is concerned, it makes no difference whether the minimum rate in a plant is 50 cents or $1.00 an hour, or whether the maximum rate for the most skilled job is $1.50 or $2.50 per hour. Whichever the rate, in the job evaluation and time and motion study processes it serves as a bench mark for determining the base rates of all intervening jobs upon which premium rates are established.

Methods of Job Evaluation

Job evaluation is the process of establishing wage differentials for the various jobs in a plant by determining their relative importance and requirements and the measure of their differences.

Distinctions in job values have always been recognized by employers, workers, and unions, as is attested by the fact that some jobs have consistently paid higher rates than others. The most common general classifications have been skilled, semi-skilled, and unskilled, although there is seldom agreement among those immediately concerned (i.e., employers and workers) when it becomes necessary to classify particular jobs on the basis of these categories.

Craft unions are inclined to ignore the semi-skilled classification altogether and to rate all jobs as either journeyman or laborer grade. However, a journeyman classification connotes all-round proficiency, usually on jobs requiring the use of hand tools, and additional classifications are implicit under most apprenticeship systems which provide graduated scales up to journeyman status.

The multiplicity of jobs[2] ensuing from the division of labor inherent in machine and factory production calls for more precise methods of determining the relative values of jobs because their distinguishing characteristics are more obscure. Also the mere fact of there being hundreds of different jobs within a plant means that no one workman can be familiar with the exact nature of all of them, and therefore inconsistencies[3] arise when reliance is placed upon the casual judgment and separate decisions of numerous persons. The primary purpose of job evaluation is to achieve consistency in the rate structure within a plant. To accomplish this, the pooled judgment of many individuals is used, and a sys-

---

[2] Here we are referring to "jobs" as distinguished from "positions." A "position" is the aggregation of duties required of one individual, whereas a "job" includes all the identical positions within the plant; there may be one person or many persons performing a particular job.

[3] During the wage stabilization program the War Labor Board found so many inconsistencies in plant wage structures that it was compelled to adopt special policies to correct what it termed wage "inequities."

tematic comparison of job attributes is substituted for the individual arbitrary decisions of numerous persons.

Several more or less distinct methods are currently in use for analyzing and evaluating jobs, some of them being more precise than others. All of them necessarily involve some degree of judgment and therefore cannot be considered infallible. The validity of their results depends upon the individuals whose judgment is used in each determination, as well as the accuracy with which each job is analyzed before the evaluation is made.

One simple method, which is feasible only in smaller plants, is to use the pooled judgment of all the plant supervisors (together with that of the union stewards in organized shops) who, after comparing all the jobs on the basis of oral or written job descriptions, list them in order of importance and then rank them into grades between the minimum and maximum wage rates already determined or agreed upon. A variant of this method is to predetermine and define a few key job grades and then assign all the other jobs to the grade which seems most appropriate. In both procedures, jobs are considered in their entirety rather than upon the basis of their various requirements or attributes, the evaluation being dependent upon narrative job descriptions, oral or written.

Much more accurate evaluations are possible when, instead of relying upon general job descriptions, which are likely to be superficial, the jobs are broken down into well-defined basic factors or characteristics such as mental and physical requirements, skill, responsibility, and experience. The evaluation can then be based either on point values which have been assigned to each factor, or on a comparison of the factors of the jobs to be evaluated with the ratings given to factors of key jobs already evaluated. Since both the point system and the comparison method are widely used in wage determination throughout industry today, it is worth while to discuss them in greater detail.

Point System of Job Evaluation

Under the point system anywhere from half a dozen to a dozen or more basic requirements are established as factors which are more or less common to all the jobs in the plant. Values or points are then assigned each factor. For some factors, e.g., "experience," the point values can be measures of specific requirements in terms of months or years, such as 2 points for jobs requiring six months' experience to attain proficiency, 3 points for those requiring a year's experience, and so forth. For other more intangible factors e.g., "skill," the point values must be defined in relative or suggestive terms, such as 1 point for jobs requiring little or no skill, 2 points for jobs in which simple tools are used and some accuracy is required, 3 points for jobs requiring a moderate need for precision or where machines must be given rather close attention.

After the point values have been defined for all the factors which are to be used in all the jobs, each job is then carefully analyzed and broken down into its several factor requirements and the proper point values are assigned according to their degree of importance. When these points are totaled, the job is evaluated; that is, its relationship to all the other jobs has been determined by analyzing its component characteristics and rating them according to established definitions.

In large plants where there are hundreds or even thousands of different kinds of jobs, the process of evaluation and rating is simplified if jobs of a somewhat similar nature are grouped into job grades or job "families" and each grade given a range of rates. Some employers and unions prefer a large number of job grades with step-up wage differentials amounting to as little as one cent. In most plants, the existing hundreds of different occupations are classified into as few as a dozen or twenty grades, with 3- or 5-cent rate intervals.

Although the ultimate objective of job evaluation is the determination of wage rates, the money value or price given the job is not an inherent part of the evaluation process. After the wage rates for a few representative jobs have been established they are used as yardsticks, and the determination of the rates for all the other jobs becomes automatic, since it is based on these point values.

To illustrate the point system process, let us assume that the job of machine lasting in a shoe factory is to be evaluated according to a comparatively simple point system. According to the procedure used (see the accompanying chart), eight factors have been selected, with a scale of 8 degrees for each factor. (In some

ILLUSTRATION OF POINT SYSTEM OF JOB EVALUATION

Job—Shoe Lasting Machine Operator

Factors	0	2	4	6	8	Numerical Rating
Education—Formal preparation to perform job.	Elementary school	2 years high school or vocational school	Graduate high school or vocational school	High school plus 2 years vocational school	Graduate college or technical school	2
Skill—Quality requirements. Extent job requires skill with hands, manipulation of machines, or handling materials; extent of precision, judgment, and accuracy required.	Little need or opportunity for care or precision	Use of simple tools; need for exactness	Automatic machine tending; moderate need for attention to quality	Quality important; intricate machines or hand tools	Great deal of accuracy required; precision tools; work from blueprints	5
Experience—Measured in terms of experience on other jobs which are necessary for promotion to this job, as well as time required for mastery of this job.	Few days	At least 6 months	At least 12 months	At least 2 years	Minimum of 4 years	7
Versatility—Number of major skills or operations required for handling job.	No major skills	1 major skill	1 major and 1 minor skill	Several different skills	Numerous different skills	2
Responsibility—In terms of costs to company to replace materials, machinery, or other equipment which might be damaged. Loss to company if poor product reaches customer.	Possibility of little loss to company	Might involve slight losses	Moderate costs to company possible	Possibility of significant losses	Possibility of serious losses	4
Resourcefulness—Extent to which ingenuity and initiative are required because of non-routine character of work or likelihood of unexpected problems arising.	None or very little	Fairly routine or follow directions	Occasional independent thinking required	Great deal of independent thinking	New problems constantly arising	3
Physical Requirements and Environment—Mental and physical fatigue involved; strength and endurance required; safety and health hazards involved in occupation or work place.	Light work, no hazards, pleasant surroundings	Standing jobs, some nervous	Moderately strenuous; slight hazards	Strenuous; fair working conditions; some hazards	Heavy work, unpleasant working conditions; hazards	5
Supervision—Number of persons for whose work, training, and conduct is directly responsible.	None	Under 6	6-12	12-25	25-50	0
						28

systems, the major factors are subdivided, each subdivision being scored. Also some systems have a different percentage distribution of points for the various factors; e.g., skill may be given a maximum total of points several times higher than that for physical requirements.) In the present illustration, the highest possible value, 64 points, could be given only to a job involving supervision of at least 25 subordinates, and requiring a person who has had a full college or technical school education and at least four years' practical experience. In addition, the job must be especially unpleasant or hazardous and require numerous skills with precision tools which, if not used properly, would entail heavy losses to the company.

There are no jobs in a shoe factory which involve the maximum degree for all 8 factors, although adequate performance on several jobs requires the maximum 8 points for one or several of the factors. In other words, in the example used in this illustration, no job would have a point value as high as 64.

In the present hypothetical shoe plant the rates of two jobs are used as yardsticks. The minimum rate for the least skilled job classification is 60 cents an hour and has been given a value of 5 points; one of the most highly skilled jobs, hand cutting, has a base rate of $1.20 per hour and has been evaluated at 35 points. Each point, therefore, has a 2-cent value (the difference between the minimum and maximum wage rates, 60 cents, divided by the difference between 5 and 35 points). The job under review, shoe lasting machine operator, is analyzed factor by factor, with a resulting total value of 28 points, which is 23 points above the minimum. The job rate for a shoe lasting machine operator therefore is $1.06 per hour, which is 23 times 2 cents plus the base rate of 60 cents.

Factor Comparison Method

Sometimes the process of evaluation is reversed by using money values instead of point values for each factor. According to this method, a selected number of key jobs whose wage rates have already been agreed upon are chosen as bench marks. These key jobs, which range from the bottom to the top of the plant's wage scale, are ranked under each of the factors in order of their relative importance; that is, under "Skill" the key job requiring the greatest skill is listed first, and under "Physical" the most strenuous job or the one requiring the greatest endurance is listed first. The established wage rate for each of these jobs is then divided among the factors in accordance with their estimated importance. For example, a key job paying $1.00 may be assigned 40 cents for skill, 30 cents for experience, 20 cents for responsibility, and 10 cents for physical requirements. After money values have been assigned to all the factors of all the key jobs, there results a series of scales to be used for evaluating all the other jobs in the plant. In other words, instead of descriptive definitions of factors as in the point method, there are series of money values in terms of key jobs against which other jobs can be compared and their factor values cross-totaled to obtain job rates.

TIME AND MOTION STUDY

Regardless of whether or not it has been "scientifically" determined, any wage rate represents a composite payment for the *kind* of work performed and the *amount* of work produced. Job evaluation, as indicated above, is a systematic method of classifying jobs and establishing rate differentials according to the kind of work done. It is not concerned with quantitative measures of performance. Entirely different means are used in the scientific determination of wages on the basis of the amount of work accomplished.

Purpose of Time and Motion Study

An individual's output per unit of time depends, first, upon the conditions and methods of work performance and, second, upon his ability and will to produce. For the first, the industrial engineer offers time and motion study to ascertain production standards, and for the second, some form of wage incentive to induce workers to meet or exceed established standards. In principle, the established standard represents the performance which an average operator can achieve with average effort and at a pace that can be maintained indefinitely.

The primary purpose of time and motion study is to discover what *is* being accomplished and what *can* be accomplished on any particular job. Since many of the conditions affecting performance lie within management's control, the initial function of time and motion study is to establish the conditions of work that will facilitate optimum output. These include such matters as the condition of tools, machinery, or other equipment, physical surroundings such as lighting and ventilation, the routing of work to the operator, and the like.

When satisfactory conditions surrounding the job have been established, the next step is to analyze the job performance itself. This is done either by means of stop-watch readings or through motion picture or micromotion analysis.

Stop-Watch Method

For stop-watch studies[4] a minute-decimal stop watch is used for timing, and an observation sheet is used for recording. A worker of average competence is selected, or several persons on the same job are observed, in order to get the average performance. In lieu of recognized "average" performance, the time study analyst may rate the skill and effort of the operator under observation in terms of the percentage of what the analyst considers to be average, and make whatever allowances are necessary when totaling the time. This is commonly called "leveling."

In the more careful time study, recordings are taken for each movement or element of each operation, rather than the over-all time for the entire operation. An element represents the smallest unit of effort or motion which can be recognized and accurately timed, and all the elements involved in the completion of one unit of work represent a work cycle. Since many elements are the same in various operations, the values of these "constant" elements, when once determined, can be used repeatedly. For example, in jobs which require the handling of similar tools or materials, the picking up of the tool or the placing of the material might be constant elements, while the motions involved in the use of the tools or materials would comprise variable elements, each depending upon the nature of the several jobs.

Different methods are used for reading the stop watch and recording the time on the observation sheet. Sometimes the watch is permitted to run throughout the observation, that is, through several work cycles, with watch readings being taken at the end of

---

[4] First used by F. W. Taylor in a steel plant in 1881.

TIME STUDY OBSERVATION SHEET

DATE
PART NAME
OPERATION

SPECIAL EQUIPMENT
(Coolant, Type Cutter, etc.)

OPER. NO. _____ MACHINE

DRAWING NO.
PATTERN NO.
ITEM NO. _____ MAT'L.
ORDER NO.
OPERATOR

TOOL NO. _____
CLOCK NO. _____ DEPT.

No.	ELEMENTS	Fr./Rev. Per Min.	Feed Ins. Per Min./Rev.	1 Reading	1 Time	2 Reading	2 Time	3 Reading	3 Time	4 Reading	4 Time	5 Reading	5 Time	Time
TOTALS														

PIECES FIN. BEFORE STUDY   INSPECTED BY   INSPECT. NET CYCLE TIME EACH _____ MIN.

FINISH TIME A.M. P.M.   CHECKED BY   FM. EFFORT & SKILL _____ % _____ MIN.

START TIME A.M. P.M.   OBSERVER   LEVELED NET _____ MIN.

OVERALL TIME   APPROVED BY   PERSONAL NORMAL _____ %

NO. OF PIECES TIMED   SPECIAL _____ %

OVERALL TIME PER PIECE   TOTAL ALLOWED TIME EACH   MIN. MACHINE CARE _____ %

TYPE OF WATCH USED   DECIMAL HOURS   HRS. TOOL CARE _____ %

SET-UP   INCENTIVE RATE $ ALLOWED TIME EACH _____ MIN.

SHEET _____ OF _____ SHEETS   P. W. PRICE OR STD. TIME _____ MIN.

each element; subtraction of the successive readings gives the time for each element. Sometimes the watch is snapped back to zero at the end of each element observed or, more commonly, at the end of each cycle. In the latter case, of course, the successive readings must also be subtracted to obtain the time for each element. Regardless of the stop-watch procedure, a half-dozen or more readings are usually made, and either the most representative as determined by the analyst is selected, or the average of all the readings is used as the final time allowance for each element.

To the total of all the element-times are added specified allowances for personal needs, fatigue, care of tools and machines, and any regular unavoidable delays or interruptions which are accepted as an intrinsic part of the operation. The allowance for personal needs is usually 4 or 5 per cent of the total time, which is equivalent to 20 minutes in an 8-hour day. Allowance for fatigue varies, of course, according to the nature of the job, and the same is true for the care of machines and tools and any other recognized allowances.

The sum of the net cycle time, less any leveling and plus all specified allowances, represents the "standard" time per work cycle or operation. "Standard" is expressed in decimal hours which can be readily translated into either a time or piece unit of meaurement for wage-setting purposes. Although "standard" is supposed to represent average or normal performance, it is usually less than the time which was taken previously to perform the operation. In other words, time and motion study almost always results in time saving or, to express it another way, in greater production per hour or day.[5]

Micromotion

Motion pictures are sometimes utilized in place of or supplementary to stop-watch studies. Micromotion study,[6] as it is called, involves the use of a motion-picture camera and a timing device

---

[5] In a study of 70 plants it was found that "standards" established on the basis of time and motion studies were 17 per cent in excess of previous production. (J. M. Nickerson, Director of the Management Consultant Division, W.P.B., before the American Society of Mechanical Engineers, December 1, 1943.)

[6] Frank C. and Lillian M. Gilbreth were the pioneers in the use of motion pictures. On the basis of such studies they determined that there were 18 elementary subdivisions or elements (which they called "therbligs") to a cycle of motions which they believed were common to all kinds of manual work. A well-known example of one of their early studies was bricklaying; they reduced the movements for laying a brick from 18 to 5 motions. In addition to micromotion, they developed what they called the chronocyclegraph technique which measures the time, speed, acceleration, and retardation, and shows the direction and path of motion in three dimensions.

which indicates the time intervals on the motion-picture film. The advantage of micromotion is that the sequence of movements and the use of the body organs (eyes, head, arms, feet) can be observed, and unnecessary, awkward, and fatiguing practices can be easily

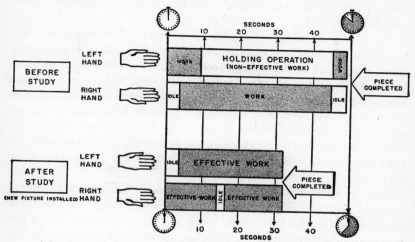

FIG. 23.   *Example of Method Improvement.*
(*Source: Albert Ramond and Associates, Inc.*)

detected (see Fig. 23). Since the motions are recorded on a film, the best methods can be "captured" for use in training and re-training. Once the best methods have been established and the motion-picture time recordings have been taken, the process of tabulating standard time for the job cycle is similar to that used with the stop-watch procedure.

TIME-WORK METHOD OF WAGE PAYMENT

The establishment of standards through time and motion study or by other means does not necessarily imply any change in methods of wage payment. Wages may continue to be a fixed sum per hour or day, with no direct or automatic adjustment of daily or weekly wages to output.

Presumably, however, an employee will not be retained if he constantly fails to meet accepted standards of output; likewise, an employee whose output is regularly above the average may receive a "merit" rate which is higher than the base rate for the job. Some plants have merit rating systems and measured production, with graduated pay according to each individual's average output. Such an arrangement approximates a wage incentive plan, although day-to-day earnings do not fluctuate automatically with daily output.

The chief advantage of the time-work method of wage payment to both employers and employees is its simplicity. It requires the least amount of bookkeeping, and the workers know exactly what their earnings are at the close of each day. Where other wage plans have supplanted payment on a time-work basis, the motive of the employer has been to provide greater inducements for increasing production. Where other types of wage payment systems have been accepted by workers, it has been because they considered that such plans offered greater possibilities for increasing their earnings.

A wage system based on the time worked is the only practical form of payment for certain kinds of jobs or under certain job conditions; for example, where unusual skills and individuality are required, or where danger of spoilage outweighs any consideration of volume of output, or where the processes or materials used are constantly undergoing change. When the exact reverse of such conditions exists, payment on an hourly basis is likewise most feasible. For example, on so-called "mechanically paced" jobs, that is, on chain assembly and automatic machine-tending jobs where the machines themselves determine output, there is no need or opportunity for reward on the basis of individual output. Incentive systems of wage payment are practical only when output can be increased by the employees' *own* effort and output can be *accurately* measured.

INCENTIVE WAGE SYSTEMS

Basically, incentive methods of wage payment are of two general types: those in which payments are directly adjusted to units of output, and those in which payments are based on a combination of time and output units according to an established formula. The first is usually referred to as straight piecework; the second, as a premium or bonus system. (Sometimes "incentive" is used to refer only to premium systems, although of course straight piecework is also a form of incentive wages.)

Straight Piecework

Under a straight piecework system a constant rate is paid per unit of output, with no specified minimum or guaranteed rates and no maximum limitations. Actually, minimum earnings must meet the legal requirements,[7] and any difference between piecework earnings and the legal minimum rate must be made up by the employer.

Payment by the piece is the oldest form of incentive wages, but it is now being replaced by other kinds of incentive systems in many plants. It has existed for many years in the clothing, shoe, hosiery, and cigar industries, as well as in rolling mills and coal mining where payment is on a tonnage basis. The methods of determining individual piece rates do not necessarily differ from those used in other forms of wage incentive systems. However, since many piecework systems antecede scientific management techniques, piece rates are less frequently determined on the basis of job analysis.

In lieu of time and motion study, each individual piece rate either is the result of employer-union bargaining or, in unorganized plants, is determined by the employer or foreman. In both situations the rates for new jobs tend to be determined on the basis of past production on similar jobs, with estimates for any new factors involved. Much of the odium which workers attach to piecework has been due to the employers' practice of cutting rates even though there has been no change in the content of the job.

Under any piecework system the rates established per unit of output include allowances for fatigue, short absences from the job for personal reasons, oiling of machines, and any other incidental duties regularly involved in the performance of the day's job. Piece rates, however, do not make provision for unusual interruptions caused by machine breakdown, delays in the flow of work, etc., and practice varies with respect to payment for such lost time. In some plants the employee is reimbursed the equivalent of his average piece-rate earnings over a fixed period of time, for example, the last pay period; in others each employee or individual job has a base rate, usually somewhat under the average earnings, which is the amount of reimbursement for "dead time."

---

[7] See chap. 14.

The basis of reimbursement for time lost on the job through no fault of the operator frequently becomes a matter of contention under any piecework system. In many plants the individual foremen exercise a good deal of discretion and there is therefore no uniform practice even within the same plant. Under collective bargaining, unions seek to have the policy standardized, the amount of discretion allowed foremen being kept to a minimum in each individual case.

Payment of a fixed rate per piece (or per unit of weight such as a ton) is the simplest form of wage incentive plan. It is relatively easy for the workers to understand; hence they can know what their daily earnings are. Unlike some other wage incentive systems, the rate per piece remains constant and earnings are in direct proportion to the number of units of output. For the employer the piece-rate system, like any other wage incentive plan, tends to reduce unit labor costs, in addition to providing an accurate measure for estimating these costs. It also provides an automatic stimulant for shop efficiency; for since pieceworkers naturally object to working conditions which hinder their maximum earning ability, they will insist that machines be kept in good condition and that there be the least possible amount of interruption in the flow of work.

Some workers favor piecework because of the relative amount of independence and freedom from close supervision such a wage system affords. So long as the quality of his work is satisfactory, a pieceworker is free from close scrutiny by his foreman and he has more latitude in his work habits than an employee who is paid, or guaranteed, a fixed wage per hour or day.

Under piecework where the total wages paid are automatically related to the total volume produced (except for legal minima), there is not the same urgency for an employer to keep to a minimum the number of persons on the job as there is under time work. For the workers, this has advantages as well as disadvantages. An employer may be prone to hire an excess number of workmen during temporary booms, which causes a reduction in the earnings possibilities of the older workers. On the other hand, during slack seasons there are likely to be fewer layoffs. In unionized plants there are generally rules to prevent excess hiring, as well as regulations pertaining to work sharing and layoff, so that work will not be spread to the point where no one is able to earn subsistence wages.

Premium Systems

There are scores of different kinds of premium or bonus systems[8] now in use and many others which have been used for a time and then discarded. The variety of types, however, is not as great as the numerous titles applied to them would seem to indicate, for many which appear to be dissimilar actually incorporate only minor variations but have been given new names, frequently the name of the engineering firm who sponsors or sells the system.[9]

No matter what name they go by, all premium systems have one distinct characteristic, namely, a guaranteed rate with premium payments for production beyond an established standard. The standard may be in terms of units of output or units of time, that is, minutes or hours. So far as the incentive feature is concerned, there is no difference in principle whether the premiums are figured on the number of pieces produced above standard or on the number of minutes or hours saved.[10] A practical advantage of the time unit as contrasted with the piece unit is that there is no necessity for changing hundreds of individual piece rates whenever general wage levels are changed.

The essential distinctions in the various incentive systems have to do with (1) the point or level of production at which premiums begin, and (2) the formula used for determining premium rates.

In all premium systems the crucial factor is where the "task" or "standard" is set; the policy adopted can tend toward either of two directions, namely, a strict standard which is difficult to

---

[8] Since the term "bonus" is more commonly used to refer to occasional payments such as Christmas bonuses and service bonuses, the term "premium" will hereafter be used in connection with incentive wage plans.

[9] One engineer who analyzed 28 different incentive systems concluded that many of the differences were unimportant and that few of the more recent, complex plans have essential or original modifications of the simpler types. (See C. W. Lytle, *Wage Incentive Plans,* The Ronald Press Company, New York, 1942.)

[10] For example, if the standard is 75 pieces an hour and the rate is 1 cent per piece, a worker who produces 100 pieces in an hour would earn a premium of 33⅓ per cent, or an hourly wage of $1. If, on the other hand, the standard is one hour for 75 pieces and a worker completed 75 pieces in 45 minutes, he would be rated as 133⅓ per cent efficient (60 minutes ÷ 45 minutes) and therefore be paid $1.00 for an hour's work.

accomplish, with high premiums for better than standard, or a lenient standard with relatively small premiums. If a very strict standard is set which can be exceeded only through the best efforts of the most competent workers, the guaranteed rate tends to become the actual earnings rate for most of the workers. If, on the

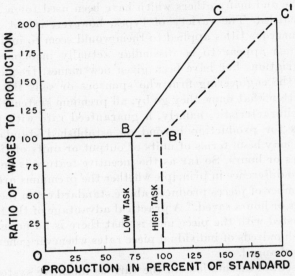

FIG. 24.   *Earning Curves for High and Low Task Standards.*

other hand, a relatively easy standard is fixed, the major portion of the total earnings of most employees on the job will consist of premium wages.

The difference in potential earning capacity under a low and high task[11] is graphically illustrated in Fig. 24, where *BC* represents the wage curve based on a relatively low standard, and B^1C^1 the curve based on a high standard. In this figure premiums are assumed to be 100 per cent; that is, workers receive a guaranteed base rate up to the established standard, and the equivalent of straight piece rates for output above standard.

---

[11] Time study analysts commonly refer to standards which they deem too low as being "loose," and workers call standards "tight" which they think are too high.

The second fundamental distinction in incentive plans has to do with the formula for the division of gains when above-standard production is attained, regardless of whether or not the established standard is high or low. In straight piecework, of course, the worker's earnings increase in direct ratio to output; that is, the premiums amount to 100 per cent of the piece rates regardless of output. Under some incentive plans, probably a minority of those currently in existence, the premium rate is either less or more than 100 per cent as output increases above standard.

Increasing the ratio of returns to the worker is obviously done for the purpose of encouraging ever higher production. Plans providing for a decreasing ratio of returns, or a declining wage curve, are based upon the principle that increased output not only is a result of the workers' efforts but is also due to improvement in working conditions for which management is responsible, and that management therefore should "share" in the gains. Also, the declining premium rates are supposed to serve as a deterrent to rate cutting by the employer, since his unit labor costs decrease as production increases.

Incentive plans which provide for graduated premium rates are referred to as "multiple piece-rate" plans; those providing for decreasing rates are called "gain-sharing systems," although workers are more likely to refer to them as "take-away" plans. The fundamental differences in the various premium systems can best be explained by brief descriptions of a few of the more important systems which illustrate general principles. Most of the incentive plans in actual use today, regardless of their names, are variations and modifications of one or more of these systems.

Differential or Multiple Piece-Rate Systems. The original incentive wage system, excluding the straight piecework already discussed, was that used by F. W. Taylor and called the "Differential Rate System." Essentially it was a modification of the straight piece-rate plan, with the important difference that it established two distinct sets of piece rates for each job—a lower piece rate when less than the established day's task was completed, and a higher rate per piece when the total output equaled or exceeded the established task. For example, if the task is 100 pieces per day, the rate per piece might be 3 cents for below task performance and 4 cents per piece for performance at or above task. Thus, to use

an extreme case, a worker would earn $2.97 a day when he pro-
duced 99 pieces, and $4 a day when he produced 100 pieces, or
approximately a 35 per cent increase in earnings for 1 per cent
more output.

The Taylor plan is frankly punitive, the lower rates being "fixed
at a figure which will allow the workman to earn scarcely an
ordinary day's pay when he falls from his maximum pace, so as
to give him every inducement to work hard and well."[12] In extenua-
tion of this harsh wage system it can be said that under the Taylor
plan for efficient management, improved working conditions facilitated better production, and increased output was not achieved
solely at the expense of greater physical effort on the part of the
workers. Many employers, however, adopted the Taylor wage
system without also putting into effect the Taylor plans for improved management.

Modifications of the original Taylor system lessen the abrupt
change in the earnings curve by substituting two or more step-ups
in piece rates. The multiple premium rate plan formulated by
D. V. Merrick, provides for the payment of three different piece
rates on the same job—a relatively low rate for performance below 83 per cent of the established task, an additional 10 per cent
premium when output is between 83 and 100 per cent of task, and
a 20 per cent premium when output is at or above task.

Gain-Sharing Plans.   The Halsey[13] Gain-Sharing Plan was the
first incentive system to provide a guaranteed rate plus a premium
for extra output. As originally conceived, existing time rates
continued to be paid for "normal" production based on average
past performance, with a premium, usually 50 per cent but sometimes less, for any time saved by the worker. In its initial form, the
Halsey plan was directed solely toward reward for extra effort,
the workers continuing to receive the same day rates for working
at their customary pace. Later, however, when time and motion
studies were substituted for average past performance as a measure of "normal," the standard time allowance tended to be lowered,

[12] Frederick W. Taylor. "A Piece Rate System," *American Society of Mechanical Engineers Journal,* June, 1895.

[13] Sometimes referred to as the Towne-Halsey plan since the engineer
Frederick A. Halsey got his idea from the profit-sharing system which Henry
R. Towne had introduced (1886) in the Yale-Towne Mfgr. Co.

with the result that better than past performance was necessary before any premiums were earned. Consequently, the 50 per cent premium actually represented a reduction in wages in relation to output. In other words, the employer shared 50 per cent of the gains resulting from an output above the standard which *he* established.

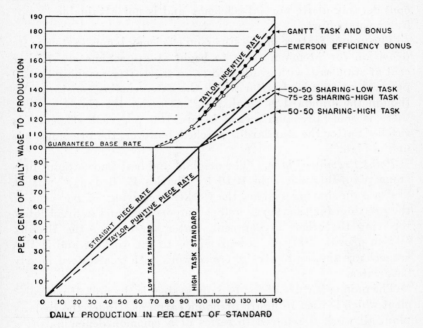

FIG. 25. *Earning Curves Under Various Incentive Plans.*

The significant difference in earnings with any gain-sharing plan based on high task performance in contrast to straight piecework is illustrated in Fig. 25.

Task and Bonus Plans. The Gantt[14] task and bonus plan combines the characteristics of both the Taylor and the Halsey systems. Like the latter it provides a guaranteed minimum wage for

---

[14] Henry L. Gantt, an associate of F. W. Taylor, introduced his system at the Bethlehem Steel Works in 1901 as a temporary measure until conditions made feasible the use of the Taylor system. The Gantt arrangement soon superseded the Taylor wage plan.

below the "task," instead of the Taylor punitive low piece rate. Above the "task" the worker receives not merely the equivalent of full piece rates instead of a portion as under the Halsey plan, but also an additional premium which essentially is comparable to the high piece rate under the Taylor plan. As an offset to the high premium rate, however, the task or standard is established considerably above normal efficiency and is not attainable except by unusual efforts.

The unique feature of the Emerson efficiency bonus system is its provision for premium rates to begin at approximately 70 per cent of standard, with graduated rates thereafter reaching to 120 per cent at standard, after which the rate remains constant. Although the standard is "high task" as under the Gantt system, there is some premium award before 100 per cent efficiency is reached; after the standard is reached, however, the premiums are not as high.[15]

Point Premium Plans. The original and best-known point premium plan, introduced in 1916 by Charles E. Bedaux,[16] was at first a gain-sharing system, the workers receiving 75 per cent of the premium for time saved and the supervisors and indirect labor receiving the other 25 per cent. Later versions of the Bedaux system provide 100 per cent premiums to the workers and in this respect are similar to straight piecework with guaranteed hourly base rates.

The unique feature of the Bedaux system is the unit of measurement which is used to figure premium earnings. Under the Bedaux plan, all work is reduced to terms of a common denominator, a minute of time called a "B," with total work performance the sum

---

[15] First put into operation by Harrington Emerson on the Santa Fe Railroad in 1904. To illustrate, assume a wage of 60 cents an hour, with 6 hours established as standard for completion of a task. If the worker completes the task in 5 hours, his earnings according to the Emerson formula would be: 60¢ × 5 hours × 120% + 60¢ = $4.20.

[16] Workers and unions who disliked all incentive systems were especially antagonistic toward Mr. Bedaux, who became their symbol for speed-up and unjust pay plans. After making a fortune in this country with his industrial engineering system, Mr. Bedaux, who had immigrated to the United States when a young man, moved back to France. After World War II broke out, the Department of Justice reported that Bedaux had close associations with Nazi officials. He was brought back to this country to face a grand jury investigation but committed suicide before the trial started.

of the B's produced within a given time. A "B" minute is composed of the relative proportion of work and rest as indicated by the requirements of the whole job. For example, time and motion study may indicate that a job takes 15 minutes of straight labor but, to be continued throughout the day, requires 5 minutes' rest, or a ratio of 3 to 1. The "B" for this job would be a minute of 45 seconds' work and 15 seconds' rest. Other jobs have other ratios, but all are measured in terms of B's; 60 B's equal the standard and premiums are based on B's above the standard.

Another well-known point method is the Haynes system. In it the standard man-minute is called a Manit, and is supposed to represent four-fifths of the amount of work that a normal person can do. Workers are paid according to the Manits produced; if 75 Manits are produced in an hour, for example, the earnings are 25 per cent above the hour base rate. As originally conceived, the Haynes system was a gain-sharing plan (50 per cent to workers, 10 per cent to supervisors, 40 per cent to the company), but it was later modified so that the full savings were paid to the workers.

Group Incentive Plans. In the foregoing descriptions it has been assumed that the output of each worker was measurable so that premiums could be computed on each individual's production. Under many conditions of production, however, it is impossible to separate the work performed by several persons in order to determine each one's contribution. Where work is closely integrated and inseparable, the joint product of a crew of workers, sometimes referred to as a "gang," is treated as a unit and the premiums are distributed to the group in proportion to their several base rates. As an illustration, if there were three members in a group whose base rates (varying according to their relative skills, etc.) were 75 cents, 90 cents, and $1 per hour and the day's group bonus amounted to $4, they would receive premiums of $1.13, $1.36, and $1.51 respectively.

PREVALENCE OF INCENTIVE SYSTEMS AND THEIR EFFECT ON WAGES

No one knows exactly how many American wage earners are now being paid on an incentive basis, but it is probable that more than half of those on production processes—as distinct from maintenance, custodial, time-keeping, and the like—are employed under some form of incentive system.

There is considerable variation in the extent to which incentive plans have been adopted in the different industries. They are almost completely absent in the construction and printing industries, although some paperhangers and lathers as well as printers[17] are on a piecework basis. Incentive systems exist in a number of shipyards and aircraft plants in the eastern section of the country, but they are almost non-existent on the west coast. Following unionization of the automobile industry in 1935–1937, time work was substituted for piecework in many plants; however, a number of plants retained or have recently established incentive systems. Payment on a tonnage basis is common in coal mining, and various kinds of premium systems are in effect throughout large sections of the electrical equipment, rubber, steel, and glass industries. Piecework prevails in the textile and clothing industries, including shoe, glove, and hat manufacturing, and is fairly common in the meat-packing, paper, leather, and machinery industries.

Reduction in manufacturing costs is of course the primary reason why employers install incentive systems. The reduction is both direct and indirect. Greater output per wage dollar is a direct saving; more effective use of machinery and equipment is an indirect economy. Furthermore, some employers claim that incentive workers need less supervision, although others have found it necessary to increase supervision and inspection to safeguard quality. Offsetting some of the savings in direct labor and machinery outlay are the overhead costs of administering incentive systems for they are always higher than a time-work pay system.

The only reason workers have been willing to accept incentive pay plans is the possibility they offer for increasing earnings. Although there are no over-all statistics to show comparative earnings of incentive versus time workers, numerous studies of particular industries and plants reveal significant differences.

One study of three industries[18] showed that average earnings

---

[17] As a result of a concerted drive by the International Typographical Union, piecework has been practically abolished among its members during the past few years.

[18] "Effect of Incentive Payments on Hourly Earnings," *Monthly Labor Review*, May, 1943.

of incentive workers ranged from 12 to 18 per cent higher than the hourly earnings of time workers in the same occupation. In more than two-thirds of the occupations in machinery manufacturing plants located in various sections of the country, the average hourly wages of incentive workers were from 10 to 30 per cent higher than the wages of time workers, and there were about the same differences for most of the occupations in cotton goods manufacturing and non-ferrous metal fabrication. Reports from individual companies during the recent war period indicated that average hourly earnings increased an average of almost 20 per cent within three months after incentive systems were installed.[19]

WORKERS' ATTITUDE TOWARD INCENTIVE SYSTEMS

As indicated earlier, the scientific determination of wage rates is concerned solely with procedures for establishing relative values of jobs and earnings in relation to output. The area within which wages can be "scientifically" determined lies within the boundaries of minimum and maximum standards already established. Since scientific wage systems are not concerned with general wage levels, they are not substitutes for, or necessarily inimical to, collective bargaining or other means for establishing general wage standards. Nonetheless, workers are concerned with scientific procedures because they vitally and directly affect the amount of wages they receive as well as the conditions under which they work.

Acceptance of Job Evaluation

In general, workers and their unions have accepted the principle of job evaluation by systematic methods. Differences of opinion arise, of course, over the particular methods used and the ratings given particular jobs. In organized plants, the unions naturally insist that the workers concerned have a voice in the evaluation process and that dissatisfactions arising over job evaluations be dealt with through the union's grievance adjustment machinery.

In small shops where there are only a few skilled occupations,

---

[19] J. W. Nickerson, *Wage Incentive Plans and Labor Management Relationship,* Management Consultant Division, War Production Board, Washington, 1944.

especially when they are under the jurisdiction of different craft unions, the various groups of workers or unions may prefer to bargain separately for each job rate.[20] Systematic job evaluation is most frequently utilized in large plants where old-time craft distinctions are no longer dominant and where there are a multiplicity of different kinds of jobs.

Opposition to Incentive Systems

Other phases of scientific wage determination, namely, time and motion study and incentive plans, have not gained the same acceptance by workers as has job evaluation. Few management policies have aroused as much controversy between employers and workers as have time and motion study and incentive forms of wage payment. Workers have vigorously and often successfully opposed the introduction of stop-watch and incentive plans;[21] where such plans have been installed over the workers' opposition there have been numerous disputes over their day-to-day administration.

The fact that incentive wages have been used successfully as rallying cries to get unorganized workers to join unions[22] is one

[20] Job evaluation undoubtedly would result in the readjustment of some existing rates which have grown up through collective bargaining by various unions. For example, in the building trades the rates for bricklayers are generally higher than the carpenters' rates, although the latter are usually required to read blueprints and assume other responsibilities in addition to their hand skills.

[21] The first major success was in 1914, when organized labor conducted a vigorous campaign against the adoption of incentive systems on government projects. Ever since 1914–1915 riders have been attached to the Army, Navy, and Post Office Appropriation Acts specifying that no part of the appropriation "shall be available for the salary or pay of any officer, manager, superintendent, foreman or other person or persons having charge of the work of any employee of the U. S. Government while making or causing to be made with a stop watch or other time-measuring device a time study of any job of any such employee between the starting and completion thereof, or, of the movements of any such employee while engaged upon such work; nor shall any part of the appropriations made in this act be available to pay any premiums or bonus or cash reward to any employee in addition to his regular wages, except for suggestions resulting in improvements or economy in the operation of any Government plant; . . ." (77th Cong., Public Act No. 441.)

[22] Long-pent-up grievances over incentive wages and speed-up in the Detroit automobile industry was a major factor in the successful unionization campaigns of 1936–1937.

In a rival union campaign at the Aluminum Corporation of America plant at Lafayette, Indiana, in 1943, the C.I.O. Aluminum Workers favored incen-

evidence that union opposition, where it exists, is not a creation of the unions themselves but rather a reflection of individual workers' attitudes. Unorganized as well as organized workers have "pegged" their production, refused to work with "pace setters," and tried other means of thwarting or controlling incentive systems. When workers are unorganized, however, their expressions of opposition must necessarily be more subtle and be made by tacit arrangement in small groups, as contrasted to the more vigorous and overt expressions and actions of union members and their spokesmen.

Some of the objections which workers have to time study and premium systems relate to the essential nature of any and all incentive plans; others have to do with particular kinds of systems and practices which are not necessarily inherent in the principle of incentive wages per se. Much of the disrepute of incentive systems is due to the practice—more common in past years than now —of cutting rates and forcing workers to speed up to make their expected earnings. Serious objections are made against the complexities and mysteries of many of the systems and the consequent inability of workers to know how their pay is figured.[23]

An understandable reluctance to accept time and motion study and wage incentives is the fear of losing one's job because of increased productivity. Employers and industrial engineers may argue that the resulting reduced costs of production will in the long run make for greater prosperity and more jobs, but workers are necessarily concerned with their own immediate situation, and their concern seems justified to them when they hear employers boast that they were able to effect "substantial" layoffs after

---

tives, while the A. F. of L. Federal Labor Union opposed them. The A. F. of L. union won, largely because of such sentiments expressed as the following: "The bonus system is a notorious design of the slave-driving piece work plan that the A. F. of L. has fought against for years. . . . Under incentives, when the machine is being repaired WHAM goes your bonus. When there is a shortage of material WHAM goes your bonus. . . . We don't want this kind of . . . company policy. . . . We want to know exactly how much we are making an hour." (War Labor Board Report.)

[23] Any unbiased person who has attempted to study the intricacies of the systems which some industrial engineers espouse will heartily sympathize with the workers' feelings in this respect. For example, one plan proposed this formula for premium payments: guaranteed day rate up to $62\frac{1}{2}$ per cent of task; 50–50 sharing from $62\frac{1}{2}$ to 100 per cent of task; 10 per cent of base rate bonus at task; above task $66\frac{2}{3}$ to $33\frac{1}{3}$ constant sharing. Let any worker, even though he be a college graduate, try to figure his pay on such a formula!

installing wage incentive plans.[24] Some of this fear is removed or at least mitigated by carefully planned transfers or by payment of dismissal wages.

Underlying all the hesitancy and objection to time study and incentive wages are the workers' instinctive aversion to and uneasiness over a purely "scientific" approach to their jobs which seems to ignore them as human beings and to treat them as abstract labor going through numerous cycles of motions.[25] This feeling is alleviated to some extent when the time study analyst adopts a human approach and when the workers concerned are allowed to have a voice in the process.

Acceptance of Incentive Plans

Although many workers and unions are strongly opposed to all forms of incentive wages, piecework and other kinds of incentive

---

[24] Examples like the following can be found in any management journal: "Labor costs reduced 75%." "Reduced force from 94 to 19." "Earnings of survivors have increased." "In slack times there is no temptation to make the job last." "In every group there are 2 or 3 men who keep the foremen informed about other workers." "Identity of interest has greatly simplified the problem of discipline."

[25] The following is illustrative of the numerous formal expressions of union opposition to incentive systems: "We are against all attempts to revive and impose on American workers the 'incentive' payment plan in any shape, manner or form. More than ever are we convinced that these 'bonus' trick systems are injurious to the best interests of labor. They are spurious panaceas aggravating rather than alleviating grievances and infections in our economic relations. . . . By adopting the incentive payment plan, American Labor will be driving its own people out of jobs. The great benefits of unionization will be discarded and destroyed. The speed at which men are asked to work properly falls within the sphere of collective bargaining. . . . Very often the lure of higher earnings is hollow. Incentive payments encourage a reckless speeding up of the workers. . . . All too often we have found that after production per worker has been increased through the speed-up, the employers have cut the rate per piece of work turned out. Here is a vicious circle. Either the worker must suffer a loss of earnings, or he must speed up still more. . . . To our profit-hungry efficiency engineers, the model worker is one who freely expends all of his surplus energy during the working hours and who utilizes his non-working hours only for recuperation and preparation for another day's work. . . . The advocates of these bonus schemes are trying hard to pit worker against worker and thus destroy collective bargaining as an instrument for assuring a just wage for the American working people. . . . The 'incentive' system is a springboard for further efforts at lengthening hours, speeding up production and putting over devious wage reduction schemes. The time to defeat these plans is now. . . . Union labor must hit back and hit back hard now." (*The Carpenter*, August, 1943.)

plans have been customary in some industries for many years, with no serious efforts made toward their elimination either before or after the plants were unionized. Incentive wages prevail in some of the most strongly organized industries, e.g., clothing,[26] coal mining, steel, and more recently the electrical equipment industry. In a number of other industries a larger proportion of the unionized than the non-union plants have incentive systems.[27]

Although some unions are unalterably opposed to all incentive systems,[28] most unions adapt their tactics to the current situation in a particular plant; if incentive wages are already in existence they accept them in principle but seek to obtain specific modifications. In some instances where unions have succeeded in abolishing incentives, they have later reversed their position and cooperated

---

[26] Piecework in the clothing, shoe, and cigar trades has its roots in the early "domestic" system of production, where work was contracted out to persons who worked at home. In such circumstances, piece rates assume the form of prices more than wages. Vestiges of this remain in small construction where jobs are let to a skilled worker who does all the work himself. Here the contract price is equivalent to wages since there is no profit element. Because of the possibility of these contract prices undercutting regular hour scales, building-trades unions normally do not allow their members to accept such contract jobs.

[27] Wage studies by the Bureau of Labor Statistics indicate that the existence of incentive systems is related more to the size of plant than to the presence or absence of unions, incentive wages being more prevalent in large plants. In Sweden, where trade unions have been firmly established for many years, piecework systems are prevalent throughout industry and even extend into the building trades, where group bonus systems exist. (Paul H. Norgren, *The Swedish Collective Bargaining System*, Harvard University Press, 1941.) In Great Britain, where unions are also firmly established, there has been a great expansion in incentive payments. The British Amalgamated Engineering Unions, which for a hundred years had opposed piecework, changed this policy as a means of increasing war production. In 1943 about 75 per cent of the direct production workers in the engineering industries were covered by incentive systems of wage payment. ("Payment by Results in British Engineering," *International Labor Review,* June, 1944.)

[28] The constitutions of a number of unions absolutely forbid contracts embodying incentive methods of wage payment, and some cite acceptance or encouragement of incentive plans as grounds for expulsion from the union. Some unions, e.g., the large U.A.W.-C.I.O., allow the continuance of plans already in existence but disallow further extension into plants now paying on a time basis. The United Steelworkers of America and the United Electrical Workers (C.I.O.) are examples of large unions which have accepted the principle of incentive wages but have taken definite steps toward obtaining "proper controls and safeguards." The latter has prepared a booklet entitled *UE Guide to Wage Incentive Plans, Time Study and Job Evaluation* for their members' use.

with the employers in getting them reestablished. The change in attitude may have resulted from competitive necessity and fear of the loss of jobs if the employer was forced out of business, or it may have been in response to the members' realization that earnings were less under time work than under the incentive system.

There are economic factors inherent in certain industries which seem to make piecework or other incentive plans the logical form of wage payment. Unions in these industries are aware of the problems and have made little effort to eliminate such plans. For example, piecework in general has been acceptable to unions in the apparel trades because of the importance of manual skill and control which results in wide variations in individual worker productivity. Thus, there are always sizable groups of faster workers who may feel that a change to time work would cause a decrease in their earnings. In addition, the apparel industries are subject to wide seasonal fluctuations in production and employment. Unions in these industries practice rigid work-sharing during slack seasons. The piecework method makes work-sharing possible, since employers are assured a fixed labor cost regardless of the amount of work to be done. These unions realize that without this fixed labor cost per unit of output, very few employers would consent to the rigid work-sharing which both workers and unions feel to be desirable in these industries. Also, these unions have adopted a policy of stabilizing labor costs among competing employers. Piecework facilitates stabilization, because unit labor costs can be determined in advance and do not depend on the relative efficiency of the individual workers or establishments.

The president of the C.I.O. has tacitly endorsed time and motion study and incentive wage plans under certain specified conditions in which there is maximum collaboration between labor and management: "Properly made and utilized they [time studies] are the most accurate and the fairest of all methods of fixing standards and for production control. . . . The fact that time study can, and often is, badly used is no argument against the method itself. The stop watch, in fact, is one of the most effective tools for union-management cooperation, because it establishes facts that cannot be gainsaid."[29]

---

[29] Morris L. Cooke and Philip Murray, *Organized Labor and Production,* Harper & Brothers, New York, 1940, pp. 117–118.

SELECTED REFERENCES

Balderston, C. C., *Wage Setting Based on Job Analysis and Evaluation,* Industrial Relations Counselors, Inc., New York, 1940.

Barnes, Ralph M., *Motion and Time Study,* John Wiley & Sons, Inc., New York, 1940.

Benge, E. J., Burk, S. L., and Hay, E. N., *Manual of Job Evaluation,* Harper & Brothers, New York, 1941.

Dickinson, Z. Clark, *Compensating Industrial Effort,* The Ronald Press Company, New York, 1937.

Gilbreth, Frank B. and Lillian M., *Applied Time and Motion Study,* Sturgis & Walton Co., New York, 1917.

Holmes, Walter G., *Applied Time and Motion Study,* The Ronald Press Company, New York, 1938.

Kennedy, Van Dusen, *Union Policy and Incentive Wage Methods,* Columbia University Press, New York, 1945.

Louden, J. K., *Wage Incentives,* John Wiley & Sons, Inc., New York, 1944.

Lowry, S. M., Maynard, H. B., and Stegemerten, G. J., *Time and Motion Study and Formulas for Wage Incentives,* McGraw-Hill Book Company, Inc., New York, 1940.

Lytle, C. W., *Wage Incentive Methods,* The Ronald Press Company, New York, 1942.

Lytle, C. W., *Job Evaluation Methods,* The Ronald Press Company, New York, 1946.

Myers, H. J., *Simplified Time Study,* The Ronald Press Company, New York, 1944.

Presgrave, Ralph, *The Dynamics of Time Study,* McGraw-Hill Book Company, Inc., New York, 1946.

Schutt, William H., *Time Study Engineering,* McGraw-Hill Book Company, Inc., New York, 1943.

Shumard, F. W., *Primer of Time Study,* McGraw-Hill Book Company, Inc., New York, 1940.

Stigers, M. F., and Reed, E. G., *The Theory and Practice of Job Rating,* McGraw-Hill Book Company, Inc., New York, 1942.

Taylor, Frederick W., *Shop Management,* Harper & Brothers, New York, 1911.

Taylor, Frederick W., *The Principles of Scientific Management,* Harper & Brothers, New York, 1911.

United Electrical Workers (C.I.O.), *U.E. Guide to Wage Payment Plans,* United Electrical Workers, New York, 1943.

13

WAGE SUPPLEMENTS

WAGES EARNED WHILE ON THE JOB REPRESENT MOST, AND FRE-
quently all, of the income which workers have at their disposal to
meet their daily costs of living and occasional vacations, as well
as sickness and other disabilities. Some workers are benefited by
payments and contributions of their employers which are not
direct payments for work performed on the job, although indirectly they represent rewards for service rendered.

These extra payments and benefits can be considered as supplements to regular wages. To the employer they are additions to
his labor costs, and to the recipients they are tantamount to wages
since they provide extra cash or benefits which otherwise would
have to be paid for out of wages. Some of the major types of extra
remuneration or benefits received by wage earners from their employers are pay for vacations and holidays not worked, sick and
old age benefits other than those provided by law, and bonuses
other than those paid as a reward for extra output or time spent
on the job.

In some instances these supplementary payments and benefits
amount to as much as 5 or 10 per cent of the total wages. However, relatively few employees benefit from all the supplementary
wage programs; a majority receive vacation pay, for example,
but only a handful receive profit-sharing bonuses.

PROFIT SHARING

Profit sharing, depending upon the hopes and fears of the
spokesman, has been variously described as a form of incentive
wages, a kind of employer welfare program, a symbol of industrial
democracy, and a beginning step toward cooperative production
and distribution. The last-mentioned were dominant when the

profit-sharing movement first started during the middle of the 19th century in France and England, and later in this country, when profit sharing was esteemed as a movement of social reform. The Christian Socialists of England and France advocated profit sharing as a countermovement to Marxian socialism, which was based upon the principle of class struggle and the final dictatorship of the proletariat. It was hailed by zealous reformers as a means for alleviating the harshness of a growing capitalistic economy, and as a panacea for eliminating employer-employee conflicts. Through the sharing of profits there would be a co-partnership of employers and employed, and the latter, with a stake in the ownership, would psychologically be transformed from wage earner to capitalist.

In this country the movement was largely fostered by employers, although the social reform aspect was not entirely absent. During the 1890's there was a periodical called the *Employer and Employed*, issued by an association for the promotion of profit sharing, whose banner was "Industrial divisions should be perpendicular, not horizontal. The workman's interest should be bound up with those of his employer." The belief of those who sponsored this movement was that employer-employee harmony should be substituted for conflict, and that this would be brought about if each company's income was shared by all who contributed to production.

Meaning of Profit Sharing

Profit sharing has been defined as "an agreement (formal or informal) freely entered into by which employees receive a share, fixed in advance, of the profits."[1] Another authority describes profit sharing as "payments in the form of cash, stock, options, warrants or otherwise, given under a predetermined and continuing policy by the management of a company to all or any group of its officers or employees in addition to their established wages or salaries."[2] These definitions exclude such extra-wage payments

---

[1] Definition formulated by the International Congress on Profit Sharing held in Paris in 1889.

[2] Bryce M. Stewart and Walter J. Couper, *Profit Sharing and Stock Ownership for Wage Earners and Executives,* Industrial Relations Counselors, Inc., New York, 1946, p. 1.

as Christmas, attendance, and other similar bonuses, sales commissions and production premiums, and insurance and pension plan payments. Some persons, however, include all such extra payments under the term of profit sharing.[3]

Profit sharing has attracted a great deal of popular interest, especially during up-trends in business prosperity. From time to time there have been organized movements to promote the voluntary adoption of profit sharing, and these have sometimes been accompanied by definite proposals for incentive taxation to encourage its wider adoption. The fact that profit sharing has received much more attention than actual experience with it would seem to warrant indicates that many persons entertain a belief (or hope) that there is merit in the principle of profit sharing and that its large-scale adoption would benefit the general economy.

The underlying principle of profit sharing is based on the belief that the present wage system is too rigid to enable employees to secure their proper share of their company's income and that profit sharing, by promoting mutuality of interest on the part of the management and workers, will tend to increase the company's income and at the same time assure its fair distribution. Actual experiences with the operation of profit-sharing plans, limited as they are, afford some indication of their results on worker morale and productivity; this will be discussed later. So far as their effect on wages and the general distribution of income is concerned, it is impossible to draw any conclusions from the meager number of plans which have been established. Therefore, this discussion will have to be largely theoretical and based on the assumption that profit sharing is generally established throughout most of industry.

Theories Pertaining to Profit Sharing

Fundamentally, the sharing of profits by labor is anomalous to all conventional theories of private capitalistic enterprise

---

[3] An instance of this is a report of the Senate Committee on Finance in 1939, which includes descriptions of every conceivable type of employer welfare program, from company restaurants to sick benefit plans, and calls them all profit sharing. The purpose of this report obviously was to commend employers for their good works at a time when employers were suffering from loss of prestige because of the great depression of the early 1930's.

which hold that profits are a reward (or price) for risk capital. According to traditional economic theories, profit sharing contradicts two basic conceptions of capitalistic production: (1) Control is not in proportion to risk in that workers share in the risks without having control over most of the risks they have to incur. (2) To the extent that profits are devoted to labor, the return to capital does not represent its "natural" reward.

Those who advocate profit sharing maintain that it serves to bolster rather than weaken capitalistic enterprise because (1) the mutuality of interest between management and worker which it engenders tends to increase the company's income and automatically assures its fair distribution; and (2) the supplementary payments afforded by profit sharing bear a definite relation to company income and obviate the necessity, when business is prosperous, of saddling the enterprise with a permanent charge of increased wages.

Profit Sharing and the Distribution of Income

In spite of its appeal as a means of a fairer distribution of income, profit sharing does not automatically resolve the problem of wages. The question remains as to *how much* of the company's profits shall be shared. Whatever the amount, it is a matter of arbitrary determination and does not represent a "scientific" evaluation of labor's versus capital's contribution to the productive process. Some existing plans specify as much as 25 per cent of the net profits of the company, but most provide only 10 or 15 per cent. The small share allotted under these plans is frequently cited as a major reason for their failure to gain the desired interest and cooperation of workers.

Just how much "reward" capital should or must receive in a competitive economy is a matter of conjecture. Let us assume that it is feasible for capital to receive a considerably smaller proportion of business income than it now does, and that stockholders are willing to share one-half of their dividends with wage earners.

In 1939 this would have meant the distribution of 860 million dollars among 7 million workers employed by incorporated manufacturing establishments. Each worker, on the average, would have received $123, or the equivalent of slightly less than an 11 per cent increase in his annual income.[4]

If the fifty-fifty sharing of dividends had taken place in 1945, approximately 1128 million dollars would have been distributed to 10.5 million wage earners employed in incorporated manufacturing establishments. Each worker, on the the average, would have received $107, which would have been equivalent to a 4.8 per cent increase in his average annual income.

These assumptions, of course, are merely suggestive and cannot take into account all the possible interacting influences. For example, if dividend payments to stockholders were reduced because of sharing with labor, corporations might lay aside less for corporate savings in order to enhance stockholder dividends. In 1945, almost half the total profits (after taxes) of manufacturing corporations were retained as savings—a much greater proportion than in prewar years. If 70 per cent had been distributed as dividends under fifty-fifty profit-sharing arrangements, stockholders would have received more and the per capita worker payment would have been $151 instead of $107. On the other hand, with the shrinkage in the investment potential of the higher-income groups as a result of the sharing of dividends, corporations might lay aside a greater proportion of their profits than they now do so that adequate capital will be assured for expansion and upkeep.

Another factor to be considered is the influence of profit sharing on prices and the total income to be distributed. If productivity is increased under profit sharing, as its advocates believe, there will be more to distribute to both stockholders and labor. However, the benefits of improved productivity *could* be passed on to consumers by lower prices. It is entirely possible that a wide adoption of profit sharing, while providing flexibility of labor income, might have the opposite effect upon the price structure; workers might

---

[4] These illustrations are necessarily confined to incorporated manufacturing establishments because no employment and wage data are available for workers employed by all kinds of corporations, and it is impossible to segregate profits from other income for non-incorporated businesses. The above profit data are from *Survey of Current Business,* April, 1946. Employment and wage data are from 1939 census and 1945 Bureau of Labor Statistics reports. It is estimated that about 90 per cent of all manufacturing employees are employed in incorporated establishments.

be inclined to join with their employers to maintain prices at fixed levels while profits were advancing.

Effect of Profit Sharing on the Wage Structure

If profit sharing were adopted generally throughout industry, it would result in two fundamental changes in the wage structure: (1) Levels of workers' incomes would be determined on a vertical basis, that is, according to each individual company's ability to pay, rather than on a broad horizontal basis as at present, with roughly similar rate structures throughout an industry or area. (2) Employees' earnings would fluctuate directly and immediately with the changing financial condition of the company.

The repercussions of such changes would be far reaching and would be reflected in labor turnover and the character of the labor force in different plants, the longevity of marginal firms, the general level of wages, and perhaps the magnitude of the business cycle curve.

Prosperous firms which regularly distributed generous profit-sharing payments would be able to obtain and keep the best workers. Most companies, however, have their ups and downs and many workers would be inclined to move from one plant to another with the fluctuations in profit-sharing payments. Marginal firms which had little or no profits to share at frequent periods would experience the greatest turnover, and this in itself would accentuate their tenuous position because of the higher labor costs resulting from labor turnover. New companies, even though they paid the going rates of wages, would be at a disadvantage in attracting the best workers unless their prospects for profits were unusually favorable.

Most advocates of profit sharing maintain that firms which have profit-sharing plans should pay the prevailing wage rates, and that profit-sharing payments are therefore additions to what workers would otherwise receive. This may be true at the present time when only a very few companies maintain such programs. If profit sharing became the general practice, however, it would have a tendency to retard advancements in wage levels. Advances in wage levels are made by first obtaining increases during prosperous years from firms most able to pay higher rates; these higher rates gradually spread until they become the prevailing rates for the industry or area. If profit sharing were in effect, the workers best able to pioneer new rate levels might not press for higher rates during prosperous years, with the result that no new wage plateaus would be established. Since profit sharing in itself offers no protection for the maintenance of existing rates during depression years, the secular trend in wage levels might actually be downward.

Employer Motives

By definition, profit sharing is a voluntary arrangement, and employers who have established profit-sharing plans have been guided by very practical as well as humanitarian motives. These may be summarized as follows:

1. To encourage employee efficiency and stimulate production. With a stake in the returns, employees will be more willing to exert themselves, prevent waste, and thus reduce labor costs.

2. To secure more flexibility in the pay roll. By sharing profits instead of increasing wages during prosperous times, management will not be saddled with high wage rates when depression comes; moreover, profit sharing can be discontinued more easily than wage rates can be reduced.

3. To avoid excess profits taxes. By distributing to employees excess profits that otherwise would be largely absorbed in taxes, management is able to cultivate employee good will at little or no cost. That this is an important motive is evidenced by the increase in the number of profit-sharing plans introduced during both world war periods when excess profits taxes were extremely high.

4. To reduce labor turnover and increase labor stability. Employees will hesitate to quit when there are prospects of receiving semi-annual or annual "dividends." Also the program will engender a feeling of belonging which will encourage stability and continued service with the company.

5. To encourage employee savings and provide employee security. A number of profit-sharing plans are tied in with savings and retirement plans.

6. To discourage unionism or at least minimize its militancy. If employees share in the profits of business, a spirit of cooperation with management will be developed which will discourage them from turning to "outside" organizations for assistance.

Union and Employee Attitudes

Although a few local unions have endorsed specific profit-sharing plans of their employers, the labor movement in this country has always viewed such plans with disfavor. Unions maintain that profit sharing is offered as a sop to workers in lieu of "good" wages and as a means of discouraging justifiable demands for wage increases. Recognizing the last-mentioned employer motive, the unions naturally think of profit sharing as a menace to worker organization and as being purposely designed to thwart their own growth and effectiveness. They maintain that, far from providing employees with a better substitute for unions, profit sharing tends to keep wages down while at the same time it encourages speed-up. Instead of promoting "democracy" in industry, the unions point out that the conditions of participation and distribution are determined solely by management and that most profit-sharing plans favor a select few instead of benefiting all the employees in the plant.

Profit sharing has never aroused the interest of the rank and file employees; they are more concerned with an assured steady income. "By its intrinsic nature, profit sharing does not commend itself to wage earners. . . . The first want of the worker is for a steady income assessed on the business as an operating cost with payment insured by a first lien on the assets. He will accept any handout from profits as so much 'gravy,' but he will not be content to depend upon such a fluctuating factor as profits for any substantial part of his regular income. Profit sharing may appeal to the gambling instinct of some wage earners, but there is no considerable body of evidence that it has any more effect in inciting them to greater effort than would a lottery ticket. . . . Unsolicited subsidiary benefits granted to employees are not valued as highly as equivalent cash benefits appearing in the pay envelope."[5]

Prevalence and Characteristics of Existing Plans

Although there has been a great deal of talk and much literature concerning the merits and possibilities of profit-sharing plans,

---

[5] Stewart and Couper, *Profit Sharing and Stock Ownership for Wage Earners and Executives,* pp. 43–44.

an inconsiderable number have been established, and a large proportion of those adopted have been discontinued after a few years' experience. Profit sharing has over a century's history, and during that time no more than 1000 or 1200 plans have been established in both Europe and the United States. A survey in 1945 revealed the existence in this country of only 70 plans which covered wage earners as well as supervisory personnel, and more than half of them had been adopted during the preceding ten years.[6] The typical plan includes about 540 employees and the total number of wage earners now employed under profit-sharing plans is probably no more than 40,000.

Profit-sharing plans differ in three major respects: (1) coverage and requirements for participation, (2) the form and time of payments, and (3) the formula or basis upon which profits are divided.

Most profit-sharing plans have eligibility requirements, most commonly a period of at least one year's service with the company; under some, the service requirements are as much as five or more years. Some are limited to particular groups of employees, whereas others include other qualifications such as good attendance records, non-participation in work stoppages, etc. A study in 1936 indicated that about 67 per cent of the total labor force of the companies having profit-sharing plans participated in them.[7]

Of the plans now in existence, about half provide that the shares in profits shall be distributed currently; the remaining are "trusteed" plans under which the shares go into a fund for later distribution under specified conditions. The latter are frequently tied in with savings and retirement plans which require employee contributions as a condition for sharing in the profits. Many also provide that shares, instead of being paid in cash, shall be distributed to the employees in the form of the company's stock.

The most important feature of any profit-sharing plan is the formula which determines the proportion of the profits that is to be distributed. More than three-fourths of the existing plans provide

[6] *Ibid.*, p. 22. There were an additional 70 plans which covered executives or managerial employees, or both.

[7] C. C. Balderston, *Profit Sharing for Wage Earners,* Industrial Relations Counselors, Inc., New York, 1937.

that a fixed percentage of net profits (most of them range from 5 to 25 per cent), after specified deductions, shall be distributed; according to the remaining plans the management arbitrarily determines each year the amount of profits which shall be shared. The basis of allocation among the participants also varies. A few plans provide for equal distribution among all the employees covered; many allocate the fund in proportion to each employee's annual earnings; under other plans the distribution is left to the discretion of management. Those which are tied in with contributory savings and retirement programs may allocate the fund on the basis of each employee's contribution.

Actual money receipts from existing profit-sharing plans are not great; in 1943 the average payment was about $266 per employee covered. Throughout their history, profit-sharing payments have averaged about 2 per cent of the pay roll, 7 per cent of the net operating profits, and approximately 10 per cent of the dividends of the companies maintaining such programs.[8]

Results of Profit-Sharing Experiments

Experiments with profit sharing have fallen far short of the expectations of the employers who have established them. To paraphrase another writer[9] on the subject: The degree of employee loyalty to a company is a result of the workers' reaction to the whole complex of situations and relations that go to make up their "job," and the establishment of profit sharing has failed to eliminate or overbalance their discontent about some other aspects of the employment situation. Employees are inclined to look upon the profits dividend as withheld wages, as something to which they had been entitled before it was given them. They never know whether there are going to be any profits or not, and when there are none they are apt to think that the books have been manipulated and the profits concealed for the benefit of the stockholders or executives.

Employee cooperation means to the average employer the dis-

[8] Stewart and Couper, *Profit Sharing and Stock Ownership for Wage Earners and Executives*, p. 38.

[9] D. D. Lescohier, *History of Labor in the United States,* The Macmillan Company, New York, 1935, pp. 376–379.

continuance of restriction of output and the manifestation of unstinted effort. But so long as piece-rate cutting and the fear of layoffs exist, workers are bound to maintain defensive attitudes, and profit sharing is not an adequate antidote to these fears, born of experience. Profit sharing has not reduced turnover. The failure of employers to couple their profit sharing with steadiness of employment, and the almost universal practice of confining benefits to those employees who have been with the company for a definite period of time, has prevented profit sharing from producing any marked decrease in turnover among the part of the labor force in which turnover is high. And when boom years come and work is plentiful, employees go elsewhere in quest of higher immediate wages in preference to an uncertain profit-sharing check at the end of the year. Moreover, the size of the profit-sharing dividend is not great enough to exercise great pressure, and many workers and unions are convinced that small profit-sharing dividends are a substitute for higher wages.

Experience with Profit Sharing

In view of the above expressions, it is not surprising to learn that actual experiments with profit sharing have proved disappointing so far as improvement in worker morale and productivity is concerned. In relatively few instances have programs for profit sharing been sufficiently successful, according to their sponsors, to warrant their continuance for considerable periods; significantly, the oldest profit-sharing plans are found in companies which have had high, steady profits over many years. Most of the plans which have been abandoned were discontinued because of the dissatisfaction which arose when profits diminished or disappeared.

Profit-sharing plans seem to be most successful in companies whose labor forces (or those sharing in the profits) are relatively small. The smaller the groups covered, the easier it has been to obtain the desired cooperation and stimulation of effort; conversely, the larger the number of participants, the less the relative effect of any one individual's efforts upon the total benefits and the less, consequently, the direct stimulation provided by profit sharing.

A recent study indicates that 60 per cent of the profit-sharing

plans in existence in 1937 had been abandoned by 1946.[10] The
reasons cited for their discontinuance were as follows:

Apathy and dissatisfaction of employees..	30 per cent of cases
Diminished profits or losses.............	22 per cent of cases
Substitution of other benefits[a]..........	13 per cent of cases
Changes in management or the discontinuance of business.................	14 per cent of cases
Government regulations[b]..............	7 per cent of cases
Unknown...........................	14 per cent of cases

[a] Presumably other benefits would not have been substituted for profit sharing if the latter had been satisfactory.
[b] Most of these were the result of the 1942 Internal Revenue and Wage Stabilization requirements.

PAID VACATIONS AND HOLIDAYS

Much more significant than profit sharing, in both monetary returns and number of persons benefited, is the current practice of
granting annual vacations and holidays without loss of earnings.
The recent movement of providing wage earners with paid vacations and holidays represents one of the most remarkable phenomena in the entire history of employer-employee relations.
Workers have probably never gained any other benefit of comparable proportion as quickly and peacefully, with less governmental assistance. Within less than a decade the granting of paid
vacations to industrial wage earners grew from a negligible to an
almost universal practice. And this was accomplished largely
through union pressure and peaceful collective bargaining; few
strikes were called and no legislation[11] was invoked to obtain the
right to paid vacations.

Prevalence of Paid Vacations

The right to annual vacations and the observance of national
holidays with no loss in salary were an almost exclusive privilege

---

[10] National Industrial Conference Board, "Experience with Profit Sharing,"
Conference Board Management Record, February, 1946. These plans included
both the deferred distribution and the annual cash payment type.

[11] This is in contrast to the British experience. Although unions and collective bargaining traditionally are stronger in Great Britain than in the U. S.,
British unions turned to their government for assistance in gaining the right
to paid vacations. In 1938 the British Parliament passed the Holidays with
Pay Act, which empowered all statutory wage-regulating authorities, such as
Trade Boards, to give directives providing vacations with pay for workers for
whom they prescribe minimum wages, and authorized the Minister of Labor to
encourage paid vacations in other industries upon the request of the workers.

of managers and supervisors and some other white-collar workers
before the middle of the 1930's. Although most factories and other
business establishments closed down on holidays, hour and day
wage earners were compelled to take this time off with loss of pay.
The taking of an annual vacation, stimulated by the widespread
use of automobiles, had become a national custom, but wage-
earners' vacations usually meant the loss of one or several weeks'
wages. In only the petroleum industry were paid vacations commonly granted production workers; there were scattered instances
among chemical, electrical machinery, food, printing, and the
large rubber industries.

One of the major objectives of unions after they gained recognition in mass-production and other industries during the 1930's
was to obtain for production workers the vacation privileges then
commonly enjoyed only by supervisory and some clerical employees. (Many of the latter who formerly were excluded have
recently gained such benefits.) The obvious fairness of their demands, together with the fact that annual vacations had become
an established custom in this country, impelled most employers to
grant the unions' demands with only comparatively mild resistance. In fact, a number of employers, for example the large steel
companies, granted paid vacations before collective bargaining
was established in their plants but while organization campaigns
were under way.

By the time the war stabilization program was inaugurated, a
majority of the factory wage earners and practically all the coal
miners, shipbuilding, non-operating railroad and city transportation employees had obtained the privilege of annual paid vacations.
With the practice fairly well established, it was feasible for the
National War Labor Board to extend the privilege to other
workers, their vacation awards frequently being in lieu of wage
increases which were not permitted under the stabilization program. Although the government, through the N.W.L.B. and its
appointed arbitrators, facilitated the granting of paid vacations
in a number of particular instances, it is probable that the extension of this policy would have taken place at about the same pace
if there had been no war with its attendant abnormal government
intervention in employer-employee relations.

At the present time almost all unionized workers, except those in the building trades and a few other seasonal occupations, and at least three-fourths of the unorganized workers, have annual paid vacation rights, under specified service and other requirements.[12]

Types of Vacation Allowances

At first, vacation privileges usually amounted to one week's vacation after one year or sometimes six months with the company. Within a short time, however, most of the vacation provisions were liberalized to include a maximum of two and sometimes three weeks. The more liberal allowances are usually graduated plans which allow the maximum vacation only to the employees who have longer periods of service, most commonly three or five years. The prevalence of the various types of vacation allowances in unionized manufacturing industries is shown in Table 24.

The 1946 agreements in coal mining provided ten days' time off with a lump-sum vacation payment of $100 to all employees with service records of a year or longer. Practically all iron-ore miners are allowed one week after three years' service and two weeks after longer service, most commonly ten or fifteen years. A majority of the non-ferrous metal miners receive a week's vacation after a year of service and two weeks after five years. Both operating and non-operating employees in the railroad industry receive a week's vacation with pay, provided they have worked 160 days within the year. Railroad clerks' and telegraphers' agreements also provide nine days' paid vacation after two years' service, and twelve days after three years.

Although a considerable number of agreements in the trucking industry allow two weeks' paid vacation after one year of service, and some provide two weeks after longer periods, a majority of the workers are allowed a maximum of one week's vacation after a year of service. In the street-railway and bus industry, the major portion of the workers receive two weeks' vacation after one year's service, although many are employed under graduated vacation plans which allow a week's vacation after service varying from six months to one year, and two weeks after service varying from two to five years.

Because the nature of their work requires prolonged absences

---

[12] Bureau of Labor Statistics, *Paid Vacations in American Industry*, Bulletin No. 811, Government Printing Office, Washington, 1945

TABLE 24.   Distribution of Manufacturing Workers by Length of Vacation and Service Requirements, 1944[13]

Length of Vacation and Service Requirements	Per Cent
Plans providing maximum vacation of 1 week	37
1 week after 6 to 10 months	1
3 days after 6 months, 1 week after 1 year	5
1 week after 1 year	28
1 week after 2 to 3 years	1
1 week after other periods of service	2
Plans providing maximum vacation of over 1 week but less than 2 weeks	1
Plans providing maximum vacation of 2 weeks	56
1 week after 6 months, 2 weeks after 1 year	2
2 weeks after 1 year	1
1 week after 1 year, 2 weeks after 2 to 4 years	3
1 week after 1 year, 2 weeks after 5 years	41
1 week after 1 year, 2 weeks after 6 to 10 years	2
1 week after 2 years, 2 weeks after 4 to 6 years	2
2 days after 6 months, 2 weeks after 6 years	3
2 weeks after other periods of service	2
Plans providing maximum vacation of 3 weeks	2
1 week after 1 year, 2 weeks after 5 years, 3 weeks after 20 years	2
Maximum not known	4
Total workers under paid-vacation clauses	100

from home, the vacation allowances for most maritime employees are comparatively liberal. Union agreements covering personnel on tankers commonly allow thirty days' paid vacation after a year of service for licensed officers, and twenty-one days after a year for unlicensed personnel. On dry-cargo ships, officers usually receive two weeks after one year, and the unlicensed personnel one week after one year and two weeks after two years' service.

In the light and power industry, the majority of the workers receive a week's vacation after a year's service but must work from two to five years to be eligible for two weeks' vacation. Most of the telephone and telegraph operating and maintenance workers are eligible for one week's vacation after one year of service, two weeks after two years, and three weeks after longer service periods. In wholesale and retail trade the most prevalent type of vacation

---

[13] From *ibid.*, p. 24.

clause is that which grants one week's vacation after one year of service, although many allow a maximum of two weeks, usually after two years' service.

Vacation pay is usually equivalent to normal or regular wages, that is, pay based on a 40-hour week, although during the war when the 48-hour week was prevalent, many employees were given vacation allowances based on the longer work period. For piece and other incentive workers, vacation pay is based on the average weekly earnings during a specified period, most commonly the month preceding the vacation or the social security quarter preceding the vacation. This form of payment includes overtime, but any absences from work during the period over which earnings are averaged are also reflected in the vacation pay. Vacation pay occasionally is computed as a percentage of annual earnings, usually 2 but sometimes 2½ per cent. Overtime earnings are generally included in the annual earnings. Of course, this method of computing vacation pay reflects absences from work during the year, although 2 per cent of the annual earnings would approximate a week's pay, provided enough overtime was worked to offset such absences.

Paid Holidays

Wage earners, unlike salaried employees, are customarily not paid for holidays not worked even though the holiday falls on a regular workday. Consequently, their weekly wages during a holiday week are substantially less than normal; over the Christmas season when lack of funds is particularly noticeable, most workers' pay envelopes contain less money than usual. If work is done on a holiday it has become almost universal to pay overtime rates, most commonly time and one-half; however, an increasing number of union agreements specify double time.

Parallel to the paid vacation movement there has been a tendency toward providing pay for holidays not worked, although this is not as common as vacation payments. Very few wage earners in unorganized plants are paid for holidays not worked, but paid holidays are common in several unionized industries (e.g., the women's clothing, bakery, wholesale and retail trade, trucking, and leather industries) and fairly common in the machinery, chemical, textile, fur, and other industries. However, although an increasing number of agreements provide for paid holidays, the practice is not general at the present time.

The number of holidays specified in union agreements varies considerably, some providing as few as two or three, and a few specifying as many as twelve or thirteen. Both the agreements which provide paid holidays and those which provide holidays without pay most commonly specify six days—New Year's Day, Memorial Day, Fourth of July, Labor Day, Thanksgiving Day, and Christmas Day. Some additional holidays frequently observed are Armistice Day, Election Day, Columbus Day, Washington's Birthday, and sometimes Lincoln's Birthday. Special local patriotic and labor holidays, as well as religious holidays, are also included in some agreements.

SPECIAL BONUSES

In addition to premiums based upon output under wage incentive plans, and premium payments for overtime work, some employees secure other types of bonuses which are not directly related to production standards or work schedules. Some of these bonuses are paid with more or less regularity from year to year; others are paid for temporary periods in recognition of abnormal or peculiar situations.

Christmas Bonuses

It has long been customary for some employers to give their employees an annual bonus immediately before the Christmas season. During prosperous times, or when excess profits taxes are unusually high, the payment of Christmas bonuses is much more widespread than at other times. When such bonuses are paid regularly each year, regardless of the economic or tax situation, the costs are considered as part of the regular operating expenses of the business; when their distribution is contingent upon the company's current financial situation, these bonuses assume the aspect of profit sharing. To employees, this difference in concept marks the difference between assurance and uncertainty of receiving a given sum of money each year. To avoid the latter, a number of unions now have Christmas bonuses included in the terms of their contracts.

The amounts of the bonuses and the eligibility requirements vary from plant to plant. Frequently one year's service with the company is a requisite, and sometimes there are additional attendance and good behavior requirements. Probably the most common type of bonus is based upon a percentage of annual wages, for example 2 per cent, and under such plans there may be no service or attendance requirements, because the amount received is automatically adjusted to the time worked. Some companies pay a uniform amount to all regular employees, irrespective of individual earnings or length of service beyond the required minimum for obtaining a "regular" status; other companies base each individual's bonus upon a fixed sum per year of service.

Employer motives for the payment of Christmas bonuses are not unlike those for profit sharing, although the practice of paying Christmas bonuses is much more general. They promote good will, loyalty, and stability among employees and also provide a means of sharing some of the company's income during prosperous times without committing the company to added costs (as would a wage increase) which would be difficult to reduce during periods when profits are not high.

War Risk Bonuses

The bonuses paid merchant seamen while a war is in progress are an illustration of a bonus paid a particular group of workers because of a peculiar and temporary work situation. The ordinary marine hazards of peacetime are regarded as part of the seafarer's calling. War entails unusual hazards, for when peaceful trade routes become the hunting grounds of enemy submarine and aircraft, every time a seaman sets forth it may be his last journey.[14]

In the First World War a bonus was paid seamen amounting to 50 per cent of the basic wages for the duration of each voyage across seas, and 25 per cent for coastwise voyages. Beginning in 1940 a series of arrangements were negotiated as the hazards of travel increased with the extension of war areas, the gradual lifting of travel bans under the Neutrality Act, and finally our entrance into the war. The last arrangement provided a bonus

[14] The Maritime Commission reported 5638 seamen on American flag vessels dead or missing from Pearl Harbor to the end of the war (release, March 1, 1946). The average employment during the war was approximately 130,000.

which was equivalent to 100 per cent of the seaman's basic wages for all transoceanic voyages, and 40 per cent for most coastwise trips. In addition there were "area bonuses" amounting to $5 a day while vessels were within specified areas (the designated areas were changed from time to time with the fortunes of war), and port attack bonuses of $125 paid each seaman when a port or anchorage was subjected to enemy attack while his vessel was in it. If his vessel was lost, the war risk bonus continued at the rate which was in effect at that time, until the seaman arrived in a port where he was no longer exposed to marine perils.

Cost of Living Bonus

Another type of bonus which is also associated with war conditions, although less directly than war risk bonuses, is the cost of living bonus. Unlike wage increases, the cost of living bonus is a lump-sum payment which is adjusted from time to time, for example every quarter, according to the rise and decline in the cost of living index and which automatically ceases when the index returns to a stated point. The purpose of cost of living bonuses is twofold: to maintain existing wage levels during a war period when there are great fluctuations in prices, and at the same time to provide workers with additional income to the exact equivalent of the increase in the cost of living.

Organized labor is opposed to the principle of cost of living bonuses for the same reason that it objects to the automatic gearing of wages to a cost of living index. During the First World War the payment of such bonuses was quite general; however, during the recent war, largely because of union influence, cost of living bonuses were rare in this country but more general in Canada.

Family Allowances

The practice of paying extra sums to heads of families according to the size of family is almost non-existent in this country but is an important feature of the wage system in some other countries.[15] In Europe, family allowance systems were an outgrowth of

---

[15] In 1929 in Germany, family allowance clauses covering 3 million workers in private industry were included in employer-union agreements. In 1930 in France, over 4 million persons in private industry were employed in enter-

the cost of living bonuses paid during the First World War and the post-war inflation period. Although they were adopted by many employers as a substitute for general wage increases, the movement was encouraged and sometimes made mandatory by various governments in order to encourage large families. In France, which is especially concerned over her decline in population, family allowances have become an integral part of the wage system. There the allowances amount to from 4 to 10 per cent additions to the worker's wage, depending upon the number of children. To meet the problem of discrimination in favor of employing workers with few or no children, the allowances are paid out of equalization funds, some of which are established on an area and some on an industry basis, to which each employer contributes according to a formula based on his total wage bill and total number of employees.

Family allowances, when part of the wage system, represent remuneration in accordance to need rather than output. The question of incorporating such allowances in the wage structure of private industry in this country has never risen and would most certainly be opposed by American labor unions.[16] Even in Europe where the need for family allowances is accepted and promoted by workers' organizations, most unions prefer and sometimes demand that such payments be integrated into social insurance systems rather than take the form of wage supplements.

EMPLOYER-FINANCED SICK BENEFIT PROGRAMS

To the extent that sick benefit and pension plans are financed by employers and have been voluntarily adopted entirely apart

---

prises which paid family allowances. The latter are still in effect and the allowances have recently been increased. In most other countries, family or children allowances are incorporated in the social security programs or are financed by grants from the general revenues of the government. In 1945 both Canada and Great Britain enacted laws to provide grants to parents of children under 16 years of age.

[16] Family allowances are paid to a considerable number of public-school teachers in this country. In an attempt to attract and maintain men in their school systems where regular salaries are low in comparison to salaries in private industry, at least 75 cities pay family allowances or married men's differentials. (Bureau of Labor Statistics, *Family Allowances in Various Countries, 1944–5*. Bulletin No. 853.)

from governmental social security programs, they can be considered as supplements to weekly wages. To the employer who finances them they represent labor costs; to unions they are a matter for bargaining along with wages; to individual workers they represent monetary benefits that are additional to the wages received for work performed. Employer assistance during periods of sickness is of two general types: (1) continuation of the payment of regular wages during all or part of the period of illness, and (2) financing of formal sick benefit plans which provide for medical care in addition to weekly cash payments.

Paid Sick Leave

The granting of sick leave without pay, but without loss of seniority or employment rights, has long been the practice with a majority of American employers and is provided for in a great proportion of current union agreements. The continuation of wage payments to production workers during periods of sickness is not common practice, although labor unions to an increasing extent are now bargaining to obtain paid sick leave for their members. At present, however, paid sick leave is the exception rather than the rule among manufacturing employees, but is fairly common among public utilities, wholesale and retail trade, telephone and telegraph, city transportation, and clerical and professional workers.

Depending upon the proportion of regular wages received, paid sick leave provisions are of three types: (1) full pay for a limited period; (2) less than full pay for a limited period, i.e., a stipulated portion of the regular wages, such as 50 or 70 per cent, or a stipulated amount, such as $10 a week or $50 a month; (3) payments to supplement group insurance or workmen's compensation benefits, such as payment of all or a portion of the regular wages during the waiting period for workmen's compensation or after insurance benefits have been exhausted.

Paid sick leave plans also vary with respect to qualifying requirements and length of leave allowances. In some instances there are fixed or uniform arrangements for all eligible employees; elsewhere there are graduated or sliding-scale arrangements which provide more generous time and wage allowances for employees with longer service. The time allowed under existing plans varies from three days per year for all eligible employees, to as much as 52 weeks under graduated plans for employees with long service records. In general, full wages are paid when the time allowed is no more than one or two weeks; but when extended time is allowed, the amount received each week is equivalent to less than full wages. Frequently a waiting period is required before payments are made in order to restrict compensation to illnesses of longer duration; sometimes, however, payments are retroactive to the beginning of the absence if the illness extends beyond the waiting period.

Sick Benefit Plans

Although some sick benefit programs, wholly or partially employer-financed, have been in existence for a long time, they have become much more numerous during recent years. The increase in the number of benefit plans is an indication of the workers' increasing consciousness of the need for protection during periods of sickness, as well as an evidence of union strength which has enabled them to obtain plans which are largely employer-financed. During the war stabilization program, a number of sick benefit plans were negotiated in lieu of wage increases, but many have been established since the ban on wage increases was lifted. Until provision for sickness insurance is incorporated in the social security program (See Chapter 27), the number of privately administered plans will no doubt continue to increase. Even with a government program in effect, unions and employers may continue to establish their own supplementary programs.

The earlier sick benefit plans, as well as a number in effect today, were voluntarily established by employers as part of their general employee welfare programs. In most cases they were jointly financed by the employer and his employees and administered through a company mutual benefit association. The mutual benefit association movement in this country began before the turn of the 20th century and grew until the depression of the 1930's. Many of these associations gradually assumed additional functions and developed into employee representation groups, or what later came to be called company unions. In addition to the mutual benefit associations, a considerable number of companies maintained group policies with commercial private insurance companies which included life insurance as well as sick benefit features.[17]

In 1938 no less than 2 million workers employed in approximately 500 plants were covered by sick benefit plans. Only about 10 per cent of these plans, however, were financed entirely by the employers; almost a half were supported entirely by the employees. Of the jointly financed arrangements, employer contributions ranged from the occasional meeting of deficits to the regular matching of employee dues.[18]

Benefit Plans Provided by Collective Bargaining

Organized labor has never wholeheartedly endorsed company-established benefit plans because it suspected that they were adopted to win employee loyalty and discourage union organization. During recent years an increasing number of unions have succeeded in having health benefit plans included in their agreements with employers. Some of these represent the substitution of contractual arrangements for already established employer plans, but many of them are new. Most of the plans negotiated through collective bargaining are financed entirely by employers, although the union maintains virtual control of their administration. A considerable number, in both unionized and unorganized shops, are underwritten by private insurance companies which assume the responsibility for determining eligibility claims and payment of benefits, although frequently the union, or the union and employer jointly, review the claims and sign drafts on the insurance company.

Most of the agreements which provide for sick benefit plans stipulate that the employer shall contribute a specified percentage of his pay roll to meet his obligations.[19] The amount ranges from 1 to 5 per cent, but most commonly is 2 or 3 per cent. In the main, the health benefit plans provided under union agreements include

---

[17] The commercial insurance companies began underwriting group policies which included both life insurance and sick benefit features about 1912.

[18] National Industrial Conference Board, Inc., *Studies in Personnel Policy, Health Insurance Plans,* Nos. 9, 10, 11, New York, 1938.

[19] According to the terms of the 1946 coal miners' agreements, 5 cents a ton on all coal produced is put into a fund for sickness, disability, death, and retirement benefits. A joint board of trustees is to determine the exact allocation of the funds and to manage the several programs.

weekly cash benefits during periods of illness and of disability caused by non-occupational accidents, and the payment of hospital and surgical expenses and, in some cases, doctors' bills. Dental care and medical preventive work, such as periodic examinations, are not commonly provided under these plans, although many large companies maintain these types of service.

Most of the plans include weekly disability benefits ranging from about 50 to 60 per cent of an employee's regular earnings or, where fixed benefits are stipulated, from $10.50 to $20 per week. (As might be expected, the benefits tend to be higher under plans negotiated in industries having relatively high wage scales.) The maximum time allowed for receiving benefits usually ranges from 13 to 26 weeks for any one continuous disability, although several plans allow continuous coverage for 52 weeks. Under almost all the plans the payment of benefits commences on the eighth day of disability in case of illness, and on the first day in accident cases.

Payments for hospital services, ranging from $4 to $5 per day for 31 days, are usually allowed for any one continuous disability, but are limited to 12 or 14 days in maternity cases or cases involving any condition resulting from pregnancy. Frequently an additional $25 is allowed for special hospital expenses. Payment for medical service is not commonly provided, although a few plans allow specified payments for doctors' services up to a maximum of 50 visits for any one disability; payment usually begins with the first treatment in case of accident, and the fourth in case of illness. Maximum surgical benefits under most of the plans range from $100 to $175, and these plans frequently furnish a schedule of surgical allowances for different types of operations. Hospitalization coverage for dependents is provided in some plans, but it sometimes entails additional contributions by the employee. Two union health benefit programs deserve special notice because of their unique methods of administration and the variety of services rendered. Both are a development of a good deal of experimentation and represent a transfer from union to employer financing within recent years.

Benefit Program of the International Ladies' Garment Workers' Union. The benefit programs currently in effect for members of the International Ladies' Garment Workers' Union are an outgrowth of the union's welfare and health programs formerly financed entirely by the members. These plans include vacation payments in addition to sick benefit payments and medical services; some also include retirement provisions, but none provide death benefits. The employer usually contributes from 3 to 4 per cent of his gross pay roll, but only part (from a third to a half) of this amount is allocated for health benefits, the rest being used to finance the vacation and retirement provisions (not discussed here).

Employers' contributions are turned over to the appropriate joint boards or locals of the union which are responsible for the administration of the programs. Under several of the more important plans, the amount of the benefit, as well as the rules and regulations under which claims are paid, is determined by a committee of employer and union representatives. In other instances the determination of benefits and other regulations is entirely in the hands of the union. Under all the plans the actual payment of claims, as well as appeals from decisions of the benefit committee, is handled through the union office.

The I.L.G.W.U. programs stress medical care, and the union has established health centers in most of the important clothing areas. The health center in New York City has been in operation since 1912, the one in Philadelphia was established in 1943, and that in Fall River was opened in 1944. Until 1943, the New York center was financed by local union contributions, any deficits being met by the International Union. Since then, a large part of this center's financial support has been derived from funds paid to the union under health insurance programs included in union agreements. The health center acts as an agency for the certification of benefit claims, its physicians making recommendations approving or disapproving cash benefit payments under the insurance program.

To be eligible for benefits, the worker usually must have been a member of the union in good standing for at least six months (in some cases nine months), and have no more than four weeks' dues unpaid. The usual allowances range from $6 to $15 weekly for from 10 to 13 weeks in any year, with payments beginning on the eighth day of illness. Hospitalization benefits are $2 to $5 a day, the time allowed ranging from 12 to 21 days. In tubercular cases, the workers are given the choice of a cash benefit payment of $200 to $250, or treatment in a sanatorium for the entire period of illness.

Benefit Program of the Amalgamated Clothing Workers. The national insurance plan of the men's clothing union is financed entirely by manufacturers and contractors, who contribute 2 per cent of their weekly pay rolls to the Amalgamated Insurance Fund, which is administered by a board of trustees composed of twelve members of the executive board of the union. Before the trustees can "enter into any insurance contract, or purchase any insurance policy, or make any change in any outstanding policy . . ." they must obtain the consent of an advisory committee composed of eleven members of the association representing the employers. The resources of the Amalgamated Insurance Fund are employed to operate the Amalgamated Life Insurance Co., a capital-stock insurance company chartered under the laws of New York State, with a board of directors composed of union and employer representatives. This company issues policies and pays the benefits to eligible members of the union who are employed by the contributing employers.

All workers in the men's clothing industry (including learners and clerks, as well as production workers) who have been members of the union for at least six months, and who have worked for an employer at least one day in each of six different months, are automatically insured. Employees are covered as long as they are employed in any shop included in the plan, and for four months after layoff from the industry; but insurance terminates upon withdrawal, suspension, or expulsion from the union.

Weekly benefits for sickness and non-occupational accidents are $12 for men and $8 for women for a maximum of 13 weeks in any 12 consecutive months (rather than for any continuous disability). For accidents resulting in disability extending over seven days or more, the payment of benefits begins the first day of the disability. In the case of illness resulting in disability lasting fourteen days or more, the payment of benefits begins on the eighth day of disability. Confinement to bed or in the home is unnecessary, but the member must be under a doctor's care and unable to work, and must have notified the office not later than twenty days after the first day of his disability. The plan includes hospitalization benefits of $5 per day for 31 days in any one year, and $25 for additional expenses.

EMPLOYER-FINANCED PENSION PROGRAMS

A generation before the inauguration of the federal old age pension program a number of employers began to accept some responsibility for caring for their aged employees. By 1934 there were several hundred company pension plans in operation and in that year employers contributed more than 100 million dollars to finance them; 120,000 former employees were receiving annual pensions.[20]

These pension programs were voluntarily established by employers who were actuated by both humanitarian and business motives. After being in business for thirty or forty years, any concern has some employees who are old both in years and in service; the company has benefited from their long years of steady, loyal service, but their weekly wages, which have probably suffered intermittent interruptions because of layoffs and sickness, have not enabled them to save for their old age. Their retirement on a pension satisfies a sense of justice and also makes possible their replacement by younger, more vigorous workers.

Inadequacy of Voluntary Plans

As an adequate pension system for the mass of industrial workers, voluntary programs operated on a company basis not only were much too limited in number but also had some inherent disadvantages. Most of these private plans required long periods of continuous service with the company as a condition of receiving pensions. Under modern industrial conditions, workers necessarily change their place of employment from time to time either because of layoffs or because they wish to better themselves, and they are therefore unable to accumulate continuous service records with a single employer. Even when the plan did not specify a definite period of service, companies which maintained pension programs

---

[20] *Monthly Labor Review,* January, 1937, p. 61.

were reluctant to employ older workers because they might soon be on the pension rolls.[21]

The most serious deficiency of private pension plans was the fact that they were voluntary and employers could terminate them at will. When a plan was terminated it meant not only that the present employees were deprived of the prospect of old age benefits but that the monthly payments ceased abruptly for those already on the pension rolls.[22] Typically the plans specified:

This pension plan has been established voluntarily by the Company; and the Company shall have, and hereby expressly reserve to themselves, the right and privilege to amend, suspend, or annul it at any time at the pleasure of the Company. The plan indicates and embodies the present attitude and intention of the Company in reference to the payment of pensions to the employees of the Company, but it is not understood or construed as ever constituting in any respect a contractual relation between the Company and any such employee.

Even though a company might not wish to terminate its pension program, the continuation of payments was contingent upon its financial condition. The pensions paid under many of the earlier plans were charged to the company's operating pay roll and thus were dependent upon current operating income. Even though the company established a separate pension fund, continued pension payments depended on its ability regularly to augment the fund. Business reverses, and especially general business depressions, have

[21] These disadvantages are inherent in any pension plan which is structurally limited to a particular class of workers, because it tends to freeze employees to their present jobs and to discourage a healthy amount of mobility. An example of this is the pension program now pertaining to schoolteachers which keeps many teachers tied to their classrooms, even though they would prefer to experiment with other kinds of employment.

[22] In 1909 Morris and Company of Chicago established a contributory pension plan. In 1923 the company sold its business to Armour and Company. At the time of the sale the company had contributed $1,250,000, employees who had not yet been put on the pension roll $916,352, and pensioners $132,000. After the sale many member employees withdrew their contributions and the reserve fell to $320,000; this was enough to continue the pensions then being paid for only fourteen months. Some of the pensioners sued Armour and Company to compel them to continue their pensions, basing their claims upon the theory that Morris and Company had entered into a contract which Armour's had taken over with the business. Their contentions were completely denied by the court. (*Agnese R. Cowles, et al., Appellants* v. *Morris and Co.,* Appellate Court, First District of the State of Illinois, December 21, 1926.)

deprived many employees of pensions which they had been led to expect would be coming to them upon their retirement.

Existing Company Plans

Experience with voluntary company pension plans has demonstrated that they alone could never be the solution of the problem of old age security for the mass of workers. The 1929 financial crisis and the subsequent termination of the employment status of millions of workers accentuated a conviction, which had been growing for many years, that more adequate measures were necessary. This resulted in the adoption of the federal old age assistance and insurance programs discussed in a later chapter.

A comprehensive government program, however, does not necessarily mean that there may not be advantages to both employers and workers in maintaining voluntary plans also. Proof of this is the increase in private pension plans since the inauguration of the federal program. At the present time probably 2 million workers, more than half of them in manufacturing, are employed in companies which maintain voluntary pension plans.[23] Since a large majority of the existing plans cover employees who are also covered by the federal program, the benefits accruing from the company plans represent additional gains.

[23] A survey in 1938 indicated that 1,693,718 employees were covered under 383 plans for which reports were available, but 132 additional plans were known to exist. Some of those reported covered, however, were not wage earners but officials and other supervisory employees. (M. W. Latimer and Karl Tufel, *Trends in Industrial Pensions,* Industrial Relations Counselors, Inc., New York, 1940.)

Another study made in 1943 was based on pension plans in 339 companies with a total employment of approximately 2½ million, but at least one-fourth of these plans covered employees earning over $3000 per year. On the average, membership in the plans included about one-half of the total employment. Two hundred of these plans had been adopted or revised during the first two years of the war. It is known that additional plans were established during the succeeding years while the wage and salary stabilization program was in effect, but many of them were confined to the higher-salaried employees. (F. Beatrice Brower, *Trends in Company Pension Plans,* National Industrial Conference Board, New York, 1944.)

In the spring of 1946 the National Electrical Contractors Association signed an agreement with the International Brotherhood of Electrical Workers providing that 1 per cent of its gross pay roll is to be allocated by employers to the existing union pension fund.

These additional benefits take various forms, depending upon the particular type of company plan in effect. Some provide that pensions shall begin at an earlier age than the minimum required by the Social Security Act; some provide supplementary benefits beginning at the same retirement age; many provide for both a lowering of the age of retirement and an augmentation of the government pension rates. Thus a majority of the newer company plans specify a "normal" rather than a compulsory retirement age, and most of them permit retirement at the discretion of the management. Most company plans also specify pension rates which, together with those specified by the federal system, increase by several hundreds of dollars the annual pensions of those covered.[24]

More than 75 per cent of the company pension plans known to be operating are contributory but these cover less than 30 per cent of the total employees covered by all company plans. Many of the largest companies[25] defray all the costs of their programs, whereas the cost of most of those in effect in smaller companies are shared equally by employers and participating employees. No information is available on the total amount of money which employers are now contributing to all types of voluntary private pension programs. Under three-fourths of the plans in operation in 1942, company contributions amounted to less than 5 per cent of their total pay rolls.[26] At the beginning of 1939 there were 80,000 or more former employees receiving pensions under company programs. During the preceding year pension payments probably totaled around 70 million dollars and the average an-

---

[24] It has been estimated that the contributory pension plans established during 1938 provide a median annual pension of $394 for a person 35 years of age, and $380 for a person 55 years of age, at entry into the plan, exclusive of benefits under the Social Security Act. Comparable amounts under the non-contributory plans are $500 for both ages. (Latimer and Tufel, *Trends in Industrial Pensions*, p. 68.)

[25] The U. S. Steel Corporation has a dual arrangement. At the end of 1945 there were 15,143 pensions in force under both the contributory and the non-contributory parts of its program. Total payments during the year amounted to almost $29,000,000 and individual payments averaged almost $35 a month, in addition to public pensions. (1945 *Annual Report* of the U. S. Steel Corporation.)

[26] Brower, *Trends in Company Pension Plans,* p. 28.

nual per capita pension was close to $800.[27] To the extent that these payments were the result of employer contributions, they can be considered as supplements to wages received for time and output on the job.

SELECTED REFERENCES

FAMILY ALLOWANCES

Bureau of Labor Statistics, *Family Allowances in Various Countries, 1944–45,* Bulletin No. 853, Government Printing Office, Washington, 1946.

Douglas, Paul H., *Wages and the Family,* University of Chicago Press, Chicago, 1925.

Vibart, H. H. R., *Family Allowances in Practice,* P. S. King & Son, Ltd., London, 1926.

HEALTH AND OLD AGE BENEFIT PLANS

Latimer, Murray W., and Tufel, Karl, *Trends in Industrial Pensions,* Industrial Relations Counselors, Inc., New York, 1940.

National Industrial Conference Board, *Health Insurance Plans,* Studies in Personnel Policy, Nos. 9, 10, 11, New York, 1938.

National Industrial Conference Board, *Trends in Company Pension Plans,* No. 61, New York, 1944.

Social Security Board, *Cash Benefits Under Voluntary Disability Insurance in the U. S.,* Bureau Report No. 6, Government Printing Office, Washington, 1941.

Social Security Board, *Prepayment Medical Care Organizations,* Bureau Memorandum No. 55, Government Printing Office, Washington, 1944.

Wyatt, Birchard E., *Private Group Retirement Plans,* Graphic Arts Press, Inc., Washington, 1936.

PROFIT SHARING

Balderston, C. C., *Profit Sharing for Wage Earners,* Industrial Relations Counselors, Inc., New York, 1937.

Bruere, Henry, and Pugh, Grace, *Profitable Personnel Practice,* Harper & Brothers, New York, 1929.

Emmett, Boris, *Profit Sharing in the U. S.,* Bulletin No. 208, Bureau of Labor Statistics, Washington, 1917.

---

[27] The annual pension was calculated by dividing the total pension payments during the year by the average number of pensioners, which, of course, is different from the number at any given date. (Latimer and Tufel, *Trends in Industrial Pensions,* pp. 35–36.)

James, Gorton, *et al.*, *Profit Sharing and Stock Ownership for Employees*, Harper & Brothers, New York, 1926.

National Industrial Conference Board, *Practical Experience with Profit Sharing in Industrial Establishments*, Research Report No. 29, Boston, 1920.

Stewart, Bryce M., and Couper, W. J., *Profit Sharing and Stock Ownership for Wage Earners and Executives*, Industrial Relations Counselors, Inc., New York, 1946.

VACATIONS

Bureau of Labor Statistics, *Paid Vacations in American Industry*, Bulletin No. 811, Government Printing Office, Washington, 1945.

Mills, Charles M., *Vacations for Industrial Workers*, Industrial Relations Counselors, Inc., New York, 1927.

National Industrial Conference Board, *Trends in Company Vacation Policy*, Studies in Personnel Policy No. 21, and *Vacation Policy and National Defense*, No. 34, New York, 1942.

14

GOVERNMENT
REGULATION OF WAGES

IT IS AN AXIOM OF A FREE, COMPETITIVE ECONOMY THAT RATES OF wages shall be a matter for the buyers and sellers of labor to negotiate between themselves. In an ideal, exactly balanced economy, the rates so determined would presumably represent the optimum for the individuals and groups directly concerned, as well as for the general welfare. But the most fundamental of all truths is that human society, although ever striving, never attains an ideal status, and that there is never an exact balance of power or influence among the several groups making up that society. It remains, then, for the sovereign power of the government to intervene in order to mitigate the effects of the imbalances and inequalities. Reluctantly, and sometimes belatedly, governments enact laws to regulate wages when conditions become sufficiently acute to cause dire distress to certain individuals, or when the welfare and economic progress of the nation itself is threatened. Not all wage legislation, it must be added, has been enacted for the common good; some laws, at least those of earlier days, were enacted to protect the interests of special groups who happened to be in control of the government.

Wage legislation is of two general types: (1) legislation which establishes certain specific rates, and (2) laws providing that already established standards shall be made generally effective, or shall be made to apply to groups which otherwise would not receive the prevailing rates. The first type may, but seldom does, incorporate the rates in the laws themselves; more frequently the laws provide for administrative agencies which determine the specific rates according to the general principles laid down in the law.

The rates established may be either minimum or maximum rates, depending upon the purpose of the legislation.

The second type of legislation accepts the reasonableness of the rates already prevailing in a particular industry or area and requires that they shall be paid throughout that industry or area, thus removing the competitive menace of employers who otherwise would pay lower rates than those paid by the majority of employers. In this country, "prevailing wage" legislation has been largely confined to the regulation of wages on public works. Most of the Canadian provinces have laws which apply the prevailing wage standard to private industry as well. The Collective Agreement Act of Quebec, for example, provides that where a collective agreement has been entered into by an organization of employees and one or more employers, either side may apply to the Minister of Labour to have the terms of the agreement[1] made binding throughout the province, or within a certain district, on all employers and employees in the trade or industry.

REASONS FOR WAGE LEGISLATION

Throughout the years, when a government has intervened to regulate the rates of wages to be paid in private industry, it has been motivated by one or more of the following principles: (1) To protect a particular group, either workers or employers, who happened at the time to be in an extremely weak bargaining position because of either scarcity or abundance in the labor market; if the legislation is to assist employers the wages will of course be maximum rates; if employees, they will be minimum standards. (2) To protect the health of particular workers by enabling them to secure subsistence living. (3) To protect the general economy by either increasing or stabilizing purchasing power, according to the need at the time. In addition, there is legislation to regulate the wages of those persons who directly or indirectly work for the

---

[1] The "Terms" cover, in addition to wages, hours and certain other working conditions. When application is made to the Minister of Labour a notice is published and 30 days is allowed for filing objections, after which an Order in Council may be passed granting the application, with or without changes as considered advisable by the Minister. The Order in Council may be amended or revoked in the same manner. Each agreement is administered and enforced by a joint committee of the parties concerned.

government; such laws are based on the principle that the government should be a "good" employer and pay at least as much as prevails in private industry.

The first of the above principles was the basis of legislation as far back as the 14th century in Great Britain and the colonial period in our own country, when laws were enacted to protect employers during times when labor was scarce. The minimum wage legislation enacted during the past generation is based in part on the first but more on the second principle. The wage rates resulting from the National Industrial Recovery Act are a spectacular illustration of governmental efforts to revive the general economy by increasing wages and purchasing power. In contrast, the wage regulations during the recent war and post-war period were directed toward preventing sharp rises in wages in order to stabilize purchasing power and prevent inflation.

Maximum Wages

Early wage legislation in Europe and colonial America reflected the interests and "needs" of the landowners and other employers of labor who were in control of the government at that time.[2] Following the Black Death in England (1348), which reduced the working population by one-half, laws were enacted to regulate wages and to prevent workers from taking advantage of the labor shortage. Throughout the Elizabethan era and almost to the close of the 18th century, the British Parliament enacted a succession of statutes empowering local officials to fix maximum prices for labor and to penalize employers who paid more, as well as laborers who asked more, than the established rates. Compliance was difficult, especially when labor was scarce and employers were willing to pay above the maximum rates rather than do without needed workmen.

Throughout our colonial period, farm and urban employers faced a scarcity of both skilled and unskilled labor. Although a continuous stream of free and indentured labor arrived on our shores, the abundance of free land induced most of them to forsake their normal occupations and to leave their masters as soon

---

[2] Until well into the 19th century, in Europe as well as the United States, the right to vote was held as a vested privilege attached to a particular status generally connected with the possession of lands and other property.

as their period of indenture was served. The town and colonial governments tried various measures for procuring needed labor[3] and keeping workmen from taking advantage of their meager numbers by charging "excessive rates." As early as 1630, Plymouth Colony and Massachusetts Bay Colony passed laws fixing maximum rates of pay in certain skilled trades as well as for "inferior" workmen. Employers were soon overbidding the rates, however, and the penalty for paying more was repealed, although workmen continued to be fined for accepting more than the fixed rates. Thereafter, the delicate problem of enforcing wage regulations was left, for the most part, to the town authorities, but they were not much more successful than the colonial governments.

Minimum Wages

The wage legislation of the 17th and the early part of the 18th century was directed toward protecting employers against "excessive" rates rather than workers against depressive rates. With the advent of the Industrial Revolution employers no longer sought to have wages fixed by statute. Accepting the principle of *laissez faire* and the demand-supply theory of wage determination,

---

[3] The tendency of craftsmen to become farmers was frowned upon in New England, since it was "more to the public welfare and the Glory of God to hold them to the trade"; it was specifically legislated against in Virginia. Agents of the Virginia Company were instructed to establish tradesmen in towns in order "to remove them from the temptation to plant on their own account." Later, after the Colonial Assembly was established, persuasive tactics were used and a law was passed which exempted "handicraftsmen" from taxation.

New England towns also made concessions in order to obtain the services of needed mechanics. If local laws limited property holding and citizenship to "freemen" and "commoners," and thus operated to exclude needed tradesmen from a town, the laws were either suspended in given cases or the town found some way to get around them. Both Boston and Charlestown in 1640 waived certain of the citizenship requirements to obtain carpenters. As early as 1635, Lynn voted to admit a landless blacksmith, and later granted him 20 acres of land, thus keeping both the blacksmith and the letter of the law requiring that residents be landholders. The town of Windsor, Connecticut, presented a currier with a house and land and "something for a shop," but it was to belong to him and his heirs only on condition that "he lives and dies with us and affords us the use of his trade." In 1656 a skilled weaver was granted "twelve acres of meadow-land and twelve acres of upland" in what afterward became the great textile center of Lowell, Massachusetts, "provided he set up his trade of weaving and perform the town's work." (Bureau of Labor Statistics, *History of Wages in the United States from Colonial Times to 1928,* Bulletin No. 604, pp. 8, 11, 46.)

the employers were mainly concerned with seeing that their government maintained a condition of "free" competition in the labor market by forbidding and discouraging workers to combine in order to raise their wages.

Opposition to this kind of government policy began to be expressed during the latter part of the 19th century, not only by wage-earning groups but by the socially-minded public, people who were concerned with the evils of wages that were insufficient to enable workers to live decently. The result was a general movement in many industrial countries toward the establishment of legal minimum levels for all workers, or at least for particular classes of workers—for example, women—who for various reasons were unable to obtain adequate wages through their own efforts. Minimum wage legislation started in New Zealand in 1894, when a compulsory arbitration law was passed which gave district boards the power to fix minimum wages. Australia followed in 1902, and in 1909 Great Britain established her trade board system for those industries or trades in which the prevailing rate was "exceptionally low as compared with that in other employments."[4] A few years later the movement for minimum wage laws began to have effect in the United States.

STATE MINIMUM WAGE LEGISLATION

Under our federal form of government it was natural that wage as well as other kinds of labor legislation should have been initiated by the state governments. Until recent years, except for labor conditions on federally financed projects, wage legislation was

---

[4] In 1918 Parliament amended the Trade Board Act of 1909, which had limited the application of trade boards to "sweated" industries, to permit the Ministry of Labour to set up a trade board in any trade in which, in his opinion, "no adequate machinery exists for the effective regulation of wages throughout the trade, and that accordingly, having regard to the rates of wages prevailing in the trade or any part of the trade, it is expedient that the principal Act should apply to that trade." By 1944 there were 52 trade boards in operation.

The arbitration boards of New Zealand and Australia, as well as the trade boards of Great Britain, do not confine themselves to minimum rates for the least skilled workers, as does most of the minimum wage legislation in the United States; they also establish minimum rates for semi-skilled and skilled occupations. Since 1938 the British trade boards have also been empowered to grant vacations with pay, not exceeding one working week in any year.

confined to state action and was built around the police powers of the state to protect the health and well-being of individuals and to safeguard them from fraudulent and unjust practices. Legislation pertaining to the rates to be paid by private employers was limited almost entirely to regulations covering women and minors on the theory that their bargaining power was inadequate to prevent oppressive wages which were inimical not only to themselves but to the general welfare. Recently, Connecticut, Rhode Island, and New York have extended their legislation to cover men. Many states in their capacity of employers have also enacted laws to regulate the wages of men, as well as women, who are employed on state-financed public works. Most of these, like the federal statutes discussed later, provide that the "going" or "prevailing" rates of wages in the locality shall be paid on state public works.

Progress of Minimum Wage Legislation

Minimum wage legislation was introduced in this country during the period of "reform" preceding the First World War. The pressure for legislation was exerted for the most part by public-spirited non-wage-earner groups who were aroused to the social evil of underpaid women workers. With a few exceptions, organized labor[5] lent only nominal support to the early campaigns and in some cases actively opposed the legislation. Indifference on the part of the unions was attributable both to their general feeling at that time that "the less legislative intervention in labor matters, the better" and to their fear that minimum wages inevitably become maximum wages and hinder collective bargaining. The National Consumers League, which spearheaded the movement for minimum wage legislation, had at first sought to improve working conditions for women and children by using the label and appealing to the public as consumers not to purchase goods which were manufactured under depressed conditions. Meeting with indifferent success through this approach, it turned to legislation.

Massachusetts enacted the first minimum wage law in 1912 and the next year eight other states followed.[6] Thereafter the move-

---

[5] The labor movement at that time was largely composed of building and metal workers and miners, almost exclusively male trades.

[6] Colorado, California, Minnesota, Nebraska, Oregon, Utah, Washington, and Wisconsin.

ment lost its momentum, although by 1923 eight additional laws had been enacted.[7] The first Massachusetts law represented a cautious step. The law was not mandatory but depended entirely upon publicity for enforcement, and the financial condition of the industry, as well as the cost of living, was taken into account in establishing minimum rates. Several of the other states, although their laws were mandatory and based solely on the cost of living concept, established minimum rates so low that they had little effect in raising wages, and fell far short of the cost of living standard as prices advanced rapidly during and after the First World War.

In all the states the operation of minimum wage laws was hampered by continued attempts on the part of employers to get them declared unconstitutional. In 1917 the question seemed to be settled when the U. S. Supreme Court sustained the favorable decision of the Supreme Court of Oregon. However, in 1923 when a new case from the District of Columbia was brought before the U. S. Supreme Court, its personnel having altered in the meantime,[8] that court held the District minimum wage law unconstitutional. The 1923 decision held that the District law conflicted with the due process clause of the Fifth Amendment because it took away the liberty of employers and workers to include any terms they wished in their employment contract. It was based on the principle that labor is a commodity and that compelling employers to pay a living wage is taking away their property rights; that

---

[7] Arkansas and Kansas in 1915, Arizona in 1917, the District of Columbia in 1918, North Dakota, Texas, and Puerto Rico in 1919, and South Dakota in 1923. The Nebraska law, however, was repealed in 1919. Texas also passed a law in 1919 but repealed it in 1921, minimum rates having never been put into operation. (U. S. Department of Labor, Women's Bureau, *The Development of Minimum Wage Laws in the U. S., 1912–1927,* Bulletin No. 61.)

[8] *Adkins* v. *Children's Hospital,* 261 U. S. 525. One justice who favored minimum wage legislation did not participate; the result was the equivalent of a five-four vote against validation. Much has been written about the timing of this case and the effect of a change in personnel on the court. It has been maintained that from the time of the enactment of the first legislation in 1912 until 1930, there were always at least five on the Supreme Court bench who were favorable to minimum wage legislation, except during the two years 1921–1923 when the District of Columbia case came up. This case took thirteen months to be decided; if it had been decided within three or four months, the usual length of time for cases, the law would have been validated since one judge who was favorable died in the meantime.

the Nineteenth Amendment put women on an equality with men, and that women are as able as men to bargain for their wages with employers; that minimum wages do not directly affect the public health and morals and therefore should not come under the exception which permits legislative interference with freedom of contract.

Following this Supreme Court decision, six additional minimum wage laws were declared unconstitutional by various state courts, and most of the remaining laws became inoperative. Some of the state commissions ceased to enforce their orders; others sought voluntary compliance but were reluctant to prosecute violations for fear their laws would be entirely nullified.[9] In order to meet the Supreme Court's objection to compulsory cost of living wages, a number of states injected a new principle into their wage determination, namely, that wages shall not be "oppressive" and shall be a "reasonable and adequate compensation for the services rendered."

It was not this new concept[10] of what a minimum wage should signify that determined its constitutionality, but a change in the spirit of the times and the personnel of the U. S. Supreme Court. In 1937 the Supreme Court sustained one of the earliest state laws (Washington) which was based on the cost of living principle.[11] In this decision the court ruled that the 1923 decision "was a departure from the true application of the principle governing the regulation of the state of the relationship of employer and em-

---

[9] Because of the "voluntary" feature of the Massachusetts law, that state's minimum wage commission was not affected by the Supreme Court decision. A state court, however, held unconstitutional the provision requiring a newspaper to publish the names of firms not paying minimum wage rates which the commission might submit. However, most of the newspapers in the state were willing to publish the names, so this decision had little actual effect upon the enforcement of the law.

[10] In 1936 the federal Supreme Court, in a case under the New York law which incorporated the principle of fair value for services rendered, declared that it could find no essential difference between the new statute and the one held unconstitutional in the Adkins case, and that "any measure that deprives employers and adult women of freedom to agree upon wages, leaving employers and men employees free to do so, is necessarily arbitrary." (*Morehead v. People ex rel. Tipaldo,* 298 U. S. 597.)

[11] *West Coast Hotel Co.* v. *Parrish,* 300 U. S. 391. This was also a five-to-four decision but in reverse to the 1923 and 1936 decisions.

ployed," that minimum wage legislation was a proper exercise of the police powers of the state because it was in the social interest to maintain the welfare of women workers, and that it did not violate liberty of contract except as is required to protect the health, safety, morals, and welfare of the people.

Coverage of Existing Laws

The Supreme Court's validation of the principle of minimum wage legislation encouraged a number of states to enact laws and put new life into old laws which had become moribund. The Massachusetts commission, for example, was empowered to issue mandatory orders instead of relying solely upon the publication of names of employers for enforcement. By 1945 there were thirty minimum wage laws on the statute books—twenty-six states and the District of Columbia, Alaska, Hawaii, and Puerto Rico.[12]

The New York, Connecticut, Rhode Island, Puerto Rico, and Hawaii acts apply to men as well as women. Most of the laws cover all minors, but the Arkansas, Louisiana, Nevada, and South Dakota acts do not cover male minors. A "minor" is defined variously as all persons under 18 years of age, or all under 21 years of age, or girls under 21 and boys under 18, or vice versa. All the laws allow the payment of less than the established minima to "any woman or minor, including a learner or apprentice, whose earning capacity is impaired by age or physical or mental deficiency or injury." Each case, however, must be approved by the proper licensing authorities.

The existing laws are broad in their coverage of industries; most of them are all-inclusive, but there are a few listed exceptions such as agriculture and domestic service. The Wisconsin and Alaska laws cover all occupations; at the other extreme is the Maine law, which applies only to fish packing. In effect, since the federal Fair Labor Standards Act establishes rates for all interstate industries, state minimum wage legislation is primarily useful in non-manufacturing industries such as retail trade, laundries and dry cleaning, hospitals, hotels and restaurants, beauty parlors, and canneries.

---

[12] Kansas, Oklahoma, and Louisiana, however, did not have rates in effect, although their laws had been in force for a number of years. (Women's Bureau, *State Minimum Wage Laws and Orders,* Bulletin No. 191.)

Procedures for Minimum Rate Determination

All but a few of the existing minimum wage laws provide for the determination of wage rates by conferences or wage boards appointed to study the various industries and make recommendations to the state agencies authorized to fix minimum wages and issue orders. In Nevada, South Dakota, Arkansas, Alaska, and Hawaii, however, the minimum wages to be paid were determined by the

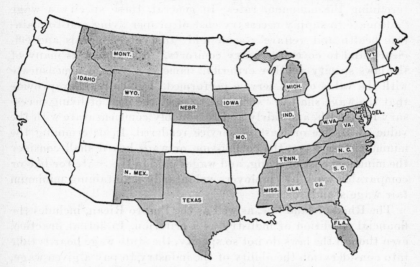

FIG. 26.   *States Without Minimum Wage Laws in 1945.*

legislatures and are specified in the laws. Rates fixed by law are much less flexible than those established by commissioners, for the latter can readily be changed as prices and other conditions change.[13] Also, where the rates are incorporated in the law there is usually no commission established to see that the law is enforced. Elsewhere, the commission that determines the rate is also responsible for the administration of the law. Under most of the commission-administered laws the minimum wage is determined for each industry separately, although orders have been issued in some states for a wide coverage of industries. Three states—Kentucky, Minnesota, and Wisconsin—have issued blanket orders in-

[13] Three legislatures—Hawaii, Nevada, and South Dakota—raised their minimum wage rates during the recent war in response to rising costs of living.

tended to apply to all industries, as well as separate orders for certain industries.

There are two very important differences with respect to the bases for determining the minimum rates, namely, whether or not the cost of living is the sole factor taken into consideration; also whether hourly or weekly rates are to be established. About half the laws provide that the cost of living shall be the basis for determining the minimum rates. In general, these specify a wage "adequate to supply necessary cost of proper living and to maintain health and welfare"; some add "to protect morals and efficiency and to cover necessary comforts." But almost as many of the laws specify another criterion, namely, a wage commensurate with the value of the service performed. Typically, they provide that the wage shall be "sufficient to meet the cost of living necessary for health, and fairly and reasonably commensurate with the value of service or class of service rendered. In determining the minimum fair wage, the commission or wage board shall consider the minimum cost of living, and wages paid in the State for like or comparable work by employers voluntarily maintaining minimum fair wage standards."

The Rhode Island law, as well as the Puerto Rican, includes the financial condition of industry as a criterion. In actual practice, even though the laws do not so specify, the state wage boards take into consideration the ability of the industry to pay a given wage, for in most cases the rates which have been established are equivalent to those already in effect in some or even a majority of firms. In considering cost of living, the wage commissions base their orders upon the needs of self-supporting women without dependents,[14] but few of the existing rates could be considered sufficient to provide a "comfortable" standard of living; the highest in 1945 was 60 cents an hour for straight time work, and most of them were 40 cents an hour or under.

Some of the more recent wage orders are not restricted to minimum rates on a straight hourly basis but also take into account the many subsidiary factors that affect a worker's wages, such as

---

[14] In 1942 a Minnesota employer contended that the State minimum wage law did not apply to a married woman partly supported by her husband and intermittently employed, but the State Supreme Court held that the law applies equally to married or single women fully or intermittently employed.

irregularity of employment, detrimental labor practices, and long hours of work. One such type of regulation provides that an employer who requires the worker to wear a uniform while on duty must furnish the uniform and must either bear the expense of laundering it or compensate the worker for doing so by paying an additional weekly sum. The evil of long over-all working hours occasioned by the split-shift arrangement has been mitigated by the requirement of a higher rate of pay on days when it occurs.

Several methods to counteract underemployment have been devised. One of these is the requirement of a higher hourly rate of pay for part-time workers. Another is the establishment of a basic minimum wage rate on a weekly basis so that the worker who is employed for less than the maximum legal work week will nevertheless receive a week's wages. "Guaranteed weekly wage provisions," as minimum wage rates established on a weekly basis are termed, have taken several forms. Some state orders require the weekly minimum wage to be paid for any work done during the week, irrespective of the number of hours. Under other orders, the weekly wage must be paid if work is performed on a certain number of days. Encouragement was given to the principle of the "guaranteed weekly wage" when the highest court of the State of New York in 1942 upheld a wage order which established a rate fixed on a weekly basis, even though only part of a week was worked. The decision stated:

. . . It is fairly to be assumed that the legislature, bent on seeing to it that women and minors should, so far as possible, receive subsistence wages for their work, appreciated that no hourly rate of wages could achieve that result unless it were multiplied by some appropriate number of hours. . . . The legislature, driving toward its plainly marked goal, would have stopped far short of that goal if it had provided for minimum hourly wages only. The accomplishment of its high social purpose required a grant of authority to the Labor Department to make such orders as would in fact be directed toward providing a living wage, not merely an hourly rate which, in most industries, would not produce a living income, unless ordered paid for a sufficient minimum number of hours.[15]

---

[15] *Mary Lincoln Candies, Inc.*, v. *Department of Labor of the State of New York*, 45 N.E. (2d) 434, December 3, 1942. The wage order in this case was for the confectionery industry; in addition to providing for a minimum wage

EQUAL PAY FOR EQUAL WORK FOR WOMEN

State minimum wage laws, as their name indicates, are designed to provide women with wage rates which will cover the costs of the barest necessities of day-to-day living. They are premised on two major distinctions between women and men workers: first, that women, or at least certain classes of women, are less able than men to bargain for adequate wages and therefore need the assistance of the government; second, that the rates established under these laws shall be based on the cost of living for a single individual, thus assuming that women have no dependents to support.[16] The philosophy underlying minimum wage laws for women is one of social welfare rather than individual justice or equity.

Another type of legislation—that prohibiting discrimination in pay because of sex—approaches the problem of wages from the standpoint of compensation for work performance and equity between groups or classes of workers, rather than of wages as a social obligation. Legislation providing equal pay for equal work removes the question of wages from one of *need* to one of *rights*. Since such laws are directed toward seeing that women secure the same pay as men when performing the same kind of work, they also assume that women's bargaining power is unequal to that of men; hence the government must intervene in order that justice shall prevail. Unlike minimum wage laws, however, their purpose is not to establish rates per se but to establish the principle of equality of rates between men and women, to substitute *job* rates for rates based on sex, and to require that wages, whatever they are, be based on job content rather than on who is doing the job.

Seven states now (1946) have laws which prohibit discrimination in rate of pay because of sex.[17] Several are limited to manufac-

---

of $14 for a full 40-hour week, it required employers to pay $10 to employees working three days or less in any week during the busy season and $7 to employees working two days or less in any week during the slack season.

[16] According to numerous studies made by the Women's Bureau of the U. S. Department of Labor, about 10 per cent of the women wage earners in this country are the sole support of families of two or more persons, and approximately 50 per cent contribute to the support of dependents.

[17] The states and the year in which the laws were enacted are: Michigan (1919), Montana (1919), Washington (1943), Illinois (1943), New York (1944), Massachusetts (1945), and Rhode Island (1946). The U. S. Civil

turing employment and others exclude domestic and agricultural occupations. Typically they read: "Any employer in this State, employing both males and females, who shall discriminate in any way in the payment of wages as between sexes, or who shall pay any female a less wage, be it time or piece work, or salary, than is being paid to males similarly employed, or in any employment formerly performed by males, shall be guilty of a misdemeanor. . . . A differential in wages between employees based in good faith on a factor or factors other than sex shall not constitute discrimination within the meaning of this act."

The enforcement of equal pay laws entails some peculiar difficulties. The administration of a minimum wage law, after the rate is once determined, is simply a matter of policing to see that no one is paid less than the specified rate, and this can be done very largely by examining employer pay-roll records. The crux of enforcing an equal pay law, on the other hand, lies in determining the comparability of work performed by men and women. Job titles on the pay-roll records may or may not indicate real differences in job content; hence the jobs themselves must be analyzed to determine their essential elements. Furthermore, there is the question of the meaning of "equal" or "similar." Suppose that a man and a woman are engaged on work which is exactly similar for the major portion of the day, but that during the day the man is required to do some heavy lifting while the woman is engaged on some light but perhaps more skillful operation. Is this "similar" work because it is identical a major portion of the day? Should the light but more skillful operation of the woman offset the heavy operation performed by the man? Suppose their work is identical throughout the day, but compliance with a state law or a union contract enables the woman to enjoy several rest periods with pay. Should this be ignored in determining equal pay rates?

Job analysis and evaluation pose many difficult problems, as has been brought out in an earlier chapter; and an equal pay law

---

Service Classification Act of 1923 definitely established the principle that federal jobs were to be paid on the basis of job elements without regard to sex. The British civil service, on the other hand, maintains a dual wage system, that is, a rate for men and a rate for women on the same job. The National War Labor Board accepted the principle of equal pay for women in their wage awards. (See "Equal Pay for Women Workers," *Monthly Labor Review*, September, 1946, p. 380.)

provides no automatic assurance that rates within any given plant will be based on job characteristics alone, and that traditional discriminatory practices will be eliminated. Nevertheless, equal pay laws establish a goal or standard and provide the means for removing some of the more obvious inequalities.

STATE WAGE COLLECTION LAWS

State governments have been concerned not only with rates of wages but also with providing workers assurance of the full benefits of the wages which they have earned. Wage collection laws are directed toward seeing that wage earners receive the full and exact amounts of money which are due them, and that their wages are paid at intervals convenient to their welfare and in a form which permits the free use of their earnings as an instrument of purchase. In order that employees may know of their legal rights, most states require employers to keep posted in conspicuous places a notice specifying the regular payday and the time and place of payment.

Legal Claims to Wages Earned

The natural presumption under a contract of employment is that wages will be paid at the time agreed upon, with final settlement at the termination of employment. No one questions a worker's right to the wages he earns, and yet for thousands of workers payday comes and goes, leaving them empty-handed. They find, too late, that their employers were financially irresponsible or careless or perhaps downright dishonest. Practically every state has passed some kind of wage collection law to protect workers against employers who fail to pay wages regularly, or who do not pay in full, or who do not pay at all. Not all of these laws are equally effective, but under the best of them tens of thousands of wage claims are collected each year, adding up to several million dollars.

The right of workmen to a prior claim to the results of their labors has long been recognized. The common law grants a lien on employers' property enforceable by sale, from the returns of which the charges of the workmen are to be paid. Practically every state has a statute defining and enforcing this right. The liens for payment of wages are given priority over other claims; and if the employer has died, become bankrupt, or otherwise is disqualified, executors as well as receivers of his estate are subject to service for such preferred claims. Subsequent to claims of the government and to the costs of administration or preservation of the estate, wage liens have preference over ordinary debts.

A major function of many state labor departments is to collect wage claims for workers and thus make it unnecessary for them to go to the expense of engaging lawyers. The procedure for the actual payment of the claim varies. Some labor departments require the employer to pay the claim to the commissioner of labor, who in turn issues a check to the complainant. This is generally recognized as the safest and surest method; if any difficulty develops over the solvency of the employer or the validity of the check, the employer is dealing with an agency of the state, not with an individual employee who may be too timid to protest. Some labor departments permit payment directly to the worker in the presence of a representative of the department, who secures the worker's receipt and files it with the docket of the case. If the commissioner decides that legal action is necessary for collection, and if the state law gives him authority, he will enter suit on behalf of the worker. If he decides that provisions of the law regulating wage payment have been violated, he will exercise his authority to enforce the law.

Wage Assignments

By necessity, families with low incomes live from "hand to mouth," and many of them are compelled (or persuaded by merchants) to buy their furniture, clothes, and other costly items on an installment basis. Also, when faced with unexpected or abnormal expenses, such as medical costs for a prolonged sickness or operation, they have no savings with which to pay their bills. In order to obtain payment, creditors may ask the courts to attach their wages by serving garnishee notices to their employers to withhold wages already due or to be earned in the future. The money is then assigned to the courts, which turn it over to the creditors.

Restrictions or prohibitions on the assignment of wages, particularly of wages not yet earned, are contained in the laws of a

number of states. Outright prohibition of assignment has been
challenged on the ground of its alleged infringement of property
rights, but some courts have upheld the prohibition of wage assignments as a desirable safeguard for those dependent upon wages
for support, and as a protection from oppression, extortion,
fraud, and the consequences of a worker's weakness, folly, or improvidence. A very common protective provision is an exemption
of a certain amount or percentage of the employee's wages from
garnishment in order to secure to those dependent upon these
wages a means of support. For example, some laws provide that
the amount garnisheed may not exceed 10 per cent of an employee's wages; others exempt 75 per cent, with a further stipulation that the exemption shall not be less than a given sum, such
as $50.

Kickback Laws

Kickback is the return or withholding of a portion of an employee's wages by his employer or foreman upon threat of losing
his job or as a bribe for obtaining a job. While instances of kick-
backs have existed in manufacturing, mining, and other industries
where foremen or "straw bosses" have demanded payments from
workers as the price of employment, the practice has been most
prevalent on public construction as a means of circumventing
wage laws. It is especially easy for contractors to demand kick-
backs during times of depression when jobs are scarce and workers
are fearful that what little income they are receiving may be taken
from them.

Several states as well as the federal government have taken
cognizance of the kickback evil by making it a misdemeanor and
subject to heavy fines. The federal law, enacted in 1934, applies
to employment financed in whole or in part by federal funds. Typical of the state laws are those of New Jersey and New York which
provide:

Whenever an agreement for the performance of personal service
requires that workmen engaged in its performance shall be paid the
prevailing rate of wages, it shall be unlawful for any person, either
for himself or any other person, to request, demand, or receive, either
before or after such workman is engaged, that such workman pay
back, return, donate, contribute, or give any part or all of such work-

man's wages, salary, or thing of value, to any person, upon the statement, representation, or understanding that failure to comply with such request or demand will prevent such workman from procuring or retaining employment. The violation of the provisions of this section shall constitute a misdemeanor; and any person who directly or indirectly aids, requests, or authorizes any person to violate any of the provisions of this section shall be guilty of a violation of the provisions thereof.

In a decision upholding the kickback law, a New York court emphasized that such a law protects the workman as well as the employers who are conducting their operations in an ethical manner with fairness and justice to their employees, because it insures parity of labor cost and thus establishes competitive equality on one of the basic calculations for those engaging the same classifications of labor.

Frequency of Pay Periods

The frequency of the payment of wages is usually determined by the contract of employment or by custom. In the United States, however, nearly all the states have enacted legislation requiring the payment of wages at some specified time—weekly, monthly, or semi-monthly. Many of the early laws applied only to certain corporations or occupations, such as mining, quarrying, manufacturing, or transportation. While this type of law still exists, the tendency in recent years has been for such statutes to apply either to all occupations or to all corporations doing business in the state. But like so many types of labor laws, the laws pertaining to the frequency of pay periods usually exclude domestic and agricultural employment.

The majority of the states specify that wages shall be paid at least semi-monthly. Only two jurisdictions (Alaska and Oregon) have provided that wages must be paid at least once a month; all the New England States, New York, and Puerto Rico require pay periods not to exceed one week. Textile employees in South Carolina are required to be paid weekly on the premises during working hours. In only four jurisdictions (the District of Columbia, Florida, Idaho, and Washington) are there no requirements for the payment of wages at specified intervals.

In order to give the employer time to make up his pay roll,

many of the laws permit a "holdover" period, some as long as 15 or 18 days. Such long "holdovers" mean that new employees are not paid for two or three weeks after starting work and that all the employees are always several weeks behind in their wage receipts. When an employee voluntarily quits his job, it is generally assumed, and sometimes stated in the statutes, that his unpaid wages do not become due until the next regular payday. Several state laws, however, require all wages due an individual who quits his job to be paid within a given time; the specified periods range from one to ten days. Some specify immediate payment if the employee has given several days' notice of his intention to quit. Requirements are much stricter in cases of discharge; a majority of the state laws require employers to pay all wages due the employee at the time and place of discharge, but a few allow the employer three or five days.

Although the provisions of the laws regulating the time of wage payment are fairly uniform, the decisions of the courts rest on such various grounds that no generalization can be made as to the degree of regulation which will be allowed. However, nearly all the court decisions were rendered years ago, and since that time many states have enacted laws the constitutionality of which has not been successfully challenged. Even in the states in which manifest declarations of unconstitutionality have been made, legislative action indicates a purpose to regulate the payment of wages, and in some instances constitutional amendments have been adopted for this purpose.

Payment in Scrip

The use of scrip, tokens, or orders in lieu of currency for the payment of wages is generally equivalent to a 10 or 20 per cent reduction in income. If the scrip is redeemed at an independent store, the store usually demands a substantial discount; when scrip is paid, however, it is usually associated with company stores and there is ample proof that the prices charged by such stores are substantially higher than those of independent stores.[18] Both payment by scrip and company stores are most frequently found in isolated types of employment such as mining and lumbering,

[18] See page 48, footnote 16.

and at railroad terminals and construction projects which are distant from urban centers.

At least 33 states now have laws governing the issuance of scrip; 16 of these states also have legislation making it unlawful to compel an employee to purchase at any particular store, and five states have provisions regulating the prices which may be charged for goods sold in company stores. (It must be remembered, however, that no laws are self-enforcing; those dealing with prices are especially ineffective if there is not vigorous and constant inspection.) The better type of laws reads as follows:

No employer shall issue in payment of wages due, or to become due, or as an advance on wages to be earned (a) any order, check, draft, note, memorandum, or other acknowledgement of indebtedness, unless it is negotiable and payable in cash, on demand, without discount, at some established place of business in the state. (b) Any scrip, coupon, cards, or other thing redeemable in merchandise, or purporting to be payable or redeemable otherwise than in money.

No employer, or agent thereof, shall compel or coerce any employee, or applicant for employment, to patronize his employer, or any other person, in the purchase of any thing of value.

FEDERAL REGULATION OF WAGES[19]

Traditionally, the federal government as a direct employer of labor has adhered to the principle of paying the "going" rate for similar work paid by private employers in the community in which the work was done. As a purchaser of goods and services, however, it is only within recent years that the government has accepted this principle; formerly, it purchased goods and services on a competitive bid basis, regardless of the wages or working conditions of those employed by the manufacturer or contractor. In 1931 the federal government first recognized a responsibility for wages paid on public works done through private contractors, and five years later legislation was enacted to cover employees engaged in the manufacture of products purchased by the government.

---

[19] Omitted from this discussion is the legislation pertaining to particular classes of workers, such as the establishment of wages under the Merchant Marine Act of 1936.

Wages of Government Mechanics and Laborers

The principle that the wages for mechanical and laboring employees of the federal government shall conform to the rates for similar work prevailing in private industry in the locality was recognized by Congress as long ago as 1862, when legislation was enacted which applied this principle to government navy yards. Since then it has been extended to similar positions in the Bureau of the Mint, Bureau of Engraving and Printing, Government Printing Office, Post Office Department, and other agencies which directly employ mechanics and laborers not covered by statutory classifications and rates under the Civil Service regulations.

In general, these government agencies have used three methods for determining specific rates: wage board procedures, administrative procedures, and collective bargaining. Under all three procedures wage surveys in the local areas are made, but from that point the methods differ in the degree to which the employees themselves, or their representatives, participate in the process of rate determination. Administrative procedures provide for the smallest degree of employee participation, since there is no formal method by which employees may offer information or protest proposed rates, prior to the promulgation of the rate schedule. The situation is quite different under the wage board procedures. These provide for public hearings prior to rate determination in order to afford employees an opportunity to introduce additional wage data or other factual materials; they also permit public hearings for appeals from proposed rates. In some instances the wage boards are composed entirely of administrative employees of the agency concerned; in other instances public or union representatives are also members.

The collective bargaining process goes furthest in the matter of employee participation, but at present this method is used only by one federal agency, the Tennessee Valley Authority, although the Government Printing Office procedure approximates collective bargaining. Under the first plan, representatives of the Authority meet once a year with the various employee unions operating through the Tennessee Valley Trades and Labor Council, and bargain on rates in accordance with those prevailing for comparable work in the area; the rates are then incorporated in a bilaterally signed agreement. In case agreement cannot be reached, the law requires that the disputed rate or rates be submitted to the Secretary of Labor for final decision. In the Government Printing Office, the rates for each of the crafts are negotiated between the Public Printer and committees representing the employees concerned, but the final determination is left to the Joint Committee on Printing (a congressional committee), and the rates established are not incorporated in bilaterally signed agreements.

Government Contract Work

In 1931 Congress passed the original Davis-Bacon Act, which covered all contracts in excess of $5000; in 1935 the law was amended to cover contracts in excess of $2000. The Act requires the payment of prevailing wage rates on all public buildings and public works, including road construction and federally aided housing projects. All laborers and mechanics employed directly upon the site of the work by either contractors or subcontractors are covered. Whenever wages are to be determined under the law, the Department of Labor requests all interested persons, including unions, employers' associations, and state labor departments, to submit information concerning the rate of wages paid on similar projects in the locality to the various classes of laborers and mechanics customarily employed on that type of work. The wage rates determined by the Department of Labor to be the prevailing rates are advertised in the specifications, are inserted in the contract, and must be posted at the site of work.

In the Public Contracts Act of 1936, known as the Walsh-Healey Act, Congress exercised its power to regulate conditions of employment when the federal government is the purchaser of the goods produced. Under this Act employees engaged on a government contract which exceeds $10,000 in value must be paid not less than the prevailing minimum wage in the industry and locality as determined by the Secretary of Labor. The Act covers all workers, except office and custodial, who are employed in or connected with the manufacture, fabrication, assembling, handling, supervision, or shipment of materials, supplies, articles, or equipment

---

[20] By a special statute, contracts for the construction of naval vessels for the Navy Department were placed under the Walsh-Healey Act.

under the contract.[20] In many cases the wage standards provided under the Public Contracts Act extend beyond the employees immediately employed on government contract work. Because employers producing for the government are generally also producing for the open market, the public contracts wages are usually paid to all employees doing similar work within the plant. In fact, a regulation stipulates that when an employee works for any part of a day in a given pay-roll period on a government contract in an industry for which a wage determination has been issued, he is entitled to at least the determined minimum wage for all hours worked in that pay-roll period or work week.

Although the Davis-Bacon and Walsh-Healey Acts are similar so far as the principle of prevailing wages is concerned, there are differences in their provisions, in addition to the size of contract which determines their coverage. Unlike the Walsh-Healey Act, the Davis-Bacon Act contains no requirements regarding hours and overtime rates, working conditions, and child labor—subjects which are discussed in a later chapter. A laborer or mechanic is covered by the Davis-Bacon Act only if he is actually employed at the site of construction. A worker is covered by the Walsh-Healey Act if he is employed by the contractor, if he is employed by a manufacturer supplying materials directly to the government under a contract awarded to a dealer, or if he is employed by one manufacturer who is doing work required under a contract awarded to another manufacturer which in the normal course of business the contracting manufacturer would have done in his own plant. Thus, employees of subcontractors are not subject to the Walsh-Healey provisions unless the subcontract is for work which, under the usual practice of the industry involved, is not subcontracted.

The Davis-Bacon Act stipulates that the Secretary of Labor shall determine the hourly rates prevailing in the immediate neighborhood of the construction site for each occupation and that these shall be the minimum rates for the various classes of laborers and mechanics. Under the Walsh-Healey Act, the Secretary of Labor determines only the prevailing minimum rate for an industry, rather than for each of the various occupations; and in most instances a single minimum rate is put into effect for an entire industry, regardless of where the goods are being produced.

Wage Regulation Under the National Industrial Recovery Act

The federal government's first and most extensive program for the regulation of wages in private industry was established under the National Industrial Recovery Act during 1933–1935, when most of the country's industries were subject to nation-wide labor standards. The N.I.R.A. was enacted for the express purpose of lifting the country out of a "national emergency of widespread unemployment and disorganization of industry." Its initial approach was "to increase the consumption of industrial and agricultural products by increasing the purchasing power," and the one way to accomplish this (in addition to providing more jobs, which was discussed in Chapter 7) was by increasing wage rates. In signing the bill, President Roosevelt said: "It represents a supreme effort to stabilize for all time the many factors which make for prosperity of the nation and the preservation of American standards. Its goal is the assurance of a reasonable profit to industry and a living wage for labor."

In order to accomplish these two purposes—a reasonable profit to industry and a living wage for labor—codes of fair competition were established for each industry; these provided, among other things, minimum rates of wages for the industry concerned. The wage provisions established by each code differed from the minimum rates provided by other laws, previously and later enacted, in two major respects: (1) The minimum rates were not always confined to the unskilled or any particular class of workers. (2) The minimum rates were not always uniform throughout the industry.

Although there were no legal restrictions against establishing rate structures to cover all classes of workers within the industry, less than 10 per cent of the codes included minimum rates for labor above the unskilled class, and more than half of these covered various branches of the clothing industry. The most that was done to protect the wages of skilled workers in the majority of the codes was to write into the labor provisions a general statement that the existing wage differentials between occupational classes was to be maintained. The clauses of the codes devoted to this purpose took many forms and did not necessarily insure equality of treatment as between codes, the terminology being so indefinite in certain cases as to permit varying interpretations. A common clause provided that "equitable adjustments" of pay schedules of employees paid above the minimum should be made, More satisfactory from the standpoint of enforcement and interpretation were the provisions whereby (1) employers were obligated to make adjustments of wages in the brackets above the code minimum so that existing differentials were maintained, and (2) wages might not be reduced, notwithstanding any reduction in the full-time working week.[21]

A number of the codes provided differential rates based upon one or more of the following: geographical area, size of locality, and sex. The definition of North and South varied considerably in the codes and led to much dissatisfaction, especially in borderline states such as Maryland, which was rated as a southern state in some codes and a northern state in others. A number of codes differentiated between eastern and western metropolitan areas, and several established one minimum rate for men and another for women. In general, the minimum rates established under the codes for unskilled men ranged from 30 cents to 40 cents an hour, the latter prevailing in over half the codes. Rates for women were about 5 cents less on the average, although most codes specified that when women did the same work as men they should receive equal pay.

Fair Labor Standards Act

After the Supreme Court in May, 1935, declared the codes of fair competition under the N.I.R.A. to be unconstitutional,[22] Congress immediately enacted several laws which preserved and strengthened some of the labor features of the codes. Thus, the Bituminous Coal Act of 1937 was a direct application to a single industry of the "fair trade practice" idea of the N.I.R.A.;[23] the National Industrial Relations Act of 1935 was, in essence, an expansion of Section 7a of the N.I.R.A.; and the minimum wage and maximum hour concepts of the N.I.R.A. were carried over into

---

[21] See chap. 16 for the hour standards provided under the N.I.R.A. codes.

[22] *Schechter* v. *United States,* 295 U. S. 495 (1935).

[23] While the Bituminous Coal Act did not include specific labor provisions, it set forth the policy of the right of collective bargaining and gave the Commission established under the Act the power to determine minimum and maximum coal prices, thus indirectly assisting workers to improve their wages. The Act expired in 1943.

the Public Contracts Act of 1936 and the Fair Labor Standards Act of 1938.

The declared purpose of the Fair Labor Standards Act is to correct and eliminate labor conditions that are detrimental to the maintenance of the minimum standard of living necessary for the health, efficiency, and general well-being of workers, without substantially curtailing employment or earning power. Under its terms a minimum wage and a maximum work week are established for employees engaged in interstate commerce or the production of goods for interstate commerce. By an administrative ruling, an employee is covered if even a small part of the goods he works on is moved in interstate commerce if the employer has reason to believe, at the time of production, that the goods will be moved across state lines or will become part of such goods (for example, buttons on shirts). Certain industries, notably farming, are specifically exempt from coverage.

The wage clauses of the Act provided for a progressive, automatic raising of minimum rates throughout all industry, as well as the raising of rates for particular industries by administrative action. The automatic increases were from the initial 25 cents an hour rate to 30 cents in 1939 and 40 cents in 1945. During the six-year interval between 1939 and 1945 the Administrator of the Act (the Wage and Hour Division of the U. S. Department of Labor) was empowered to appoint industry committees, composed of equal numbers of representatives of employers, employees, and the public, which could recommend—and the Administrator could then establish—a minimum wage not to exceed 40 cents for the entire industry concerned, or for reasonable classifications within the industry, provided such classifications were not based solely on a regional basis or on age or sex. The industry committees were instructed to recommend the highest minimum wage for the industry, having due regard to economic and competitive conditions which would not substantially curtail employment in it. Among relevant factors to be considered were wages established by union agreements and wages paid by employers who voluntarily maintained standards.

The Fair Labor Standards Act was unprecedented in that it provided for minimum wage rates for all classes of workers (except those in local, intra-state occupations over which the federal government cannot under the Constitution exercise control). When enacted, it covered between 12 and 13 million workers, more than two-thirds of whom were engaged in manufacturing. Almost 700,-000 workers were directly benefited when rates were automatically raised to 30 cents an hour in October, 1939.[24] When the six-year interval was provided in the Act for the automatic increase from 30 to 40 cents an hour, war conditions were not contemplated. As it happened, before the close of 1941 wage orders had been issued by the Administrator covering the majority of industries in which a substantial number of workers were earning less than 40 cents an hour; and long before the time for the general automatic raise in October, 1945, the 40-cent minimum had been established for all industries covered by the Act.

WARTIME REGULATION OF WAGES

Remembering the serious inflation which took place during the First World War and its accompanying post-war collapse, the Administration undertook vigorous measures to control prices during World War II. Incorporated in the general stabilization program were regulations pertaining to changes in wage rates.

Although the National War Labor Board during its first ten months of existence[25] had no authority over wage adjustments voluntarily agreed upon by employers and employees, in the settlement of wage disputes which were referred to it the Board was guided by the Emergency Price Control Act enacted a few weeks after Pearl Harbor which provided: "It shall be the policy of those departments and agencies of the government dealing with wages, within the limits of their authority and jurisdiction to work toward a stabilization of prices and cost of production." Accordingly, in its first test case the Board laid down a principle which it followed throughout the war, namely, that wage rates should not be automatically adjusted to increases in living costs, although increases might be allowed "to the extent that it can be done without inflationary effects."[26]

---

[24] "Two Years of the Fair Labor Standards Act," *Monthly Labor Review,* September, 1940, pp. 551 ff.

[25] See chap. 20 concerning the Board's activities in industrial disputes.

[26] International Harvester Company case decided April 15, 1942 (1 W.L.B. 112, p. 120).

During 1941 and the spring of 1942, however, general wage increases had been secured by workers in most industries, and prices had advanced. To counteract this trend, the President on April 27, 1942, outlined a seven-point stabilization program which stated that "wages in general can and should be kept at existing levels," with "due consideration to inequalities and the elimination of substandards of living."[27] It was under this basic rule that the National War Labor Board decided the Little Steel case[28] the following July. This decision established what afterward was called the "Little Steel" formula, namely, a 15 per cent allowable increase in wages above those existing in January, 1941, to cover the rise in the cost of living between that date and May, 1942, at which time general wage levels (and prices) were to be frozen. Thereafter the Board adhered to the 15 per cent maximum in all dispute cases submitted to it except those involving "inequities" and "substandards of living."

In spite of the measures taken after the announcement of the President's seven-point program, the cost of living and particularly the cost of food continued to rise, and numerous wage increases were voluntarily made by employers, largely because of the rapidly increasing demand for labor. On October 2, 1942, Congress passed the Stabilization Act, which authorized the President to issue a general order stabilizing prices, wages, and salaries that affected the cost of living, such stabilization so far as practicable to be on the basis of the levels which existed on September 15, 1942. This Act prohibited, for the first time, voluntary wage increases; and Executive Order 9250, issued under the Act, provided that no increases (or decreases) in wage rates should thereafter be made without the approval of the National War Labor Board. The Board, furthermore, was to allow only such increases as were "necessary to correct maladjustments or inequalities, to eliminate substandards of living, to correct gross inequities or to aid in the effective prosecution of the war."

---

[27] The "points" in addition to wages included the levying of heavy taxes and the foregoing of high profits, industrial and agricultural price ceilings, rent control, purchase of War Bonds, rationing of all scarce commodities, control of credit and of installment buying.

[28] *In re Bethlehem Steel Corporation, Republic Steel Corporation, Youngstown Sheet and Tube Co., Inland Steel Co., and United Steelworkers of America (C.I.O.), 1 W.L.B. 325.*

Between the passage of the Stabilization Act and March, 1943, the cost of living and hourly earnings continued slowly to rise, causing the Administration growing concern. On April 8, 1943, the President issued Executive Order 9328, the so-called "hold-the-line" order. The Little Steel formula was incorporated in this Order and the Board was forbidden to make any further wage adjustments except to correct substandards of living. The effect of this was to remove the Board's capacity to change the Little Steel formula (which it had hinted it might do if the cost of living continued to rise) and to forbid wage increases to correct inter-plant inequalities beyond the minimum of the "sound and tested going rates for comparable occupations in the given labor market area."

From the spring of 1943 until the defeat of Japan there were no changes in the policies and rules of wage stabilization; in other words, the principle was maintained that general wage rate levels were not to rise higher than 15 per cent above the January, 1941, levels, although individual increases were allowed under certain specified conditions. One of these conditions was the existence of substandard wages, and employers were permitted to raise wages up to 50 cents an hour without prior approval from the Board. In dispute cases, however, the Board did not always specify as much as 50 cents. Another exception was to correct gross inequities in a plant's wage structure by job evaluation and reclassification. To effectuate this, the Board adhered to the principle that job classifications should be based on job content, that equal pay should be assured for equal work within a plant, and that collective bargaining processes should be used to the fullest extent in solving job classification problems.

Organized labor strenuously objected to the wage ceilings imposed by the Little Steel formula on the grounds that consumers' prices were not being controlled as rigidly as wages. Labor maintained that the cost of living had advanced much higher than the official index indicated. Although non-partisan investigations did not substantiate labor's contention that the government index was grossly inaccurate,[29] it was generally conceded that prices were

---

[29] A joint A. F. of L.–C.I.O. report maintained that the cost of living had advanced 43.5 per cent between January, 1941, and December, 1943, whereas the Bureau of Labor Statistics index showed only 23.4 per cent. During this con-

rising and that the actual cost of living was indirectly increased as a result of the deteriorated quality of some goods and services, and the necessity for workers to purchase higher-priced goods because of the disappearance of low-priced items from the stores.

Post-War Stabilization

Although wage rates did not advance during the war as rapidly as did prices, average weekly earnings, as a result of overtime pay, shift premiums, upgrading of workers, and other war conditions, increased more than the cost of living.[30] These war-time factors disappeared on V-J Day and the government was faced with the alternative of (1) returning to a basic wage structure which in terms of real wages was lower than had existed before the war, or (2) allowing a higher level of wage rates in keeping with the higher price levels. On the assumption that the profit position of industry as a whole was sufficiently high to absorb some increase in wages without price advances, wage controls were lifted a few days after the defeat of Japan. According to Executive Order No. 9599 (issued August 18, 1945), unions could again bargain with employers for their rates, and employers could grant increases so long as they did not result in price increases. After a trial period of six months at the higher rates, however, employers were privileged to request higher price ceilings to meet increased labor costs.

The unions immediately inaugurated a vigorous campaign for higher wages; many of them, particularly the C.I.O. unions, demanded 30 per cent increases. The government fact-finding boards, which were established to investigate a number of the major cases, recommended a little better than half that amount, but employers

---

troversy a number of committees investigated the figures published by the Bureau, including one appointed by the American Statistical Association and one appointed by the War Labor Board at the request of the President. The majority opinion was that the Bureau's figures accurately measured the prices of goods, but that 3 or 4 points might well be added to the index to offset the effects of quality deterioration in goods and services furnished consumers during the war. (See *Report of the President's Committee on the Cost of Living,* Government Printing Office, Washington, 1945.)

[30] Average weekly earnings for manufacturing workers were 70 per cent higher in the summer of 1945 than in January, 1941, and just before the defeat of Germany they were almost 80 per cent higher. Prices of consumers' goods in large cities had increased slightly more than 30 per cent by the end of the war. (See Fig. 20.)

were insistent that they could not grant even that much without price adjustments. As a result of the stalemate, which caused prolonged and widespread strikes "serious enough to threaten our economy with almost complete paralysis,"[31] wage regulations were restored. By an order issued in February, 1946, employers could immediately request a price adjustment to cover wage increases, but the latter had to be approved by the reestablished Wage Stabilization Board. The Board was authorized to grant increases not only to remove inequities and to correct substandards of living, but also to correct any disparities between wage rates and the cost of living.

The government price control program was virtually abandoned when Congress refused to extend the existing Office of Price Administration law and enacted much more limited price controls in July, 1946, although the Wage Stabilization Board was not formally abolished until the following winter.

SELECTED REFERENCES

Anderson, George, *Fixation of Wages in Australia,* Macmillan & Co., Ltd., Melbourne, 1929.

Armstrong, Barbara, *Insuring the Essentials,* The Macmillan Company, New York, 1932.

Bureau of Labor Statistics, *Handbook of Labor Statistics,* Vol. II, 1941 ed., *Wages and Wage Regulation,* Government Printing Office, Washington.

Burns, Eveline M., *Wages and the State,* P. S. King & Son, Ltd., London, 1926.

Commons, John R., and Andrews, John B., *Principles of Labor Legislation,* Harper & Brothers, New York, 1936.

Dickinson, Z. Clark, *Collective Wage Determination,* The Ronald Press Company, New York, 1941.

Division of Labor Standards, U. S. Department of Labor, *Wage Payment and Wage Collection Laws,* Bulletin No. 58, Government Printing Office, Washington, 1943.

Lyon, L. S., Homan, Paul T., Terborgh, George, Lorwin, L.L., Dearing, C. L., and Marshall, L. C., *The National Recovery Administration,* Brookings Institution, Washington, 1935.

---

[31] President's message announcing Executive Order 9697 on February 14, 1946.

Millis, H. A., and Montgomery, R. E., *Labor's Progress and Problems,* McGraw-Hill Book Company, Inc., New York, 1938.

National War Labor Board, *Wage Report to the President,* February 22, 1945, Government Printing Office, Washington.

Sells, Dorothy, *British Wage Boards,* Brookings Institution, Washington, 1939.

Senate Committee on Education and Labor, *Equal Pay for Equal Work for Women,* 79th Congress, Hearings on S-1178, Government Printing Office, Washington, 1946.

Women's Bureau, U. S. Department of Labor, *State Minimum Wage Laws and Orders,* Bulletin No. 191, Government Printing Office, Washington, 1942.

15

HOURS OF WORK

THE TWO MOST IMPORTANT WAYS IN WHICH WORKERS ARE ABLE TO receive benefits from technological advancement are increased "real" wages and reduction in hours of work. The level of wages and the length of working hours prevailing in any country are a measure of its workers' standard of living and an indicator of its industrial and political development. Without the aid of power machinery, the great mass of people must not only subsist on the bare essentials, but spend most of their waking hours eking out their meager subsistence; without the benefit of democratic participation in their country's government, workers are deprived of the means of obtaining their share of the comforts and leisure resulting from the use of labor-saving machinery.

Reduction in hours of work can take various forms. Annual vacations and holidays without loss of pay, discussed in an earlier chapter, represent one variant of reduced work schedules. The weekly work time can be shortened by a reduction in either the days per week or the hours per day worked. The religious heritage of Europe and the western hemisphere has caused Sunday to be considered a day of rest throughout most of the Christian era, and in many countries there are also numerous other religious holidays on which no work is done.[1]

---

[1] The Christian Sunday is a development of the Hebrew Sabbath, whose origins lie in antiquity. (*Shabbath* means rest.) The Roman emperor Constantine enjoined a Sunday rest from labor in 321 A.D., and during medieval times fines were imposed upon laborers who worked on Sundays. However, Sunday as a day of rest has not always been strictly observed. In continental Europe it has been customary for retail and service shops and even manufacturing plants to remain open on Sundays. In 15th- and 16th-century England, Sundays and religious holidays were quite generally ignored, but in 1677 the Sunday Observance Act was enacted; this forbade all "tradesmen, artificers, labourers, or other person whatsoever" from carrying on their usual businesses under penalty of fine. In this country the influence of the Puritan movement

With one day of rest in seven provided for most industrial workers, the movement for shortening the work schedules was for many years confined to obtaining a reduction in the daily hours of work. It was not until the 1920's that serious consideration was given to reducing the number of work days per week.

HOURS OF WORK IN EARLIER TIMES

During the Middle Ages, primitive lighting arrangements and the danger of fire limited the workday to daylight hours, and in many cities night work was officially prohibited. The eight-hour day was more or less customary for tradesmen, and according to some authorities was required under the rules of most of the gilds. Legend attributes to King Alfred the Great the saying "Eight hours' work, eight hours' sleep, eight hours' play, make a just and healthy day." As centralized governments dominated by landholders became more powerful, decrees were enacted to lengthen the workday. During the 15th and 16th centuries England passed a number of laws specifying that during the summer all laborers must work from 5 A.M. to 8 P.M., with two hours for meals and rest. By the end of the 17th century, the hours of craftsmen had been extended, but except for agricultural labor during the growing season, the workday was seldom longer than ten hours.

The introduction of power machinery toward the end of the 18th century proved to be more of a curse than a blessing for many workers. Instead of labor-saving machinery reducing their hours of labor, the workdays were lengthened; instead of bringing comfort and leisure to their families, women and children were forced to labor long hours in unsanitary factories and mines.

caused a virtual cessation of all forms of employment on Sunday, and practically all states now have laws restricting various kinds of employment on that day.

Communist Russia has made a number of experiments with the length of the work week. As a means of breaking traditional religious practices and giving workers more rest days, the six-day week was substituted for the seven-day week early in the regime. In 1929, in order to keep plants in continuous operation, the five-day week was introduced; it consisted of four days of work and one day of rest, with rotation of rest days. In 1931 the six-day week was reestablished (five days' work and one rest day) and during World War II the traditional seven-day week was resumed.

One of Mussolini's "improvements" was the abolition of many of the religious holidays which had prevailed in Italy, although Sunday was retained.

Hours were longer than under handicraft production because employers insisted that when they invested money in machines, the machines must be kept working as long as possible, and since the work was purely mechanical the last hour of the day was as valuable as the first. Because the operation of the machines required little or no skill, children as young as six or seven years of age could attend them; in the textile industries especially, the labor of children and women was preferred to that of adult males.[2]

During the early 1800's the factory hours in Great Britain, the only industrialized country at that time, were as long as 19 and 20 a day and 90 to 100 a week. In 1842 the working day in English mines was 14 to 15 hours, not only for men but for women and children who were used in hauling coal. Obviously no human being could withstand such work hours for long; but the supply of labor was plentiful and employers were not concerned with child mortality or premature physical breakdowns.[3] People interested in the national welfare, however, became concerned about the effects of long hours of labor, and between 1802 and 1832 Parliament enacted legislation prohibiting night work by children and restricting their hours to 12 actual working hours a day. In 1848 a 10-hour day was legally established in England for all industrial labor.

When power looms and improved spinning machinery changed textile manufacturing in the United States from a domestic to a factory industry, long hours and child labor became as prevalent as in England. The use of women and children was looked upon as an unqualified good which made possible the development of manufacturing without taking men from agriculture. According to Alexander Hamilton, it made women and children "more useful

---

[2] Said the man who first applied power to the weaving of woolen cloth in this country: "The saving in operating 60 looms by water instead of the old way, by hand, amounted to about $40 per day. Besides this saving, we got rid of 60 weavers, the most of them men who in those bygone days were intemperate and exceedingly troublesome, and substituted for them 30 girls, who were easily managed and did more and better work." (Manuscript diary of Joshua Aubin, quoted in Bureau of Labor Statistics, *History of Wages in the U. S. from Colonial Times,* Bulletin No. 604, p. 86.)

[3] The cotton factories in the Lancaster and Yorkshire districts were worked largely by pauper children from London and other towns who were brought in in cartloads. The atrocities visited upon these boys and girls, housed in horribly overcrowded and unsanitary dormitories and literally driven to death in the mills, form one of the darkest chapters in the history of childhood.

than they otherwise would be" and enabled them to escape the evils of idleness and destitution.[4] Children as young as seven years of age were employed in American textile mills ; in 1832 at least two-fifths of all persons working in New England factories were between seven and sixteen years of age; they worked never less than 10, seldom less than 12, and often 14 or 15 hours per day.[5]

In 1840 the normal work week in Massachusetts textile mills was 84 hours ; two years later this was reduced to 78 hours for women and, by legislation, to 60 hours for children under twelve years of age. Men continued on the 84-hour schedule until 1850, when their time was also shortened to 72 hours. During the 1850's the 66-hour week was adopted for women in the New England textile mills, although 72 hours prevailed in New York mills until 1867 and in Carolina mills as late as the 1880's. In other occupations, even among the skilled trades, the hours were equally long. Many printers and machinists worked 14 hours a day, 84 hours a week, until almost the middle of the 19th century ; the work schedule for most bakers was 12 to 14 hours a day, seven days a week. Building tradesmen worked from sunup until sundown, which meant long hours during the summer months but shorter hours during the winter.

A HUNDRED YEARS' CAMPAIGN
FOR SHORTER HOURS

Long hours of work were not endured without protest. As early as 1791 some Philadelphia carpenters went on strike for a 10-hour

---

[4] *Report on Manufactures,* 1791, p. 29; quoted in Bureau of Labor Statistics, *History of Wages,* p. 85.

[5] Many of the New England textile manufacturers maintained company boarding houses for their "mill girls," who lived under a rigorous paternalism which controlled working conditions and "not only regulated the dwelling places and food of their operatives but dictated the time of going to bed and the rules of social intercourse. . . . In one of the early factory tracts, issued by the Female Labor Reform Association of Lowell, complaint is made of the wearisome extent of corporation control. At the close of the day's work, the operative was said to be watched to see that her footsteps did not 'drag beyond the corporation limits' and whether she wished it or not she was subjected to the manifold inconveniences of a large crowded boarding house where, too, it was said that the price paid for her accommodation was so utterly insufficient that it would not insure to her the common comforts of life." (Bureau of Labor Statistics, *History of Wages,* p. 88.)

day. When they lost the strike, in retaliation they organized a cooperative and contracted for jobs 25 per cent below the current
rate established by the master carpenters.[6] In 1822 the journeymen millwrights and machinists of Philadelphia "met at a tavern,
and passed resolutions that ten hours of labor were enough for one
day, and that work ought to begin at 6 A.M. and end at 6 P.M.
with an hour for breakfast and one for dinner."[7] Two years later
"female weavers" struck with men contract workers in Pawtucket,
Rhode Island, to resist an increase in hours; this was the first
known strike in this country in which women participated.[8] A
year later there was a general strike of Boston carpenters for a
10-hour day, and in 1828 textile workers in Paterson, New Jersey,
Philadelphia, and Boston went on strike in protest against long
hours and low pay.

In 1835 the carpenters, masons, and stonecutters of Boston
joined in a strike for a 10-hour day which won sympathy among
workers throughout the country. Trade unions from various cities
sent them money and passed resolutions to stand by the "Boston
House Wrights" who, "in imitation of the noble and decided stand
taken by their Revolutionary Fathers, have determined to throw
off the shackles of more mercenary tyrants than theirs."[9] That
same summer the Paterson textile workers demanded that their
day be reduced to 10 hours, and in Philadelphia both building-
trades mechanics and factory workers joined in a mass movement
for a 10-hour day. It was reported in the newspapers at the time
that groups of different crafts quit work, organized processions,
and marched through the streets with fife and drum and flags.
"Our streets and squares are crowded with an idle population. . . .
Our buildings are at a stand-still and business generally is considerably impeded."[10] These demonstrations definitely turned the tide
in favor of shorter hours; several cities established the 10-hour day

---

[6] John R. Commons, and associates, *History of Labour in the United States*,
The Macmillan Company, New York, 1918, vol. i, p. 110.

[7] John B. McMaster, *History of the People of the U. S.*, D. Appleton & Company, 1914, vol. v, p. 84.

[8] Bureau of Labor Statistics, *Strikes in the U. S., 1880–1936*, Bulletin No.
651, pp. 14 ff.

[9] Quoted in John R. Commons and associates, *History of Labour in the
United States*, vol. i, p. 389, from *Pennsylvanian*, Philadelphia, July 31, 1835.

[10] Bureau of Labor Statistics, *Strikes in the U. S.*, p. 15.

for public servants and a number of private employers were forced to follow.

The campaign for shorter hours, which was to last more than a hundred years, was on. First to be attacked was the prevailing "sun-to-sun" workday. After the 10-hour day was won, the fight continued for an eight-hour day and then a five-day week. But progress was by no means uniform throughout all the trades or areas of the country. Long after the 10-hour day had been gained in some trades, the 12- and 13-hour day persisted elsewhere. Thirty years after many of the organized journeymen craftsmen had gained a 48-hour week, many other workers were on a 60- or 65-hour or longer work week. Industry by industry, plant by plant, the struggle went on, with successive reductions from one plateau to another. Sometimes gains were not spread even throughout a single plant but were confined to particular groups of employees. One of the significant effects of craft union bargaining was the lack of uniform hour standards within a single company.

Unlike wage changes, which are generally in small units and take place at frequent intervals, changes in work schedules are seldom in smaller units than hours, and a change once made is effective for a period of years. By and large, the 10-hour campaign which began during the 1830's lasted until the middle of the 1890's; on its heels was a quarter century's struggle for the eight-hour day, then the 44-hour week, followed by the relatively sudden and general adoption of the 40-hour week.

Let us consider in more detail how these improvements in this very important phase of labor standards were brought about—the arguments used, the obstacles overcome, and the general economic environment in which they were put into effect.

Arguments Used

During the hundred-year campaign for shorter hours of work, many reasons were advanced to encourage and justify changes in work schedules. Some of the arguments used were purely economic; others were premised on human justice and social welfare. As circumstances changed, the grounds for shorter hours shifted; somewhat different arguments were used to get a reduction from the 48- to the 40-hour week than had been used to change the 72- and 80-hour week. In any particular instance, numerous reasons were usually presented in order to assure both the employer and the public that the proposed reductions were practicable so far as business operations were concerned, as well as desirable from the standpoint of the workers.

During the time when the excessively long 14- and 15-hour day was in effect, the demand for shorter hours was based upon the workers' right to the enjoyment of some leisure and the need for time for civic activities. "Work from 'sun to sun' was held to be incompatible with citizenship, for it did not afford the workman the requisite leisure for the consideration of public questions, and therefore condemned him to an inferior position in the state."[11]

In the general movement for the 10-hour day the argument for leisure time for self-improvement and participation in civic affairs continued, but the effect of long hours upon health was also stressed. Statements from medical authorities were advanced citing the relation of fatigue to susceptibility to disease, accidents, and nervous exhaustion. Interested persons outside the labor movement, as well as labor itself, argued the point of general welfare by stressing the nation's interest in preserving the health of wage earners and maintaining a wholesome family life, possible only when the head of the family had some time to spend with his family. (As will be seen later, employers countered this last argument by saying that workers did not use their leisure profitably and that leisure for "the laboring class" endangered their morals and the public welfare.)

As technology advanced, economic reasons came to the fore, although the factor of nervous fatigue resulting from the use of rapid and complex machines was also mentioned. T. V. Powderly, Grand Master Workman of the Knights of Labor, compared factory work with office work as justification for the eight-hour day: "No one thinks of requiring the bank clerk to work ten hours or even eight. His mind could not stand the strain. The work of the future will be scientific in its nature and will call for more exercise of brain than of the hand. . . . No longer strength but skill is required and no man or woman can work as long at an occupation which requires skill as at one which calls for no experience of the mental process. . . . Brain work will soon be required in all call-

---

[11] Commons and associates, *History of Labour in the United States,* vol. i, p. 170.

ings and . . . the hours of labor should be reduced to the eight-hour standard."[12]

In its cruder form, the economic basis for shorter hours assumed a share-the-work-argument; if hours were reduced more jobs would be available.[13] When this argument was originally used, organized labor was willing to accept reduced hours with a commensurate cut in weekly wages on the theory that the shorter day would decrease the supply of labor and thus enable workers eventually to raise their wage rates. This belief gave rise to the famous union doggerel framed by the wife of Ira Steward, the Boston machinist who devoted his life to the eight-hour-day movement:

> Whether you work by the piece,
> Or work by the day,
> The longer the hours,
> The shorter the pay.

As the increased productivity resulting from technological improvements became more apparent, organized labor changed its position and demanded reduced hours with no reduction in weekly wages, that is, shorter hours accompanied by increased hourly rates.

The argument for shorter hours *and* increased pay assumed two aspects, one remedial and the other preventive. Fundamentally, both stemmed from the same premise, but the emphasis in approach shifted according to the economic situation at hand when the hour issue was under consideration. When unemployment was widespread, shorter hours were demanded to offset the effects of machine production. Samuel Gompers, when president of the American Federation of Labor, maintained on numerous occasions that the ever-increasing inventions and improvements in methods had rendered hundreds of thousands of wage earners superfluous and that "so long as there is one man who seeks employment and cannot obtain it, the hours of labor are too long."

Shortening hours to reduce unemployment was a very practical

[12] T. V. Powderly, in *North American Review*, April, 1890, p. 467.
[13] Reduction in hours does not necessarily create additional employment opportunities. Even without mechanical improvements, shorter hours frequently result in increased individual efficiency sufficient to maintain former production with the same number of workers. (See *Monthly Labor Review*, November, 1933, pp. 1032 ff.)

argument; but organized labor, as well as others, have also contended that shorter hours are a means of preventing unemployment. The line of reasoning is that with both shorter hours and increased wages, workers have more leisure to develop wants and also the money with which to satisfy them, and this creates additional markets, stimulates production, and thus creates more jobs. In other words, shorter hours *and* increased wages serve to balance consumption and production, a theory which has been discussed in some detail elsewhere in this volume.

EMPLOYER OPPOSITION

Reduction in work schedules can be achieved by three means: through pressure of organized labor, through legislation, and by voluntary action of employers. These have not always operated as discrete forces, however, and most improvements in hours have been the result of interacting influences. Labor unions have been instrumental in getting hour legislation enacted, and legislation, once enacted, has aided unions in obtaining further improvements. Public opinion has been an important factor in many instances, but unions have played a major role in arousing public opinion. In many cases of seemingly voluntary reduction of hours by employers, the impelling reasons have actually been to thwart the unionization of their plants or to ward off threatened strikes. In plants where both men and women are employed, legislation restricting the hours of women has encouraged a general reduction in work schedules in order to maintain a uniform flow of work.

In spite of the apparent logic that the use of labor-saving machines should result in shortening the hours of human labor, reductions in work time with a few notable exceptions have been obtained only after prolonged struggles and against bitter employer opposition. At every stage employers have contended that the proposed new restriction of hours would deprive them of all margin of profit, lower the wages of their employees, raise the price of their commodities, and make it impossible for them to meet competition in this country or from foreign countries.

To bolster their arguments, employers have offered "conclusive" evidence that the then existing hours resulted in maximum efficiency. Decades after many unions had won an eight-hour day and at a time when they were successfully negotiating the 44-hour week, studies financed by manufacturers[14] indicated that the nine-hour or longer day represented the optimum work schedule. An investigation of the shoe industry in 1918 concluded that, under the given operating conditions, maximum efficiency was impossible under less than a 52-hour week. A study of the silk industry fixed the point of maximum output between 50 and 54 hours. A similar report for wool plants, while admitting that reduction in hours with increase in output might be expected in large plants, stated that reduction to a 54-hour schedule involved a loss of output in the majority of cases. Investigation of cotton manufacturing plants led to the same unfavorable conclusion, that reduction from 58 or 56 to 55 or 54 hours a week had, in the great majority of cases, been followed by a decreased output. Significantly, conclusions about the metal manufacturing industry, in which unions had gained an eight-hour day in some plants, were neither so definite nor so unfavorable; they admitted that the 48-hour week had proved to be practicable in a considerable number of plants, but that there was no clear-cut line below which reduction in hours led to a uniform change in efficiency.

Fear of increasing the costs of production, of course, was the basis for employer opposition to reduced hours, although some employers freely admitted that after experimenting with shorter hours their unit labor costs had not advanced and indeed had declined. In opposing reduction of hours, however, employers have not always confined themselves to strictly business reasons. According to many of their statements, they have been equally concerned about the morals and legal rights of their employees. When the 10-hour day was up for discussion in 1870 an owner of a bleachery stated that he had "invariably noticed that when men are kept at work until 10 P.M. they live in better health, as they keep indoors instead of sitting around doors smoking."[15]

In opposing an eight-hour bill in 1902, the president of the National Association of Manufacturers denounced it as a socialistic

---

[14] The National Industrial Conference Board, which is supported by its members, most of whom at that time (1918–1919) were manufacturers and manufacturers' associations. The above statements are from their *Research Reports,* Nos. 4, 7, 12, 16, 18, and 32, as summarized by Marion C. Cahill, *Shorter Hours,* Columbia University Press, New York, 1932, pp. 248–249.

[15] Massachusetts Bureau of Statistics of Labor, *First Annual Report,* 1870, pp. 223–224.

and artificial measure which controverted the inalienable right of the individual to use his time as he saw fit.[16] Less than twenty years ago, another president of the same Association, in expressing his opposition to the five-day week, stated:

"Six days shalt thou labor and do all thy work." So reads the fifth of the great commandments and for sixty centuries it has been accepted as the divinely prescribed standard of economic effort. It is the perfectly fixed basis of human achievement and social contentment. . . . These constant attempts to amend the decalogue and to adapt by alterations the moral law to the appetites developed by easy and loose living constitute the outstanding peril of our unprecedented prosperity.

More leisure is sought, it is said, to provide larger opportunities for the cultural processes. Let it not be forgotten in this connection that there is quite as close relationship between leisure and crime as between leisure and culture. When, therefore, we reflect upon the black, appalling fact that ours is the most crime-ridden nation on earth, as well as the easiest living, should we not conclude that it would be well for us to curtail some of the opportunities for culture already perverted to criminal uses?[17]

Upon another occasion, happily unaware of the business collapse and subsequent "reforms" which were to take place within a few years, the same spokesman for this manufacturers' association expressed gratification that the workers' time was fully taken up with their jobs: "They [the working masses] have for the most part been so busy at their jobs that they have not had time to saturate themselves with false theories of economics, social reform, and of life. They have been protected in their natural growth by the absence of excessive leisure. . . . I do not, therefore, share the view that leisure as an end is a worthy or desirable aspiration. . . ."[18]

The Steel Industry

The reduction in hours which took place in the 1920's in the steel industry reveals the influence of public opinion upon employer

---

[16] D. M. Parry, *Disastrous Effects of a National Eight-Hour Law,* pamphlet, 1902.

[17] Quoted in L. T. Beman, *Five Day Week,* H. W. Wilson Company, New York, 1928, p. 65.

[18] John E. Edgerton, National Association of Manufacturers, 34th Annual Convention *Proceedings,* 1929, p. 23.

policy. Steelworkers at that time were unorganized and the change in hours was largely the result of an aroused public opinion, prodded, it is true, by an unsuccessful strike by the workers. Since steelmaking is a continuous-process industry, the shortening of hours necessitated the employment of additional crews and an entire rearrangement of work shifts which, from the management's side, presented a more complex undertaking than a mere curtailment in the number of hours of plant operation.

In 1900 practically every ton of pig iron and steel produced in the entire world was made by men working in doubled shifts of 12 hours each, having neither Sundays nor holidays the year round. Earlier, some plants in the United States had worked on a three-shift, eight-hour basis, but because of competition had been forced to go on the two-shift schedule. The now defunct Amalgamated Association of Iron and Steel Workers during the 1880's had been successful in getting Sunday off for its members, except those at blast furnaces; but after the loss of the Homestead strike of 1892 the employers were in complete control and the seven-day week, 12-hour day became universal. In 1910 the excessive hours, as well as other evils in the steel industry, were brought to public attention through a study made by a private agency,[19] and following a strike at the Bethlehem mills that same year a government investigation was undertaken which also stirred up public opinion. These investigations revealed that in contrast to the general tendency in other industries toward decreased hours, in the great basic steel industry only 14 per cent of the employees worked less than 60 hours per week, and almost 43 per cent worked 72 hours and over per week.[20]

These reports and the adverse public opinion they aroused caused the U. S. Steel Corporation to appoint a committee to "consider what, if any, arrangement with a view to reducing the twelve-hour day insofar as it now exists among the employees of the subsidiary companies is reasonable, just and practicable." Very little resulted from these investigations, although some workers were taken off the seven-day week; since their rates were not

---

[19] The well-known Pittsburgh survey under the Russell Sage Foundation. See John A. Fitch, *The Steel Workers,* The Survey Associates, New York, 1910.

[20] U. S. Senate, *Report on Conditions of Employment in the Iron and Steel Industry,* 1911, vol. i, p. xvi. The investigation was conducted by the Department of Labor.

adjusted, this resulted in a 14 per cent loss in wages. The corporation in 1913 asserted that it could not eliminate the 12-hour day until its competitors did likewise, but it tabled a resolution which proposed cooperation to this end by the entire industry.[21]

During the First World War, with its pressure for production and the decreased supply of labor, the question of shortening hours receded into the background. The general strike in 1919 brought the issue to the public attention once again, and again investigations and publicity on the part of private groups provided the impetus for action. After investigation, the Inter-Church World Movement[22] indicated that average hours in the industry were actually longer than before the war and that over 52 per cent of the employees of the U. S. Steel Corporation were on 12-hour shifts. The Federated American Engineering Societies, on the basis of an investigation of the three-shift operations in a number of continuous-process industries, found "no outstanding obstacle" to putting the steel industry on an eight-hour day and estimated that the change would entail only a 3 per cent increase in costs.[23]

The industry's answer to these reports was that the elimination of the 12-hour day was not feasible at the time, that such a step would increase the cost of production 15 per cent and require 60,000 additional workers, and that the 12-hour day was not of itself an injury to the employees physically, mentally, or morally. This adverse answer from the Steel and Iron Institute was bitterly attacked by the general public, and within a few months the industry reversed its decision, indicating that it would begin the total elimination of the 12-hour shift, with compensatory wage rate increases. There were some immediate effects from this change of policy, and average hours in the steel industry declined. In spite

[21] Cahill, *Shorter Hours*, p. 210.

[22] The Commission of Inquiry, Inter-Church World Movement, *Report on the Steel Strike of 1919*, New York, 1920, pp. 49, 71. This Commission was composed of representatives of Protestant, Catholic, and Jewish churches.

Although the 1919 strike was primarily for union recognition, the prevailing long hours were a major cause of the discontent. Before and during the strike the employers, under the leadership of Elbert H. Gary of the U. S. Steel Corporation, persistently refused to talk to the union committee and declined offers made by both the Inter-Church World Movement and the Senate Investigating Committee to appoint a mediator or arbitrator. The strike was an absolute failure.

[23] Federated American Engineering Societies, *The Twelve-Hour Shift in Industry*, E. P. Dutton & Co., New York, 1922.

of the change to the three-shift basis, however, relatively long hours continued in the steel industry until the 1930's. In 1929 more than one-half of the blast furnace employees regularly worked a seven-day week; although 73 per cent had a work week of 60 hours or less, more than 11 per cent were still working from 72 to 84 hours a week.[24]

The Five-Day Week Issue

While the majority of employers held firmly to their belief that the 50- and 54-hour week represented the shortest practicable work schedule, a few employers began to adopt the five-day week during the 1920's. The same research agency which in 1919 had found the 54-hour week necessary to maximum efficiency in several industries stated ten years later that "the 5-day week has passed from the status of a vague future possibility to that of an accomplished fact in several hundred establishments."[25] Most of these plants, however, were small, and more than half were unionized clothing shops.

It was quite a different matter to have the five-day week introduced into a great mass-production industry, and there was a great deal of consternation among employers when Henry Ford adopted it in 1926. (In 1914 he had introduced the eight-hour day at the time when the nine- and ten-hour day was common throughout most manufacturing industries.) Ford gave as his reason for instituting the shorter week the necessity for providing workers with more leisure time so that they would be better consumers. In his announcement he said:

The harder we crowd business for time the more efficient it becomes. The more well-paid leisure workmen get the greater become their wants. These wants soon become needs. Well-managed business pays high wages and sells at low prices. Its workmen have the leisure to enjoy life and the wherewithal with which to finance that enjoyment.

The industry of this country could not exist long if factories generally went back to the 10-hour day, because the people would not have the time to consume the goods produced. For instance, a workman would have little use for an automobile if he had to be in the shops

---

[24] *Monthly Labor Review,* June, 1930, pp. 183 ff.

[25] National Industrial Conference Board, Inc., *The Five-Day Week in Manufacturing Industries,* New York, 1929, p. 7.

from dawn until dusk. And that would react in countless directions, for the automobile, by enabling people to get about quickly and easily, gives them a chance to find out what is going on in the world—which leads them to a larger life that requires more food, more and better goods, more books, more music—more of everything.

Just as the 8-hour day opened our way to prosperity, so the 5-day week will open our way to a still greater prosperity. . . .

Ford was careful to state that reductions in hours could be premature for certain industries at certain times:

Twenty years ago, introducing the 8-hour day generally would have made for poverty and not for wealth. Five years ago, introducing the 5-day week would have had the same result. The hours of labor are regulated by the organization of work and by nothing else. It is the rise of the great corporation with its ability to use power, to use accurately designed machinery, and generally to lessen the wastes in time, material, and human energy that made it possible to bring in the 8-hour day. . . . Further progress along the same lines has made it possible to bring in the 5-day week. . . . In the old days a man had to work through a long day in order to get a bare living. Now the long day would retard both production and consumption.

Prophetically, he added,

At the present time the fixing by law of a 5-day week would be unwise, because all industry is not ready for it, but a great part of industry is ready, and within a comparatively short time I believe the practice will be so general in industry that it can be made universal.[26]

The response to this unprecedented action by one of their number was unfavorable, to say the least. Many employers questioned Ford's sincerity, maintaining that he adopted the shorter week because his business had declined and the five-day week was merely a share-the-work device. Elbert Gary, who a few years before had maintained that it was impossible to eliminate the seven-day week in the steel industry, now extolled the six-day week and quoted the Bible as opposing a five-day work-week: "Six days shalt thou labor, and do all thy work. The reason it didn't say seven days is

---

[26] *Monthly Labor Review,* December, 1926, pp. 11–12. Quoted from an interview by Samuel Crowther appearing in the *World's Work,* October, 1926.

that the seventh is a day of rest and that's enough."[27] The National Association of Manufacturers opposed the five-day week for the very reason Ford advocated it, maintaining that "it would create a craving for additional luxuries to occupy the additional time."[28]

This was only a few years before the business collapse in 1929. When the 40-hour week was recommended as a means of recovery from this depression, much of the former opposition of employers disappeared.

UNION PRESSURE FOR REDUCED HOURS

Many persons other than wage earners have been interested in the question of working hours and upon occasion have assisted in getting them reduced. But it has been the workers themselves, through their unions, who are chiefly responsible for the fact that weekly hours of work have been reduced by one-half during the past hundred years. In their efforts to shorten their hours of labor, workers have used every tactic and means at their disposal. They have appealed to the general public as well as bringing pressure upon employers through peaceful negotiations and, when necessary, through boycotts, strikes, and threatened strikes.

The benefits from union action have not been confined to union members. Union influence has been an important factor in hour legislation which has benefited non-union as well as union workers, and the downward trend in hours resulting from collective bargaining has spread into the unorganized industries. Although the work week for unorganized workers was generally four to six hours longer than that in unionized trades until the leveling effect of recent legislation, the trend of hours for the former was likewise downward, although at a different level.

Legislation Versus Direct Action

Historically, the labor movement in this country has relied more upon its own bargaining strength than upon legislation to obtain shorter hours of work in private industry. At times, particular unions and individual spokesmen of the labor movement have agi-

---

[27] *Monthly Labor Review,* December, 1926, p. 16.
[28] New York *Times,* October 21, 1926.

tated for hour legislation, but throughout the years the dominant attitude has been one of preference for bringing pressure upon employers through direct action and negotiation. Although this attitude changed somewhat during the 1930's when organized labor became a vigorous supporter of hour legislation, the unions have not accepted the hours standards established through legislation as the final word but are continuing to bargain for "better" hours than those provided by existing laws.

In the early days of the labor movement, some union leaders placed more emphasis upon the ballot and political action than upon bargaining for improved hours. Following the Civil War, when the demobilization of soldiers caused widespread unemployment, various local unions throughout the country took an active part in the formation of Eight-Hour Leagues.[29] In 1866 a general convention of union and Eight-Hour League delegates declared "That the first and grand desideratum of the hour, in order to deliver the labor of this country from thralldom, is the enactment of a law whereby eight hours shall be made to constitute a legal day's work in every State of the American Union." In order to obtain an eight-hour day there was talk of forming a separate political party. "The time has come when the workingmen of the United States should cut themselves aloof from party ties and predilections, and organize themselves into a National Labor Party, the object of which shall be to secure the enactment of a law making eight hours a legal day's work by the National Congress and the several state legislatures. . . ."[30]

This eight-hour movement was sponsored as much by reform elements outside the labor movement as by union leaders. The great reformer, Wendell Phillips, was a prominent leader; he maintained that long hours were the root cause of unemployment and other social evils, and that hour legislation was necessary to obtain justice and equality of opportunity for workingmen by giving them time for intellectual development. This concerted movement for eight-hour legislation soon collapsed, however, many of the original

---

[29] The Eight-Hour League movement started in Boston and spread rapidly to the Middle West and even to New Orleans and San Francisco. Some of the scattered Leagues united; the Grand League of Illinois, for example, had over twenty subordinate leagues in that state. (Commons and associates, *History of Labour in the United States,* vol. ii, pp. 91 ff.)

[30] *Ibid.,* vol. ii, pp. 95 ff.

sponsors turning to monetary reform (cheap money and low interest rates) to secure "the natural rights of labor."[31]

When the Knights of Labor was established during the 1870's it adopted the eight-hour-day slogan, but its leaders never vigorously supported legislation or any specific program for obtaining it. According to the Grand Master Workman there were other more basic problems than that of hours: "Hours of labor will be reduced in vain where hundreds of thousands seek for employment as a result of unjust taxation and speculative landholding"; the panacea, according to him, was education to prepare for the eight-hour day in the future and "cooperation by which machines will be made the slave of man, not man kept in attendance on the machine."[32]

From the date of its formation, the American Federation of Labor made the eight-hour day its rallying cry, but it early adopted the policy of direct action rather than legislation, except for particular groups of workers. In order to have the government set a good example to private industry, the A. F. of L. has always sponsored and fought for legislation to cover the hours of labor of public employees; it has also endorsed hour legislation for women and minors, and upon occasion has supported legal hour limitations for men engaged in especially hazardous and unhealthy occupations such as mining. For private employment in general, the official policy of the A. F. of L., until very recent years, has been opposition to hour legislation but a persistent campaign for reduced hours through collective bargaining.

There were several reasons for this attitude. In the first place, the leaders of the A. F. of L. were convinced that the prospects for obtaining general legislation were illusory and that efforts in this direction were therefore a waste of time. Also they believed, as did most of the public, that even if hour laws were enacted they would be declared unconstitutional by the courts.[33] Efforts to obtain

---

[31] Fundamentally, this monetary reform movement was directed toward making it possible for every wage earner to become his own boss, either by having his own business or through cooperative enterprises.

[32] T. V. Powderly, Knights of Labor *Proceedings,* September, 1886, p. 40.

[33] See the next chapter. As an illustration of the unpredictability of events, an unbiased student of the hour problem said, as late as 1932, "The powers of the Federal Government to legislate on the question of hours are distinctly limited by the Constitution. . . . A general federal hours' statute is a Utopian hope." (Cahill, *Shorter Hours,* pp. 21–22.)

adequate enforcement of the few laws that had been enacted to cover public employees was disappointing, to say the least; hence experience seemed to justify the belief that ". . . it is useless to wait for legislation in this matter. A united demand for a shorter working day, backed by thorough organization, will prove vastly more effective than the enactment of a thousand laws depending for enforcement upon the pleasure of aspiring politicians, of sycophantic department officials."[34]

A major reason for organized labor's opposition to hour legislation was its fear that it would lead to a decreasing interest in unions, that if the eight-hour day was given to all workers, unorganized as well as organized, there would be little inducement or need for workers to belong to unions. This fear was expressed by President Gompers at the 1914 convention when a large faction of the delegates was pressing for legislative action: "If we can get an eight-hour law for the working people, then you will find that the working people, themselves, will fail to have any interest in your economic organization, which even the advocates declare essential in order that such a law can be enforced." Gompers also expressed two all-pervading fears of labor at that time. The first, based on experience with "anti-labor" decisions of the courts, was that hour legislation might be distorted through judicial interpretation in such a way as to interfere with the liberties of workers; the second, that legal minimum standards might become maximum standards and that a general eight-hour law might preclude unions from ever gaining shorter hours.

These objections to legislative measures for the improvement of hours (which applied to other aspects of work conditions as well as hours) sprang from the weak position of organized labor at that time. Experience has proved that these fears are unfounded and that the presence of labor legislation does not remove the need for, or the workers' interest in, union organization. Laws are not self-enforcing, and legislatures appropriate money and see that adequate enforcement is provided only when there is persistent prodding by influential and articulate groups of voters. This is especially true of labor laws because individual workers, without the protection of unions, will not report employer violations for

---

[34] Federation of Organized Trades and Labor Unions, *Proceedings* (1884), pp. 10–11. In 1886 this organization became the American Federation of Labor.

fear of losing their jobs. An outstanding illustration of the degree of enforcement during periods of relatively weak, compared to strong, union influence is revealed in the history of the Federal Eight-Hour Law, discussed later.

Progress Through Collective Bargaining

When the American Federation of Labor was formed in 1881, union members almost without exception were working 10 hours a day for six days a week. A very few had gained the 48-hour week, and a few were on 70- and 72-hour week schedules. The 12- and 13-hour day, however, had almost disappeared in the unionized trades, although it was still prevalent among unorganized workers. One of the first matters discussed by the newly established Federation was the feasibility of a nation-wide strike for an eight-hour day. A formally authorized nation-wide strike never matured, but hundreds of local unions called strikes and held public demonstrations on May Day, in 1886, which received a great deal of publicity and in some cases, notably in Haymarket Square, Chicago, resulted in violence.[35]

As a result of this agitation, a few locals secured reductions in hours; but, on the whole, the A. F. of L. leaders considered this initial mass movement a failure so far as the immediate objective of the eight-hour day was concerned.[36] Thereafter, the Federation substituted the salient for the mass movement tactic, that is, carefully planned successive drives by individual trades, accompanied by a great deal of publicity, speechmaking, etc. The carpenters' union, which was strongest and which had already accumulated a fund for this purpose, took the initiative. Within a year their con-

---

[35] On May 3 police had fired into an assembly of strikers at the McCormick Harvester Works, killing four and wounding many more. During a protest meeting held the following day there was a bomb explosion attributed to anarchists which killed or wounded several hundred workers and scores of policemen. Eight union leaders were convicted; four were hanged, one committed suicide. The other three, sentenced to life imprisonment, were freed by Governor Altgeld.

For an account of the strikes and demonstrations during this eight-hour-day campaign, see Cahill, *Shorter Hours,* pp. 154–159.

[36] Samuel Gompers attributed the failure of the campaign to the Haymarket affair. "The effect of that bomb was that it not only killed the policeman, but it killed our eight-hour movement for that year and for a few years after, notwithstanding we had absolutely no connection with these people." (*Industrial Commission Report VII,* p. 623.)

certed campaign resulted in an eight-hour or at most a nine-hour day in a number of cities. According to the original plan, the coal miners were to follow the carpenters, but the United Mine Workers found themselves too weak at this time to face the determined opposition of the United Coal Operators and decided not to strike.

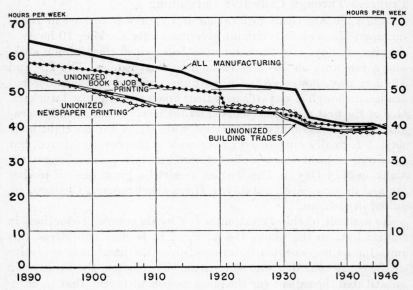

FIG. 27.   *Trends of Average Weekly Work Schedules, 1890–1946.* (*For years prior to 1907, the estimates are based on data in* History of Wages in the U. S.; *after 1907, on annual reports of the Bureau of Labor Statistics.*)

Because of the prolonged depression which began in 1893, no more industry-wide drives were undertaken until 1900, when the granite cutters called a general strike for an eight-hour day and won a complete victory for their members. In 1904 the Typographical Union inaugurated its successful nation-wide movement for an eight-hour day, many of its locals having gained a nine-hour day a few years previously.[37] One organized trade after an-

---

[37] The Typographers had a special reason for pressing for a shorter workday, namely, the introduction of the linotype machine which was causing widespread unemployment throughout the craft. Instead of fighting the new machine and allowing it to be taken over by unskilled labor, the Typographical

other carried on its drive, and as soon as a local won a 48-hour week, pressure continued for a 44-hour week. But success was not uniform even within the same trade; in some cities the 60-hour week remained in force several years after the 44-hour week' had been established in other cities in the same trade. By and large, however, there was usually a lag of only a few years before each successive downward revision for a given trade was obtained in all the cities in which the union functioned.

When the First World War began in Europe, most of the organized building-trades workers and newspaper printers were on a 44-hour week, and the book and job printers, brewery workers, and engineers had obtained a 48-hour week. A majority of the unionized metal workers and bakers, on the other hand, were on a nine-hour-day schedule, while most unionized teamsters and truck drivers worked 10 hours a day and longer. In 1915, when employment was rising as a result of war orders from abroad, the machine trades started a movement for an eight-hour day, 48-hour week, which extended into many industries after our entry into the war. In 1921 the book and job printers, after numerous strikes, gained a 44-hour week, as did most of the metal workers a few years later. Unionized truck drivers did not fare so well, however. As late as 1930 three out of four truck drivers were working more than 58 hours a week, and the normal work week of one out of four was 60 or more hours.

Union organization before the middle 1930's was confined very largely to skilled craft workers, and the normal work week for most manufacturing employees consisted of 50 hours or more. The men's clothing industry was fairly well organized and the Amalgamated Clothing Workers had obtained a 48-hour week in many of the large clothing centers in 1916; ten years later half the unionized shops were on a five-day week. Most of the organized fur workers and many of the women's garment workers in New York had also obtained a 40-hour week by this time.

Hours Provisions in Union Agreements

Several years before the 40-hour week became effective under the provisions of the Fair Labor Standards Act (see the next

Union accepted the innovation subject to the proviso that it be operated by union men and be regarded as a means to "secure decreased hours of labor at a fair rate of wages." (See Cahill, *Shorter Hours*, pp. 175 ff.)

chapter), most union agreements specified a normal work week
of 40 hours. Before the legal 40-hour week became effective, unionization had expanded into the mass-production industries, and the
hour standards provided in collective bargaining contracts signified the prevailing work week for most semi-skilled and unskilled
workers, as well as the skilled crafts. Important exceptions were
employees in retail trade and the service industries which were not
extensively unionized.

Although there was no effort to reduce work time during World
War II, prior to its outbreak a number of unions had succeeded
in negotiating work weeks of less than 40 hours. According to
union agreements in effect in 1946, most of the organized glass,
rubber tire, and men's clothing workers were on a 36-hour week,
although in the first two industries overtime premium rates were
provided after 40 hours. The 35-hour week prevailed in the
women's clothing, fur, and hat industries and in coal mining; the
37½-hour week was common in newspaper publishing. Many of
the building-trades unions had obtained 30- and 35-hour weeks.

During the war, as indicated later, longer hours were actually
worked than were specified in union agreements. The hours thus
specified refer almost without exception to the maximum number
which may be worked at regular rates of pay. Very few agreements,
and then only when unemployment exists in the trade, prohibit
working longer hours provided overtime or penalty rates are paid
for work beyond the specified hours. The most common overtime
rate is time and one-half the regular rate; some agreements establish double rates for all overtime, and many more require double
or even triple rates for Sunday and holiday work or for overtime
exceeding 10 or 12 hours in any day.

Since the legal adoption of the 40-hour week, most unions thus
far have directed their attention toward establishing a normal
work week consisting of eight-hour workdays from Monday
through Friday. The Fair Labor Standards Act establishes no
daily maximum, and in the absence of agreements to the contrary,
the 40 hours specified in the Act can be spread over six or seven
days or telescoped into fewer than five days without the payment
of overtime rates for longer than eight hours. A majority of agreements now provide for the payment of overtime rates after eight

hours' work in any day. In order to protect the five-day week, most agreements outside the continuous-process industries also require overtime pay for work done on Saturday, even though Saturday work does not involve working beyond 40 hours. Thus, if time has been lost during the week because of holidays, lack of work, machine breakdowns, and so forth, Saturday make-up time must be paid for at overtime rates. Many agreements exclude continuous-process and maintenance workers from Saturday penalty rates, although such rates must be paid for all the time worked in excess of 40 hours during any week.

ACTUAL WORKING HOURS

Thus far we have been discussing daily and weekly scheduled hours, that is, normal full-time hours, which usually designate the maximum number of hours of work allowable at regular or straight-time wage rates. The actual hours worked differ significantly from the scheduled hours or standard work time. The actual working hours during any period reflect time lost because of absenteeism and part-time employment; they also include overtime or hours in excess of the regularly scheduled time. Workers are interested in reducing their normal or scheduled hours of work, but they are also concerned when their actual working hours fall below scheduled hours since this represents underemployment and loss of wages.

The actual hours worked are one of the basic measures of industrial activity and manpower utilization as well as an indicator of the trend of scheduled working time. The relationship between scheduled hours and actual hours varies greatly among different groups of workers and, more especially, during different periods and under different economic conditions. The number of hours worked per week by any group of workers under normal conditions usually averages about two hours less than their scheduled weekly hours, owing to loss of time for such causes as personal absences, turnover, imbalance in production between different plant departments, and machinery breakdowns. When part-time employment is widespread, the discrepancy between the actual hours and the scheduled hours is, of course, much wider. In reverse, during periods of extraordinary production needs, such as the recent war, the actual hours are considerably longer than the normal scheduled hours.

Trend in the Actual Hours Worked

At the beginning of the First World War, the scheduled work week for three-fourths of all manufacturing wage earners was 54 or more hours, and for almost one-third the normal work week was 60 or more hours. In southern manufacturing, the normal work week for at least 60 per cent of all employees was 60 hours or more. Throughout the country, the 10-hour day six-day week prevailed for almost half of all employees engaged in textile, leather, and paper manufacturing; many steel, lumber, and sugar refinery workers were employed 72 hours or longer a week.[38]

The hours of work were greatly reduced for most workers, union and non-union, during the First World War, when employers were forced to compete for labor in a tight market. Many 60-hour-week schedules were reduced to 54 hours, and in response to government as well as union pressure many war industries adopted a basic eight-hour day.[39] During the war period the proportion of factory wage earners with a scheduled work week of 48 hours or less more than quadrupled, and the proportion with

---

[38] Data for the remainder of this chapter are from the regularly published monthly employment reports of the Bureau of Labor Statistics and from a special report, "Hours of Work in Manufacturing, 1914–43," in *Monthly Labor Review*, April, 1944.

[39] Owing to a complicated legal situation, some government contracts for war materials provided for an eight-hour day with time and a half for overtime, whereas contracts for other types of products set no limits on the hours employees might be required to work at straight time. The resentment and feeling of injustice which this situation engendered led to many labor troubles. Extension of the eight-hour standard therefore became a major objective of the War Labor Policies Board after it was established in May, 1918, to unify the government's labor policy, although the Board was concerned not so much with reducing the net working time as with establishing standards as to straight-time and overtime hours. The Board created machinery for enforcing the basic eight-hour day in plants with contracts specifying this standard, and tried, with some success, to obtain voluntary adherence to the eight-hour principle where it was not legally applicable. In addition, the Navy Department, the U. S. Shipping Board, and other government agencies favored the six-day week and urged employers to restrict Sunday work to cases of emergency. The National War Labor Board, established in April, 1918, to adjust labor disputes, also provided for a basic eight-hour day and six-day week in many of its awards.

schedules of 54 or more hours declined by half. These reductions in scheduled hours caused a drop in the average hours worked between 1914 and 1919 from 51 to less than 48 a week, even though pressure for production encouraged overtime and reduced part-time to a minimum.

During the early 1920's the Saturday half holiday was introduced in many manufacturing plants and the 50-hour week became typical. Also many steel mills and other continuous-process industries, in which the 12-hour day had persisted, changed from a two- to a three-shift basis; this resulted in a cut in the average full-time work of steelworkers from over 63 hours in 1922 to 55 hours two years later. For all manufacturing wage earners the average hours worked had declined to approximately 45 and for coal miners to around 33 in 1924, having been much lower during the depression of 1920–1921. The hours worked by a majority of wage earners remained practically the same from 1924 to 1930. Most unions were very weak and were therefore unable to obtain reduced schedules even in plants and trades where the 60-hour week remained in force. Because business activity was at a relatively stable level, there were no marked over-all fluctuations in the actual hours worked.

With the depression years of the 'thirties came a radical change in the level of working hours throughout American industry. In the five years from 1929 to 1934, average weekly hours in manufacturing dropped 25 per cent. Most of the decrease took place between 1929 and 1932, reflecting the great amount of part-time employment created by the decline in business activity and by the accompanying share-the-work programs. When a maximum work week of 40 hours was established for most branches of manufacturing during 1933 and 1934 under the National Recovery Administration codes,[40] the average weekly hours were already below the 40-hour level in many industries. In textiles and a few other industries where large proportions of the employees were still working more than 40 hours a week in 1932, the N.R.A. brought a considerable drop in average weekly hours. Many workers in "sweat-

---

[40] Of 558 master codes, all but 41 specified a maximum work week of 40 hours or less, though often there was provision for longer hours in a limited number of peak weeks or for the averaging of hours over specified periods of time.

shop" garment factories also benefited by a reduction in their exceedingly long working hours, although in the regular garment factories the average weekly hours were low because of extensive part-time employment.

Following the invalidation of the N.R.A. codes in 1935 there was a tendency to lengthen the work week. Before it was well under way, the greatly increased strength of labor unions and the influence of the Fair Labor Standards Act initiated a new trend toward a shorter work week. Nevertheless, in 1938 more than 60 per cent of all wage earners in manufacturing and the principal non-manufacturing industries were employed on weekly schedules exceeding 40 hours a week. When the 40-hour provision of the Fair Labor Standards Act became effective in October, 1940, the work schedules of nearly 2 million workers, out of the 12½ million wage earners covered by the Act, called for more than 40 hours a week.[41]

The actual hours worked fluctuated considerably during the late 1930's, reflecting business conditions. For example, during the recession year of 1938, the average hours worked in the steel, automobile, and rubber industries dropped to 32 a week but increased again with the resumption of business activity the following year.

In direct contrast to the trend in weekly hours during the First World War, the Second World War witnessed the sharpest rise in weekly hours of which there is a record. In spite of this rise, however, the average work week during the peak of World War II was at least six hours less than during World War I. During World War I the drop was from a pre-war average of more than 51 hours per week, whereas during World War II the rise was from an average of around 38 hours per week.

At the beginning of the war program President Roosevelt issued an order that all statutory provisions affecting the hours of labor and the payment of overtime should be observed. In line with this policy, the 48-hour week was generally adopted throughout the war industries, with eight hours and overtime rates in conformity with union agreements and the Fair Labor Standards Act. During 1944, the peak production year of the war period, the actual hours

---

[41] *Monthly Labor Review,* December, 1940, p. 1469.

worked by all manufacturing employees averaged slightly more than 45 a week.

Immediately following the close of the war, the actual time worked by manufacturing employees declined four hours a week on the average. In spite of the termination of war production, however, the actual hours during the first half of 1946 averaged one hour more than the scheduled hours. This was due to the continuation of a large amount of overtime in the metal and machinery industries which were producing tools and equipment for consumer goods industries.

SELECTED REFERENCES

Beman, L. T., *The Five Day Week,* H. W. Wilson Company, New York, 1928.

Bureau of Labor Statistics, *History of Wages in the United States,* Bulletin No. 604, Government Printing Office, Washington, 1934.

Cahill, Marion C., *Shorter Hours,* Columbia University Press, New York, 1932.

Commons, John R., and associates, *History of Labour in the United States,* The Macmillan Company, New York, 1918, vols. i, ii.

Federated American Engineering Societies, *The Twelve-Hour Shift in Industry,* E. P. Dutton & Co., Inc., New York, 1922.

Florence, P. Sargent, *Economics of Fatigue and Unrest, and the Efficiency of Labor in Industry,* Henry Holt & Company, Inc., New York, 1924.

Frankfurter, Felix, and Goldmark, Josephine, *The Case for the Shorter Work-Day,* National Consumers League, New York, 1916.

Gompers, Samuel, *Seventy Years of Life and Labor,* E. P. Dutton & Co., Inc., New York, 1925.

Interchurch World Movement, *Public Opinion and the Steel Strike,* Harcourt, Brace & Company, Inc., New York, 1921.

Lescohier, D. D., and Brandeis, Elizabeth, *History of Labor in the U. S.,* The Macmillan Company, New York, 1935, vol. iii.

National Industrial Conference Board, *The Five-Day Week in Manufacturing Industries,* New York, 1929.

Webb, Sidney, and Cox, Harold, *The Eight Hour Day,* Walter Scott, London, 1891.

16

GOVERNMENT REGULATION OF HOURS

LAWS FOR THE REGULATION OF HOURS OF WORK HAVE BEEN directed toward four general ends and have assumed two distinct characteristics. The several purposes are indicated by the groups of employees covered: workers directly or indirectly employed by the government; women and children; men engaged on occupations which are especially hazardous either to themselves or to the public; and finally, all workers, regardless of sex or age, kind of employer or employment.

Hour legislation for workers employed on public works and public contracts is an expression of the government's willingness to exercise its prerogatives as an employer of labor to establish certain labor standards. Laws for particular classes of workers and occupations in private industry represent the community's willingness to assume a measure of responsibility for the health and safety of the workers concerned as well as the general public. While health and safety have also been factors in the enactment of general hour laws, economic motives have been predominant, as is evidenced by the circumstances of their passage.

In addition to the groups of workers covered, there is a basic distinction in the types of hour laws which have been enacted; this is of major importance because of their effect upon business operations and, under certain circumstances, upon the national welfare. Hour laws differ fundamentally according to whether they fix an absolute limit on the number of hours which may be worked, or whether they establish a standard and require the payment of extra wages or penalty rates for work beyond the specified standard.

444

Laws which are primarily for the purpose of protecting the health and safety of individuals are designed to place absolute limits on allowable work time. Based on the assumption that longer hours are injurious to the particular workers concerned, or might jeopardize the public safety, they seek to prohibit altogether the working of longer hours than those specified in the law. Actually, however, most of them permit longer hours under specified circumstances, usually designated as "emergencies." If "emergency" is interpreted in the narrow sense to refer to fires, floods, or other "acts of God," the hours specified in the statute virtually fix an absolute limit on working time. On the other hand, if "emergency" can be interpreted to mean a "business emergency" such as a rush of work to fill an order or to save perishable goods, the statutory hours, of course, are not the actual maximum hours worked at all times.

General legislation covering all classes of workers has been directed more toward discouraging long hours of work than prohibiting them altogether. This is achieved by the establishment of a standard number of hours and requiring the payment of penalty rates for hours worked beyond the established standard. It allows flexibility in working time to take care of production needs which would not usually be classified as "emergency," and at the same time the penalty rates serve as a deterrent to excessive or unnecessary long hours. Moreover, this type of law is relatively easy to enforce. Longer hours are not absolutely forbidden when extra production is needed or wanted, and most employers would rather pay the extra wages than run the risks of violation. Also, employees are more likely to report violations in order to collect their overtime rates.

The merits of a "normal hours" law with penalty rates for overtime, in contrast to a rigid ceiling on hours, were amply demonstrated during World War II. Since there were no legal restrictions on the actual hours of labor, schedules could be arranged to take care of production requirements. At the same time, the overtime rates helped to boost weekly earnings when the cost of living was rising. The hours as well as the overtime feature of the laws made for flexibility in work schedules and income when both were needed.[1]

[1] In contrast to the federal hour laws in this country was the legislation

HOUR LEGISLATION AND THE COURTS

Legislative and judicial action on the regulation of hours during the past hundred years reveals the same gradual shift in position as has taken place with respect to other phases of labor conditions. During the early years of the movement it was a question of legislative acceptance of a responsibility to shorten the hours of work of wage earners; later the issue hinged more upon judicial application of hour legislation to the principles of freedom of contract and police powers of the state. As early as the middle of the 19th century legislators in various states began to respond to public opinion and pressure by enacting laws to regulate the hours for particular groups of workers whose situation seemed to warrant such protection from their government. But many of these laws were invalidated by the courts, and other proposed laws were kept off the statute books for fear of adverse decisions by the courts. It is only within comparatively recent years that government regulation of hours of work has found judicial acceptance.

Principle of Freedom of Contract

The principle of freedom of contract used by the courts in invalidating hour and other labor legislation was based on the Fourteenth Amendment of the Constitution, enacted after the Civil War for a very different purpose, which says, "No state shall deprive any person of life, liberty, or property without due process of law." The courts held that labor is property and that therefore a laborer has a right to sell his labor and to contract with his employer like any other property owner; hence any laws to regulate labor interfere with the individual's property rights or "freedom of contract."

Counterarguments, which finally became decisive, held that labor is not property; that the individual worker actually has little choice or freedom in his employment contract but "obeys the compulsion of circumstances"; and that the police power of the state

---

enacted in France just prior to the outbreak of the recent war, which placed rigid restrictions on the number of hours which could be worked. Many persons questioned the merit of this legislation when France was forced to make a desperate effort to increase production for national defense.

for the protection of health, safety, and welfare is paramount to an individual's freedom of contract. Let us review briefly the evolution of legislative and judicial opinion and action as they pertain to the regulation of hours of work.

As early as 1847 New Hampshire passed a general 10-hour law and during the following decade six other states passed similar legislation. After the Civil War, as a result of vigorous campaigns by labor and reform leaders, a number of states passed general eight-hour laws. By the end of the century hour legislation had been enacted in seventeen states, most of which established the eight-hour standard. These laws, however, had almost no effect upon working hours, and labor denounced them as "frauds on the laboring class." There were two reasons for their ineffectiveness. In the first place, they included an important qualification, namely, "unless otherwise stipulated by the contracting parties"; and the courts almost always assumed that where more than the statutory hours were being worked, this had been agreed upon by the employer and his employees. In the second place, either the laws carried no provision for enforcement or, if penalties were provided, they could be invoked only if the employer "willfully" violated the law or, according to some of the laws, if it could be proved that he "compelled" his employees to exceed the legal limit. Compulsion on the part of the employer was never realistically interpreted to mean that a request by an employer actually becomes a demand when he has the right to discharge.

These early hour laws were based on the principle that labor legislation should not curtail individual liberty to contract, and their constitutionality was never questioned. But when Nebraska in 1891 passed a law which provided extra compensation for work beyond eight hours a day for all classes of laborers except farm and domestic workers, the State Supreme Court held it unconstitutional on two grounds: first, that it made an unjustifiable distinction between classes of labor by exempting farm and domestic workers, and second, that it infringed upon freedom of contract. By this decision the court rejected the concept of "reasonable classification" of coverage, which is a fundamental presumption for many types of laws; it also assumed that individual workers exercised liberty in their employment contracts and it refused to allow the police power of the state to interfere in any way with that assumed liberty.[2]

Almost a quarter of a century elapsed before the highest court in the land was called upon to decide the constitutionality of a similar general hour law covering both men and women. In the meantime, most of the hour laws which were enacted were of limited coverage, that is, confined to particular classes of workers or kinds of occupations.

Decisions on Hour Laws for Women

For many years state legislation confined to the regulation of hours of women did not fare much better at the hands of the courts than general hour legislation. The one exception was in Massachusetts, whose State Supreme Court upheld a 10-hour law enacted in 1874 which covered women and minors employed in factories. The Massachusetts courts never invoked the freedom of contract theory but held that there "can be no doubt that such legislation may be maintained either as a health or police regulation, if it were necessary to resort to either of those sources of power."[3]

In contrast to Massachusetts was the situation in Illinois, where an eight-hour law for women employed in factories and workshops was enacted in 1893. Two years after its enactment the Supreme Court of Illinois declared the law unconstitutional, under both state and federal constitutions, on the grounds that it discriminated against factories and against women. It held that women "have a natural equality with men and no distinction may be drawn between them with respect to power of engaging to labor," and that the law violated the Fourteenth Amendment by depriving individuals of property without due process of law. The court held that limitation of this right can be justified only by some special condition, and there was "no reasonable ground . . . for fixing upon eight hours in one day as the limit within which a woman can

---

[2] *Low* v. *Rees Printing Co.*, 41 Neb. 127 (1894).

[3] *Commonwealth* v. *Hamilton*, 120 Mass. 383 (1876). Another Massachusetts law in 1892 reduced the weekly hours for factory women to 58, in 1908 to 56, and in 1911 to 54. In 1900 women employed in stores were brought under state regulation.

work without injury to her physique, and beyond which, if she works, injury will necessarily follow."[4]

At the time this decision was rendered there were thirteen women's hour laws on state statute books; but after their constitutionality was questioned, little or no effort was made to enforce them outside of Massachusetts. Nevertheless, proponents of hour regulations were able to get laws enacted in several other states, including two important states—Pennsylvania (1897) and New York (1899)—which established the 60-hour week for factory women and in some cases for women in mercantile establishments.

The cloud of uncertainty as to the constitutionality of such laws was removed in 1908 when the Supreme Court of the United States sustained an Oregon law which prohibited women from working in any mechanical establishment or factory or laundry more than 10 hours during any one day. The highest court held that this was justifiable class legislation because it was obvious that "the two sexes differ in structure of body, in the functions to be performed by each, in the amount of physical strength, in the capacity for long continued labor, particularly when done standing, the influence of vigorous health upon the future well-being of the race, and self-reliance which enables one to assert full rights, and in the capacity to maintain the struggle for subsistence. This difference justifies a difference in legislation and upholds that which is designed to compensate for some of the burdens which rest upon her."[5]

Seven years later the United States Supreme Court reaffirmed and extended its acceptance of hour regulation for women when it validated an eight-hour day, 48-hour week California law. Concerning the complaint that the law infringed upon freedom of contract, the court said: "As the liberty of contract guaranteed by the Constitution is freedom from arbitrary restraint—not immunity from reasonable regulation to safeguard the public interest—the question is whether the restrictions of this statute have reasonable relation to a proper purpose. Upon this point, the recent decisions of this court upholding other statutes limiting the hours of labor of women must be regarded as decisive." With re-

---

[4] *Ritchie* v. *People,* 155 Ill. 98 (1895).
[5] *Muller* v. *Oregon,* 208 U. S. 412 (1908).

gard to the specified length of the day, the court said: "It is manifestly impossible to say that the mere fact that the State of California provides for an eight-hour day, or a maximum of 48 hours a week, instead of 10 hours a day and 54 hours a week, takes the case out of the domain of legislative discretion. This is not to imply that a limitation of the hours of labor of women might not be pushed to a wholly indefensible extreme, but there is no ground for the conclusion here that the limit of the reasonable exertion of protective authority has been overstepped."[6]

Between the time of these two important decisions a number of states had enacted legislation to regulate, and in some cases to prohibit, night work for women. Massachusetts was the first; its 1890 law forbade the employment of women in factories between 10 P.M. and 6 A.M., and this was supplemented in 1907 by a law prohibiting their employment in textile mills after 6 P.M. The organized male textile workers fought vigorously for this law in order to force the mills to abandon the practice of regularly keeping their mills working during the evening by evading the maximum hour law, that is, employing for evening work women who had already worked the maximum number of hours in other mills during the day. The courts had held that this dual employment was not a violation of the maximum hour law.

The night work laws of other states were not vigorously enforced for a number of years because of their questioned constitutionality, especially after 1907, when the New York Court of Appeals invalidated the New York night work prohibition law. In 1915, however, the New York court reversed its earlier decision, largely because of the evidence presented which was based on case histories of women night workers and medical testimony on the effects of night work. The medical testimony was to the effect that all night work, whether carried on regularly in night shifts or irregularly in the evenings, causes loss of sleep and sunlight; that during the night, the processes of tissue repair are in the ascendent and this is one reason why loss of sleep at night is so detrimental to the organism; that lack of privacy and quiet for sleep in the day, especially in workers' homes, also causes loss of sleep

---

[6] *Miller* v. *Wilson*, 236 U. S. 373 (1915).

and this is accentuated in the case of women who spend much of the day in housework instead of sleep.[7]

The New York decision virtually established the constitutionality of night work legislation for women, although it was not finally confirmed by the Supreme Court of the United States until 1924.[8]

Regulation of Hours on Public Works

The constitutionality of protective laws for persons employed directly by the government was never questioned, on the principle that the state itself is a proprietary power. However, there was a good deal of litigation and various determinations by state courts and the Attorney General of the United States before the legality of hour regulation for people indirectly employed on public contract work was finally established.

As early as 1840, President Van Buren issued an Executive Order establishing the 10-hour day in government navy yards, and various cities during subsequent years enacted ordinances establishing the 10-hour and later the eight-hour day for municipal workers. The first legislation covering public contract work was enacted by New York in 1853. In 1868 Congress passed an eight-hour law for federal public works and California passed a similar statute. None of these laws or those enacted later by several other states were enforced, most of the state courts holding them unconstitutional on much the same grounds as hour laws for private employment.

In 1899 the Kansas Supreme Court broke precedent by ruling that there was "no infringement of constitutional rights" in the application of an hour law covering contract work, since "there can be no compulsion of a contractor to bid upon public work, nor is the laborer bound to take employment from a person having such a contract."[9] The United States Supreme Court used much the same language when it upheld the state court's decision and

---

[7] *People* v. *Charles Schweinler Press,* 214 N. Y. 395 (1915). The evidence presented was the report of the Factory Investigating Commission. See Josephine Goldmark, *Fatigue and Efficiency,* Russell Sage Foundation, New York, 1912.

[8] *Radice* v. *New York,* 264 U. S. 292 (1924).

[9] 61 Kan. 275 (1899).

emphasized that ". . . it belongs to the State, as the guardian and trustee for its people, and having control of its affairs, to prescribe the conditions upon which it will permit public work to be done on its behalf, or on behalf of its municipalities. . . ."[10]

Attitude About Hours on Hazardous Work

In its decision on public contract employment, the Supreme Court explicitly ignored the question of whether or not the work involved was dangerous to life or injurious to health. State courts which had held general hour laws for adult men to be an infringement upon freedom of contract were inclined to be more favorable to laws covering particular occupations which involved hazards either to the public safety or to the men employed in them. When the states began to enact laws limiting the hours of work of city streetcar operators and railroad workers, the state courts usually declared them constitutional. Likewise, federal legislation regulating the hours for railroad workers was upheld by the Supreme Court of the United States as a safety measure "to reduce the dangers [to life and property] incident to the strain of excessive hours of duty."[11]

The question of hour regulation on hazardous work first came to the courts' attention as an issue involving the health and safety of the men employed in the occupations, rather than the danger to public safety. In 1898 the Supreme Court of the United States sustained a decision of Utah's highest court on the validity of an eight-hour law for miners and smelters. This decision greatly extended the police power of the state when it held that the right of contract "is itself subject to certain limitations which the state may lawfully impose in the exercise of the police power. . . . While this court has held . . . that the police power cannot be put forward as an excuse for oppressive and unjust legislation, it may be lawfully resorted to for the purpose of preserving the public health, safety or morals, or the abatement of public nuisances, and a large discretion is necessarily vested in the legis-

---

[10] *Atkin* v. *Kansas*, 191 U. S. 207 (1903).

[11] *Baltimore and Ohio Railroad Co.* v. *Interstate Commerce Commission*, 221 U. S. 612 (1911). A few years later the Supreme Court held that a state statute with higher standards than the federal hours of service act was void so far as interstate transportation was concerned. (*Erie Railway Co.* v. *New York*, 233 U. S. 671 [1914].)

lature to determine, not only what the interests of the public require, but what measures are necessary for the protection of such interests. . . . While the general experience of mankind may justify us in believing that men may engage in ordinary employments more than 8 hours per day without injury to their health, it does not follow that labor for the same length of time is innocuous when carried on beneath the surface of the earth. . . ."

The decision also acknowledged the unequal relationship between employers and employees: ". . . the proprietors of these establishments and their operators do not stand upon an equality, . . . their interests are, to a certain extent, conflicting. The former naturally desire to obtain as much labor as possible from their employees, while the latter are often induced by the fear of discharge to conform to regulations which their judgment, fairly exercised, would pronounce to be detrimental to their health. In other words, the proprietors lay down the rules and the laborers are practically constrained to obey them. In such cases self-interest is often an unsafe guide, and the legislature may properly interpose its authority."[12]

This decision was specific in its reference to the hazards of mine employment and settled the question of the legality of hour legislation for occupations in which the hazards to health are obviously greater than in the general run of occupations. Just where the dividing line between extraordinary and ordinary hazards of employment was to be drawn was not specified. The same court a few years later held invalid a New York 10-hour law for bakers on the ground that baking was not dangerous enough to be regulated, in spite of the evidence cited as to the heat and dust-laden atmosphere connected with it. The court held in this instance: "We think that there can be no fair doubt that the trade of a baker, in and of itself, is not an unhealthy one to that degree which would authorize the legislature to interfere with the right to labor, and

---

[12] *Holden* v. *Hardy*, 169 U. S. 366 (1898). This case was brought to the attention of the courts by the Utah Federation of Labor, when Holden, a mine owner, insisted on working his miners 10 hours a day. It is reported that the State Attorney General refused to prosecute or to prepare a brief for the prosecution of this violation of the state law, saying, "There are two classes of citizens in Utah, those who pay taxes, and those who do not; and in this case those who pay taxes don't want such a law, and I don't propose to spend their money to defend it." (*American Federationist,* vol. v, pp. 23–24.)

with the right of free contract on the part of the individual, either as an employer or employee. . . . Statutes of the nature of that under review, limiting the hours in which grown and intelligent men may labor to earn their living, are mere meddlesome interferences with the rights of the individual."[13]

Acceptance of Legality of General Hour Laws

In spite of this decision, there was a gradual tendency to broaden the coverage of hour laws and to base their legality upon general health grounds rather than specific hazards. In 1912 a southern state, Mississippi, passed a law establishing a maximum 10-hour day for all employees in manufacturing. The Supreme Court of that state declared this a reasonable act within the police powers of the state because ". . . the present manner of laboring, the use of machinery, the appliances, requiring intelligence and skill, and the general present-day manner of life which tends to nervousness, it seems to us quite reasonable, and in no way improper to pass such a law so limiting a day's labor." In commenting upon the principle of liberty of contract and the inalienable rights to labor—which were always brought up by those opposed to regulation—the court said prophetically: "Some day, perhaps, the inalienable right to rest will be the subject of litigation; but as yet this phase of individual liberty has not sought shelter under the state or federal constitutions."[14] Further recognition of the state's right to enact general hour legislation was made that same year when Ohio amended its constitution to give the legislature power to regulate the hours of labor for men as well as women.

The final test on state hour legislation of a general character was the favorable decision by the U. S. Supreme Court on an Oregon law enacted in 1913, which stated that the working of any person in a factory for more than 10 hours in one day was "injurious to the physical health and well-being of such person, and tends to prevent him from acquiring that degree of intelligence that is necessary to make him a useful and desirable citizen of the State." The law, however, allowed three hours per day overtime at time-and-a-half rates. The Supreme Court held that this law

---

[13] *Lochner v New York,* 198 U. S. 45 (1905).
[14] 102 Miss. 802 (1912), and 103 Miss. 263 (1913).

was not an unreasonable or arbitrary regulation, and made no reference to the Lochner case in which it had arrived at the opposite conclusion.[15]

This affirmation of the right of the states to regulate the hours of men as well as women was considered a major turning point by those who had been seeking such legislation for many years. So far as the enactment of new state laws was concerned, however, it brought no results. The ensuing decade (the 1920's) was not conducive to reform, especially in labor matters.

It was almost a quarter of a century after the decision on the Oregon law before the highest court was again called upon to consider the legality of general hour legislation. This time it was federal and not state legislation, and the question of constitutionality rested upon the interpretation of the power of the federal government to regulate interstate commerce, rather than upon the freedom of contract of individuals versus the police power of the states.

In 1941 the Supreme Court of the United States upheld the constitutionality of the Fair Labor Standards Act of 1938 on the ground that Congress has the power to prohibit the shipment in interstate commerce of any goods in the production of which any worker was employed in violation of the wage and hour requirements of the Act. The court maintained that its previous decisions (citing those mentioned above) made it no longer open to question that it is within the legislative power to regulate hours of labor. Regarding coverage of the Act, "interstate commerce" in this and later decisions has been given a very wide application to include any employer who manufactures or deals in products, any portion of which he has reasonable expectation may be shipped across state lines, as well as any employment incidental to the manufacture and delivery of such goods.[16] This judicial recognition that work hours in private industries could be regulated by the federal government represented a milestone in constitutional law.

---

[15] *Bunting* v. *Oregon*, 243 U. S. 426 (1917). A very exhaustive brief was prepared for this case which is published in book form. See Felix Frankfurter and Josephine Goldmark, *The Case for the Shorter Work-Day*, National Consumers League, New York, 1916.

[16] *United States* v. *F. W. Darby Lumber Co.*, 61 Sup. Ct. 451 (1941).

FEDERAL HOUR LAWS

From the foregoing it is evident that the federal and state hour laws now on the statute books did not, like Pallas Athene, spring full-grown but rather were the result of decades of agitation and an outgrowth of numerous legislative and judicial decisions. The far-reaching provisions of the Fair Labor Standards Act had their roots in previously enacted state legislation and represent a culmination of public and congressional discussions extending over many years.

At least twenty years before this law was passed, bills had been introduced in Congress to establish the eight-hour day in all plants engaged in producing articles entering interstate commerce. When the constitutionality of such proposed legislation was questioned, there was frequent mention in Congress of a constitutional amendment to permit such legislation. Final action was not taken, however, until after the country had experienced its most severe business depression. The influence of the hour regulations included in the codes of fair competition under the National Industrial Recovery Act, as well as the hour limitations adopted under the various work relief programs, paved the way for permanent legislation.

Significant of possible future trends is the fact that during the business depression which provided the "climate" for the passage of the Fair Labor Standards Act, a number of bills were introduced in both houses of Congress "to prevent the shipment in interstate commerce of any article, in connection with which persons are employed more than five days per week or six hours per day."[17] Thus, several years before the 40-hour week became a legally established standard, serious consideration had been given to a 30-hour week requirement.

Let us review, briefly, the major provisions of the hour laws now in effect on the federal statute books as well as in the various states.

Public Contracts Act

As early as 1868 the federal government enacted an eight-hour-day law for workers employed on federal public works, but this

---

[17] Quoted from the thirty-hour week bills introduced by Senator Black in 1933 and 1935.

was never seriously enforced. In 1892 another law was passed which limited work on federal public contracts to eight hours a day except in case of "emergency." Since the term "emergency" was never clearly defined, the eight-hour limit was easily avoided. The act was materially strengthened in 1913 by an amendment which provided that every contract to which the federal government is a party shall contain a provision that no laborer or mechanic in the employ of the contractor or subcontractor shall be required or *permitted* to work more than eight hours in any calendar day except when the President of the United States has suspended the hour limit during a national emergency, such as a war. In such emergencies, time-and-one-half rates are provided for work in excess of eight hours.

This national eight-hour law does not apply to contracts for the purchase of supplies by the government, nor does it cover workers employed on the production of goods which the government buys in the open market. It was not until 1936 that the latter type of employment was brought under hour regulation. The so-called Walsh-Healey Public Contracts Act provides for a basic eight-hour day and 40-hour week on all contracts entered into by the United States government for the manufacture or furnishing of materials, supplies, etc., in excess of $10,000. Overtime is permitted, provided that time-and-one-half regular rates are paid for daily or weekly overtime, whichever results in the greater compensation. This Act also prohibits the employment of boys under 16 and girls under 18 years of age, and specifies that the goods purchased by the government shall not be manufactured under conditions that are dangerous or unsanitary to the health and safety of the workers.

Transportation Workers

There are a number of laws which regulate the hours of workers engaged in interstate and foreign transportation, including railroad, maritime, motor vehicle, and air. In some cases the allowable hours are specified by statute, but in other cases the statutes empower regulatory agencies to establish hour standards.

In 1907 a law was enacted by Congress in which the hours of employees engaged in or connected with the movement of trains across state borders were limited to 16 consecutive hours, and the hours of employees not connected with the movement of trains (dispatchers and telephone and telegraph operators) were limited to nine a day in offices which were continuously open, and to 13 in offices which were open only during the day. The Adamson Act of 1916 provided a basic eight-hour day for railroad trainmen for the purpose of computing compensation, that is, overtime rates.[18]

The hours of employees "whose activities affect the safety of the operation of motor vehicles" engaged in interstate transportation are controlled by the Interstate Commerce Commission. According to its regulations, no driver is permitted to drive more than 10 hours in the aggregate without having at least eight hours off duty, and no driver is permitted to remain on duty more than 60 hours in any period of 168 consecutive hours (seven days) or more than 70 hours in any period of 192 consecutive hours (eight days). In the event of adverse weather, road, or traffic conditions, driving is permitted up to 12 hours a day. These regulations are the maximum allowable hours established for purposes of safety. The agreements negotiated by employers and unions generally provide for a 40- or 48-hour basic week, with overtime rates in excess of these hours.

According to legislation enacted in 1936 and 1938, licensed officers and sailors on oceangoing and Great Lakes merchant vessels are on a three-watch basis when at sea, and on an eight-hour day when in safe harbor. Under its power to make safety regulations, the Civil Aeronautics Board has prescribed a maximum eight-hour day, 30-hour week for first pilots on commercial planes.

---

[18] The basis of computing pay for operating railroad employees is frequently a matter of dispute when new contracts are being negotiated, largely because of the operators' contention that the formula has become obsolete since trains have been speeded up considerably beyond the average mileage existing when the basis of computation was originally formulated. The railroad unions contend that this speed-up has caused a greater nervous strain and therefore the original formula is justified. According to the agreements in effect in 1945, road service employees are paid either for a specified number of miles or for a specified number of hours. The basic daily rate in freight service is paid for 100 miles or less, or eight hours or less, on the assumption of an average speed of 12.5 miles per hour—not actual speed on the road but speed in the sense of elapsed time between terminals. Engine service employees on passenger trains are paid the basic daily rate for 100 miles or less, or five hours or less. Train service employees on passenger trains are paid the basic daily rate for 150 miles or less, or 7.5 hours or less. The assumed speed in terms of elapsed time is in both cases 20 miles per hour. Overtime compensation for road service employees begins when the hours worked or the miles run in a day exceed the specified limits.

If a flight exceeds eight hours, a rest period is required of at least eight hours, or twice the number of hours flown since the last rest period. As in the case of other transportation employees, more favorable hours may be established by collective bargaining.

Fair Labor Standards Act

The most far-reaching legislation in the United States regulating the hours of work in private employment is the Fair Labor Standards Act of 1938, sometimes called the Wage and Hour Law. As indicated in Chapter 14, it was enacted subsequent to the invalidation of the National Industrial Recovery Act and was designed to continue and extend the hour provisions (and other labor standards) included in most of the codes of fair competition.

The hour clause of the Fair Labor Standards Act establishes a maximum work week, but not a daily maximum, for employees engaged in interstate commerce and in the production of goods for interstate commerce. The law provides for the payment of time-and-a-half rates for all hours worked in excess of the maximum specified, but does not limit the number of hours any individual may actually work or the hours a plant may remain open. It provided for a three-step downward revision of hours: a maximum of 44 hours a week during the first year, 42 hours during the second year, and 40 hours beginning October, 1940.

Employees of retail or service establishments, the greater part of whose business is intra-state, are excluded, as are farm laborers and employees engaged in the first processing of milk, cotton, and certain other agricultural products. For other agricultural processing industries, such as canning, a 12-hour day, 56-hour week is allowed during a total of 14 work weeks in any one year. Another exception is employees in manufacturing or any industry working under collective agreements which provide an absolute maximum of 1000 hours' work in 26 weeks, or a guarantee of 2000 hours' employment during any 52-week period. Under such contracts employees may work up to 12 hours a day or 56 hours a week before the payment of overtime begins. This clause was inserted in the Act to encourage guaranteed employment contracts, but it has been little used up to the present time.[19]

---

[19] See chap. 7.

STATE HOUR LEGISLATION

Since the passage of the general 10-hour laws by Mississippi
and Oregon in 1913, previously mentioned, only one state, North
Carolina, has enacted similar legislation to cover the general employment of both men and women.[20] Almost all the state hour laws
now in effect cover specific occupations or are limited to women
and minors. While the passage of the federal Fair Labor Standards
Act has removed some of the incentive for the enactment of state
legislation, it must be borne in mind that state legislation covering
particular groups of employees usually establishes maximum
allowable work time, in contrast to the federal law which permits
an unlimited number of hours provided overtime rates are paid
after 40 hours' work a week.

Laws Covering Men

For the most part, state laws regarding the working hours of
men apply only to those engaged on public works, or in the transportation industry where public safety is directly affected, or in
those employments considered particularly dangerous or unhealthy to the workmen. Laws limiting the hours of labor on public works have now been enacted by more than one-half of the states
as well as Alaska, Hawaii, and Puerto Rico. All these laws provide
for an eight-hour day and most of them cover all contracts
financed by the state or its political subdivisions, although a few
limit the coverage to public contracts of the larger cities in the
respective states. Approximately two-thirds of the states have
adopted hour laws covering employees engaged in city and other
intra-state transportation; most of them fix a maximum of 10 or
12 hours of continuous work and require a period of rest before
resumption of duty.

In private employment where public safety is not directly concerned, hour laws for men are limited principally to workers in
mines, smelters, and related industries. Over a dozen states have
laws regulating the hours of labor of some or all classes of work in
these industries, a majority limiting the hours to eight a day. Several states have laws regulating the hours of labor of employees

---

[20] While these laws are general in their coverage, they specifically exempt certain occupations.

working under compressed air; these laws provide a schedule showing the pressure, shifts, and intervals of rest between shifts for each 24-hour period, thereby prohibiting any overtime work.

In addition to the laws enacted especially for persons engaged on hazardous work, men are also included in the coverage of a few state laws which were primarily directed to the protection of women. For example, men are included in the Arizona law covering laundries, the Montana eight-hour law for retail stores and restaurants, and the Maryland, South Carolina, and Georgia laws placing a 10-hour limit in cotton and woolen manufacturing establishments.

Limitations on Hours for Women

Since the passage of the Fair Labor Standards Act, state legislation covering the hours of work for women is especially pertinent with respect to intra-state occupations, such as retail trade, laundries, restaurants and hotels, and other commercial service industries. In 1946 only six states and Alaska and Hawaii had no laws regulating the number of hours of work for women in one or all of these occupations. Over half the state laws establish eight hours a day, or 48 hours a week or less, as the maximum time a woman may be employed in one or more industries. Nine or more hours a day are permitted by the other state laws, although overtime rates must of course be paid after 40 hours a week in occupations covered by the Fair Labor Standards Act.

Most hour laws for women include other provisions in addition to prescribing the maximum number of daily or weekly hours. About half provide for one day of rest in seven in some or all industries; well over half specify that meal periods varying from twenty minutes to one hour must be allowed, and several require rest periods of ten minutes after a work period of four consecutive hours. Fifteen state laws prohibit night work for women in certain industries or occupations, and several others which permit longer hours for day work limit night work to eight hours.

Table 25 lists the maximum hour provisions in the various state laws for occupations which are largely intra-state and in the main not covered by the Fair Labor Standards Act. A few state laws include manufacturing and other types of employment covered by the Fair Labor Standards Act, but these hour provisions are not shown in the table. Many of the laws exempt certain occupations which are also not covered by the Fair Labor Standards Act. Where the law specifies different standards for different industries, the highest standard—that is, the shortest maximum work period—is shown in the table.

TABLE 25.　State Hour Laws for Women, 1946
Maximum Legal Hours in Industries Other than Manufacturing[a]

8-Hour Day, 44-Hour Week	8-Hour Day and/or 48-Hour Week	9-Hour Day and/or 54-Hour Week	10-Hour Day, 54- or 55- Hour Week	10 Hours or More per Day 57- or 60-Hour Week	No Limitations
Oregon	Arizona	Arkansas	Delaware	Kentucky	Alabama
Pennsylvania	California	Idaho[d]	New Jersey	Maryland	Alaska
	Colorado	Maine	South	Mississippi	Florida
	Connecticut	Michigan[e]	Dakota	South	Georgia
	District of	Minnesota[f]		Carolina	Hawaii
	Columbia	Missouri		Tennessee	Indiana
	Illinois	Nebraska			Iowa
	Kansas	New			West
	Louisiana	Hampshire[g]			Virginia
	Massa-	Oklahoma			
	chusetts[b]	Texas			
	Montana	Vermont			
	Nevada	Wisconsin[h]			
	New Mexico				
	New York				
	North Carolina[b]				
	North Dakota[c]				
	Ohio				
	Puerto Rico				
	Rhode Island[b]				
	Utah				
	Virginia[b]				
	Washington				
	Wyoming				

[a] Occupational coverage of the state laws varies as between states; the provisions shown here are for industries largely intra-state in character and not covered by the Fair Labor Standards Act. However, many of the laws exclude specified occupations which are local in character. Where the law specifies different standards for different industries, the highest standard (that is, the shortest maximum work period) is shown.
  [b] Nine-hour-day maximum.
  [c] Eight-and-one-half-hour-day maximum.
  [d] No weekly maximum.
  [e] Ten-hour day permitted.
  [f] No daily maximum.
  [g] Ten-and-one-fourth-hour-day maximum.
  [h] Fifty-hour weekly maximum.

CHILD LABOR REGULATION[21]

In this country, as in most foreign countries, children were the first workers for whom protection of the state was sought and to some extent attained. It was early recognized that there was no single solution of the child labor problem and that adequate protection for children necessitated a number of diverse requirements, namely, (1) a minimum age below which they should not be allowed to work; (2) a minimum of education which they should acquire before entering employment; (3) a maximum number of hours for their employment; and (4) regulations to protect them against especially hazardous or unhealthful occupations.

Out of these four elements and the attempts to enforce them there has developed a variety of statutes containing age and hour limitations, lists of hazardous employments, and provisions as to documentary proof of age and the issuance and use of employment certificates.

Early Efforts to Regulate Child Labor

Laws relating to child labor were enacted in the six New England States in the middle of the 19th century, and by the end of that century 28 states had some kind of protection for child workers. Most of these laws set a minimum age of 12 years and a maximum workday of 10 hours for children employed in manufacturing.

In 1904 a National Child Labor Committee composed of private citizens was formed, and it undertook a campaign to abolish child labor throughout the country. Largely through its efforts, existing state laws were improved and additional states enacted legislation. In spite of its work, however, only nine states had met all of the Committee's standards ten years after it was organized. The standards included a minimum age of 14 years for employment in manufacturing and 16 years for employment in mining; and for children between 14 and 16 years of age a maximum workday of eight hours, prohibition of night work, and documentary evidence of age.

[21] The author is indebted to Elizabeth Sands Johnson of the Division of Labor Standards, U. S. Department of Labor, for the information in this section. For an historical account of child labor legislation, see her chapter in D. D. Lescohier and Elizabeth Brandeis, *History of Labor,* The Macmillan Company, New York, 1935, vol. iii.

Attempts to Obtain Federal Regulation

Not satisfied with the slow progress of state-by-state legislation, the National Child Labor Committee turned to Congress for action. In spite of the expressed opposition of southern cotton mill manufacturers and other employers, a federal law was enacted in 1916 which made it unlawful to ship in interstate commerce any products which were produced in violation of the specified standards pertaining to the labor of children.

This Act was declared unconstitutional in 1918, by a five-to-four decision of the Supreme Court, on the grounds that the federal government could not use its commerce power to regulate child labor. A second federal law was enacted a few months after this decision; it imposed a tax of 10 per cent on the net profits of any concern employing children in violation of the standards established in the Act. In 1922 this law also was declared unconstitutional, the court holding that the taxing powers of the federal government could not be used for child labor regulation purposes.

Advocates of federal child labor legislation thereupon turned their attention to getting an amendment to the federal Constitution. Despite much opposition, Congress in 1924 passed a resolution for a proposed amendment which provides: "The Congress shall have power to limit, regulate, and prohibit the labor of persons under 18 years of age."

Up to 1946, only 28 states had ratified the proposed constitutional amendment, but the Fair Labor Standards Act includes provisions concerning child labor employed in the production of goods shipped in interstate commerce. The Act prohibits the employment of children under 16 years of age in manufacturing, mining, and the operation of power-driven machinery. In other occupations children between 14 and 16 years of age may be allowed to work by special certification. The Act also prohibits the employment of children between the ages of 16 and 18 in occupations which are especially hazardous. These provisions are strengthened and supplemented by the various state laws which are now in effect.

State Child Labor Laws

Every state at the present time has a child labor law regulating the conditions under which employers may hire children and young people, and also a compulsory school attendance law requiring children of certain ages to attend school. However, child labor laws vary considerably as to both the occupations to which they apply and the standards they set up for the employment of minors. Some laws apply to all gainful occupations, others exempt agriculture or domestic service, and still others apply only to specified industries, such as factories or stores. Children who sell or distribute newspapers or other articles on the streets, or work as street bootblacks, are usually subject to special street-trades regulations.

To facilitate enforcement, child labor laws usually require the issuance of employment certificates or work permits which certify that the persons to whom they are issued have met all the requirements of the child labor law regarding going to work. The certificates are usually issued by the superintendent of schools, thus providing an opportunity for the schools to find out why the child is leaving school and seeking employment. Some laws require that the child must pass a physical examination showing that he is fit for the intended work. Under most laws these certificates or permits must be kept on file by the employer while the young worker is employed by him. Age and employment certificates issued under state child labor laws are accepted as proof of age under the federal Fair Labor Standards Act.

Most of the state laws now on the statute books for the regulation of the employment of minors were enacted before the passage of the Fair Labor Standards Act and the Public Contracts Act. For employment covered by these Acts, the standards established by them prevail where state legislation is less restrictive. A number of states, however, have enacted laws which establish higher standards than those provided by the federal legislation. An association composed of state and federal labor officials of the United States and Canada has adopted certain standards for the employment of minors which they would like to see incorporated in the legislation for all the states. How far this has been attained is indicated by the tabulation on page 466, which shows that fewer than one-half of the states have established 16 years as the minimum age for employment during school hours, only one-fourth have maximum 8-hour day and only two maximum 40-hour week laws for all minors under 18 years of age.

Major Standards Recommended by the International Association of Governmental Labor Officials for State Child Labor Legislation and the Extent to Which Existing State Child Labor Laws Meet These Standards

	I.A.G.L.O. standards	Extent to Which State Child Labor Laws Meet I.A.G.L.O. Standards. Wartime Relaxations not Shown
Minimum age	*16 years*, in any employment in a factory; 16, in any employment during school hours; 14, in non-factory employment outside school hours.	17 states meet this standard in whole or in part (Conn., Fla., Ga., Ill., La., Mass., Mont., N. J., N. Y., N. C., Ohio, Pa., R. I., S. C., Utah, W. Va., Wis.)
Hazardous occupations	*Minimum age 18* for employment in a considerable number of hazardous occupations. State administrative agency authorized to determine occupations hazardous for minors *under 18*.	Few, if any, states extend full protection in this respect to minors up to 18 years of age, though many state laws prohibit employment under 18 in a varying number of specified hazardous occupations. 20 states and D. C. have a state administrative agency with such authority (Ariz., Colo., Conn., Fla., Kans., La., Mass., Mich., N. J., N. Y., N. C., N. Dak., Ohio, Okla., Oreg., Pa., Utah, Wash., W. Va., Wis.)
Maximum daily hours	8-hour day for minors *under 18* in any gainful occupation.	12 states and D. C. have an 8-hour day for minors *of both sexes* under 18 in most occupations (Calif., La., Mont., N. J., N. Y., N. Dak., Ohio, Oreg., Pa., Utah, Wash., Wis.) 7 other states have this standard *for girls* up to 18 (Ariz., Colo., Ill., Ind., Nev., N. Mex., Wyo.)
Maximum weekly hours	40-hour week for minors *under 18* in any gainful occupation.	2 states (N. J., Wis.) have a 40-hour week for minors *under 18* in most occupations; 4 states (La., Oreg., Pa., Utah) a 44-hour week for such minors. 1 of these states (Wis.) has a 24-hour week for minors *under 16;* 4 other states (Fla., N. C., R. I., W. Va.) a 40-hour week, and 5 others (Ga., Miss., N. Mex., N. Y., Va.) a 44-hour week for such minors.

Major Standards Recommended by the International Association of Governmental Labor Officials for State Child Labor Legislation and the Extent to Which Existing State Child Labor Laws Meet These Standards

	I.A.G.L.O. standards	Extent to Which State Child Labor Laws Meet I.A.G.L.O. Standards. Wartime Relaxations not Shown
Work during specified night hours prohibited	13 hours of night work prohibited for minors of both sexes *under 16* in any gainful occupation.	12 states meet or exceed this standard, at least for most occupations (Iowa, Kans., Ky., N. J., N. Y., N. C., Ohio, Okla., Oreg., Utah, Va., Wis.)
	8 hours of night work prohibited for minors of both sexes *between 16 and 18* in any gainful occupation.	10 states and D. C. meet or exceed this standard, at least for most occupations (Ark., Calif., Conn., Fla., Kans., La., Mass., N. J., Ohio, Wash.).
Employment certificates	Required for minors *under 18* in any gainful occupation.	21 states and D. C. require employment or age certificates for minors *under 18* in most occupations (Calif., Conn., Fla., Ga., Ind., La., Mass., Mich., Mont., Nev., N. J., N. Y., N. C., Ohio, Oreg., Pa., Tenn., Utah, Wash., Wis., and, where continuation schools are established, Okla.). One state (Ala.) requires such certificates for minors *under 17*. (A few of these states require certificates for minors 18 years of age or over, at least in certain occupations.)

U. S. Department of Labor, Washington
Child Labor and Youth Employment Branch, Division of Labor Standards
July 16, 1946

SELECTED REFERENCES

Cahill, Marion C., *Shorter Hours,* Columbia University Press, New York, 1932.
Children's Bureau, U. S. Department of Labor, *Why Child Labor Laws?* Publication No. 313, 1946.
Commons, John R., and Andrews, John B., *Principles of Labor Legislation,* Harper & Brothers, New York, rev. ed., 1936.
Frankfurter, Felix, and Goldmark, Josephine, *The Case for the Shorter Work-Day,* National Consumers League, New York, 1916.

Goldmark, Josephine, *Fatigue and Efficiency,* Russell Sage Foundation, New York, 1912.

Lescohier, D. D., and Brandeis, Elizabeth, *History of Labor,* The Macmillan Company, New York, 1935, vol. iii.

Moulton, Harold, and Levin, Maurice, *The Thirty-Hour Week,* Brookings Institution, Washington, 1935.

Women's Bureau, U. S. Department of Labor, *History of Labor Legislation for Women in Three States,* Bulletin No. 66, 1929.

Women's Bureau, U. S. Department of Labor, *The Effect of Labor Legislation on the Employment Opportunities,* Bulletin No. 65, 1928.

PART THREE

LABOR UNIONS AND LABOR-MANAGEMENT RELATIONS

GROWTH OF THE AMERICAN LABOR MOVEMENT

THE URGE TO COMBINE WITH OTHERS FOR MUTUAL PROTECTION AND advancement is an inherent characteristic of human nature. In every form of society persons of similar economic pursuits and needs have tended to unite into associations for the purpose of promoting their common interests. The nature of these associations, and the methods pursued, differ according to the particular needs and desires of the members; they are also affected by legal and other forms of social control.

A labor union has been defined as "a continuous association of wage-earners for the purpose of maintaining and improving the conditions of their employment."[1] Spontaneous strikes and rebellions of oppressed and dissatisfied workers are as old as history itself, but labor unions are a product of comparatively modern times, since by definition they imply a wage system and more or less permanent and formal organizations of workers. Although there is no generic connection between the modern labor union and the medieval craft gild, there are significant similarities, as to both purposes and the methods by which these purposes were carried out.

The medieval gilds were based on a feeling of scarcity of opportunity. To protect their interests, the gilds brought influence upon the government to forbid anyone from practicing a trade who was

---

[1] Sidney and Beatrice Webb, *History of Trade Unionism,* Longmans, Green & Co., London, 1911.

not a member of the gild, and through their strict apprenticeship regulations and their restrictions of "foreigners" from other localities they saw that too many did not become gild members. Their work rules included quality standards to protect them from the competition of inferior workmanship, daily hours were limited, and night and holiday work was forbidden. The gilds, like many labor unions today, also performed certain fraternal functions such as providing financial aid in time of sickness or death of their members.

The medieval gild, however, was composed of both masters and journeymen and there was no conflict of interest between the two because the journeyman was serving a master only temporarily; in a few years he would also be a master and any advantages which he might gain from his master he would in turn have to give to his journeymen. The gild system was concurrent with an economy of local markets and no capital outlay except a few tools and a limited supply of raw materials. The gild was a group of craftsmen banded together for mutual protection and control of the local market. When the market was extended and more capital was needed to care for short credits and finished stock, the industrial grouping changed. The journeyman's opportunity for becoming a master grew more limited, and the great bulk of workers ceased to be independent producers who owned their tools and materials and themselves disposed of the product of their labor. The journeymen came to constitute a distinct and permanent class, and many of them formed gilds of their own as their masters gradually converted the craft gilds into merchant-employer gilds.

The use of power machines and the factory system widened the gap between employers and workers. The factory system, because of the increasing amount of capital required, necessitated combinations of capital resources which were legalized into corporations. The collective action of capital and management extended beyond the confines of a single corporation and found expression in trade and manufacturers' associations, chambers of commerce, and other permanent and *ad hoc* combinations to promote and protect the interests of the investors and managers of capital.

In response, ever seeking a semblance of equality in the bargaining relationship, workers' organizations have expanded both horizontally and vertically. Local unions of skilled craftsmen have grown into national and international unions; workers of all crafts in an industry have united into industrial unions; both craft and industrial unions have formed city, state, and national federations or councils.

EARLY ORGANIZATIONS

Although machines and mass production have materially influenced the growth and character of labor organizations, labor unions preceded the factory system. The earliest labor organizations, and some of the strongest today, were established in the skilled handicraft trades. The first organizations of labor in this country appeared among the carpenters, shoemakers, printers, and tailors in the east coast cities during the 1790's. These craft societies bargained over wages and hours, demanded closed-shop conditions, engaged in strikes, boycotts, and picketing, paid strike benefits, regulated apprentices, and employed "walking delegates" to see that the terms agreed upon were enforced. These early workingmen's societies were local in scope, although there was some interchange of information among the societies of a given trade, and some concerted effort to deal with the problem of traveling journeymen who competed with resident workers.

Experiments Early in the 19th Century

As the local craft societies became more numerous and active, more united efforts were made to alleviate some of the worst ills which beset the workingmen of that day. The various societies in the different cities united into "trades' unions" to provide common support during strikes, and frequently maintained a common strike fund accumulated through per capita taxes from each member society. Paralleling these city combinations, local societies of shoemakers, printers, carpenters, and weavers united into what they called "national" organizations, although in reality their membership was limited to the larger eastern cities. During the "wild-cat" prosperity and rising prices of the middle 1830's, members of these city and craft organizations formed a National Trades' Union. All these organizations, in addition to seeking improvements in wages and hours, were concerned with broad

social reforms such as free public schools, abolition of imprisonment for debt, and elimination of property qualifications for
voting.

The national organizations as well as most of the local unions
collapsed during the panic of 1837 and the ensuing years of business dislocations. New workingmen's organizations appeared
during the 'forties, but these were concerned more with cooperatives, land reform, and general social improvement programs than
with bargaining with employers. Numerous local trade unions
came into existence with the general expansion of industrial activity and the rising prices that followed the discovery and use of
California gold. In contrast to the workingmen's associations
established in the 'forties, the major concern of these local unions
was bargaining for better wages and hours. It was during the
1850's that several of our present-day national unions had their
beginnings—the typographers, hat finishers, machinists and blacksmiths, and molders. All the labor organizations suffered a serious
setback in the depression which began in 1857 when unemployment
and wage cuts affected union treasuries and morale.

Post-Civil War Developments

Within a few years after the outbreak of the Civil War, many
new local organizations and several national unions came into
existence as a means of combating the soaring prices that resulted
from the issuing of "greenbacks" and the lag in wage increases.
There was a further interest in organization after the close of the
war, when returning soldiers found that their skilled hand jobs had
been supplanted by factory and machine production, when existing
work standards were being menaced by the influx of immigrants
willing to work for low wages, and when improved railroad transportation made it possible for goods manufactured in low-cost
areas to be brought to higher wage markets.

Most of the organizations which emerged during the decade following the Civil War were craft unions. A progenitor of the
modern industrial union was the Knights of St. Crispin, a shoe
workers' union founded in 1869 for the purpose of protecting
journeymen against the influx of "green-hands" into their industry. With its 50,000 members, it was probably the largest

union in existence at that time, but within a decade the Crispins disintegrated because of drastic wage cuts and the introduction of new machinery which they were unable to prevent.

After several attempts to unite the numerous national and local organizations, the National Labor Union was formed in 1866; it was a loose federation of trade unions and of some reform organizations which were not strictly concerned with labor problems. At first it directed its chief attention toward obtaining an eight-hour day but later it turned more and more to political action and began to espouse varied kinds of reform measures, social and fiscal. Thereupon many of the trade unions became dissatisfied and withdrew. The National Labor Union finally disbanded in 1872, after an unsuccessful attempt to form a National Labor and Reform political party.

The Order of the Knights of Labor

To circumvent employers' lockouts and black lists, workers were led to meet secretly and to organize a type of association so clothed in ritual, sign grips, and passwords that "no spy of the boss can find his way into the lodge room to betray his fellows." One of these organizations was the Noble Order of the Knights of Labor, which was established by some Philadelphia tailors in 1869. Soon the tailors were joined by shoemakers (mostly remnants of the St. Crispin lodges), carpenters, miners, railroadmen, and other organized and unorganized workers.

During the 1880's the Knights of Labor, having revoked its secrecy features, grew into a spectacular mass movement which included workers of all trades and degrees of skill. Discontented farmers, professional persons, and even some employers responded to its appeal for the amelioration of the hardships of the common man under the rallying cry, "An injury to one is the concern of all." The general and far-reaching aim of the Order was the substitution of a cooperative society for the existing wage system, which it hoped could be attained through education and legislation. More immediately, it sought improvement in wages and hours and the abolition of convict and child labor.

Structurally, the Knights of Labor was composed of local assemblies (organized along either craft or mixed lines), combined into district assemblies[2] which had sole authority within their respective jurisdictions; at the head was the General Assembly, with "full and final jurisdiction." These mixed assemblies bargained with employers and conducted strikes, frequently calling out workers in various trades to aid strikers in a given trade or plant. Through these mixed assemblies, the superior bargaining power of the skilled workers could be utilized to help the unskilled workers.

The Knights of Labor reached its peak following the southwest railroad (Gould system) shopmen's strike in 1885, when for the first time officials of a large corporation met with and negotiated an agreement with the organization. This success brought enthusiastic response from workers throughout the country, and the Knights of Labor membership increased sevenfold within one year. By the autumn of 1886 the Order had over 700,000 members in more than 5500 local assemblies—the equivalent of almost 10 per cent of the total industrial wage earners.[3]

Its day of power was brief. Railroad strikes in 1886 met with disastrous defeat, and the united opposition of employers caused the failure of numerous strikes for an eight-hour day which resulted in the disintegration of entire assemblies. Most important was the disaffection of most of the skilled workers, who were leaving the mixed assemblies in the Knights and forming trade unions. By 1900 the Order had practically ceased to exist as a national movement, although a number of local and district assemblies remained active for several decades.

The Knights of Labor was the first national labor organization in this country to be active for more than a year or two and its influence extended beyond its immediate membership and beyond

---

[2] Opposition by some of the trade groups to the mixed district assemblies forced the Knights of Labor to allow these groups to organize into district and national trade assemblies. Thus the telegraphers and the window glass and shoe workers finally obtained national craft autonomy, although the general officers of the Knights of Labor did everything they could to discourage trade autonomy.

[3] Grand Master Workman Powderly said regarding this: "In 1885 we had about 80,000 members in good standing: in one year the number jumped to 700,000, of which at least 400,000 came in from curiosity and caused more damage than good." (Terence V. Powderly, *The Path I Trod,* Columbia University Press, New York, 1940.) The newspapers at that time, greatly alarmed over the popularity of the mass movement, quoted a membership of 2½ million.

the years of its active national existence. Its chief contribution was education. The workers learned the strength and weaknesses of the one-big-union type of organization, and the general public, as never before, was made conscious of the bitter discontent which existed among large sections of industrial wage earners.

THE AMERICAN FEDERATION OF LABOR

The conflict of interest between skilled craftsmen who worked with tools and the mass of semi-skilled and unskilled wage earners led in 1881 to the formation of the Federation of Organized Trades and Labor Unions, which in 1886 became the American Federation of Labor. Samuel Gompers of the Cigarmakers' Union was elected the first president of the Federation and continued in that office, with the exception of one year, until his death in 1924. In contrast to the mixed assemblies of the Knights of Labor, complete autonomy was retained by each organized craft in the American Federation of Labor. Each national union (international if it included Canadian locals) had its own constitution, its own rules for internal government, and its own procedures for dealing with employers. In no case were outsiders—that is, persons not working at the trade but in sympathy with the union's aims—admitted to active membership.

General Policies of the A. F. of L.

For fifty years the American Federation of Labor was not only the dominant but practically the sole spokesman of the organized workers in this country. During this half century, while sweeping and fundamental changes were taking place in the nation's economic and industrial life, it maintained a consistent course of action and almost never deviated from the general policies adopted during its formative period.

The Federation was established at a time when many persons, both wage earners and intellectuals, believed that the ultimate solution of labor's problems was the elimination of employer-employee classes altogether through the substitution of a new industrial order of producers' cooperatives or socialism.[4] This could

[4] Although Marxian socialism had a considerable following, there were many other proposed schemes whereby workers would share in the ownership, man-

be achieved only through the solidarity of all workers, skilled and unskilled alike, who would not only engage in piecemeal efforts with individual employers, but also use their united economic and political strength to gain basic and general reforms throughout the industrial system.

The emergence of the A. F. of L. represented a decisive defeat for the one-big-union idea by which the superior strength and strategic advantages of the skilled workers could be used economically and politically to benefit the entire working class. Not only was the Federation founded upon the principle of craft autonomy, but it early adopted the policy of concentrating its efforts on the economic front and relegating political action to a minor role. Instead of engaging in political campaigns to obtain laws for the general improvement of working conditions, the A. F. of L. and its affiliated unions preferred to rely solely upon collective bargaining with employers. The only governmental assistance they sought was legal protection against actions of employers and public officials (such as court injunctions) which interfered with their freedom to exert the maximum economic pressure to gain better terms in their trade agreements. This was early demonstrated in the methods used to obtain the eight-hour day, discussed in Chapter 16.

The rise of a labor movement such as the American Federation of Labor resulted in the exclusion of an ever-increasing number of industrial workers from the benefits of unionization. Although the Federation from time to time made efforts to organize particular groups of factory workers, it received lukewarm support and sometimes opposition from its affiliated craft unions, which feared a dilution of their bargaining strength. The A. F. of L. type of organization had its advantages, however, for it was no doubt its limited coverage of skilled crafts which enabled it to carry on dur-

---

agement, and profits of business. Similar philosophies were popular among workers in European countries. The French term for labor union, *syndicat,* implies direct action through general strikes and violence, if necessary, to establish control over the means and processes of production—a theory which the French labor movement later abandoned. For a more adequate discussion of this period, see Selig Perlman, *History of Trade Unionism in the United States,* The Macmillan Company, New York, 1923, and Harry A. Millis and Royal Montgomery, *Organized Labor,* McGraw-Hill Book Company, Inc., New York, 1945, vol. iii.

ing periods when other forms of organization were unable to survive.

In contrast to the experience of unions during previous depression periods, the unions affiliated with the American Federation of Labor made substantial gains during the prolonged depression of the 1890's. On the return of business prosperity at the beginning of the present century, there was a further expansion in union organization and in collective bargaining. In the foundry and machinery industries, industry-wide bargaining was established between the unions and the employers' associations. In 1902, with the assistance of a federal government commission, collective bargaining arrangements were begun in the anthracite areas.

Membership in the American Federation of Labor increased from 350,000 in 1899 to over 1,675,000 in 1904, and some two dozen new national and international unions were established. By 1904 there were no less than 90 stable national unions, most of which, except the railroad and postal unions, were affiliated with the American Federation of Labor. With the exception of the mine, brewery, garment, textile, and shoe workers, practically all of them were craft unions. In the local organizations of the garment, textile, and shoe unions, moreover, craft distinctions were usually followed.

Employer Opposition

While the skilled workers in industries characterized by hand tools and small employers were able to establish new unions, factory and mill workers were facing the powerful opposition of large corporations which were assuming an ever-increasing importance in American industry. The American Railway Union was virtually extinguished after the strike in 1894 in which it faced the combined opposition of the Pullman Company and the Railway Managers' Association.[5]

Two years previously the Amalgamated Iron and Steel Workers, the most powerful trade union in existence at the time, had suffered a disastrous defeat in its strike at Homestead, Pennsyl-

---

[6] The Pullman strike is significant in labor history because of the numerous injunctions issued by the federal courts upon the initiative of the Department of Justice, and because President Cleveland sent United States troops to Chicago in spite of the protest of the governor of the state.

vania, against the Carnegie Steel Company in protest against a wage reduction. Thereafter one large mill after another was put on a non-union basis. After the formation of the United States Steel Corporation in 1901 and its adoption of a vigorous anti-union policy,[6] the once strong Iron and Steel Workers' Union was practically eliminated from all the major steel concerns in the country.

The influence and prestige of one large corporation were instrumental in driving unionization from the steel industry; in industries made up of many independent companies the employers combined into trade associations to combat the unions. Such organizations as the National Founders' Association, the National Metal Trades' Association, and the Structural Erectors' Association not only refused to enter into agreements with unions but engaged in activities directed toward their complete destruction. Local employers' associations and "citizens' alliances" also came into existence, their chief function being to break up strikes and otherwise aid employers who were having labor difficulties. In 1902 there was organized the American Anti-Boycott Association, a secret body of manufacturers who sought to attack unions through the courts.[7] About the same time the National Association of Manufacturers, originally organized for purely trade purposes, began to combat trade unions, chiefly through political and legislative means.

Paralleling these positive and belligerent campaigns against unions was the indirect effect of scientific management which was then being popularized by Frederick Taylor and his followers. Scientific management cut into union morale in two ways: The unions' opposition to its implied speed-up and the lessening of job opportunities through improved processes caused many employers

---

[6] A congressional investigating committee, ten years after the adoption of this policy, said: "The great bulk of American union laboring men in the iron and steel industry understood they were not wanted at the works of the U. S. Steel Corporation. The process of filling the places of these union laborers is interesting and important. . . . Southern Europe was appealed to. Hordes . . . poured into the United States. They . . . knew absolutely nothing about iron and steel manufacture but they were sufficient to fight the labor unions." (House of Representatives, 62nd Congress, 2nd Session, Report No. 1127, p. 128.)

[7] Among the many cases this Association took through the courts was the famous Danbury Hatters' case discussed in chap. 21.

to increase their determination to do away with the unions. Second, the wage incentive plans tended to discourage group loyalties and solidarity by encouraging individual workmen to seek better wages through their individual effort on the job, rather than through collective bargaining. The welfare programs which some employers were just beginning to adopt were a further means of winning employees away from "outside" unions.

LABOR DURING WORLD WAR I

The American Federation of Labor's prompt assurance of cooperation with the government upon its entry into the First World War smoothed the way for the expansion in union organization which followed. In March, 1917, almost a month before the United States declared war, representatives of most of the unions met in Washington, where they voted unqualified support to the government and drew up a statement of labor's war policy. This statement expressed the demand that the organized labor movement be recognized by the government as the representative of all wage earners, including those "who have not yet organized," and that organized labor be given representation in all agencies determining and administering policies of national defense.

Government Labor Policy

The principle of labor representation on government committees was accepted. Never clearly defined was the policy with respect to organized labor's status in private industry—even in those industries upon which the government was directly dependent for carrying on the war. The Council of National Defense accepted the principle adopted by its labor advisory committee,[8] that "neither employers nor employees shall endeavor to take advantage of the country's necessities to change existing standards." The Secretary of Labor explained this as meaning that "where efforts to organize the workers are not interfered with and where a scale of wages is

---

[8] The Council of National Defense was established by the Army Appropriation Act of December, 1916. Early in 1917 an advisory committee on labor was established with Mr. Gompers as chairman; it consisted of over a hundred representatives of labor, capital, and members of organizations interested in social and industrial problems, as well as government officials and specialists.

recognized that maintains the present standard of living . . . for the time being no stoppage of work should take place for the purpose of forcing recognition of the union." The National War Labor Board, which was established in the spring of 1918, adopted a more positive policy, namely, that "the right of workers to organize in trade unions and to bargain collectively, through chosen representatives, is recognized and affirmed. This right shall not be denied, abridged, or interfered with by the employers in any manner whatsoever."

Accompanying this positive declaration, however, was the statement that "the workers, in the exercise of their right to organize, shall not use coercive measures of any kind to induce persons to join their organizations, nor to induce employers to bargain or to deal therewith." Another statement specified that employers were not required to deal with union representatives who were not employees of the company unless this had been the practice previously. This latter provision opened the way for the rapid growth of employees' works councils, which became a formidable rival of trade unions. These works councils (later more generally called employee representation plans or company unions) multiplied rapidly, some being installed by employers to avoid dealing with trade unions, others being established by award of government boards as an expedient compromise with firms which would have no other form of collective dealing.

In spite of this encouragement of the works councils, distinct advantages to trade unions resulted from the adoption of the principle of collective bargaining by this first National War Labor Board. With jobs plentiful enough to remove the fear of discharge and with sufficient grounds for discontent to encourage workers to seek to better their wages and hours, the established unions were able to carry on successful organization drives. Except in the steel industry, the unions connected with most of the industries important to the war effort made significant gains. The building- and metal-trades unions expanded and, on the intervention of the government, recognition was obtained from the large meat packers. The seamen were successful in getting agreements everywhere except on the Great Lakes, and the bituminous coal miners were able to extend their central competitive agreement into other areas. The shipbuilding unions obtained recognition, and the railroad brotherhoods were equally successful during the period the government took over the operation of the railroads.

Industrial Workers of the World

While the American Federation of Labor and the railroad unions were making notable gains, the war witnessed the virtual disappearance of the rival labor movement which had been active during the decade preceding the war, the Industrial Workers of the World. This organization, formally launched in 1905, was a "one big union" made up of the Western Federation of Miners[9] and the hitherto unorganized migratory workers of the wheat fields and lumber camps of the Northwest. It was a direct-action movement which was opposed to the signing of collective bargaining agreements with employers. Although its long-time program sought the substitution for the existing government, of a workers' society in which the unions would own and operate all industry, its immediate efforts were directed toward improving conditions on the job.

At first largely confined to the unskilled workers of the West and Middle West, in 1912 the Industrial Workers of the World expanded into the East, especially among the foreign-born, low-wage textile workers. These campaigns, however, resulted in no lasting organizations. In the West, the I.W.W. remained active although its ranks were depleted by group secessions and the withdrawal of prominent leaders.

As a consequence of its anti-war position, the members of the I.W.W. were suspected and accused of acts inimicable to the pursuit of the war program, although the organizers maintained that their numerous strikes were directed toward improving working conditions. Through action on the part of both the federal Department of Justice and local governments, most of its leaders were imprisoned and its headquarters were closed subsequent to

---

[9] A metal miners' union organized in 1893. Its many bitter strikes against strongly organized employers who frequently had the active support of their local government had made many of its members anti-government. The more conservative faction gained control of the union in 1907 and the Western Federation of Miners withdrew from the Industrial Workers of the World. For more complete information on this movement, see Paul F. Brissenden, *The Industrial Workers of the World, a Study in American Syndicalism*, Columbia University Press, New York, 1920.

our entry into the war. In the Northwest logging camps, where it had been most active, a representative of the War Department was successful in replacing the I.W.W. with an organization composed of both workers and employers—the Loyal Legion of Loggers and Lumbermen—which remained in existence for more than twenty years.

STALEMATE OF THE 'TWENTIES

The close of the war in 1918 brought an end to active government participation in labor relations, as well as the unions' release from the wartime restraints. With the continued expansion in business and the rise in living costs following the signing of the Armistice, workers continued to join the unions in increasing numbers. In 1919 and 1920 more than one and a half million joined the various unions, bringing the total membership to over 5 million. This represented a peak not surpassed until 1937.

Post-War Adjustments

The unions' efforts to expand collective bargaining and raise wages led to many bitter disputes. The industrial unrest and the difficulties incident to getting industry back on a peacetime basis caused President Wilson in October, 1919, to call a conference of representatives of employers, labor, and the public to "discover such methods as had not already been tried out of bringing capital and labor into close cooperation." The conference immediately split on the question of collective bargaining and trade unions. Mr. Gompers submitted an eleven-point resolution, the first of which was the right of wage earners to organize into unions and to bargain collectively. The employer group adopted a resolution including "the right of employers to deal or not to deal with men or groups of men who are not their employees," stating that the arbitrary use of collective bargaining "was a menace to the institution of free peoples." The representatives of the public endorsed the principle of collective bargaining but insisted that employee representation groups be included as proper collective bargaining agencies. Unable to arrive at any common agreement on the fundamental basis of all employer-employee relations, the conference broke up within a few days.

The Open-Shop Movement

Following this conference, employers throughout the country started a movement to destroy unionism. Manufacturers' associations, boards of trade, chambers of commerce, builders' associations, bankers' associations, so-called "citizens' associations," and even a farmers' organization—the National Grange—united in a program, which they called the "American Plan," to save workers from "the shackles of organization to their own detriment."[10] Open-shop organizations existed in practically every industrial center in the country; in addition to conducting "patronize the open-shop" campaigns, these organizations extended direct aid to employers such as maintaining black lists of union members and furnishing money, spies, and strikebreakers to employers involved in strikes.

Union after union lost its war and post-war gains under the combined onslaught of the anti-union drives and the wage cuts introduced during the post-war depression of 1921–1922. Early in 1921 the "Big Five" packing companies declared that they no longer would be bound by the union agreement and the labor administrator they had reluctantly accepted during the war, and the packing industry once again became open shop. A few days prior to the expiration of the seamen's agreement in 1921, the United States Shipping Board and private shipowners demanded the abolition of the three-watch system and the withdrawal of union preferential hiring. The two-month strike following this demand was lost; seamen returned to the 12-hour day, 84-hour week, and the once powerful seamen's union was soon reduced to less than one-fifth its former size.

Even the strongly organized building trades did not escape the anti-union drives. When the building-trades' unions in San Francisco rejected a wage reduction, employers conducted a general lockout until the workers returned under open-shop conditions. In Chicago, a citizens' committee organized by the Illinois Manufacturers' Association and the Chicago Chamber of Commerce was successful for several years in compelling unions and builders to maintain an open shop and to accept the wage rates determined by an arbitrator.

---

[10] From a statement of policy of the American Bankers' Association in the magazine *Industry,* January 1, 1921.

Efforts to break up the unions failed in a few industries, notably in the book and job printing industry and in the New York men's and women's clothing industry, where the unions were forced to engage in prolonged strikes in order to maintain their collective bargaining relations.

In spite of occasional victories for the unions, the employers' open-shop drives, aided by the post-war depression, resulted in large losses to organized labor. Union membership dropped from a peak of over 5 million in 1920 to 3½ million in 1924 and, contrary to all similar experience in the past, continued to decline after the return of business prosperity.

Welfare Capitalism

The chief reason for the absence of trade union growth during the 1920's was the failure to organize the expanding mass-production industries. New machines and processes were substituting semi-skilled machine tenders for skilled craftsmen working with tools. The bulk of the trade unions were composed of skilled craftsmen, and few of them made any serious attempts to broaden their field of interest to include the new type of factory worker. Whole industries, such as automobile and rubber, remained untouched; in others, such as steel, electrical products, furniture, and glass manufacture, only a fraction of certain groups of skilled workers belonged to any union.

Even if energetic organizing efforts had been undertaken, the response of many of these workers at that time might have been lukewarm, especially those in the newer expanding industries where relatively high wages were paid and where increasing production softened the incidence of technological displacements. The comparatively high wages received by these workers were not diluted by rising costs of living, for the prices which workers paid for what they bought remained stable through this period. If there had been a marked increase in the cost of living, no doubt many of the unorganized workers would have sought the assistance of already established unions or formed new ones, just as they had in the past when prices were rising.

It was in these industries, characterized by large corporations, that management was most active in the adoption of programs which many employers felt made unions unnecessary. The 'twenties marked the peak of welfare activities, when employees' pension plans, group life insurance, and medical services were offered as security against the unavoidable hazards of life, when professional personnel managers were engaged to handle the grievances and problems arising on the job, and when plant baseball teams, glee clubs, and dances provided recreation off the job. To create an attitude of partnership with management, employee stockownership was encouraged and sometimes required.[11]

As a further substitute for trade unions, a number of employers established works councils or employee representation plans. The number of workers covered by such plans increased from less than 700,000 in 1922 to over 1,500,000 in 1928.[12] Many of these company unions were established after an unsuccessful strike by trade unions. Shop councils were established on the Pennsylvania and a number of other railroad systems following the shopmen's strike in 1922; the General Electric Industrial Representation Plan was established in 1924, following numerous strikes of the metal workers' unions; and some of the larger New England textile mills adopted employee representation plans as an aftermath of strikes by the textile unions.

Union-Management Cooperation

In response to the challenge offered by personnel managers and by company unions, a number of the trade unions adopted programs of union-management cooperation. The first such plan on a broad basis was entered into by the Baltimore and Ohio Railroad and the Machinists' Union soon after the railroad shopmen's strike in 1922, and was later accepted by other shop crafts and several other railroad systems not already entrenched in company unionism. The cooperative machinery provided for local, regional, and system joint committees of union representatives and super-

---

[11] The National Industrial Conference Board (*Employee-Stock Purchase Plans in 1928*) estimated that in 1928 over a million employees owned or had subscribed for over a billion dollars' worth of securities of the companies by which they were employed. In over 315 companies which reported having employee-stockownership plans, 30 per cent of the employees were stockholders. All the employees of the Firestone Tire and Rubber Company, and 70 per cent of those of the International Harvester Company, owned company stock.

[12] National Industrial Conference Board, *Collective Bargaining Through Employee Representation*, New York, 1933.

visors, which not only handled employee grievances but discussed all questions and problems relating to the greater efficiency and improvement of railroad service. Similar arrangements were entered into by the Association of Street and Railway Employees and the Philadelphia Rapid Transit Company whereby, under the Mitten Plan, the union shared with management the responsibility for promoting efficiency and reducing operating costs.

The Amalgamated Clothing Workers' Union was an outstanding example of a union's willingness to share in management responsibility. Employers were persuaded to allow union experts to go into the shop in order to reorganize the flow of work, subdivide processes, establish production standards, and even substitute machines for hand labor. When such innovations resulted in reductions of the staff, dismissal wages were sometimes provided for the employees laid off; in other instances, such workers were transferred to other plants by the union's centralized hiring hall. In addition to these aids for improving the competitive position of individual firms, the union sometimes loaned money to enable employers to stay in business.

Another instance of union-management cooperation took place in the coal industry. As an aftermath of a bitter strike in the Colorado coal fields in 1927, the United Mine Workers accepted the offer of one of the companies, the Rocky Mountain Fuel and Iron Company which was friendly to union organization, to cooperate with management in order to obtain maximum efficiency so that the company might compete successfully with neighboring non-union mines which paid lower wages. Later, cooperative relations progressed to such an extent that the union undertook sales promotion campaigns to bring more business to the company.

Union motives for entering into cooperative plans with management were twofold. They believed that efficiency provided the key to higher wages, and they also hoped that their endorsement of such programs would encourage non-union employers to welcome unionization. During this period when the unions were unable to win new members through the customary organization drives, many of them adopted the "front-door" approach; that is, organizers went directly to employers and sought closed-shop contracts in return for promises of a more efficient and stable work force.

Left-Wing Movement

Although most of the union leaders during the 'twenties were sufficiently satisfied with the existing role of organized labor not to depart from their customary methods and policies, many workers inside and outside the movement felt that more aggressive action was needed toward union expansion and the betterment of working conditions. Capitalizing on this discontent, some left-wing groups, dominated by the Communist party, formed the Trade Union Unity League in 1928. During the next few years this League organized a number of industrial unions, the most important being in the mining, textiles, and needle trades.

The National Miners' Union was active during the coal strikes in 1931, especially in and around Harlan County, Kentucky. Most of these coal strikes ended in defeat, the few settlements which were made being negotiated with the older United Mine Workers. The National Textile Workers' Union conducted a number of organization strikes among southern textile workers, the best known of which occurred in Gastonia, North Carolina. The establishment of a Needle Trades' Workers Industrial Union marked the culmination of years of bitter strife in the Ladies' Garment Workers.

Although the Trade Union Unity League was active in certain areas, its total membership was probably never over a hundred thousand. In 1934 the League dissolved as a separate organization, and most of its members reentered their respective unions.

REVIVAL UNDER THE NEW DEAL

From a low ebb of less than 3 million members in 1933, labor has developed into a dynamic and expanding movement that includes about 14 million members. While a favorable government has made possible the expansion which has continued almost without interruption since 1933, the workers themselves have been responsible for the actual growth in numbers and influence. Given an even break by the law and courts, large masses of workers have shown a spontaneous desire toward an organized effort to improve their condition of life, and vigorous labor leadership has come to the fore.

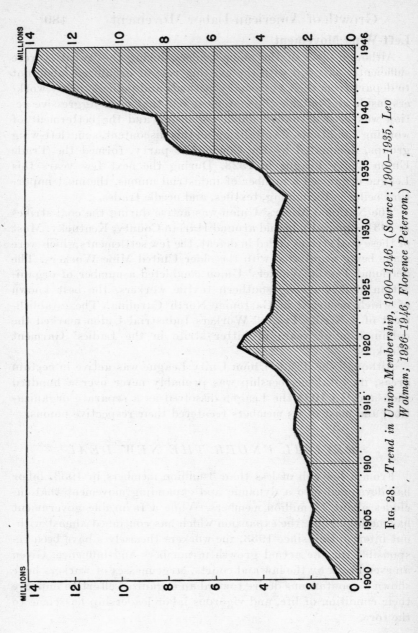

FIG. 28. *Trend in Union Membership, 1900–1946. (Source: 1900–1935, Leo Wolman; 1936–1946, Florence Peterson.)*

The National Industrial Recovery Act

The National Industrial Recovery Act provided that each industry establish codes of fair competition which were to include minimum working standards. Labor was given only an advisory status in the preparation of the codes, although in a few instances, such as clothing and mining, the union representatives were active in determining the labor terms and in seeing that they were enforced. A majority of the codes, however, were prepared with a minimum of worker participation.[13]

Of vital significance to organized labor was Section 7a of the Act, which required that each code contain the provision that "employees shall have the right to organize and to bargain collectively through representatives of their own choosing, and shall be free from the interference, restraint, or coercion of employers . . . in the designation of such representatives. . . ." Labor boards were created to handle disputes arising over the interpretation of this section and to conduct elections to determine bargaining representation.

A wave of union activity followed in the wake of the passage of the National Industrial Recovery Act. Much of this was the result of the planned efforts of unions which sought to organize the open-shop areas in their industries. In many non-union industries and regions, however, the urge to organize emanated from the workers themselves, with union organizers in many instances unable to keep up with the demands made upon them. The biggest gains were made by the mine workers' and the men's and women's clothing unions. For the Amalgamated Clothing Workers the increase represented the regaining of depression losses and some extension into previously unorganized areas. But both the Mine Workers and the Ladies' Garment Workers had suffered such severe losses during the 'twenties that the gains made under the National Industrial Recovery Act signified the virtual revival of these unions.

As a result of the twenty-two months' activity under the Act, membership in American Federation of Labor unions increased

---

[13] After a code was drawn up by the proper trade association, public hearings were held by the Code Administrator, at which any labor representative could appear. As a further protection, a Labor Advisory Board, appointed by the Secretary of Labor, was responsible for seeing that every labor group affected, organized or unorganized, was represented at such hearings.

over 40 per cent; in 1935, for the first time since 1922, their total paid-up membership exceeded 3 million. The Railroad Brotherhoods, benefiting from the 1934 amendment to the Railway Labor Act, also expanded. Organized labor as a whole not only recouped its depression losses and regained some of the following it had lost during the 1920's, but began to enter a few of the hitherto non-union industries. Scattered local unions appeared among the mass-production industries and even among white-collar and agricultural workers.

Company Unions Under the National Industrial Recovery Act

During this time of union revival and expansion, many employers were active in setting up their substitute for trade unions, namely, company unions. Although Section 7a was interpreted by labor to mean the legal right of being represented by unions which were coextensive with employers' trade associations, many employers insisted that dealing exclusively with their own employee representatives fulfilled the requirements of the law about bargaining collectively and that the workers' freedom "from interference, restraint, and coercion" did not preclude assistance from employers in establishing and maintaining company unions. Accordingly, employee representation plans which had been formed before the depression and had become moribund were revived, and new ones were established. Trade associations and employers' counselors not only prepared model plans for their clients, but maintained experts to assist companies in getting them started and keeping them active.

By the spring of 1934, probably one-fourth of all industrial workers were employed in plants which maintained company unions.[14] Almost two-thirds of these unions were established while the National Industrial Recovery Act was in force—a majority of them after a strike had taken place or a trade union had made headway in the plant. Most of the larger steel, rubber, petroleum, and chemical companies had company unions, as well as many of the utility companies and manufacturing concerns of all kinds. A good deal of the time of the National Recovery Administration labor boards was devoted to the disputes arising from the conflict-

---

[14] See Bureau of Labor Statistics, *Characteristics of Company Unions*, Washington, 1935.

ing claims of unions and employers over the interpretation of Section 7a with respect to company unions.

Growth of Unions Under the National Labor Relations Act

The protections afforded labor under the National Industrial Recovery Act had become sufficiently acceptable to induce Congress, a few months after the Supreme Court's invalidation of that Act, to enact the National Labor Relations Act, which guarantees employees "the right to self-organization, to form, join, or assist labor organizations, to bargain collectively through representatives of their own choosing, and to engage in concerted activities for the purpose of collective bargaining or other mutual aid or protection." But passage of a law does not always insure immediate observance, and for almost two years the operation of this Act was seriously impeded by the resistance of many employers who were firmly convinced that the Act would be invalidated in the courts. Its constitutionality was affirmed by the Supreme Court in April, 1937, and a number of Supreme Court decisions thereafter have clarified the coverage of the Act and strengthened the power of the board created to enforce it.

The National Labor Relations Act signified governmental assistance of the first magnitude to organized labor. Union membership more than doubled during the first five years after its passage —from about 3¾ million in 1935 to 8½ million in 1940.

National unions successfully entered the mass-production industries such as the steel, automobile, rubber, and electrical products industries. Workers in industrial centers in the southern states, as well as in many of the smaller communities in the northern states, were aroused to trade union consciousness for the first time. Union organization made some headway among agricultural hired laborers, sharecroppers, and cannery workers. Coal miners were organized in sections where formerly employer hostility, aided by local government officials, had been an effective barrier against unionization. Interest in organization extended into certain groups of white-collar workers, such as newspaper reporters, as well as office workers and retail clerks in some cities. Unions expanded among federal government workers and were established for the first time for many state and local government employees.

These organization drives were accompanied by many strikes, some of which were called as a means of rallying workers to the unions, while others were resorted to when employers refused recognition after the union had obtained majority representation. Most of these strikes took the conventional form of a walkout with picketing. A considerable number, however, were sit-down strikes and these received a great deal of adverse public criticism.

THE CONGRESS OF INDUSTRIAL ORGANIZATIONS

Concurrently with the passage and validation of the National Labor Relations Act, momentous changes had taken place within the labor movement itself. Since the beginning of the labor movement there have been differences of opinion as to whether unions should be organized along occupation or craft lines, or whether they should be coterminous with the industries concerned. The American Federation of Labor unions were predominantly craft organizations, although some were established on an industrial basis and others gradually expanded their coverage to include most or all of the employees within a plant or industry regardless of occupation.

When the organization of the mass-production industries was undertaken during the National Recovery Administration, the issue of craft versus industrial unionism became acute. At the 1934 A. F. of L. convention a resolution was adopted which recognized that there had been "a change in the nature of the work performed by millions of workers in industries which it has been most difficult or impossible to organize into craft unions." The same resolution stated, however: "We consider it our duty to formulate policies which will fully protect the jurisdictional rights of all trade unions organized upon craft lines." The controversy came to a head at the 1935 convention, when the industrial union resolution was defeated and when jurisdiction coextensive with the industry was denied the rubber, automobile, radio, and other unions.

A month after this convention the presidents of eight A. F. of L. unions created a Committee for Industrial Organization "for the purpose of encouraging and promoting the organization of the unorganized workers in mass-production and other industries upon an industrial basis." During the ~~ensuing~~ months other A. F. of L. unions joined the Committee, and membership was later augmented by new groups which had never before been organized, as well as unions not affiliated with the A. F. of L.

The A. F. of L. interpreted the formation of this Committee as "dual in character and as decidedly menacing to its success and welfare." Persons within and outside the labor movement, including the Secretary of Labor and the President of the United States, attempted to heal the breach, but without success; and in May, 1938, the unions participating in the Committee were expelled from the A. F. of L. A few months later, the 32 international unions, together with the city and state bodies then forming the Committee for Industrial Organization, met in constitutional convention and established the Congress of Industrial Organizations.

The formation of the Congress of Industrial Organizations caused a spectacular growth in unionization of the mass-production industries. But the dynamics and influence of the new labor movement extended beyond its immediate membership. Many of the older craft unions, responding to the challenge of the newer unions, extended their jurisdictions to include semi-skilled and un-skilled workers and in many plants functioned as industrial unions.[15] Likewise the boldness and vigor displayed by some of the new leaders in the C.I.O. have influenced other union leaders to strive for greater gains for their members. Of momentous significance, not only to labor but to the country at large, has been the change which the C.I.O. has wrought with respect to workers' participation in politics and governmental affairs.

The C.I.O. and Political Action

From the date of its formation, the A. F. of L. has followed a non-partisan political policy of supporting its friends and opposing its enemies regardless of their party affiliations. This non-partisanship is based on the belief that (1) partisan politics might create dissension among its members and turn their attention away from trade union matters, (2) neutrality is more effective for obtaining political concessions since competing candidates must bid

---

[15] When the craft unions first began to enroll production workers and others who had not served an apprenticeship, they were sometimes classified as "B" members without full voting rights. This policy has been largely discontinued.

for the members' support, and (3) labor should not run the risk of identifying itself with any particular party because it would lose all its political influence if that party should be defeated.[16]

In contrast to this traditional policy of the American labor movement, the C.I.O. is convinced that vigorous activity in political affairs is necessary if labor is to retain and increase its economic gains. In 1936 various C.I.O. unions, joined by several A. F. of L. unions, established a Labor's Non-Partisan League which campaigned for the reelection of the New Deal administration. Subsequently, New York unions took an active part in the American Labor party, although many withdrew in the spring of 1944 on the grounds that the Communists had gained control.

The impetus for direct political action on a national scale was strengthened during 1943, when widespread expressions in the daily press, state legislatures, and Congress aroused fears that the New Deal labor gains were in jeopardy.[17] To assure the continuation of the New Deal program, both national and international, the C.I.O. established a Political Action Committee which carried on an unprecedented educational program that is generally believed to have had a major influence on the outcome of the 1944 elections.

Subsequently, the Political Action Committee continued to be a very active force in primary and election campaigns, as was

---

[16] While non-partisanship has been the guiding rule of the A. F. of L., upon a few occasions it has endorsed particular presidential candidates, and a number of its affiliated organizations from time to time have actively sponsored political parties and occasionally have gone so far as to advocate a separate labor party. Samuel Gompers, first and long-time president of the A. F. of L., actively participated in the Democratic party campaign in 1908 after he was repulsed by the Republicans in his efforts to obtain relief from the courts' use of the Sherman Anti-Trust Act and injunctions in labor disputes. He continued to support the Democratic party, although less actively, until 1924 when, in protest against the conservative platform and candidate this party had chosen, he persuaded the A. F. of L. Executive Council to endorse a new third party—the Progressive party, which also received the official support of the railroad brotherhoods in that election. Prior to this, in 1919–1922, a number of A. F. of L. state federations in the Middle West had identified themselves with the Farmer-Labor party, which was successful in a number of state and local elections.

[17] In 40 state legislatures bills were introduced to restrict various activities and practices of labor unions, although only eleven of these bills actually became law during the year. See chap. 21. In Congress the Connally-Smith War Labor Disputes Act was interpreted by unions as anti-labor.

evidenced by the daily press notices which commonly designated candidates according to whether or not they had Political Action Committee endorsement.

UNION ACTIVITY DURING WORLD WAR II[18]

All branches of organized labor took an active part in many phases of the war production program. At the outset, President Roosevelt indicated that the safeguards afforded labor by the National Labor Relations Act, the Fair Labor Standards Act, and the Public Contracts Act were not to be sacrificed but rather to be utilized to strengthen morale and improve productive efficiency. Organized labor was represented on the Council of National Defense established in May, 1940; when the Office of Production Management was created in January, 1941, a labor representative was appointed as associate director, and in a later reorganization a labor representative served in the dual capacity of vice-chairman of both the War Production Board and the War Manpower Commission.

Maritime unions cooperated with the Maritime Commission and the Labor Department in working out plans for war risk insurance, as well as means for manning newly acquired merchant vessels. The building and metal trades and other unions assisted in supplying skilled workers as instructors in the newly established training centers. The Treasury Department sought the assistance of the unions in the sale of war bonds. Under the auspices of the War Production Board, labor-management committees were established in hundreds of plants for the purpose of "meeting such problems as the maximum war use of the equipment and manpower of every shop and factory, the spreading of war orders, the orderly transfer and retaining of workers for war jobs, the conversion of strategic war materials, as well as many other questions." A large majority were in unionized plants where union members served as the employee representatives on the joint committees.

Direct participation in government administration was pro-

---

[18] For an account of the various activities and problems of organized labor during the war, see *Labor Relations and the War*, American Academy of Political and Social Science, November, 1942, Philadelphia; also Labor Research Association, *Labor Fact Book*, International Publishers, New York, 1943, vol. vi.

vided in the tripartite National War Labor Board which was established in January, 1942, as a "supreme court for labor disputes." So long as this Board confined its activities to the original purpose, organized labor enthusiastically endorsed it as an example of voluntary cooperation by management, labor, and government. There was considerable dissatisfaction, however, after the Board was given responsibility for administering the wage stabilization program (in September, 1942). On the whole, cordial relations with organized labor were maintained by the War and Navy Departments, both of which employed labor relations experts at their Washington headquarters, as well as in the important production centers, to plan and direct labor policies and assist in settling differences between unions and military authorities. As a morale builder, union leaders were taken to training centers and foreign combat areas to see how guns and ammunition were being used and to gain firsthand knowledge of war production needs.

POST-WAR STRAINS

When the last bomb was dropped over Japan the semblance of union-management cooperation which had been fostered during the war disappeared in large sections of our industry. Workers had become more and more restive under the wage stabilization program, and when overtime and other war bonus payments ended they were determined to have their wage rates increased. Moreover, they insisted that employers, with their accumulated war profits and bright outlook for an era of high production, could afford pay increases without jeopardizing the price stabilization program. The employers, on the other hand, contended that this was impossible and gave as one reason the decline in worker efficiency which they stated had taken place during the war years when jobs were plentiful.

Underlying the wage disputes was the old, unresolved issue of what constitutes the necessary functions and prerogatives of management, and to what degree and along what lines workers shall participate in the making and administration of plant policies. Concretely, this is a question of the interpretation of collective bargaining, and many employers who asserted they were in favor of the principle of collective bargaining were nevertheless in wide disagreement with their unions over important matters pertaining to shop management.

With the hope that some workable solution of these major issues could be found, President Truman called a Labor-Management Conference on Industrial Relations in November, 1945. After several weeks' discussion, the conference adjourned with no agreement between management and labor on the issue, as stated in the agenda, of "management's right to manage." This conference was a disappointment insofar as it was unable to achieve any meeting of minds on the major specific problems facing industry and labor. In contrast to the similar conference after the First World War, however, there was no disagreement over the principle or right of collective bargaining per se, and some constructive recommendations were made for the improvement of collective bargaining contracts and the settlement of plant grievances.

The discontent of workers was expressed in the numerous and prolonged strikes which took place during the winter and spring of 1945–1946. The strikes resulted in a general lifting of wage levels, but this was a Pyrrhic victory because price controls were simultaneously relaxed and the cost of living advanced. Not only was organized labor unsuccessful in its efforts to maintain existing price controls, but Congress enacted practically none of the legislation which the unions sponsored as a means of smoothing the transition from a war to a peacetime economy and improving the general condition of all workers. Proposed bills to guarantee full employment, raise the minimum legal wage level, liberalize and extend the coverage of social security and unemployment benefits, provide health insurance and housing programs, and retain the Employment Service in the federal government were either rejected entirely or amended to such a degree that they had little resemblance to the original measures which organized labor had sponsored.

Frustrated at the Capitol in Washington, organized labor reacted in two directions. Both the A. F. of L. and the C.I.O. undertook union organization drives in the southern states in order to increase their membership and influence in an area where "anti-labor" sentiment was strong, and both groups also intensified their general political activities.

Organized labor emerged from the war with more than 13¾ million members. At least a third of the country's population lived in families whose wage earners were members of labor unions. Although less than half of the total employed wage earners were dues-paying members, union strength was greater than this pro-

TABLE 26.   Labor Union Membership, 1900–1946[19]

Year	Average Annual Membership	Year	Average Annual Membership
1900	868,500	1923	3,622,000
1901	1,124,700	1924	3,536,100
1902	1,375,900	1925	3,519,400
1903	1,913,900	1926	3,502,400
1904	2,072,700	1927	3,546,500
1905	2,022,300	1928	3,479,800
1906	1,907,300	1929	3,442,600
1907	2,080,400	1930	3,392,800
1908	2,130,600	1931	3,358,100
1909	2,005,600	1932	3,144,300
1910	2,140,500	1933	2,973,000
1911	2,343,400	1934	3,608,600
1912	2,452,400	1935	3,890,000
1913	2,716,300	1936	4,700,000
1914	2,687,100	1937	7,400,000
1915	2,582,600	1938	8,000,000
1916	2,772,700	1939	8,200,000
1917	3,061,400	1940	8,500,000
1918	3,467,300	1941	10,500,000
1919	4,125,200	1942	12,000,000
1920	5,047,800	1943	13,500,000
1921	4,781,300	1944	13,750,000
1922	4,027,400	1945	13,600,000
		1946	13,800,000

portion would seem to indicate, because most of the members were employed in the basic industries. A large majority of the workers employed in manufacturing, transportation, mining, and construction were union members, whereas a minority of those employed in the service and clerical occupations and in agriculture belonged to labor unions.

During the decade preceding the close of the war, union membership had increased threefold and collective bargaining had be-

[19] 1900–1935 figures by Leo Wolman, in Bulletin No. 68, National Bureau of Economic Research, New York, 1937; figures for 1936–1946 are estimates by the present author.

come the prevailing practice throughout most of the major industries. Collective bargaining was protected by law and endorsed by most sections of the general public.[20]

In spite of all the progress which American labor unions have made during recent years, they face many problems and uncertainties; some of these are discussed in Chapter 22. Before they can be understood, it is necessary to know more about the mechanics and policies of union organizations and existing collective bargaining procedures, matters which are discussed in succeeding chapters.

SELECTED REFERENCES[21]

Bonnett, Clarence E., *Employer's Associations in the United States,* The Macmillan Company, New York, 1922.

Brooks, R. R. R., *When Labor Organizes,* Yale University Press, New Haven, 1937.

Commons, John R., and associates, *History of Labor in the United States to 1896,* The Macmillan Company, New York, 1918.

Galenson, Walter, *Rival Unionism in the United States,* American Council on Public Affairs, Washington, 1941.

Gompers, Samuel, *Seventy Years of Life and Labor,* E. P. Dutton & Co., Inc., 1925.

Green, William, *Labor and Democracy,* Princeton University Press, Princeton, 1939.

Harris, Herbert, *American Labor,* Yale University Press, New Haven, 1939.

Logan, H. A., *History of Trade Union Organization in Canada,* University of Chicago Press, Chicago, 1928.

Lorwin, L. L. *The American Federation of Labor,* Brookings Institution, Washington, 1933.

Marquand, H. A., *Organized Labor in Four Continents,* Longmans, Green & Company, Inc., New York, 1939.

---

[20] The value of a free labor movement to a democracy was emphasized when the State Department and our military forces encouraged and facilitated the rebuilding of labor organizations in occupied Germany and Japan. Faced with the responsibility of building democracies in foreign lands, government authorities who previously had been indifferent to labor unions were brought to the realization that a free labor movement is one of the major pillars of a democracy.

[21] In addition to the general titles listed here, the student is referred to the numerous books dealing with particular unions.

Millis, Harry A., and Montgomery, Royal, *Organized Labor*, McGraw-Hill Book Company, Inc., New York, 1945, vol. iii.

Perlman, Selig, *History of Trade Unionism in the United States*, The Macmillan Company, New York, 1923.

Perlman, Selig, and Taft, Philip, *History of Labor in the United States, 1896–1932*, The Macmillan Company, New York, 1935, vol. iv.

Saposs, David J., *Readings in Trade Unionism*, Doubleday-Doran & Company, Inc., New York, 1926.

Slichter, Sumner H., *Union Policies and Industrial Management*, Brookings Institution, Washington, 1941.

Walsh, J. Raymond, *CIO Industrial Unionism in Action*, W. W. Norton & Company, Inc., New York, 1937.

18

UNION STRUCTURE AND
INTERNAL GOVERNMENT

"ORGANIZED LABOR" REFERS TO THOSE WORKERS WHO HAVE COM-
bined into organizational units of one kind or another for the purpose of improving their economic condition. The "labor movement"
connotes the unified purpose, activities, and aspirations of such
workers. Neither term relates specifically to the structural arrangements by which workers group themselves, although such
arrangements are the basic elements of any general movement,
since its character and effectiveness are influenced strongly by its
internal mechanism and rules of operation.

Organized labor is a composite of different types and hierarchies
of organizations with varying kinds of relationships and lines of
control. At the base are the local unions to which every member
belongs and to which he pays his dues. These local unions have
lateral and vertical affiliations, the most important of which are
the national unions. The national unions, in turn, may be federated
with other national and international organizations.

FEDERATED ORGANIZATIONS

Most labor unions at the present time are affiliated with either
the American Federation of Labor or the Congress of Industrial
Organizations, although there are important exceptions. A number of railroad and government workers' unions, for instance, have
never belonged to the federated groups. Several other unions have
at various times belonged to either the A. F. of L. or the C.I.O.
but for some specific reasons have withdrawn or been expelled.

The major functions of the federated organizations, both the

A. F. of L. and the C.I.O., are (1) to promote the interests of workers and unions before the legislative, judicial, and administrative branches of government; (2) to expand union organization, both directly and by assisting their member unions; (3) to provide research, legal, and other technical assistance to their members; (4) to publish periodical journals and other literature dealing with economic problems and general matters of interest to labor; (5) to represent and promote the cause of labor before the general public; (6) to determine the jurisdictional boundaries of their affiliated unions and to protect them from dual unionism; and (7) to serve as spokesman for their unions on international affairs, especially international labor movements.

Historically and structurally the A. F. of L. and the C.I.O. are agents of their constituent organizations, having only such powers and engaging in only such activities as have been assigned to them by their affiliates. Although the C.I.O. tends to assert more control over its affiliated unions than does the A. F. of L., neither federated organization has any direct authority over the internal affairs or activities of its member unions so long as they do not impinge upon the jurisdiction of another affiliated union. The federated organizations' only actual power is that of expulsion from the central body.

The annual conventions, attended by delegates from each affiliated unit, are the supreme lawmaking bodies of both organizations. Decisions and instructions of the conventions are carried out by the executive councils, and the responsible administrative agents are the general presidents and secretary-treasurers. Most of the revenue for the support of the A. F. of L. and the C.I.O. is derived from per capita taxes and from portions, usually one-half, of the initiation fees charged new members. The tax of the A. F. of L. amounts to 2 cents per member per month for unions having up to 200,000 members, and $1\frac{1}{2}$ cents per member for unions in excess of 200,000. The C.I.O. tax is 5 cents per month from each member.

Departments of the American Federation of Labor

Since most of its constituent unions are industrial in character, the C.I.O. has not found it necessary to establish departments through which the various craft unions can seek to settle their

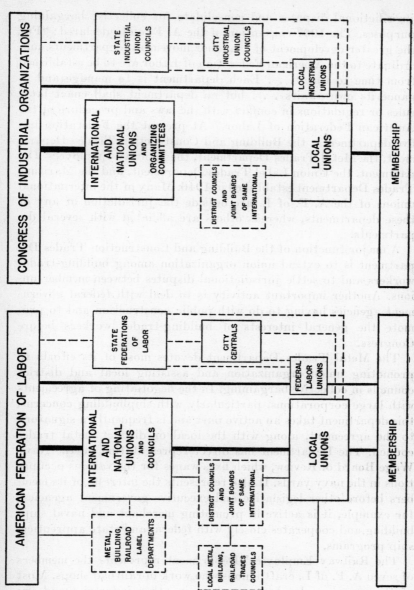

Fig. 29. Structure of U. S. Labor Organizations.

jurisdictional disputes and consolidate for collective bargaining purposes. The 1907 convention of the A. F. of L. declared: "For the greater development of the labor movement, departments subordinate to the American Federation of Labor are to be established from time to time. . . . Each department is to manage and finance its own affairs . . . but no department shall enact laws, rules or regulations in conflict with the laws and procedure of the American Federation of Labor." At present the Federation has five departments: the Building and Construction Trades Department, the Metal Trades Department, the Railway Employees' Department, the Union Label Trades Department, and the Maritime Trades Department established in 1946. Many of the international unions of the A. F. of L. are outside the jurisdiction of any of these departments, whereas others are affiliated with several departments.

A major function of the Building and Construction Trades Department is to extend union organization among building-trades workers and to settle jurisdictional disputes between member unions. Another important activity is to deal with federal government agencies having to do with public construction and to promote the general interests of building-trades workers before Congress.

The Metal Trades Department devotes most of its efforts to promoting union organization and assisting local and district councils in collective bargaining. In the negotiating of agreements with large corporations, particularly with shipbuilding concerns, this department takes an active part and is frequently a signatory to the agreement, along with the local or district metal trades council. The Department has direct representation on the Navy Wage Board of Review, which fixes wages for the various occupations in the navy yards. It also represents the interests of its members before other legislative and executive government agencies; for example, it is active in promoting merchant and naval shipbuilding and cooperates closely with federal and state apprenticeship programs.

The Railway Employees' Department represents the members of seven A. F. of L. craft unions who work in railroad shops. Most of these unions also have members in other industries and are therefore affiliated with the Building and Construction and the Metal Trades Departments. The Railway Employees' Department organizes what is known as "system federations," which are composed of all its members in the various craft unions working for the same carrier or railroad company. The Department maintains general supervision over the activities of the system federations, and sanction must be obtained from it on all proposed agreements with employers as well as contemplated strike action. Jurisdictional disputes between the crafts and concerted demands for wage increases are referred to the Department for action. Any grievance which cannot be settled by the system federation involved is referred to the Department, which decides whether or not it should go to the Railway Adjustment Board. Only the Department may invoke the services of the National Mediation Board (see Chapter 20).

The Union Label Trades Department is composed of all the affiliated A. F. of L. unions which use labels, cards, buttons, or other insignia to designate the products or services of their members. The purpose of the union label is to promote union organization and union standards of workmanship by appealing to the consumer. The label is especially designed to channel the purchasing power of union members, who make up a large portion of the consuming public, into buying union-made goods and services. The Department conducts advertising campaigns, issues union label directories, and in union conventions and literature urges members and their families to patronize union goods.

City and State Central Bodies

International unions are primarily concerned with protecting and improving the working conditions of members within their particular trades or industries. To take care of the many matters of common interest to workers in all trades, and to provide a means for a united effort for the general improvement of conditions of labor, unions representing different trades and industries affiliate for concerted action. The A. F. of L. and the C.I.O. represent such affiliations at the top level. Locally, there are the city centrals, which are affiliates of all A. F. of L. local unions within the city, and the city industrial councils to which the C.I.O. locals belong. On the state level are the A. F. of L. state federations and the C.I.O. state industrial councils.

The city organizations are composed of representatives from all the member local unions; the state organizations include delegates from the city organizations as well as from all the affiliated local unions in the state. Membership in the city and state organizations is optional with the locals, although most of them belong. However, no local which does not belong to an international affiliated with the A. F. of L. or the C.I.O., as the case may be, may belong to their respective city and state organizations. The state federations and state industrial councils are concerned chiefly with legislative and educational matters. They hold annual conventions in which programs of general interest to all the workers in the state are formulated, initiate legislation and appear before state legislatures, and in various ways promote organized labor's interests before the public.

The A. F. of L. city centrals go by various names such as Trades and Labor Assembly, Trades and Labor Council, Central Labor Council, Central Labor Union. The city bodies of the C.I.O. are officially called "City Industrial Union Councils." In contrast to the state organizations, these city organizations deal more on the economic front, serving as clearinghouses for the locals and assisting them in dealing with employers. Most of them issue weekly or monthly papers which give the local labor news as well as important items concerning unions and workers generally. They are the agencies which, next to the local unions, touch the individual workers most closely.

INTERNATIONAL UNIONS[1]

The international and national unions are the autonomous, self-governing units of the labor movement. Even though an inter-

---

[1] Labor organizations in this country are commonly called "international" unions because most of them have some members in Canada as well as in the United States. A majority of their constitutions describe their coverage as extending throughout "the United States, its territories and possessions, and Canada," although some specifically cite Alaska, Hawaii, Puerto Rico, and the Canal Zone as well as continental United States and Canada. The constitutions of some unions, especially the railroad and maritime organizations, add Newfoundland and Mexico and a few indicate "North America" or "Central and South America" or "the entire Western Hemisphere." Even though their constitutions may designate broad coverage, few if any of the standard labor unions at the present time have locals outside the United States and her possessions, and Canada.

For the sake of brevity and because of its general usage in trade union circles, the author throughout this volume uses the term "international" when referring to any of the bona fide labor unions in this country.

national union is affiliated with a larger body such as the A. F. of L. or the C.I.O., it retains its independence as a self-governing organization so far as its internal affairs are concerned. Even with respect to outside activities, the international union exercises wide latitude. It may, for instance, on its own initiative sponsor political programs and legislative measures so long as such endorsements do not violate the fundamental principles and policies of the general labor movement with which it is affiliated.

The chief functions of the international are to extend union organization throughout the trade or industry over which it has jurisdiction in order that uniform working standards may be obtained, to advise and assist its locals in negotiating agreements with employers and to see that such agreements are adhered to, and to participate in the program of the federated organization (A. F. of L. or C.I.O.) to which it is affiliated. Many of the internationals maintain staffs of economic and legal advisers to assist their locals as well as their own officers; practically all publish weekly or monthly periodicals for distribution to their members.

The methods by which the international accomplishes its purposes vary according to the rules and traditions of the union, its leadership, the condition of the industry, and the general economic situation at any particular time. Under some circumstances, for example, the international may deal directly with an employer or an employer's association, although usually the local union is the active party in negotiating agreements. Some internationals require their locals to obtain permission from their international officers before a strike may be called; others merely lay down rules such as requiring a majority vote of the members affected before a strike is called. However, if the local expects financial aid from its international in the form of strike benefits, the approval of the international officers is always necessary.

Number and Size of International Unions

There are at present about 170 labor organizations whose jurisdictions are broad enough to justify their being called international or national unions; of these, approximately 100 are affiliated with the A. F. of L. and 40 with the C.I.O. Several of the non-affiliated unions have at one time belonged to either the A. F. of L. or the C.I.O. but for various reasons have withdrawn or been suspended. Most of them, including eight of the railroad unions and six organizations of government workers, have always had an independent status.

International unions vary in size from fewer than a hundred to almost a million members. Differences in size may be due to the jurisdictional character of the union, the extent to which it has been able to organize the trade or industry in which it has jurisdiction, and the number of workers employed in the trade or industry. In general, unions covering entire industries, or several categories or trades, tend to be larger than those confined to single crafts.

Practically all the ten unions which now have fewer than a thousand members are confined to particular skilled trades, some of them trades that are now becoming obsolete. The six unions with over a half million members, on the other hand, include employees in all or most of the occupations within an entire industry or even several industries; the Automobile, Aircraft, and Agricultural Implement Workers, as its name implies, covers three expanding industries. The United Steelworkers covers workers in both steel and aluminum production and fabrication plants. The United Mine Workers includes not only bituminous and anthracite miners but workers engaged in coal processing, chemical, and other industries. Although the Brotherhood of Carpenters and Joiners, the Association of Machinists, and the Brotherhood of Teamsters, Chauffeurs, Warehousemen, and Helpers originally were confined largely to particular groups of workers, they now accept persons employed in all or most of the occupations in related industries and plants.

Craft Versus Industrial Unions

The kind and variety of occupations and workers included in a union's jurisdiction have far-reaching effects on employer-union bargaining relations, on interunion relations, and upon the size and character of the union itself. What the jurisdiction of a union is at any given time is determined by the union, subject to the approval of its affiliated body. Insofar as it does not trespass upon the claimed jurisdiction of any other union affiliated with the same general organization (that is, the A. F. of L. or the C.I.O., whichever the case may be), a union may expand its coverage at will.

Likewise, it may choose not to include certain occupations or groups of workers. In the case of an unaffiliated or independent union, the only limitation on its jurisdiction is its ability to enlist the support of the workers it wishes to have as members.

While the constitutions and sometimes the names of the unions are designed to indicate their claim to coverage, jurisdictional lines are never fixed or settled over a long period of time. Unions tend to respond to the changes taking place in industry itself, and in a dynamic industrial situation there necessarily are frequent amalgamations as well as divisions, transfers, and expansions of jurisdictions. Realignments in the corporate or managerial units of business, increasing mechanization, and changes in materials and processes bring about conditions which call for adjustments in union jurisdiction. Such changes are likely to create potential areas of conflict between unions, resulting in jurisdictional disputes and rival and dual unionism. One of the major concerns of organized labor has been to find ways and means of settling amicably these recurring problems of adjustment to changes in business structure and processes. If the adjustment is too delayed or is not sufficiently adequate, it may jeopardize the very existence of a union; it may even cause serious defections or upheavals in the entire labor movement, such as took place when the C.I.O. was formed.

To indicate their general type of jurisdiction, unions are sometimes referred to as being either craft or industrial in character. A strictly craft union consists of workers who have undergone an apprentice training and whose acquired skills enable them to carry through to completion a particular process usually requiring manual dexterity with tools. A craft union crosses industry lines—that is, it has members in various industries—since industries producing entirely different commodities or services include some processes or occupations which are similar. In contrast, an industrial union is identified with a particular industry and covers all the workers, skilled and unskilled, who are employed in that industry.

As a matter of fact, few unions at the present time fall within either of these extreme categories of craft versus industrial organizations, and no two persons would classify existing unions alike. One example of a craft union is the Brotherhood of Loco-

motive Engineers. Illustrations of unions whose jurisdictions cover
entire industries are the clothing and textile unions. A number of
unions are multicraft; that is, they include several parallel and
somewhat related occupations. Usually they represent an amalga-
mation of two or more unions which in some instances is indicated
by their name—for example, the Bricklayers, Masons and Plaster-
ers International Union. Some unions, including the six largest already mentioned, can be termed multi-industrial since they include
within their jurisdiction workers engaged in all occupations in
several different industries.

Not only do unions readjust their jurisdiction from time to
time in respect to industrial changes, but the same union may
function on a craft basis in some branches of an industry and as
an industrial union in others. The Brotherhood of Carpenters and
Joiners, for example, operates as a craft union in building construction and as an industrial union in logging camps and furniture plants. This union is sometimes referred to as a "vertical"
union because its jurisdiction is built around the commodity wood
—from the tree to lumber to building and furniture. The Meat
Cutters and Butcher Workmen functions as a craft union in local
retail stores but as an industrial union in the packing industry.
The Brotherhood of Electrical Workers and the Association of
Machinists operate as craft unions in railroad shops and outside
construction work but are frequently organized on an industrial
basis in manufacturing plants.

Internal Government

The supreme authority and sole legislative body of all international unions is the general convention, which is composed of delegates from all the local organizations. Because of the importance
of conventions as the final authority on all union matters, the frequency and regularity with which they are held, the distribution of
voting power, and the manner in which officers are elected are important criteria of a union's democratic administration. Ever-
tighter control by a few officers inevitably results, for instance,
when conventions are postponed from year to year and when the
attending delegates are predominantly the paid organizers or representatives chosen by the officers.

A majority of the international unions hold conventions either annually or biennially and most of the others hold conventions every three or four years. Several unions, mostly with small memberships, hold conventions every five years or only upon a referendum vote of their members.

Every international has a general executive board, chosen at the convention, which is responsible for the administration of the union's affairs and which serves as an appellate body on matters referred to it by the locals as well as the individual members. Although not the same in all unions, most general executive boards have the responsibility and authority to issue and withdraw local charters and to repeal any local's by-laws which do not conform to the international constitution; to remove any officer for incompetence or non-performance of duties and to fill the vacancy until the next convention; to take charge of the affairs of any local when it is decided that this is necessary "to protect or advance the interests of the union"; to pass upon all claims, grievances, and appeals from locals and other subordinate bodies; to reverse or repeal any action of any international officer; to select auditors for the auditing of books, and to prepare the report for the forthcoming convention; to supervise the policies and publication of the official journal; to determine the amount and methods of bonding all the officers who handle union funds, and to levy assessments in accordance with the terms of the constitution.

The general president is necessarily vested with the chief responsibility for the day-to-day conduct of the union's affairs. As in any other organization, the actual powers and influence exercised by an elected leader depend about as much upon the will and ability of the person holding office as upon the authority formally granted by the constitution. Through the prestige of his office, as a presiding chairman and ex officio member of committees, the union president has great influence in determining what and how matters are discussed and voted upon at executive board meetings and general conventions. As administrator of the union's day-to-day activities, his decisions and course of action vitally affect not only the internal affairs of the union and its members but also public opinion. In most unions the president's decisions are subject to the approval of the executive board and appeal to the convention; a few unions give their presidents final authority on many matters of basic policy.

LOCAL ORGANIZATIONS

To the union member, his local union is his point of contact with the other organized workers in his trade or industry; it is the agency to which he pays his dues and expresses his demands for better working conditions, and through which he seeks settlement of his grievances and participates in the union's broader political and economic programs. Most generally it is the local union that deals with employers for its members, although the international union may assist in particularly difficult or important situations.

There are at present approximately 60,000 local unions in the United States, ranging in size from a dozen to over 100,000 members. Locals may be organized on an occupational or craft basis, or on a plant or multiplant basis. The unit of organization of a local does not necessarily parallel the jurisdictional boundaries of its parent body; e.g., many locals of the clothing and other industrial unions are organized on a craft basis. Locals for each craft covering numerous employers in the same city or area are common in the building, printing, metal, and trucking industries. Railroad locals are organized on a craft basis by railroad systems. In manufacturing, locals confined to single plants are most common in unions whose jurisdictions cover all the occupations in an industry. However, there are some large locals which cover workers in a number of manufacturing establishments in the same city and industry that are sometimes referred to as amalgamated locals.

Internal Government of Locals

Local unions are necessarily subordinate to their international organization and must abide by its constitutions and convention rulings. Membership qualifications, area and trade jurisdiction, and methods of suspension and expulsion of members are among the matters subject to control by the international. Within these limits, however, the day-to-day policies and activities of the local union are determined by its membership. For example, the constitution of most internationals specifies the election procedure and the various officers which their locals are required to maintain, but both the choice of individuals for these offices and their pay are determined by the locals.

Although subject to the rules of the international, each local has a voice in the formulation of these rules and policies through representation at the general convention. The number of delegates which a local may send to the convention, the highest governing body of the union, is dependent upon its paid-up membership as prescribed in the international's constitution. Even though not specified in the constitution, the president of the local is ordinarily selected as a delegate and is accompanied by others elected by the members if the local is of sufficient size to permit more than one delegate.

In large locals, one or more of the elected officers may devote his full time to union affairs. In small locals the elected officers usually continue to work at their trade and receive no regular salary from the union; the presidents and vice-presidents are generally paid a few dollars for each meeting over which they preside, and the secretary-treasurers are paid a few hundred dollars a year for keeping the books. In addition to the regularly elected officers, most unions have so-called "business agents" who are full-time paid employees of the locals with no definite term of office, thus providing continuity to the local's activities. Most business agents have served as officers of the local and have been experienced workers in the industry, and thus know the language of the trade.

The monthly or semi-monthly meeting of the local is the medium through which the membership controls the policies and activities of the union. As with other kinds of voluntary organizations, many unions experience great difficulty in getting full attendance at meetings. Although poor attendance is no indication of lukewarm loyalty to the union, as is evidenced by the wholehearted response during a crisis such as a strike, nevertheless the character and effectiveness of a union are strongly influenced by the attendance at local meetings, since control of any organization's affairs inevitably goes to the few faithful attendants and they may or may not be representative of the entire membership. In order to insure maximum attendance and avoid complaints from members that measures were adopted about which they had no knowledge, many unions require their members to attend all or a specified minimum number of meetings a year and impose fines for unexcused absences, with possible expulsion for repeated absences.

Joint Boards and Councils

Joint boards and trades councils are combinations of locals having jurisdiction in related trades or the same industry. In some unions they are referred to as joint boards, while in others they are called city or district trades councils. Whatever their title or exact geographical coverage, their primary purpose is to secure united action in collective bargaining and uniform working conditions within the same industry in a given city or area. With most unions it is mandatory to have a joint board or council whenever the union has a given number (usually three or more) of locals in the city or area, and most internationals require all their locals within the community to belong to the council after it is once established.

There are two types of joint boards or councils: (1) those composed of locals of the same international, usually referred to as joint boards; and (2) those composed of locals of different internationals having jurisdiction over allied trades in the same industry, usually referred to as trades councils.

In the clothing and textile industries, as an example, the joint boards are made up of locals of the same internationals. Although these internationals are industrial in character, their locals may be organized on a craft basis, on a plant basis, by section of the industry, or they may be "mixed," i.e., include workers in various occupations within the industry. The joint boards may represent all or most of the various craft and mixed locals in the entire industry in a city or region. In a large clothing center, there may be joint boards for different branches of the industry, such as knit goods, dresses, coats and suits, custom tailoring, neckwear, etc. Similarly, the Teamsters joint councils may be composed of locals covering distinct types of trucking or delivery service—for example, milk delivery, department store or parcel delivery, heavy trucking, and moving vans.

The printing, building, and metal-trades councils are made up of locals belonging to the several unions whose jurisdictions cover allied crafts. City allied printing trades councils, for example, include the locals of the five allied printing trades unions (the Typographical, Pressmen, Bookbinders', Stereotypers' and Electrotypers', and Photo-Engravers' unions). The building and metal-trades councils are also composed of the locals in the various crafts of the same industry. Once a joint board or district council has been

established, the internationals involved require all their locals in
the area to belong, in order to promote harmony among the different crafts within a community as well as to obtain unified action
with employers.

MEMBERSHIP RULES

In any trade or industry in which labor organizations are active,
every worker and employer is directly or indirectly affected by the
rules and regulations having to do with the acceptance and retention of members in the union. In all plants where collective bargaining exists, the non-union employee as well as the union member
is bound by the terms of the contract negotiated by the union. If a
non-union employee is dissatisfied with those terms and decides to
join the union in order to bring about changes in the employment
contract, he immediately becomes interested in the union's qualifications for acceptance.

Membership rules are of paramount importance in the trades
and plants whose contracts require union membership as a condition of employment. Under such closed or union-shop agreements,
members already employed are interested in the rules for maintaining good standing, and applicants and potential applicants
for positions are concerned with the union's entrance requirements.
The employer also is vitally interested because his choice of workers, and perhaps even the number he may employ, is affected by
the union's regulations pertaining to the admission, transfer, and
expulsion of members.

The aim of a union generally is to take in as many as possible
of those employed within its jurisdiction. Although some unions
may place certain restrictions on the acceptance of candidates for
employment, the tendency is in the opposite direction, since it is
the chief aim of the unions to expand their membership by accepting any and all persons who can liberally be interpreted as being
employed in the trade or industry over which they have jurisdiction.

The broad provisions specified in the international unions' constitutions necessarily allow wide latitude in practice within any
local organization. Also, of course, a local union may be able to
circumvent the spirit if not the letter of its international's consti-

tution. For example, the constitution may specify that there shall be no discrimination as to race, but the members of a local organization may have a tacit understanding among themselves not to recommend anyone of the colored race for membership. Likewise, a broad requirement that all applicants must be "of good moral character" may be interpreted variously upon different occasions.

Restrictions on Membership

The attitude of unions on citizenship, sex, and racial requirements has been dominated by the fear that recent immigrants, women, and Negroes are a competitive menace to the wage and working standards which the unions have already obtained or hope to gain. Throughout the years there have been conflicting opinions within the labor movement as to the best course to follow—whether to debar these groups from membership and seek to keep them out of the trade altogether, or allow them to join the union and thus reduce the hazard of having entrants into the trade accept jobs under competitive non-union conditions. Negroes and immigrants, for example, have frequently been employed for strikebreaking and anti-union purposes[2] and women have been hired for wages which are far below union standards.

Most generally, the unions have deemed it wisest in the long run to alleviate the competitive menace of persons willing to accept jobs at low standards by taking them into the unions. A majority of the international unions, both A. F. of L. and C.I.O., are non-restrictive. A number of unions, especially those established at the time of the heavy influx of immigrants into this country, specify that members shall be citizens or at least have applied for their first citizenship papers. Although a dozen of the craft unions restrict membership to males, most of these are in building and other trades where few if any women are employed.

Provisions with respect to political beliefs and affiliations have always presented a delicate problem to unions. The American labor movement has never formally aligned itself with any political party, pursuing instead the policy of endorsing or condemning

---

[2] Notable examples were the use of Negro strikebreakers in the Illinois Central Railroad shopmen's strike in 1911 and the longshoreman and railroad strikes in the early 1920's, and the importation of Negroes in the West Virginia coal fields during the 1920's.

candidates for public office upon their individual voting records on matters which concerned unions and workers generally. In line with this traditional policy of political non-partisanship, the unions have adhered to the general principle that there should be no political qualifications or requirements for individual members.

An important qualification of this general expression of political freedom is specified in some union constitutions and implied in others, namely, that members shall not be identified with any political program that is considered inimical to the present form of American democracy. Thus, a number of constitutions state: "No person shall be excluded by reason of his religious belief or political affiliation *provided* he is not a member of any organization hostile to the American form of government." In contrast to such qualified statements are provisions in many constitutions which specify that persons shall be accepted into the union "regardless of nationality, race, religious or political beliefs or affiliations." The absence of a qualified statement in a union's constitution, or a provision which seemingly places no restrictions upon political action, does not in itself indicate that the union will accept or retain individuals who engage in activities commonly considered to be contrary to American union philosophy. It may merely indicate that no situation or problem has arisen in the union which has caused it to incorporate a specific restriction in its constitution.

By and large, labor unions have been much more liberal in their attitude toward accepting Negroes into membership on an equal basis than have most other groups in this country, including churches and educational and professional organizations. Racial equalitarianism has been the policy adopted by most of the labor movement since the earliest times. For many years after its formation the A. F. of L. insisted that all its affiliated unions eliminate color restrictions in their constitutions in line with its declared policy that "working people must unite and organize irrespective of creed, color, sex, nationality or politics."[3] Much like the initially declared policy of the A. F. of L. is the stated object in the present C.I.O. constitution, namely, "to bring about the effective organiza-

[3] *Convention Proceedings,* 1897, p. 82. For a detailed discussion of the practices and policies of unions with respect to Negroes, see Herbert R. Northrup, *Organized Labor and the Negro,* Harper & Brothers, New York, 1944.

tion of working men and women of America regardless of race, creed, color, or nationality."

The precepts adopted at conventions, however, have sometimes been ignored or been abandoned altogether, at the insistence of rank-and-file members. Not many years after its formation, the A. F. of L. began to admit unions with color restrictions, and its present constitution does not mention membership qualifications. Although the matter is left to each of its constituent unions, when an affiliated international refuses to accept Negroes, the A. F. of L. frequently organizes them into locals (federal labor unions) directly under its jurisdiction.

While none of the C.I.O. internationals have adopted any restrictive rules against Negroes, its officers in a number of instances have had to bring pressure upon their local groups not to deny Negroes the full benefits of union membership and rights established by collective agreements, particularly with reference to upgrading and seniority. In an effort to overcome such prejudices, the C.I.O. and a number of its internationals have established special committees on non-discrimination for the purpose of conducting educational campaigns and investigating and correcting specific instances of discrimination against Negroes.

At present, the absolute exclusion of Negroes by constitutional provision exists only among some of the railroad unions. Although none of the constitutions of other unions explicitly bar Negroes from membership, some allow them an auxiliary status only, and many of their locals exclude them. In some instances restrictions are placed on the kinds of occupations the colored members may pursue, although such restrictions may not appear in the constitutions.

Suspension and Reinstatement

After once joining a union a member is expected to continue his membership as long as he is employed in the industry or trade within the union's jurisdiction. For that reason the term "resignation" is seldom if ever used by unions. If a member changes jobs but remains in the trade or industry over which his union has jurisdiction, he obtains a transfer; if he retires or changes his occupation to one outside the jurisdiction of his union, he applies for an honorable withdrawal or retiring card. Any separation from the union other than honorable withdrawal or transfer is cause for suspension—for example, dues delinquency or, as happens infrequently, violation of union rules.

Union constitutions generally provide that if a member fails to pay his dues for a certain length of time—most commonly two to six months—he is automatically suspended. If a member works for an employer who has a checkoff arrangement with the union, dues paying automatically continues for the duration of his employment with that employer. In some plants which do not have the checkoff, union officers are privileged to collect dues in the work place or at the factory gates on payday. Elsewhere it is the responsibility of each individual member to go to the local union headquarters to pay his monthly or weekly dues.

Requirements for the reinstatement of suspended members vary. In unions with low initiation fees, where there is no closed or union-shop agreement, members may be inclined to allow their dues to lapse if rejoining at any time is too easy. Such lapses in membership tend to take place after a wage increase or other improvement in working conditions has been obtained or, conversely, during times when the union is not able to gain immediate benefits for its members. In unions with relatively high initiation fees, the membership is more likely to be stable, since the cost of reestablishing good standing more than offsets the continued payment of dues.

As a deterrent to frequent lapses in membership, most unions require the full payment of all back dues and assessments, in addition to a specified reinstatement fee, especially if the member has been continually employed in the interim. In some cases the reinstatement fee, or rejoining fee as it is sometimes called, is less than the original initiation fee; where the latter is nominal, the reinstatement fee is likely to be somewhat higher. Some unions make no distinction but require their suspended members to pay the regular initiation fee in addition to all back dues and assessments. A few require no payment of back dues or assessments but have a relatively high reinstatement fee, for example, as much as $30 or $50.

Expulsion

While expulsion for causes other than non-payment of dues is infrequent, it nevertheless is a serious matter and may prove a hardship in individual cases. This is especially true where unions have closed or union-shop agreements with most or all employers in the industry or locality, for in this case expulsion from the union is tantamount to depriving a member of employment in his trade. Unions naturally consider as the most serious offenses the actions by individuals or groups which jeopardize the union's existence or prestige, such as instigating internal factional disruption, promoting or aiding a rival union, or going to court about internal union matters. Here, of course, unions face the same problem as does any political or other organism, namely, the inherent contradictions of group solidarity versus individual freedom.

In their day-to-day functioning, unions and their officers are continually faced with the problem of how to impose the discipline that is necessary for effective group action and at the same time preserve maximum individual freedom of speech; how to maintain organizational cohesion and unity of purpose and at the same time retain sufficient flexibility to permit group protests which might result in changes in the customary procedures. Permissible grounds for expulsion and the methods by which it is consummated are important criteria of the way a union seeks to reconcile the necessities of efficient administration with maximum freedom of expression and action on the part of its members.[4]

Although some union constitutions do not specify particular causes for expulsion, all of them carefully outline the procedure to be used when charges are brought against a member. In many of them the grounds for expulsion are described in such general terms as "violation of union rules" or "continued offense against the union." A number add to these general expressions such specific offenses as intemperance or selling alcoholic beverages (common among railroad unions), accepting a job declared unfair by the union, working in a non-union shop, strikebreaking or, conversely, going out on strike without the sanction of the union. Essentially, such constitutional provisions are designed to permit expulsion only when basic union rules are violated.

In contrast are the provisions in a number of constitutions that

---

[4] For a discussion of intra-union controls and discipline, see Philip Taft, "Judicial Procedure in Labor Unions," *Quarterly Journal of Economics*, May, 1945.

itemize numerous causes for expulsion which, if enforced, might result in the expulsion of a member who openly voiced dissatisfaction or sought to solicit votes for a change in the union's program or officers. Such potential infringements on the members' freedom of speech generally turn on such clauses as "making untruthful statements," "impugning the motives of officers," "misrepresenting the union and its officers." Obviously such clauses are subject to various interpretations under given circumstances. Their potential dangers are greatly mitigated, if not eliminated, if the accused members are insured a fair trial before heavy fines or expulsion is imposed. With few exceptions, the constitutions of international unions provide for open hearings for trial and at least a majority —more generally two-thirds—vote of the local membership, and progressive appeal from local union's action to the international president, the general executive board, and finally to the international convention, or, in a few instances, to a referendum vote of the entire membership.

Foremen and Supervisors

The question of whether or not to allow or require foremen and supervisors to belong to unions has always been a troublesome problem to all parties concerned—management, unions, and the foremen themselves. Most foremen have been promoted from the machine or work bench and in organized shops were of course union members. If they belonged to unions which maintain old age and sick benefit plans, they naturally do not want to lose these benefits toward which they have contributed for many years. Even more important, perhaps, is the risk of losing their seniority rights and the privilege of bumping[5] when they are no longer needed or wanted as foremen. This hazard is increased in seasonal industries where workmen are promoted to foremen during peak seasons and return to the machine or bench during dull seasons.

For an increasing number of foremen the desire to belong to a

---

[5] "Bumping" implies displacement of someone with less seniority. In most instances bumping according to seniority is confined to employees covered by the employer-union agreement. However, in some plants where foremen are not union members, special clauses have been negotiated which give displaced foremen the right to return to their former or to similar jobs according to their seniority standing before promotion to the foremanship or, in some cases, according to their accrued seniority including the time spent as foreman.

union is the same as it is for workers, namely, to exert group pressure in order to improve their economic status. This is especially true where foremen find that as a result of assuming their new duties and responsibilities their hours are longer and their pay little more, and sometimes less, than those of some of the employees who work under them. The desire of foremen to organize into unions is increasing in large mass-production industries where the authority and prestige of the foreman's position have depreciated to the point where he participates very little, if any, in formulating company policies and is given limited leeway in applying such policies in his particular bailiwick. One among hundreds of others of the same status in the company, he is almost as anonymous to the top management as the rank-and-file workers and thus feels that he has little chance for any individual redress of grievances.

So far as union policy is concerned, some of the oldest unions have always favored the practice of having their foremen retain their membership because, as members, they serve to insure adherence to the union's work rules and in dealing with the higher management they can sympathetically interpret union aims and policies. Many unions, on the other hand, have been reluctant to allow members who have been promoted to foremen to continue their membership, and much less willing to accept as members foremen who were not previously members. This policy is based on the belief that the inherent nature of a foreman's job makes him an instrumentality of management in dealing with labor and that there can be no satisfactory commingling of management and union functions. Furthermore, many union members fear the dominant role foremen might take in union affairs if they were permitted to be active members; foremen necessarily have leadership qualities which other members feel might be exercised at union meetings to the disadvantage of the rank and file. It is for this reason that a number of the unions which allow foremen to be members place some restrictions upon their participation in union affairs.

The alternative, however, is not necessarily between foremen not belonging to any union and being members of the union to which the men under them belong, for foremen may be organized into unions confined to persons of their own rank. There are several long-established craft unions that are composed solely of foremen

and supervisors in particular industries; during recent years
several foremen's unions have been established whose jurisdictions
are not confined to one industry as are the older supervisors' organizations. The largest of these is the Foremen's Association of
America, organized in Detroit in 1941.

FINANCES AND DUES

While the total amount of money which passes in and out of all
union treasuries currently amounts to several hundred million
dollars a year, the reserve on hand at any given time in most
unions averages not more than $2 or $3 per member. A substantial
portion of the total income of many unions is paid out in death,
old age, and disability benefits to individual members. The bulk, of
course, is used to advance the general economic interests of the
millions of workers who support the unions and to promote legislation and other measures which will improve the well-being of all
workers, non-union as well as union.[6] In union bookkeeping the
furtherance of these activities is chargeable to general administrative and organizing expenses.

Costs of Administration

On an average, over the years, the greatest items of expense to
unions are the salaries and traveling expenses connected with
administration and organization work, although at certain times
other expenditures may be much greater.[7] The number of full- and
part-time persons on a union's staff will vary not only in relation
to the size of the organization but also in accordance with the activities conducted by the union at any particular time. During an
active membership campaign a union will employ additional or-

---

[6] For example, wage and hour legislation, and safety, health, and social security programs, both federal and state. Not only does organized labor employ
economists, lawyers, and others to take an active part in promoting such legislation, but representatives of the unions are frequently called upon to serve on
tripartite advisory committees and in other ways to assist in the effective administration of the laws. To the extent of the cost of these salaries and other
expenses, the dues-paying members of unions are bearing the costs of benefits
which are shared by all workers affected by the legislation, non-union as well
as union.

[7] A prolonged strike, for example, may involve many times the outlay of ordinary administrative expenses, in addition to loss of dues.

ganizers; if engaged in litigation or negotiating an agreement involving the preparation of a good deal of statistical and legal data, extra lawyers and economists will be employed. Unions which engage in benefit programs must employ actuaries and accountants to administer these activities.

Since practice varies as to the relative amount of the services performed by the international office and its locals, the comparative costs as between international union administration and local union administration are not uniform. In most of the internationals the only elected officers who are paid on a full-time basis are the president and secretary-treasurer. The amounts of their salaries are usually specified in the union's constitution and are determined by convention vote, although some unions also require a majority referendum vote of the membership to change salaries.

The amount of the salaries paid the union's staff personnel conforms with that paid by private industry and the government for similar or comparable work. With respect to the salaries of the elected officers, union practice differs not only according to the union's ability to pay but also according to its general theory of remuneration for such officials, as well as the attitude of the membership toward the particular person holding the office. Some unions, for example, base the salaries of their officers at about or slightly above the highest level of wages earned by their members at their trades. Other unions feel that the prestige and effectiveness of their officers are enhanced if their salaries approximate those received by the employer representatives with whom they deal. In many instances the salary paid a particular president or other official is a token of recognition and appreciation of his long service rather than an established remuneration for the office as such. The salaries of a large majority of union presidents range from $5000 to $10,000 a year; about a dozen receive from $12,000 to $15,000, and at least seven receive from $20,000 to $30,000. In general, the salaries of the full-time vice-presidents and secretary-treasurers are about 20 per cent less than that of the presidents.

Dues and Assessments

Members contribute to the support of their unions by payment of (1) membership dues, usually on a monthly basis; (2) special assessments, usually for some particular purpose; (3) initiation fees when they first join the union, and reinstatement fees if they have withdrawn or allowed their membership to lapse and seek to rejoin. On rare occasions fines may be levied upon members, but these are disciplinary measures and not for revenue purposes.

All money is collected by the local unions, either directly from the members or through the employers when unions have checkoff arrangements. The locals, in turn, forward certain specified sums to their international and the other organizations with which they are affiliated, such as local joint boards, city centrals, and state federations. The amounts going to the federated bodies are usually limited to a few cents per capita taxes a month.

The large majority of union members are now paying dues of $2 a month, although a number are paying only $1.50. Some are paying as much as $3 and $4 a month, and a few are paying $5 or more a month. These latter, almost without exception, are highly skilled craftsmen. In several unions the dues are levied in accordance with earnings—for example, 2 per cent of the weekly wages of each member.

None of the "low dues" unions maintain old age or other pension activities, although some carry group life insurance or maintain burial funds that pay a few hundred dollars upon the death of a member. In most of the unions which have dues as high as $3 or more a month, a substantial portion of the funds collected are used to finance benefit programs such as old age, sickness, and disability pensions. A number of these unions have two classes of membership, beneficial and non-beneficial; where the first class of members may pay dues of $3 or more, the dues of the non-beneficial are $1 or $1.50 a month. The latter members are usually engaged in the less skilled occupations, or persons who were middle-aged or over before they were taken in as members.

On occasion the money received from regular dues may be insufficient to meet all the union's current or anticipated expenses. A union may decide to engage in an intensive organizing drive; its funds may have been depleted because of a prolonged strike or unusually heavy outlays for unemployment and disability benefits; or it may vote to make a contribution to a benevolent cause. For such contingencies a single assessment may be levied upon each member, or a specified assessment may be levied for a given number of months.

Assessments may be levied by the international office, in which case all members of the union pay alike; or they may be levied by individual locals, in which case only the members of the particular locals are affected. Most commonly, assessments may be levied only after a two-thirds favorable referendum vote of the membership affected. Some constitutions impose a limitation even with referendum voting, for example: "not to exceed $2 a year" or "not more than 5 cents in any one month"; and a few prohibit special assessments under any circumstances. On the other hand, in a number of unions the general executive board is given wide latitude and has authority to levy special assessments "whenever necessary" or "whenever necessary to met an emergency."

Initiation Fees

A large majority of the present union members paid a fee of $2 to $5 when they were initiated into their unions, although a considerable number, especially those in the skilled trades belonging to craft unions, paid higher initiation fees—most commonly $10 to $25. Some have paid as much as $50; in a few locals, initiation fees run as high as $200 to $300, with a few instances of $500 or more. Initiation fees, unlike dues, are not levied primarily for the purpose of revenue, and the income from such fees is irregular. During periods of stabilized membership little is received in initiation fees, no matter how high the individual fee may be; during periods of expanding membership, as under wartime production, the initiation fees amount to considerable sums.

Unions which charge relatively high initiation fees regard them in the nature of a fine as well as a means of membership control. They maintain that the older members who have contributed many years to supporting the union have enabled the unions to obtain higher wages and better working conditions than would have existed if there had been no unions. Since newcomers to the trade profit by these hard-won gains, the older members consider initiation fees a reimbursement for past services of the union, a method by which the new members share the cost of improved working conditions which they did not assist in procuring. This is evidenced in the practice of some unions of differentiating between the amount of fee charged those joining before a contract with the employer is signed and those joining after union conditions are established.

Historically, high initiation fees have been a means of controlling the intake into the union as well as into the trade. (To the extent that the union has closed-shop agreements with employers, control of entrance into the trade or industry is of course automatic with control of admission into the union.) Unions which charge high initiation fees justify them on the grounds that they tend to stabilize employment for their members by acting as a deterrent to large influxes of new workers into the trade during temporary booms ; for once new members are accepted, they not only share in the job opportunities during the temporary boom, but also claim rights to jobs when these become scarce. These unions contend that, if the need for extra workers is confined to one locality, their unemployed members elsewhere should be transferred, and that if it is a general but short-time boom the available jobs should be stretched over a longer period for those already in the trade rather than have new members taken in. Unions which charge extremely high initiation fees claim that such fees are seldom if ever actually paid by anyone, but that they are a device for keeping out newcomers.

Financial Records

Provisions for the auditing of accounts and the reporting of the union's finances to the members are an important part of every union constitution. The constitutions of the internationals not only specify the method and frequency of auditing and reporting the internationals' accounts, but also contain regulations concerning their locals' financial records.

Almost all unions require an auditing of funds by certified public accountants at least once a year ; many specify a quarterly or semi-annual audit. The auditor's annual or biennial report is generally incorporated in the executive board's report to the convention and is published in the convention proceedings. Frequently the entire report or an abbreviated summary is published in the union's journal or in a special bulletin for distribution among the members. In response to recent public interest[8] in union finances, a number of unions have adopted the policy of issuing the reports of their certified public accountants in pamphlet form for general

---

[8] Several states have enacted laws which, among other measures, require unions to submit detailed financial reports to designated state agencies. See chap. 21.

distribution. As in business and other organizations, the practice varies with respect to the amount of detail covered in the published reports. Some of the financial reports of unions are brief and general, whereas others cite all items of receipts and disbursements, the reports covering as much as fifty or sixty printed pages.

SELECTED REFERENCES

Harris, Herbert, *American Labor,* Yale University Press, New Haven, 1929.

Hoxie, R. F., *Trade Unionism in the United States,* D. Appleton-Century Company, Inc., New York, 1923.

Johns Hopkins University studies on *American Trade Unions,* Johns Hopkins Press, Baltimore, 1912.

Johnson, Julia E., *Industrial versus Craft Unionism,* The H. W. Wilson Company, New York, 1937.

Lorwin, L. L., *The American Federation of Labor,* Brookings Institution, Washington, 1933.

Peterson, Florence, *American Labor Unions,* Harper & Brothers, New York, 1945.

Peterson, Florence, *Handbook of Labor Unions,* American Council on Public Affairs, Washington, 1943.

Seidman, Joel, *Union Rights and Union Duties,* Harcourt, Brace & Company, Inc., New York, 1943.

Wolman, Leo, *Ebb and Flow in Trade Unionism,* National Bureau of Economic Research, New York, 1936.

19

COLLECTIVE BARGAINING

THE PRIMARY PURPOSE OF LABOR UNIONS IS TO NEGOTIATE WITH employers for the purpose of establishing the terms and conditions under which their members shall be employed. The employer-union agreement represents the consummation of these negotiations. A bilaterally signed agreement indicates that civil rights have been introduced into industry and that the personal, one-sided rule of managers has been replaced by rules and terms in whose making all concerned have had a voice.

A mutual agreement entered into by an employer and a union, like other contracts, is an expression of the various rights, duties, and privileges of those covered by the agreement. On the employee side, the contracting party is the union which a majority of the employees have chosen to represent them.[1] While no law requires employers and employees to agree on any particular terms, once they have reached an understanding the union may require the employer to sign a written agreement.[2] Such agreements are enforceable in the courts like any other contracts.

The manner in which agreements are negotiated, the variety of subjects covered, and their substantive contents vary greatly between industries and within any industry, for the process and results of collective bargaining are necessarily influenced by many factors—general economic conditions, as well as the situation of a particular employer, his attitude toward the union and collective

---

[1] According to law, the terms of the agreement cover minority non-members in the bargaining unit (if such exist), as well as the union members. See the next chapter for a discussion of the National Labor Relations Act.

[2] According to the judicial interpretation of the N.L.R.A., employers are required to enter into signed agreements once the terms of an agreement have been negotiated; in other words, a unilateral statement of employment policy does not fulfill the requirements of collective bargaining.

bargaining, the strength of the union and the ability of its negotiators, and the desires and determination of its members.

Regardless of their specific terms, all employer-union agreements
include two fundamental features, namely, the substantive provisions covering work conditions and the status of the union, and
the rules of procedure for settling questions or disputes over the
interpretation and application of the terms of the agreement. The
latter are of major importance because no formalized body of
regulations can cover the minutia of day-to-day work conditions
or forestall varying interpretations when applied to specific situations. Furthermore, business is a dynamic process; hence contingencies arise which could not be foreseen at the time the agreement
was signed.

The machinery provided in union agreements for the settlement
of grievances and disputes is discussed in the next chapter; here we
are concerned with the process of the negotiation of agreements
and their substantive contents.

THE BARGAINING UNIT

The unit of bargaining has a direct influence on the degree of
standardization of wages and working conditions within an industry or area. Whether collective bargaining takes place between
individual employers and local unions, or through associations of
employers to cover large segments or an entire industry, very
largely determines whether the terms of employment are uniform
or dissimilar. As already discussed in the chapters on wages, standardized wage rates (or other matters involving costs) tend to be
what the marginal employer in the industry can afford, and there
are advantages and disadvantages to everyone concerned in having
a uniform level throughout the industry, or variations based on
individual employers' ability to pay.

The policy of a union and of the employers in any industry with
respect to the bargaining unit may vary from time to time and
from area to area. Among the factors which affect the union's
policy regarding bargaining with an individual employer or on a
wider basis are the strength of the union, the number of employers
and the degree of centralized control in the industry, the size of
the establishments and their proximity to each other, and their

relative prosperity. If a few employers are especially prosperous, the union may wish to bargain with them separately and use these agreements as a vanguard for negotiating agreements elsewhere in the industry.

The willingness or reluctance of employers to bargain collectively on a wide basis depends largely upon their competitive situation. If labor costs are an important factor in selling costs, the employers who are paying relatively high wages may wish to have the entire competitive market under the same or similar agreements. On the other hand, some employers consider it advantageous to pay better than prevailing rates in order to be able to attract the best workers, and therefore do not welcome standardized wages even though they would entail no advance in their own rates.

In general, unions are more favorable to bargaining on an industry-wide basis than are employers, and the tendency in recent years is in that direction. Unions feel that united action throughout an industry will result in generally higher standards than could be obtained through piecemeal bargaining with individual employers. Some employers, on the other hand, are opposed to industry-wide bargaining in principle and in practice. To them it appears to be one more step away from individual plant control and the intercompany distinctions which promote competition. Many of these same employers, however, have also expressed opposition to a firm's paying higher than the prevailing rates "just because it is more prosperous than its competitors and can afford to do so."

Bargaining with Individual Employers

In spite of the current trends toward wider bargaining units, most of the agreements now in effect are made in the name of a single company and the local union to which its employees belong. If a local union includes members who work for different companies, the agreement will be signed by the union on behalf of the members employed by the particular company. If all the employees in a plant belong to a single local union, one agreement results. If, however, the employees are organized into separate unions according to craft or occupation, each union may either sign a separate agreement with the employer or jointly negotiate and sign a single agreement. Joint bargaining on the part of craft unions may strengthen the bargaining power of the individual crafts and from the employer's point of view eliminates the necessity for extended negotiations with several unions, each of which represents only part of his employees.

In the case of large corporations with a number of plants, the various local unions may sign jointly with the central office of the corporation. In this way, a single agreement may cover plants in widely separated geographical areas. Even when each local union negotiates separately with each plant management, the substance of the various agreements for all the corporation's plants may be similar. In the case of multi-plant corporation and industry-wide agreements, the national office of the union may take a prominent part in the negotiations. Generally the corporation-wide agreement establishes the relationships of the parties, the general wage levels, and the machinery and procedure for further negotiations. Many subjects, including individual wage rates, are then negotiated locally between the various plant managements and the local unions.

Industry-Wide Bargaining

There are only a few instances of formal industry-wide bargaining in this country, although what approximates it obtains in a number of industries. A necessary corollary to such a bargaining unit is a wide degree of organization among both employers and employees throughout the industry. Until the past decade few industries were widely unionized, and in only a few industries were most or all the employers members of employers' associations.[3] Instances of industry-wide bargaining which have been in effect for many years are found in the pottery, glass (except several of the largest companies), wallpaper, and elevator manufacturing industries. Even in these industries, however, wage rates are sometimes negotiated locally.

In anthracite mining a single agreement is signed to cover all mines, and in recent years the equivalent of industry-wide bargaining has existed in bituminous coal mining, where the separate agreements expire on the same date. Once the terms for the most im-

---

[3] The employers' associations with which unions negotiate are usually not the regularly established trade associations which deal more with marketing, public relations, style problems, etc., than with labor relations.

portant producing areas have been agreed upon, the other districts proceed to sign agreements with virtually identical general terms but with specific wage rates that are adapted to local conditions.

The traditional bargaining unit in railroad transportation is the individual railroad company or system, with each of the operating crafts (trainmen, engineers, etc.) negotiating separate agreements with the various systems, and the maintenance employees (shop crafts) negotiating joint agreements with each system. Although the agreements continue to be signed by each railroad system, during recent years it has become the practice to negotiate major questions of wages, vacation allowances, and general working rules on a national scale. After a two-day strike in May, 1946, when the government took over the railroads, the same wage increase was granted to all railroad workers even though all the unions had not presented a united appeal.

Several factors have promoted or encouraged industry-wide bargaining within recent years. The gradual expansion and increased strength of labor unions have facilitated their ability to obtain a larger unit basis, and at the same time have induced employers to unite for mutual protection in their dealings with the unions. Another influence was the government's wage program during the war period, for it directly and indirectly tended to establish uniform terms of employment within an industry or at least within an area.

One of the basic provisions of the Wage Stabilization Program was the removal of "inequalities" in wages within industries and areas in order to reduce labor turnover and eliminate competitive bidding for workers. More important than the leveling of specific wage rates was the change in the pattern of collective bargaining resulting from the operation of the stabilization program. Both employers and unions found it feasible to centralize their research facilities and employ "experts" to present their cases when wage adjustments were subject to complicated formula and applications for changes had to be accompanied by detailed factual data, and perhaps oral hearings at Washington. It became the tendency to talk and negotiate in terms of industries rather than of individual concerns.

This was exemplified in the steel industry where disputes were presented to and settled by the National War Labor Board either on an outright industry-wide basis or for important segments of the industry, with the understanding that the remainder of the industry would also accept the awards. This also took place in the shipbuilding, meat-packing, automobile, and other industries.

The maritime industry presents a vivid illustration of the evolution of industry-wide bargaining as a result of union pressure. During the period between the two World Wars when there was no effective unionization, each shipping company and longshore contractor established their own rates and terms of employment. But the new unions which were organized during the 1930's insisted upon dealing with employers on a port-wide and later on a coast-wide basis. In 1946 virtual industry-wide bargaining was effected when the C.I.O. maritime unions formed a Committee for Maritime Unity and, after a threatened general shipping strike, obtained a settlement covering all their members on all three coasts. (The agreement, however, did not cover A. F. of L. seamen or C.I.O. seamen on the Great Lakes.)

Bargaining for Geographical Areas

When a number of companies in an area who are engaged in the same industry have signed agreements, a frequent development is the formation of an employers' association to represent the unionized firms in that area and industry. This has been the development of collective bargaining relations in the various branches of the clothing industry in the major centers. In this industry, when an agreement is entered into by an association of employers on behalf of its members, the agreement generally specifies that the terms are applicable to all the association's members. Some agreements, however, provide that terms are binding only upon the members who ratify it or who authorize the association to enter into such an agreement. There may be a requirement that the union shall be furnished a copy of the authorization or of the names of the companies ratifying the agreement, in order that it may know which employers are bound by the terms. Resignation, suspension, or expulsion from the association usually does not relieve an employer from his obligation to abide by the agreement.

In the men's and women's clothing, men's hats and millinery, and fur industries, there is highly developed industrial relations machinery in each of the metropolitan areas which are important as producing centers. These unions and employers' associations customarily make use of permanent impartial chairmen to administer the agreement. In addition, joint trade boards, stabilization commissions, and other similar union-management bodies are frequently established to deal with particular problems that arise from time to time. The employers in a given city are usually organized into more than one association within each of the garment industries. The basis of distinction is both the price line of the product and the classification of employers—that is, jobbers, contractors, inside manufacturers.

In the hosiery industry a bargaining relationship of several years' standing exists between the Full-Fashioned Hosiery Manufacturers and the Federation of Hosiery Workers. The employers' association, originally covering only Philadelphia mills, now covers a major part of the northern section of full-fashioned hosiery manufacturers. In the textile industry there are association agreements between the Textile Workers' Union and the silk and rayon mills in the Paterson, New Jersey, area. A joint arrangement of longer standing exists for the dyeing and finishing of textiles in non-integrated mills.

The pulp and paper industry, though dealing elsewhere on the basis of individual companies, in the Pacific Northwest is combined into the Pacific Coast Association of Pulp and Paper Manufacturers, which deals with the two paper unions jointly. The dominant method of bargaining in the organized section of the lumber industry is through employers' associations in a producing area. For intercity trucking, the Teamsters' Union usually negotiates with employers' associations whose operations cover several states; one of the largest is the Midwest Agreement, which covers over-the-road hauling in twelve North Central States.

In many other industries and trades characterized by numerous small establishments within a city, collective bargaining has been conducted with associations of employers in that city. In many cases the associations are formal organizations whose officers have power to bind all the members to the agreed terms of employment. In other cases the employers may unite informally and perhaps only for the duration of the bargaining conferences. In some instances the lack of a continuing employers' association makes no difference in the actual negotiation of the agreement, but considerably complicates its enforcement. Several industries in which the predominant method of dealing is with city-wide associations are brewing, retail trade, baking, printing and publishing, restaurants, local trucking, and barber shops.

The Building Trades

More city-wide association bargaining is found in building construction than in any other single industry. Almost half the building-trades agreements are negotiated by permanent associations of contractors and individual unions. Usually, after the agreement between the union and the association has been consummated, non-association contractors are offered agreements containing identical terms, with the exception that some of the joint machinery for settling disputes between the union and association members is of necessity modified. In a few instances, advantages are given to association members, such as a provision that they shall have preference in obtaining union workmen. However, in a number of cases, non-members of the contractors' association are required either to join the association before signing the agreement or else to pay the association, or the joint board of the association and the union, an amount of money equivalent to the association membership fee.

A number of building-trades agreements are negotiated by the individual unions with temporary associations of contractors through joint committees appointed for that purpose. Under such circumstances the accepted terms are incorporated either in a single agreement which each employer signs, or in separate identical agreements signed with each employer. Where there is neither a permanent nor a temporary association of employers, the individual building-trades local, often after obtaining tacit acceptance from some of the leading contractors, prepares a contract that is automatically accepted by each unionized firm in the locality. Frequently there is no regular agreement that includes all the usual provisions. Instead, the employers either sign a memorandum or orally give affirmation to pay a specified wage and abide by the working rules of the union.

"Standard" Agreements and Union Labels

In the absence of association bargaining, unions often achieve standardization of wages and working conditions on an industry-wide or market-wide basis by negotiating nearly identical agreements with individual employers. Ordinarily, the individual employers with whom such agreements are negotiated are confined to an industry or trade in a metropolitan area. This is true not only of the retail and service industries but, in some centers, of manufacturers whose products flow into interstate markets.

A degree of uniformity is sometimes effected by having the international union office exercise control over local agreements, such as requiring its approval of them or issuing standard agreements or union-label and "shop-card" agreements. Generally, provisions dealing with apprentices, arbitration, and membership status are standardized and enforced on an industry- or trade-wide scale more often than are provisions regarding wage rates, hours, and working conditions.

The common practice in regard to the approval of local agreements is to have the union constitution require that agreements shall not be considered finally ratified until approved by the international union office. As an incentive toward standardization, some unions make available to their locals printed forms of agreements to be negotiated with local employers. These forms, or "standard" agreements, contain the minimum requirements that have been adopted through convention action (usually appearing in the constitution and by-laws) and have blank spaces in which locally negotiated wage rates, hours, and working conditions may be inserted.

Similarly, the internationals often issue standard union-label agreements that set forth the minimum terms under which employers may use the label. Supplemental agreements establishing local wage rates and working conditions are negotiated. Since the use of the union label is strictly under the control of the international, a measure of uniformity may be achieved among employers who sign the label agreement.

Local unions in some retail and service trades often secure standardization throughout the city by the use of the union-shop card. To secure a shop card the employer agrees to observe the minimum standards of the international and, in addition, the local's wage rates, hours, and working rules. Changes in local working conditions are negotiated in joint conferences between the locals and the employers. In the absence of an employers' association, a local may adopt a change by a vote of the membership and merely advise the employers regarding it. The shop-card and union employees may then be withdrawn from employers who do not conform to the new rules.

THE BARGAINING PROCESS

Annual negotiations between employers and unions are most frequent, even though the agreements do not always specify that they are to be in effect for only one year. Many agreements are of indefinite duration but are subject to renegotiation upon notice by either party. Some agreements are negotiated for periods of two or more years without privilege of alteration. Although the longer period may seem to insure greater stability in the employment relationship, if drastic economic changes occur in the meantime, either the employer or the workers may find it difficult to abide by the contract. Numbers of strikes and lockouts have taken place as a result of "frozen" wage rates which were agreed upon some time before a rise or fall in prices and the cost of living occurred.

Regardless of the period the agreement is to remain in effect, most agreements require the party which wishes it changed or terminated to notify the other party thirty or sixty days in advance of the expiration date so that new terms can be negotiated without interruption of the contractual relationship. Union members usually do not continue working after the expiration date, although if negotiations are not concluded the old contract may be extended, frequently with the provision that new terms are to be made retroactive.

Union Procedure

The effectiveness of a union in negotiating agreements depends considerably on the composition and experience of its bargaining committees. Union negotiations usually are conducted by officers of a local union or of a joint board or district council, although the international representatives may be consulted for advice prior to or during the negotiations, or they may participate directly in the bargaining, especially with the larger employers. These international representatives generally have major responsibility in

regional or industry-wide negotiations and in bargaining with a
large corporation for an agreement covering many plants.

A union chooses its strongest leaders for the task of negotiating
either a new agreement or a renewal. Ordinarily, these leaders are
the president and other elected officers, although other union representatives may be put on the negotiating committee or a special
committee may be selected. If the union employs a business agent,
he is usually a member of the committee and may play a primary
role in negotiations.

There are several ways in which the members of a union may
exercise control over negotiations. First, the members of the negotiating committee are elected or appointed by officers who are
themselves elected by the members ; second, the demands to be made
upon the employer may be submitted for approval to the members
prior to the negotiations ; third, the tentative agreement reached
with the employer may be submitted to the members for ratification,
and the members of the negotiating committee may be required to
defend the results of their bargaining and explain why any compromises were made.

When the bargaining involves an employers' association or a
large corporation and a number of local unions, it is common for
each local to recommend the terms it desires to be included in the
agreement to a joint conference of representatives from all the
locals. This conference, in consultation with the international
officers, decides the exact nature of the demands to be made, and
it may elect a negotiating committee. Any agreement reached with
the employer is then submitted to the local unions for ratification.

Employer Procedure

The negotiating machinery on the employer's side depends
largely on the size of the company and whether or not the employer is a member of an employer's association. A small owner-
employer who is not a member of an association usually bargains
directly with union representatives, although he may enlist the
aid or advice of his lawyer. Where there are many small employers
within a producing area, an employers' association, as already
indicated, may function as the bargaining agent for the member
employers. Negotiations may be conducted by the secretary and

the executive officer of the association, or a special committee of member employers may be appointed. After the agreement has been drafted it may be signed by the executive officer or negotiating committee for the association, or each employer member may affix his signature.

In large companies the negotiating process depends upon the corporate structure. In some instances the plant manager may negotiate final terms, frequently with the aid of the industrial relations director. In other cases, when the agreement is negotiated by the branch manager, it does not become final until it is approved by the corporation's central office. Elsewhere, the central office negotiates directly with the union either one agreement to apply uniformly over all its plants or different agreements for its various plants. The latter, however, is infrequent unless the plants are engaged in different types of work or the employees belong to different unions.

Outside Aid

Either or both parties may seek outside help in reaching an agreement, especially if there is a stalemate in the direct negotiations and a work stoppage is threatened or has taken place. Employers, and to a less extent unions, may hire lawyers to assist them in drawing up their agreements, although many prefer not to emphasize the legalistic approach to agreement negotiations. This can be avoided, of course, if the lawyer has had industrial relations experience as well as training in economics and law.

If the employer refuses to negotiate with a particular union on the grounds that a majority of his employees do not belong to it, recourse may be had to the National Labor Relations Board if the company is engaged in interstate business or, if intra-state, to state labor relations boards where they exist; these agencies hold elections or otherwise decide whether or not the union should be certified as the exclusive bargaining agency.[4] If a controversy arises over the specific terms to be incorporated in the agreement, either party may ask help from the federal or state conciliation

---

[4] For railroad and airline employees the National Mediation Board determines the bargaining agency. See Herbert R. Northrup, "The Appropriate Bargaining Unit Question Under the Railway Labor Act," *Quarterly Journal of Economics*, February, 1946.

service. Since the conciliator has no legal powers of compulsion, his effectiveness is dependent entirely upon the prestige of his office, the assistance he can render by reason of his knowledge of the facts involved, his skill as a negotiator, and the willingness of the parties to compromise or come to terms.

If the conciliator's recommendations are not acceptable to one or both parties, they may decide to submit the issue to an arbitrator for final decision. On the other hand, either party may decide to use its economic strength to obtain its terms, and a strike or lockout may be called. Under such circumstances, the final terms of settlement are dependent largely upon which side is able to hold out longer, although an important factor is the pressure of public opinion, especially in work stoppages which result in inconvenience to the public. For every agreement that has been negotiated after a strike or lockout, thousands have been negotiated peaceably with no stoppage of work.

Factual Aids to Bargaining

The need and use of factual data in determining the terms and conditions of employment are increasing in importance as economic relationships grow more complex and collective bargaining processes become more extensive. Knowledge and mutual acceptance of specific facts remove many areas of conflict between employers and employees and minimize many others. The maximum use of all available data and the diligent search for additional facts indicate mature rational bargaining.

Knowledge of given facts, however, never automatically resolves all employer-worker differences. Beyond the point where all the parties connected with an enterprise are interestd in its maximum prosperity, there remains the basic question of how the gross income of the enterprise shall be distributed. Similarly, although management and workers may agree in principle that standards of efficiency must be maintained, there still exist differences as to the relative value of specific efficiency methods. As aptly summarized by one who has observed the collective bargaining procedure: "While factual collective bargaining tends to develop a smoothly functioning employer-union relationship, it guarantees no millennium. Divergent interpretation of jointly determined fact will still provide disagreements. Conflicts of interest will continue to exist.

Nevertheless, it seems beyond doubt that a factual basis for negotiations is an essential requirement for a mature system of collective bargaining."[5]

The parties negotiating an agreement must necessarily rely upon various kinds of data in making their determinations. Financial records of the company, economic data on the industry, wages and working conditions prevailing elsewhere, prices and cost of living, and other related matters are taken into consideration to a greater or lesser extent whenever a new agreement is negotiated.

The employer in some respects is in an advantageous position with regard to factual data to support his claims. It is difficult if not impossible for the union to know the exact condition of the company's finances. On the other hand, a union that is national in scope can collect data from all its locals and thus be informed about the wages and working conditions throughout the unionized section of the industry. Employers' associations could also obtain from and disseminate information through their members, but in this country, at the present time, few of the established trade associations deal with problems of collective bargaining. Not all the unions maintain research facilities, but the number is increasing and at present research to facilitate collective bargaining is fairly common on both the union and the employer side.

PROVISIONS IN LABOR AGREEMENTS

An employer-union agreement may be a document of half a dozen typewritten pages or a 50-page printed booklet, although most agreements are 15 or 20 pages in length.[6] The extremely

[5] Neil W. Chamberlain, *Collective Bargaining Procedures,* American Council on Public Affairs, Washington, 1944, p. 98.

[6] The merits of long versus short agreements are a frequent subject of discussion, especially at management conferences. Professor Slichter has made this interesting comment:

"A large proportion of our trade agreements are too long and complicated and contain too many rules. . . . When one picks up a British trade agreement, one finds it is just about as long as one of ours, but the length comes not from shop rules, but rather from the fact that the agreement spells out in considerable detail how cases shall be handled, where they shall go first, where next, where next, and where ultimately. If one may contrast in general terms the policies represented by the British trade agreement and the American, one may say that the Americans are more disposed to rely upon the legislative method —the method of a definite rule spelled out in advance—and that the British are

long agreements include occupational wage listings and detailed work rules, whereas the shorter agreements are confined to statements of policy and general rules of procedure, with the further specification that other documents, such as the company's book of rules and the union's constitution and by-laws, are to be observed.

Regardless of their length, all agreements cover five major issues: (1) the type of recognition afforded the union; (2) basic wages and hours, including overtime and other items affecting earnings; (3) seniority rules; (4) work rules, including health and safety measures; and (5) procedures for settling disputes arising during the life of the agreement, as well as the procedure to be followed in opening negotiations for a new contract. These procedural provisions are discussed in the next chapter.

The specific provisions in employer-union agreements vary not only because of the necessary differences due to the nature of the industry or occupation covered and the customs and trade practices which have developed through the years, but also because of many dynamic influences such as the general economic situation prevailing at the time the agreement was negotiated, the competitive position of the particular industry or employer, the bargaining strength of the union, the desires of the employer and union members, the skill of the negotiating parties and the factual evidence each has presented during the negotiations, the presence or absence of governmental regulations, and the pressure of public opinion.

Union Status

One of the first and most important parts of any agreement is that which outlines the basic relations between the employer and the union, namely, the degree of recognition extended, the membership status of present and newly hired employees, dues collection, the union's use of bulletin boards, and related matters.

---

more disposed to rely upon the administrative method—the method of settling individual cases in the light of particular facts. The British method is more flexible and more adaptable to a rapidly changing world. It is less likely to bind both sides by rules which later become obsolete and a handicap to each, but which are difficult to abolish because they have created vested interests among the workers or even among the employers." (Sumner H. Slichter, "The Contents of Collective Agreements," *Society for the Advancement of Management Journal*, January, 1938, p. 13.)

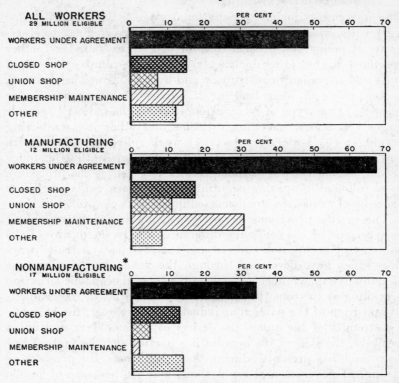

* COAL MINING IS ALMOST 100 % UNDER UNION SHOP AGREEMENTS; PRACTICALLY ALL RAILROAD WORKERS ARE COVERED BY AGREEMENTS BUT THESE AGREEMENTS, IN ACCORDANCE WITH THE RAILWAY LABOR ACT, DO NOT SPECIFY UNION SHOP CONDITIONS.

Fig. 30. *Type of Union Recognition of Workers Covered by Agreements in 1945.* (*Source*: Monthly Labor Review, *April, 1946.*)

The degree of recognition may vary from a closed shop to recognition of the union as the sole bargaining agent, which is the minimum legal requirement under the N.L.R.A. Under a "closed-shop" provision all employees covered by the agreement must be members of the union, and in addition all new employees must be hired through the union or be members of it at the time of employment. While a "union-shop" agreement also requires all permanent employees to be union members, the employer has complete control over the hiring of new workers; if they do not already belong to the union a probationary period is usually allowed before they are required to join.

Under a maintenance-of-membership provision, joining the union is optional; but after an employee once joins he must retain his membership for the duration of the agreement, otherwise he is subject to discharge. Some agreements which include no union membership requirements encourage membership by providing preferential treatment to members, such as specifying that nonmembers shall be the first to be laid off and the last to be reemployed.

Clauses concerning the collection of union dues may specify that the employer shall deduct them from the pay of all union members (automatic checkoff), or from employees who request this form of collection (individual authorization), or from delinquent members only. If the checkoff is not provided, the agreement may allow union officials access to the plant for the purpose of collecting dues, or grant the union the right to set up a booth on company premises to collect dues on payday.[7]

Almost half of the 14 million workers employed under agreements during 1945 were covered by closed- and union-shop provisions. More than half these workers were employed in manufacturing plants; almost a million were construction workers, a half million were truck drivers, another half million were miners, and the rest were in trade, service, and amusement industries. Almost 30 per cent of all the workers employed under agreements were covered by clauses requiring persons who join the union to maintain their membership for the duration of the agreement; less than one-fourth were not required to be union members as a condition of being hired or continuously employed.[8]

Almost 5½ million workers in 1945 were employed under agreements which provided some form of checkoff for union dues; most of them provided for an automatic checkoff, although a considerable number specified that checkoffs might be made only upon individual written authorization of the employees. Most of these

---

[7] Permission to collect union dues, distribute union literature, and carry on other union activities on company property but outside of work hours—for example, during lunchtime—has been ordered by the National Labor Relations Board under certain circumstances, viz., where plants are located at a distance from cities or where the employees' homes are scattered over wide areas, thus making it difficult for the union to get in contact with its members or prospective members except at their work places.

[8] *Monthly Labor Review*, April, 1946.

agreements provided the full checkoff of "all dues and assessments" levied by the union, although some specified a maximum amount or "regular dues only."

Wage and Hour Provisions[9]

Practice varies widely with respect to the amount of detail with which wage matters are treated in union agreements. In the case of small shops, the agreements may include itemized wage lists for each occupation; agreements for larger plants may specify minimum and maximum rates for the major job categories, or merely give a minimum learner or common labor rate. Where wage incentive plans exist, the agreements may specify the base or guaranteed rates and outline the conditions under which new production standards and piece rates are to be established.

Some agreements specify the form—cash or check—and frequency of wage payment. Other wage provisions relate to differential rates for night or hazardous work, guaranteed pay for reporting at the regular time and finding no work to do, pay when transferred to a different job, deductions for damaged work or for equipment used, etc. A few agreements, as indicated in Chapter 7, provide for lump-sum payments, or the payment of regular wages for a given number of weeks, in case of dismissal from the job through no fault of the employee.

Seldom do union agreements contain absolute restrictions on the number of hours employees shall be permitted to work, but almost without exception they provide penalty or overtime rates for all hours worked in excess or outside of the regular schedule. Most agreements establish both daily and weekly hour maxima— for example, eight hours per day and 40 hours per week—although penalty rates are not paid twice for any given hours of overtime. Many agreements provide penalty rates for Saturday and Sunday work, even though such work does not represent overtime. Special rates are also provided for second- and third-shift work, that is, nightwork, although these rates are usually only 5 or 10 per cent higher than the regular day rates, in contrast to the time and a half or double time paid for overtime and week-end work.

---

[9] See chaps. 13 and 15 for more detailed information on hours, vacation, and sick benefit provisions in agreements.

Seniority Rules[10]

Since seniority is a measure of a claim to a job, the clauses dealing with seniority are of major importance to both the employer and the employees concerned. Practically all agreements contain detailed rules specifying how seniority is acquired—on a plant-wide, department, or occupational basis, or a combination of any of these—as well as how such rights are applied and lost.

Most union agreements provide that layoffs are to be made on the basis of strict seniority, employees with the shortest service record being laid off first, although some specify that the employer may retain a given nucleus of "indispensable" employees regardless of seniority. In order to preserve continuity in the grievance adjustment personnel, many agreements specify that union stewards shall be placed at the top of their respective seniority lists and thus be the last to be laid off.

Reemployment is of course in reverse order to layoff, those with the greatest seniority being the first to be reinstated when work picks up. Some agreements establish a maximum period of layoff—for example, one year—during which seniority rights are retained, although many agreements explicitly or implicitly allow the retention of seniority rights for an indefinite period until such time as the employer is able to offer a suitable job or the employee obtains work elsewhere.

Many agreements which apply straight seniority to reductions in force and reemployment do not recognize an employee's length of service as the sole or primary consideration when promotions are made; in other words, seniority may govern only in the case of employees whose skill and ability are relatively equal. Some agreements, however, go further by providing that the oldest employee in point of service shall be given an opportunity to qualify for a promotional vacancy and that if, after a fair trial, he cannot qualify, the next in line shall be eligible, and so on.

Work Rules

In addition to the above provisions, and those relating to dispute and grievance adjustments discussed in the next chapter, union agreements contain clauses outlining specific work rules as

---

[10] See chap. 8 for reasons for seniority rules.

well as provisions concerning health and safety matters. Owing to the tendency of some employers in the past to use physical examinations as a means of discriminating against union members, and also because of the fear of depriving persons of needed employment, some agreements prohibit physical examinations as a condition of hiring, or during the period of employment. An increasing number, however, provide entrance examinations and periodical checkups thereafter, although many permit appeal to the family doctor in case of an adverse report from the company physician. Where examinations are provided, most agreements specify that they shall be at company expense.

Most agreements contain only general provisions concerning safety and sanitation, although a few of them go into much detail, especially in the case of hazardous occupations or where the public safety is at stake. Since most state workmen's compensation laws require the reporting of accidents by the employer, most agreements do not mention this, although conformity to the law is commonly specified. Some agreements provide for a special safety committee, which may be a joint management-union committee or one composed solely of union members. An increasing number of agreements, particularly those covering "dirty occupations" in which the workers must change from their street clothes, require the furnishing of shower baths, lockers, and dressing rooms.

Work rules necessarily differ for different industries and plants, and there is wide variation in practice as to the amount of detailed instructions included in agreements. A complete outline of the plant's working rules rarely appears, although existing company and union rules may be incorporated by reference. Aside from matters of discipline, clauses in agreements may state rules concerning apprentices and learners, the size of work crews and work loads, the distribution of work among employees, subcontracting and working on non-union materials, the use of the union label and bulletin boards, the treatment of special groups such as handicapped or aged employees, the care and use of machinery, and the making of time and motion studies. Although some agreements include explicit statements pertaining to the prerogatives of management, in most of them such matters are implied rather than specifically mentioned.[11]

---

[11] See chap. 22 for discussion of management prerogatives.

EXTENT OF COLLECTIVE BARGAINING

The expansion of collective bargaining roughly parallels the growth of union membership, although the actual number of employees covered by collective agreements is not identical with union membership in three major respects: (1) There are scattered union members working for employers with whom agreements have not yet been negotiated although presumably they will be negotiated whenever a majority of the employees join the union. (2) As indicated above, agreements cover all the employees in the bargaining unit; only under closed- and union-shop agreements, in which all employees are required to belong to the union, would coverage be identical with union membership. In other plants agreement coverage would be more extensive than union membership. (3) There are thousands of government employees—federal, state, and municipal, including schoolteachers—who are union members but who are not working under the usual type of bilateral agreement existing in private industry.

Agreement Coverage

Almost 14 million workers, or approximately 50 per cent of all employees in private industry in 1945, were working under the terms of union agreements. About 70 per cent of manufacturing wage earners as a whole were covered by union agreements, and in such industries as aluminum fabrication, automobiles and airframe, men's clothing, non-ferrous metal smelting and refining, shipbuilding, and basic steel, over 90 per cent were covered. Almost all the mine, maritime, commercial construction, and railroad workers, and over 90 per cent of those in the local bus and street railway, airline, trucking, and telegraph industries were employed under union agreements.

Collective bargaining is not extensive in the clerical, professional, and service occupations except in the amusement and railroad industries. Practically all professional actors and musicians, as well as the clerical and supervisory personnel on the railroads, are employed under union agreements. In contrast, agreements cover less than 10 per cent of the clerical and professional workers in manufacturing, financial, and wholesale and retail trade establishments.

TABLE 27. Proportion of Wage Earners Under Union Agreements in 1945[12]

MANUFACTURING INDUSTRIES

80–100 Per Cent	60–80 Per Cent	40–60 Per Cent	20–40 Per Cent	1–20 Per Cent
Agricultural equipment. Aircraft and parts. Aluminum. Automobiles and parts. Breweries. Carpets and rugs, wool. Cement. Clocks and watches. Clothing, men's. Clothing, women's. Furs and fur garments. Glass and glassware. Leather tanning. Meat packing. Newspaper printing and publishing. Non-ferrous metals and products. Rubber products. Shipbuilding. Steel, basic. Sugar, beet and cane.	Book and job printing and publishing. Coal products. Electrical machinery, equipment, and appliances. Machinery and machine tools. Millinery and hats. Paper and pulp. Petroleum refining. Railroad equipment. Rayon yarn. Steel products. Tobacco products. Woolen and worsted textiles.	Baking. Canning and preserving foods. Dyeing and finishing textiles. Flour and other grain products. Furniture. Gloves, leather, and cloth. Hosiery. Jewelry and silverware. Knit goods. Leather luggage, handbags, novelties. Lumber. Pottery, including chinaware. Shoes, cut stock, and findings. Stone and clay products.	Beverages, non-alcoholic. Chemicals, excluding rayon yarn. Confectionery products. Cotton textiles. Paper products. Silk and rayon textiles.	Dairy products.

NON-MANUFACTURING INDUSTRIES

80–100 Per Cent	60–80 Per Cent	40–60 Per Cent	20–40 Per Cent	1–20 Per Cent
Actors and musicians. Airline pilots and mechanics. Bus and streetcar, local. Coal mining. Construction. Longshoring. Maritime. Metal mining. Motion-picture production. Railroads—freight and passenger, shops and clerical. Telegraph service and maintenance. Trucking, local and intercity.	Radio technicians. Theater—stage hands, motion-picture operators.	Bus lines, intercity. Light and power. Newspaper offices. Telephone service and maintenance.	Barber shops. Building servicing and maintenance. Cleaning and dyeing. Crude petroleum and natural gas. Fishing. Hotels and restaurants. Laundries. Non-metallic mining and quarrying. Taxicabs.	Agriculture. Beauty shops. Clerical and professional, excluding transportation, communication, theaters, and newspapers. Retail and wholesale trade.

12 *Monthly Labor Review*, April, 1946, p. 568.

SELECTED REFERENCES

Bureau of Labor Statistics, U. S. Department of Labor, *Union Agreement Provisions*, Bulletin No. 686, Washington, 1942.

Bureau of National Affairs, Inc., *Collective Bargaining Contracts*, Washington, 1941.

Carroll, Mollie Ray, *What Is Collective Bargaining?* Longman, Green & Company, Inc., New York, 1939.

Cooke, Morris L., and Murray, Philip, *Organized Labor and Production*, Harper & Brothers, New York, 1946.

Golden, Clinton S., and Ruttenberg, Harold S., *The Dynamics of Industrial Democracy*, Harper & Brothers, New York, 1942.

Greenman, Russell L., and Elizabeth B., *Getting Along with Unions*, Harper & Brothers, New York, 1947.

Harbison, Frederick H., *Seniority Policies and Procedures as Developed Through Collective Bargaining*, Princeton University Press, 1941.

Hill, Lee H., and Hook, C. R., *Management at the Bargaining Table*, McGraw-Hill Book Company, Inc., New York, 1945.

Lieberman, Elias, *Collective Labor Agreements, How to Negotiate and Draft the Contract*, Harper & Brothers, New York, 1939.

Metcalf, Henry C., *Collective Bargaining for Today and Tomorrow*, Harper & Brothers, New York, 1939.

Pierson, Frank C., *Collective Bargaining Systems*, American Council on Public Affairs, Washington, 1942.

Slichter, Sumner H., *Union Policies and Industrial Management*, Brookings Institution, Washington, 1941.

Smith, Leonard J., *Collective Bargaining*, Prentice-Hall, Inc., New York, 1946.

Twentieth Century Fund, *How Collective Bargaining Works*, New York, 1942.

Twentieth Century Fund, *Trends in Collective Bargaining*, New York, 1946.

20

LABOR DISPUTES

SO LONG AS FREE MEN AND WOMEN ENGAGE IN ECONOMIC UNDER-takings, there will always be disputes between employers and employees. A complete absence of disputes for any period of time would indicate a condition of absolute dominance of one group and abject servility of the other, a situation which makes for stagnation rather than progress. Likewise, the total elimination of inter-union controversies could be attained only by stifling natural, and in some instances desirable, expressions of group rivalry.

Disputes need not lead to work stoppages, however, and maintaining the privilege and right to engage in strikes and lockouts does not mean that efforts should not be made to prevent them from occurring. The peaceful[1] settlement of labor disputes is the goal of government, employers, and unions alike, and all have taken measures toward this end. What these are and why they do not always succeed will be discussed in this chapter; further proposals for solutions will be discussed in Chapter 22.

TYPES OF DISPUTES

Employer-employee disputes fall into four general categories: (1) those caused by the conflicting interpretation or the non-observance of the terms of the employer-union agreement; (2) jurisdictional disputes between two or more unions as to which shall have jurisdiction over certain jobs or kinds of work; (3) those concerning conditions of employment—wages, hours, working rules, etc.—when such matters have not already been agreed

---

[1] The term "peaceful" is used in the popular sense of settlement before the occurrence of a strike or lockout. This use of the word is somewhat misleading, however, because it implies that strikes and lockouts are in themselves turbulent when in fact most of them involve no display of violence.

upon and the terms embodied in a collective agreement; (4) disputes concerning the bargaining agent, union recognition, and other issues connected with collective bargaining per se.

Each of these types of disputes is basically different and each requires a different approach for satisfactory settlement. The signing of an agreement by an employer and a union automatically removes some of the major causes of conflict—the matter of union recognition has been settled and the questions of basic wages, hours, and working rules have been agreed upon. Although the establishment of such a contractural relationship does not entirely remove the possibility of disputes, they should not develop into strikes and lockouts if the agreement also provides adequate adjustment machinery and if all parties are willing to use the specified procedures. Likewise, unions have established various means for the adjustment of jurisdictional disputes although these have not always prevented strikes from taking place.

Most disputes arise over the terms to be included in new agreements—that is, wages, hours, and working conditions—as well as over the question of union recognition. For the final determination of such issues there are usually no prearranged contractural procedures because these matters involve the essence of collective bargaining. When collective bargaining fails or threatens to fail, government agencies are widely utilized for both conciliation and final determination.

UNION RULES CONCERNING STRIKES

Practically every union constitution contains some statement regarding the calling and conduct of strikes. In general, the purpose of such clauses is to minimize hasty and ill-advised action and to provide financial aid and insure maximum success once a strike is called. In considering the purpose and character of strike clauses in union constitutions it should be remembered that any organization's formally adopted rules may not be adhered to by all its members at all times. Just as individuals may ignore or violate civil laws, so members of unions may on occasion engage in strikes contrary to their unions' regulations. Such stoppages the unions themselves call "illegal" and in some cases fines are imposed upon members who instigate them.

Rules for Calling a Strike

In order to call a strike the majority of unions require a two-thirds affirmative vote of the membership affected, and sanction by the international president or general executive board. Some unions permit the calling of a strike by a majority vote of the local membership, whereas others require a three-fourths vote. Many stipulate that the vote shall be by secret ballot at a special meeting of the members which has been announced a given number of days in advance, and which is attended by at least one-fourth of the total membership affected. Some unions require the presence of an international representative at the local meeting when a strike vote is to be taken.

While such rules prevail, in the building-trades and some other unions the local business agent is sometimes given authority to call "job" or "shop" strikes when in his opinion the agreement is being violated. But if such strikes will affect the members of other unions as well as his own, approval of the local or district trades council or joint board is required.

Although almost all unions require the sanction of the general executive board or the international president before a strike may be undertaken, in practice this sanction is usually effective only so far as financial aid is sought and obtained from the international. Some unions specifically limit the sanction requirement to strikes which the international is to finance, and in such cases the local union's vote to call a strike is final if the membership does not expect to receive strike benefits or other aid from its international office. On the other hand, the locals of some unions are absolutely forbidden to engage in any strike without approval of the international office; otherwise they may be suspended.

In some situations the general executive board (or the international president) is authorized to take the initiative in calling strikes, with or without a vote of the local membership. Whether so defined or not, the circumstances under which the international office is empowered to call a strike on its own initiative are usually confined to situations which violate a basic principle of the union and thus jeopardize its existence. A few unions, for example, permit the international executive board to call a strike whenever "necessary to defend the organization" or "to protect the union's jurisdiction," in a "great emergency," or, more particularly, "where members are working on struck work."

Rules for Terminating a Strike

Unions which require a three-fourths vote of the members to call a strike usually require only a majority vote for its termination. As with the calling of a strike, the authority of the general officers to end it varies in the different unions. In some instances the international president has the power to call off a strike whenever in his judgment it is to the best interests of the union to do so. More generally the termination of a strike is dependent on the vote of those immediately involved, although the influence of the international officers usually has considerable weight. In all cases, so far as the continuance of strike benefits is concerned, the international officers have the final word.

Strike Benefits

The calling of a strike is a serious matter to the workers and union concerned, for it means loss of earnings and union dues and perhaps substantial cash outlays from the union treasury. As indicated in Chapter 25, only a few states pay unemployment compensation during strikes and lockouts, and then only under restricted conditions. Although the unions' ability to pay strike benefits when needed varies greatly, practically all of them seek to maintain a reserve to finance strikes which is most commonly called the "defense fund."

The amounts in these defense funds naturally fluctuate, depending both upon the provision made for maintaining them and upon the necessity for withdrawals at any particular time. Some union constitutions specify that a certain portion of the regular dues shall be regularly deposited in the defense fund, while others specify a minimum amount which shall be maintained; if the fund falls below the specified amount, the treasurer is authorized to levy special assessments. When separate funds are not maintained and strike benefits must be paid from the general fund, the drain upon the treasury during a prolonged strike may jeopardize other activities of the union.

The amount of weekly benefits paid individual members while

out on strike is by necessity based on minimum subsistence needs during the period of loss of wages. Few unions pay more than $10 or $15 a week per member; and in strikes involving large numbers, as in the mass-production industries, grocery allowances or commissaries may be provided in lieu of individual cash payments. Usually benefits do not begin until after a strike has been in progress for at least two weeks, and many unions place a limit on the maximum number of weeks in which benefits may be paid, regardless of the duration of the strike. In any case, of course, actual payments are contingent upon the condition of the union's treasury when the strike occurs.

JURISDICTIONAL DISPUTES

Disputes between two or more unions over the right to do certain jobs or kinds of work are frequently the most baffling of all labor disputes to resolve.[2] Stemming from the craft form of organization, jurisdictional disputes are by-products of the continual changes in machinery, methods, and materials that take place in a dynamic industrial economy. Each such change causes the elimination of certain kinds of occupations or types of jobs and the substitution of others.

Conflicts arise when a union seeks to continue its jurisdiction over the function performed, regardless of the new materials or processes which may be introduced, or when a new process arouses a desire for a new craft autonomy. Thus the Carpenters' Union has had many disputes with the Sheet Metal Workers, Structural Iron Workers, and Machinists, as steel and other metals were substituted for wood for essentially the same function. The Bricklayers have clashed with the Glaziers when glass blocks were substituted for bricks and stone. The discovery of acetylene torches not only brought disputes between the Blacksmiths and Machinists but gave rise to a new Welders' Union which is now in conflict with the older metal-working unions. The introduction of the offset

2 There is a distinct difference between jurisdictional disputes and disputes between rival unions. As is explained later, a dispute between rival unions is likely to be brought before a labor relations board, since it is a matter of determining which union a majority of the workers in a certain trade or plant wish to have represent them.

process in printing occasioned an unresolved conflict between the Lithographers, Pressmen, and Photo-Engravers unions.

One of the major functions of the American Federation of Labor is to determine the jurisdictional boundaries and to resolve the disputes of its affiliated unions. A prime motive in the establishment of its Building and Construction Trades Department was to settle the ever-recurring conflicts of jurisdiction among the building-trades unions. At certain times, on a national scale as well as in some of the larger cities, the contractors and unions have established joint machinery for the handling of such disputes.

Under the present procedure of the Building Trades Department, both claimants to a job submit their briefs to the local building-trades council, which forwards them to the president of the Building Trades Department in Washington. This officer, after consulting with the international president of the unions concerned, renders a "spot" decision which covers the specific job in dispute. The case is then handed to a permanent national referee who is empowered to award the specific type of work permanently to the union which he believes has the greatest right to do it. During these proceedings, stoppages are prohibited and the union in possession of the work continues to do it until the final decision is rendered.

In spite of the machinery which the A. F. of L. and its affiliated organizations have established, numerous jurisdictional disputes occur which not only inconvenience employers and the public but frequently disrupt union affiliations. In numbers of instances, unions have severed their connections with the A. F. of L. because of unfavorable decisions regarding questions of jurisdiction. Recent examples are the Brewery Workers, who are in conflict with the Teamsters, and the Machinists because of their long-standing grievances against the Carpenters' union. After withdrawal from the A. F. of L., unions are of course not subject to its prescribed adjustment machinery or jurisdictional mandates. The Machinists' withdrawal from the A. F. of L. in 1945 not only eliminated the interunion machinery for the settlement of their disputes with the Carpenters, but opened the door for the Teamsters to assume jurisdiction over garage mechanics, thus providing additional areas of conflict.

In principle, jurisdictional disputes by their very nature are best settled by the unions themselves. However, they are the kind of disputes with which the general public has least patience; therefore they are most likely to come under the control of legislation if union methods prove inadequate Recently, several states have enacted laws to control jurisdictional strikes. As an example, a Minnesota law enacted in 1943 empowers the Governor to appoint a labor referee in jurisdictional disputes which involve strikes, boycotts, or picketing; and pending the referee's decision it is illegal to picket, strike, or boycott a place of business. Currently, work stoppages resulting from jurisdictional and rival union disputes comprise only about 3 or 4 per cent of the total strikes and lockouts which take place throughout the country.

SETTLEMENT OF DISPUTES UNDER EMPLOYER-UNION AGREEMENTS

Experience with collective bargaining has led to a general acceptance of three essentials for the adjustment of disputes which arise under an employer-union agreement: (1) union-management negotiations, beginning with the foreman in charge of the shop or department where the dispute originates and proceeding up to the highest officials of the company; (2) if such negotiations fail to secure an adjustment, appeal to an impartial outside agency or individual; and (3) restriction on strikes and lockouts until these other means of settling the dispute have been exhausted.

Union Representatives

The workers usually select their own representatives to negotiate with management when a dispute arises. The most common procedure is for the employees in a shop, or in each department of a large plant, to elect one of their own group to serve as shop chairman or steward who acts as their representative in the initial handling of a grievance. In large plants the chairman or steward may function with a shop committee composed of the shop chairmen elected from the various departments. Occasionally the shop officers may be appointed by the local union rather than being elected by the members of the local who work in the particular shop.

An employee with a grievance generally goes directly to his shop steward, who proceeds to negotiate with the foremen; in some plants, however, there are optional arrangements. The aggrieved employee may take up the matter with his foreman first and refer it to the shop steward only if he cannot obtain a satisfactory settlement, or he may ask the steward to accompany him to the foremen, or he may turn the matter over to the steward immediately and take no active part himself in the negotiations. Unions prefer to be a party to the negotiating procedure from the start, in order to insure uniform enforcement and interpretation of the terms of the agreement and general working rules.

Under the terms of many agreements, the stewards and members of the shop committees are placed at the top of the seniority list of the plant or department in which they work. This serves as an inducement to assume the responsibilities of a stewardship, removes fear of discriminatory dismissal because of action taken in connection with the work of a steward, and safeguards continuity in grievance adjustment personnel. Some companies pay stewards their regular wages for the time spent in adjusting grievances, although some limit such compensated time to a specified number of hours per week or only to meetings called by the management. In other cases stewards are reimbursed from union treasuries for loss of wages.

In the building-trades and a few other unions, the shop chairman or steward performs a less important function. He may handle some negotiations with the foreman, but the major burden of enforcing the agreement provisions falls upon the business agent. Although the steward is responsible for securing compliance with the terms of the agreement on a particular job, the business agent has this responsibility for all the employers in the same industry throughout the city. The business agent is a paid, full-time officer elected by the members of the local or appointed by a designated union official. He is not an employee of any of the work places covered by the union agreement, but he usually has a knowledge of the industry through previous employment. In order to function, the business agent must be able to enter the plants under his jurisdiction during working hours and check up on working conditions at firsthand.

Depending upon the character of the industry as well as the

bargaining tradition of the union, the appeal of a dispute to the higher company officials may be handled by the officers of the local union, or provision may be made for the active participation of regional or international officers in the final stages of the joint negotiations. Locals organized on a city-wide basis, or including many small work places in a given area, ordinarily settle their grievances without reference to their international officers, the business agents dealing with the necessary officials of the companies.

On the other hand, unions in large industrial corporations often reserve the higher stages of grievance appeals to their regional or international representatives. This may be done to take advantage of the more skillful bargaining ability of the higher union officials or because the physical location of the corporation's central office, removed from the site of production, makes it difficult for the local union leaders to handle negotiations. Furthermore, when a grievance case reaches the highest company officials, the decision may involve an important principle of union-management relations, applicable to more locals than the one originally involved in the dispute.

When a case goes to arbitration, the union ordinarily selects the worker representative on the arbitration committee. Whether the union representative is selected by the membership or appointed by a union official or committee varies with local practice. In either case the choice usually falls upon an individual with considerable union experience.

Employer Representatives

The employee's immediate supervisor is ordinarily the first negotiator on behalf of the employer in dispute negotiations with the union. In small establishments, the owner himself may handle the initial negotiations; in large industrial concerns the foreman, the department superintendent, the division superintendent, and the plant manager are in turn responsible for dealing with the union. Personnel or labor relations officers, where these are employed, usually take an active part when appeal is taken beyond the foreman, although in some instances the personnel office is involved only after negotiations with the departmental officials have failed to secure a settlement.

In a number of industries, agreements are made with associations of employers which are city-wide, regional, or nation-wide in scope. Although these associations are at times established solely for the purpose of negotiating new agreements, they may also serve as enforcement agencies; in this case the association officials help to settle disputes which arise between the union and any employer who is a member of the association. These association officials are elected by the member firms and, like business agents of the union, are experienced in the industry and familiar with its problems.

Arbitration Provisions

The great majority of employer-union agreements make provision for the arbitration of disputes arising over the interpretation or application of the agreement in the event the parties to the dispute are unable to settle the matter. In the few agreements which do not provide for arbitration, there may be provision for referring the dispute to a state or federal agency for conciliation or mediation. Although this brings the assistance and prestige of experienced negotiators into the proceedings, it does not automatically provide a decision which must be accepted.

The most common form of outside reference is through the selection of an impartial chairman by a committee on which both sides are equally represented. The chairman may be selected to function with the committee from the beginning, or he may be added only after the joint committee has failed to make an adjustment. Some agreements do not leave the selection of an arbitrator until any dispute gets to the stage of arbitration, but specify an individual who is to act as arbitrator as needed throughout the life of the agreement.

When the agreement covers more than a single city, joint machinery may function over a wide area; and when agreements cover virtually the entire industry, the joint machinery operates for the entire industry. For example, the agreement in the pottery industry refers disputes to a standing committee composed of representatives of the association and the union. For many years there has been a permanent board of conciliation in the anthracite industry which has research and administrative functions in addition to settling disputes arising under the agreement. Highly developed joint machinery is found in the garment industry where, because of the nature of the industry which is characterized by seasonal fluctuations, style changes, complex piece-rate structures, and subcontracting, the day-to-day settling of these problems is necessary to insure a smoothly functioning employer-union relationship.

As a rule, unadjusted disputes may be referred to arbitration upon the request of either the employer or the union; in practice, this insures automatic arbitration whenever a dispute is not mutually resolved. Under the terms of a few agreements, both parties must agree to have the matter referred to arbitration; this means that the party satisfied with the *status quo* is able to prevent recourse to arbitration. Since it is usually the union that is seeking redress, under the latter type of arbitration referral the union must either decide to accept the management's decision or resort to economic pressure and call a strike.

The arbitrators hold hearings, take testimony, and occasionally make independent investigations of the facts. In order to avoid unnecessary delays, a time limit is generally set for each step in the process—the selection of arbitrators, the conduct of hearings, and the rendering of decisions. The decision of the arbitrator is, of course, final and binding on both parties. Its enforcement may be secured through resort to the strike or lockout, non-compliance being the only occasion when stoppages of work are not considered a violation of the agreement. Arbitrators' decisions have occasionally been taken to the courts for enforcement, although workers usually prefer to use the strike in preference to long-drawn-out litigation. Whenever the agreement is made with an employers' association, the association officials are held responsible for the compliance of member companies.

GOVERNMENT AGENCIES FOR SETTLING DISPUTES

Government agencies for the adjustment of labor disputes are of two general types: (1) mediation and conciliation agencies, which have no legal power to compel acceptance of their recommendations and which may not even have a legal right to intervene if the parties to the dispute do not request their assistance; and

(2) boards and commissions, which are empowered to administer and enforce specific laws concerning employer-employee relations and working conditions.[3]

Federal Conciliation Service

The present United States Conciliation Service was established under an act passed in 1913, which created the United States Department of Labor, providing among other things that "the Secretary of Labor shall have the power to act as mediator and to appoint commissioners of conciliation in labor disputes whenever in his judgment the interests of industrial peace may require it to be done." The conciliation commissioners are engaged in efforts to settle questions in dispute before strikes and lockouts occur, or to bring the latter to a speedy settlement if they have already begun. The Conciliation Service may enter a case at the request of either party to the dispute, or at the request of some representative of the public, such as a mayor, governor, or Congressman. It may also intervene upon its own motion, but this is done only in the more serious disputes when it is believed that the public interest is in jeopardy.

Although the original Act gave them power to mediate in any kind of dispute, the conciliation commissioners have no power of coercion or means to enforce their recommendations. Acceptance of the conciliator's service is optional, and his recommendations may or may not be adopted. The results he obtains are dependent entirely upon the prestige of his office, the assistance he can render by reason of his knowledge of the facts involved in the dispute, his skill as a negotiator, and the willingness of the opposing parties to come to an agreement.

The Conciliation Service is primarily concerned not with the rights and mechanics of collective bargaining as such, but with the disputes which arise over the terms to be included in a col-

---

[3] In time of war the government must take unusual measures to minimize strikes which interfere with war production. During both the World Wars, National War Labor Boards were established as supreme tribunals for the adjustment of disputes. In case of non-compliance with the Boards' decisions, the plants were taken over by the government. For a full account of the World War II Board's activities, consult *The Termination Report of the National War Labor Board*, U. S. Government Printing Office, Washington, 1946. See also Joseph Shister, "The National War Labor Board: Its Significance," *Journal of Political Economy*, March, 1945.

lective agreement or the interpretation and application of the provisions of the agreement after it is once made.[4] The Service is also frequently called upon to settle jurisdictional disputes, most of these being in the construction industry.

A commissioner of conciliation has no set formula of procedure when he is called in to help settle a dispute. Whenever possible, he tries to get the parties concerned to discuss their differences in conference, in which case he acts as a conciliator. Frequently, especially during the early stages, either or both parties refuse to meet together. He then acts as a mediator, holding separate conferences with the respective sides, adjusting the minor points of misunderstandings or differences, and getting each side to agree upon what major points can or shall be further negotiated. If either or both sides still refuse to discuss these major points together, the commissioner may draft a plan of settlement independently and submit it to the parties as a recommendation, or he may obtain the approval of both sides to have the matter arbitrated. He may be asked to select an arbitrator, or the parties may request him to serve as arbitrator. As an arbitrator, his decisions are final and must be accepted by both parties in accordance with their voluntary agreement to accept such arbitration.

Fact-Finding Boards

Immediately after the termination of the National War Labor Board and the wartime wage stabilization program in August, 1946, fact-finding boards were established to settle wage disputes in a number of important industries. Their functions were to determine the facts in each dispute and make recommendations for settlement within the reconversion wage-price policy of the government.[5] In essence, their function was the quasi-judicial one of

---

[4] In many of the European countries before the recent war there were special legal and quasi-legal arrangements for the arbitration of disputes arising over the interpretation of an agreement, called "disputes on rights," and the conciliation or arbitration of disputes over terms of a new agreement, called "disputes on interests."

[5] For a discussion of the basic wage problems with which these boards were faced and their general recommendations, see H. M. Douty, "Wage Policy, and the Role of Fact-Finding Boards," *Monthly Labor Review*, April, 1946; John T. Dunlop, "Fact-Finding in Labor Disputes," *Academy of Political Science Proceedings*, May, 1946, Vol. xxii, No. 1; Bryce M. Stewart and W. J. Couper, *Fact Finding in Industrial Disputes*, Report No. 11, Industrial Relations Counselors, Inc., New York, 1946.

applying this policy in specific instances, with reliance upon public opinion to force the conclusion of employer-union agreements on the basis of recommendations made. Usually the boards held informal public hearings in which all the parties concerned had full opportunity to present oral information and submit written briefs. During the course of the proceedings, the unions and employers were encouraged to resume collective bargaining; but if their efforts failed, the issues were referred back to the boards.

When the first boards were appointed, many non-partisan persons were hopeful that the fact-finding principle would prove to be not only the panacea for the settlement of existing strikes but a forerunner of procedures to be used in future employer-union disputes. There was discussion about incorporating the fact-finding method in legislation applicable to all industry similar to that already enacted for the railroad industry.

These hopes were soon dashed by the reaction of employers and unions, both of which opposed the principle of compulsory fact-finding by government boards. Fundamental to adequate fact-finding in a wage dispute is knowledge of a company's financial condition, but employers expressed vigorous opposition to having "outsiders" examine their books.[6] The attitude of most of the unions as well as the employers was that the "fact-finding procedure and its many varieties and forms hinder rather than help the promotion of industrial peace. They place a premium on the professional technicians who in their role of outsiders make

---

[6] When this issue first arose, President Truman said: "In appointing a fact-finding board in an industrial dispute where one of the questions at issue is wages, it is essential to a fulfillment of its duty that the board have the authority, whenever it deems it necessary, to examine the books of the employer. That authority is essential to enable the board to determine the ability of the employer to pay an increase in wages where such ability is in question. Ability to pay is always one of the facts relevant to the issue of an increase in wages. This does not mean that the Government or its fact-finding board is going to endeavor to fix a rate of return for the employer. It does mean, however, that since wages are paid out of earnings, the question of earnings is relevant." The President's statement also declared that the information obtained from the books of an employer should not be made public.

The test case came in the General Motors' dispute in 1945–1946, in which the union was insistent that the company could afford a wage increase without increasing the prices of its products. The company refused to allow the fact-finding board to examine its books and withdrew from the hearings in protest against the board's decision to consider the question of the company's ability to pay as one factor in its wage recommendation. The strike was finally settled by allowing both a wage increase and a price increase.

judgments unrelated to the operating experience of workers or employers. They provide an entering wedge for the usurpation by government fiat of the private responsibility of adjusting the work arrangements in the light of the practical relationship between workers and employers."[7]

In spite of the expressed opposition to fact-finding as a permanent procedure, most employers and unions cooperated with the boards established during the post-war emergency when strikes were paralyzing industry and halting reconversion to a peacetime economy. These boards were effective in settling a number of particular disputes, as well as in establishing a wage pattern which served as a guide for the peaceful negotiation of numerous other employer-union agreements. As a result of this experience, it is probable that many employers and unions will voluntarily use fact-finding boards in the future, although neither wish to have it made compulsory.

National (Railroad) Mediation Board

Labor relations on the railroads at the present time are governed by the 1943 amendments to the 1926 Railway Labor Act. These created a three-man National Mediation Board appointed by the President, and a National Railroad Adjustment Board consisting of 18 carrier representatives and 18 union representatives. The Adjustment Board, with headquarters in Chicago, is divided into four separate divisions, each of which has jurisdiction over a distinct class of employees, namely, train and yard service, shop crafts, and so forth.

In this arrangement for handling labor relations on the railroads, a clear distinction is made with respect to the basic differences in the character of labor disputes, that is, those over the interpretation and application of existing agreements, and those over the terms of a new agreement—wages, hours, and working conditions—and questions concerning bargaining units and representation agencies.

The Adjustment Board handles disputes "growing out of grievances or out of the interpretation or application of agreements

---

[7] President William Green of the American Federation of Labor, in testimony before a special committee of the House Labor Committee on July 1, 1946.

concerning rates of pay, rules, or working conditions." Its deci
sions may be enforced by civil suits in federal district courts. If
the bipartisan board is unable to agree, it must appoint a referee;
if it cannot agree in a selection, the National Mediation Board
appoints the referee.

The National Mediation Board intervenes in the other two
classes of disputes. By holding elections or by other means it
certifies who shall represent the workers in their collective bargaining;[8] on request of either party to a dispute involving changes
in pay, rules, or working conditions, or on its own motion in
cases of emergency, it intervenes and through mediation attempts
to bring about an agreement. If its mediating efforts fail, the
Board endeavors to induce the parties to submit their controversy
to arbitration, the arbitration board to be selected by the parties
concerned. If they cannot agree on the selection, the Board is
authorized to name the members of the arbitration board.

If arbitration is refused by either party and the dispute should
"threaten substantially to interrupt interstate commerce to a
degree such as to deprive any section of the country of essential
transportation service," the Board is required to notify the President, who may appoint an emergency board to investigate the
facts and report thereon within thirty days. During this time no
change, except by agreement, may be made by the parties to the
controversy in the conditions out of which the dispute arose. The
law does not require compliance with the recommendations of the
emergency board, although the publication of the findings makes it
difficult for either party not to follow its suggestions.

As was evidenced by the two-day strike in the spring of 1946,
the present machinery for settling disputes on the railroads does
not provide an absolute guarantee against strikes. Nevertheless,

---

[8] The National Mediation Board certifies the union receiving the majority
vote in an election within an "appropriate" unit. While the Board takes into
consideration the customary practice of the union or unions involved, in many
cases involving rival claimants it must define jurisdictional boundaries in order
to determine the appropriate bargaining unit. During the ten years that the
National Mediation Board has been responsible for certifying collective bargaining agencies in the railroad industry, it has disposed of more than a thousand representation disputes, of which over one-third involved two or more
rival unions. See Herbert R. Northrup, "The Appropriate Bargaining Unit
Question Under the Railway Labor Act," *Quarterly Journal of Economics,*
February, 1946.

thousands of grievances and controversies have been adjusted; and the present railroad mediation machinery is probably as effective as could be devised, short of drastic legal prohibitions accompanied by severe penalties, the merits of which are discussed in a later chapter.

National Labor Relations Board

The National Labor Relations Board is a non-partisan, quasi-judicial board of three members, appointed by the President, to develop and administer the National Labor Relations Act.

In pursuance of the provisions of the Act, the Board's activities are of two general types: (1) determining and certifying employees' collective bargaining agents, and (2) preventing employers from engaging in unfair labor practices. The Board is empowered upon complaint to investigate charges of unfair labor practices, to hold formal public hearings, to issue subpoenas requiring the attendance and testimony of witnesses and the production of any written evidence, to issue cease and desist orders from unfair labor practices, to determine the appropriate bargaining unit (that is, whether single or multiple plant or company, craft, or department unit, etc.), and to conduct elections or otherwise to determine which union, if any, a majority of the employees have selected as their bargaining agent. Upon occasion it must decide whether a group of employees may change their union affiliation.

The orders of the Board are not self-enforcing. To secure compliance, the Board must petition the appropriate Circuit Court of Appeals and file with it the record taken before it. The court is authorized to make a decree enforcing, modifying, or setting aside the Board's order in whole or in part. In like manner, any person aggrieved by a final order of the Board may obtain a similar review by filing in the appropriate Court of Appeals a petition that the order be modified or set aside.

According to the Board's recent annual reports, an average of more than 9000 cases are filed with its national and regional offices each year—about twice as many representation as unfair labor practice cases. Various unions are certified in an average of about 4000 plants or bargaining units each year, and remedial action against employer unfair labor practices has been effected in approximately 2000 cases a year. In less than a hundred instances

annually has it been necessary for the Board to resort to court
action for enforcement of its orders.

State Conciliation Services

State machinery for the adjustment of labor disputes ante-
dates the Federal Conciliation Service; that in Massachusetts and
New York for instance, has been functioning since 1886. The
concern of most state governments with employer-employee relations, however, has fluctuated with the increase and decline of
labor disputes, and in only a few states has there been any continuing consistent program for the prevention and settlement of
strikes and lockouts. More generally, when there has been a sharp
rise in union activity and workers have shown a disposition to
make known their discontent and desires, the state government
has hastily passed legislation in an attempt to meet the situation.
During periods when there have been few disputes, such legislation
has been all but forgotten.

With the recent increase in union activity and industrial disputes, a number of states have enacted labor relations acts more
or less similar to the National Labor Relations Act, as well as
laws which require a specified number of days' notification to a
state agency before stoppages of work may take place.[9] None of
the latter makes arbitration mandatory, and a strike or lockout
may be called after the notification period if a settlement satisfactory to both parties has not been effected.

There is a great deal of variation among the several state mediation agencies in mechanical arrangements, legal powers, and the
financial and moral support given them. The most common arrangement is for the conciliation service to be a unit in the state
labor department or industrial commission, the conciliators usually having other duties when not engaged in settling disputes. A
number of states have tripartite boards appointed by the governor.
While these may be permanent boards, in some instances the individual members serve only upon occasion and are paid on a per
diem basis. In only a few of the more inportant industrial states
are there full-time conciliation and arbitration boards. Several
states have no permanent machinery but provide that the labor department or the governor shall appoint a conciliation committee

[9] See chap. 21.

as the occasion arises or when there is a particularly grave dispute.

The procedure in some states resembles the federal arrangement by sharply differentiating disputes arising over questions of union organization and collective bargaining from those arising over questions of wages, hours, and working conditions. The former are handled by state labor relations boards with quasi-judicial powers, while the latter come under the state conciliation service. In other states which have labor relations laws there is no such distinction; the same agency attempts to settle all kinds of disputes, those arising from unfair labor practices and union organization as well as those arising from specific terms of employment such as wages and hours.

Most generally the state agency intervenes only upon the request of one or both parties to the dispute, although a few of the laws specify that the agency shall on its own motion investigate disputes whenever "public interest is material." Some of the laws require that a minimum number of persons, usually ten, must be involved in a dispute before the state agency shall intervene. Others specify that there shall be state intervention only when asked by a designated number of private citizens, local government officials, the employer, or a majority of the employees involved in the dispute.

Since the Kansas experiment in 1920, discussed in Chapter 22, no state has attempted to compel the parties to a dispute to accept the recommendations of the conciliation agency unless they have agreed beforehand to abide by its determinations. In some instances, a degree of pressure is exerted by permitting or requiring the board to publish a written report with recommendations. A few laws specify that if conciliation fails and the parties refuse to arbitrate, the state agency shall request a sworn statement from each party regarding the facts in dispute and their reasons for not arbitrating, the statement to be for public use. Several state laws go still further by providing that the state board shall prepare and publish its findings, and place the blame by designating which party is mainly responsible for the existence and continuance of the dispute. Such provisions for bringing the pressure of public opinion upon the situation are as far as any of the existing state laws have gone to compel acceptance of the recommendations made by their conciliation agencies.

If the parties to a dispute voluntarily agree to have the state board act as arbitrator, the law usually specifies that the awards shall be binding. After arbitration is once accepted, strikes and lockouts are generally forbidden during the time of investigation, and the board is usually given power to subpoena books and records and to require the desired persons to appear as witnesses. In practice, this subpoena power is seldom used, even in the states which have the greatest number of disputes and the most active arbitration agencies.

WORK STOPPAGES RESULTING FROM DISPUTES

In spite of all the machinery for adjusting employer-worker controversies when they first arise, many of them are not settled before a strike or lockout takes place. Impartial observers are prone to think that work stoppages due to labor disputes are not only wasteful but unnecessary; that if a dispute can be settled after a strike or lockout occurs it could just as well have been settled without a stoppage. This may be true in some cases, but the fact is that in many instances different terms of settlement are obtained following a work stoppage than would have been effected without the stoppage. It is this prospect and the hope of obtaining more favorable terms which induce workers (or an employer in the case of a lockout) to undergo the hardships and inconveniences of a cessation of work.

Significance of Strike Action

Because of the relatively strong bargaining position which the employer usually has in the bargaining relationship, most work stoppages take the form of strikes rather than lockouts by employers. Most generally, it is the employees who must take overt action to obtain new terms of employment or to protect existing standards. The employer needs only to announce that he will not raise his wages or intends to reduce them, and his proposals will automatically *go into effect* unless his employees protest.[10] Work

[10] Technically, the distinction between a strike and a lockout depends on the party which actually initiates the stoppage, but in actual experience it is frequently impossible to make a distinction. For example, an employer says he

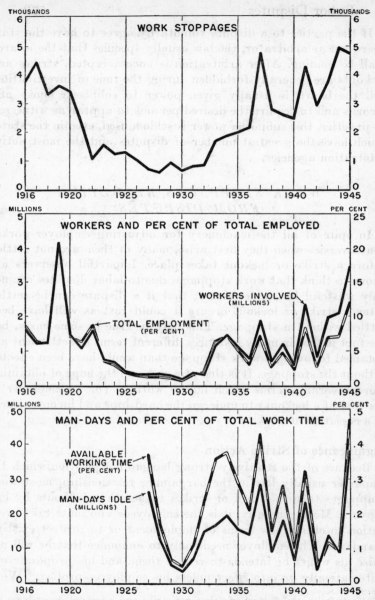

FIG. 31. *Number of Work Stoppages, Workers and Man-Days of Work Involved, 1916–1945.* (*Source:* Monthly Labor Review, *April, 1946.*)

stoppages due to labor disputes, therefore, are conceived of and generally referred to as strikes.

A strike is an evidence of discontent and an expression of protest; it is an overt act by which workers seek to better their condition or mitigate a worsening of conditions. While a strike indicates dissatisfaction, it is also a manifestation of hope. Workers driven to the point of despair, either because of fear of retaliation or because of the general hopelessness of their economic situation, seldom indulge in such overt acts as strikes; their protests must necessarily take the form of sabotage or of a listless slowing down on the job.

A strike is a temporary stoppage of work for specific reasons, entered into with the expectation that work will be resumed when a settlement is effected. The strikers retain their status as employees, with the right to return to their jobs when they have reached a mutual agreement over the matters in dispute or, if unsuccessful, when they are willing to return to work on the terms offered by the employer, provided that he continues to carry on his business. Although some strikes arise over internal shop matters, most of them have broader implications and are directed toward a change in basic working conditions or in employee-employer relationships.

Major Causes of Work Stoppages

Very few work stoppages are the result of only one or even two causes. In most cases the issues are many and complex; sometimes the immediate issue which brought on the stoppage is of less importance than other matters which caused a cumulative dissatisfaction extending over many months or even years. With the warning that its classification of stoppages should be considered only proximate, the United States Bureau of Labor Statistics groups them all into five main categories[11] according to the major

---

cannot operate a plant unless wages are reduced. The workers refuse to accept the reduction and the plant shuts down and reopens a month later at the reduced wage. Here the employer sought to enforce terms upon the workers, who at first refused to accept them. On the other hand, a union may announce certain terms which it says must be adopted as a condition of continued work by its members; work ceases when the employer refuses to accept those terms. In both cases, the workers would claim that these stoppages were lockouts, whereas employers would probably call them strikes.

[11] Prior to 1942, only three categories were used; during 1942–1944 four cate-

issues involved: (1) wages and hours, (2) union organization, wages, and hours; (3) union organization; (4) other working conditions such as seniority, work load, shop rules, etc.; (5) inter-union and intra-union matters, including sympathy and jurisdictional strikes.

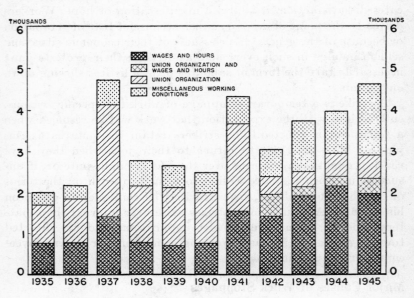

FIG. 32. *Number of Work Stoppages, by Major Issues Involved in Disputes, 1935–1945. Prior to 1942, the "union organization" category includes work stoppages in which the issues of union recognition and wages and hours were involved. (Source:* Monthly Labor Review, *May, 1946.)*

Fig. 32 graphically reveals the changing proportion of stoppages due to various major issues involved. For five years following the passage of the National Labor Relations Act, approximately half of all the work stoppages resulted from disputes in

gories, and beginning in 1945 five categories. During the years when there was no separate category for the combined union organization and wages and hours issues, these strikes were classified in either the wages and hours or the union organization category, depending upon which issue appeared to be more important. Likewise, prior to 1945, interunion and intra-union disputes were classified under the "miscellaneous and other" category.

which the major issue was union status; most of them were for union recognition or the union shop, and some were in protest at discrimination against union members. During the recent war and post-war period, wage issues were predominant and relatively few stoppages were caused by controversies over union recognition, especially after the War Labor Board adopted the policy of granting maintenance-of-membership awards and thus assured unions a measure of security. Second to wage disputes during the war were disputes over internal shop conditions and policies, including such matters as supervision, discipline, work load, shift assignments, and physical and safety conditions. Many of these grievances were the direct effect of war conditions when the presence of large numbers of inexperienced supervisors as well as workers, crowded work rooms and multiple-shift arrangements, coupled with the fatigue and strain of long hours, inadequate housing, and transportation, brought on work stoppages which would not normally have occurred.

Kinds of Strikes

A large majority of work stoppages result from disputes between individual employers and their employees and take place when one party makes definite demands on the other. Some stoppages, such as jurisdictional disputes, quarrels between rival unions or factions within the same union, and sympathetic protests, are not directly due to controversies between workers and their immediate employers.

In the usual jurisdictional dispute the employer is passive; the quarrel is solely between worker groups who have no grievance against their employer, although in some cases he very obviously has an interest as to which union does a particular piece of work because of the differences in wage rates. Disputes between rival unions are somewhat different. In these cases a second group with similar trade jurisdiction seeks to displace a union which has already been recognized by the employer. (Since they are the result of dualism in organization, the rival unions usually do not belong to the same federated group, that is, the A. F. of L. or the C.I.O. Sometimes neither union is affiliated with either group.) While the immediate issue causing the stoppage of work appears to be the rivalry of two factions of workers, the employer is nevertheless an integral factor in the situation. The very fact that there are two rival unions fighting for the allegiance of his employees generally signifies the discontent of one group of workers with the terms which its union has obtained from him, and the hope that the other union can secure better terms.

A sympathetic or general strike represents another situation in which the dispute is not primarily one between an employer and his own employees. In a so-called sympathetic strike, an individual employer may not be responsible for any of the dissatisfactions which bring about the stoppage; it is called for the purpose of demonstrating the solidarity of workers and broadening the group pressure upon the employer against whom there is a strike for specific cause. Sympathetic strikes are not common; they have never amounted to as much as 1 per cent of the total stoppages in any year. Since they usually involve breaking the no-strike provision in employer-union contracts, they are resorted to only in extreme cases when the union or union standards appear to be in jeopardy throughout the trade.

A sympathy strike is generally confined to one or a few employers engaged in the same or a related industry to that of the employer with whom the workers are in dispute. A "general strike" refers to a stoppage of work by all or a large majority of the workers in different industries within one community. Not more than a half dozen general strikes have taken place during the history of this country. All of them have been confined to single cities and have been called in sympathy with particular groups of strikers or in protest against some action taken by city authorities.[12]

In this respect American experience thus far differs from that of some other countries where general strikes that included workers in all the industries throughout the country have occurred. In France, before World War II, several such strikes were called in protest against government actions. The most notable general strike is the one which took place in 1926 in Great Britain, in which all organized workers, including government employees, quit work in sympathy with the striking coal miners.

---

[12] One recent city-wide strike took place in Rochester, New York, in May, 1946, when members of over a hundred locals, including A. F. of L. and C.I.O. affiliates as well as independent unions, stopped work for 24 hours until city officials *agreed to deal* with a union of municipal employees.

Sit-Down Strikes

Among the most dramatic, and to many people most alarming, strike phenomena in recent years were the so-called sit-down strikes which took place during 1936–1937. Sitting at one's work place but refusing to work was not an entirely new technique for dissatisfied workers to use in their efforts to force better working conditions from employers. It is not unusual for small groups of workers in unorganized as well as unionized shops to stop work but remain at their work places until a particular wage rate or other grievance is settled. Such stoppages usually last only an hour or two. In previous years, however, they had seldom occurred in mass-production industries where an interruption by a few employees immediately affects the flow of production throughout the entire plant.

The 1936–1937 wave of sit-down strikes was unprecedented both in magnitude and in the unique characteristic that the workers stayed in the plants day and night for extended periods.[13] Although they were the manifestation of spontaneous protests by groups of workers in various individual plants rather than a planned, integrated movement, they nevertheless represented a focal reaction to the accumulated impact of many forces, political and economic, national and international. Significantly, most of these sit-down strikes were vanguards of unionization rather than acts of already organized workers, and took place in plants and industries in which employers had long opposed collective bargaining.

In the background were the long years of employer absolutism in labor relations and the many jobless months during the worst years of the depression in 1930–1933. In the foreground were the newly aroused hopes and expectations inspired by the New Deal government and the National Labor Relations Act. The numerous and dramatic sit-down strikes which were taking place in France, and the "stay-down" strikes occurring in Hungarian, Polish, and

---

[13] In 525 of the 6912 strikes during these two years, workers stayed in the plants one or more working days. There were also numerous unrecorded sit-down strikes which lasted only a few hours. In about half the 525 officially recorded sit-down strikes, workers stayed in the plants for one or more nights— in a few cases as long as several weeks. Sit-down strikes reached their peak in March, 1937, when 170 occurred. By the end of the year they had practically disappeared. (*Monthly Labor Review*, August, 1938, p. 360.)

Welsh coal mines, no doubt had their effect on the psychology of the workers in the United States; moreover, there is some evidence that the philosophy of passive resistance personified by the Gandhi movement in India also had its influence.[14]

Although the sit-down strikes were a radical departure from the traditional behavior of American workers, they did not represent a revolutionary movement; they were not founded on Marxian doctrines or the syndicalist philosophy of the I.W.W. Even in the minds of their most ardent advocates there was no intention of seizing employers' property permanently in order to operate the plants, and the "guarding" from within was conceived merely as a substitute for the outside picket line to keep employers from operating their plants until the grievances were settled. Ideological defenders maintained that the right "to hold" the work place was a natural corollary to the worker's right to his job; since the skill of the worker in running a machine is a property right that has no value apart from the machine, workers have the right to protect this asset, and to do so it might be necessary for them to remain at the machine or in the plant. The sit-down strikers themselves, however, gave little thought to the principles at stake as they vigorously utilized this new-found weapon to gain immediate concessions from employers (and incidentally got a good deal of emotional release from the novel dramatic experience).

Responsible union leaders never approved this method of striking, for very practical reasons. In addition to their fear of the consequences of public disapproval, the "wildcat" nature of this form of strike action imperiled the unions' influence upon the workers themselves. By their very nature such strikes are not compatible with stable collective bargaining relationships for they enable a few workers, without notice to the union or to the employer, to tie up operations in entire plants. When they occur in organized plants, they represent a rebellion against the union as

---

[14] The prolonged depression had incited many young "intellectuals" to thinking about methods of protest against economic and political injustices, and some of them became deeply impressed by the Hindu Nationalists' passive resistance technique. Some of these young people, who directly and indirectly had some influence on labor activities during these years, recommended the sit-down method in preference to the traditional picket strike as being a more passive form of protest. However, not all the sit-down strikes turned out to be as peaceful as the name implies.

much as against the employer because they antithesize the orderly grievance adjustment procedures established by the union's contract with the employer.

Frequency of Work Stoppages

The prevalence of strikes, as well as their immediate causes, varies with the conditions existing at any given time. The general economic and labor market situation, the attitude of the public and the government, the strength of union organization, the employers' willingness and ability to allow unrest to reach the state of strike action all have their influence. Historically, strikes have tended to diminish when business activity declined and job opportunities were scarce, and to increase during periods of business prosperity, especially when the revival of business was accompanied by rising prices. History may not always repeat itself, however. Conceivably, the unions could be sufficiently entrenched in the nation's economic and political fabric so that workers would not feel it necessary to accept without protest the distress and reverses they formerly suffered during business depressions.

Unfortunately, there are no statistical records of work stoppages prior to 1881.[15] Available records show that following the depression of the middle 1880's the number of strikes almost trebled, declined during the depression of the 1890's, and more than doubled on the upturn of business at the beginning of the century. With the rise in prices and expansion in business during the First World War, strikes increased greatly, reaching a peak in number in 1917 although more workers were engaged in strikes during the post-war year 1919. Thereafter strike activity subsided sharply and remained at a low level during the 'twenties as well as during the depression of the early 'thirties. The reasons for the comparatively few strikes in the "prosperous" 1920's have been suggested in earlier chapters. Although substantial numbers of workers suffered from job insecurity, low wages and long hours, prices were fairly stable, unions were very weak, and the general political atmosphere was not conducive to open protests by wage earners.

---

[15] Strike statistics between 1880 and 1927 are very incomplete; no data of any kind were collected for the years 1906–1913 inclusive. For details about strike statistics and the history of strike activity, see Florence Peterson, *Strikes in the United States, 1880–1936,* Bureau of Labor Statistics Bulletin No. 651, Government Printing Office, Washington, 1937.

TABLE 28.   Work Stoppages Due to Labor Disputes, 1916–1946[18]

Year	Number	Workers Involved		Man-Days Idle		Indexes (1935–1939 = 100)		
		Number	Per Cent of Total Employed[a]	Number	Per Cent of Available Working Time[b]	Strikes and Lockouts	Workers Involved	Man-Days Idle
1916	3,789	1,599,917	8.4	c	c	132	142	c
1917	4,450	1,227,254	6.3	c	c	155	109	c
1918	3,353	1,239,989	6.2	c	c	117	110	c
1919	3,630	4,160,348	20.8	c	c	127	370	c
1920	3,411	1,463,054	7.2	c	c	119	130	c
1921	2,385	1,099,247	6.4	c	c	83	98	c
1922	1,112	1,612,562	8.7	c	c	39	143	c
1923	1,553	756,584	3.5	c	c	54	67	c
1924	1,249	654,641	3.1	c	c	44	58	c
1925	1,301	428,416	2.0	c	c	45	38	c
1926	1,035	329,592	1.5	c	c	36	29	c
1927	707	329,939	1.4	26,218,628	0.37	25	29	155
1928	604	314,210	1.3	12,631,863	.17	21	28	75
1929	921	288,572	1.2	5,351,540	.07	32	26	32
1930	637	182,975	.8	3,316,808	.05	22	16	20
1931	810	341,817	1.6	6,893,244	.11	28	30	41
1932	841	324,210	1.8	10,502,033	.23	29	29	62
1933	1,695	1,168,272	6.3	16,872,128	.36	59	104	100
1934	1,856	1,466,695	7.2	19,591,949	.38	65	130	116
1935	2,014	1,117,213	5.2	15,456,337	.29	70	99	91
1936	2,172	788,648	3.1	13,901,956	.21	76	70	82
1937	4,740	1,860,621	7.2	28,424,857	.43	166	165	168
1938	2,772	688,376	2.8	9,148,273	.15	97	61	54
1939	2,613	1,170,962	4.7	17,812,219	.28	91	104	105
1940	2,508	576,988	2.3	6,700,872	.10	88	51	40
1941	4,288	2,362,620	8.4	23,047,556	.32	150	210	136
1942	2,968	839,961	2.8	4,182,557	.05	104	75	25
1943	3,752	1,981,279	6.9	13,500,529	.15	131	176	80
1944	4,956	2,115,637	7.0	8,721,079	.09	173	188	51
1945	4,750	3,467,000	12.2	38,025,000	.47	166	308	224
1946[d]	4,700	4,650,000	15.2	113,000,000	1.50	164	413	667

[18] From Bureau of Labor Statistics, Department of Labor. Statistics include all strikes and lockouts which lasted one day (or shift) or longer and involved 6 or more workers.

[a] "Total employed workers" as used here includes all workers except those in occupations and professions where strikes rarely if ever occur. In general, the term "total employed workers" includes all employees except the following groups: government workers, agricultural wage earners on farms employing less than 6 workers, managerial and supervisory employees, and certain groups which because of the nature of their work cannot or do not strike (such as college professors, clergymen, and domestic servants). Self-employed and unemployed persons are, of course, excluded.

[b] "Available working time" was estimated for purposes of this table by multiplying the average number of employed workers each year by the number of days worked by most employees during the year.

[c] Not available.

[d] Preliminary estimates.

The first year of recovery and the impetus for increased union activity resulting from the National Industrial Recovery Act doubled the number of strikes in 1933–1934. They again increased more than twofold in 1937, when the great mass-production industries were unionized. Despite government efforts to forestall work stoppages during the recent war, there were a considerable number of strikes, but most of them were of short duration and a large proportion of the time lost was concentrated in the coal mining industry. According to official records, there were 14,731 work stoppages lasting a day or longer between Pearl Harbor and V-J Day. These stoppages involved over 6½ million workers and 36⅓ million man-days of idleness, which amounted to slightly over one-tenth of 1 per cent of the total work time.[16] Almost 40 per cent of the total idleness resulted from strikes of the coal miners.

A few weeks after the cessation of hostilities in August, 1945, there was a sharp increase not only in the number of work stoppages but also in their extent and duration. Whereas most of the stoppages during the war were small, spontaneous strikes, many of them over minor issues which could be quickly settled, the stoppages after V-J Day involved fundamental issues of wages in relation to prices and profits. With the elimination of overtime and night shifts, and the downgrading from high-wage war jobs, workers experienced substantial reductions in their take-home pay, although prices and cost of living were rapidly rising.[17]

Practically all the major industries experienced strikes which caused cessations of work throughout the industries, and many of these strikes were long and stubborn, requiring direct intervention by the President. In two critical stoppages during the spring of 1946, a strike which completely tied up railroad operations for two days and a five-week miners' strike, the government took over the industries under the President's war-time powers and made settlements. The coal mines were shut down again in November when the union demanded that its contract with the government be reopened in order to permit negotiations for higher wages. The government, maintaining that the contract it had signed six

---

[16] *Monthly Labor Review,* May, 1946, p. 723.

[17] Until the close of the war, base rates were controlled by the "Little Steel" formula which permitted rates to be 15% over their 1941 levels, although cost of living had advanced at least 30 per cent during this period. See chap. 10 concerning wage rates and "real" wages.

months previously was in force for the period of government operation of the mines, refused to reopen negotiations. The miners returned to work (December 7th) after heavy fines were levied against the union for violation of a government injunction to call off the strike.[18]

SELECTED REFERENCES

Adamic, Louis, *Dynamite, the Story of Class Violence in America,* The Viking Press, New York, 1931.

Bing, A. M., *Wartime Strikes and Their Adjustment,* E. P. Dutton & Co., Inc., New York, 1921.

Braun, Kurt, *The Settlement of Industrial Disputes,* The Blakiston Company, Philadelphia, 1944.

Brooks, Robert R. R., *Unions of Their Own Choosing: An Account of the N.L.R.B.,* Yale University Press, New Haven, 1939.

Galenson, Walter, *Rival Unionism in the United States,* American Council of Public Affairs, Washington, 1941.

Kaltenborn, Howard S., *Governmental Adjustment of Labor Disputes,* The Foundation Press, Inc., Chicago, 1943.

Kellor, Frances, *Arbitration in Action,* Harper & Brothers, New York, 1941.

Lapp, John A., *Labor Arbitration, Principles and Procedures,* National Foremen's Institute, Inc., Deep River, Conn., 1942.

Levinson, Edward, *I Break Strikes: The Technique of Pearl L. Berghoff,* Robert M. McBride & Co., New York, 1935.

National War Labor Board, *The Termination Report of the N.W.L.B.,* Government Printing Office, Washington, 1946.

Peterson, Florence, *Strikes in the United States, 1880–1936,* Bureau of Labor Statistics Bulletin No. 651, Government Printing Office, Washington, 1937.

---

[18] See p. 653, note 17. The injunction raised the issue as to whether or not the Norris-LaGuardia Act was applicable to government operations. The Federal District Court held that the Act did not deprive the government of injunctive relief, and fined the union $3,500,000 and President John L. Lewis $10,000 for contempt of court. The case was immediately referred to the Supreme Court which, by a 5-to-4 decision, held that the Act did not prohibit injunctions in labor disputes where the government functions in the capacity of an employer. The Supreme Court, however, reduced the fine against the union to $700,000, but the fine against Lewis personally was upheld. The Court did not have before it the question of whether or not the agreement was reopenable and therefore made no finding on this point. (*United States* v. *United Mine Workers,* No. 759, U. S. Sup. Ct., March 6, 1947.)

Spencer, William H., *The National Railroad Adjustment Board,* University of Chicago Press, Chicago, 1938.

Twentieth Century Fund, Inc., *Labor and the Government,* McGraw-Hill Book Company, Inc., New York, 1935.

Twenty Years a Labor Spy, by GT 99, Bobbs-Merrill Company, Indianapolis, 1937.

Updegraff, C. M., and McCoy, W. P., *Arbitration of Labor Disputes,* Commerce Clearing House, Inc., Chicago, 1946.

Yellen, Samuel, *American Labor Struggles,* Harcourt, Brace & Company, Inc., New York, 1936.

21

LEGAL FOUNDATIONS OF COLLECTIVE BARGAINING

COLLECTIVE BARGAINING BY DEFINITION SIGNIFIES THAT THE TERMS and conditions of employment are negotiated through combinations of workers. Inextricable from the law of collective bargaining, therefore, are the laws pertaining to labor unions and their activities. Legislation which protects or restricts labor organizations include not only laws which are specifically directed toward unions, but also general laws which are applicable alike to members of unions and all other persons.

The legal keystone of employer-union relations in this country is the same basic civil rights of freedom of speech and assembly, prohibition against involuntary servitude, and protection of life, liberty, and property, that are provided in our Constitution for all our citizens. Similarly, unions and their members are subject to the same regulatory laws pertaining to conspiracy, sedition, violence, racketeering, and other criminal acts which apply to all other citizens. For many years organized labor was guided solely by the judicial interpretation and application of these general protections and regulations. During recent years, in recognition of the peculiar needs and position of wage earners in the modern industrial economy, the federal government and most of the states have enacted laws which pertain particularly to collective bargaining and labor organizations.

When applied to specific employer-union situations, both the general and the specific labor laws are subject to varying interpretations, and judicial decisions through the years have shown little unanimity or consistency of opinion. The higher courts have differed from the lower courts in interpreting the same case, and many important cases have been finally decided by a close margin in a given court. Moreover, like all other human institutions, law is dynamic and not fixed for an indefinite period of time; new legislation is enacted and interpretations of existing laws are revised with the changing times, in response to public opinion or shifts of the court personnel.

Because of these varying and ever-changing decisions by the judicial and administrative agencies throughout the land, as well as the great variety of laws on the statute books of the various states, it is impossible in this brief summary to give a definitive statement of the present law of collective bargaining and related activities. The best that can be done is to indicate some of the broad principles and the major federal statutes and opinions of the United States Supreme Court, with incidental reference to particular state laws and state court decisions. To do this it is necessary to make passing reference to the developing concepts represented in the court decisions throughout the years. Although some of these earlier decisions have been superseded by statutory laws, many of them represent the latest word on particular issues and may assume importance whenever the appropriate occasion arises, even though they may seem to be dormant at a given time. Furthermore, the recently enacted statutory laws can be understood and appreciated only in the light of the common law which preceded them.

LEGAL RESTRICTIONS

The Doctrine of Conspiracy

American law on collective bargaining and union activities developed out of the earlier English common and statutory laws, which held that the mere existence of combinations of workers was a conspiracy and therefore illegal. During the 18th century, Parliament enacted a series of statutes which forbade various groups of workers to enter into combinations to raise their wages or lessen their hours, and condemned offenders "to hard labour or the common gaol without bail or mainprize." The British court attitude at that time was typified by a statement in connection with the conviction of some tailors who had attempted to raise their wages by concerted action: "The illegal combination is the gist of the offense, persons in possession of any articles of trade may sell them at such prices as they may individually please, but if they confederate and agree not to sell them under certain prices, it is a conspiracy; so every man may work at what price he pleases, but a combination not to work under certain prices is an indictable offense."[1]

The essence of the conspiracy doctrine is that a number of persons acting in concert or combination possess powers to do wrong which an individual does not possess; in other words, an act which is lawful for an individual is not lawful if done by a number of persons acting together. There is also a crime of conspiracy when a group have agreed to undertake a wrongful act even though they have not yet accomplished it. When applied to formal organizations such as labor unions, the conspiracy doctrine was further extended to hold that if one or several persons in the combination do an illegal act, all the other members are equally responsible even though they had no knowledge of the act.

The first application of the conspiracy doctrine in this country was invoked in 1806 against some Philadelphia shoemakers,[2] who, according to the prosecution, ". . . did combine, conspire, confederate and unlawfully agree together that they . . . should not work and labor but at certain prices . . . to the damage, injury and prejudice of the masters employing them, . . . did agree that each and every one of them would prevent by threats, menaces and other unlawful means, other workmen from working and laboring. . . ." The defendants, on the other hand, maintained that

---

[1] *Rex* v. *Journeymen Tailors of Cambridge* (1721). The British Combination Acts of 1799 and 1800, which outlawed all concerted action by workers and employers, were essentially a confirmation of the British common law which was centuries old. These Combination Acts were repealed in 1824 but, following a wave of strikes during subsequent months, they were largely reestablished in 1825. In 1867 the Old Masters and Servants Act was repealed. This Act provided that a master could be sued only civilly for breach of contract with an employee, whereas workmen could be proceeded against criminally and imprisoned. During the 1870's most of the British common law pertaining to trade unions was replaced by statute law. An Act of 1906 extended further legal protections to union activity. The 1927 Trade Unions Act, enacted after the 1926 general strike, imposed some restrictions upon union organizations and their activities, but this Act was repealed in 1946.

[2] Statements concerning these shoemakers' trials are taken from J. R. Commons, *Documentary History of American Industrial Society*, Arthur H. Clark Company, Cleveland, 1910, vols. iii, iv.

". . . if a single individual has the right to refuse to work for a certain wage, a number can unite for the same object. . . . That a menace is not indictable; that if any employer suffer inconvenience or mischief in consequence of his journeymen being seduced or driven from his employment he has his remedy by civil action in which he may recover damages . . . that since they did not use physical violence in preventing non-members from working, but only refused themselves to work for the same employer, this was not an offense or crime."

Action was brought under the English common-law doctrine of criminal conspiracy. At that time there was a great deal of contention as to whether any of the English common law should be extended to this country. The Jeffersonian Democrats were strongly opposed to it, but the Federalists, who controlled the courts, were favorably disposed toward English judicial precedent. Conviction followed the judge's charge to the jury, which stated: "A combination of workmen to raise their wages may be considered in a two-fold point of view; one is to benefit themselves . . . the other is to injure those who do not join their society. The rule of law condemns both. If the rule be clear we are bound to conform to it even though we do not comprehend the principles upon which it is founded. We are not to reject it because we do not see the reason of it."

As a result of the influence of the Jeffersonians, the judiciary shifted its point of emphasis in a similar case a few years later when the court's charge to the jury said nothing about the illegality of combinations as such, but referred to the case as a "combination to secure increases in wages by *unlawful means*," defining the latter as anything of a "nature too arbitrary and coercive."

The famous *Commonwealth* v. *Hunt* decision in 1842 marked a definite departure from earlier and later expressions of the court. Chief Justice Shaw in this case recognized the area of conflict within which organized labor might strive to attain union objectives and even indicated that a strike for a closed shop is a lawful means to that end: "The manifest intention of this Association is to induce all those engaged in the same occupation to become members of it. Such a purpose is not unlawful. We think that associations may be entered into, the object of which is to adopt measures that may have a tendency to impoverish another, that is, to diminish his gains and profits, and yet, so far from being criminal or unlawful, the object may be highly meritorious and public spirited."

The *Commonwealth* v. *Hunt* decision was largely ignored as legal precedent by other judges, who continued for many years to consider as criminal conspiracies any combinations of workers to prevent others from accepting employment on any terms they might see fit. The effect of this doctrine was somewhat softened by several state laws enacted during the 1860's which legalized combinations of workers formed for the purpose of improving working conditions.

Restraint of Trade Doctrine

Closely allied to the common-law concept of criminal conspiracy as applied to labor unions was the doctrine of restraint of trade. This doctrine was based on the philosophical premise of the natural right of every person to dispose of his own property and labor as he pleased, free from the dictation of others. As applied to employer-labor relations it meant that an employer had a right to buy his labor in the cheapest market and that each individual laborer was entitled to sell his labor on whatever terms he saw fit to accept.[3] In most labor cases brought before the courts the decision rested upon what the particular court considered to be unlawful coercion by unions to obtain workers' participation in acts directed toward what they deemed to be "unreasonable" ends.

The common law of restraint of trade was reinforced by statute with the passage of the Sherman Anti-Trust Act in 1890 in response to popular demand for regulation of monopolies and "trusts." The Act states that "every contract, combination in the form of trust or otherwise, or conspiracy, in restraint of trade or commerce among the several states, or with foreign nations, is hereby declared to be illegal."[4] Under the Act the courts were able to impose increasing restrictions on the activities of unions, largely

---

[3] See pp. 635 ff. for a discussion of this principle as applied to the union shop and the "right to work."

[4] At the time of its passage, the Act was generally thought to have no application to labor unions, but some of the first cases decided by the courts under the Act had to do with labor disputes. See Edward Berman, *Labor and the Sherman Act,* Harper & Brothers, New York, 1930.

through the legal identification of "trade" and "property" with "good will" and the right to do business. Under this concept, an employer had a right to unhampered access to the commodity and labor market and therefore legal protection against boycotts, picketing, and other acts of unions which might hinder him from selling his product or prevent him from getting new employees to take the place of strikers.

The first serious application of the Sherman Anti-Trust Act to unions was in the Danbury Hatters' case in 1908,[5] in which the court held the individual members of the union responsible to the full amount of their individual property for triple damages to the company because of the union's nation-wide boycott against the company. In another case a few years later the Supreme Court held that a nation-wide boycott conducted through the American Federation of Labor against the Buck Stove and Range Company was in violation of the Sherman Act, and forbade the officers of the A. F. of L. to speak or write anything in furtherance of the boycott.[6] In essence, these decisions meant that even peaceful persuasion and peaceful assembly were illegal if they resulted in curtailment of trade and impairment of the "good will" of business.

Organized labor, construing these decisions as indicating that any union activity might be interpreted as illegal restraint of interstate trade, undertook a vigorous campaign to have unions exempted from the provisions of the Sherman Act. It thought it had won with the passage of the Clayton Act in 1914, which it optimistically hailed as "Labor's Magna Charta."

The Clayton Act declares that the "labor of a human being is not a commodity or article of commerce," and provides that the anti-trust laws shall not be construed to forbid the existence of labor organizations or to restrain their members from carrying out the "legitimate objects" thereof, that no injunction shall prohibit the quitting of work, the refusal to patronize, peaceful picketing, or peaceful persuasion, whether these acts are done "singly or in concert." The Act further provides for a jury trial for persons accused of violating injunctions by acts indictable as criminal offenses.

In actual operation, the Clayton Act did not exempt labor from

---

[5] *Loewe* v. *Lawlor*, 208 U. S. 274 (1908) and 235 U. S. 522 (1915).

[6] *Gompers* v. *Buck Stove and Range Company*, 221 U. S. 418 (1911).

the anti-trust law and the most important provisions of the Act were construed by the courts as having made no change in the law as previously interpreted. This was revealed in a number of important decisions made by the Supreme Court during the 1920's.[7]

Four cases dealt with boycotting and picketing. In the Duplex Printing Co. case the court held that the Machinists union's efforts to get printing companies not to buy Duplex presses was illegal because threats had been used and the aim was to injure the company. In the American Steel Foundry and the Truax cases the court held that more than one picket at each factory gate was unlawful because it constituted intimidation and violated the constitutional guarantees of liberty and property, although the court explicitly said that the number of permissible pickets depends upon the circumstances of each particular case. The Coronado and Red Jacket Coal cases involved the application of the Sherman Act to strikes, and again brought up the question of the suability of unions. In these decisions the Supreme Court held that unions could be sued even though unincorporated, and that inasmuch as the union's actions against the companies were for the purpose of stopping production of non-union coal and preventing its shipment into other states, they constituted illegal interference with interstate trade.

The Bedford case in 1927 had to do with the union's refusal to allow its members to work on non-union material, and the court's decision was one of the most severe it had ever handed down. In this instance no boycott was attempted by the union against the firm's products; neither did the union picket non-union men. The strike was confined to members of one national union, and the union's efforts were directed solely toward peacefully persuading its own members to abide by their union rule of not working on non-union material. The Supreme Court held that this was a course of conduct which directly and substantially curtailed or threatened to curtail the natural flow of interstate commerce, and

---

[7] *Duplex Printing Company* v. *Deering,* 254 U. S. 349 (1921); *American Steel Foundries* v. *Tri-City Central Trades Council,* 257 U. S. 184 (1921); *Truax* v. *Corrigan,* 257 U. S. 312 (1921); *Coronado Coal and Coke Co.* v. *United Mine Workers,* 259 U. S. 344 (1922) and 268 U. S. 295 (1925); *United Mine Workers* v. *Red Jacket Coal & Coke Co.,* 18 Fed. (2nd) 839, certiorari denied, 275 U. S. 536 (1927); *Bedford Cut Stone Company* v. *Journeymen Stone Cutters' Association,* 274 U. S. 37 (1927).

that even though the ultimate aim was a benefit to the union and no illegal tactics were used, the organization was guilty of conspiracy to restrain trade.

Rights of Liberty and Property Doctrine

The Fourteenth Amendment to the Constitution provides: "No State shall make or enforce any law which shall abridge the privileges or immunities of citizens of the United States; nor shall any State deprive any person of life, liberty or property, without due process of law, nor deny any person within its jurisdiction the equal protection of the laws."[8] Two fundamental concepts have influenced the courts when applying this amendment to employer-labor disputes: First, the right to engage in business is property, and employers therefore should be guaranteed protection against abuse not only of their physical property but also of their "good will" and their means of carrying on business. Second, workers and employers must be treated with formal "equality" by the law; as long as the worker is free to quit for any or no reason the employer must be free not to hire him or to fire him for any or no reason. Such a concept, of course, completely ignores the basic economic inequality between employers and workers, and considers a large corporation (which is a combination of capital) to have the same status as an independent owner-employer.

The right to hire and fire at will provides one of the most direct methods of combating labor unions and collective bargaining. It permits the use of employer black lists, "yellow-dog" contracts, discriminatory discharges, and the hiring of strikebreakers. In recognition of the essential injustice accruing from such unrestrained powers, many states early enacted laws making it a criminal offense for employers to dismiss employees or discriminate against prospective employees because of union membership or activity. Almost uniformly these state laws were held unconstitutional by the courts prior to the enactment of federal legislation in 1932.

---

[8] The Fourteenth Amendment was adopted in 1868 to protect the rights of the freed Negroes. Its use by the courts in labor cases is an outstanding illustration of a diversion of the original purpose of statutory law; for fifty years it was used by the courts against union activities and the general improvement of working conditions, as already indicated in Chaps. 14 and 16.

The first important case involving the constitutional right of an employer to dismiss an employee for any reason whatsoever, including union affiliation, was directed against the federal Erdman Act of 1898, which forbade discriminatory discharge of railroad employees. In the Adair decision, the Supreme Court said:

While . . . the rights of liberty and property guaranteed by the Constitution against deprivation without due process of law, is subject to such reasonable restraints as the common good or the general welfare may require, it is not within the functions of government—at least in the absence of contract between the parties—to compel any person in the course of his business and against his will to accept or retain the personal services of another, or to compel any person against his will, to perform personal services for another. The right of a person to sell his labor upon such terms as he deems proper is, in its essence, the same as the right of the purchaser of labor to prescribe the conditions upon which he will accept such labor from the person offering to sell it. So the right of the employee to quit the service of the employer, for whatever reason, is the same as the right of the employer, for whatever reason, to dispense with the services of such employee. . . . In all such particulars the employer and the employee have equality of right, and any legislation that disturbs that equality is an arbitrary interference with the liberty of contract which no government can legally justify in a free land."[9]

Outstanding as a device to prevent unionism and obstruct collective bargaining has been the "yellow-dog" contract. Although varied in form, such a contract in substance obligates the employee not to join a union or engage in strikes or other union activities. In turn the employer gives the worker employment either for a definite period of time or at will. In 1915 the Supreme Court held that a state statute which forbade the use of yellow-dog contracts was unconstitutional, when, in the *Coppage* v. *Kansas* case, it stated: "Under constitutional freedom of contract, whatever either party has the right to treat as sufficient ground for terminating employment, where there is no stipulation on the subject, he has the right to provide against by insisting that a stipulation respecting it shall be the sine qua non of the inception of the employment, or its continuance if it be terminable at will. It fol-

---

[9] *Adair* v. *United States,* 208 U. S. 161 (1908).

lows that this case cannot be distinguished from *Adair* v. *United States*."[10]

In practice, the yellow-dog contract operates most effectively as a bar to unionization when the injunction is utilized to protect it from threatened breach. The use of the injunction for this purpose was brought to the attention of the Supreme Court when the United Mine Workers of America attempted to unionize the non-union coal-mining area in the West Virginia Panhandle where employees had signed such contracts. In this case, *Hitchman Coal & Coke Company* v. *Mitchell*,[11] the Supreme Court enjoined the organizers from soliciting membership. The injunction was based upon the well-established doctrine that action will lie against the person who persuades either party to a contract to breach it. The Hitchman case was the first important application of this doctrine to the anti-union contract.

Theory and Use of Injunctions

Concomitant with the legal identity of *business* with *property* was the use of injunctions in labor disputes. Injunctions were sought by employers primarily to protect their rights to do business, in other words, to prevent obstruction of the sale of their goods and of their access to the labor market. The police and criminal laws provide protection against damage to physical property and violence in labor disputes, but employers sought injunctions to restrain workers from engaging in boycotts, picketing, and other acts which interfered with business operations, even though such acts were unattended by violence or damage to physical property.

The use of injunctions in labor disputes can best be understood by reference to the principles of equity which are supposed to govern the courts in issuing them. Injunctions[12] are orders issued

---

[10] *Coppage* v. *Kansas,* 236 U. S. 1 (1915). In this instance a railway employee was discharged for refusing to sign a pledge to withdraw from the Switchmen's Union when withdrawal meant a sacrifice of insurance benefits to the amount of $1500. On the basis of this and other evidence, the Kansas Supreme Court held the exaction of the pledge to be coercion, but the United States Supreme Court reversed the decision of the Kansas court.

[11] 245 U. S. 229 (1917).

[12] The injunction originated centuries ago in the British Courts of Chancery. Unlike the experience in the United States, the use of injunctions in labor disputes has been very infrequent in England.

by judges commanding individuals to do or to refrain from doing certain acts. Violation of an injunction constitutes contempt of court, and the judge who grants the injunction has the power and discretion to fine or imprison anyone who violates it. Injunctive relief is supposed to be an extraordinary measure to be used only when there is "inadequate remedy at law," that is, when civil action for damages will not provide full redress either because of the defendant's financial inability to make restitution, or because damage is threatened which is irreparable owing to the nature of the thing harmed. A basic principle of equity is that anyone who seeks injunctive relief must come into court "with clean hands"; that is, he must himself be guiltless of unlawful conduct in connection with the dispute. Another principle is that an injunction should not be granted if it would result in greater loss to the defendant than to the complainant. As originally used, injunctions were *served* individually and were not binding upon anyone who did not receive a notice.

The traditional principles guiding the issuance of injunctions were radically changed by the courts when applied to labor disputes. The majority[13] were granted with no notice to those against whom they were directed, and no hearing at which labor's side of the case could be presented and evidence shown as to whether the employer came before the court "with clean hands." The employers' mere statements were accepted as sufficient, without substantiating proof; and the employers' applications frequently included every possible restriction upon workers' activities that they believed could be of advantage to them. Employers were not required to post bonds or forfeits, and injunctions were granted on trivial pretexts, with no consideration as to the relative losses which they might cause the complainant and the defendant. Furthermore, they were not always limited to the short period of the strike or lockout; permanent injunctions were sometimes issued which re-

---

[13] A study of 118 applications for injunctions presented to federal courts between 1901 and 1928 found that seventy of them were *ex parte,* and in only twelve cases did employers bring records or witnesses to substantiate their statements. See Felix Frankfurter and Nathan Greene, *The Labor Injunction,* The Macmillan Company, New York, 1930; Cleon O. Swayzee, *Contempt of Court in Labor Injunction Cases,* Columbia University Press, New York, 1935; E. E. Witte, "Injunctions in Labor Disputes in the United States," *International Labour Review,* March, 1930.

strained unions and workers from engaging in activities that otherwise would have been lawful.

An injunction might be worded in general and vague terms so that the workers could not know in advance whether or not they were violating some of its provisions. This is especially serious when one realizes that violation of injunctions entails risks not present under civil and criminal law. Instead of trial by jury with an opportunity to secure change of venue if desired, a violator of an injunction is tried and punished by the judge who issued the injunction. In many labor injunctions, the evidence was in the form of affidavits, with no witnesses appearing to support the charges, and the accused was not furnished counsel or given the opportunity of listening to evidence presented by the accusers.

Probably the greatest travesty of equal rights before the law resulted from the blanket labor injunctions which prohibited lawful as well as unlawful acts and restrained not only the actual defendants but also "all persons combining and conspiring with them and all other persons whomsoever." This was the coverage in the famous Debs case[14] in 1895, which provided the pattern for numerous injunctions thereafter. In the Railroad Shopmen's strike in 1922 injunctions restrained many specified individuals "and all their attorneys, servants, agents, associates, members, employers; and all persons acting in aid or in conjunction with them." Persons were forbidden "in any manner by letters . . . word of mouth, oral persuasion, or suggestion, or through interviews to be published in newspapers or otherwise in any manner whatsoever, encourage, direct or command any person . . . to abandon the employment of said railway companies . . . or to refrain from entering the service of said railway companies. . . ."[15]

"Government by injunction," as it was referred to by labor, prevailed for almost fifty years.[16] During this time organized labor

---

[14] 158 U. S. 564. The occasion was a strike of the American Railway Union against the Pullman Company, which was held to be a conspiracy in restraint of trade and a menace to the public welfare.

[15] 283 Fed. 479 (1922); Final, 290 Fed. 978 (1923).

[16] The use of injunctions in the United States began in the 1880's, but almost half of the total number were issued between 1920 and 1930. The exact number which were sought for and issued is not known, but one of the leading authorities reports knowledge of over 2000. Of these, approximately 75 per cent were in state courts and 25 per cent in federal courts. State courts granted 88 per cent and denied 12 per cent which were applied for, and the federal courts;

made relief from injunctions its foremost legislative demand. It thought that Section 20 of the Clayton Act afforded such relief, and in the American Foundries case in 1921 Chief Justice Taft stated that it was "clear that Congress wished to forbid the use by the Federal courts of their equity arm to prevent peaceable persuasion by employees, discharged or expectant, in promotion of their side of the dispute, and to secure them against judicial restraint in obtaining or communicating information in any place where they might lawfully be." In the *Truax* v. *Corrigan* case decided a week later, however, he delivered another opinion in which a provision in the state statute similar to that in the Clayton Act was declared unconstitutional because the state's supreme court had interpreted its law to legalize picketing in any form, provided violence was not used.

Following this decision the use of injunctions increased (more than a thousand were issued by state and federal courts during the ensuing decade), and labor and friends of labor sought congressional action. Bills were introduced annually, and finally in 1932 a federal anti-injunction act passed Congress and was signed by President Hoover. By this time twelve states had already enacted laws regulating the issuance of injunctions but they had proved notoriously ineffective because of the courts' interpretations.

LEGAL PROTECTIONS FOR COLLECTIVE BARGAINING

The legal status of collective bargaining at the beginning of the 1930's has been described thus:

The workers were free to bargain collectively; their right to organize and bargain collectively was recognized and repeatedly affirmed by legislatures and by courts. Their right to strike was also recognized, though, as we have seen, it was by no means unqualified. But the rights of employers and non-union workers were also recognized and affirmed.

granted 94 per cent of all applications. (E. E. Witte, *The Government in Labor Disputes,* McGraw-Hill Book Company, New York, 1932, p. 84.) See the bibliography on injunctions in labor disputes in *Monthly Labor Review,* September, 1928, pp. 201–220.

Non-union workers had the right to get and hold jobs; employers had the right to use yellow-dog contracts, to hire and fire for any or no reason, and to organize company unions. They also had the right of access to the commodity and labor markets, the right to operate their plants, and the general right to do business.

Now these rights of workers and employers were bound to come into conflict. And the courts who were supposed to enforce the rights of both groups very frequently had to decide which rights to enforce. On the whole, their decisions in such cases tended to favor the employers, largely because their rights were better understood by lawyers and judges, and were more susceptible of protection through court proceedings.

The right to bargain collectively certainly includes the right to join a union. Yet the protection of this right by forbidding discriminatory discharges and yellow-dog contracts was held to be an infringement of the employer's right to hire and fire. . . . While the courts enforced yellow-dog contracts which enabled employers to maintain *shops closed to union labor,* they often held illegal strikes to secure *shops closed to non-union labor.* Again, collective action by workers cannot be effective unless it extends beyond the confines of a local craft union. Yet the courts, ignoring economic realities, condemned many kinds of sympathetic action on the ground that these workers had no legitimate interest in the dispute.

Collective action by workers is more likely to interfere with the rights of the public than are the methods which employers use to combat it. Pickets must use the streets, agitation may lead to violence; but the firing of employees or the procuring of new ones is but an incident to the regular conduct of business. Hence the courts were more likely to interfere with the activities of workers.

Injunctions theoretically could be used to protect workers' rights as well as employers'. But the injunction can only be used to protect property rights from irreparable injury. For the most part, workers' rights were not recognized as property rights which could be protected in this way. . . . Thus in actual practice the law operated to protect those employers who strove to prevent organization among their workers, who refused to bargain collectively, or who were trying to break a strike. The workers had the right to bargain collectively, but in seeking to achieve this end they were allowed to use only those methods which did not interfere with the rights of employers and of non-union workers.[17]

---

[17] J. R. Commons and J. B. Andrews, *Principles of Labor Legislation,* Harper & Brothers, New York, 1936, pp. 417–419.

Norris-LaGuardia Anti-Injunction Act

Collective bargaining received its first substantial protection and encouragement from federal legislation[18] with the passage of the Norris-LaGuardia Act in 1932. The Act declared the workers' right to self-organization and collective bargaining to be the public policy of the United States by these significant statements:

Whereas under prevailing economic conditions, developed with the aid of governmental authority for owners of property to organize in the corporate and other forms of ownership association, the individual unorganized worker is commonly helpless to exercise actual liberty of contract and to protect his freedom of labor, and thereby to obtain acceptable terms and conditions of employment, wherefore, though he should be free to decline to associate with his fellows, it is necessary that he have full freedom of association, self-organization, and designation of representatives of his own choosing, to negotiate the terms and conditions of his employment, and that he shall be free from the interference, restraint, or coercion of employers of labor, or their agents, in the designation of such representatives or in self-organization or in other concerted activities for the purpose of collective bargaining, or other mutual aid or protection. . . .[19]

The formal title of the law is the Federal Anti-Injunction Act, but its provisions extend beyond the regulation of the issuance of injunctions. Specifically, the Act provides that United States

---

[18] Six years previous to the Norris-LaGuardia Act, the railroad workers had been given legal protection against interference in their self-organization. The 1926 Railroad Act forbade "interference, influence, or coercion exercised by either employers or employees over the self-organization or designation of representatives by the other," and it was under this law that the first important judicial decision as to the legal status of company unions arose.

In a wage dispute between the Texas and New Orleans Railroad Company and the Brotherhood of Railway Clerks, the union claimed that the company created a company union by compelling its employees through intimidation to join that organization. The Supreme Court found the company guilty and affirmed the constitutional validity of congressional action granting railroad workers the right to be free from interference in organization and in designating representatives for collective bargaining. (281 U. S. 548, 1930.)

The Railroad Act of 1926 was strengthened and clarified by amendments in 1933 and 1934 and now has substantially the same provisions for railroad workers as the National Labor Relations Act does for other workers, with this major exception, that the railroad employers and unions may not negotiate closed union-shop agreements.

[19] 47 U. S. Stat. 70 (March 23, 1932), Section 2.

courts[20] may not issue injunctions against the normal and peaceful activities connected with industrial disputes and that injunctions may be granted only after open hearings. It also relieves officers and unions of liability for unlawful acts of its members, and makes unenforceable in federal courts individual contracts (yellow-dog contracts) in which the employee promises not to join any labor organization.

Because of the limitations on injunctions in labor disputes, the Act's definition of "labor dispute" has far-reaching effects. "Labor dispute" is broadly defined to include any controversy concerning terms and conditions of employment, or concerning the representation of persons in negotiating terms of employment "regardless of whether or not the disputants stand in the proximate relation of employer and employee"; a person is "participating or interested in a labor dispute" if he "is engaged in the same industry, trade, craft or occupations, in which the dispute occurs, or has a direct or indirect interest therein, or is a member, officer or agent of any association composed in whole or in part of employers or employees engaged in such industry, trade, craft or occupation."

Encouragement Under the New Deal

Although the Norris-LaGuardia and the Railroad Acts foreshadowed the legislation which was to come, the New Deal's influence on the progress of collective bargaining amounted to much more than placing additional and strengthened laws on the statute books. Experience with similar state legislation at the hands of the courts in the past made for a good deal of skepticism regarding the outcome of the Norris-LaGuardia Act at the time it was enacted. It was not until after the Supreme Court in 1937 had taken cognizance of the change in public opinion which had occurred under the New Deal that any labor legislation was reasonably secure from judicial invalidation.[21] Just a year previously it

---

20 Similar restrictions have been imposed upon some state courts by a number of state laws which follow the general pattern of the Norris-LaGuardia Act.

21 For an account of President Roosevelt's efforts "to pack the Supreme Court," the student is referred to the daily press and journals during the spring of 1937. Regardless of the merits of his proposals, there is no doubt that his *threat* to increase the personnel of the court caused a drastic change in the attitude of its members toward all types of labor legislation—wage and hour

had stated that "the relation of employer and employee is a local relation and consequently beyond the scope of Federal jurisdiction . . . the relation of employer and employee, at common law, is one of domestic relations . . . the powers which the general government may exercise are only those specifically enumerated in the Constitution, and such implied powers as are necessary and proper to carry into effect the enumerated powers. . . ."[22]

The first legislative protection for collective bargaining under the New Deal was incorporated in Section 7a of the National Industrial Recovery Act, which borrowed much of its language from the public policy declaration of the Norris-LaGuardia Act. This section required that each code of fair competition contain the provision that "employees shall have the right to organize and to bargain collectively through representatives of their own choosing, and shall be free from interference, restraint, or coercion of employers . . . in the designation of such representatives. . . ." The wording of Section 7a was sufficiently vague and general, however, to permit company unions to thrive as much as bona fide labor unions.[23] Nevertheless, the experience under the N.I.R.A. facilitated the enactment of more adequate legislation when this Act was invalidated by the Supreme Court.[24]

---

controls as well as protection for collective bargaining. In the spring of 1937 the Supreme Court declared three important types of labor legislation to be constitutional, namely, the National Labor Relations Act, the Social Security Act, and the Washington State minimum wage law for women. The preceding year it declared unconstitutional not only the labor provisions of the National Coal Conservation Act, but also the New York state minimum wage law which was similar to the Washington law. Actually, the change in opinion of the court during these few months represented a change in attitude on the part of only one or two justices, most of the cases in both years being five-four decisions.

[22] *Carter* v. *Carter Coal Co. et al.,* 298 U. S. 238 (1936). This decision invalidated the 1935 National Bituminous Coal Conservation Act and, in effect, held that Congress has no power to regulate wages, hours of labor, and working conditions in an industry not directly engaged in interstate commerce; it declared that "mining is not interstate commerce, but, like manufacturing, is a local business."

[23] See Bureau of Labor Statistics, *Characteristics of Company Unions,* Bulletin No. 634, Government Printing Office, Washington, 1938.

[24] When the labor provisions of the N.I.R.A. are under consideration it must be remembered that the other clauses of the Act providing for codes of fair competition accorded certain rights of collective action to employers which were long forbidden under the anti-trust laws. It was the price-fixing and similar features of the Act which were the points at issue before the Supreme

The National Labor Relations Act

The National Labor Relations Act (Wagner-Connery Act) was approved in May, 1935, and its constitutionality was affirmed by the Supreme Court in April, 1937. The Act declares that "employees shall have the right to self-organization, to form, join, or assist labor organizations, to bargain collectively through representatives of their own choosing, and to engage in concerted activities, for the purpose of collective bargaining or other mutual aid or protection."

To protect these rights, certain enumerated unfair labor practices are forbidden:

Employers must not interfere with, restrain, or coerce employees in the exercise of their right to self-organization, to form, or join labor organizations, to bargain collectively through representatives of their own choosing.

They must not dominate or interfere with the formation or administration of any labor organization or contribute to the financial or other support of it.

They must not discriminate in hiring, discharge, or any condition of employment to encourage or discourage membership in any labor organization.

They must not discharge or otherwise discriminate against employees who file charges or give testimony under the Act.

They must not refuse to bargain collectively with representatives of employees designated in accordance with the Act.

The Act provides for a non-partisan board whose duties are twofold: (1) to aid in the free selection of employee representative agencies by holding elections or otherwise determining the choice of the majority of the workers in an appropriate bargaining unit; and (2) to prevent unfair labor practices and to see that employers bargain "in good faith," once the representative agency has been determined.

The determination of the bargaining unit has an important bearing on the outcome of the election and the subsequent bargaining relations. Several state laws (see below) provide that where the majority of employees of a particular craft shall so decide, the

---

Court in the Schechter case (295 U. S. 495, 1935). See L. L. Lorwin and Arthur Wubnig, *Labor Relations Boards,* Brookings Institution, Washington, 1935, for an account of the activities of the labor boards established under the N.I.R.A.

board shall designate that craft as the bargaining unit. The National Labor Relations Act leaves it to the board to decide in each case. Some of the factors which guide the N.L.R.B. in determining the coverage of the appropriate bargaining unit are the past record of collective bargaining in the industry, locality, and plant; the present wishes of the parties concerned; and what the board itself considers will best secure for the employees the full benefit of their right to collective bargaining.

State Labor Relations Acts

Determination of the coverage of the National Labor Relations Act rests upon the interpretation of the federal power to regulate industrial situations which affect the free flow of commerce among the several states and territories. The Supreme Court has interpreted the term "affecting commerce" to include all manufacturing plants, any part of whose products are procured from or sold in other states; mining, newspaper offices, and telegraph services; public utilities which supply any service to interstate industries; retail establishments which sell as little as 1 per cent of their products across state lines; and maintenance employees working in buildings occupied by offices of companies engaged in interstate commerce. The Act, however, specifically excludes agricultural labor and domestic servants.

Despite this broad coverage of the N.L.R.A., many wage earners are employed in occupations which are definitely intra-state and for these workers several states enacted "Little Wagner" acts soon after the passage of the N.L.R.A. Later, several amended their acts to make them radically different in some respects from the federal model. The chief revision has been to add certain union activities as "unfair labor practices"—provisions which are considered by labor to jeopardize rather than to protect the rights of organized labor as is the purpose of the N.L.R.A.

In 1946 five states had labor relations acts which closely followed the federal act—New York (1937), Massachusetts (1937), Utah (1937), Rhode Island (1941), and Connecticut (1945). All these laws prohibit the same unfair labor practices by employers, and several go further by specifically outlawing black lists and espionage—actions which are also illegal by implication under the N.L.R.A. although not specifically mentioned. Provisions for the determination of bargaining agencies are likewise similar to those in the N.L.R.A., except that most of the state acts specifically permit (but do not require) elections upon the request of the employer as well as upon the petition of a union, and also specify that a craft unit shall be designated as an appropriate bargaining unit if a majority of the employees of the craft so request.[25]

In addition to these five state laws there are several others which are sometimes referred to as labor relations acts although they differ from the federal Act by placing restrictions on employees and unions as well as upon employers. Among these, the Pennsylvania act deviates least, the most important difference being that it designates sit-down strikes and intimidation or coercion by threats of harm on the part of employees as unfair labor practices.[26] The Michigan law, enacted in 1939, includes similar unfair labor practices provisions for employees but also requires a waiting period after notification to the state board before a strike may take place—thirty days' notice for strikes "affected with a public interest" and five days for all others. The Michigan law has no provision for the determination of bargaining agencies although it includes the usual prohibitions against employer interference and discrimination.

The Minnesota law, enacted in 1939 and amended in 1943, includes a number of restrictions on employee and union activities, whereas the unfair labor practices specified for employers are extremely limited. Although it prohibits employers from engaging in espionage and black lists, it does not specifically prohibit them from dominating and interfering with labor organizations or refusing to bargain collectively; at the same time it specifically says employees may refrain from organizing or bargaining collectively. The Minnesota act not only includes unfair labor practices for employees similar to the Pennsylvania and Michigan acts, as well as waiting periods for strikes (thirty days for those affecting the public interest and ten days for all others), but also places restrictions on strikes, picketing, boycotts and jurisdictional disputes.

---

[25] These latter provisions conform to the general practice of the National Labor Relations Board even though the federal law includes no such specific requirements. See above.

[26] The original 1937 Pennsylvania act was similar to the N.L.R.A. but was amended in 1939 and 1943. The Massachusetts, Wisconsin, and other state laws also prohibit sit-down strikes.

A strike may not be called unless it has been voted for by a majority of the voting employees in the bargaining unit affected. At plants where a strike is in progress a majority of the pickets must be employees of the establishment, and in secondary strikes only one picket is allowed at any entrance of a plant whose employees are not on strike. Interference with the free and uninterrupted use of streets and highways is unlawful, and unions are prohibited from hindering the transportation, production, processing, and marketing of farm products, or conspiring to injure any processor or marketing organization by secondary boycotts or other means in order to coerce or damage farmers.

The Wisconsin Employment Peace Act,[27] like the Minnesota law, includes provisions intended to protect the interests of farmers and the rights of employers and individual workers, as much as organized workers. Individual workers are given the express right to refrain from organizing and bargaining collectively, and unions are forbidden to "coerce or intimidate" them or their employers in order to induce them to become members of unions. Agreements requiring union membership, that is, closed-shop and maintenance-of-membership agreements, are forbidden unless approved by two-thirds of the voting employees, provided the two-thirds constitutes a majority of the employees in the bargaining unit. Also "all union agreements" may be terminated if the union "unreasonably" refuses to enroll any employee covered by the agreement. The checkoff is permitted only upon individual authorization of employees; mass picketing and secondary boycotts are forbidden; and no strikes, picketing, or boycotts are allowed unless voted for by a majority of the employees of the company against whom such action is taken. Employees engaged in the production, harvesting, or processing of agricultural products must give ten days' notice of intent to strike.

In 1943 Kansas and Colorado enacted laws which follow the pattern of the Wisconsin law but include many additional provisions regulating the internal government of unions.[28] In 1945 Hawaii and Puerto Rico also enacted laws modeled after the Wis-

---

[27] The Wisconsin Employment Peace Act enacted in 1939 replaced a 1937 labor relations act modeled after the federal Act. Amendments were made in 1943 and 1945.

[28] See p. 611.

consin act in that they recognize equally the right of employees to organize and bargain collectively or to refrain from such activities, and list an equal number of unfair labor practices for both employers and employees.

In the five states which have laws similar to the N.L.R.A., there is little opportunity for conflict between the federal and state laws. In the last group of states mentioned, however, there may be conflicts with the federal Act, although some of these laws specify that their coverage excludes employees covered by the N.L.R.A. Others have no such limitations. Wisconsin, for example, has maintained that under the police powers of the state its law is all-inclusive; and in several test cases involving mass picketing, the Supreme Court has upheld the state's power to regulate matters which directly affect the public safety and the use of public thoroughfares. But the Supreme Court has also held that any state order which deprived a union or employees of rights specifically guaranteed by the federal Act would be set aside.[29]

Espionage and Anti-Strikebreaking Legislation

Among the more unsavory practices which employers have resorted to in their efforts to combat union organization has been the use of spies and professional strikebreakers,[30] and these ac-

[29] *Allen-Bradley Local, United Electrical, Radio and Machine Workers* v. *Wisconsin Employment Relations Board,* 315 U. S. 740 (1941); *Hotel and Restaurant Employees* v. *Wisconsin Employment Relations Board,* 315 U. S. 437 (1941).

[30] The distinction between a professional strikebreaker and what is commonly called a scab should be kept in mind. The latter refers to a non-union employee who continues to work for an employer whom the union has designated as "unfair," or who accepts employment during a labor dispute with the intention of remaining as a permanent employee. A professional strikebreaker is an outsider who has no intention of becoming a permanent employee and usually is not competent to perform the job; his purpose is to fill the job only during the labor dispute.

For authentic information about the use of spies and strikebreakers, see the Reports of the Senate Committee on Education and Labor (LaFollette Committee), 74th, 75th, and 76th Congresses, pursuant to S. Res. 266 (74th Congress), which are incorporated in twelve reports published by the Government Printing Office. Some of the titles are *Labor Policies of Employers' Associations, Industrial Espionage, Strikebreaking Services, Private Police Systems, Report on the Chicago Memorial Day Incident.*

See also Sidney Howard, *The Labor Spy* (1924); Leo Huberman, *The Labor Spy Racket* (1937); Jean E. Spielman, *The Stool Pigeon* (1923); Edward Levinson, *I Break Strikes* (1935); Clinch Calkins, *Spy Overhead, the Story of*

tivities have had important repercussions upon the attitude and behavior of workers and unions. Commented one authority a few years ago: "The labor spy is the most hated, by workingmen, of all beings. . . . What organized workingmen believe about the spy system is almost incredible. They feel that spies are everywhere and that they have a hand in practically every union activity. Labor men are forever trying to discover whether their fellow officers in unions are spies, and they are never sure that they have got rid of all of them. Plus this suspicion, they entertain resentment not only against the spies and the detective agencies, but against the employers who in the last analysis•are responsible for their existence. This feeling of suspicion and resentment is a far more potent cause of violence than even the direct incitement to acts of lawlessness by the spies and strike guards furnished by detective agencies, of which there is considerable evidence."[31]

Industrial espionage was widespread in American industry for many years, and many "reputable" employers who boasted about the "one big family" relationship in their plants apparently saw nothing incongruous in the presence of company spies. Some large companies hired their spies directly, and in some plants the so-called labor relations director was actually the head of the company's espionage system. Most employers used outside services; one of the major functions of some employers' associations was the furnishing of spies and strikebreakers to their members, and a number of detective agencies maintained "industrial departments" which provided spy service to employers on a contract basis, including inside operatives, guards, strikebreakers, and "missionaries" to visit the homes of strikers and further "back-to-work" movements.[32]

Industrial Espionage (1937); C. E. Bonnett, *Employers' Associations in the United States* (1922).

[31] E. E. Witte, *The Government in Labor Disputes,* pp. 188–189.

[32] One of the earliest occasions when a private detective agency was used in industrial disputes was during the Homestead, Pennsylvania, strike in 1892, when several hundred guards supplied by the Pinkerton Agency participated in riots in which scores of strikers were killed and injured. The use of private detective agencies for industrial espionage became widespread during the First World War and the 1920's; many companies had continuing contracts with detective agencies to furnish inside operatives, even though no strikes were threatened in their plants. Their duties are described as follows:

"The inside operatives carry on the work of industrial espionage while work-

Much of the violence which has accompanied strikes and picketing has been caused by the presence of professional strikebreakers who sometimes were instructed to "stir up trouble" in order to create a situation which would make it easy for the employer to get an injunction to forbid picketing. Even if they were not under specific instructions to foment violence, the character of the men employed to do such work made it inevitable that violence would occur.[33]

Largely as the result of pressure from organized labor, a number of states have enacted legislation requiring detective agencies, and in some cases the individual operatives, to be licensed. Pennsylvania enacted a law in 1937 which makes it a misdemeanor for any person, firm, or corporation "not directly involved in a labor dispute or lockout" to recruit any persons to take the place of employees in an industry where a strike or lockout is in effect. Utah requires every person to register with the State Industrial Commission before starting work for an employer whose employees are on strike.[34] A New York law enacted in 1938 makes it unlawful for a detective agency to furnish strikebreakers and strike guards or to engage in industrial espionage.

In 1936 the federal government took action to control the use of strikebreakers when it enacted a law, strengthened by an amend-

---

ing for the client employer under assumed names as ordinary mechanics or workmen. . . . They do their daily work and draw pay checks like other workmen, and their fellow employees and immediate superiors—often the superintendents themselves—have no inkling that they are spies. But every day they make a report to the detective agency, and this agency in turn reports to the employer. Practically never do the operatives report directly, the roundabout method of reporting being represented to the employer as necessary to preserve secrecy, but it is no doubt primarily resorted to to enable the home office to make the employer think that he is getting a valuable service . . . it is an almost invariable practice of the inside operatives to join the union. The great detective agencies seem to have membership cards in all unions. . . . The spies attend all union meetings and take an active part in all union affairs . . . they create strife within the union, arouse racial hatreds, and spread suspicion." (*Ibid.*, pp. 185–186.)

[33] Mr. Burns, of the W. J. Burns Detective Agency, himself said of spies and strikebreakers that "as a class they are the biggest lot of blackmailing thieves that ever went unwhipped of justice." (*Ibid.*, p. 188.)

[34] As required by the Wagner-Peyser Act, the U. S. Employment Service does not refer an applicant to a position involving a strike or lockout without first notifying him verbally and in writing of the existence and nature of the dispute.

ment in 1938, which makes it a felony for any person "to transport or cause to be transported in interstate or foreign commerce any person who is employed or is to be employed for the purpose of obstructing or interfering by force or threats with (1) peaceful picketing by employees during any labor controversy affecting wages, hours, or conditions of labor; or (2) the exercise by employees of any of the rights of self-organization and collective bargaining."[35]

This act goes no further than to forbid the importation of strikebreakers. Although not specifically mentioned, espionage is outlawed by the National Labor Relations Act, which forbids employers to interfere with labor organizations. At the present time (1946) there is no federal legislation outlawing industrial spies or private armed guards (except for protection against theft), although bills to that effect have been introduced into Congress.[36] As a result of the sensational exposures at the LaFollette Committee hearings in 1937, most of the large private detective agencies announced that they were discontinuing their "industrial departments," and there is no doubt that the practice of industrial espionage has greatly lessened although there has been evidence of the use of armed strikebreakers in at least a few industrial disputes within very recent years.

PRESENT LEGAL STATUS OF UNION ACTIVITIES

In spite of the fact that the federal government has assumed jurisdiction over many phases of employer-labor relations, much remains in the hands of the state and local governments, and there is wide divergence among them as to the manner in which they exercise their authority in labor matters. Not only do the state laws vary, but on any single day numerous different opinions may be handed down by the various lower courts with respect to similar situations and points at law. Although ultimate decisions of va-

---

[35] 49 Stat. 1899 (1936) as amended, 52 Stat. 1242 (1938).

[36] In 1942 Senators LaFollette and Thomas introduced such a bill, but Congress adjourned without taking action. This bill was an outcome of the LaFollette hearings (see footnote 30). Among its provisions were the outlawing of private armed guards with criminal records hired to attack strikers, the use and possession of explosives during labor disputes, and the use of spies.

lidity rest with the Supreme Court, only a relatively few cases are ever processed through the judicial hierarchy, with the result that in a majority of specific employer-labor crises, state laws and lower court decisions are controlling.

The following is a brief summary of federal and state legislation and significant court decisions in effect at the close of 1946. At that time there was a good deal of discussion about the kinds of labor regulatory laws which the 80th Congress might enact during the ensuing months.

Recent State Legislation

It is impossible in these few pages to give an adequate summary of the laws pertaining to unions which are now on the statute books of the various states. One fact should be noted. With a very few exceptions, the state laws which have been enacted since 1937 tend to restrict rather than to protect union activities and collective bargaining. Most of these restrictive laws, some of which are extremely drastic, have been enacted by southern states where there has been a vigorous and concerted campaign to outlaw many traditional practices of unions. A dozen states now have restrictive legislation of varying degrees, and in several instances it has taken the form of constitutional amendments.[37]

These laws not only place stringent limitations on activities having to do with employer-union relations but also include rules pertaining to internal union affairs. For example, Florida, Colorado, and Texas have imposed regulations on the holding of union elections, the tenure of office of union officials, and the amount of dues and assessments which unions may levy. These same states and Massachusetts, Alabama, Idaho, Kansas, and South Dakota, have enacted laws requiring labor organizations to register with the state and to make annual detailed reports on their finances and membership, and the names and salaries of their officers, which in most instances are open to the public. Some of these acts also require union business agents to obtain annual licenses; under the

---

[37] Bills which were almost exactly similar were introduced in most southern and in some northern state legislatures during 1941–1945, but many of them were defeated in the legislatures or vetoed by the governors. In the South especially, the legislation was championed by an organization known as the Christian American Association.

Florida law, for example, a license is contingent upon ten years' residence in the state and "good moral character" as determined by the governor, the secretary of state, and the superintendent of education.

Other state regulations apply to collective bargaining and strike activity. Arizona, Florida, Nebraska, South Dakota, and Virginia have so-called "right-to-work" laws which, in effect, forbid closed or union shop agreements. In a half dozen states secondary boycotts are outlawed and picketing is restricted as, for example, "in a manner not to prevent ingress and egress" or "to prevent employees' right to work," or in such a way as "to prevent any person from engaging in a lawful occupation."

A number of these state laws, in whole or in part, are now being appealed in the courts and some sections have already been invalidated. The Idaho Supreme Court has declared unconstitutional the provisions of the Idaho statute which require unions to file financial statements and which outlaw picketing of agricultural premises. The United States Supreme Court has ruled that the provision of the Texas law which requires union organizers to register with the secretary of state before soliciting members is contrary to the constitutional right of freedom of speech and assembly when applied to a union leader addressing a union membership rally.[38] With respect to the Florida licensing law, the Supreme Court has declared that it restricts the "full freedom" of choice in the selection of bargaining representatives and thus is repugnant to the guarantees in the National Labor Relations Act; therefore the state has no right to enjoin a union which refuses to comply with the registration requirement.[39] The Colorado act of 1943 which required compulsory incorporation of labor organizations, as well as the filing of annual reports, was declared unconstitutional by the state supreme court a year after it was enacted.

Application of the Sherman Act to Union Activity

Labor unions are subject to the Sherman Anti-Trust Act, but in two important decisions the Supreme Court has drastically restricted the application of the Act so far as union activities are concerned.

---

[38] *Thomas* v. *Collins,* 323 U. S. 516 (1944).
[39] *Hill* v. *Florida,* 325 U. S. 538 (1944).

In the Apex case[40] the court recognized that all combinations of workers necessarily restrain competition since they curtail competition among employees and tend to eliminate wage differences. But they are not thereby unlawful. Nor are strikes which obstruct the shipment of goods across state lines in violation of the Sherman Act, even though they result in violence and destruction of property; the latter are punishable under state and local criminal laws but not under the Sherman Act. The only type of interference with interstate commerce which is outlawed by the Sherman Act is the suppression of competition by monopolizing a supply of goods, controlling its price, or discriminating between purchasers—in other words, interference with trade in a commercial sense where there is an actual or intended or direct effect upon prices and price competition.

In a later case involving a boycott and picketing in connection with a jurisdictional dispute, the Supreme Court emphasized its restricted concept of the applicability of the Sherman Act to union activity. In the Hutcheson case, the court held that activities which are not enjoinable under the Clayton and the Norris-LaGuardia Acts are not subject to the Sherman Act. In holding that peaceful picketing and boycotting cannot be enjoined or prosecuted, even though the immediate issue is a jurisdictional dispute in which the employer is not directly involved, the court stated, ". . . whether trade union conduct constitutes a violation of the Sherman Law is to be determined only by reading the Sherman Act and Sec. 20 of the Clayton Act and the Norris-LaGuardia Act as a harmonizing text of outlawry of labor conduct. . . . So long as a union acts in its self-interest and does not combine with

---

[40] 310 U. S. 469 (1940). The Apex Hosiery Company maintained a non-union shop. When the American Federation of Hosiery Workers were refused recognition they ordered a strike and Philadelphia members of the union seized the plant and locked the doors against the owners and employees for six weeks. The employer sued for triple damages under the Sherman Act and the District Court awarded judgment against the union officers and strikers in the sum of $712,000. The Circuit Court of Appeals reversed the decision on the grounds that the union had not intended to restrain interstate commerce, and the Supreme Court upheld this decision with regard to the application of the Sherman Act but condemned the stay-in strike and stated that the civil and penal laws of the state had been violated. Some months after this decision the company recognized and signed an agreement with the union and the damage suit was settled out of court.

non-labor groups, the licit and the illicit (under Sec. 20 of the Clayton Act) are not to be distinguished by any judgment regarding the wisdom or unwisdom, the rightness or wrongness, the self- ishness or unselfishness of the end of which the particular union activities are the means."[41]

While the above decisions allow unions wide latitude when acting unilaterally for their own interests, unions are nevertheless sub- ject to the Anti-Trust Act when acting in concert with employers to create business monopolies and to control the marketing of goods and services. In the Allen Bradley case the Supreme Court held that the union as well as the employers had violated the Sher- man Act when they banded together to monopolize the entire New York City market for electrical goods by boycotting out-of-city and non-union products. The court stated that an employer and a union may lawfully agree that the employer will not buy goods manufactured by companies which did not employ the members of the union; nevertheless, they may not become "copartners" to de- stroy competition even though the union action is for the purpose of furthering the interests of the union members.[42]

Unions and Anti-Racketeering Legislation

A racketeer is defined by Webster as "one who singly or in com- bination with others extorts money or advantages by threats of violence or unlawful interference with business." A number of states have legislation which variously defines and outlaws racket- eering, and in 1934 a federal anti-racketeering act was enacted. In a case involving New York City truck drivers, the Supreme Court held that this Act was not applicable to a labor union's efforts to get jobs for its members, even by threats of violence; that the union's insistence that the employer pay the equivalent of union wages to the union is not racketeering if the members are ready

---

[41] 312 U. S. 219 (1941). In this case the Brotherhood of Carpenters had en- gaged in picketing and boycotting a brewery in an effort to compel it to hire carpenters instead of machinists to erect some machinery. The Supreme Court in effect sustained the carpenters in their historical jurisdictional fight with the machinists, and this decision had a bearing on the withdrawal of the Ma- chinists union from the A. F. of L. See p. 559.

[42] *Allen Bradley Co.* v. *Local #3, Brotherhood of Electrical Workers,* 325 U. S. 797 (1944).

and able to do the work even though an employer prefers to hire someone else.[43]

Considerable dissatisfaction was expressed over this court decision, and in 1946 the Hobbs bill was enacted; this makes it a felony to obstruct, delay, or interfere "by robbery or extortion" with the movement of any goods in interstate commerce. Although Congress undoubtedly had certain union activities in mind, and organized labor unsuccessfully fought the passage of the Act, it remains to be seen what construction the courts will give it. When President Truman approved the bill, he specifically stated that he understood it was not to "interfere with the rights of unions in carrying out their legitimate objectives . . . that nothing in the bill shall be construed to repeal, modify, or affect the legislative safeguards which Congress has established for the protection of labor. . . ."[44]

Legality of Strikes and Lockouts

The legal right to strike has been unquestionably established in this country under common law and the Thirteenth Amendment, which prohibits involuntary servitude. This right has been reinforced and protected by recent law as well as judicial decisions.

---

[43] *United States* v. *Local 807*, 315 U. S. 521 (1941). The Supreme Court's decision stated that the intent of Congress in enacting this law was to eliminate the levy of blackmail upon industry, especially small shops which had been at the mercy of organized gangs of bandits. The case which came before the court involved New York City truck drivers who insisted that they be employed to drive out-of-city trucks into the city where they were unloaded. If truck owners were unwilling to change drivers at the city limits, the New York drivers insisted that they be paid the equivalent of a day's wages for each out-of-city truck unloaded in New York City. When out-of-city truckers resisted, the New York drivers in some instances forced their claims by acts of violence.

[44] As an aftermath of the many strikes which took place immediately following the close of World War II, Congress passed a bill (Case bill) which would have imposed severe restrictions on many traditional union activities. President Truman vetoed this bill and the Hobbs Act was approved more or less as a compromise. After its passage the Teamsters Union asserted that it did not deprive its members of their right to get union drivers on all trucks entering New York City. While the bill was under consideration, labor claimed that it would permit anti-labor judges to interpret union fees as "extortions," union hiring halls as a "job racket," organizing campaigns as "coercion," wage raises gained through strikes as "extortion," picketing as the use of "force," and name calling as "violence."

Such legal protections have been extended by both the federal Anti-injunction and the National Labor Relations Acts to include disputes in which those involved may not "stand in the proximate relation of employer and employee," that is, secondary or sympathetic strikes.

At common law the courts placed fewer limitations on lockouts by employers than on strikes by employees. Lockouts could be practiced by those personally concerned without any legal restrictions as to motive or possible result, except that in a few instances the courts held lockouts in violation of agreements to be unlawful. Although an unwilling employer could not be coerced to participate, a voluntary association of employers could engage in a lockout irrespective of the number of plants or workers involved. Recent statutory laws have placed a severe restriction upon employers' rights to engage in lockouts—employers may no longer engage in lockouts in order to discourage or interfere with the self-organization of their employees. In disputes over the terms to be included in an agreement, however, employers have the legal right to engage in lockouts just as employees may engage in strikes.

Although workers have the legal right to quit work, this does not necessarily mean that all strikes are legal, or that persons cannot be prohibited from inducing others to go on strike under particular circumstances, or that employers may not refuse reemployment to individuals who have committed illegal acts during the course of a strike. Fraud and violence, of course, are as unlawful in labor disputes as elsewhere. There is a long judicial history on the question of the legality of strikes per se regardless of purpose, the legality of strikes for only "lawful purposes," what constitutes lawful conduct of strikes, and other matters pertaining to strikes and lockouts, only a few of which can be discussed here.

One kind of strike has been unequivocally outlawed, namely, the sit-down or stay-in strike. In 1939 the Supreme Court declared that sit-down strikes were a "high-handed proceeding without a shadow of legal right" and that employers had the right to discharge sit-down strikers.[45] Preceding and following that decision

---

[45] 306 U. S. 240 (1939). In the Fansteel Metallurgical Corporation case the employer was found guilty of unfair labor practices and the N.L.R.B. had sought to have some sit-down strikers reinstated. The majority of the court re-

a number of states enacted laws which specifically ban sit-down strikes or make them an unfair labor practice under their labor relations acts.

Legality of Picketing

Picketing is the presence of one or more persons at the approach to a work place during a labor dispute for the purpose of (1) informing the public and employees that a strike exists or that the employer is on the union "unfair" list, (2) persuading workers to join or continue the strike or boycott, (3) preventing persons from entering or going to work. Secondary picketing refers to the picketing of an employer not directly involved in the labor dispute but connected through ownership or business dealings with the employer with whom the union is in dispute.

The right to picket stems from the constitutional right of free speech and assembly. Based on this right alone, all peaceful picketing would be lawful. But the inherent nature of picketing necessarily causes impingements upon the personal and property rights of others, and the courts are frequently called upon to weigh the relative rights of all the parties concerned, including the general public, and to decide whether or not picketing in a given situation should be restricted or prohibited altogether. Decisions of the various courts are not always consistent; it is probably true that in no other area of labor activity is there as much diversity of legal opinion and practice as there is with respect to picketing.

---

versed the board's decision because of the nature of the sit-down strike. While the minority opinion of the court agreed with the majority in disapproving the sit-down strike, it did not consider such conduct sufficient cause to deny strikers reinstatement since management and labor had both erred.

During the wave of sit-down strikes in 1937, a number of judges refused to issue injunctions to have the employees evicted, and several issued injunctions restraining companies from evicting sit-down strikers. One law-school dean is reported to have held that "the sit-down strike did not constitute trespass so long as the property was occupied in good faith awaiting the adjustment of differences growing out of the industrial relation." Another dean observed that "the history of our law is replete with illustrations of the creation of new rights." The legality of the sit-down strike "will depend in part upon the emphasis that law will give to the concept of property and its inviolability in its industrial and corporate setting to economic pressure of this type—and in part, perhaps, on the capacity of our law to devise new concepts and mechanisms to meet the needs out of which this type of economic pressure had been born." (Louis Stark, "Sit-Down," *Survey Graphic,* June, 1937.)

This is illustrated by a few cases decided during the spring of 1946.[46] (Any other period would reveal the same diversity.)

The New Jersey Court of Chancery held that mass picketing, whether peaceful or otherwise, which prevented free access to the company's property worked an irreparable injury to the owner; that regardless of the state's anti-injunction law "the complainant needs the protection of the court and is entitled to it by the established principle of equity." In contrast, a state District Court of Colorado declared that the state legislature could not prohibit mass picketing, even in cases of secondary boycott, because all peaceful picketing is an exercise of the right of free assembly. On the same day that the Colorado decision was handed down, a Philadelphia judge issued an injunction limiting the number of pickets at a strike-bound plant to ten at each gate, although there had been no violence during the previous mass picketing. The Supreme Court of Pennsylvania, in a similar situation, held mass picketing to be equivalent to a sit-down strike and therefore illegal, declaring that "seizure of plants is as effective by refusing entry through the gates as from inside the plant; a change in techniques did not change the end result, which was to deny the employer the use of his property until he acceded to the union demands."

Two Superior Courts in California have given opposite opinions on that state's Hot Cargo Act, which forbids secondary picketing. The Los Angeles court said the act was constitutional because secondary picketing limits the right of free speech only to the extent of preventing abuses; but the parallel court in San Diego maintained that the act was unconstitutional because it outlawed peaceful picketing for a lawful purpose.[47]

Recent decisions of the United States Supreme Court have tended to hold that all peaceful picketing is a lawful expression of the right of free speech; that the merits of the dispute itself, or whether or not the picketing is confined to the place of business where the dispute exists, has no bearing upon the rights of workers to advertise their grievances through picketing.

The right to picket for a closed-union shop, even when the

---

[46] Cases cited in *Monthly Labor Review*, May, 1946, pp. 762–763; June, 1946, pp. 923–925.

[47] *Union Ice Co.* v. *Sales Drivers Union* (March 18, 1946); *Ramser* v. *Van Storage* (April 30, 1946).

pickets are non-employees, has been upheld by the Supreme Court when the picketing and attendant publicity were not malicious and did not misrepresent the facts of the controversy.[48] However, the Supreme Court has also said that under certain circumstances where there is no logical relationship between the place of picketing and the scene of the dispute, the state has the right to protect innocent third parties and to restrict the scene of picketing to the place where the labor dispute takes place.[49] If for physical reasons, however, it is impossible to picket those against whom there is a dispute, then picketing at the next logical place of business is permissible.[50]

Legal Status of Collective Agreements

The end purpose of most union activity is to negotiate contracts with employers. Although there is no legal compulsion for employers and unions to agree upon the substantive terms of a contract, once the terms have been mutually agreed upon, the National Labor Relations Act requires that they be embodied in a bilater-

---

[48] In the *Senn* v. *Tile Layers Protective Union* case (1937) the Supreme Court went far in legalizing a strike for a closed shop when it withheld injunction relief from an employer who refused to sign an agreement with a union whose rules would have prevented him from working along with his men. The Court in a five-four decision held that there was a reasonable ground for the presumption that the closed shop and the union rule prohibiting employers from working were necessary to maintain standards, and that it would have been discrimination against other employers if the union had not enforced its rules in this case.

[49] *Carpenters* v. *Ritter's Cafe*, 315 U. S. 722 (1942). The owner of a restaurant had contracted to have another building constructed which had no relation to his restaurant, and the contractor used non-union labor. The carpenters picketed not only the construction project but also the restaurant. The restaurant employees and delivery drivers, although belonging to different unions, refused to go through the carpenters' picket line, and the owner obtained an injunction against the restaurant picketing which the carpenters appealed.

[50] *Bakery and Pastry Drivers* v. *Wohl*, 314 U.S. 704 (1942). New York bakery drivers started to picket bakeries which were selling their products to peddlers who in turn sold them to retailers. The union maintained that the peddlers, by working seven days a week for a small margin of "profit," were tearing down union standards and depriving union drivers of employment. The state courts issued an injunction against the picketing on the technical ground that no labor dispute existed between the drivers and the bakeries since employees of the bakeries were not involved in the dispute. The Supreme Court brushed aside this point and said the union had a right to publicize its difficulty with the peddlers by picketing; since it could not picket the peddlers directly because they moved around, the bakeries were a logical site for the picketing.

ally signed agreement.[51] The enforceability of such agreements is not as definitely established by law as is the legal requirement that they be in written form. There is no federal statute specifically defining the legal status of collective bargaining agreements and only a few states have laws pertaining to their enforceability.[52] However, there have been numerous court decisions relating to the legal status of various terms of agreements, only the general outlines of which can be indicated here.[53]

In earlier times the courts were inclined to view contracts with unions as one-sided gentlemen's agreements on the part of employers, not as legally binding contracts. Modern agreements include mutual rights and obligations. In return for certain wages or other specified benefits, the union members assume certain responsibilities such as the maintenance of work standards, observance of procedures for handling disputes and grievances, etc. Such agreements, voluntarily negotiated without duress or misrepresentation of material fact, the courts have come to consider as legally binding and enforceable.

Employer-union agreements, like any other private contract, may not include provisions contrary to law or public policy. Thus, an employer and a union may not enter into an agreement which results in monopolistic price fixing or which provides for wage rates, hour schedules, or other conditions of employment that do not meet the standards established by federal and state laws.

If a collective agreement prohibits strikes and lockouts during the entire life of the agreement, or calls for certain preliminary

---

[51] This legal right was affirmed by the Supreme Court in *H. J. Heinz* v. *N.L.R.B.*, 311 U.S. 514 (1941), when the court maintained that the signed written agreement was the final step in the bargaining process and therefore a requirement under the N.L.R.A. after the terms of an agreement have been mutually agreed upon.

[52] Violation of a collective bargaining agreement is specified as an unfair labor practice in at least a dozen states. In 1940 California amended its labor code to provide that collective agreements shall be enforceable at law or in equity, and New York amended its civil practice act to make written arbitration agreements legally enforceable.

[53] There are numerous articles in the various law journals which discuss the legal status of collective agreements. Among them are "The Enforcement of Collective Labor Agreements: A Proposal," by Harry D. Wolf, in *Law and Contemporary Problems,* Spring, 1938; "Union Agreements: A War Weapon," by David Ziskind, in *University of Chicago Law Review,* October, 1942.

steps before a stoppage of work may take place, the courts may give damages for the breach of such a provision, or grant injunctions against acts necessary to effectuate the stoppage. Although the courts may not compel people to work, they may restrain them from interfering with the work of others, and union leaders may be ordered to refrain from calling a strike in violation of an agreement. Similarly, the employer may not be compelled to continue his business, but if he stays in business he may be ordered to employ certain individuals or not to discharge certain employees, to pay certain wages, to refrain from moving his plant, or to do other things required by the agreement.

SELECTED REFERENCES

Berman, Edward, *Labor and the Sherman Act,* Harper & Brothers, New York, 1930.

Bureau of National Affairs, *Labor Relations Reference Manual* (continuing series), Washington, D. C.

Commons, J. R., and Andrews, J. B., *Principles of Labor Legislation,* Harper & Brothers, New York, 1936.

Frankfurter, Felix, and Greene, Nathan, *The Labor Injunction,* The Macmillan Company, New York, 1930.

Gregory, Charles O., *Labor and the Law,* W. W. Norton & Company, Inc., New York, 1946.

Landis, James M., and Manoff, Marcus, *Cases on Labor Law,* The Foundation Press, Chicago, 1942.

McCracken, Duane, *Strike Injunctions in the New South,* University of North Carolina Press, Chapel Hill, 1931.

Mason, Alpheus T., *Organized Labor and the Law,* Duke University Press, Durham, 1925.

Millis, H. A., and Montgomery, R. E., *Organized Labor,* McGraw-Hill Book Company, Inc., New York, 1945, vol. iii.

Raushenbush, Carl, and Stein, E., *Labor Cases and Materials,* F. S. Crofts & Co., New York, 1941.

Reed, George L., *Law of Labor Relations,* Soney and Sage Co., Newark, 1942.

Silverberg, Louis G. (ed.), *The Wagner Act: After Ten Years,* Bureau of National Affairs, Washington, 1945.

Swayzee, Cleon A., *Contempt of Court in Labor Injunction Cases,* Columbia University Press, New York, 1935.

Teller, Ludwig, *The Law Governing Labor Disputes and Collective Bargaining,* 3 vols., Baker, Voorhis & Company, Inc., New York, 1940.

Twentieth Century Fund, *Labor and the Government,* McGraw-Hill Book Company, Inc., New York, 1935.

Witte, Edwin E., *The Government in Labor Disputes,* McGraw-Hill Book Company, Inc., New York, 1932.

22

INDUSTRIAL RELATIONS PROBLEMS

LABOR ORGANIZATIONS HAVE EXISTED IN THIS COUNTRY FOR MORE than a hundred years, but prior to the 1930's labor unions were limited almost entirely to the skilled crafts, and collective bargaining took place between relatively small employers and small groups of workers. It is only within recent years that we have experienced the pervasive influence of unionization upon our general economy and upon employer-worker relations.

Although the principle of collective bargaining is now widely accepted as a permanent arrangement in our industrial life, it is also generally recognized that many complex problems accompany strong unionization throughout our major industries. Some of these unsolved problems pertain to internal union administration; many have to do with the area and processes of collective bargaining and their effect upon the management of industry; others relate to union activities which directly involve the public convenience. The preceding chapters were primarily concerned with explaining existing conditions and their historical development. In the following pages we shall briefly discuss the principles and issues underlying a few of the major problems and controversial questions connected with management-union relations.

COLLECTIVE BARGAINING AND MANAGEMENT EFFICIENCY

The substitution of collective bargaining for an employer's authoritarian control of working conditions signifies the introduction of democratic procedure in industry. It also raises additional and unique problems, the impact of which extends far beyond the individual business enterprise or employer (and stockholders) and workers directly involved. As with democracy in political government, rules and laws cannot be enacted with the promptness and arbitrary single-mindedness of purpose as they can under a totalitarian government. Neither can they be enforced with the same rigidity and ruthlessness.

Democracy implies sympathetic consideration of the interests of all persons and groups. Participation of many people in the formulation of policies and rules usually entails delays; ultimate decisions inevitably represent compromises; and enforcement must frequently be tempered by other considerations than rigid obedience to the letter of the law or one person's interpretation of the law.

Business enterprises, like governments, must, however, have rules and competent administration; otherwise there would be chaos and anarchy. Since many individual and group interests are divergent, these rules cannot fit or please all the persons who must abide by them. The interests of workers and employers are never identical except in the limited, though important, sense that both have a concern in the continuance and prosperity of the enterprise. In the very nature of the case, employers and workers approach their tasks from different angles and with different "stakes."

In one important respect the management of a business enterprise is different from a political government. Theoretically at least, in a democratic government those who are responsible for making and administering the laws are coextensive with those who live under them. It is a government *by* the people and *for* the people. A business concern, however, must recognize the interests and desires not only of those directly engaged in the enterprise (managers, stockholders, and employees) but also of the customers who buy its goods and services. In a competitive enterprise system a business concern must produce what consumers want and at a price at which they will buy; and under normal conditions in a buyers' market there is active competition among business concerns for the consumer's dollar. This competition is not limited to concerns producing the same kinds of goods and services but extends across industrial lines. Coal must compete with oil; railroads must compete with bus and air transportation; laundries and beauty parlors must compete with mechanical home appliances which perform the same functions.

The ultimate test of any employer or union policy, or of their collective agreement on policy, is whether in the long run it helps or hinders the production of goods and services which can be sold in a competitive market. This is not to say that workers should be willing to accept any wages or working conditions which will make it easy for their employer to sell his products by undercutting his competitors. Just as the employer will not long continue in an unprofitable business, so workers may prefer the risks and hardships resulting from the closing down of a business rather than accept work conditions which they consider unduly onerous. It is to the long-time interest of workers, as well as of the general public, that reasonable working standards not be sacrificed even though a particular employer and group of workers may suffer loss of business and jobs.

The crux of the problem in any given situation is, what are reasonable standards, and do any given rules and standards actually promote or harm the business? In most instances the impact of a policy or work rule cannot be immediately and conclusively determined; it cannot be proved that a specific condition has caused or will cause a business to decline or progress; it cannot always be foreseen whether or not a certain work rule or policy will promote or hinder maximum employment. The immediate short-time effect of the adoption of a policy or work rule may be entirely different from its broader and ultimate effect, and the latter may not be anticipated or recognized by the parties directly concerned when the policy or rule is adopted.

Management Prerogatives Versus Collective Bargaining

Many employers who have conceded, or at least accepted, the principle of collective bargaining for the determination of wages and general terms of employment are opposed to having work rules and plant policies established through the process of union-management negotiation. They contend that employers cannot properly carry out their managerial functions if they are deprived of their "right" to make decisions and enforce policies necessary for the efficient conduct of the business. They term these functions "management prerogatives" which cannot be shared by unions if the business is to operate successfully.

The issue has its philosophical as well as its practical aspects. One doctrine to which most employers adhere holds that, under common law and the employer-servant relationship, management retains all the authority and right to run its business as it sees fit except with regard to the specific matters which it has relinquished to joint management-union control. According to this concept, collective bargaining is a retreat from the preexisting legal and moral rights of employers. Therefore, management must exercise caution and not yield too much to collective bargaining, which deprives management of its "natural" and proper functions and is likely to interfere with the efficient operation of the business.

In contradistinction to this doctrine is the concept that management operates as a trustee for all those affected by the enterprise—those who furnish the capital, those who furnish the labor, and those who buy its products. According to this theory, collective bargaining is a *way* of managing and not a concession on the part of the owners or managers of capital. Collective bargaining, accordingly, does not imply a retreat from inviolate rights but only a change from former or customary procedures. Implied in this theory is the expectation (and hope) that the balancing leverage of collective bargaining will serve in the long run to promote the interests of owners, workers, and consumers.

Determination of Work Rules. In specific terms, those who believe that collective bargaining represents a negative influence on good management maintain that the employer should have the sole right to control the hiring and assignment of the work force, to establish job and quality standards, and to determine such matters as the processes and equipment to be used, the inventories and reserve funds to be maintained, the location of plants, and the subcontracting of work.

Unions, on the other hand, claim that all these activities affect job and working conditions, that the workers have a stake in their outcome and should therefore have a voice in their determination. For example, the questions of plant relocation and the subcontracting of work not only affect the job security of people already on the job, but influence general wages throughout the industry. If branch plants are established in low-wage areas or work is subcontracted to non-unionized plants, those employed in higher-wage union plants may eventually lose their jobs because of competitive costs, and working standards throughout the industry will inevitably decline. Earlier chapters have shown how the workers' interests—employment, wages, and other conditions of work—are affected by changes in methods of production, job evaluation, and rate-fixing methods.

Even if it is conceded that workers have an immediate interest in plant policies and rules, does it necessarily follow that it is feasible to submit these matters to collective bargaining? If the processes and decisions of collective bargaining interfere with management's efficiency, will not the workers as well as the employers and the general public suffer in the long run? The standard of living of workers, like that of everybody else, rests upon efficient management and high productivity. Restrictive work rules, like high tariffs, may benefit particular groups at the expense of the general welfare.

So-called "restrictive" work rules or "feather-bedding" places arbitrary limits on the amount of individual output, requires the employment of excess workers, or causes duplication of work. Examples commonly cited are the rules of the musicians' union which require radio stations to engage "live" musicians, even though their services are not needed because of the use of recorded music;[1] the "laws" of the typographical union which require the resetting of any type borrowed or purchased from another shop, and which stipulate that only journeyman printers may clean up

---

[1] In 1946 Congress passed the Lea Act which, among other regulations, forbids strikes to force radio stations to employ "stand-by" musicians. A few months after its passage a federal judge held the Act invalid on the ground that it violated the First, Fifth, and Thirteenth Amendments of the Constitution. In his ruling the judge held that "The Fifth Amendment imposes a restriction upon Congress, not specific, but equally effective as to arbitrary classification. This statute could be used to deprive the members of the musicians' union of the right to quit work collectively as a means of enforcing their demands with reference to the making of a new contract. All other employes of this country have the right to quit work collectively in order to use their bargaining power; they have the right to strike in order to enforce their demands.

"The guarantee of peaceful picketing is found in the specific guarantee of freedom of speech by the First Amendment; the guarantee of freedom to withdraw from employment or refuse to accept employment is found in the specific guarantees of the Fifth and Thirteenth Amendments."

type and perform other tasks which employers think unskilled labor could do just as well; and the rules on the railroads which require full crews for certain jobs which the operators contend could be done by fewer workmen.[2]

The reasons for union work rules are understandable. In some cases they are invoked for the health and safety of union members, as for example the rules pertaining to the use of poisonous materials. Most generally, however, they are for the purpose of prolonging jobs, and thus assume the aspect of "make-work" or "feather-bedding." While it is natural for workers, like any other persons, to take measures which will protect and promote their particular interests, it is nevertheless true that rules which artificially limit performance are a deterrent to economic progress. They are prejudicial to the long-time interests of both workers and the general economy, and provide no constructive answer to the problem of job insecurity.

Restrictive work rules are most likely to be adopted when unions take unilateral action, that is, when they adopt specific rules by a membership vote, or authorize their officers to prescribe rules which all union members and employers with unionized shops must abide by. When these rules are established by unions which also control the labor market as a result of closed-shop agreements, they take the form of monoply controls. They are not exposed to the give-and-take of annual collective bargaining in which consideration can be given to new or special situations.

Most unions do not attempt to establish specific work rules by unilateral action but seek to obtain them through collective bargaining, either by having them incorporated in the written contracts with employers, or by having a general clause in the contract requiring the mutual consent of the employer and union before there can be any change in existing rules and policies. Many employers are opposed to having policies and work rules come within the purview of collective bargaining. As a matter of principle, however, it can be argued that there is no more justification for denying workers a voice in the determination of any policies affecting employment conditions than there is for

---

[2] For additional examples, see Corwin D. Edwards, *Public Policy Toward Restraints of Trade of Labor Unions*, rebutted by Edwin E. Witte in *American Economic Review*, March, 1942, pp. 432–459.

depriving employers of the opportunity to bargain over rules promulgated by unions.

The entire history of unionism is a step-by-step admission of workers into the area once held to be the sole prerogative of management. The employers who now object to union participation in the formulation and execution of work rules hold much the same attitude as those who formerly opposed the determination of wages through collective bargaining. Industrial democracy implies jointly established terms of employment conditions. The problem of management is how best to function within the framework of these terms even though they remove certain functions from its sole competence.

Acceptance of the principle that collective bargaining is feasible for all matters affecting working conditions does not imply that the collective bargaining process always results in the wisest decisions, or that it is necessary to utilize it upon all occasions. Customarily, the workers and their unions do not care to intervene or participate in management's financial, marketing, or general engineering policies. It is only when job security and employment standards are threatened that the unions become interested in the broader phases of management.

Concern in the formulation of company policies, however, does not necessarily imply day-to-day participation in the execution of these policies. "Democratic administration does not mean wide, general voting on all sorts of operating and technical issues. . . . It does not mean that at numerous levels of administrative action the administrator shall be elected by those whose work he oversees. . . . It does not mean that in committees we talk ourselves into inaction because talk is easier than actual productive work. . . . Democratic organization does mean a clear distinction between policy making and policy execution. It means that the process of determining purposes, policy and method is advisedly seen as shared, and the process of oversight and direction is seen as unified and single." [3]

Control over the Work Force. The right of an employer to hire and discharge, to transfer and promote, whenever and whomever he wishes has been traditionally accepted by employers as

---

[3] Ordway Tead, *Democratic Administration,* Association Press, New York, 1945.

one of the fundamental prerogatives of management. Employers have considered that their right to select, reject, and discharge their employees as they deemed advisable was as necessary to good business operation as their freedom to buy and sell goods in the open market. Not to be able to choose freely whom he should employ, not to be able to lay off anyone at will, was tantamount to management chaos. Although the "enlightened" employer in the interests of good morale might use the weapon of discharge sparingly, his power and right to dismiss workers for any reason were seldom questioned.

In contrast, a fundamental tenet of unionism is that the individual worker is entitled to his job so long as it exists and he is willing and able to do it; and that job rights are not lost when employees temporarily cease work (strike) in an effort to improve their working conditions. Furthermore, union philosophy incorporates the principle that unions have the right to reserve jobs over which they have jurisdiction for the exclusive benefit of their members, or at least that their members shall have first claim to the available jobs.

Labor bases its claim on the principle that jobs inherently belong to the workers. In former years, as independent artisans who owned their own tools, the workers individually or collectively maintained job control. The fact that technology has deprived them of the tools of production does not divest them of their claim to jobs, for this right follows the job regardless of changing methods of production. According to this premise, workers are entitled to demand the adoption of regulations which they feel will provide the most equitable arrangements for job tenure. Just as the capital used in the enterprise belongs to the stockholders, so jobs or job tenure rights belong to the workers; and the managers of industry must accept both labor and capital on the terms which each offers.

With these opposite claims regarding one of the fundamental elements of manager-worker relationships, it is not surprising that conflicts have arisen as the growing strength of unions enabled them to demand the wider adoption of their principles and rules pertaining to job tenure. Laying aside the theoretical or moral rights claimed by either labor or the employers of labor, let us consider some of the practical problems as they affect the process of management. Specifically, does the adoption of union demands regarding the hiring and firing of employees cause a deterioration in management's efficiency and thus increase the costs of production? Does the quality of goods and services suffer when management does not have a free hand over the composition of its work force? Are there advantages to management as well as to labor in having formalized rules and methods substituted for personal judgment or preferences in the selection and control of the work force?

The individual worker's job security is protected by provisions in employer-union contracts which specify that length of service shall be the sole or major determinant in layoffs and rehiring. As a safeguard against arbitrary discharge, unions usually insist that the possible causes for discharge be clearly defined in the contract, and that an employee's supervisor must not have the final decision; in other words, an accused employee must be given the opportunity to obtain the intervention of his union and have his case appealed to the highest management authority and perhaps to outside arbitration.

To a disinterested person, these protections against unjust and hasty discharge seem reasonable. In effect, they are not unlike the procedures followed by a few employers before their plants were unionized. In the vast majority of unorganized plants, however, the workers have no protection against the whims and prejudices of employers and their foremen. There have been numerous cases where employees with many years of faithful service have been fired arbitrarily because of some minor infraction of a rule. An impatient and angry foreman has sometimes interpreted an employee's answer in self-defense to a criticism as an "act of insubordination" calling for discharge.

In many instances of this kind, the higher-up management has disagreed with the foreman's action, as did he himself after his temper cooled; but seldom was the discharge reconsidered, regardless of the injustices wrought the worker and the cost to management of losing an experienced employee. To a dictatorial management, it is more important to uphold the prestige and power of the foreman than to rectify a mistake, no matter how much hardship it causes the worker and his family.

Employers who place major reliance upon discharge as a

weapon with which to maintain discipline and quality of workmanship have naturally resented the intrusion of restrictions upon their absolute powers to discharge at will. Most employers, however, recognize the justice of the protections which organized workers have demanded. Their only objections are that the appeals procedure is too time-consuming and that the unions are prone to be unduly solicitous in protecting their active members.

Effect of Seniority Rules. The use of seniority rules as a basis for layoffs, and particularly for promotions and job assignments, presents more complex problems than the establishment of fixed rules for discharge. Unlike discharge, the selection of workers to be laid off (or promoted) is not an employer-employee issue alone; it also involves the question of choice or preference *among* workers. It is not a question as to whether or not A should be discharged, but as to whether A *or* B should be laid off when work is slack, or whether A *or* B should be promoted to a better job. Moreover, the "bumping" process required by seniority rules for layoffs frequently involves shifting and demoting many more persons than the number actually laid off.

In essence, seniority rules connote the substitution of another kind of yardstick than relative merit and proficiency for the obtaining and holding of jobs. While the oldest worker in point of service may be the best qualified, it can also be true that a junior employee will have superior or potentially superior qualifications. If the latter happens to be the case, the application of strict seniority rules means the difference between having the most able worker on the job or one with mere passing attainments.

Management contends that seniority rules have a two-way impact on plant efficiency. Not only may less competent employees be appointed (or retained) on particular jobs, but the general application of the seniority criterion offers little inducement for individuals to attain their maximum efficiency; when job security and promotions are primarily dependent upon the mechanical operation of seniority rules, the ambition to excel is minimized, with a consequent leveling influence throughout the entire work force.

Unions and workers argue that seniority rules have the opposite effect, that the feeling of security and fair play engendered by them improves morale and encourages good performance.

Furthermore, even though an employer (or his foreman) does not consciously practice discrimination, human judgment is fallible; and in the absence of fixed rules employees who are good self-advertisers rather than good workers are likely to receive preferential treatment.

Seniority versus individual merit as a basis for preferment is an age-old issue which is not confined to industrial workers or employer-union relations. It exists in our military forces and in our halls of Congress ;[4] in both places seniority largely prevails. If the agencies which are responsible for the defense of our country and for the laws which control our political life function under the seniority system, it would seem to be feasible for private business. But employers who have come to accept the principle of seniority for the rank and file of jobs insist that individual ability and other factors should be given dominant consideration in the selection of persons for supervisory jobs and other work requiring special skills. Here is where the greatest contention exists at the present time.

Union-Management Cooperation

The fact that workers (or their representatives) have a voice in making and administering plant rules does not necessarily mean that decisions must be made in an atmosphere of conflict or that they must be the result of compromises by opposing forces. In many areas of employer-worker relations, union-management cooperation may be substituted for collective bargaining, which is essentially a competitive process. Instead of conflict there can be collaboration and a mutual effort to achieve jointly desired ends.

Union-management cooperation represents maturity in the employer-worker relationship, although it does not eliminate the need for collective bargaining. As has been aptly said:

There are some problems, notably wage negotiation, which are likely to remain matters for collective bargaining regardless of the degree of cooperation which exists between a union and management.

There is nevertheless some shift as the development process takes place. Some of the things which were originally dealt with through

---

[4] Seniority along party lines is the basis of selecting the chairmen of the congressional committees which exercise powerful control over the bills introduced in and passed by Congress.

collective bargaining come in time to be dealt with cooperatively. For example, a great many grievances come to be handled in time by cooperative means. As the union and management deal with each other, and as mutual trust and confidence begin to develop, there comes a gradual recognition that the real aim of a grievance procedure is the solution of common problems to the mutual satisfaction of all concerned. . . . In many cases the basic desires of the two parties are found not to be incompatible. When this occurs, the settling of a grievance becomes a cooperative procedure in which both sides attempt to find a solution which is mutually satisfying. To the extent that this happens, the grievance procedure becomes a cooperative process rather than one of collective bargaining. There are some grievances, of course, which involve conflict of interest or desire, and these cannot be handled cooperatively.

It is perfectly possible for union and management to cooperate on some things and to compete on others. What is not possible is for them to compete and to cooperate at once with respect to the same problem. Matters for collective bargaining, involving conflict, cannot at one and the same time be matters for cooperation, involving mutual aid.[5]

There are potential pitfalls in union-management cooperation as well as possibilities for constructive accomplishments. As long as a cooperative endeavor is confined to methods for improving internal plant efficiency, the result can be beneficial to everybody —employer, workers, and the public. But if, to promote the success of the enterprise, this cooperation extends into controlling competition, fixing prices, or retarding innovations, the result can be detrimental to the public interest and may be in violation of the anti-trust laws.

For example, unions have cooperated with the coal and railroad industries in opposing the use of pipe lines from the natural gas fields of Texas to northern and eastern parts of the country, and in opposing the development of the St. Lawrence Waterway. There have been instances in the construction industry where local unions have joined with employers in boycotting materials from other areas in order to promote "home" industries, even though such materials were produced under union conditions elsewhere. In some cases employers have accepted collective bargaining for

---

[5] Irving Knickerbocker and Douglas McGregor, *Union-Management Cooperation: A Psycnological Analysis,* Series 2, No. 9, p. 5, Massachusetts Institute of Technology, Cambridge.

the primary purpose of obtaining union support in their efforts to forestall or discourage competition, for they realize that public opinion is more responsive to workers' protests about loss of jobs than to employers' arguments about loss of business.

Union-management cooperation carried to its extreme limits could lead to a corporative society in which the general economy would be divided along industry lines. Horizontal class competition between employers and employees would give way to vertical competition in which the employers and workers within each industry (or plant) were united to promote the interest of their particular industry or enterprise.

THE "RIGHT TO WORK" AND THE UNION SHOP

The principle that an individual's preference not to belong to a union or engage in union activities should not be a deterrent in finding or holding a job is usually expressed in legislative proposals and laws which read variously as follows:

No person may be denied employment and employers may not be denied the right to employ any person because of that person's membership or non-membership in any labor organization.

It shall be unlawful, singly or in concert, to interfere with another in his exercise of the right to work.

Every person has the right to work, and to seek, obtain and hold employment, without interference with or impairment or abridgement of said right because he does not belong to or pay money to a labor organization. Anything done or threatened to be done which interferes with, impairs, or abridges said right is unlawful.

The purpose of legislation of this kind is to outlaw employer-union contracts which require union membership as a condition of employment, and to prohibit picketing and other union action which make it difficult or embarrassing for non-union workers to accept or continue their employment. Such blanket restrictions for workers engaged in interstate industries are counter to the National Labor Relations Act and the Anti-Injunction Act as they read in 1946.

Opponents of such legislation also maintain that the restrictions are unconstitutional because they violate the guarantees of free speech and union property rights inherent in contracts with employers. Its proponents, while admitting that it nullifies certain provisions in existing federal labor laws, hold that it conforms to the best traditions of our Constitution and Bill of Rights because it affords protection against union coercion and intimidation.[6]

The Right-to-Work Theory

A policy of protection for non-union workers and the open shop is based on the assumption that any person should be able to engage in lawful work anywhere and under any conditions he chooses, and that any employer should be able to hire anyone he chooses. Exalted into a principle, it is expressed as a duty of government to protect the inalienable right of an individual to work—a right which is as fundamental as his right to quit work, and as sacred as the right to "life, liberty and the pursuit of happiness."

Although much of the support for restrictive union legislation comes from groups which before the enactment of the National Labor Relations Act were opposed to collective bargaining of any kind, these groups now maintain that they do not object to the principle of collective bargaining but merely to its misuse. Workers, they say, have a right to select an agent of their choosing and to ask this agent to bargain in their behalf. But when a majority of the employees designate a bargaining agent, they have no moral right, and should have no legal right, to act for the minority who wish to bargain for themselves. They maintain that to force workers to join and pay dues to a union in order to obtain and hold a job is repugnant to every instinct of liberty, and is a form of human bondage because it infringes upon the individual's right to work under whatever conditions he chooses.

Regardless of the merits or deficiencies of the closed or union shop or other requirements for union membership, there are obvious loopholes in the "right-to-work" argument as a reason for restricting union job control. An inalienable right is one which cannot be taken away; but no proponent of this argument goes

---

[6] Although the issue has come to the attention of the lower courts, the United States Supreme Court has not yet (1946) ruled on it.

so far as to say that jobs should always be guaranteed to those who seek work, and that no one should be dismissed from a job he wishes to retain. It could just as well be argued that unions protect the right to work rather than deny it, for some of the major planks in collective contracts are the job protection clauses concerning layoffs and discharges. In the absence of collective bargaining, all the rights an individual worker has under the law and under our present industrial system is the right to go from employer to employer in search of work and to accept any job which may be offered on the terms and conditions prescribed by the employer.

Job Holding and Union Membership Rules

The fact that a collective bargaining contract requires union membership as a condition of employment does not in itself deny anyone the right to work; it merely superimposes another requirement upon the employee in addition to those prescribed unilaterally by the employer. However, if the union is unwilling to allow certain individuals to become members, or makes the cost of membership prohibitive, the requirement of union membership for holding a job is tantamount to depriving persons of jobs.

There are two reasons why a union may deny membership privileges: First, certain people may be unacceptable, and second, there may be an actual or potential surplus of workers in the trade. Where union-shop conditions prevail throughout most of a trade or industry, non-union members are at a definite disadvantage when jobs are scarce. Fundamentally, however, it is job scarcity rather than union membership requirements which deprive them of the "right to work." In the choice between members and non-members for the limited number of available jobs, the unions naturally feel that those who have fought and sacrificed to improve working conditions should have preference. Non-union applicants who are debarred, and employers who naturally prefer to select their employees in a highly competitive labor market, are inclined to regard this as the union's monopoly of jobs, even though the union is not responsible for the scarcity.

Effect of Restrictive Membership Rules. Certain persons may be deprived of jobs because of restrictive union admission rules or because they are personally unacceptable to the union. As was indicated in Chapter 18, very few unions follow the policy of restricting membership either by specific rules of admission or through exorbitant initiation fees; most of them automatically accept all applicants who are employed or are seeking employment within their respective jurisdictions. A few unions, on the other hand, deny membership to Negroes and some exclude persons of specified political beliefs, such as communists. Within recent years several states have enacted laws against union membership discrimination, and most people are in accord with the general principle embodied in such legislation.[7]

Any union may object to having a certain individual as a member because of actions or attitudes which it considers inimical to its interests. There may be a suspicion, and perhaps evidence, that he is anti-union and a "stooge of the boss" who will use his membership for purposes of spying or disrupting the union. On the other hand, he may have been a loyal member who for conscientious reasons objected to certain union rules and policies and was expelled when he refused to abide by them. Also, as with any kind of organization composed of human beings, personal prejudices and

---

[7] The 1937 Wisconsin Employment Peace Act states that a union may be deprived of a closed-shop agreement if it refuses to enroll any employee of the employer. A 1940 New York statute specifically forbids any labor organization in that state to deny membership because of race, color, or creed, makes violation a misdemeanor, and provides a fine of $100 to $500 to be recovered by the person discriminated against. A 1941 Pennsylvania statute excludes unions which restrict membership because of race, creed, or color, from the benefits of the state Labor Relations Act. A 1941 Kansas law prohibits any union from acting as a collective bargaining representative which discriminates against or excludes from' membership any person because of race or color, but this law excludes railroad and airline unions where race discrimination is most prone to exist. A 1941 Nebraska law forbids racial discrimination in collective bargaining but does not refer directly to union membership.

Up to the present time (1946), the courts have generally ruled that complete responsibility rests with the unions so far as their membership rules are concerned, even though membership restrictions might hamper or debar certain workers from jobs. Typical is a California court decision in 1944, which said, ". . . A voluntary organization may prescribe conditions upon which membership may be acquired and upon which it may continue and rules of conduct for members. The court is without power to enforce admission of members to a voluntary association. Membership is not a right that may be granted independently . . . but is a privilege that may be withheld or accorded on such terms as the association [union] sees fit to impose." (California Superior Court, Los Angeles County, *Blackeney* et al. v. *California Shipbuilding Corporation* et al., August 7, 1944.)

animosities may cause some persons to be kept out, or expelled, in spite of all the safeguards provided in union constitutions.

A union's refusal to accept or retain certain people as members is a delicate problem which involves the question of what is considered reasonable or justifiable motives. A member may refuse to obey a union rule which many persons, inside and outside the union, might also consider unwise; but if the majority of the members have voted for the rule, or have voted for the officers who interpret it, union discipline requires compliance by all.

Union Monopoly and the Majority Rule

Essentially, the issue of union status within a plant involves individual or minority rights as opposed to majority rule. According to the present laws, a union must have been designated by a majority of the employees concerned before it is permitted to become their bargaining agent. To argue that the union so designated has no right to act for the minority who wish to bargain for themselves may be compared to saying that the minority of citizens who lost in a political election should not have to abide by the laws enacted by the successful majority, or that a minority of stockholders should be allowed to interpose in the management of a corporation.

This analogy could be extended further in defense of the union shop by arguing that just as the unsuccessful citizens' minority must continue to help support the government and pay the taxes levied by the party in power, so the minority of non-member employees should share in the costs of collective bargaining. If wages and other work standards achieved through collective bargaining could be applied only to union employees, it could be maintained that those who do not choose to pay union dues should not have to do so in order to hold their jobs. Since two different wage and other standards within the same plant are obviously impractical, it would seem logical that all who secure benefits from the union should share the financial burden of its maintenance.

Dangers of Union Monopoly. In addition to partisan and specific objections to union membership as a condition of employment, there is opposition which stems from a general fear that the union shop leads to union monopoly of jobs and dictatorship of working conditions. Accompanying this fear is a desire to keep the status of unions in a fluid condition, thus enabling employees to enter or leave at will, or to change their allegiance from one union to another.

Union monopoly can be as inimicable to the public interest as any other type of monopoly, but a closed or union shop does not necessarily signify union monopoly. Those who speak of union monopoly usually think in terms of a strongly entrenched clique of union officers who, because of compulsory membership requirements, are enabled to exercise despotic power over workers and employers alike. This is possible if the union ceases to be democratically governed and if the circumstances of its jurisdiction (for example in highly specialized trades and professions) make it possible for it to maintain control over the entire potential labor market.

There is an opposite danger in the closed- or union-shop arrangement than the possibility of over-aggression and tyrannical control, namely, apathy. The avowed purpose of a union shop is to provide union security and eliminate the necessity for continual membership drives during which skeptical and indifferent employees must be won over by tangible evidence of the union's accomplishments. This challenge is minimized when full membership is automatically assured through union-shop agreements, with the result that union leaders may become less alert in promoting their members' welfare. Taking advantage of this all-too-human reaction to "security," some employers have accepted union-shop agreements in order to obviate what they call "popularity contests," in which the union must promise better working conditions in order to win new members and hold dissatisfied members who otherwise would transfer allegiance to a more aggressive union.

Safeguards Against Union Monopolies. A union can be said to be monopolistic when there is not free access to membership and when it has ceased to be the instrument of expression for the majority of those who work under the agreements it negotiates. A union cannot accurately be called monopolistic when it maintains an open door for all eligible members, when there is full participation by all members in the administration of its activities, and when it is possible for employees to change their union affiliation whenever a majority so desire. The latter involves the delicate problem of rival unions, and the policies of the National Labor Relations Board and similar state agencies with respect to employee elections for the determination of bargaining agents.[8] Safeguards against union monopoly of jobs and union leader dictatorship lie in the unions' internal rules and procedures and in the mechanism provided for determining the majority choice of any group of employees.

REGULATION OF LABOR UNIONS

The presence of the union shop or its equivalent throughout large sections of industry, as well as the general expansion in union membership and power, has brought forth many proposals and some laws for the regulation of labor unions. Some of these proposals emanate from persons who are unsympathetic toward labor and who frankly or covertly seek laws which will curb the effectiveness of organized labor. Some, however, come from people who are staunch supporters of collective bargaining and who feel that certain forms of regulation will improve the conduct of labor unions and thereby strengthen their position in the economy. Organized labor itself opposes government regulation; it maintains that unions are voluntary associations and that whatever changes or improvements are needed should come from within, through self-discipline and joint cooperation with industry.

Proposals and laws for regulating labor unions and labor relations are of two general types: those which are concerned with the internal workings of the union, such as membership rules, the election and authority of officers, and dues and finances; and those which are concerned with union activities directly affecting employers and the public, such as strikes, picketing, and boycotts. We can discuss only briefly some aspects of a few of these proposals.

---

[8] The National Labor Relations Board presently follows the policy of allowing the employees in any bargaining unit to petition for a new election toward the closing date of an existing contract, or a year or more following a previous election. If the insurgent group fails to win the election, the employees may not be discharged because of their activities on behalf of the rival union, even though the original union has a closed-shop contract and has expelled them because of their attempt to change the bargaining agent.

Incorporation of Unions

Compulsory incorporation of labor unions has been advocated as a means of increasing labor's responsibility and of making unions "amenable to the law and liable for wrongful acts." It is argued that business incorporates and is financially responsible for any damage it may commit, and that unions should be forced to undertake similar obligations. Specifically, it is maintained that incorporation would make unions more responsive to the Anti-Trust Act, and that it would prevent racketeering and would restrain union officers and members from committing other acts for which they could be sued for damages.

The opposite view holds that the corporate device is not adaptable to union organization and will not fulfill the purposes desired by its sponsors.[9] Organized labor interprets compulsory incorporation as a movement to destroy unions, and cites the following arguments:

1. Business is not required to incorporate. Businessmen are free to operate either as individuals, as copartnerships, or as voluntary associations. Combinations of businessmen, such as trade associations, are not required to and do not incorporate.

2. The purpose of the incorporation of business is to *limit* liability, not to establish it, and members of incorporated businesses can escape personal liability. The incorporation of trade unions seeks to *establish* liability in such a way as to hold the central organization responsible for the irresponsible acts of individual members who may actually be

---

[9] In the 19th century, organized labor favored incorporation as a countermove to the conspiracy laws which followed the general strikes of 1877. It was also felt that incorporation would give legal recognition to the right to organize. A federal incorporation law was passed in 1886 which permitted trade unions to incorporate in the District of Columbia and other federal territories. Subsequently several unions incorporated. After the Taff-Vale decision in England in 1901 (which held that a union was subject to a civil suit for damages performed by an individual member and that its funds were attachable to satisfy claims), the attitude of organized labor changed to opposition. The 1886 incorporation law was repealed in 1932, largely on the grounds that it was being used by beneficiary societies carrying on an insurance business.

The latest instance of union incorporation legislation was a law passed by Colorado in 1943 which required every labor organization in the state to incorporate. This law was invalidated by the state supreme court in 1944 on the grounds that it infringed on the constitutional right of assembly. Some states, for example Illinois, specifically exclude labor unions from their incorporation laws.

serving as spies, provocateurs, and strikebreakers for the employers.

3. Businesses are set up for the purpose of making profits. Trade unions are non-profit organizations.

4. Incorporation will not stop racketeering. Unions as such are not parties to racketeering; when unscrupulous officers engage in such practices it is not on union instructions and is generally done in collusion with employers. Moreover, racketeering might easily be extended through the device of paper corporations and dummy officers.

5. Union incorporation would restrict the right of workers to organize. A hostile political regime might refuse to grant a union a charter or might delay permission until the workers' enthusiasm to organize had waned.

6. Incorporation might restrict normal union activities. When applying for a charter the union would have to ask the right to engage in each particular activity, and a hostile government could refuse to grant some of the rights requested. At any time—for example, during a strike—a judge might decide that the union was deviating from the exact provisions in its charter and might suspend or cancel it, attach the union's books and funds, and appoint a receiver to run its affairs. Even if a higher court later reversed this action, the strikebreaking purposes of the lower court would have been achieved.

Aside from the fears of organized labor, union incorporation raises a number of legal questions.

1. Should only the national union be incorporated or should each local be incorporated? If the various locals of a national union are required to incorporate under different state laws, will this not in effect destroy the national organization? If only national unions are required to incorporate and a pro-labor state legislature passes an incorporation law giving wide permissive powers to trade unions, will not all the national unions be inclined to incorporate in that state? (An analogy is the inclination of business to incorporate in the state of Delaware.)

2. Under the law of agency, would a national union be responsible for a local union's actions which it did not authorize? Would either a local or a national union (or both) be responsible for the unauthorized acts of its individual members? The general principles of agency make an organization liable only for authorized or ratified acts of its agents. Should unions have to assume a greater degree of liability than is imposed on other organizations?

3. How would the incorporation law define a trade union? How would it distinguish between this type of voluntary association and, for example, the American Medical Association or the National

Grange, which perform protective functions for their members similar to those performed by labor unions?

4. The capacity for perpetual succession is a distinguishing feature of corporations, with rights and duties descending upon its successive members. If a majority of the members of an incorporated union desired to change its affiliation, could the minority continue under the old charter and retain the union's funds and assets? Would incorporation not tend to freeze the *status quo* and prevent changes in policy in response to the changing needs and desires of new generations of members?

It is apparent from the above that compulsory incorporation of labor unions may create more problems than it can resolve. For that reason, many persons who seek changes in union practices advocate laws directed to specific ends, rather than compulsory incorporation.

Regulation of the Internal Government of Unions

Those who sponsor legislation to regulate the internal affairs of labor unions give as their primary purpose the protection of workers against unfair union rules and unscrupulous union officers, although they also indicate that employers and the public will benefit from such regulation. The specific forms of the remedies offered indicate the areas in which those who advocate regulation believe that some unions, at least, have failed to represent the will and desires of the workers whose interests they are supposed to promote.

Union Democracy. A common criticism is that the rank-and-file members do not participate sufficiently in the conduct of their union's affairs and that dictatorial powers rest with the officers. This raises the question of how much democracy is possible and desirable in unions—an age-old question common to all types of organizational and community life. Most union constitutions, as indicated in Chapter 18, provide the mechanism for maximum participation of the members, although the basic laws of a few unions permit and encourage highly centralized officer control. Under the former as well as the latter, however, personal domination by a few leaders frequently exists.

The reasons are twofold. The leaders naturally are better informed about conditions within and outside the union and can take prompt and decisive action as issues arise. Furthermore, the majority of the members prefer to have their officers assume most of the responsibility for deciding and administering union policy. Like the ordinary stockholder in a business corporation or the average taxpayer in any community, most union members are willing to have their elected leaders assume full authority as long as they "deliver the goods."

As one student of labor unions observed some years ago, "While unionism as a whole is the spontaneous outcome of the conditions, needs and problems of the workers, the rank and file in general are not in a condition to formulate methods for meeting needs or solving problems, and, apart from the direction of competent leaders, have not the intelligence to combat employers successfully. . . . Only when the union is weak and the leaders unsuccessful do the rank and file take control."[10] Just as the inertia of citizens results in domination by machine politics and sometimes corruption in city government, so the unwillingness of union members to spend time and effort on union affairs makes it possible, if not necessary, for a few leaders to assume dictatorial control.

Can this human weakness of indifference and inertia be remedied by law? Some governments penalize citizens for not voting and some unions fine members for non-attendance at meetings. Presumably, there could be laws to require union members to take an active part in the government of their organizations, and to require unions to hold meetings and conventions at frequent intervals in which officers would be elected and policies decided by secret ballot. Such legislation might correct certain evils existing in some unions but it would most certainly open the way for government regulation of many other kinds of private organizations. The ultimate result could be a totalitarian government that would reach into every phase of economic and social activity. Many persons believe that the better answer is the exposure of specific evil practices to the "court of public opinion," and reliance upon remedy from within the unions.

Protection Against Expulsion. Reform from within is con-

---

[10] R. F. Hoxie, *Trade Unionism in the U. S.,* D. Appleton & Company, Inc., New York, 1923, p. 177. See also Norman Thomas, "How Democratic Are Labor Unions?" *Harper's Magazine,* May, 1942.

tingent upon the ability of any member or group of members to criticize the actions of their union or its officers without fear of reprisal. The difficult problem for the union is to distinguish between sincere criticism and an effort to disrupt the union, especially when there is a suspicion that the criticism emanates from "stooges of the boss." It might well be argued that, regardless of motive, members should have some protection against arbitrary expulsion, at least where union-shop conditions exist and expulsion means the loss of a job. Under the latter circumstances the issue goes beyond internal union government; it affects the employer as well as the means of livelihood of members and their families, and comes within the purview of union contracts.

Protection need not take the form of legislative definition of members' rights, but guarantees due process for accused members. Persons expelled from unions now have recourse to the courts, and in a number of instances the courts have ordered the reinstatement of members who were expelled for violating union rules which the courts considered unconstitutional, for bringing suit for the restoration of misappropriated funds, and for other reasons.[11] Restoration through the courts is costly, however, and therefore most union members are reluctant to invoke judicial procedures.

A practical alternative would be the requirement that union-shop contracts include the provision that expelled members have the right to appeal to arbitration where it is provided in the agreement, and otherwise to the courts. The former is usually preferable because industrial arbitrators are more familiar with union and labor relations problems than the average judge.

Regulation of Union Finances

Proposed measures and laws pertaining to union finances are directed toward two purposes: to regulate the amount of dues and fees which unions levy upon their members, and to safeguard and restrict the use of union funds. The expressed motive for regulations of this kind is to protect workers from excessive charges; but underlying this is fear, on the part of employers and others,

---

[11] The reader is referred to a discussion of this subject by John P. Troxell and David A. McCabe in the *American Economic Review*, March, 1942, pp. 460–489.

of the increased power which ample treasuries would give the unions.

There is considerable opposition, for example, to union expenditures for political purposes; it is argued that unions, like business corporations, should not be allowed to make contributions to political parties or candidates.[12] Whether or not it is to the best interests of all concerned for unions to make such contributions is debatable, but comparing them to corporation contributions is a specious analogy so long as there are individual stockholders who are able to make political contributions as large as most unions can afford to make. As far as equalizing political influence is concerned, it could logically be argued that no individual's contribution to political campaigns should exceed the amount which an average worker could afford to make.

Criticisms with respect to union levies pertain more to initiation fees than to regular monthly dues. Only the craft unions, and not all of them, charge more than a few dollars for joining. Although there are understandable reasons why these unions have relatively high initiation fees, as is indicated in Chapter 18, there are instances in which the fees have exceeded amounts which most people would consider reasonable. There was adverse criticism during World War II when some unions were able to collect large sums of money from the thousands of new members employed under union-shop agreements in war industries. The unions' answer to this criticism claimed that this was an abnormal situation and that industry also received large returns from war contracts.

In spite of instances of exceedingly high fees, the advisability of legal restrictions is questionable. The kinds and amount of services which unions render their members vary greatly and no uniform scale of fees could reasonably be applied. It would seem

[12] The British experience with union political contributions is pertinent. The British Trade Union Act of 1913 authorized unions to spend money for any political purposes for which a majority of the members voted, and all members automatically contributed except those who individually refused. The Trade Disputes Act of 1927 reversed the method of collection by specifying that each member must individually authorize the union to use his contribution for political purposes. The Conservative party was in power in 1927 and the purpose of this provision was to check the political development of the British Trade Union movement. It is significant that less than twenty years after the passage of the Act the Labor party gained control of the government.

that the members themselves are the best judges of the financial needs of their unions and the expenses they should incur and that external regulations should be confined to procedural arrangements, namely, the requirement that dues and fees, as well as union expenditures, shall be approved by a secret vote of the members.

STRIKE REGULATION[13]

When labor unions are weak, employer-labor disputes are localized and affect relatively few persons. When there are strong unions in the important base industries, their conflicts with employers can disturb the general economy and affect the well-being of the entire population of this nation, and even foreign countries. Thus, the stronger and more active the labor movement becomes, the greater are the demand and need for finding means to avoid work stoppages, especially in the major or key industries.

The problem is, what effective means does a democratic society have for maintaining industrial peace when the parties directly involved in a controversy approximate equality in bargaining strength? Can legislation put an end to strikes and lockouts? Because of the nature of the problem they attempt to remedy, laws to discourage or prohibit work stoppages must restrict certain actions of workers and their unions. Will such laws thereby tip the scale in favor of employers, and ultimately destroy the equilibrium necessary for effective collective bargaining?

In considering the causes and social effects of industrial disputes, the inherent disadvantageous position of workers in relation to their employers and the public must ever be kept in mind. Employers are able to improve their economic condition—that is, increase their profits—without consulting their employees or inconveniencing the public by lockouts. Workers cannot improve or even maintain the existing standards without the approval of their employer; and if he refuses to raise the standards or insists upon lowering them, the only recourse open is to strike. In other words, the workers must resort to overt action that causes in-

---

[13] The complex and controversial problem of labor disputes obviously is one which requires more than a few pages to be discussed with any degree of adequacy. The student is urged to supplement his study with further reading in current labor and management journals as well as the books listed at the end of this and preceding chapters.

convenience to the public (as well as to themselves and the employer) in order to obtain conditions of work not readily granted by their employer.

Moreover, the protests and struggles of workers must be carried on in the open. A few employers can meet quietly in a New York office and decide upon a labor policy which will affect hundreds of thousands of workers. The public may never know that there has been any concerted action on the part of these employers, but it is well aware of any concerted action of the employees when they protest the working conditions resulting from this agreed-upon policy.

The inherent inequality in the strategy available to employers in contrast to that available to workers must always be kept in mind in any consideration of laws to bring about "equality" in the employer-employee relationship. The present discussion, however, is concerned not primarily with the rights of employers versus those of workers, but rather with a consideration of the means available for protecting the general welfare against the impact of disputes between the two groups. Because these disputes stem from varied causes and circumstances, there can be no generalization about methods for handling all employer-worker conflicts. The remedies and methods for mitigating their effects upon the public, whether by law or private arrangement, must be fitted to the circumstances attending the various kinds of disputes. The proposed remedies must also take into consideration the merits and deficiencies of alternative measures.

Compulsory Arbitration

The most plausible-sounding remedy for strikes and lockouts is compulsory arbitration. Many well-meaning persons who want to be fair to both employers and workers argue that their differences should be settled by impartial agencies authorized to make decisions which the parties to the dispute must accept as final. Comparison is frequently made to the functions and powers of courts which settle civil disputes and impose penalties for violation of the laws.

This comparison between courts and compulsory arbitration of industrial disputes has only limited validity. It is inappropriate in the majority of disputes which have to do with the terms and conditions of employment to be included in employer-union contracts; it might have some cogency with respect to the enforcement of the terms in existing contracts. Courts function under laws which express the will of the people; the courts merely interpret and apply these laws in individual situations. The people of this country have never expressed their will in legal code as to how the income of business should be distributed between the owners of capital and labor, and how much should be laid aside for future investment. In settling a wage controversy, therefore, there are no laws upon which to base decisions. In the absence of a public mandate as to what are "fair" profits, "just" wages, and "reasonable" working conditions, compulsory arbitration forces the parties involved in the dispute to accept decisions based solely upon what individual arbitrators deem to be expedient.

Arguments Against Compulsory Arbitration. Employers and unions[14] concur in their opposition to compulsory arbitration, although their opinions may be expressed somewhat differently. Both fear government control of labor standards and the injection of politics into labor disputes which attends arbitration by government mandate. When wages and other working conditions are determined by labor courts or other government agencies, both labor and management must rely upon political action to protect their interests. Inevitably, compulsory arbitration leads to a labor versus a conservative (employer) political party alignment, for whichever group controls the government also controls the conditions under which industries and unions operate.

Under compulsory arbitration litigation supplants collective bargaining, with employers and unions directing their major efforts toward securing favorable decisions from government tribunals instead of trying to arrive at mutually satisfactory terms

---

[14] In some countries—for example, Australia—organized labor favors compulsory arbitration. Significantly, the consequences of compulsory arbitration mentioned in this section have occurred in Australia. For information about actual experiences with compulsory arbitration, see Orwell de R. Foenander, *Toward Industrial Peace in Australia* and *Solving Labor Problems in Australia,* Melbourne, 1941; W. Rupert Maclaurin, "Recent Experience with Compulsory Arbitration in Australia," *American Economic Review,* March, 1938, pp. 65–81; E. J. Riches, "The Restoration of Compulsory Arbitration in New Zealand," *International Labor Review,* December, 1936; E. E. Witte, "Experience with Strike Legislation Abroad," *Annals of American Academy of Political and Social Science,* November, 1946.

through direct negotiations. Every arbitration hearing tends to become a battle of wits in which bitterness is intensified as each side inveighs against the other in order to impress public opinion as well as the arbitrators.

Compulsory arbitration promotes standardization of employment conditions through entire industries and areas. The awards of arbitration tribunals tend to become binding upon an entire industry, thereby changing the work standards of those who have not come before the tribunals to argue in support of their interests. Under some compulsory arbitration systems in other countries, the industry-wide application of decisions is required by law. Even though not specifically required, the proneness of courts and similar bodies to base their decisions upon precedents tends toward standardization.

Compulsory arbitration does not prevent strikes, as is evidenced by the strike records where this procedure exists.[15] Only a totalitarian government can eliminate strikes, and even these governments cannot prevent slowdowns whose cumulative effects may cause greater losses in production than complete, but brief, work

---

[15] Australia and New Zealand, for example, continue to have many strikes, although compulsory arbitration has been established for many years.

In the United States, as is well remembered, there were many strikes during the recent war period, although what amounted to compulsory arbitration in war industries was provided in the War Labor Disputes Act which gave the War Labor Board authority to "decide the dispute" and order the "terms and conditions . . . governing the relations between the parties."

The only peacetime experience this country has had with statutory compulsory arbitration was that of the Kansas Court of Industrial Relations, which functioned from 1920 to 1923. This court was given jurisdiction in disputes arising in the public utilities, coal, food, and clothing industries, wherein strikes were altogether prohibited. The three-man court appointed by the governor had power to fix wages and conditions of employment in these industries. Labor, particularly the Kansas district of the United Mine Workers, bitterly opposed the establishment of the court. Several of the union leaders were given jail sentences when they defied the anti-strike clause of the Act by calling a number of strikes. Some employers also refused to put into effect its wage and hour decisions. The United States Supreme Court sustained these employers, holding that the fixing of wages and hours, rules and regulations by such an agency was contrary to the due process clause of the Fourteenth Amendment in that it "curtailed the right of the employer, on the one hand, and of the employee, on the other, to contract about his affairs." Before even the first of the Supreme Court decisions was rendered, the Industrial Relations Court had practically ceased to function, because of the increasing opposition and indifference of employers, workers, and public. In 1925 it was abolished.

stoppages. In a democratic country people cannot be compelled to work, and public opinion will not long support a law which requires an army to enforce it, and jail penalties or even fines for thousands of persons. And there is ample evidence that sanctions against a few union leaders will not cause the rank-and-file employees to return to work. On the contrary, such a step sometimes tends to increase their class-consciousness and their loyalty to their leaders.

Agreement Observance

To argue against compulsory arbitration for settling disputes over terms of employment does not preclude the possibility of mandatory arbitration of disputes after the employer-union contract has been negotiated. Theoretically, there should be no work stoppage where employer-union contracts provide that either party may appeal grievances to arbitration. When work stoppages occur, they usually signify violation of the terms of the agreement, for arbitration provisions are generally accompanied by no-strike clauses. As is indicated in Chapter 20, a majority of the existing agreements have arbitration clauses; but according to some, arbitration is permissive only, and in others the consent of both parties is required. Obviously, the latter clauses provide no effective alternative to strikes and lockouts.

"Illegal" Strikes. Most stoppages occurring while agreements are in effect are spontaneous actions of the rank-and-file workers and are not authorized by the union. (They are commonly referred to as "wildcat" or "quickie" strikes.) But the union must be held responsible to the extent that its officials do not exert all possible pressure to get their members back to work and do not discipline them for the unauthorized stoppage.

It is not always easy for union officials to do this, however; moreover, it must be remembered that it is much easier for management to fulfill its side of the contract than for labor. As one authority on labor problems has observed: "Business has a far more monolithic structure than unions. Top management has absolute control and has far less to do to keep the stockholders satisfied than a labor leader who must meet his men on a day-to-day basis. . . . The top executives have merely to pass the word down the line. But labor has to depend on the loyalty of many men to abide by a decision with which many of them may not even agree."[16]

The Problem of Interpretation of Agreements. Work stoppages during the term of an agreement involve the question of liability for breach of contract. Inextricably tied in with the question of agreement observance are the problems connected with the interpretation and application of the agreement in particular situations. When stoppages occur under no-strike agreements, workers usually claim that the employer (or his foreman) had already violated the agreement and that the strike, in reality, was for the purpose of obtaining observance.

No matter how carefully an agreement is phrased, there can always be differences of opinion with respect to the meaning of certain clauses when applied to specific conditions.[17] Furthermore, no agreement can foresee and cover all the contingencies which may arise in the day-to-day operation of a business enterprise. Honest differences of opinion as to the meaning of particular clauses are bound to occur.

In practice, agreement observance demands the subordination of claims *under* the agreement to an over-all loyalty *to* the agreement itself. Even though employer-union agreements are legally enforceable contracts, neither employers nor unions find the ordinary judicial processes practical in most situations involving questions of breach of contract. A wildcat strike, for example, is usually ended long before the issue could be settled in court, and with its termination the employer and the workers usually want to forget about it instead of renewing the ill feelings by rehearsing the entire affair before a court.

One method of encouraging observance of employer-union contracts would be to include in the National Labor Relations Act a provision that agreements which include "reasonable" provisions for arbitration of disputes and penalties for violation of the

---

[16] E. Wight Bakke, in *Labor and Nation,* June–July, 1946, p. 23.

[17] An outstanding example was the controversy with respect to the termination clause in the agreement negotiated by the government in May, 1946, with the United Mine Workers. Presumably, the best lawyers in the government and the union drew up the agreement, but when the crisis came six months later there were diametrically opposed views among the legal fraternity on the issue of how and when the agreement could be terminated. The basis of this disagreement, which is identical to that in many other cases, was the question of which of two clauses superseded the other.

agreement could be filed with an appropriate government agency which would thereupon assume responsibility for enforcing the agreement.

"Reasonable" arbitration provisions would include time limitations for the submission and disposition of arbitration cases, requirements pertaining to the method of selecting arbitrators and hearing procedures, and the amount and kind of penalties to be imposed for violations. The exact type of arbitration and penalty provisions would be left to employer-union negotiations in each case, with the government agency merely passing upon their "reasonableness" before the agreement was filed for enforcement purposes.

Such a procedure, in effect, would be compulsory enforcement of voluntary arbitration. The privilege of having the agreement become enforceable under the aegis of the government could be used as a bargaining factor; for instance, employers might be willing to grant a higher wage rate or a more liberal vacation allowance if they had assurance that there would be no work stoppages during the term of the agreement, or that proper penalties would be invoked if a stoppage took place.

Settlement of Jurisdictional Strikes

The preceding discussion had to do with disputes between employers and employees over the terms and conditions of employment. There are other causes for work stoppages which may call for different kinds of treatment. Among these are strikes over union jurisdiction; here the quarrel is solely between unions who have no immediate dispute with the employer.

Jurisdictional disputes are basically different from rival union disputes. In the latter, the issue involves the question of which one of several contending unions shall have the right to represent a given group of *workers*, an issue which can be solved by holding an employee election. In a jurisdictional dispute it is a question of which union has the right to control the *jobs*, and this cannot be determined by holding an election of the employees who happen to be doing the jobs. If these workers do not belong to the union which is finally awarded jurisdiction, they may be displaced, although the victorious union may (but does not always) allow them to transfer their membership and continue on the job.

Because jurisdictional disputes usually take place between unions belonging to the same labor federation (most frequently the American Federation of Labor), it would be best if they could be settled within the labor movement. Although the A. F. of L. has been able to settle many of the jurisdictional quarrels which have arisen among its affiliated unions, it has been far from successful in preventing jurisdictional strikes. Its decisions almost always favor the union which controls the most votes in the Federation, and frequently the smaller defeated union severs its connection with the parent body and continues the fight as an independent organization.

Arbitration of Jurisdictional Strikes. Since jurisdictional strikes are the result of conflicting claims to property rights over jobs, it is not illogical to suggest that they be handled differently from disputes between employers and workers over the terms and conditions of employment. Furthermore, restrictions against stoppages of work during jurisdictional disputes need not be predicated upon forcing workers to remain on the job against their will because one of the conflicting groups of workers is always anxious to do so.

Although no law can prohibit jurisdictional disputes from arising, legislation could be enacted to compel the contending unions to submit their dispute to an impartial agency *before* engaging in a jurisdictional strike or boycott. The National Labor Relations Board, or some other designated government agency, could be empowered to serve as arbitrator in threatened jurisdictional strikes, the unions involved having the option of choosing their own arbitrator or the government agency. Meanwhile, however, work stoppages and boycotts involving questions of jurisdiction could be forbidden and penalties imposed upon the unions or union members who engage in activities leading to such strikes or boycotts.

Strikes in Public Utilities

Some persons who are not inclined toward legislative action against strikes in general nevertheless favor the control of strikes in industries having a "public interest." The difficulty is to determine what industries and occupations should be included in the category of "public interest" when considering the alternative (compulsory arbitration) for free collective bargaining. So far as the convenience and welfare of the public are concerned, a prolonged shutdown of the coal mines, or stoppages in the telephone or any of the transportation industries, including trucking, can be almost as serious as strikes in the power, light, and water industries.

The arguments against compulsory arbitration are as pertinent to these industries as to all others, with the possible exception of the non-competitive public utilities which come under the purview of federal, state, and municipal regulatory commissions. Where rates (prices) and profits are subject to government control, it could be argued that wages and other work conditions affecting costs could also be controlled by the same commissions. Such an extension of government regulation must of necessity lead to a large measure of government control of the management of these enterprises. To illustrate: In considering the question of a wage increase, the regulatory commission might reasonably conclude that an increase was possible if certain cost-saving machinery and other improvements were installed. The logical outcome would be government-imposed changes in the methods of operation and management.

In the public interest, to avoid cessation of vital services, it might be deemed advisable for the government to assume control of the management of public utilities. The important thing to keep in mind is that such control is an inevitable outcome of the outlawing of strikes and the imposition of its necessary corollary, compulsory arbitration or government determination of the terms of employment. Even under actual or virtual government control, however, there is no absolute assurance that strikes will not take place. This brings up the basic problem involved in any restrictive measures designed to control the actions of large masses of people.

FUNDAMENTAL TESTS FOR EVALUATING REGULATORY LAWS

The most immediate and practical test for appraising the value of any legislation is: Can the law be enforced and will the given regulation accomplish its intended purpose if it is enforced?

With respect to labor regulatory laws, it must ever be kept in mind that workers in a free country cannot be forced to work and that it is utterly impractical to write laws whose enforcement depends upon the power of the government to put thousands of persons in jail. The problem of the enforcement of any law which large masses of people consider unfair and inimical to their interests is an entirely different matter than the enforcement of a law to control misdemeanors of individuals. Moreover, adherence to fiat rules does not always result in correcting the situation which the law was intended to rectify. If persons who feel that they have a just cause or grievance are deprived of one means to obtain their ends, they will seek other methods.

A second test is: Will the imposed regulation endanger the liberties which are the cornerstone of our democracy and the freedoms which are essential to our competitive enterprise system? It is not alone a question of preserving the fundamental rights of workers as citizens, important as that is. Laws to regulate the activities of labor unions will inevitably have far-reaching effects upon the whole nation's way of life because regulations enacted for one group, or for one purpose, tend to become precedents and are gradually applied to others. Business has on occasion opposed laws to regulate labor unions because of its fear that similar regulations would be applied to trade associations.

The fundamental principles in a democracy are individual liberty and equality of opportunity. These are in themselves self-conflicting. Equality is a matter of relationships, and whenever the government seeks to establish a situation which will promote equality it must necessarily impinge upon the liberties of those who already enjoy the superior opportunities or stronger positions. Democracy in a capitalistic society can exist only when there is approximate balance of power among the major economic groups. Any measures which weaken the labor movement automatically tip the scales in favor of organized capital (whether it be a single corporation or an aggregate of incorporated businesses), even though the measures are imposed for the ostensible purpose of protecting individual liberties.

This does not imply that the government, as the spokesman and protector of our entire political economy, should not establish certain rules by which all groups shall operate. But these rules or laws must be based upon a realistic conception of the inherent

658 Survey of Labor Economics

inequality existing between business corporations and individual employees, or even combinations of employees within single plants.

SELECTED BOOKS[18]

Daugherty, Carroll R., *Labor Problems in American Industry,* Houghton Mifflin Company, Boston, 1941.

Garland, J. V., *Federal Regulation of Labor Unions,* The H. W. Wilson Company, New York, 1941.

"Labor Relations and the Public," *Annals of the American Academy of Political and Social Science,* November, 1946.

Lester, Richard A., *Economics of Labor,* The Macmillan Company, New York, 1941.

MacDonald, Lois, *Labor Problems and the American Scene,* Harper & Brothers, New York, 1938.

Mathewson, Stanley B., *Restriction of Output Among Unorganized Workers,* The Viking Press, Inc., New York, 1931.

Metz, Harold W., *Labor Policy and the Federal Government,* Brookings Institution, Washington, 1945.

Nyman, R. C., and Smith, E. D., *Union-Management Cooperation in the "Stretch Out,"* Yale University Press, New Haven, 1934.

Owen, William V., *Labor Problems,* The Ronald Press, New York, 1946.

Patterson, S. Howard, *Social Aspects of Industry,* McGraw-Hill Book Company, Inc., New York, 1943.

Seidman, Harold, *Labor Czars,* Liveright Publishing Corporation, New York, 1938.

Stein, Emanuel, Davis, Jerome, *et al., Labor Problems in America,* Farrar & Rinehart, Inc., New York, 1940.

Taft, Philip, *Economics and Problems of Labor,* Stackpole Sons, Harrisburg, Pa., 1942.

Toner, Jerome L., *The Closed Shop,* American Council on Public Affairs, Washington, 1942.

Watkins, Gordon S., and Dodd, Paul A., *The Management of Labor Relations,* McGraw-Hill Book Company, Inc., New York, 1938.

Yoder, Dale, *Labor Economics and Labor Problems,* McGraw-Hill Book Company, Inc., New York, 1939.

SELECTED PERIODICALS

Advanced Management. Journal of the Society for the Advancement of Management, Inc., New York. Monthly.

[18] See also the books listed in preceding chapters in Part III.

American Federationist. American Federation of Labor, Washington, D. C. Monthly.

Conference Board Management Record. National Industrial Conference Board, New York. Monthly.

Executive Labor Letter. National Foremen's Institute, Deep River, Conn. Weekly.

Industrial Relations. The Dartnell Corp., Chicago. Monthly.

Labor and Nation. Inter-Union Institute, Inc., New York. Bi-monthly.

Labor Report. Prentice-Hall, Inc., New York. Weekly.

Labor Supervision. Bureau of National Affairs, Inc., Washington, D. C. Weekly.

Monthly Labor Review. Bureau of Labor Statistics, U. S. Department of Labor, Washington, D. C.

Personnel. American Management Association, New York. Bi-monthly.

Union News Service. Congress of Industrial Organizations, Washington, D. C. Weekly.

Weekly News Service. American Federation of Labor, Washington, D. C. Weekly.

PART FOUR

SOCIAL SECURITY

SOCIAL SECURITY: PRESENT AND FUTURE

EVERYONE WHO WORKS FOR HIS LIVING, WHETHER IN INDUSTRY, commerce, or agriculture, faces the risk that his earnings will be cut off at a time when there is still urgent need for them. Even in the most prosperous times, individuals become too old to work; they become unable to work because of injuries or sickness; they die without having been able to make adequate provision for the support of their families. Those who work for wages and salaries are confronted by the additional risk of involuntary unemployment.

When earnings stop, some substitute is necessary, because individual savings alone are frequently not sufficient to fill the gap. Relatively few persons earn enough during their entire working lifetime to permit the accumulation of savings adequate for the years which follow retirement. If earnings are cut off prematurely and unexpectedly, particularly during the period when a worker is young and his family responsibilities are greatest, there may have been neither time nor opportunity to accumulate any savings. In the past, the only recourse for families faced with the necessity of finding income to substitute for the breadwinner's earnings was for the mother to leave her family or for the children to leave school and accept gainful employment, or for the family to turn to relatives, to friends, or to charitable organizations.

This country embarked upon its first large-scale program to fill these gaps in income security in 1935, with the Social Security

---

[1] The author is indebted to Wilbur J. Cohen, Assistant Director of Research and Statistics, of the Federal Social Security Administration for chaps. 23, 24, 25, and 27.

Act. Previously, there had been no continuing[2] government-sponsored programs to assist workers and their families during times of emergency, except some state programs that provided compensation for industrial injuries.

The term "social security" in its broadest aspect covers programs of employers, workers, and other private groups, as well as government activities. However, it is customarily used in a more limited sense to mean the various government-sponsored insurance, assistance, and welfare programs designed to provide benefits and services to the aged, the sick and disabled, the unemployed, and widows and children.

The term "social security" originated in the United States and was first used in 1935 but is now used throughout the world. The term "social security" is broader than "social insurance" because it also encompasses non-insurance programs, such as public medical services, children's allowances, and non-contributory pensions, and such related programs as workmen's compensation. Private insurance, employer and union insurance plans, and compulsory social insurance plans may resemble each other in one way or another. In many cases private plans become incorporated in public plans or there are mixed arrangements as under workmen's compensation. For these reasons the more general term "social security" is useful, particularly when reference is made to the varying plans of different nations and the evolving trends both in the United States and abroad.

Social security programs for workers and their families have an impact on wages, prices, profits, savings, incentives for work, regularization of employment, and employer-labor relations. Thus social security is a vital phase of labor economics.

GENESIS OF SOCIAL SECURITY

The origin and development of social security as part of the field of labor economics has several aspects. The desire of the individual for some measure of security is a basic reason for the organization of unions as well as for various collective activities

---

[2] As indicated in chap. 7, government-administered emergency relief programs were in operation when this Act was passed, and local and state governments had undertaken emergency relief measures on occasion in the past.

of employers and consumers. Social security programs are a particular form of collective action which individuals, unions, and employers in many nations have found meet a need that is not satisfactorily handled solely by individual action.

Gradual Acceptance of Public Responsibility

The initial impetus to the modern development of social security plans was given in 1883 when Chancellor Bismarck of Germany inaugurated a social insurance program in order to stave off a growing trend toward socialism. The adoption of health and unemployment insurance in Great Britain some twenty-five years later stimulated activity in the United States for similar programs as part of a general program for labor legislation.

The search for security is not a new aspiration for the individual or a new responsibility for government. While objectives have not changed, new ways and means have been applied to the timeless quest for security. In earlier days the son's responsibility for the care of his parents was the most important method of providing security for the aged. But as the relentless forces of industrialism swept forward, it became inevitable that the responsibility of the individual must be supplemented by the affirmative responsibility of the whole community. Early American social services were, on the whole, limited in scope, local in character, and usually negative in spirit. When we view them in perspective we see an evolution from a local, voluntary, privately provided set of services to a network of services that is for the most part publicly supported and administered. Once health, education, and job placement, for example, were looked upon as exclusively private responsibilities of the individual. Today, there are public school and public health activities and a nation-wide system of public employment offices, all of which have come to be accepted as part of the general community's social services.

The main body of British and American social security services evolved from three main sources: the poor law, public education, and labor legislation. The care of needy individuals and universal public education saw the earliest applications of the fundamental principle of community responsibility for social services which could not be provided adequately on an individualistic basis. This principle has merely been applied in more extensive and diversified ways as time has progressed and as new social problems have been recognized by the community. Social insurance and related services have become one of the significant modern social inventions and eventually have grown to be important in all countries of industrial status.

In the United States public responsibility for new social security services developed somewhat later than in Europe. At first compulsory workmen's compensation legislation was opposed, as was the extension of free public employment offices, as an unnecessary interference with the freedom of the employer and the employee. Old age pensions were opposed because they might discourage thrift and promote indolence. Unemployment insurance was opposed on the grounds that it would encourage unemployment.

But the catastrophic world-wide depression of the early 1930's brought new insights into an old problem. By 1937 Mr. Justice Cardozo, with general public acceptance, could say in his memorable decision upholding the constitutionality of the federal old age insurance plan in the Social Security Act: "Needs that were narrow or parochial a century ago may be interwoven in our way with the well-being of our nation. What is critical or urgent changes with the times. The purge of nation-wide calamity that began in 1929 has taught us many lessons. Not the least is the solidarity of interests that may once have seemed to be divided."

THE SOCIAL SECURITY ACT

The Social Security Act of 1935 was the immediate outgrowth of President Roosevelt's message to Congress on June 8, 1934, in which he painted in broad, bold strokes a picture of existing needs and forthcoming developments, saying: ". . . We are compelled to employ the active interest of the Nation as a whole through government in order to encourage a greater security for each individual who composes it."

The President created a Committee on Economic Security to study the entire problem of social and economic security and make recommendations to him. This Committee's basic recommendations were embodied in the Social Security Act of 1935.

Social Security Act of 1935

The 1935 Act made provision for four major types of programs. First, it provided federal grants to the states for three forms of public assistance: to the needy aged, the blind, and dependent children. Second, it provided a tax program which encouraged states to enact unemployment insurance laws and expand their employment services. Third, it established a federal system of old age insurance for persons working in industry and commerce. Fourth, it provided additional federal funds for the extension of state public health and rehabilitation facilities and for the development of state maternal and child health and welfare programs.[3]

Thus, the Social Security Act aimed to attack the problem of insecurity on two fronts: first, by providing safeguards designed to reduce dependency through the operation of old age and unemployment insurance, the expansion of employment services, and public health, vocational rehabilitation, and maternal and child health and welfare services; second, by providing more adequate relief for existing needs of persons already aged, blind, or dependent in childhood. The only program in the legislation solely administered by the federal government was federal old age insurance. All the other programs provided for state administration with financial aid from the federal government.

It was almost two years after the passage of the Social Security Act that the U. S. Supreme Court upheld its constitutionality. On May 24, 1937, the court in two separate decisions upheld the constitutionality of the provisions of the federal law relating to both old age and unemployment insurance.

Amendments to the Social Security Act, 1939–1946

In 1939 the Act was amended to expand the federal old age insurance system to include monthly survivors' benefits to widows, children, and dependent parents. This changed the character of

---

[3] The original provisions in the Social Security Act of 1935 have in the meantime been changed in the following respects: The federal social insurance premiums were incorporated in 1939 in the Internal Revenue Code; the federal grants to states for vocational rehabilitation were incorporated in 1943 in a separate law; and the federal grants to states for public health services were incorporated in 1944 in the Public Health Service Act.

the benefits from an individual to a family basis. The 1939 amendments also liberalized benefits in the early years of the program
and provided for benefit payments to begin in 1940 instead of
1942. In addition, coverage was extended under the federal old age
and survivors' insurance system to seamen, bank employees, and
employed persons sixty-five years of age or over. Bank employees
were also brought under unemployment insurance. On the other
hand, the exclusion of "agricultural labor" was so broadened as
to exclude an additional 600,000 individuals from the protection
of both insurance systems.

While Congress has not enacted any major substantive changes
in the Social Security Act since the 1939 amendments, it has enacted a number of separate laws affecting the program. Legislation was passed in several successive years by which the old age
insurance premiums were frozen at the 1 per cent rate each on
employers and employees, although a provision was added to the
law authorizing an appropriation, whenever it might become
necessary, from the general revenues of the federal Treasury, of
"such additional sums as may be required to finance the benefits
and payments provided" by the insurance program. The sections
of the law providing that the rates go to $2\frac{1}{2}$ per cent each in
1948 and to 3 per cent each in 1949 were retained.

In 1943 legislation was enacted to enable seamen employed by
the federal government during the war to continue being covered
under the federal old age and survivors' insurance program rather
than under the separate system for federal employees. Later, in
1946, the Federal Unemployment Tax Act was amended to include maritime employment.[4]

In 1944 Congress adopted a provision calling for loans to state
unemployment insurance funds which might run low. In the same
year it passed the Servicemen's Readjustment Act, popularly
known as the "G.I. Bill of Rights," which, among other things,
provides unemployment insurance benefits to servicemen. This
law relieved the states of the financial obligation, undertaken by

---

[4] As benefits under regular state coverage which were established as a
result of the law are not payable immediately, the law also provides for
benefits during a temporary period up to June 30, 1949, under a new title
of the Social Security Act, "Reconversion Unemployment Benefits for Seamen."

most of them in their unemployment insurance laws, of paying benefits to servicemen with credits under the state law at the time of their entry into military service. Two years later, provisions were made with respect to certain veterans who die within three years after discharge. In general, the provisions guarantee survivors of veterans who are not entitled to compensation from the Veterans' Administration, the same survivors' benefits they would have enjoyed had the veteran died fully insured under the insurance program.

Public Assistance

The 1935 Social Security Act included federal grants-in-aid to the states for cash assistance to three needy groups: the aged (65 and over), the blind, and dependent children. The original law provided that the federal government would pay one-half of all expenditures which a state makes to assist these three groups. In 1946 the federal share, for the aged and the blind, was increased to two-thirds of the state's expenditures of the first $15 paid per month, and one-half the balance. For children, the federal payments were increased to two-thirds of the first $9 paid by the state for each child per month, and one-half the balance. However, for aged and blind persons, the federal grant is limited to $25 per individual per month, and for dependent children to not more than $13.50 for the first child and $9 for each additional child in the family.

Each state in order to receive federal funds must have a plan approved by the Social Security Administration. In addition to certain requirements relating to methods of administration and financing, the state program must provide that it is in effect throughout all the political subdivisions of the state; and the state agency, in determining need, will take into consideration any other income and resources of an individual claiming assistance; that each individual denied assistance will be given an opportunity for a fair hearing before the state agency; that there will be safeguards which restrict the use or disclosure of information concerning applicants and recipients to persons directly connected with the administration of assistance.

In June, 1946, all the states and Alaska, Hawaii, and the District of Columbia had established programs for old age assistance; all but one had plans for aid to dependent children; and all but four were administering federal-state programs for aid to the blind. Over 2 million aged persons and 750,000 children were receiving assistance. About 55,000 blind persons were being assisted under federal-state programs, in addition to over 15,000 blind persons receiving aid from programs in three states not financed from federal funds.

Assistance levels vary greatly among the states. In June, 1946, the average monthly payment for old age assistance ranged from a low of less than $12 a month in Kentucky to over $53 in Washington. For aid to the blind the average payment ranged from $13 in Kentucky to over $59 in Washington. For aid to dependent children the range in these same two states was about $22 to $99 per family. For general assistance, the range was from less than $10 in Mississippi to over $52 in Washington.

The objective of the individual assistance payment is to supply the difference between any income or other resources the needy person himself has and the amount the state agency finds necessary to meet his requirements. Lack of funds, however, has made it necessary for some states to limit the amount payable to any person or family, however great the need. Other states have had to disregard such requirements as medical care in determining the amount of the assistance payment; still others have applied a uniform limit to the proportion of the recipient's needs which the assistance payment can meet—for example, some allow the recipient only two-thirds or three-fourths of the amount which the state agency finds he needs.

Since the federal funds granted for state public assistance programs under the Social Security Act depend on the amounts which each state appropriates for federal matching, proportionately more federal aid goes to the wealthier states than to those in which resources are least and the need is greatest. The ten states which had the highest per capita income in 1944 had 36 per cent of the population of the country and received 40 per cent of the total amount of federal grants-in-aid for public assistance from February, 1936, through December, 1944. The ten states with the lowest per capita income in 1944 had 18 per cent of the population and received only 8 per cent of these federal funds. The total amount of public assistance payments in 1944,

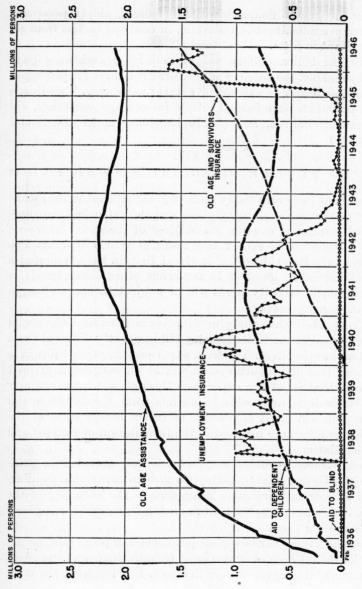

FIG. 33. *Social Insurance Beneficiaries and Public Assistance Recipients Under the Social Security Act, February, 1936, to July, 1946. (Source: Federal Social Security Administration.)*

including programs financed without federal aid, represented about $22 per inhabitant in Colorado, in contrast to less than $5 per inhabitant in fifteen other states.

Nearly one billion dollars was expended for assistance payments throughout the country in 1945 for the three special types of public assistance, as well as for general assistance. Two-thirds of these payments were federal grants for old age assistance, aid to dependent children, and aid to the blind under the Social Security Act.

THE FUTURE OF SOCIAL SECURITY

Throughout the world today there is great interest in the establishment of new social security plans and the extension, improvement, and revision of existing plans. Most of the social insurance laws of Europe will be recast as a result of World War II. The adoption of the Beveridge plan[5] in Great Britain has stimulated a review of the entire question in numerous other countries. It is clear that social security plans will be subject to many changes during the coming years.

It is very likely that forty or fifty years from now the social security system of the United States will be greatly different from the system now in effect. Yet from experience in other fields it is safe to say that the future system will be an outgrowth of past experience, that is, of the experience through which we are now going. While it is impossible to outline what the future social security plan will be, it is possible to review briefly some of the major issues which are involved in the formulation of present and future legislation.

Although social security in general is now accepted in principle in the United States, there still remain many sharp differences of opinion on particular issues such as the adequacy of the benefits, the costs and methods of financing them, and the methods of administering them.

Opinions on these various questions depend in large part on attitudes on the relation of government to individuals and the effect of governmental programs on individuals. For instance, the most

---

[5] See Sir William Beveridge, *Social Insurance and Allied Services,* H. M. Stationery Office, London, 1942.

general criticisms of social security are that it makes people dependent upon government, stifles initiative, incentive, and thrift, increases bureaucracy, and levies a cost on the producers of goods for the benefit of non-producers which retards production.

A detailed examination of each of the criticisms would necessitate an extensive analysis of both economic and political theories as well as an evaluation of actual experience in the operation of social security plans in the United States and abroad. It may be said, however, that despite criticisms and difficulties social security plans throughout the world have continued to expand. No country which has adopted such a system has ever abandoned it.

A major argument against compulsory social insurance is that "once it has been accepted that compulsion may be laid upon the individual to improve his life, on the ground that his voluntary efforts to improve it himself are unsatisfactory, there is no logical place to stop short of minding his life from birth to death."[6]

An opposite point of view states: "There should be neither conflict nor confusion between social security, properly defined, and that type of security which comes from the exercise of personal industry and thrift. While the one represents the basic protection which can safely be provided through Government programs set up by society at large, the other gives the individual the right and the opportunity to raise himself and his family to such a level of security as his industry and thrift dictate. They complement each other rather than conflict with each other."[7]

A basic problem of our time is how to maintain maximum freedom in our economic life and also provide security for the individual and his family. There are those who believe that in relieving and protecting the individual against economic hazards we discourage individual initiative and responsibility, and thereby increase dependency. But there is also ample evidence to support the belief that destitution feeds upon itself and carries in its train evils that increase already existing complex social and economic problems. Social security is designed to set up certain protec-

---

[6] National Industrial Conference Board, "American Affairs," April, 1946; published in *Congressional Record,* May 23, 1946, p. A-3081.

[7] Joint report of the American Life Convention, the Life Insurance Association of America, and the National Association of Life Underwriters, Chicago, 1945.

tions for those in distress and thus restore their hope and their faith and make them self-respecting, self-sustaining, and valuable members of society. In achieving this goal, many controversial problems are encountered.

Adequacy and Costs of Benefits

The most important element in any public discussion of the adequacy of social security benefits is the amount of benefits to be provided to individuals. There are, however, other important questions such as eligibility for benefits, their duration, and related problems which also bear upon the adequacy of the protection.

From time to time questions are raised as to whether payment of a maximum unemployment benefit of $20 to $25 a week retards the worker's incentive to become reemployed. Similar problems also arise, but are not so apparent, with respect to the aged, the blind, the disabled, and widows and dependent children. Numerous proposals have been made by various groups for payment of benefits to the aged as high as $200 per month, although this amount exceeds the average normal income of large numbers of persons.

The level of the benefits raises implications of the relationship of social security benefits to private insurance and other forms of voluntary protection. It also raises the question of how much the program will cost, and how much of the income of its producing members the nation wishes to earmark for social security purposes. For instance, the initial cost of a $40 per month pension for all persons age 65 or over would be about 5 billion dollars per year. By 1960, the cost would reach 6.5 billion annually, and 9 billion by 1980.

When the social security program was first established much emphasis was placed on providing benefits—both unemployment and old age—which preserved the individual's equity in relation to his contributions. Under old age insurance, the person's entire contributions were returned to his estate if he died prior to age 65, even though he left no immediate survivors. Under unemployment insurance, the benefits were related almost exactly to the individual's previous wage. During recent years the emphasis has begun to move away from too close reliance on "individual equity" toward the direction of "social adequacy." The elimination of the return of contributions under old age insurance in 1939, and the substitution of survivors' insurance, are one indication of this trend. The addition of dependents' benefits under unemployment insurance is another.

Some people who maintain that social security benefits should meet a test of "social adequacy" also believe that all benefits should be the same for all persons on the grounds that such a system would be more equitable and simpler to administer, and would eliminate the need for any reserve funds. Under such a plan the benefits would have no relation to wages. Those who oppose such a flat-rate plan believe that it would inevitably result in the elimination of the contributory insurance features of the program. Since there is objectively no way of arriving at agreement as to what constitutes "social adequacy" in determining the level of benefits, the opponents of the flat-rate plan believe that it would introduce uncertainty and dissatisfaction on the part of many beneficiaries.

The premium rates which workers, their employers, and the self-employed would pay for comprehensive social insurance protection would depend, in part, on the policy adopted with respect to government participation in the program through general revenues. If the coverage of the system is extended to the entire working population or to most of it, a government contribution from general revenues is consistent with sound fiscal policy. The proposal advocated by organized labor for a comprehensive social insurance program, which contemplates an eventual government contribution of about a third of the costs of the program, proposes a premium of 4 per cent of wages and salary to be paid by workers, with a like amount to be paid by their employers. Under this proposal the self-employed, who would not be insured against unemployment or temporary disability but would assume responsibility for the combined employer-employee premium for the benefits to which they are entitled, would pay a premium of 5 per cent of their earned income.

Any consideration of whether the population as a whole or any group in it can afford to pay the costs of a comprehensive social security program must recognize that these are by no means entirely or even largely new costs. The costs of old age, sickness, and unemployment are met, whether through individual sacrifice to pay large doctor bills or to support an aged parent, through taxation to finance relief programs, or otherwise. A social security program provides a more orderly and equitable method of meeting these costs; its expenditures represent chiefly a redistribution among people and over periods of time.

Federal Versus Local Responsibility

A further question arising in the administration of various social security benefits is the desirable relation between the federal government, on the one hand, and state and local governments, on the other. In 1935, Congress decided that because of the extensive movement of workers from one state to another during their working lifetime, it would be very impractical to establish insurance programs dealing with long-time risks, such as old age insurance, on a state-by-state basis. Permanent disability insurance also involves the same long-run building of rights to and duration of benefits. Accordingly, discussions concerning its adoption generally agree that it should also be administered by the federal government as part of the federal old age and survivors' insurance system.

On the other hand, a good deal of controversy has centered around the question of the appropriate governmental unit for administering unemployment insurance. A similar controversy exists with respect to the administration of a governmental system of health insurance. The general arguments in favor of a single national system of social insurance hold that there would be a rational relation between the various benefits, one system of wage records, contributions, simplified administration, and lower administrative costs. In addition, those who favor a national system believe that problems arising out of unemployment and ill health are not confined to state lines, and that pooling the financial risks in a single national system, rather than dividing them into 51 separate state and territorial systems, would be a much more rational approach to a problem of national dimensions.

Proponents of a national system of social insurance contend that it would be quite possible, and desirable, for its administration to be highly decentralized through extensive use of regional and field offices and advisory councils made up of representatives of labor, employers, and the public. This would permit achieving the advantages both of a nationally coordinated and organized system, and of intimate local contact with the actual beneficiaries of the program. Also, it would be quite consistent, under such an arrangement, to make full use of the services and facilities of state and local health and other agencies so that the actual day-to-day detailed administration would be a cooperative undertaking at all levels of government.

Relation of Social Insurance to Private Plans

The inadequacies of existing social security laws have given rise to the supplementation of benefits by private arrangements, such as those provided by unions, employers, and consumers' groups, and through collective bargaining. Some of these plans have been adopted as a stopgap, with the intention that they will be either abandoned or integrated into the social security program as the latter is expanded and further developed. Some private plans, on the other hand, are advocated for the purpose of discouraging the adoption of a general compulsory social insurance program. This is true of those advocating voluntary hospitalization insurance, voluntary medical care, and private disability insurance.

Life insurance companies have been the notable exception to the rule that existing private groups will oppose the enactment and improvement of the social security benefits with which they are directly concerned. This is because the existence of either old age or life insurance benefits under social security does not prevent life insurance companies from selling insurance, but actually gives them a sales argument for encouraging individuals to buy more private insurance. Because these insurance companies sell little or no permanent disability insurance they do not oppose the principle of amending the law to cover such benefits under the old age and survivors' insurance program. But accident and health insurance companies oppose social security programs for temporary disability and health insurance, because the introduction of such insurance would curtail their activities in this field.

Attitude of Organized Labor Toward Social Insurance

Organized labor at the present time strongly supports the principle of compulsory social insurance for all the major risks. This was not always true, however. At a conference on social insurance in 1916, Samuel Gompers, then president of the American Federation of Labor, endorsed compulsory workmen's compensation and old age pensions but opposed compulsory health and unemployment insurance. He stated that the introduction of such compulsory insurance "means that the workers must be subject to examinations, investigations, regulations and limitations. Their activities must be regulated in accordance with the standards set by Governmental agencies. To that we shall not stand idly by and give our assent."[8] In other speeches he also implied that such insurance might undermine union activity and divert attention from its main efforts at improving wages, hours, and working conditions.

Although a number of the individual unions and state federations of labor had placed themselves on record in favor of compulsory social insurance, the A. F. of L. did not officially modify its position until its 1932 convention. At that time, after lengthy debate, the convention endorsed state unemployment insurance "and the supplementing of such state legislation by federal enactments."[9] Specific endorsement of health and disability insurance followed during the next few years.

Although the Federation orginially endorsed separate state unemployment insurance programs, in 1935 William Green, president of the A. F. of L., supported a federal unemployment insurance plan as a member of the Advisory Council on Economic Security. After the United States Supreme Court validated the Social Security Act in 1937, the Federation actively supported an outright federal unemployment insurance system. Organized labor's endorsement of a federal compulsory social insurance system for all risks, including health insurance, did not take place until 1943 when both the American Federation of Labor and the Congress of Industrial Organizations sponsored the Wagner-Murray-Dingell bill[10] in the United States Congress.

The present attitude of organized labor toward social security is that a sucessful first step has been taken. Workers have become

---

[8] Bureau of Labor Statistics, *Bulletin No. 212,* p. 845.
[9] *Report of Proceedings of the 52nd Annual Convention of the American Federation of Labor,* 1932, pp. 141, 325–360.
[10] See chap. 27.

familiar with and have endorsed the social insurance principle of pooled risks to lessen individual hardship. They retain self-respect under a system which collects premiums in the years when they have earnings and entitles them to benefits when earnings stop. The most frequently expressed argument by labor organizations in support of social insurance is that the worker's right to protection is clear and undeniable; benefits are paid without regard to other resources and without a "needs" test. Because benefits are related to past earnings, they help families to maintain a standard of living approaching the standard they had when they were receiving current earnings. Also emphasized is the fact that the premiums which a worker pays give him a more direct and a stronger interest in the program than he would have if he were paying the same amount in the form of general taxes on his income or property. This view is accompanied by the belief that a program in which workers have a direct interest or "stake" is less apt to be subjected to changes which will endanger their rights as future beneficiaries.

Widespread endorsement of the principle of social insurance to compensate for the wage loss which results from the worker's unemployment, old age, or death indicates that organized labor believes that social insurance methods should be used in extending comparable protection to groups of workers not now covered, and in broadening the programs to include protection against other insurable risks. When the insurance programs have more extensive coverage and have been in existence for many years, relatively few families will be without protection; nevertheless, there will always be some individuals not able to do gainful work and hence share in social insurance protection. For those who cannot be covered by insurance programs, and for members covered by the insurance system who have special needs which require supplementation of their benefits, organized labor has urged an improved public assistance program as an essential part of a comprehensive social security setup.

Attitude of Employers

In general, employers' organizations did not take an official position for or against compulsory social insurance prior to 1935, although two decades earlier they had urged that employees as well as employers contribute to workmen's compensation. The Committee on Economic Security appointed to its Advisory Council several employers who supported the Committee's proposals for unemployment and old age insurance. While the National Association of Manufacturers opposed the legislation in Congress, the National Retail Dry Goods Association supported it.

In 1938 representatives of employers signed a unanimous report, with representatives of organized labor and the public, urging extension and improvement of the compulsory federal old age insurance program. At the present time the national employer and labor organizations are in general agreement on certain specific social security recommendations such as extension of coverage. However, there continues to be disagreement on such issues as labor's demand for the establishment of a federal system of unemployment insurance, the elimination of experience rating in unemployment insurance, the enactment of compulsory health insurance, and the increase in the amount of the various insurance benefits, problems discussed in more detail in the following chapters.

FULL EMPLOYMENT AND SOCIAL SECURITY

It is sometimes stated that social security would be unnecessary if arrangements could be worked out to assure all workers an annual wage or guaranteed employment. It is extremely doubtful, however, that the problem of needy individuals and families could be eliminated entirely, even under conditions of full employment with reasonably high wages. While steady jobs at high incomes would help greatly in reducing the amount of need and destitution, the income of many families would still be reduced or cut off entirely by the premature death, permanent disability, sickness, or old age of the wage earner. Some wage loss from unemployment occurs even during periods of full employment. As indicated in Chapter 5, it is inevitable that even under the most favorable conditions a certain number of persons at any given time will be temporarily without jobs.

The old age insurance provisions in the original 1935 law were written as part of a general plan to encourage the retirement of older people from the labor market so as to lessen the competition for jobs. However, the existing level of benefits has not been high enough to encourage many persons to withdraw voluntarily. The available information indicates that most individuals prefer to work if they are physically capable of doing so, and retire only when circumstances require them to do so, or when they have built up sufficient income in addition to their insurance benefits.

From time to time various proposals have been made to expand the social security benefit programs in order to insure the purchasing power necessary for a full employment economy. One view holds that if we have full employment we can and should provide generous social security benefits as part of a program of high labor standards and humanitarianism. Another view maintains that continued full employment cannot be assured without substantial disbursements under governmental programs, and that it is necessary, therefore, that social security payments substantially exceed the income specifically levied for that purpose in order to offset deflationary tendencies in our economy. These views affect the problems relating both to financing the benefits and to their coverage, amount, and character.

A comprehensive social security program would contribute toward full employment in a number of ways. It would reduce or remove the economic barrier to the withdrawal from the labor market of such groups as the aged, the disabled, and women with young children. It would increase job opportunities in the fields of public and private health. Unemployment insurance facilitates labor mobility, which is necessary to full employment. An even more important aid in maintaining full employment would be the effect of a comprehensive system of social security on the total demand for goods and services.

Effect of Social Security on Sustained Purchasing Power

The payment of social security benefits to persons whose income has been cut off or who are in need has the effect of placing purchasing power in the hands of families, many of whom would otherwise lack it. This purchasing power will normally be spent promptly for consumers' goods. Such additions to consumer demand will in turn give employment to many individuals who otherwise might not have jobs.

The effects of social security payments upon purchasing power will be of special significance in periods when there is a tendency for consumer demand and employment to decline. It is inherent in the very nature of a social security program that the total income exceeds disbursements in periods of high employment and that disbursements to individuals and families increase in periods when economic activity slackens. Thus, social security benefits serve to provide something in the nature of a floor under purchasing power if a shrinkage in the latter threatens. A comprehensive system of social security provisions, therefore, can contribute a great deal toward stabilizing consumer demand and, in turn, minimizing rapid and wide fluctuations in national income and employment.

Whether or not social security can produce a permanent increase in the effective demand for consumers' goods will depend upon the relationship at any time between total payments to individuals and the total amount and sources of the revenues of the social security system. In periods when part of the payments is financed from the reserves or from general revenues which do not themselves curtail consumption, the net effect of the payments will be to increase the total amount of consumer purchasing power. To the extent, however, that the contributions and taxes used to finance the benefits themselves curtail consumption, they serve to offset the stimulating effects of the payments. The net over-all economic effect of the program on consumer demand will depend, therefore, upon the relationship existing at particular times between payments that increase purchasing power and contributions, and taxes that decrease it.

The frequency and effects of the common economic hazards would be less under full employment and, in turn, the cost of providing protection against these hazards would be lower than otherwise. The cost of social security would be lower both absolutely and in relation to the income out of which it is financed. Hence, under a full employment economy, the nation can afford a better and more comprehensive system of social security than might otherwise be possible.

SELECTED REFERENCES

Abbott, Grace, *From Relief to Social Security,* University of Chicago Press, Chicago, 1941.

Altmeyer, A. J., "Social Insurance," in *Social Work Year Book, 1947*.

Annual Reports of the Social Security Board, Government Printing Office, Washington.

Armstrong, Barbara N., *Insuring the Essentials*, The Macmillan Company, New York, 1932.

Beveridge, Sir William, *Social Insurance and Allied Services*, H. M. Stationary Office, London, 1942.

Chamber of Commerce of the United States, *Social Security in the United States; Chamber Policies and Report of Committee on Social Security*, Washington, 1944.

Cohen, Wilbur J. (ed.), *War and Post-War Social Security*, American Council on Public Affairs, Washington, 1942.

Harris, Seymour E., *Economics of Social Security*, McGraw-Hill Book Company, Inc., New York, 1941.

International Labour Office. *Approaches to Social Security: An International Survey*, Studies and Reports, Series M (Social Insurance), No. 18, Montreal, 1942.

Meriam, Lewis, *Relief and Social Security*, Brookings Institution, Washington, 1946.

Millis, Harry A., and Montgomery, Royal E., *Labor's Risks and Social Insurance*, McGraw-Hill Book Company, Inc., New York, 1938.

National Planning Association, *Joint Statement on Social Security by Agriculture, Business and Labor*, Washington, 1944.

Social Security in America: The Factual Background of the Social Security Act as Summarized from Staff Reports to the Committee on Economic Security, Government Printing Office, Washington, 1937.

U. S. Congress, *Issues in Social Security: A Report to the Committee on Ways and Means of the House of Representatives by the Committee's Social Security Technical Staff Established Pursuant to H. Res. 204, 79th Cong., 1st. Sess.*, Government Printing Office, Washington, 1946.

24

OLD AGE AND SURVIVORS' INSURANCE

AS LATE AS 1929 ONLY TEN STATES HAD ENACTED OLD AGE PENSION laws, and of these only two (Montana and Wisconsin) were actually paying pensions even in a few counties. Elsewhere in the country old persons without income or support from their families or from private charity were sent to the county poorhouses.[1] During the years 1930–1934 at least thirty additional states enacted pension laws; and with the federal grants provided by the federal Social Security Act, old age assistance programs were expanded throughout the country. Payments provided by these programs are made on the basis of individual need and are financed from general revenues of the federal government and from state and local revenues.

The federal Social Security Act of 1935 also established an insurance program which, as it matures and expands in coverage, should decrease the necessity for public assistance or pensions. The benefits of the federal insurance system are of two broad types: survivors' benefits and retirement benefits. The survivors' benefits, in effect, are a form of life insurance.[2]

---

[1] Brandeis, Elizabeth, *History of Labor,* The Macmillan Company, New York, 1935, vol. iii, pp. 614–616. One of the arguments used in getting state pension acts was that pensions cost less than poorhouse maintenance. In California in 1931 the average annual pension was $275 compared with $484 per poorhouse inmate; in Massachusetts, $312 compared with $539; in New York, $303 in contrast to $406.

[2] The Social Security Act of 1935 (effective January 1, 1937) provided for a federal insurance plan only with respect to old age. Survivors' insurance was added to the Act in 1939 and benefits became payable in 1940.

The protection afforded by survivors' benefits is equivalent to more than 50 billion dollars of term life insurance. This amount of protection is more than

According to the 1946 law these insurance programs are financed through premiums of 1 per cent on the wages of employees and 1 per cent on the employer's payroll, making 2 per cent in all. The premiums are limited, however, to the first $3000 of wages received by an employee from an employer in a year. They are scheduled to increase to 2½ per cent each in 1948 and to 3 per cent each in 1949 and thereafter.

As of June, 1946, over 1,500,000 individuals were receiving regular monthly benefits amounting to over 360 million dollars per year. In addition, there were 815,000 insured persons aged 65 and over who were fully insured and eligible to draw their benefits when they stopped working. By 1960 it is estimated that there will be about 5 million persons, and by 1980 about 10 million, drawing old age and survivors' insurance benefits.

KINDS OF BENEFITS PROVIDED

Seven kinds of benefits are provided under the existing legislation:

1. Primary insurance benefits are payable to each insured worker who has reached the age of 65 and is not receiving wages of $15 per month or more from employment covered under the insurance plan.

2. A wife's insurance benefit of one-half the primary benefit is payable to the wife of any insured person receiving benefits if the wife is 65 years old or over. This benefit is in addition to the benefit payable to the insured worker.

3. A widow's insurance benefit of three-fourths of the primary benefit is payable to the widow of an insured man when she reaches age 65. The benefit is payable whether the husband dies before or after the age of 65.

4. A widow's current insurance benefit of three-fourths of the primary benefit is payable to the widow of an insured person who has a child or children under the age of 18 in her care.

5. A child's insurance benefit of one-half of the primary benefit is payable to each unmarried child under the age of 18, if the

---

that in effect in any single life insurance company in the world and is equal to about one-third of the life insurance in force in all private companies in the United States.

parent is entitled to a primary old age benefit, or was insured and has died, irrespective of age.

6. A parent's insurance benefit of one-half of the primary benefit is payable to either or each of both parents of an insured individual who died and left no widow or child under the age of 18. The benefit is payable if the parent was chiefly dependent upon and supported by the deceased individual at the time of his death. It commences at age 65.

7. Lump-sum death payments are payable in the case of individuals who die and leave no surviving widow, child, or parent eligible to monthly benefits at the time of his death. This is intended for burial expenses.

COVERAGE OF INSURANCE PLAN

Contributions are collected and benefits are payable on the basis of employment covered by the insurance system. In general, workers in industry and commerce are covered; but self-employed businessmen and farmers, agricultural laborers, domestic servants, employees of non-profit institutions, federal, state, and local governmental employees, railroad employees, and certain other groups are excluded from the system at the present time.

In an average week in 1944, about three-fifths of all gainfully employed civilians had jobs covered by the insurance program. Of the excluded, about 8 million were in agriculture, as either farm owners or farm employees; about 4½ million were self-employed outside of agriculture; over 5½ million were Government employees (about half federal, and the other half state and local government employees); approximately 1,400,000 were on jobs covered by the railroad retirement system; and about 1,800,-000 were in domestic service, non-profit organizations, and other excluded services.

The total number of persons affected during an entire year by the jobs included and excluded from the insurance system is much greater than the number at any one time. During a year, millions of workers shift between covered and non-covered employment. Because of mobility of employment, some persons earn credits under more than one retirement system during a year, whereas others fail to earn enough credits under one—or even any—re-

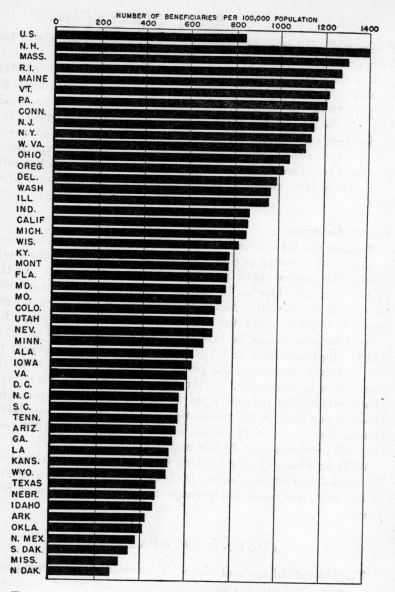

NUMBER OF BENEFICIARIES PER 100,000 POPULATION

FIG. 34. *Number of Beneficiaries on the Old Age and Survivors' Insurance Rolls per 100,000 Population, by State, December 31, 1944. (Source: Federal Social Security Administration.)*

tirement plan. Approximately 73,200,000 living persons had by January 1, 1946, earned some credits since wages became subject to the insurance plan on January 1, 1937. However, of this number only 41,500,000 were insured under the program on January 1, 1946. Of the 31,700,000 living uninsured workers, some had left the labor force after a short period of employment; included here are married women, students, and handicapped workers. A large proportion of the total uninsured, however, represents persons who do no work regularly in covered employment but rely on earnings from employment not covered by the insurance program.

Future Coverage

Because the old age and survivors' insurance program has been in operation a short period, the number of insured individuals among the present aged population is relatively small. As the system becomes older an increasing proportion of the aged will be eligible for benefits. About 15 per cent of the present aged group is eligible; after the program has been in operation for several decades it may be expected that some 60 or 70 per cent will be eligible, even if no additional occupations are covered by the program. Moreover, the proportion of aged persons in the population is increasing. At the beginning of 1945, there were about 10,000,000 persons aged 65 and over; they represented about 7 per cent of the population. On the basis of population trends, there may be 22 million aged 65 and over by 1980, and they will comprise some 14 per cent of the population.

With no change in the existing coverage or benefit structure, the annual expenditure for benefits is estimated to increase fivefold in the next ten years and perhaps twentyfold in the next fifty years.

AMOUNT OF BENEFITS

The federal old age and survivors' insurance plan incorporates two principles, namely, individual equity and social adequacy. Benefits are determined on the basis of the relationship of past earnings, but the short-time and low-wage earner receives proportionately greater protection. Persons with dependents also receive additional benefits. However, practically everyone, regardless of his level of wages or the length of time during which he has contributed, receives more by way of protection than he could have purchased from a private insurance company at a cost equal to his own contributions. This is possible because a large proportion of the employers' contributions are utilized to pay benefits to those retiring in the early years of the program, and to low-wage and short-time workers and to persons with dependents.

TABLE 29.   Examples of Monthly Retirement Old Age and Survivors' Insurance Benefits

Average Monthly Wages of Insured Person	Monthly Benefit				
	Worker, 65 and Over	Worker and Wife, 65 and Over	Widow, 65 and Over	Widow and One Child	One Child or One Parent
10 years' coverage:					
$ 50...................	$22.00	$33.00	$16.50	$27.50	$11.00
100...................	27.50	41.25	20.63	34.38	13.75
150...................	33.00	49.50	24.75	41.25	16.50
250...................	44.00	66.00	33.00	55.00	22.00
20 years' coverage:					
$ 50...................	$24.00	$36.00	$18.00	$30.00	$12.00
100...................	30.00	45.00	22.50	37.50	15.00
150...................	36.00	54.00	27.00	45.00	18.00
250...................	48.00	72.00	36.00	60.00	24.00
30 years' coverage:					
$ 50...................	$26.00	$39.00	$19.50	$32.50	$13.00
100...................	32.50	48.75	24.38	40.63	16.25
150...................	39.00	58.50	29.25	48.75	19.50
250...................	52.00	78.00	39.00	65.00	26.00
40 years' coverage:					
$ 50...................	$28.00	$40.00	$21.00	$35.00	$14.00
100...................	35.00	52.50	26.25	43.75	17.50
150...................	42.00	63.00	31.50	52.50	21.00
250...................	56.00	84.00	42.00	70.00	28.00

TABLE 30.   Examples of Lump-Sum Death Payments

Years of Coverage	Average Monthly Wages of Insured Person			
	$ 50	$100	$150	$250
10	132	165	198	264
20	144	180	216	288
30	156	195	234	312
40	168	210	252	336

The various monthly insurance benefits range between a minimum of $10 and a maximum of $85. The amount paid each insured individual depends upon the amount of wages he has received in covered employment since the insurance plan first became effective, and the length of time he was covered by the system. Table 29 shows illustrative monthly retirement and survivors' benefits which are payable, and Table 30 shows illustrations of the lump-sum death benefits, which may range from a minimum of $60 to $300 or more.

Method of Computing Benefits

In computing the amount of each individual's monthly benefits, the primary insurance benefit is computed as follows: 40 per cent of the first $50 of average monthly wages plus 10 per cent of any average monthly wage above $50 but not over $250, plus 1 per cent of this sum for each year in which the individual had $200 or more in covered wages. This is the monthly benefit payable to each insured individual age 65 and over, and all other payments are based upon this primary benefit. Wives, children, and dependent parents who are eligible for monthly benefits receive one-half of the primary amount; widows receive three-fourths. Several persons in a family may receive benefits at one time, but the family total may not exceed twice the primary benefit.

The following illustrates how the law works in the case of a worker employed in covered jobs over a ten-year period who earns total taxed wages sufficient to give him an "average monthly wage" of $100 when he becomes 65 and retires or dies: 40 per cent on the first $50 of his wages is $20, to which is added 10 per cent of the next $50, which amounts to $5. Since he has been in the system ten years he is entitled to an additional 1 per cent for each year; this is 10 per cent of $25, or $2.50. This makes a total of $27.50 per month which he will receive as old age insurance. When his wife reaches age 65 she will receive an additional 50 per cent; this will make a total benefit of $41.25 payable to him and his wife. If he dies, his widow will receive three-fourths of the amount he received, or $20.63, in monthly benefits for the rest of her life.

If, on the other hand, this worker had died in early life, say at age 40, leaving his widow with two small children, a benefit of $20.63 would be payable to her, plus $13.75 for each child, making a family total of $48.13 per month. If one of the children reached the age of 18, died, or married, his widow would still receive her three-fourths of the primary benefit, plus one-half for the other child. When that child ceased to be eligible for benefits, the widow's current insurance·benefits would stop, until and unless she became eligible for monthly benefits again at the age of 65.

Value of Benefits

The value of retirement benefits in an individual case and the amount of insurance protection afforded the family of a deceased insured person depend upon numerous factors, such as the wage of the retired or deceased individual, the longevity of his survivors, and similar factors. If an insured worker with an average monthly wage of $200 dies after being covered for ten years, leaving a widow with two children about eight years old, the benefits could continue for ten years, making a total of over $8000. If the children were still younger and the payments continued for fifteen years, the total life insurance payable to the family in the form of monthly survivors' benefits would be $12,000. If the value of the monthly benefit payable to the widow when she reaches age 65 is included in these calculations, the total protection afforded can exceed $15,000. The value of a $40-per-month retirement benefit will amount to nearly $5000 in the case of a man who lives for ten years after retirement. For a man and wife who receive a combined benefit of $60 per month for fifteen years, the value of such a benefit will exceed $10,000.

The average long-time value of the old age and survivors' insurance protection is estimated to range between 4 and 7 per cent of pay rolls. Assuming that the average cost is likely to be approximately 5 per cent of pay rolls, about 4 per cent would represent the average cost of the benefits to aged persons and 1 per cent the cost of current benefits to survivors. From the standpoint of the contributions made by the worker alone, the value of the benefits, particularly during the early years of the insurance system, is greatly in excess of the protection that could be afforded by purchasing similar protection from a private insurance company.

Benefits for retired workers at the end of 1945 averaged about $23.50 per month. The average for men was $24.50, and for

women, $19.50. The average benefit for various family groups is
shown in Table 31, along with the number of families and beneficiaries receiving benefits at that time. For widows, the average
monthly benefit was $20.20. For a family consisting of a widow
and three or more children it was $50.40.

TABLE 31. Number of Beneficiaries and Amount of Monthly Old
Age and Survivors' Insurance Benefits as of December 30, 1945[3]

Family Classification of Beneficiaries	Number of Families	Number of Beneficiaries	Average Family Benefit
Total...............................	837,200	1,288,100	....
A. Families of workers in receipt of benefits.....	5,182,000	6,909,000	....
1. Worker only:			
Male..............................	2,783,000	2,783,000	$24.50
Female............................	710,000	710,000	$19.50
Total.............................	3,493,000	3,493,000	$23.50
2. Worker and wife......................	1,591,000	3,181,000	$38.50
3. Worker and 1 or more children...........	98,000	231,000	$40.20
4. Worker, wife, and 1 or more children.....	1,000	3,000	a
B. Families of beneficiaries surviving deceased insured workers..........................	3,190,000	5,973,000	....
1. Widow only..........................	986,000	986,000	$20.20
2. Widowed mother and 1 child............	618,000	1,236,000	$34.10
3. Widowed mother and 2 children.........	349,000	1,046,000	$47.70
4. Widowed mother and 3 or more children...	191,000	776,000	$50.40
5. Children only........................	989,000	1,867,000	$22.90
6. One or more parents, aged 65 or over.....	57,000	62,000	$14.10

ª No average shown because there were too few cases.

ELIGIBILITY FOR BENEFITS

In order to be eligible for these various insurance benefits,
individuals must be insured in accordance with requirements of
the law which prescribes the areas of employment covered. In general, anyone is fully insured for all benefits under the system if he
has been in covered employment roughly half of the time. The law
measures the insurance status of each individual in terms of
calendar quarters (three-month periods), which is the time period
for which each employer reports the wages paid each employee
and sends in the contributions for the insurance program.

Each person must earn wages of at least $50 in half of the

[3] *Social Security Bulletin,* June 30, 1946, p. 31.

quarters up to age 65. There is a minimum of 6 quarters and a maximum of 40 quarters. In other words, when an individual has earned $50 per quarter—that is, $16.67 per month—in 40 quarters (equivalent to ten years) he is fully insured for all benefits. A person may be eligible for certain survivors' benefits, however, if the deceased wage earner was only "currently" insured. Thus, if he earned at least $50 in 6 out of the last 12 quarters prior to his death, his widow and children would be eligible for monthly survivors' benefits. The eligibility requirements for old age retirement insurance increase progressively, as the insurance system matures, up to the 40-quarter maximum which will be reached at the end of the year 1956.

Specific Requirements

In addition to being insured, an individual must also meet certain other requirements under the law in order to receive benefits.

A worker's retirement benefit and the benefits for his wife and children are not paid for any month during which the worker earns more than $14.99 in covered employment. Also, survivors' benefits are suspended for any month in which the person receiving the benefit earns more than this sum on a covered job. However, a child's benefits continue even though the mother earns more than $14.99 a month in covered employment, and a widow's benefit continues even when her child earns more than this sum on a covered job.

There are other circumstances under which benefits are not paid. Thus they stop for a woman when she remarries or is divorced (unless she has earned them on her own account). A child's benefits end when he leaves school (if he is over 16), or if he is adopted by a close relative, or marries.

A beneficiary may go on and off the benefit rolls from time to time, as work opportunities, health, and other circumstances affect him. He may, however, work at a job not covered by this insurance program, or he may run a business of his own, and continue to receive his benefits, no matter how much he earns.

Old age and survivors' insurance benefits usually extend for long periods. This is because the family income may stop permanently or for a long time when the breadwinner becomes too old to work or dies. Generally speaking, retired workers, their aged wives, aged widows, and parents 65 years old or over, receive monthly benefits until death. Children may receive them until they are 18; and their mothers, if under 65, until the youngest child is 18.

ADMINISTRATION OF THE PROGRAM

The existing federal old age and survivors' insurance system consists of two parts: Title II of the Social Security Act, which provides the benefits and is administered by the Social Security Administration through the Bureau of Old Age and Survivors' Insurance; and the Federal Insurance Contributions Act of the Internal Revenue Code, which levies the premiums and is administered by the Bureau of Internal Revenue of the Treasury Department.[4] The revenue received goes into the federal Treasury, and an amount equivalent to the contributions received is deposited automatically in the Federal Old Age and Survivors' Insurance Trust Fund, which is supervised by a Board of Trustees consisting of the Secretary of the Treasury, the Secretary of Labor, and the Federal Security Administrator. Reserves of the insurance program are invested in U. S. government bonds.

Employers send their contributions and those they have collected from their workers to the Collector of Internal Revenue every three months, together with a report listing the name, social security account number, and wages of each individual employed during the particular quarter. These records are then sent to the

---

[4] The language in the law administered by the Bureau of Internal Revenue is exactly the same as that in the law administered by the Social Security Administration so far as the employments covered and excluded and the definition of wages and related terms are concerned. However, the two agencies have not always agreed on how to interpret the same language in particular cases. In general, the Bureau of Internal Revenue has adopted a strict construction of the law as a tax law, whereas the Social Security Administration has adopted a broader interpretation as part of the general principle that in doubtful cases the intent of Congress was to enable persons to be covered by the insurance program. One solution of the existing problem would be to center administrative responsibility for both functions in one agency. Another would be to retain in the Bureau of Internal Revenue the responsibility for collecting contributions, but to make the Social Security Administration responsible for interpreting the coverage provisions of the two laws. Another suggestion is that when the two agencies have differences of opinion, they submit them to a third party such as the Attorney General for final determination.

Social Security Administration, which maintains records for each individual by means of a mechanical bookkeeping system. The Bureau of Old Age and Survivors' Insurance maintains nearly 450 full-time local field offices throughout the United States and in Hawaii and Alaska, where individuals may file their claims for benefits. In addition, there are 1500 localities in which the personnel from adjacent field offices holds office hours at regular intervals in some public building such as the post office.

Monthly payments are retroactive, but for not more than three months prior to the month of filing. Thus if a claim is not filed until the fourth month after the month of the insured person's death or retirement, one month's payment is lost. A claim for the lump-sum death benefit must be made within two years after the death of the insured person.

If the claim is a proper one under the law, it is approved and certified for payment and the United States Treasury then mails out the benefit checks. If the claimant is not satisfied with a decision, either because his claim has been disallowed or because he believes an error has been made in calculating his benefit, he may have his case reconsidered by the Bureau of Old Age and Survivors' Insurance or reviewed by a referee, or both. If he chooses to have his case go to a referee and is not satisfied with the decision, he may ask for review by the Appeals Council of the Social Security Administration in Washington. If still not satisfied, he may take his case to the federal courts.

MODIFICATIONS OF THE EXISTING PROGRAM

Numerous suggestions have been made for modification of the existing federal old age and survivors' insurance program. The most sweeping of them would provide for the establishment of a national pension of a uniform amount to be financed from a general federal tax levied on either all gross incomes, the value added by manufacture, or some similar basis. Other variations of these proposals would provide for the continuation of an insurance plan but have it superimposed on some general pension plan. Such proposals have been introduced in the Congress for over ten years, but Congress has not taken favorable action on any proposals for the adoption of any general social security plan financed through a special social security income tax like that in existence in New Zealand and Australia.

Many bills have been introduced in the Congress to improve, extend, or modify the provisions of the existing law, particularly by broadening the coverage, increasing the amount of the benefits, adding permanent disability insurance benefits, and modifying the financing provisions. Extended disability is the most important type of protection not provided in the existing old age and survivors' insurance program. In its effect on the individual and the family, extended disability represents premature retirement. According to the present law, a person who becomes permanently disabled must wait until age 65 to draw old age insurance benefits or must die in order for his family to receive survivors' insurance benefits. An extended period of disability may result in a substantial decrease in old age benefits or in total loss of the insured status.

Suggested programs for disability insurance are discussed in Chapter 27. Other recommendations for changes in the existing insurance law are along the following lines.

Changes in Coverage

Of all the issues in social security, there is none on which there is greater unanimity of opinion than the desirability of extending the coverage of the insurance plan. Self-employed persons, agricultural laborers, and domestic servants were excluded from the original program in 1935 primarily because of administrative difficulties. Railroad and federal government employees were excluded because they were covered by special retirement plans. Employees of state and local governments were excluded primarily for constitutional reasons relating to the difficulty involved in taxing a state or local government as an employer. Non-profit institutions were excluded because of the belief that coverage for social insurance purposes might impair the tax-exempt status of these institutions, the separation of church and state, and the freedom of educational institutions from federal interference.

These fears and difficulties have largely disappeared as a result of ten years of actual operation of the social security program. Seamen who were excluded by the 1935 law because of "administrative difficulties" were included in 1939 without any difficulty. Bank employees were also included in 1939. Certain federal employees working on the Bonneville dam were included in 1945. An overwhelming proportion of the employees of religious, educational, charitable, and similar non-profit institutions, as well as the institutions themselves, now favor coverage under the insurance plan.

Most foreign social insurance plans did not cover self-employed persons at the time that the Social Security Act was drafted in 1935, and there had been little thought of and experience with the methods which might be used to cover this group under the old age insurance plan in the United States. Subsequent developments, however, have indicated that most self-employed persons desire old age and survivors' insurance protection. The owner of a business large enough to be incorporated acquires protection as an officer of the corporation, but the owner of a small unincorporated concern has no such advantage. Moreover, many self-employed persons work as wage earners at times but fail to build up and maintain an insured status because their income from self-employment is not credited toward this status. According to the Social Security Administration, the experience gained in the administration of the present law makes it possible to develop adequate methods for meeting the problems involved in covering the self-employed.

Special retirement systems now cover approximately two-thirds of all public employees, and those employees thus covered are opposed to being brought under the federal old age and survivors' insurance program. While it would be possible to revise these special retirement systems so that the benefits would be superimposed on those payable under the basic social insurance system, such a revision is a complicated process and would of course have to be made in such a way as to increase, not reduce, the total protection afforded to public employees.

In the case of federal employees, if agreement could be reached as to the necessary adjustments in the existing federal retirement systems, at least the federal employees who are not protected by an existing retirement system could be covered under the basic old age insurance system. In the case of state and local employees, the Social Security Administration has indicated that it sees no major administrative difficulties in permitting the governmental

units which employ sufficient numbers of people to be covered
voluntarily, provided there are proper safeguards to protect the
social insurance system against adverse selection.

Agricultural Labor and Domestic Service

The principal reason for the exclusion of agricultural labor
and domestic service was the administrative difficulty arising from
the large number of small employers involved and the fact that
most of these employers do not keep books and would have difficulty in making reports. On the basis of various studies, the
Social Security Administration has said that it is administra-
tively feasible to extend coverage to these groups through the use
of a stamp-book system. Under such a system each employee
would receive a stamp book in which his employer would place
stamps to evidence contributions made by himself and the employee. In rural areas the employer could purchase these stamps
from the mail carrier, and in urban areas they could be purchased
at post offices.

If the Congress does not consider it advisable to extend coverage to all agricultural workers, the Social Security Administration has recommended that at least the language of the present
exclusion relating to "agricultural labor" be modified to make certain that this exclusion applies only to the services of a farm
hand employed by a small farmer. The wording of the present law
relating to agricultural labor excludes large-scale commercial and
industrial operators who employ 600,000 to 700,000 individuals
during the course of a year.

Many of these excluded workers are not engaged in "agricultural labor" in the usual sense of the term. Many of them
work in towns and cities and are engaged in processes identical
with or similar to those performed by workers in factories and
industries now covered by the insurance program. For instance,
more than 15,000 of the workers excluded by the agricultural
clause are carpenters, painters, engineers, bookkeepers, accountants, and the like. About 10,000 more are employed in grain
elevators, and some 40,000 work in cotton gins. Another 125,000
persons so excluded are employed at the peak of the season in
packing fruits and vegetables. Thousands of people employed by
large-scale business firms (such as chain stores or commission

houses) which purchase and harvest the entire crop of many farmers are also excluded. The extension of coverage to these quasi-industrial and commercial employees would not raise any of the problems which arise in connection with coverage for the ordinary farm worker.

Suggested Changes in the Amount of Benefits

The federal old age and survivors' insurance benefits now being paid are determined by provisions of the law which were enacted in 1939. The Social Security Administration constantly studies and recommends changes in the existing law; in general, these would increase the proportion of the average monthly wage to be paid as benefits and would make the average monthly wage formula more representative of actual earnings during periods of employment in covered jobs. For example, it has recommended that the benefit should replace 40 per cent of the first $75 (instead of the present $50) of the average monthly wage, and 10 per cent of the remainder up to $300. This would result in an increase in the primary benefit of at least $7.50 per month for persons earning an average monthly wage of over $75, and an increase of about one-fourth to one-third of 1 per cent in average benefits. The revised formula would be of special importance to beneficiaries with low average earnings, and it has already been incorporated in the 1946 amendments to the railroad program for survivors' insurance benefits.

The Social Security Administration also has recommended that the wage base for both contributions and benefit-computation purposes be raised from $3000 to $3600. The railroad retirement program already has a $3600 maximum. Such a change would recognize the general increase in wage levels and would result in benefits that represent a somewhat larger proportion of the wage loss actually sustained by families in the middle income brackets. Certain items of income such as tips and dismissal wages which are not now considered "wages" under the definition in the act, should be included as wages, so that the base for benefits would represent the worker's actual earnings from employment.

Certain changes in the provisions governing minimum and maximum benefit amounts have also been suggested. A reasonable standard of adequacy would seem to require for an eligible worker a higher minimum benefit than the present $10 a month, even though most workers have earnings that qualify them or their survivors for more than the minimum amount. Organized labor is now seeking to have the $10 minimum increased to $20.

At present, the maximum total amount payable to a worker and his dependents is $85 a month, twice the primary benefit amount, or 80 per cent of the average monthly wage of the insured worker, whichever is least. The Administration has recommended that the $85 maximum limit be raised and that the second limitation of twice the primary benefit (which limits the amount payable to a worker with dependents) be eliminated. Organized labor has recommended that the maximum be increased to $120 per month. The chief effect of these changes would be to provide more adequate benefits in the case of a widow with several children.

Suggested Changes in Eligibility Requirements

If the insurance system is amended to provide broad extension of coverage, it will be necessary to adjust the eligibility requirements and the method of determining the average monthly wage upon which benefits are based, so that the newly insured groups will not be unduly disadvantaged because of their late entrance into the system. As the law now stands, beginning with 1957 it would take any person the equivalent of ten years in covered employment to qualify for old age retirement benefits. Even at the end of ten years his average monthly wage could be one-half the average wage per month earned by him during that time because his total wages would have to be averaged over the entire period since January 1, 1937, namely, twenty years or more. These defects can be remedied in various ways. One proposal is that a person not otherwise fully insured would be so insured if he were in covered employment for five out of the ten years immediately preceding his death or retirement. His average wage could also be adjusted appropriately so that he would not be unduly disadvantaged by his late entrance into the system.

The question of lowering the retirement age is frequently discussed, and proposals have been advanced to reduce the age from 65 to 60, and in some cases to 55. Several factors, especially the costs involved, are brought forward in public discussions in this connection. It has been estimated that reducing the age requirement from 65 to 60 would in itself increase costs about 50 per cent. A second consideration is whether it is more desirable to provide benefits first for individuals permanently disabled at any age. Also, there is the question whether normally it is desirable to encourage the early retirement of persons who are still able to work.

These considerations all have controversial aspects and a complete examination of them cannot be made here. However, there seems to be general agreement that for women the age requirement should be reduced from 65 to 60 because women usually retire from gainful employment at an earlier age than men. Furthermore, wives are ordinarily younger than their husbands. Of the married men who reach age 65 each year, less than 20 per cent have wives who also have reached this age. The age requirement is lower for women than for men in many of the social insurance programs of foreign countries, and also in many of the retirement systems established in this country by various state and local governments and private concerns.

Under the existing law, benefits are not paid for any month in which the beneficiary earns more than $14.99 in covered employment. The amount of permissible earnings could well be increased, at least to $30 a month, without fear that beneficiaries will encroach on the job opportunities open to regular full-time workers.

Another problem under the existing insurance program arises out of the fact that in determining who shall receive insurance benefits a decision must be made in each case as to who is the "wife," "widow," or "child" of the insured worker. Under the existing law, such matters are determined by the federal agency in accordance with state laws, which vary widely on such points as marital and family relationships. A woman who is a "wife" or "widow" in one state will be eligible to draw insurance benefits, whereas a woman in another state, under identical circumstances, is not considered a wife or widow and so is ineligible to receive benefits. In some states illegitimate children cannot draw insurance benefits on the basis of their father's insurance rights, but in other states they can.

Under a national insurance program such variations result in inequities when all the persons covered are contributing at the same rate. Some improvement can be achieved by making

special provisions in the federal insurance law to permit payment
of benefits to many women and children who are now not eligible
for them. A complete solution to the problem would necessitate
repealing the requirement that state laws shall determine the
marital and family relationships for insurance purposes. This
would require writing into the federal law detailed provisions on
matters customarily handled by the states, and there is no general agreement on what are the most desirable provisions to be
included in a federal law.

Proposals for Changes in Financing

It has been estimated that the most probable range in the
average long-run cost of the existing federal old age and survivors' insurance benefits is 4 to 7 per cent of covered pay rolls.
Such actuarial estimates must be presented within a wide range
since no one can accurately predict future economic conditions,
mortality rates, population growth, retirement rates, and many
other factors upon which these estimates must be based.

One pertinent fact, however, has become apparent which may
modify the original calculations. According to the method of
computing primary benefits under the present law (40 per cent
of the first $50 of average monthly wages and 10 per cent of the
remaining amount up to $200 additional), an individual always
receives a larger benefit as his wages increase, but this benefit
represents a smaller proportion of his wages.[5] As a result, as the
average wages of insured persons increase, the relative costs of the
present benefits decrease as a pay-roll percentage. At the present
time, the average wages of people contributing to the insurance
system are substantially higher than those assumed when the
actuarial cost estimates were made in 1939. This single factor
results in a reduction in the relative costs of the insurance plan.
In addition, comprehensive coverage would extend to all the wages
of many individuals who are already covered by the insurance
system part of the time, thus increasing their taxable wages and
reducing the relative cost of the insurance plan. On the other

---

[5] For instance, the individual whose average wages are $100 per month re-
ceives a basic old age insurance benefit of $25 per month, or 25 per cent; the
person who earns $250 per month receives $40 per month, which represents 16
per cent.

hand, improvements will undoubtedly be made in the insurance program from time to time which will increase costs.

A major question of policy in all social insurance is how the costs should be shared as between employers, employees, and the government. Some persons, as already indicated, believe that all the costs should be met out of general governmental revenues. Others who favor a contributory social insurance plan believe that there should be a three-way division of costs, but there is no general agreement as to the exact amount to be contributed by each of the three parties. A further question arises as to the timing of any governmental contribution in relation to other fiscal policies.

The original 1935 law was passed by Congress on the assumption that only employers and employees would contribute to the insurance plan. Because of this fact the contributions had to be sufficient to produce a large reserve fund which would yield enough interest to make up the difference in the long run between annual benefit disbursements and current contributions. Thus, under the original plan it was estimated that in a year when the annual cost of benefits was 10 per cent of the total pay rolls, the interest on the reserve fund would be equivalent to 4 per cent of pay rolls. The other 6 per cent would be derived from contributions shared equally by employers and employees.

The primary justification for this financing arrangement was that the government should not contribute to a limited coverage plan. It was argued that if the government contributed out of its general revenues to the insurance system, taxpayers not covered under the system (such as farmers and small businessmen and others) would be paying part of the cost of insurance protection without receiving any direct benefits themselves.

In 1944 Congress amended the law to authorize the federal government to contribute to the insurance system out of its general revenues. Since the existing contribution rates have been more than sufficient to pay current benefits, such payments have been unnecessary up to the present time. Whether and when such payments will be necessary depends on the decision of Congress as to the rate of contribution it will levy on employers and employees, and the changes it makes in the existing benefits under the program.

Another factor hindering the possibility of obtaining an early contribution to the system from the government is the level of the debt resulting from World War II. It is usually argued that the government should use any excess funds either to pay off this debt or to reduce general taxes. It is likely, therefore, that no contribution will be made to the insurance program until the contributions from employers and employees are above the 1 per cent rate and the benefit costs are substantially higher. Continued collection of contributions without improvement in the benefit aspects of the program will also increase the reserve fund. Available estimates indicate that, if there are no important changes in the present program, the reserve fund may double in the next ten years or so.

RAILROAD EMPLOYEES RETIREMENT AND SURVIVORS' INSURANCE

The old age retirement, survivors', and permanent disability insurance program for railroad employees differs in a number of respects from the general insurance program for other workers under the Social Security Act. The benefits and contributions are higher under the railroad program, and permanent disability benefits are payable under it but not under the social security program. While monthly survivors' benefits first became payable in 1940 under the federal Old Age and Survivors' Insurance Law, similar benefits under the railroad program first became payable in 1947.

The railroad retirement program also provides benefits based upon past railroad service prior to the effective date of the law, provides for the continued payment of pensions previously granted under separate employer plans, and pays benefits on retirement from the railroad industry, or last employment, rather than from general work. Comparable provisions are not found in the general Old Age and Survivors' Insurance Law.

The benefits under the railroad retirement law are paid to an individual reaching retirement age irrespective of the length of time he has been covered by the railroad plan. The retirement benefit, of course, would be small if he had only a brief period of employment in the railroad industry. In general, benefits under the railroad retirement law are higher for long-time permanent railroad employees than for employees in similar circumstances in other industries covered by the Social Security Act. But individuals with brief periods of employment receive larger monthly benefits under the latter law than under the railroad law because of the different formulas specified in the two laws for computing retirement benefits.

The railroad plan does not make attainment of age 65 an absolute requirement for obtaining a retirement benefit as does old age and survivors' insurance. A railroad employee can receive a retirement annuity at the age of 60 if he has had thirty years of service or is totally disabled. If he is disabled for any regular employment and has ten years of service he can receive benefits even prior to age 60.

The railroad plan does not limit the maximum retirement benefit payable to any person. The benefit is therefore limited only by length of service and amount of wages earned in the railroad industry. A railroad employee, for instance, who had worked for forty years on the railroads after 1936 could receive an annuity of $120 per month if his monthly railroad wages averaged $200, and $160 per month if his monthly railroad wages averaged $300. The maximum monthly payment under old age and survivors' insurance, as already indicated, is $85.

TABLE 32.   Illustrations of Retirement Benefits for Railroad Workers

Average Monthly Earnings	Years of Railroad Employment			
	10	20	30	40
$ 50.00	$10.00	$20.00	$ 30.00	$ 40.00
100.00	17.50	35.00	52.50	70.00
200.00	30.00	60.00	90.00	120.00
300.00	40.00	80.00	120.00	160.00

The average cost of the benefits of the present railroad retirement program over a long period of time is estimated to be between 8 and 14 per cent of pay rolls. On June 30, 1946, the railroad retirement reserve fund was slightly in excess of 650 million dollars. Since 1936, when the first benefits were paid, over 1 billion dollars has been paid out. In 1938–1939, benefit payments were equal to 98 per cent of contribution collections. While the percentage dropped sharply during the war, it is expected that benefit payments will rise sharply in the future. About 185,-000 persons were drawing monthly benefits in June, 1946.

SELECTED REFERENCES

Annual Reports of the Railroad Retirement Board, Government Printing Office, Washington.

Annual Reports of the Social Security Board, Washington, Government Printing Office.

Benedict, Murray R., *A Retirement System for Farmers,* National Planning Association, Washington, 1946.

Corson, John J., "Old Age and Survivors Insurance," in *Social Work Year Book 1945.*

Epstein, Abraham, *Insecurity: A Challenge to America,* Random House, Inc., New York, rev. ed., 1938.

Harris, Seymour E., *Economics of Social Security,* McGraw-Hill Book Company, Inc., New York, 1941.

Meriam, Lewis, *Relief and Social Security,* Brookings Institution, Washington, 1946.

National Planning Association, *Joint Statement on Social Security by Agriculture, Business and Labor,* Washington, 1944.

Parker, James S., *Social Security Reserves,* American Council on Public Affairs, Washington, 1942.

Social Security, A Statement by the Social Security Committees of American Life Convention, Life Insurance Association of America, National Association of Life Underwriters, Chicago, 1945.

Stewart, Maxwell, *Social Security,* W. W. Norton & Company, Inc., New York, 1939.

U. S. Congress, *Issues in Social Security: A Report to the Committee on Ways and Means of the House of Representatives by the Committee's Social Security Technical Staff Established Pursuant to H. Res. 204, 79th Congress, 1st Sess.,* Government Printing Office, Washington, 1946.

25

UNEMPLOYMENT
INSURANCE

THE EXISTING FEDERAL-STATE PROGRAM OF UNEMPLOYMENT IN-
surance is an outgrowth of the 1935 Social Security Act, but this
Act did not directly establish a system of unemployment insurance. The Act gave impetus to state legislation by imposing a
federal tax on pay rolls against which employers were permitted
to offset the major portion of the contributions they made under
their state unemployment insurance laws. Since employers in
states which did not enact appropriate insurance laws were liable
for the full federal tax, there was every inducement for the speedy
establishment of state programs.[1] Less than two years after the
passage of the Social Security Act, unemployment insurance laws
were on the statute books of all 51 jurisdictions, including the 48
states, Alaska, Hawaii, and the District of Columbia.

REQUIREMENTS UNDER FEDERAL LAWS

The basic federal legislation, as amended in 1939 and 1944,
provides for a 3 per cent tax on pay rolls against which employers are permitted to offset as much as 90 per cent of their
federal liability in accordance with the contributions they paid
under state laws, or from which they were excused through opera-

[1] Before 1934, when President Roosevelt created the Committee on Economic Security to study social security problems and recommend legislation,
Wisconsin was the only state which had an unemployment insurance law, and
benefits were not yet payable under that law. Between January, 1935, when
the President transmitted the Committee's report to the Congress, and August
of that year, when the Social Security Act became law, four states enacted
unemployment insurance laws in anticipation of federal enabling legislation.
By June, 1937, all the states had such laws.

tion of the experience rating provisions of those laws. The federal
government uses 10 per cent of the employer tax to reimburse the
states for the cost of administering their programs.[2]

In order for an employer to receive credit against the 3 per
cent tax, his state unemployment insurance program must be administered by such methods as the federal Social Security Administration finds to be reasonably calculated to insure full benefits
to workers when due. These include the establishment and maintenance of personnel standards on a merit basis for persons in
charge of the program, and the making of such reports as the
Social Security Administration may require.

In addition, the federal laws include some specific requirements,
among which are: (1) All benefits must be paid through public
employment offices. (2) All money withdrawn by the state from
the state unemployment fund must be used solely for the payment
of insurance benefits. (3) Benefits must not be denied by a state
to any individual for refusing to accept work, (a) if the position
offered is vacant because of a labor dispute, (b) if the wages,
hours, or other conditions of work are substantially less favorable
to the individual than those in similar work in the locality, (c) if
as a condition of employment the individual is required to join
a company union or to resign from any bona fide labor organization.

Aside from these general federal requirements, the various
states are entirely free to establish whatever type of program
they wish so far as coverage, eligibility conditions, benefit provisions, and financial and other arrangements are concerned. Although many provisions in the various state plans are similar,
each one differs in some important way. This is indicated by the
summary of the significant provisions of the 51 state and territorial laws given in Table 33, as well as by the following discussion
which is necessarily limited to general comparisons and contrasts
and a few of the problems arising from the operation of numerous
autonomous programs.

---

[2] The federal tax and other unemployment insurance provisions are incorporated in two different laws, namely, the Federal Unemployment Tax
Act, which is part of the Internal Revenue Code, and the Social Security Act,
which is administered by the Social Security Administration. Railroad workers,
as explained later in this chapter, are covered by a separate federal law.

TABLE 33. Major Provisions of State Unemployment Insurance Plans, June 30, 1946

State	Size of Firm Covered	Waiting Period (Weeks)	Weekly Benefits		Maximum Weeks Payable	Maximum Total Benefits	Average Weekly Benefit, January–March, 1946	
			Minimum	Maximum			Amount	Per Cent of Average Weekly Earnings, January–March, 1946
Average, 51 states	..	..	$4	$20	..	..	$18.79	42
Alabama	8	1	8	25	20	$400	17.30	51
Alaska	1	2	8	25	25	625	15.71	32
Arizona	3	1	5	15	14	210	14.66	34
Arkansas	1	1	3	15	16	240	12.50	41
California	1	1	10	20	23.4	468	19.34	37
Colorado	8	2	5	15	16	240	14.06	34
Connecticut	4	1	8	28	20	440	21.28	45
Delaware	1	1	7	18	22	396	16.54	37
District of Columbia	1	1	6	20	20	400	17.62	43
Florida	8	1	5	15	16	240	14.41	38
Georgia	8	2	4	18	16	288	16.18	49
Hawaii	1	1	5	25	20[a]	500	22.64	53
Idaho	1	2	5	18	17	306	16.44	44
Illinois	6	1	10	20	26	520	18.88	39
Indiana	8	1	5	20	20	400	18.92	43
Iowa	8	2	5	18	18	324	16.26	43
Kansas	8	1	5	16	20	320	15.32	38
Kentucky	4	1	5	16	20[a]	320	12.55	33
Louisiana	4	1	3	18	20	360	16.27	44
Maine	8	1	5	20	20[a]	400	16.32	40
Maryland	1	0	7	20	26	520	19.14	47
Massachusetts	1	1	6	25	23	575	19.52	45
Michigan	8	1	10	28	20	560	21.15	42
Minnesota	1	2	7	20	20	400	17.07	42
Mississippi	8	2	3	15	14[a]	210	13.32	44

[a] Indicates uniform duration of benefits.

TABLE 33. Major Provisions of State Unemployment Insurance Plans, June 30, 1946—(Continued)

State	Size of Firm Covered	Waiting Period (Weeks)	Weekly Benefits		Maximum Weeks Payable	Maximum Total Benefits	Average Weekly Benefit, January–March, 1946	
			Minimum	Maximum			Amount	Per Cent of Average Weekly Earnings, January–March, 1946
Missouri	8	1	$3	$20	20	$400	$16.32	40
Montana	1	2	5	15	16ᵃ	240	13.70	36
Nebraska	8	2	5	18	18	324	16.58	41
Nevada	1	1	8	18–24	20–15	360	18.27	38
New Hampshire	4	1	6	20	20ᵃ	400	13.71	37
New Jersey	4	1	9	22	26	572	20.60	42
New Mexico	2	1	5	15	16	240	13.51	36
New York	4	1	10	21	26ᵃ	546	19.61	38
North Carolina	8	1	4	20	16ᵃ	320	12.54	39
North Dakota	8	1	5	20	20ᵃ	400	17.26	48
Ohio	3	2	5	21	22	462	19.15	42
Oklahoma	8	1	6	18	20	360	16.91	40
Oregon	4	1	10	18	20	360	16.86	37
Pennsylvania	1	1	8	20	20	400	18.25	44
Rhode Island	4	1	6.75	18	20.25	364.50	17.45	41
South Carolina	8	1	4	20	16ᵃ	320	14.29	47
South Dakota	8	1	6	15	20	300	13.20	38
Tennessee	8	1	5	15	16ᵃ	240	13.69	38
Texas	8	1	5	18	18	324	16.15	40
Utah	1	1	5	25	18.4ᵃ	460	23.99	59
Vermont	8	2	6	20	20ᵃ	400	17.15	44
Virginia	8	1	5	15	16	240	13.20	36
Washington	1	1	10	25	26	650	21.17	45
West Virginia	8	1	8	20	21ᵃ	420	16.81	37
Wisconsin	6	2	8	20	23	460	18.04	41
Wyoming	1	2	7	20	20	400	19.07	45

COVERAGE OF UNEMPLOYMENT
INSURANCE PROGRAMS

About 44 million persons earned some wage credits in employment covered by state unemployment insurance systems in 1944,
and 3 million earned wage credits under the separate federal
system for railroad workers. However, large groups of workers
still have no protection when they are unemployed. Among the
most important groups excluded are workers employed in small
establishments, employees of the federal government, agricultural
workers, and employees of non-profit institutions. Congress extended the coverage of unemployment insurance to seamen in
1946.

Substantially the same groups are included and excluded from
coverage under unemployment insurance as under the federal old
age and survivors' insurance program, although in some respects
the coverage of unemployment insurance is broader and in one
respect it is narrower. A number of states include some types of
"industrialized" farm labor which is excluded from federal old
age insurance; most states have a broader coverage so far as
salesmen are concerned; one state (New York) covers domestic
employees when the employer hires four or more domestics; and
one state (Wisconsin) covers certain types of state and local
public employees. On the other hand, all the employees in small
firms are covered under the old age program, whereas most state
unemployment insurance laws still exclude some such firms. In
total, the federal old age and survivors' insurance system in a
year covers about 3 million more members of the labor force than
the state unemployment insurance programs.

The federal unemployment tax applies only to industrial and
commercial employers of eight or more workers. Most states
originally limited coverage to employers subject to the federal
tax, but later many of them extended their coverage provisions.
At the end of June, 1946, 22 states still excluded all workers in
firms with less than eight employees, and only 16 states covered
all employers of one or more employees. The workers excluded
by the size-of-firm provisions are in the same occupations and
industries as those who are covered, and in many cases they are

employed by a fluctuating group of marginal employers who go in and out of business and thus present special risks for their employees. Employers of workers in agriculture, domestic service, non-profit institutions, and the government are also exempted from the federal unemployment tax and their employees are almost wholly excluded from the state programs.

BENEFIT PROVISIONS

Eligibility Requirements

Although the benefit provisions of the state laws vary greatly, they follow a general pattern. To be eligible for benefits, a worker must be involuntarily unemployed, able to and available for work, and registered at a local public employment office, and he must not refuse suitable work. Such provisions, although varying in form and interpretation, are found in all unemployment programs and are designed to insure that only genuine unemployment is compensated.

In addition to these qualifications, a worker must have had a certain length of time or been paid a certain amount of wages in covered work during a recent past period, usually called "the base period." These work or wage requirements in the state laws are of three general types: (1) One state (Wisconsin) expresses eligibility on the basis of length of employment, its requirement being 14 weeks of employment within the preceding 52 weeks. (2) Flat amounts in dollars of earnings are specified in 19 state laws, the amounts ranging from $100 to $300 in a one-year period. (3) Variable amounts in dollars of earnings, depending upon the weekly benefit of the individual, are required by 31 states. A few of these states also require some employment or earnings within a particular period of time. Thus, in some states if a person's weekly benefit amount is $5, he must have earned 30 times that amount in wages in a prior period, usually about a year; if his benefit is $20 per week he must have earned $600. On the other hand, the District of Columbia provides an eligibility requirement of 25 times the weekly benefit amount but limits this to a maximum of $250; this results in a variable requirement for those with benefits under $10 per week, and a flat requirement for those receiving more than this amount.

Waiting Periods

All the state laws but one (Maryland) provide for a waiting period, usually a week or two of unemployment, between the filing of a claim for benefits and the time at which they begin to be payable. This period is designed to give the administrative agency time to process the claims and, by preventing payment of benefits for very short periods, to conserve funds for claimants who suffer longer periods of unemployment. As the states have acquired facility in processing claims and have accumulated substantial reserves, the need for a long waiting period has disappeared, and many states have reduced the length of the period originally provided under their laws. At the end of June, 1946, 13 states still required a two-week waiting period. Even with a single week, the claimant's first benefit check ordinarily does not reach him until the end of his third week of unemployment, that is, a week after the end of his first compensable week of unemployment.

Amount of Benefits

Benefits are usually related to weekly wages in a recent period of employment. In general, under the original laws framed in 1935 and 1936, benefits were intended to replace about half the weekly wage loss, up to the maximum benefit amount, suffered by an individual when he is totally unemployed. This was based on the principle that the weekly benefit should be less than the wages received when he is employed full time in order to provide financial inducement to take a job when one is available. Benefits for partial unemployment are provided in all states but Montana, and all the laws include provisions for minimum and maximum benefits.

The weekly benefits provided under state laws have risen since the early days of the program because of the rise in weekly earnings as well as the liberalization of benefit provisions. State averages vary greatly; in 1945, for example, an average of $11.21 per week was paid for total unemployment in South Dakota, in contrast to $22.76 in Utah. In the United States as a whole, average weekly benefits for total unemployment have been as follows:

Year	Amount	Year	Amount
1940	$10.56	1943	$13.84
1941	11.06	1944	15.90
1942	12.06	1945	18.93

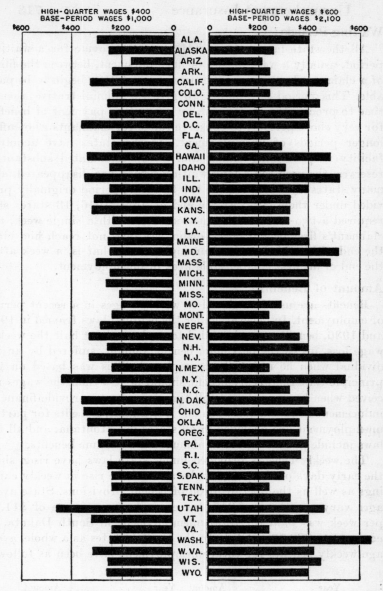

Fig. 35. *Maximum Potential Amounts Payable for Unemployment Benefits During a Year Under State Laws as of June 30, 1945, to a Worker with Specified Wage Credits.* (*Source: Federal Social Security Administration.*)

The major purpose in establishing maximums for weekly benefits is to husband the limited funds. Current maximums under the state laws, however, reduce the rights of a very high proportion of workers and result, for many, in benefits that are considerably less than half their weekly wages. Although the level of maximum benefits has been raised in many states, at the end of June, 1946, 10 states still provided for total unemployment no benefits exceeding $15 a week. Because the maximums have not risen in line with increases in weekly earnings, a large proportion of payments have been made at the maximum. In 1944, nearly three-fifths of all such payments were the maximum specified in the respective state laws, and in some states this was true of 90 per cent of all payments.

For most workers receiving the maximum, the benefits are far less than 50 per cent of their previous earnings. On the average, it is estimated, workers eligible for the maximum amount under state laws are receiving only about 42 per cent of their previous earnings; for some higher-paid workers the proportion is nearer 15 or 20 per cent. The existing maximums have no uniform relationship to state wage levels. Maximum benefits are higher in Alabama and Georgia than in Montana and South Dakota. As shown in Table 33, average benefits in Alabama represent about 51 per cent of average wages, and in Georgia about 49 per cent. The benefits in these two southern states, in relation to wage levels, are among the highest in the country.

Duration of Benefits

Since the major objective of unemployment insurance is to bridge the gap between jobs, the duration of benefits is the most important single element in the benefit formula.

In 36 states the duration of benefits is related to the amount of employment or earnings of the worker in a previous period within the specified maximum duration. The other 15 jurisdictions provide a uniform duration of benefits; that is, any worker who qualifies for benefits may receive up to the maximum provided in the state law if he continues to be unemployed. Recent legislative changes have tended to widen the differences among the states. The maximum potential duration of benefits under the state laws at the end of June 30, 1946, is shown in Table 34.

TABLE 34. Maximum Duration of Unemployment Benefit Periods
According to Number of States

Maximum Duration of Benefits for Total Unemployment (in Weeks)	Number of States with Specified Type of Duration Provisions	
	Uniform	Variable
14	1	1
16	5	7
17	0	1
18–19	1	3
20	6	15
21	1	0
22	1	2
23	0	3
26	1	4

In states with variable duration provisions, many workers who meet the earnings requirement under these laws are eligible for a far shorter period than the maximum duration. In 1941, the last pre-war year and one with fairly high employment, nine states whose provisions related benefit duration to the individual's previous earnings provided an average potential duration of less than 11 weeks for all eligible claimants. For at least 25 per cent of the eligible claimants in nine states, the potential duration for drawing benefits was less than 8 weeks. In contrast, in no state with uniform duration of benefits were the benefits so limited.

A large proportion of claimants are ordinarily still unemployed when they exhaust their benefits rights. In a rather good year like 1941, about half of all the eligible workers failed to be re-employed before their benefit rights expired, and in five states the proportion was at least 60 per cent.[3]

Annual Benefits

The wide differences among the states in duration of benefits, in maximum benefit amounts, and in other elements in the benefit formula, result in great variations in the total amount that a worker in given circumstances can receive in a year.

---

[3] In 1927, after many years of experience with variable duration, the British abolished their ratio rule, under which 1 week of benefits had been paid for each 6 weeks of contributions. Until September 1939, any eligible worker could receive benefits for as many as 26 weeks; then duration was increased to 30 weeks a year.

Under the state laws as of June 30, 1946, the $260 that New York State may pay during a year to a worker who barely qualifies for benefits is greater than the maximum that 10 states pay to any worker, whatever his past earnings. For example, for a worker who has earned $1500 in his base period and $500 in the high quarter of that period, the maximum that he can draw in benefits in a year ranges among the states from $210 to $546; weekly benefits vary from $15 to $28; and their potential duration ranges from 14 to 26 weeks. Similar disparities exist for workers at other wage levels.

RIGHTS OF INTERSTATE WORKERS

With a system administered under 51 different jurisdictions, particular questions arise with respect to workers whose jobs carry them across state lines. The problem of covering interstate workers has been partly solved by employment being defined in all state laws so that all the services of an interstate worker for one employer are usually covered in the state in which he will be most likely to seek benefits if he becomes unemployed. Certain types of employment, however, do not lend themselves to this simple solution. The employer who sends out work crews for a few months first in one state and then in another, cannot easily decide to what state or states he should pay contributions. If he pays the wrong state, he must obtain a refund and must also pay his delayed contributions, plus interest, to the right state. Differences in interpreting the various state laws sometimes result in overlapping claims by two states for the same service, and in gaps whereby some service is not covered by any state.

Most state laws provide that their administrative agencies may enter into reciprocal arrangements under which all services performed by an individual for one employer can be covered under one state law, at the request of an employer, in order to provide continuity of coverage for the workers and reduce the employer's reporting requirements. Not all of the states, however, have adopted a uniform arrangement simplifying the handling of such requests. As a consequence, workers who have benefit credits in more than one state may not be eligible in any state, or may receive smaller amounts because of the division of their wage credits.

On the other hand, if a worker's earnings in each of two or more states qualify him for benefits and if he remains unemployed and otherwise eligible, he may collect benefits, one at a time, from every state in which he is qualified. Thus some long-unemployed interstate workers may draw more in total benefits than they could if their wage credits were all in one state. Because of the differences in state laws and the order of drawing interstate benefits, some claimants are forced to forego relatively high benefits until they have exhausted their lesser benefits in another state, and sometimes their rights to the higher benefits lapse before the smaller benefits are exhausted.

Because of the differences in provisions and interpretation of the various state laws, and because only the state in which the benefit rights accrue can determine an interstate claim, it is more expensive to process interstate claims than others. Special interstate units have consequently been established in state administrative offices to make types of decisions which local offices usually make for other claims. One of the most difficult decisions in determining an interstate claim concerns the availability of the claimant for work, for in each case it is necessary to decide whether the specific circumstances require that the claimant be available for work *in* the locality in which he is filing, or in the state *against* which he is filing his claim.

Interstate claimants have the same rights as intrastate claimants to appeal from a decision on their claims. As a practical matter, however, it is usually not possible for a claimant to travel to the state where his appeal will be heard, and hence it is very difficult for interstate claimants to obtain "a fair hearing." To overcome this difficulty, special methods have been adopted more or less generally, whereby a referee of a distant state examines a claimant filing in that state and reports the facts to the state which makes the decision on his benefit rights. This procedure is complicated by the difference in provisions and interpretation of the state laws on all points that may lead to an appeal.

DISQUALIFICATION FROM BENEFITS

The purpose of unemployment insurance is to pay benefits only to genuinely unemployed workers who are actively in the labor market; hence all the laws impose certain disqualifications designed to insure that objective. Thus, disqualifications from benefits are imposed when a worker has quit his job voluntarily without good cause or has been discharged for misconduct connected with his work, when he is engaged directly in a labor dispute, or when he refuses to accept suitable work. During recent years, amendments to many of the original state laws, however, have shifted the emphasis from paying benefits to workers unemployed through no fault of their own, to paying only when the employer is responsible for their unemployment. Moreover, the disqualification provisions have tended to shift from postponement of benefits for a certain number of weeks following the worker's disqualifying act, to the drastic penalty of canceling part or all of his benefit rights. Furthermore, many special grounds for disqualifications have been added to state statutes.

The disqualification provisions in state unemployment insurance laws raise some of the most baffling problems connected with the program, because they involve elements of discretion and judgment. While the amount and duration of benefits have an important bearing on employment and labor standards, these elements are determined basically by the specific provisions of the law itself. But in deciding whether a worker is eligible for benefits when he leaves "suitable work" voluntarily without "good cause," fails to "accept suitable work" when offered to him, is "not available" for work, or is unemployed because of a "labor dispute," there is substantial room for discretion on the part of the state agency in developing general standards and in ruling on individual cases.

Quitting for Personal Reasons

In January, 1938, all but seven states had disqualifications which resulted only in postponement of benefit rights. By January, 1946, however, 19 additional states had included disqualifications which cancel part or all of a worker's benefit rights. When these rights are canceled because of a disqualifying act, not only is the worker deprived of benefits for the period following his act, but also, if he becomes unemployed in the future, he may find that even though he is in no way responsible for losing his last job, he has little or no benefit rights on which to draw. Such disqualifications may nullify duration provisions.

Eighteen states provide that benefits are not payable when an

employee leaves his job voluntarily "without good cause attributable to the employer." In all but two of these states, personal
reasons such as illness in the family, inability to find satisfactory
housing, or transportation difficulties, are not sufficient to enable
a worker to draw benefits, nor is leaving voluntarily to find a better job a satisfactory reason.

By law or in administration, some states have automatically
tended to disqualify certain groups of workers such as students,
married women, or pregnant women, irrespective of the circumstances of the individual claimant. In many states, however, the
circumstances in each case are examined to determine the facts
concerning the claimant's actual availability for employment.
About half the states disqualify persons receiving old age insurance payments or workmen's compensation, although in most
cases the state pays the difference between these payments and
the unemployment insurance benefit, if the latter is larger. A
number of states also disqualify workers when they are receiving
vacation allowances, dismissal wages, or payments under an employer pension plan.

The severity of the disqualification provisions resulted in large
part as a consequence of experience rating. The employer to
whose account the benefits are charged quite logically objects to
having them paid to persons who left his employ for reasons not
due to the job itself, even though the reason may have been compelling, such as serious sickness in the home. The employer whose
insurance charges are such as to keep him from securing a tax
reduction becomes interested in limiting the amount of compensated unemployment chargeable to him, particularly in those
cases where he cannot do much to stabilize employment because
he finds that the causes of unemployment in his business are
largely beyond his control.

In an effort to counteract this tendency and encourage the
states to make changes in the disqualification provisions in their
laws, the Social Security Administration has recommended that
disqualifications for voluntary quitting and refusal of suitable
work take the form of a postponement, not a cancellation, of
benefit rights; that the "good cause" which justifies voluntarily
leaving a job should include good personal causes as well as "good
cause attributable to the employer"; and that disqualifications

should apply only to leaving voluntarily without good cause, refusal to take suitable work, labor disputes, and discharge for misconduct.

Suitable Work

In determining whether work is suitable for an individual the states take into account such factors as the degree of risk involved to his health, safety, and morals, his physical fitness and earlier training, his experience and prior earnings, the length of his unemployment, his prospects for obtaining work in his customary occupation, the distance of the available work from his residence, and his prospects for obtaining local work. The weight given to each of these factors varies from state to state and from case to case within a state.

Many times decisions in individual cases relate to the rules of labor organizations, such as whether a claimant is subject to disqualification for refusing work when its acceptance would be a violation of union rules and jeopardize his union status. In determining whether a worker has "good cause" for leaving voluntarily or refusing an otherwise suitable job, the state agency must appraise the personal circumstances surrounding the case. Such cases frequently involve questions of the care of children, change in place of residence because of marriage, illness of a member of the family, housing and transportation, and similar factors.

Unemployment Due to Labor Disputes

All state laws have some provision for refusing payment of benefits when the worker is unemployed because of a labor dispute. The specific provisions of the laws vary from state to state, as do the interpretation and administration of the provisions.

The most common provision, found in nearly two-thirds of the laws, specifies that an unemployed individual shall not be entitled to receive a benefit for any week in which his unemployment is the result of a stoppage of work due to a labor dispute in the establishment, or at any other premises, in which he is or was last employed. However, he may receive benefits if it is shown that he is not participating in or directly interested in the labor dispute, and if he does not belong to a grade or class of workers of which there were members employed at the premises at which the stoppage occurs, any of whom are participating in or directly interested in the dispute. The other general type of law, found in about 13 states, disqualifies a worker if his unemployment is due to a labor dispute "in active progress" at the establishment at which he is employed.

Both types of laws raise difficult problems of interpretation. In the first type, such terms as "the grade or class of workers," "stoppage of work," and "participating or directly interested" in the labor dispute have been interpreted differently by various states. The second type of law gives rise to frequent differences in interpretation as to when a labor dispute is still in "active progress."

Four states provide that after an extended waiting period benefits are payable to workers still unemployed because of a labor dispute: Tennessee and Pennsylvania after a waiting period of 4 weeks, New York after 7 weeks, and Rhode Island after 8 weeks. Other states have provisions in their laws which allow payment of benefits under certain other circumstances. Thus, Arkansas, Kentucky, Ohio, and several others provide that workers may draw benefits if unemployed as a result of lockouts. West Virginia laws impose no disqualification if the employees are required to accept wages, hours, or working conditions less favorable than those prevailing for similar work in the locality, or if employees are denied the right of collective bargaining, or if an employer shuts down his plant or dismisses his employees in order to force a wage reduction or changes in hours or working conditions. Arizona, Arkansas, Montana, and Utah have provisions that permit payment of benefits if the labor dispute is due to the employer's failure to conform to state or federal laws relating to wages, hours, or working conditions.

EXPERIENCE RATING

Selection of the sources and methods of financing the federal-state program grew chiefly out of the desire for the immediate enactment of state laws in a period of widespread unemployment. The federal unemployment tax was imposed to stimulate the enactment of state unemployment insurance laws, to raise money for the administration of the laws, and to insure that employers who contributed under a state unemployment insurance law would not suffer unfair interstate competition while the program was developing.

But the method of financing the program was also influenced by concepts taken over from workmen's compensation, which at the time were generally assumed to be applicable to unemployment insurance. This led to the inclusion in the law of provisions for experience rating.

Purpose of Experience Rating

Provisions for experience rating (originally called merit rating) established methods of adjusting an individual employer's contribution rate in accordance with some measure of his own unemployment risk. This is in contrast to adjusting all employers' contributions on some general state or national basis independent of the individual employer's experience. At the present time the federal law permits states to utilize individual employer experience rating but does not permit them to adjust rates on a flat state-wide basis.[4]

Experience rating is based on the theory that unemployment is largely within the control of individual employers and that the cost of unemployment benefits should be allocated to the particular employer responsible for it. Since the incentive of lowered tax rates under workmen's compensation laws has stimulated employers' efforts to prevent accidents, it is assumed that the same methods can be used to encourage programs for the prevention of unemployment. One effect of experience rating in the unemploy-

---

[4] During the hearings on the original Act, the House Ways and Means Committee deleted provisions for additional credit for reduced rates based on the individual employer's experience with unemployment. The Senate subsequently adopted this provision, and the House in conference concurred in its inclusion.

Controversy over the relative merits of experience rating and uniform tax contributions is still active. For opinions on both sides, see Paul A. Raushenbush, "The Wisconsin Idea: Unemployment Reserves," *Annals of the American Academy of Political and Social Science,* November, 1933; E. E. Witte, "Experience Rating and Other Forms of Incentive Taxation to Promote Employment," *Proceedings of the 34th National Conference of the National Tax Association,* 1941; Elizabeth Brandeis, "The Employment Reserve Type of Unemployment Compensation Law," *Law and Comtemporary Problems,* January, 1936; and I. M. Rubinow, *State Pool Plans and Merit Rating,* in ·*ibid.*

ment insurance program has been to emphasize the use of the tax provision to encourage employers to do everything in their power to prevent unemployment, and to ignore the problems arising out of interstate competition when different rates are applicable to employers throughout the country.

Experience Rating in Operation

At the end of 1945, experience rating was in operation in 45 states, representing more than four-fifths of all the covered workers in the country. Although experience rating was originally conceived as a device to encourage employers to stabilize employment, it has come to be more of a means for obtaining tax reductions. This is indicated by the fact that at the beginning of the program (1937), rates above the standard were provided in the experience-rating provisions of 30 of the 40 state laws, whereas at the end of 1945 only 17 of the 45 states that had adopted it had provisions for increasing the rates of employers with relatively poor employment experience.

In states with experience rating in 1945, the employer contribution rate averaged about 1.5 per cent, in contrast to the standard rate of 2.7 per cent. In that year alone, employers in these states saved 624 million dollars, or more than 40 per cent of the total amount that would have been received under the federal-state system if all states had had the normal rate. Since most states use

TABLE 35.   Effect of Experience Rating on Employer Contributions and Total Revenues for Unemployment Insurance[a]

Year	No. of States with Experience Rating	Average Employer Contribution States with Experience Rating	Average Employer Contribution All States	Reduction in Revenue as Result of Experience Rating (in Millions)	Percentage Reduction in Revenue
1941	17	2.17%	2.58%	$ 53	5%
1942	34	1.81	2.57	265	20
1943	40	1.77	2.04	404	25
1944	42	1.60	1.80	567	35
1945	45	1.50	1.60	624	41

[a] During 1939 experience rating was in effect only in Wisconsin, and in 1940 in only three additional states. Total savings to employers during these two years was about 10.5 million dollars. The above data were furnished by the federal Social Security Administration.

the amounts of benefits paid to former employees as a major element in computing an employer's index of his unemployment experience, and since benefit payments declined greatly during the war years, existing experience-rating formulas automatically resulted in reducing employer contribution rates during this period. These declines obviously were the result not of employers' efforts to stabilize employment, but of the nation's participation in the war.

Rate reductions have been granted to a steadily increasing proportion of employers eligible for rate modification. In 1941, only 55 per cent of such employers received reduced rates; by 1945, over 90 per cent had reduced rates. In 1941, the rates of 41 per cent of all rated employers were below 1.9 per cent, in contrast to more than 75 per cent of such employers in 1944.

The inverse relationship between contribution rates and the business cycle has concerned various state agencies. During 1943, ten states with experience rating (Alabama, Florida, Illinois, Iowa, Maryland, Minnesota, Missouri, Ohio, Oklahoma, and Wisconsin) enacted provisions for "war risk" contributions under which employers whose pay rolls had expanded greatly during the war were taxed at higher rates than would normally have been assigned them under the regular experience-rating provisions of their laws. Wisconsin also assessed a special rate of 0.5 of 1 per cent on all subject employers as a special post-war fund. In assessing this special tax, Wisconsin indicated a desire to build up its fund at a time when employers were best able to bear the burden so that rates would not increase as rapidly as they otherwise would when employment declined, benefit loads increased, and employers were less able to pay increased taxes.

Effect of Experience Rating on Various State Tax Rates

As long as the benefit formulas and methods of determining employer contribution rates vary from state to state, employers in the same industry with similar employment records will have different contribution rates if they happen to be located in different states. At present (1946), the rates applicable to such employers range from 0.1 of 1 per cent in the District of Columbia to 2.7 per cent in Kentucky, New Hampshire, and Oregon. Average employer tax rates differ markedly among the states, as is shown in Table 36.

TABLE 36. Average Employer Tax Rates Under Various State Experience-Rating Provisions

Average Employer Tax Rate	Number of States with Experience Rating in Operation				
	1941	1942	1943	1944	1945
All states....................	17	34	40	42	42[a]
Less than 1.0................	0	1	1	3	7
1.0–1.4.....................	2	1	7	10	11
1.5–1.9.....................	4	18	15	16	14
2.0–2.4.....................	8	12	14	12	10
2.5 and over................	3	2	3	1	0

[a] Data not available for three states: Louisiana, Michigan, and Nevada.

By and large, a greater proportion of employers in the normally stable industries such as finance, insurance, and real estate have received reduced rates than in such unstable industries as construction and mining. Within a given industry, however, there are great variations among the states. In mining, for example, 99 per cent of Alabama's rated employers, in contrast to only 19 per cent of North Carolina's, had reduced rates in 1944. In construction, 96 per cent of Texas' rated employers but only 14 per cent of North Dakota's had rate reductions. In manufacturing, nearly all of Delaware's rated employers but only about half of Idaho's received reduced rates. Similar situations exist in every industry.

TABLE 37. Proportion of Rated Employers Receiving Varying Rates in 42 States, 1944

Industry	Rates		
	Below Standard	Standard	Above Standard
Mining	72.0%	19.3%	8.7%
Construction	62.0	25.4	12.6
Manufacturing	82.4	14.0	3.6
Transportation, communication, and other public utilities	87.4	10.6	2.0
Wholesale and retail trade	87.9	10.0	2.0
Finance, insurance, and real estate	92.3	6.2	1.5
Service	84.5	12.3	3.2
Miscellaneous	24.9	24.9	7.8

EMPLOYEE CONTRIBUTIONS

The federal tax is limited to employers, and the state legislatures are left to decide whether or not a state law shall require contributions from employees. On July 1, 1946, employee contributions for unemployment insurance were required in only Alabama and New Jersey. In both states the rate is 1 per cent of wages up to $3000, except that in Alabama employee contributions are reduced if the employer's contribution is reduced because of experience rating.

At one time or another nine states collected contributions from employees for unemployment insurance: Alabama, California, Indiana, Kentucky, Louisiana, Massachusetts, New Hampshire, New Jersey, and Rhode Island. Employee contributions in Rhode Island and California at the present time are allotted to cash sickness benefits administered by the state unemployment insurance agencies.[5]

The decline in the number of states requiring employee contributions is due to several reasons. For one, up to the present the favorable financial condition of the funds has made them unnecessary. Also, employee contributions conflict with the principle of experience rating. The inclusion of such contributions indicates the "social" insurance basis of unemployment insurance and tends to make experience rating inconsistent with its major premises, namely, that it provides an incentive to employers to stabilize employment, and that it automatically results in an allocation of the cost of unemployment in the price of particular products. There is also the practical consideration that it is confusing and difficult to reduce employee contributions in relation to the reduction of the employer's contribution, whereas a flat rate for employees seems inconsistent with a varying rate for the employer.

ADMINISTRATION OF UNEMPLOYMENT INSURANCE

Under the Social Security Act, the administration of unemployment insurance rests with the states. The state governments alone

[5] Under the terms of the Social Security Act Amendments of 1946, the states are permitted to withdraw from the Federal Unemployment Trust Fund any amounts contributed by employees and to use them for cash sickness or disability benefits. See chap. 27.

deal directly with the contributors to the state program and with the beneficiaries. They keep all the records necessary to determine benefits, engage and pay the administrative personnel, determine the policies and procedures that govern them in their duties, and exercise complete administrative responsibility over their work.

Federal responsibility is vested in two agencies: the Social Security Administration and the Bureau of Internal Revenue. The latter determines what employers are subject to the Federal Unemployment Tax Act and collects this tax from such employers. The Social Security Administration has broad administrative powers to determine whether or not a state unemployment insurance law and its administration are such as to enable employers in the state to obtain credit against the federal tax. It also allocates grants to the states to meet the entire expense of administering their programs. The total amount to be used for this purpose depends in the first instance on the sums appropriated by Congress each year, but the amount allocated to any one state represents the Administration's estimate of what, within the limits of the appropriations, is necessary for the proper and efficient administration of its program. Except for certain emergency relief activities during the depression of the 1930's, unemployment insurance and the related employment service program are the only examples of complete federal assumption of costs of a wholly state-administered undertaking. In other instances in which the federal government has participated in financing state services, federal grants have been contingent upon state participation, usually on a matching basis.

Problems of Dual Administration

Our present federal-state arrangement for unemployment insurance presents some peculiar administrative problems, both for employers who pay the taxes and for the government agencies concerned with collecting and allocating the funds.

The federal government collects the federal unemployment tax from employers having eight or more employees, with certain exceptions; and each state collects any additional contributions required from other employers under its own law. Each agency—federal and state—is responsible for determining liability according to the detailed provisions of its own law, collecting taxes, keeping the necessary accounts and records, and, to a greater or lesser extent, auditing employers' pay rolls. Even if the state laws should follow the coverage provisions of the Federal Unemployment Tax Act uniformly, there would still be differences in both interpretation and decisions between federal and state authorities.

Most employers are now subject to federal contributions for old age and survivors' insurance, the federal unemployment tax, and one or more state taxes for social security purposes. Some small employers must make contributions to the federal old age and their own state unemployment insurance programs, but are not subject to the federal unemployment tax, since it is limited to employers of eight or more workers. Even when an employer is taxable by both the state and federal governments, not all his employees are necessarily covered under both laws, and the amount of wages on which the tax is based may differ because of differences in the definition of wages and the treatment of tips and gratuities.

An interstate employer may be required to report in several states on different forms and in accordance with different instructions. He is not always certain in which state a given worker is covered; he may pay contributions on an employee in one state and then have to pay in a second state for the same individual, obtaining a refund from the first state. Under experience rating, an employer may have a different tax rate in each of several states.[6] Among the states there are scores of variants in coverage provisions based on the number of employees or the amount of

---

[6] At present, an employer subject to only one state law makes four quarterly contribution and wage reports to the state or, in a few states, four quarterly contribution reports and an annual report of the wages paid each employee. Under the Federal Unemployment Tax Act he also makes an annual tax return to the Collector of Internal Revenue, on which he lists for credit his contributions under the state laws and the contributions for which he obtained additional credit because of experience rating. Simultaneously, he makes four quarterly tax and wage reports to the Collector of Internal Revenue under the Federal Insurance Contributions Act—in all, at least nine reports during the year. For interstate employers, the preparation of the annual tax returns becomes progressively more burdensome as the number of state laws to which they are subject increases. Various efforts have been made to simplify and unify the wage record problems of state agencies and the wage-reporting problems of employers. For example, a uniform definition of employment has been generally adopted which is designed to prevent the payment of contributions for a multi-state worker to two or more states and to cover him in the state where he is most likely to look for a job when he becomes unemployed.

pay rolls, or both; in the definition of agricultural labor and other excluded occupations; in the definition of "employees"; and in provisions for including subsidiary companies as a unit for the purpose of determining coverage, or for including employees of contractors or subcontractors with those of the employer who hires the contractor.

While the 100 per cent federal grant of administrative funds has undoubtedly saved many state systems from being crippled by limited state resources or appropriations, this provision raises difficult problems for both federal and state agencies. It is the responsibility of the Social Security Administration to determine the amount of funds "necessary" for 51 different jurisdictions of different sizes with differing laws and different administrative organization, methods, and procedures. Some states have special provisions for seasonal workers. Most states have experience rating provisions; others do not. Among those that have such provisions, there is wide diversity in the records and personnel required to administer them.

Broad variations in administrative costs result from differences such as these, even in jurisdictions with similar statutory provisions and comparable work loads. Since the state bears none of the cost of administration, it lacks the customary incentive to economy. The federal agency, on the other hand, is required to grant the amount necessary for the proper and efficient administration of the state law without the authority to determine economical and efficient operating methods. Nevertheless, to carry out its responsibilities for allocating federal funds, the Social Security Administration must establish some standards to govern the manner and object of the expenditure of federal funds. In applying fiscal and business management standards in any state, recognition is given to the practice generally prevailing in other departments of that state. For states that have no "prevailing practice," the federal Administration has established limitations on the amount used for certain purposes, with the result that a state's employment security agencies are frequently subject to standards that are not required for other departments of its government. Inevitably the imposition of such standards has caused irritation and difficulty, since they seem to dictate the manner of state administration.

MODIFICATION OF THE EXISTING PROGRAM

The state unemployment insurance programs today are far more effective in many respects than those under the initial state laws. Nevertheless, it is generally agreed that there are important limitations in the protection afforded American workers, particularly in a period of serious unemployment. Some of the present defects of the unemployment insurance program could be removed without modifying the existing federal-state system, either by state legislative action alone, or by the combined action of the states and the federal government. Certain other shortcomings could be remedied by changing the existing type of system, but still keeping it on a federal-state basis. The most far-reaching recommendation for change is that a single national system be substituted for a state-by-state system.

State Versus National System

Advocates of a national system of unemployment insurance believe that only such a system can cope with the problems caused by the mobility of population which has characterized economic development in the United States, by averting the need for complicated and costly provisions for workers who move across state lines. A national system could insure that workers and employers in like circumstances will receive like treatment, regardless of the state in which they are located, and could both free employers from the interstate competition which results from differences in contribution rates and eliminate the duplication of reporting. At the same time payments to beneficiaries, since they are based on prior earnings, would be adjusted automatically to differences in prevailing wage levels in various parts of the country.

Those who advocate a national system of unemployment insurance also cite general economic arguments to support their point of view. In their opinion, the depression of the 1930's and World War II demonstrated that mass unemployment and full employment are no respecters of state lines. In the years ahead, national policy on such matters as reciprocal trade agreements, taxation, and interest rates will affect levels of employment and unemployment throughout the country. Their major argument is that neither single states nor employers can control the underlying forces that make for full employment or, conversely, for long lines of jobless outside employment offices. While the character of the risk of unemployment differs greatly from state to state, in accordance with the state's natural resources and its type of economic development, a national system of unemployment insurance, coordinated with national economic policy, would place the resources of the whole country behind a united program of protection for all the nation's workers and employers.

A number of groups, including most state administrators of unemployment insurance and employers' organizations, are strongly in favor of continuing the state-by-state operation of unemployment insurance. They argue that this system affords opportunity for the various states to experiment with different types of provisions, thus permitting any state to adopt the one that proves most effective and best suited to its particular needs. They also maintain that a state program can be more responsive to the interests and wishes of the persons immediately concerned than is possible under national administration. In their opinion, unemployment is a local as well as a national problem, and it must be handled in each individual case on a local basis. They believe that there is no evidence that unemployment insurance benefits would be more adequate on a national than on a state basis.

In response to these arguments, advocates of a national system of unemployment insurance claim that the experience during the first decade of the program has not shown wide or effective use by the states of their opportunities for individual experimentation, and that changes in the state laws have had little consistent relationship to particular economic or other conditions within the state or to improvements demonstrated elsewhere. Moreover, they do not believe that operations under a state program are adapted more closely to the interests of the population served than would be the case under a national system with decentralized administration, such as exists in the operation of the old age and survivors' insurance program.

Most of the controversy between advocates of a state system and those who favor a national system arises out of differences of opinion concerning the desirability of experience rating. Almost universally, those who favor a national system are opposed to experience rating, whereas those who favor the state system also favor experience rating. Although the controversy over this point is a separate issue, from a practical point of view it is impossible to disregard it in discussions of unemployment insurance. If, because of other developments, experience rating should cease to be an issue, it is likely that much of the existing controversy on the respective merits of a state versus a national system would be settled.

Liberalization of Benefits and Coverage

There are other basic differences in addition to the question of a state versus a national system of unemployment insurance. It probably is to be expected that in a program so directly related to such dynamic problems as employment and unemployment there is as yet no general agreement on such questions as the amount and duration of benefits and the methods of financing unemployment insurance.

The provisions in the various state laws are constantly being changed and, as indicated previously, there are great differences in them. At the present time, the Social Security Administration is recommending that benefits be payable for as long as 26 weeks to any worker who is eligible for them and who continues to be unemployed; that the maximum weekly benefit be at least $25 a week, including provision for dependents, for workers whose prior earnings entitle them to the maximum; that the waiting period be only one week in a benefit year; that definitions of good cause for leaving voluntarily and refusing suitable work include good personal reasons, as well as those attributable to the job or the employer; and that disqualification for these causes and for discharge or misconduct entail merely postponement of benefits for not more than four weeks, without cancellation of benefit rights or reduction of the amount.

The problem of extending coverage under unemployment insurance to all persons who work for a living is undoubtedly more difficult than it is under federal old age and survivors' insurance. Small firms now excluded by federal and some state laws could easily be included by amendment of the laws; many states already cover all small firms, and their experience indicates that such firms can be covered. Coverage of non-profit institutions would not raise any administrative problems. Coverage of such groups as agricultural laborers and domestic employees raises difficult problems of determining when such persons are "unemployed," and it is doubtful whether the existing eligibility and benefit provisions would be satisfactory for them without modification. The extensive interstate movement of large numbers of migratory agricultural laborers would be difficult to treat simply and equitably on a state-by-state basis.

With respect to financing unemployment insurance, the important question is whether the program should be financed entirely from employer contributions or shared by contributions from employees and general tax revenues. In view of the fact that under a majority of the state programs the financing of unemployment insurance is connected with experience rating, there is little likelihood of a basic change in one aspect without a change in the other. Organized labor has taken the position that if a single national system is established without experience rating, it would be possible to have employees contribute equally with employers for unemployment insurance. The rate of contribution to finance unemployment insurance on a long-run basis is still largely an undetermined matter. Judging from the experience of the past ten years and employment prospects for the immediate future, the present standard 3 per cent contribution is more than sufficient to finance the existing level of benefits for a substantial period of time.

RAILROAD UNEMPLOYMENT INSURANCE

Under the Social Security Act of 1935 railroad employees were covered by the 3 per cent federal tax against which employers were allowed certain credits for contributions paid into state unemployment insurance funds. In 1938 Congress passed a law which withdrew these employees from the state systems and placed them under a single federal unemployment insurance law. In 1946, as explained in Chapter 27, the definition of unemployment in the law was broadened to include unemployment resulting from temporary personal disability.

Although the provisions of the railroad unemployment insurance law are similar in many respects to most state unemployment insurance laws, there are several major differences. There is no experience rating for adjusting railroad employers' contributions such as exists under most state laws for other employers, nor is there any employee contribution such as is provided in a few state laws. The railroad law, in effect, provides benefits up to a maximum of 26 weeks, with a minimum weekly benefit of $8.75 and a maximum of $25. The amounts payable are determined at flat rates per day in accordance with the individual's annual earnings.

TABLE 38. Benefits Under the Railroad Unemployment Insurance Law, 1946

Annual Railroad Wages	Unemployment Benefit		Maximum in Benefit Year
	Daily	Weekly	
$ 150 to $ 199.99	$1.75	$ 8.75	$227.50
200 to 474.99	2.00	10.00	260.00
475 to 749.99	2.25	11.25	292.50
750 to 999.99	2.50	12.50	325.00
1000 to 1299.99	3.00	15.00	390.00
1300 to 1599.99	3.50	17.50	455.00
1600 to 1999.99	4.00	20.00	520.00
2000 to 2499.99	4.50	22.50	585.00
2500 and over	5.00	25.00	650.00

The railroad unemployment insurance law contains several provisions with regard to qualifications and disqualifications for receiving benefits which are not found customarily in state laws. Among other provisions, the railroad law specifies that no work shall be deemed suitable, and benefits shall not be denied a worker for refusing to accept work, if: (1) Acceptance of the work would require him to engage in activities in violation of the law or which, by reason of their being in violation of reasonable requirements of the constitution, by-laws, or similar regulations of a bona fide labor organization of which he is a member, would subject him to expulsion from such labor organization; or (2) acceptance of the work would subject him to loss of substantial seniority rights under any collective bargaining agreement.

SELECTED REFERENCES

Annual Reports of the Social Security Board, Government Printing Office, Washington.

Atkinson, Raymond C., *The Federal Role in Unemployment Compensation Administration,* Social Science Research Council, Washington, 1941.

Bigge, G. E., "Unemployment Insurance," in *Social Work Year Book 1947.*

Gray, Herman, *Should Unemployment Insurance Be Federalized?* American Enterprise Association, Inc., New York, 1946.

Meriam, Lewis, *Relief and Social Security,* Brookings Institution, Washington, 1946.

National Planning Association, *Joint Statement on Social Security by Agriculture, Business and Labor,* Washington, 1944.

National Resources Planning Board, *Security, Work, and Relief Policies* (78th Congress, 1st Session, House of Representatives, Document No. 128, Part 3) Government Printing Office, Washington, 1943.

Social Security, A Statement by the Social Security Committees of American Life Convention, Life Insurance Association of America, National Association of Life Underwriters, Chicago, 1945.

Social Security in America: The Factual Background of the Social Security Act as Summarized from Staff Reports to the Committee on Economic Security, Government Printing Office, Washington, 1937.

"Unemployment Compensation," *Yale Law Journal,* Vol. 55, No. 1, 1945.

U. S. Congress, *Issues in Social Security: A Report to the Committee on Ways and Means of the House of Representatives by the Committee's Social Security Technical Staff Established Pursuant to H. Res. 204, 79th Cong., 1st Sess.,* Government Printing Office, Washington, 1946.

26

WORKMEN'S COMPENSATION

INSURANCE AGAINST DISABILITY INCURRED FROM INDUSTRIAL HAZards is the oldest form of social security in this country. Its broad title, workmen's compensation, is evidence that when the program was initiated early in this century there was little thought or expectation that other forms of social insurance for workers would be adopted.

Workmen's compensation laws are designed to give an injured worker prompt medical care and money payments at the cost of the employer, and with a minimum of inconvenience to the worker. Before these laws were passed the only recourse an injured worker had was court appeal, and if he sued his employer for damages he had to prove that the employer was negligent. The employer, on the other hand, had as his defense contributory negligence, the assumption of risk, and the fellow-servant rule. The court remedy was slow, costly, and uncertain. Few cases were ever won by the workmen, and the great majority of industrial injuries and deaths were never brought to the courts.

Under the compensation law, the question of fault or blame for the accident is not raised, since the cost of work injuries is considered part of the expense of production and most employers are insured for the amounts paid. Injured workers are thus spared the difficulties and delays of court procedure.

DEVELOPMENT OF WORKMEN'S COMPENSATION LAWS

Late in the nineteenth century, the mounting toll of work accidents caused by the rapid mechanizing of industry focused attention on the plight of the injured workers, who were seldom able to recover damages for their disabilities and often became charges upon public or private charity. The first legislation providing benefits for work injuries in this country was enacted in Maryland in 1902, but this law was declared unconstitutional after less than two years' operation on the ground that it deprived both the employer and the employee of trial by jury and conferred judicial functions upon an executive officer. In 1908 the federal government passed a compensation law covering certain of its employees.[1] The following year Montana enacted a law to cover coal miners. Although this law provided for compulsory employer and employee payment of the tax, it permitted the injured worker to ignore the compensation provisions and sue the employer under common law. The state court declared the law unconstitutional because of this double obligation upon the employer. In 1910 New York passed a comprehensive law without the common-law liability feature, but it also was declared invalid by the highest court in that state.

In spite of these adverse judicial decisions, 10 states enacted compensation laws in 1911, and 20 more, in addition to Alaska, Puerto Rico, and Hawaii, did so during the following five years.

In 1917 all doubts as to the constitutionality of workmen's compensation laws were removed when the United States Supreme Court in a series of decisions upheld the three prevailing types of laws: the compulsory, the elective, and the compulsory with an exclusive state fund.[2] During the next two years, eight more states enacted compensation laws and many of the earlier laws were strengthened by extending their coverage and liberalizing their benefits. Workmen's compensation legislation suffered the same fate as other kinds of labor legislation during the 1920's; only two new state laws, one for the District of Columbia, and one for longshoremen were enacted. During the 1930's all the remaining

---

[1] Prior to the passage of this act it was only by special act of Congress that a federal employee could recover compensation for injuries. This first law was very limited in its coverage; more adequate laws for federal employees were enacted after 1916.

[2] *N. Y. Central Railroad Co.* v. *White*, 243 U. S. 188 (1917); *Mountain Timber Co.* v. *State of Washington*, 243 U. S. 219 (1917); *Hawkins* v. *Bleakly*, 243 U. S. 210 (1917).

states but one passed compensation legislation; Mississippi was the only state which had no such law as late as 1946.

Purpose of Workmen's Compensation

Sponsors of workmen's compensation legislation in the earlier years cited five results which they hoped such legislation would accomplish. More recently, two additional goals have been sought. In all their variations, workmen's compensation laws in general are designed to:

1. Furnish certain, prompt, and reasonable compensation to the victims of work accidents and their dependents.

2. Free the courts from the delay, cost, and criticism incident to the great mass of personal injury litigation heretofore burdening them.

3. Relieve public and private charity of much of the destitution due to uncompensated industrial accidents.

4. Eliminate economic waste in the payments to unnecessary lawyers, witnesses, and casualty corporations, and the expense and time loss due to trials and appeals.

5. Supplant concealment of fault in accidents by a spirit of frank study of causes, thereby lessening the number of preventable accidents and reducing the cost and suffering thereunder.

6. Provide for immediate and adequate medical treatment when the injury occurs.

7. Provide for rehabilitation of workers who, because of their injuries, are no longer able to follow their former occupations.

COVERAGE OF WORKMEN'S COMPENSATION LAWS [3]

In spite of the fact that practically all the states as well as the federal government have compensation laws, less than 50 per cent of the wage earners of the country are now protected by these laws. This is due to coverage limitations in the laws and to the

[3] All the statistical data on workmen's compensation in this chapter are from *State Workmen's Compensation Laws as of June 1, 1946*, Report No. 78, published by the Division of Labor Standards, U. S. Department of Labor, Washington.

adoption, by more than half the states, of an elective rather than a compulsory system.

Elective and Compulsory Coverage

Compensation laws may be classed as compulsory or elective, depending upon the degree of constraint to which employers are subjected to accept the provisions of the law. A compulsory law is binding upon every employer and employee within its scope; there is no choice. Under an elective act, employers and employees have the option of either accepting or rejecting it. In case the employer rejects, the customary common-law defenses in injury litigation are usually removed; if the employee rejects, the workmen's compensation principle of liability of the employer without regard to fault is not applicable to an action for damages. In practice, employees rarely reject coverage except where employers have urged it or made it a condition of employment.

As in shown in Table 39, 26 of the workmen's compensation laws are compulsory and 27 are elective. Many of the elective laws are compulsory as to some employments, such as "hazardous" occupations; on the other hand, some of the compulsory laws are elective or voluntary as to employers who have very few employees.

Exempted Occupations and Industries

The largest group of wage earners deprived of workmen's compensation protection by specific exclusion in state laws is agricultural workers; other specific exclusions apply to domestic servants, casual workers, and employees of charitable institutions. Exclusion of farm labor is due mainly to the opposition of farmers to compensation coverage. A step toward inclusion is the coverage, in some states, of mechanized or power operations, especially when the operation is for gain and not carried out in the course of a farmer's own production routine. The California law is applicable to a farmer whose pay roll has been more than $500 in the preceding year unless he elects not to be covered.

In most of the states, farmers may voluntarily come under the compensation law by insuring and posting notice of acceptance; but in Alabama and Oklahoma the exclusion is such that only liability, not workmen's compensation insurance, can be obtained.

TABLE 39.   Coverage and Insurance Requirements of Workmen's Compensation Laws in 1946[4]

States	Coverage		Insurance Requirements		
	Employees Exempted Who Have Fewer Than[a]	Occupational Diseases Covered	Compulsory or Elective[b]	State Funds, Exclusive or Competitive	Private Companies or Self-Insurance
Alabama	8 employees	None	Elective	....	Either
Alaska	3 employees	None	Compulsory	....	Either
Arizona	3 employees	35	Compulsory	Competitive	Either
Arkansas	5 employees	15	Compulsory	....	Either
California	....	Full coverage	Compulsory	Competitive	Either
Colorado	4 employees	21	Elective	Competitive	Either
Connecticut	5 employees	Full coverage	Elective	Competitive	Either
Delaware	3 employees	16	Compulsory	....	Either
District of Columbia	....	Full coverage	Compulsory	....	Either
Florida	3 employees	Full coverage	Elective	....	Either
Georgia	10 employees	14	Elective	....	Either
Hawaii	....	Full coverage	Compulsory	....	Either
Idaho	....	11	Compulsory	Competitive	Either
Illinois	....	Full coverage	Compulsory	....	Either
Indiana	....	Full coverage	Compulsory	....	Either
Iowa	....	None	Elective	....	Either
Kansas	5 employees	None	Elective	....	Either
Kentucky	3 employees	Silicosis & gas	Elective	....	Either
Louisiana	....	None	Compulsory	....	Either
Maine	6 employees	13	Elective	....	Either
Maryland	....	39	Compulsory	Competitive	Either
Massachusetts	4 employees	Full coverage	Compulsory	....	Either

[a] There are no exemptions in 24 laws so far as size of company is concerned. Most of the states which exempt small employers permit them voluntarily to accept compensation coverage. In some states the exemptions do not apply to certain hazardous occupations.

[b] Some elective laws are compulsory for certain occupations and some of the compulsory laws are elective for employers with a very few employees.

[4] Adopted from Tables 1, 2, and 3 in *State Workmen's Compensation Laws as of June 1, 1946*.

TABLE 39. Coverage and Insurance Requirements of Workmen's Compensation Laws in 1946 (*Cont.*).

States	Coverage		Insurance Requirements		
	Employees Exempted Who Have Fewer Than [a]	Occupational Diseases Covered	Compulsory or Elective [b]	State Funds, Exclusive or Competitive	Private Companies or Self-Insurance
Michigan	8 employees	Full coverage	Compulsory	Competitive	Either
Minnesota	....	Full coverage	Compulsory	....	Either
Mississippi	....	None	....	....	....
Missouri	11 employees	Full coverage	Elective	Competitive	Either
Montana	....	None	Elective	....	Either
Nebraska	....	Full coverage	Elective	....	Either
Nevada	....	None	Elective	Exclusive	....
New Hampshire	5 employees	None	Elective	....	Self-insurance
New Jersey	....	13	Elective	....	Either
New Mexico	4 employees	30	Elective	....	Either
New York	4 employees	Full coverage	Compulsory	Competitive	Either
North Carolina	5 employees	25	Elective	....	Either
North Dakota	....	Full coverage	Compulsory	Exclusive	....
Ohio	3 employees	Full coverage	Compulsory	Exclusive	Self-insurance
Oklahoma	2 employees	None	Compulsory	Competitive	Either
Oregon	....	Full coverage	Elective	Exclusive	....
Pennsylvania	....	12	Elective	Competitive	Either
Puerto Rico	3 employees	17	Compulsory	Exclusive	....
Rhode Island	4 employees	31	Elective	....	Either
South Carolina	15 employees	None	Elective	....	Either
South Dakota	....	None	Elective	....	Either
Tennessee	5 employees	None	Elective	....	Either
Texas	3 employees	None	Elective	....	Private companies

[a] There are no exemptions in 24 laws so far as size of company is concerned. Most of the states which exempt small employers permit them voluntarily to accept compensation coverage. In some states the exemptions do not apply to certain hazardous occupations.

[b] Some elective laws are compulsory for certain occupations and some of the compulsory laws are elective for employers with a very few employees.

TABLE 39. Coverage and Insurance Requirements of Workmen's Compensation Laws in 1946 (Cont.)

States	Coverage		Insurance Requirements		
	Employees Exempted Who Have Fewer Than[a]	Occupational Diseases Covered	Compulsory or Elective[b]	State Funds, Exclusive or Competitive	Private Companies or Self-Insurance
Utah..............	3 employees	27	Compulsory	Competitive	Either
Vermont...........	8 employees	None	Elective	....	Either
Virginia...........	7 employees	46—all permissible	Compulsory	....	Either
Washington........	....	Full coverage	Compulsory	Exclusive	....
West Virginia......	....	Silicosis only	Elective	Exclusive	Self-insurance
Wisconsin.........	3 employees	Full coverage	Compulsory	Exclusive	Either
Wyoming..........	....	None	Compulsory	Exclusive	....
United States:					
Longshoremen's Act...	....	Full coverage	Compulsory	....	Either
Civil employees......	....	Full coverage	Compulsory	c	....

[a] There are no exemptions in 24 laws so far as size of company is concerned. In some states the exemptions do not apply to certain hazardous occupations. Most of the states which exempt small employers permit them voluntarily to accept compensation coverage.

[b] Some elective laws are compulsory for certain occupations and some of the compulsory laws are elective for employers with a very few employees.

c By direct appropriation of Congress.

The laws of Ohio and Puerto Rico provide compulsory coverage for agricultural labor for employers with three or more workmen; the Hawaii law is compulsory for all agricultural employees.

In general, the legal obstacles to the inclusion of agriculture apply also to domestic service. Examples of steps toward workmen's compensation for domestic servants are the California provision covering employees working over 52 hours a week and the New York provision covering domestic servants employed a minimum of 48 hours per week in cities of 40,000 or more. The laws of Connecticut and New Jersey cover domestic service, but the Connecticut law is applicable only to employers of five or more servants, and in New Jersey the employer is not required to insure. Casual employments are excluded from coverage under all the workmen's compensation laws except in Alaska, Kansas, Kentucky, Louisiana, Maine, New Hampshire, New York, Oklahoma, Oregon, Washington, and West Virginia, and under the Longshoremen's Act. The term "casual" employment is not readily defined but it generally refers to employment which is not usual in the course of the employer's business, that is, not regular or periodical.

Two important groups of wage earners not covered by any type of workmen's compensation are railroad workers and seamen. Although state legislation is impracticable for these two groups, federal legislation would no doubt be favorably considered if these workers urged its enactment. Up to the present time, these groups have preferred to recover damages for work injuries on their ability to prove negligence on the part of their employers[5] rather than accept payments prescribed by compensation laws.

Numerical Exemptions

In addition to the exclusion of designated industries, there are other restrictions which deprive substantial numbers of workers

---

[5] The federal Employer's Liability Act of 1908 for railroad workers, and the Seamen's Act of 1915 and the Merchant Marine Act of 1920, strip the employers of their customary common-law defenses, such as the fellow-servant rule, and enable railroad workers and seamen to recover damages upon proof of negligence on the part of any agents or employees of the employer, or when any prescribed safety provisions have been violated, regardless of whether or not the injured person was guilty of some negligence himself. See Max D. Kossoris and Joseph Zisman, "Workmen's Compensation for Seamen," *Monthly Labor Review,* June, 1946.

from receiving compensation when disabled in the course of their employment. Some of the state laws limit their coverage to so-called "hazardous" employments, and often employers having fewer than a specified number of employees are exempted.

In 28 states, Alaska, and Puerto Rico, employers of less than a stipulated number of employees are exempt from compensation coverage requirements, although most of the acts permit voluntary acceptance. As is shown in Table 39, the number of employees for exemption ranges from 2 to as many as 10 or 15, although most acts specify from 3 to 5. In some of these laws the numerical exemption does not apply to certain occupations such as mining, building construction, logging, and other especially hazardous employments.

Hazardous Employments

In 12 states (Illinois, Kansas, Kentucky, Louisiana, Maryland, Montana, New Mexico, New York, Oklahoma, Oregon, Washington, and Wyoming) the compensation laws apply mainly to listed "hazardous" or "extra-hazardous" employments. The use of these terms was an expedient adopted in the early days of workmen's compensation legislation to meet the risk that such laws might be held unconstitutional by the courts. However, it has long been known that this device is not needed to assure constitutionality, and its retention in some states is a major obstacle to the wide coverage of workers.

In a few of the states with this type of coverage the list of hazardous industries is comprehensive. In New York it is so complete that most employments are covered. However, even in the states where it is fairly complete, difficulties of interpretation arise because the laws in some cases contain both specified and general provisions.

INJURIES AND DISEASES COVERED

Compensation laws are limited, not only as to persons and employments included, but also as to injuries covered. No state holds an employer responsible for every injury received by his employees. Some injuries are compensable and others are not. Workmen's compensation laws are not designed to provide general ac-

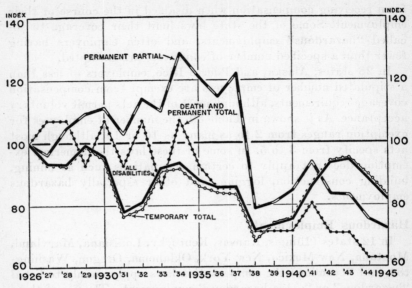

Fig. 36. *Industrial Injury Frequency Rates in Manufacturing, 1926–1945. 1926 = 100. (Source: U. S. Bureau of Labor Statistics.)*

cident and health insurance and, if strictly interpreted, cover only disabilities received in the course of employment and as a natural consequence of it. The usual definition of a compensable disability is one "arising out of and in the course of employment."

Occupational Diseases

Most of the compensation acts contain specific limitations of one or two kinds, the first relating to the conditions under which the injury was sustained, and the second relating to the nature of the injury, that is, whether sudden and violent or gradual in onset and effects. Sudden and violent injuries are usually called injuries by accident, or traumatic injuries. An industrial injury that is gradual in onset is classified as a disease. The latter is covered by the compensation act in some jurisdictions, but in others it is not compensable. However, the distinction between the terms "accident" and "injury" has been blurred by varying interpretations. For example, lead poisoning has sometimes been construed to be an "accidental" injury. Such interpretations have been made in applying the law to individual cases rather than establishing a general rule.

An increasing number of states are mitigating this confusion by covering specific occupational diseases; others go further by providing "blanket" coverage and broadening the definition of "injury" to include any mental or physical harm to an employee caused by accident or disease growing out of and incidental to his employment. According to their 1946 laws, as shown in Table 39, the laws of 16 states, the District of Columbia, Hawaii, and the two federal laws, covered all occupational diseases; 17 other states and Puerto Rico covered a varying number of listed diseases; and 11 states (including Mississippi, which has no workmen's compensation law of any kind) had no provision for occupational diseases.

BENEFIT PAYMENTS

The benefit scale is the heart of any compensation system, for upon its adequacy rests the injured worker's chance for decent maintenance during helplessness, and the protection of his dependent family from destitution or a lowered living standard. The amount of money that injured workers receive under the different acts is determined by the rate, usually a percentage of the wage; the term or period of payment; the weekly maximum; and the aggregate maximum. The amount and method of payment also differ according to the type of injury. The acts prescribe certain payments in case of death and in case of permanent total disability, and also have specific provisions covering permanent partial disability and temporary total disability.

Waiting Period

All the states except Oregon provide that during a specified period of time immediately following the injury, compensation shall not be paid. This "waiting time" ranges from a minimum of one day to a maximum of ten days, with the majority of the states requiring a seven-day waiting period. Most of the laws provide that if the disability continues for a certain number of weeks, the payment of compensation is retroactive to the date of injury. The waiting period relates only to cash compensation; both medical and hospital care are provided immediately when needed.

Weekly Compensation Based on Wages

Except in a few states which pay fixed sums, the scale of weekly compensation is based upon a percentage of the worker's earnings. Among the different states, payments to disabled persons vary from one-half to two-thirds of their wages; Wisconsin pays as much as 70 per cent. In case of death, about the same amounts are paid to widows with children, but where there are no dependent children the payments are usually less; in some states the equivalent of only a third of the deceased's wages is paid to a childless widow.

Workers or their survivors do not necessarily receive the amount indicated by these percentages, for in most states there is a limitation on the maximum amount of weekly benefits; in some cases it varies with the number of the workers' dependents. Only two states (California and Connecticut) provide a maximum as high as $30 a week; in 18 others the maximum is less than $20 a week. Although minimum amounts are also provided, this floor under compensation payments in a majority of the states is ineffective if the actual wages of the disabled person were less than the specified minimum. As is indicated in Table 40, most of the specified minimum weekly benefits are much less than is required for bare subsistence; in cases of prolonged disability at least, the workers and their families must seek assistance elsewhere.

Medical Benefits

All the compensation acts require that medical aid be furnished to injured employees. In the early legislation this provision was narrowly restricted as to the monetary cost or the period of treatment, or both. In the later development of the acts such absolute restrictions have been changed in many cases, either by providing for unlimited benefits or by authorizing benefits in addition to the initial maximum upon the approval of the administrative authority. Forty-two acts require the employer to furnish artificial limbs and other appliances.

Death Benefits

Methods for determining compensation for death vary considerably and do not in all cases depend upon the fact that the deceased was a source of support to his legal beneficiaries. Most of the compensation laws base death benefits on the average weekly wages of the deceased workman, but in Oregon, Washington, West Virginia, and Wyoming a flat pension is paid. Oklahoma pays no death benefits. The Arizona, Nevada, New York, North Dakota, Oregon, Washington, West Virginia laws, and the United States Civil Employees' Act include provisions for benefits to be paid to a widow for life, or until remarriage, and in the case of children until a specified age is reached. The other states limit the period or total amount of payments. In a majority of states death benefits are limited to payment over a specified period ranging from 260 to 600 weeks, but in some cases payments to children continue until they reach 16 or 18 years of age. Some of these states, as well as several others which have no time limitations, limit the maximum amount which may be paid. The total maximum amounts range from $3500 in Puerto Rico and Vermont to $9000 in Alaska.

Permanent Total Disability

In 16 states[6] and also under the federal act for compensating injuries to civil employees, life benefits are paid for permanent total disability. In the other states the payments are limited as to time or amount, or both. The time periods range from 260 to 1000 weeks, and the money limitations from $5000 to $12,000. The federal Civil Employees' Act, and also the laws of Arizona, Hawaii, and Nevada, provide additional payments for an attendant if one is required.

In some states the payments are different for single and married persons, with additional amounts for dependent children. For example, in Idaho the maximum weekly payment for a single employee is $14, whereas a married employee may receive $16, with $1 per week additional for each dependent child subject to a total maximum of $20 per week.

---

[6] Arizona, California, Colorado, Idaho, Illinois, Massachusetts, Missouri, Nebraska, Nevada, New York, North Dakota, Ohio, Oregon, Washington, West Virginia, Wisconsin.

Second Injuries

When an employee has sustained an injury involving the loss of a bodily member and loses another as a result of a second industrial injury, he may become permanently and totally disabled, thus increasing disproportionately the amount of workmen's compensation to be paid. All the compensation laws except those of Alabama, Louisiana, New Hampshire, Vermont, and the United States Civil Employees' Act contain provisions regarding the payment of compensation in such cases.

Some of the laws limit the amount paid the worker to the usual award that would be paid for an injury of the type last received, regardless of the actual disability resulting from the combined injuries. But under more advanced legislation, payment is made for the final disability resulting from the combined injuries. However, if the cost of such compensation is imposed upon the latest employer, handicapped persons may find it difficult to obtain employment. To meet such problems, "second-injury funds" have been created, so that if a second injury occurs the employer has to pay only for the last one, yet the employee is compensated for the disability resulting from the combined injuries; the remainder of the award is paid from the fund.

Permanent Partial Disability

Permanent partial disabilities are classified as specific or schedule injuries, such as the loss, or the loss of use, of an arm or finger, and "non-schedule" injuries or those of a more general nature, as, for example, disability caused by injury to the head or back. The measure of such compensation is usually a stated number of weeks, but under the laws of Alaska, Washington, and Wyoming the payments are fixed sums, and in California they are based upon degrees of total disability.

The laws of 45 states and also those of the District of Columbia, Hawaii, Puerto Rico, and the United States Longshoremen's Act have established schedules stating the number of weeks during which compensation shall be paid for specified injuries. The principles underlying this arrangement are that it is to the advantage of the worker to know definitely what aid to depend upon after an injury, and that it will encourage him to adjust himself to his handicap and recover his place in industry within a given

TABLE 40. Workmen's Compensation Benefits for Temporary Total Disabilities, June 1, 1946[7]

State	Maximum Percentage of Wages	Maximum Weekly Payment	Minimum Weekly Payment	Time Limit	Amount Limit[a]
Alabama	65	$18	$5 (actual wage if less)	300 weeks	$ 5,400
Alaska	65			Period of disability	
Arizona	65			433 weeks	
Arkansas	65	$20	$7	450 weeks	7,000
California	61¾	$30	$6.50	240 weeks	6,000
Colorado	50	$14	$5	Period of disability	
Connecticut	50	$30	$7	520 weeks	15,600
Delaware	60	$21	$8 (actual wage if less)	500 weeks	10,500
District of Columbia	66⅔	$25	do	Period of disability	7,500
Florida	60	$22	do	350 weeks	5,000
Georgia	50	$20	$4 (actual wage if less)	...do	7,000
Hawaii	66⅔	$25	$8 (actual wage if less)	Period of disability	7,500
Idaho	60	$14; $16 for married employee, plus $1 for each child, maximum $20.	$8; $10 for employee with children.	400 weeks; thereafter $8 per week.	
Illinois	65	$18; $19.20 if 2 children; $21.60 if 3; and $24 if 4 or more children.	$9.	Period of disability	6,600
Indiana	55	$20.08	$11 (actual wage if less)	500 weeks	7,500
Iowa	60	$18	$8 (actual wage if less)	300 weeks	5,400
Kansas	60	$18	$6	416 weeks	7,488
Kentucky	65	$18	$5	520 weeks	9,000
Louisiana	65	$20	$3 (actual wage if less)	300 weeks	6,000
Maine	66⅔	$21	$7	500 weeks	7,500
Maryland	66⅔	$23	$10 (actual wage if less)	312 weeks	3,750

[a] Total maximum payments computed where not stipulated by law.
[7] U. S. Department of Labor, Division of Labor Standards.

TABLE 40. Workmen's Compensation Benefits for Temporary Total Disabilities, June 1, 1946 (*Cont.*)

State	Maximum Percentage of Wages	Maximum Weekly Payment	Minimum Weekly Payment	Time Limit	Amount Limit[a]
Massachusetts	66⅔	$25; plus $2.50 for each dependent; total benefits limited to weekly wage.	$15 (actual wage if less)	Period of disability	$10,000
Michigan	66⅔	$21	$10	500 weeks	10,500
Minnesota	66⅔	$24	$10 (actual wage if less)	300 weeks	7,200
Missouri	66⅔	$20	$6 (actual wage if less)	400 weeks	8,000
Montana	66⅔	$15; $17 if one dependent; $18 if 2; $19 if 3; $20 if 4; $21 if 5 or more dependents.	$8	300 weeks	6,300
Nebraska	66⅔	$18	$6 (actual wage if less)	...do...	5,400
Nevada	66⅔	$18.46, plus $2.31 for total dependents residing in the United States.	$6.92	433 weeks	8,000
New Hampshire	50	$21	$3	300 weeks	6,300
New Jersey	66⅔	$25	$10	...do...	7,500
New Mexico	60	$18	$10 (actual wage if less)	550 weeks	9,900
New York	66⅔	$28	$12 (actual wage if less)	Period of disability	5,000
North Carolina	60	$21	$7	400 weeks	6,000
North Dakota	66⅔	$20, plus $2 for each child under 18, maximum $30.	$9	Period of disability	......
Ohio	66⅔	$24.50	$10 (actual wage if less)	312 weeks	4,200
Oklahoma	66⅔	$21	...do...	300 weeks	6,300
Oregon	66⅔	$15; $17.31 if married; $19.61 if one child; $21.92 if 2 children; $24.23 if 3 children; $26.54 if 4 or more children.	$6.92 (actual wage if less)	Period of disability	......

a Total maximum payments computed where not stipulated by law.

State	Maximum Percentage of Wages	Maximum Weekly Payment	Minimum Weekly Payment	Time Limit	Amount Limit[a]
Pennsylvania	66⅔	$20	$10 (actual wage if not under $5)	500 weeks	$10,000
Puerto Rico	50	$15	$3	104 weeks	1,560
Rhode Island	60	$20	$12	1,000 weeks	12,000
South Carolina	60	$25	$5	500 weeks	6,000
South Dakota	55	$15	$7.50 (actual wage if less)	312 weeks	4,680
Tennessee	60	$18	$7 (actual wage if less)	300 weeks	5,400
Texas	60	$20	$7	401 weeks	8,020
Utah	60	$22.50 plus 5 per cent for each child (not to exceed 5).	$10 (actual wage if less)	313 weeks	8,500
Vermont	50	$20	$10 (actual wage if less)	260 weeks	5,200
Virginia	60	$20	$6	500 weeks	7,800
Washington		$11.54; $13.85 for married employee plus $3.46 for youngest child; $2.31 for next child; $1.73 for each additional child.[b]		Period of disability	
West Virginia	66⅔	$18	$10	156 weeks	2,808
Wisconsin	70	$25.90	$8.75	Period of disability	
Wyoming		$12.69; $15.23 for married employee, plus $2.54 for each child; total maximum $27.92[c]		do	
United States:					
Civil employees	66⅔	$26.92[c]	$18.46	do	
Longshoremen	66⅔	$25	$8 (actual wage if less)	do	7,500

[a] Total maximum payments computed where not stipulated by law.
[b] Special schedule of monthly payments for first 6 months of disability for married or widowed employee ranging from $22.50 for childless woman whose husband is not an invalid, to $75 for married workman or widow with two children, plus $7.50 for each additional child. Additional allowance for constant attendant if necessary.
[c] Additional compensation for constant attendant if necessary.

period of time. Moreover, there are federal-state provisions for "rehabilitation" in the form of retraining, education, or placement and job guidance, to help the injured person find suitable work before the period of compensation elapses.

Temporary Total Disability

The great majority of compensation cases involve temporary disability, which ends with the cure of the injured person and his return to work, or, where the effect of the injury is continuing, with a determination by the compensation authority that the disability is permanent. The benefits for temporary total disability provided by the various laws are shown in Table 40.

ADMINISTRATION OF WORKMEN'S COMPENSATION LAWS

There are two broad phases of workmen's compensation administration, namely, arrangements for insuring compensation risks and methods for adjusting individual claims. There are many problems and differences of opinion with respect to both.[8]

State and Private Insurance

To make certain that benefit payments will be made when due, the states require that the covered employer shall obtain insurance or give proof of his qualifications to carry his own risk. The latter is known as self-insurance.

At the time the early compensation laws were enacted, private insurance carriers were insuring employers against losses through litigation under the common law and the employers' liability acts. Since the workmen's compensation laws were designed to displace the common-law and statutory basis for litigation, the continuation of private insurance arrangements for covering workmen's compensation risks was a natural development. In most of the states today, the employer is permitted to insure with private insurance companies. State insurance systems exist in 18 states and Puerto Rico; in some of these the system is called "exclusive" be-

---

[8] Much of the material in the following pages is from Marshall Dawson, *Problems of Workmen's Compensation Administration*, U. S. Bureau of Labor Statistics, Bull. No. 672, Washington, 1940.

cause employers are required to insure their risks in the state
fund. There are competitive state funds in 11 states; in them employers may choose whether they will insure their risks through the
state fund or with private insurance companies, or qualify as
"self-insurers" with the privilege of carrying their own risks. The
insurance requirements in the different acts are shown in Table 39.

Among those responsible for the administration of workmen's
compensation, there are differences of opinion as to the relative
merits of state versus private insurance systems. Criticism of the
latter is based on the refusal of insurance companies to accept
bad or unwanted risks; under a social interpretation of workmen's
compensation the worst as well as the best risks require insurance
and humane service. Also there is frequent concern regarding a
private company's continued solvency. Regardless of the adequacy
of the benefits provided in a law, the benefits are jeopardized if
employers are insured by a company which may become insolvent
and unable to pay claims when due.

Fears regarding deficiencies on the part of private insurance
systems have led to the establishment of state funds, sometimes
exclusive and in other cases as a competitor of those furnished
by the private companies. However, there is also criticism with
respect to state systems. Those in existence have been handicapped because of their dependence upon legislative appropriations for administrative support, complicated claims procedure
and recourse to court appeals, political turnover of administrators, and salaries which are inadequate to obtain technically qualified personnel.

In the United States the experience with different methods of
insuring injury risks has not yet been such as to convince the
various state legislatures that any one method is superior to the
others, and there is no immediate prospect of a uniform adoption
of one type of system.

Claims Administration

In establishing the workmen's compensation system, one of the
main purposes was to provide a prompt, simple, convenient, and
inexpensive method of settling the claims of injured workers. This
purpose has not been completely realized in the states, although the
system has conclusively demonstrated its superiority over the for-

mer common-law and statutory "liability" remedies in the courts.

The main methods of settling workmen's compensation claims are: by direct settlement, by the agreement system, and by the hearing system. Six states (Alabama, Louisiana, New Hampshire, New Mexico, Tennessee, and Wyoming) still provide court procedure. Court procedure is a survival of the earlier practice and it has been generally recognized that courts are not properly equipped to render the type of service needed for workmen's compensation administration because of the many correlated responsibilities involved.

Under the direct-settlement plan, employers or insurance companies begin payment to the injured worker on their own initiative, subject to a supervisory check by the proper state agency. The injured worker is not asked to sign any papers other than receipts for the money he is paid, nor does he have to agree to anything. He does not have to make any bargain whatever with the employer or insurance carrier; the law specifies what he is entitled to receive, and if he does not get it the state agency is supposed to correct the discrepancy either by checking on reports and receipts or by holding conferences or hearings attended by the interested parties.

Under the agreement system the employer or insurance carrier has the injured worker agree to a certain settlement. Payment is then made to him, either immediately or after approval of the settlement by the state agency. In the case of lax or inadequate supervision by the state agency, gross abuses may arise under either the direct-settlement or the agreement system. Investigations have shown that workers have lost millions of dollars annually because of inadequate supervision of claims adjustments by private companies.[9]

In theory, the most complete supervision of claims adjustment conceivable would be automatic open hearings held by the state

---

[9] The best-known examples of studies of claimants' losses on settlements are the Connor investigation in New York and the 1934 Pennsylvania survey. The investigation by Jeremiah F. Connor was made in 1919, but similar conditions as to inadequate supervision are still found in a number of states. See U. S. Bureau of Labor Statistics, Bull. No. 275, p. 117; Walter F. Dodd, *Administration of Workmen's Compensation,* Commonwealth Fund, New York, 1936, p. 108; Pennsylvania Department of Labor and Industry, Special Bulletin No. 40, Pt. I–b, 1934.

agency on every injury case. This would provide the worker with ironclad protection against an unjust settlement. In practice the disadvantages of such a system for all cases are: the workers' loss of time and money in attending hearings; delays and continuances arising from congested hearing dockets; the pressure of minor cases, making it difficult for the referees to give adequate consideration to the serious injury cases; inconvenience to physicians having to attend the hearings; and expense to the employers and insurance carriers for attendance or representation.

There is a system which is a compromise between a direct-settlement or agreement system with inadequate supervision by the state, and a universal hearing system. Under it, uncontested cases are settled directly, but under close supervision by the state agency, and contested cases are settled after open hearings.[10] Following the initial settlement there is a systematic plan for investigating and following up cases in which there is a probability that injured employees are entitled to increased compensation.

REHABILITATION OF INJURED WORKERS

When the first workmen's compensation laws were enacted, the main task in the minds of the legislators was to find a way to provide prompt medical and financial aid to injured workmen. These laws gave great impetus to the safety or accident-prevention movement, because the excessive number and severity of accidents meant high insurance costs to the employer. As a result of the operation of these laws a definite money value was set upon the loss of a worker's limb or life, and humane sentiments were thus reinforced by economic considerations. The work of the compensation agencies was expanded to include either direct activity in accident prevention or cooperation with state and private agencies interested in that task. But even with accident-prevention work and medical and financial aid, the program of service for victims of industrial accidents was incomplete.

Following World War I there was a growing feeling that injured workers should be put on the same basis as wounded soldiers

---

[10] Wisconsin is usually cited as a good example of this method. See A. J. Altmeyer, *The Industrial Commission of Wisconsin,* University of Wisconsin Studies in the Social Sciences and History, No. 17, Madison, 1932.

and given equal opportunities for restoration to vocational activity. As a rule, the early compensation acts provided meager financial benefits and limited medical aid. The compensation often stopped before the worker's reemployment began. Liberalizing the financial benefits did not completely fill the gap. If the workman was to be restored as nearly as possible to his condition before he was injured, it was evident that something more than a pension was needed. He must be refitted for an active, productive life, instead of being left a dependent invalid.

A few states, acting independently, took steps to include rehabilitation in the scope of the service rendered their injured workers. But the support of this work was uncertain because of fluctuations in state appropriations. The necessity for federal cooperation in the program was recognized.

In 1920, in response to this need, a federal Vocational Act was passed which provided federal grants to states for the vocational rehabilitation of disabled persons, whatever the cause of their disability. Federal appropriations were increased in the 1939 Social Security Amendment, and in 1943 the federal program was expanded to provide for remedial treatment as well as for job training. Under the 1943 statute, federal grants cover the entire administrative cost of approved state vocational rehabilitation programs, and half the expense for rehabilitating individuals.[11]

Since the inauguration of federal aid, many states have improved and expanded their programs in order to make their rehabilitation service practical and effective for persons disabled as a result of industrial accidents. This cooperation in rehabilitation is the newest and one of the most promising phases of workmen's compensation programs, and the degree to which it succeeds is one measure of the efficiency of workmen's compensation administration. However, many of the states have not taken full advantage of their opportunities under the federal-state cooperative plan. Their rehabilitation agencies are undermanned or unsatisfactorily staffed, and the instruments and facilities available are relatively meager. In only a few states, such as Rhode Island, are there

---

11 The Barden-LaFollette Act of 1943 is not confined to industrial workers but covers rehabilitation of all civilians. It provides for payment of the entire expense of vocational rehabilitation for persons injured in non-military war service.

reasonably adequate clinical facilities or curative centers, with full-time programs for the rehabilitation of injured workers.

ACCIDENT STATISTICS

Current statistics on accidents prove the need for workmen's compensation and its allied programs for accident prevention and rehabilitation. Every year between one and one-half and two million wage earners[12] are disabled in this country because of work injuries. Each year approximately 12,000 of these injuries result in death, and 1500 cause permanent total disability. More than 75,000, on the average, cause partial disability of a permanent nature, such as the loss of a limb, hand, or eye. In the majority of cases, the injured workers recover completely after short or prolonged medical treatment; the average time lost per temporary disability amounts to 16 or 17 days.

The total time lost as a result of industrial injuries amounts to more than 40 million man-days per year, or the equivalent of the full-time employment of about 150,000 workers. These estimates of lost time make no allowance for the future economic losses occasioned by deaths and permanent impairments. If these were included, the total economic loss caused by work injuries during the year 1945, for instance, would have amounted to more than 231 million days, or the full-time annual employment of about 770,000 workers.

Longshoring is the most hazardous industry so far as partially disabling work injuries are concerned. After an investigation of conditions among longshoremen in 1942, a government report stated:

Despite the fact that every one connected with the longshore industry seems fully aware that this is one of the most hazardous of all industries, there is little evidence of any serious attempts to carry on a safety program. . . . Particularly on the South Atlantic and Gulf Coasts, safety-code provisions are seldom followed. Hardly any of the contract stevedores maintain any accident records beyond those which are legally required for workmen's compensation purposes. . . .

---

12 An estimated additional 400,000 self-employed persons are injured during the course of their work. These statistics do not include accidents, in the home or elsewhere, not connected with gainful employment.

In spite of the fundamental and seemingly obvious necessity for maintaining first-aid facilities where injuries are known to occur, it was frequently found that not even a first-aid kit was provided. In only a very few instances was there a first-aid room with a trained attendant in charge. The use of personal protective equipment is almost unknown. Goggles and respirators are used only when the work is such that it would be physically impossible to carry on without them.[13]

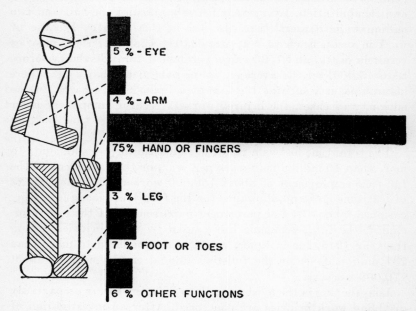

FIG. 37.   *Industrial Injuries According to Part of Body Affected, 1945. (Source: U. S. Bureau of Labor Statistics.)*

More fatalities occur in coal mining than in any other industry. During recent years, between 1600 and 1900 miners have been killed each year and about 90,000 have suffered injuries, many of them of a permanent nature. The miners' situation is aggravated by the fact that workmen's compensation is not compulsory in a number of coal-mining states and many miners receive no compensation during a period of disability, nor do their families receive benefits in case of fatal injuries. In Kentucky, for ex-

[13] *Monthly Labor Review,* January, 1944, p. 1.

ample, workmen's compensation was not made compulsory until 1946, after expressions of public indignation aroused by an accident in which 24 lives were lost. The question of safety rules was one of the issues in the prolonged coal strike during the spring of 1946. When the government took over the mines it established a uniform safety code for government-operated mines which previously had been under the various state safety codes, some of which were fairly adequate but many of which were not only inadequate but poorly enforced.

The accident rate for loggers and sawmill workers is also extremely high, and that for truck drivers is far above the average. Although the accident rate in the steel industry, especially in foundries, is relatively high, hazards have been greatly reduced during recent years as a result of safety education campaigns and the enforcement of safety rules.

TABLE 41. Disabling Work Injuries to Employees, 1939–1945[14]

Year	Total	Fatalities	Permanent Total Disabilities	Permanent Partial Disabilities	Temporary Total Disabilities
1939	1,430,300		15,000[a]	94,600	1,320,700
1940	1,696,900		16,600	80,600	1,599,700
1941	1,983,400		17,500	91,800	1,874,100
1942	1,834,600	13,400	1,400	80,800	1,739,000
1943	1,961,400	13,400	1,400	86,900	1,859,700
1944	1,802,100	11,200	1,400	76,000	1,713,500
1945	1,600,900	11,300	1,500	70,100	1,518,000

[a] Separate figures for these two classifications are not availiable before 1942.

SELECTED REFERENCES

Dawson, Marshall, *Problems of Workmen's Compensation Administration*, U. S. Bureau of Labor Statistics, Bull. No. 672, Government Printing Office, Washington, 1940.

Dodd, Walter F., *Administration of Workmen's Compensation*, Commonwealth Fund, New York, 1936.

Heinrich, H. W., *Industrial Accident Prevention*, McGraw-Hill Book Company, Inc., New York, 1946.

[14] Annual reports of the U. S. Bureau of Labor Statistics. The data do not include industrial injuries to self-employed workers, which average about 400,000 a year.

Hess, Gaylord R., *Medical Service in Industry and Workmen's Compensation Laws,* American College of Surgeons, Chicago, 1946.

Horovitz, Samuel B., *Injury and Death Under Workmen's Compensation Laws,* Wright and Potter Printing Co., Boston, 1944.

International Labour Office, *Evaluation of Permanent Incapacity for Work and Social Insurance,* Social Insurance Reports No. 14, 1937, Montreal, Canada.

Judson, Harry H., and Brown, James M., *Occupational Accident Prevention,* John Wiley & Sons, Inc., New York, 1944.

Kessler, H. H., *Accidental Injuries: The Medical Legal Aspects of Workmen's Compensation and Public Disability,* Lea & Febiger, Philadelphia, 1931.

McBride, Earl D., *Disability Evaluation,* J. B. Lippincott Company, New York, 1936.

Proceedings of the International Association of Industrial Accident Boards and Commissions, published annually by the Division of Labor Standards, U. S. Department of Labor, Washington, D. C.

Sappington, C. O., *Essentials of Industrial Health,* J. B. Lippincott Company, New York, 1943.

27

HEALTH AND DISABILITY INSURANCE

THERE ARE FOUR MAJOR CONTINGENCIES WHICH AFFECT THE SE-
curity of income of workers and their families and over which
they have little or no personal control: forced retirement because
of old age, lack of available or suitable jobs, death of the wage
earner, or his inability to work because of sickness, accident, or
other physical impairment. At the present time social security
measures are least adequate for the last-mentioned situations, in
spite of the fact that thousands of families every year suffer privations because of a reduction in or the total loss of income as a
result of physical disabilities of their wage earners.

Although compensation is afforded substantial numbers of
workers who become disabled because of injuries sustained in the
course of their employment, relatively few workers in this country are insured for cash income or medical expenses for non-
industrial sickness and injury. Some groups of workers are
covered by private health benefit programs provided by their
employers or through collective bargaining,[1] and some through
private cooperative organizations. The only government-sponsored disability insurance programs in effect during 1946 were
one covering railroad workers and two state programs in Rhode
Island and California.

NEED FOR HEALTH INSURANCE

Health insurance was one of the earliest forms of social insurance established in foreign countries and today is the most

[1] See chap. 13.

prevalent form of social insurance in operation throughout the world. Of the major industrial countries, only the United States and Canada have no system of compulsory health insurance or comprehensive public medical care. In spite of the current absence of a comprehensive health insurance program, government responsibility for medical care is not new or unknown in the United States. The health functions of state and local governments go back to the very beginning of the country. The federal government provides hospitalization and other types of medical care for seamen, veterans, Indians, members of the armed forces, and certain other groups.

In earlier times illness and health were considered the primary responsibility of the individual and his family, and of state and local governments. With new scientific discoveries in medicine, the industrialization of the economy, and the concentration of the population in urban areas, there arose a growing concern with health matters among workers and their families, as well as among numerous professional groups such as doctors, social workers, and others concerned with the public welfare. The frequent necessity for depending upon charity or relatives during periods of prolonged illness, and the inadequate medical care for large sections of the population, have aroused public interest in ways and means of protecting the general health and providing an income to those physically unable to work.

The Movement for National Health Insurance

The movement for compulsory health insurance in the United States began before the First World War, during a decade of awakening public interest in several forms of social and labor legislation. After that war, during the apparent "permanent prosperity" of the 1920's, public concern for health insurance, like that for other labor legislation, waned. Interest was revived during the early 1930's, because of the widespread hardships resulting from the depression and the release of the reports of the Committee on the Costs of Medical Care.

The Committee on the Costs of Medical Care was a non-governmental group which was "organized to study the economic aspects of the prevention and care of sickness, including the adequacy, availability, and compensation of the persons and agencies concerned."[2] Its studies, based on a comprehensive survey in 1927–1932, indicated that although illness rates are not markedly different among families at different income levels, the amount of medical care received varies considerably with economic circumstances. Specifically, its studies revealed that almost 50 per cent of the members of low-income families received no medical, dental, or eye care during the year, in contrast to 14 per cent of those at the highest income levels. Translated into three important types of services received by families at different income levels, as shown in Table 42, the study showed that persons in well-to-do families had twice as many physicians' calls and at least four times more dental and eye care than persons in the majority of wage-earners' families.

TABLE 42.   Family Income and Medical Care Received per Year[3]

| Family Income | Services Received per 100 Persons | | |
	Physicians' Calls[a]	Dental Cases[b]	Refractions or Glasses
Less than $1200	217	12	25
$1200–$2000	227	19	25
$2000–$3000	251	25	40
$3000–$5000	300	35	54
$5000–$10,000	398	52	90
$10,000 or more	532	87	160

[a] Home, office, and clinic calls.
[b] Each course of dental care is counted as a single case.

In 1935, President Roosevelt's Committee on Economic Security included in its report various proposals for health insurance, but no further action was taken, largely because of the opposition of the American Medical Association. Shortly there-

[2] This Committee was composed of about 50 physicians, economists, public health workers, and representatives of the general public, and its work was financed by a number of philanthropic foundations. Its research staff conducted a five-year survey, the results of which were published in 28 documents. The summary and analysis of the factual data appear in *Costs of Medical Care* by I. S. Falk, C. R. Rorem, and Martha D. Ring; the final report and recommendations appear in *Committee on the Costs of Medical Care*, Report No. 28. Both volumes were published by the University of Chicago Press, Chicago, 1932.

[3] Based on 8639 white families surveyed for twelve consecutive months during 1928–1932. *Costs of Medical Care*, p. 599.

after President Roosevelt appointed another (interdepartmental) Committee on Health and Welfare. A bill to carry out this Committee's recommendations was introduced in Congress in 1939 but was never voted on. World War II temporarily postponed further legislative interest in these proposals for a federal-state system of medical care.

In 1943 Senators Wagner and Murray and Representative Dingell introduced in Congress a comprehensive social security bill, including a health insurance program to be administered by the federal government. This was the first time that important health insurance legislation was introduced, with the endorsement of organized labor, which provided for administration by the federal government. The same general proposal, with various changes and improvements, was reintroduced in succeeding sessions of Congress.

In 1945, President Truman sent to Congress a special message on national health—the first time in the nation's history that a President had devoted an entire message to a comprehensive national health program. The message made recommendations for a fivefold program: the construction of hospitals and related facilities; the expansion of public health and maternal and child health services; government aid for medical education and research; the prepayment of the costs of medical care through a comprehensive health insurance program; and insurance benefits for the loss of wages from sickness and disability. In support of his recommendation for health insurance, President Truman said, in part:

Everyone should have ready access to all necessary medical, hospital, and related services. I recommend solving the basic problem by distributing the costs through expansion of our existing compulsory social insurance system. This is not socialized medicine. A system of required prepayment would not only spread the costs of medical care, it would also prevent much serious disease. . . . This health fund should be built up nationally in order to establish the broadest and most stable basis for spreading the costs of illness and to assure adequate financial support for doctors and hospitals everywhere. If we were to rely on State-by-State action only, many years would elapse before we had any general coverage. . . . Medical services are personal. Therefore, the nationwide system must be highly decentralized in administration.

The local administrative unit must be the keystone of the system so as to provide for local services and adaptation to local needs and conditions. People should remain free to choose their own physicians and hospitals. . . . The legal requirement on the population to contribute involves no compulsion over the doctor's freedom to decide what services his patient needs. People will remain free to obtain and pay for medical service outside of the health-insurance system if they desire, even though they are members of the system; . . . Likewise physicians should remain free to accept or reject patients.

Following the President's recommendations for a comprehensive national health program, Congress appropriated some money for federal grants-in-aid to the states for the construction of hospitals and the establishment of mental health services. Increased appropriations were also made to permit the expansion of maternal and child health services. But no action was taken by the 1946 Congress toward establishing either a national health or a disability insurance program. Organized labor and a number of other groups had made strenuous efforts to secure favorable congressional action but they had been opposed by organized medicine and some employers' groups.

CONTROVERSIAL ASPECTS OF A NATIONAL HEALTH PROGRAM

Although there is great interest in health and health insurance in the United States, the methods to be adopted for dealing with these problems are still a highly controversial subject. In view of this fact, some common understanding of the controversial terms and ideas is essential to a proper understanding of the subject.

Health insurance in other countries usually covers both medical services and cash payments for wage loss due to sickness or disability. In the United States, however, these two aspects of a health program have been considered separately. Consequently, health insurance customarily applies only to medical services or medical costs, and the term "disability insurance" applies to cash payments for loss of wages during the period of disability. Undoubtedly, the reason for this separate consideration has been the fact that the organized medical profession has vigorously opposed compulsory insurance with respect to medical services or costs, whereas it has gone on record in favor of compulsory insurance to provide benefit payments during periods of disability.

In public discussions health insurance is frequently confused with socialized medicine. Health insurance is primarily a method of prepaying the costs of medical care, with free choice of doctor by the patient and free choice of patient by the doctor. Under socialized or state medicine, doctors are employed by the government, usually on a full-time salaried basis; there is little or no free choice by either patient or doctor. Medical care for veterans in veterans' hospitals, and state or local medical care for the tubercular and the insane can be considered as socialized or state medicine. In reality, medical care has always had a social or socialized aspect because of the public responsibility for the care of some groups, and the public employment of doctors and other professional persons in public hospitals.

Several countries already have in operation, and others are contemplating putting in operation, a general system of socialized or state medicine. A more proper term would be "public medical care" to parallel the use of the term "public education," since there is much similarity in the basic principles of both services. Although the U.S.S.R. is usually considered the outstanding example of public medical care, New Zealand, Australia, and Chile also have similar programs, and Great Britain and Sweden are preparing to inaugurate them in the near future.

The major issues in the United States revolve around whether medical care shall be guaranteed to all persons in a community as a matter of right, and whether in doing so, either through compulsory insurance or otherwise, the conditions regarding the selection of physicians will be so modified that the program will involve a basic change in the existing methods of medical practice.

Opposition to Compulsory Health Insurance

The chief opposition to compulsory governmental health insurance has come from the American Medical Association, which officially speaks for most of the physicians throughout the country, although some individual doctors and local medical groups have expressed opinions contrary to that of the national organization. The Association has recently endorsed voluntary health insurance plans but vigorously opposes a compulsory program administered by the government. Summarizing its objections, a representative of the Association has said: "Voluntary health plans will, if given the opportunity, do the job, and do it better than Government-controlled plans can do. These plans, which already include a very large number of persons, are in accord with our traditional emphasis on personal responsibility, prudence, foresight, and thrift. They have an American dignity which is lacking in the regimentation of compulsory health insurance. They can be and are more economically administered, they can and do give better medical care, and they will be and are supported by thousands of physicians who are bitterly and unalterably opposed to Government-controlled medicine."[4]

The attitude of the American Medical Association on compulsory governmental disability insurance is different from its attitude on compulsory governmental health insurance. For a number of years the Association has endorsed proposals for providing social insurance benefits in case of disability. Payment of such benefits, of course, would enable people to pay their doctors' bills. It would also encourage them to see a doctor promptly when they became sick, since medical certification is needed to claim benefits. In this way the health of the patient and the financial status, both his own and the doctor's, would be improved.

The United States Chamber of Commerce statement of policy on insurance matters, adopted in 1946, summarized its opposition to an insurance plan for temporary disability and also medical care costs, as follows:

Legislation, either by the federal government or the states, that is designed to extend the government-operated Social Security System to the accident and health, hospitalization, and medical care field is strongly opposed. Such action is in direct competition with services and benefits now provided by private initiative and tends toward direct governmental control and supervision over physicians, hospitals, and all other groups providing medical care.

If, in any state, the public interest requires that sick benefits be more widely provided, such insurance may be provided on principles

---

[4] Hearings on S.1606, National Health Program, before the Senate Committee on Education and Labor, 79th Congress, 2nd Session, 1946, p. 627.

similar to the workmen's compensation laws, which are preferable to government expropriation of this field of service. Such insurance should be carried with private insurance companies which have demonstrated that they can administer insurance plans more efficiently than government and free from political influence, and at low cost."

Arguments for Health Insurance

Those who advocate compulsory health insurance believe that neither the course of present developments in this country, nor the experience of other countries which have tried voluntary health insurance, gives any indication that comprehensive and adequate arrangements to insure medical costs can be made in any way except through a compulsory insurance system. The principal limitations of voluntary plans, they point out, have been inadequacy of coverage, restrictions on services, limitations on membership, failure to relate contributions to ability to pay, relatively high costs, and lack of consumer or public representation in management.

Advocates of health insurance maintain that health insurance would enable self-supporting families to pay for and obtain needed medical services without any important alteration in the present form or organization of medical practice. Moreover, families dependent on public funds could be covered through payment of contributions on their behalf by the agencies administering public assistance, so that the needy individual would receive care in the same way in which self-supporting persons receive it —without the stigma and inadequacy of the present "poor-law medicine."

According to the Social Security Administration, the much-advertised fears of "socialized medicine," "regimentation" of physicians and patients, loss of the patient's freedom to choose his doctor, and deterioration of the quality of the care, can be made wholly groundless. A system of health insurance can and should be so designed as to avoid these disadvantages. By making these services readily available to those who need them, the quality and effectiveness of service may be improved, and the incomes of doctors and hospitals may be better and more secure. If, at the same time, professional education, research, and the construction of needed facilities are aided financially, progress in medicine and improvement in our national health can be greatly accelerated.

In recommending the establishment of a health insurance plan, the Social Security Administration has stated that it would be simplest, most economical, and most effective to establish comprehensive protection through federal legislation, while providing authority to utilize state agencies and other local facilities. It recommends that administration of benefits be so decentralized that all the necessary arrangements with doctors, hospitals, and others would be worked out on a local basis, the general pattern of these arrangements being developed with the collaboration of professional organizations and with careful regard for regional, state, and local circumstances. Local needs and interests would be protected by having the local, state, and federal policies and operations in each area of administration guided by advisory bodies representing those who pay the insurance contributions and those who provide the services.

It has been estimated by the Social Security Administration that contributions equivalent to about 3 per cent of the annual earnings would pay for adequate basic medical and hospital services for both workers and their dependents. A more comprehensive system would cost the equivalent of about 4 per cent. These costs would be less than the present average expenditure of families in the low-income groups.

DISABILITY INSURANCE

As already indicated, "disability insurance" refers to cash payments for loss of wages due to disability, in contrast to "health insurance" which refers to payments for medical services. Disability insurance is usually discussed from two approaches, temporary and permanent, although the line of distinction cannot be consistently maintained in all cases. Disability which at first seems temporary may become permanent. Many disabilities may last for a year or two but may not be permanent. It has become more or less common practice to identify temporary disability with the first six months of disability; disability extending beyond this period is usually considered permanent.

Insurance for Permanent Disability

The federal old age insurance program has opened a way to employees in industry and commerce whereby they, with the help of their employers, can provide an income for themselves after they retire from gainful work. But no similar protection is available to the worker forced to leave gainful employment because of permanent disability. If chronic disability cuts short the usefulness of the breadwinner, it is still primarily the responsibility of his family to provide for him. Since the disabled person may need medical and nursing care in addition to maintenance, the burden of disability is generally heavier than that created by old age.

Experience under the older retirement laws of this country indicates that it is sound to keep the retirement age flexible, and that it is feasible to combine an old age retirement system with a system of insurance against chronic disability. The purpose of both systems is to enable workers with reduced earning capacity to retire from gainful work, and to fill the vacancies created by their retirement with workers of unimpaired efficiency.

Even though the principle of insurance for permanent disability is accepted, there are practical problems of administration and financing. It raises such questions as the extent to which the benefit provisions of old age and survivors' insurance are applicable to a system of disability insurance, what new provisions would be needed, and in what respects the present law would need to be changed so that the combined insurance system against the risks of old age, disability, and death could be soundly and effectively integrated.

The most important and also the most difficult question concerns the types of disability which should come within the purview of a new law. The purpose of a disability insurance system is to grant a benefit to workers who are forced to leave gainful employment for long periods of time or permanently because of loss of, or substantial reduction in, earning capacity due to illness, loss of limb, or other impairment of body or mind. This is similar to the purpose of old age insurance, which pays benefits to insured workers from the time of retirement to the date of death. Because disability insurance requires the payment of benefits over long periods of time, it can be, and often has been, fitted into old age retirement systems.

A six-month waiting period would exclude most disabilities of a temporary character, although some last more than six months. If disability benefits are to be restricted to persons who suffer a chronic disability or one presumably long-continued or permanent, a prognosis of the disability must be made after expiration of the six-month waiting period and at stated times thereafter.

Relationship to Workmen's Compensation

The state workmen's compensation laws provide compensation for workers whose earning capacity has been impaired by injuries sustained in the course of employment, and some laws also provide benefits for workers suffering from occupational disease. If duplication of benefits is to be avoided, the general disability insurance system must include a provision which draws a clear division line between these two systems, both of which serve the common purpose of replacing at least a portion of the wages lost because of disability.

The lack of uniformity in workmen's compensation provisions, as indicated in the preceding chapter, makes it difficult to establish a uniform division between workmen's compensation and disability insurance. There are, however, various alternative ways in which the two systems can be related to each other.

One possibility would be to exclude from the disability insurance system all disabilities arising out of or in the course of employment, leaving the compensation of such disabilities to the states. Although this would preclude duplication of benefits actually or potentially payable under workmen's compensation, it has a number of drawbacks. Except in the states with the most liberal workmen's compensation laws, there would be a gap between disability insurance and workmen's compensation coverage or protection. A disabled worker might be disqualified under the disability insurance law because federal officers found that the origin of his disability was connected with his work. Yet he might fail to qualify for workmen's compensation under the state law, because his type of employment was excluded from the state system, or because his right to it was exhausted, or because the state agency had determined that the disability was not due to his employment. Also, he might live in the one state (Mississippi) which as yet has no workmen's compensation law.

The task of determining whether a given disability arose out of or in the course of employment is often difficult and complex, as is well known from experience with workmen's compensation. Even after all the necessary care had been exercised, a worker might be denied benefits under both systems because the federal agency decided that his disability was work-connected, and the state agency decided the contrary. Or duplicate benefits might be paid if the federal agency determined that the disability was of non-industrial origin, and the state found that it did arise out of or in the course of employment. These difficulties could be eliminated by providing that benefits under the federal law would be payable in those cases in which the state authorities held that the disability was not covered by the state law. Such a provision would, of course, make the application of the federal law dependent on the action of state legislatures and administrative agencies in determining the extent to which state workmen's compensation laws cover industrial disabilities.

An alternative policy would be to allow disability benefits to all eligible workers who were disabled within the meaning of the law, even if the disability was of industrial origin. The connection between the worker's disability and his employment would not need to be investigated, but a worker might receive two benefits, one from the federal government, the other from the state workmen's compensation insurance. The combined benefits might exceed the limits usually incorporated in social insurance laws to keep payments below the wages earned from gainful employment. Some arrangement would have to be worked out to insure that the combined benefits did not exceed the wages earned by the worker before he became disabled. This might be achieved by adjusting the disability insurance benefits, if the worker is eligible for workmen's compensation and if the combined benefits exceed a specified limit.

Certification and Rehabilitation

As used in a social insurance law, the term disability is not purely a medical concept. Unless the disability results in economic loss, it is not compensable under the insurance system. In the certification of disability, a medical examination determines the physical and mental condition of the claimant for benefits; but the economic loss resulting from disability must be measured by an administrative officer familiar with the conditions of the labor market, and conversant with the practices of employers in hiring, or refusing to hire, persons with physical or mental impairments. The determination of disability, therefore, is the result of the combined judgment of the physician and the labor-market or employment agent.

The provision of a small cash income for the worker who has lost his earning capacity assures him basic security, and for the worker whose invalidism is total and incurable this is the best that can be done for him. There is general agreement that the problem of chronic disease should be attacked simultaneously from another front. Not only are the prevention of invalidism and the restoration of working capacity more valuable than cash benefits from the point of view of the worker and of society, but they may also result in considerable savings for the insurance system through the removal of persons from benefit rolls. Many disabled individuals suffer from conditions which can be arrested or remedied, in part or in whole, if proper care and treatment are furnished; and the insurance system should make funds available for necessary treatment and care if there is a reasonable likelihood that the worker may once more become capable of earning his living.

Physical rehabilitation prolongs and restores the earning capacity of insured workers. Vocational rehabilitation utilizes the remaining earning capacity of a person who can no longer pursue his ordinary occupation. The value of rehabilitation programs for disabled people is attested by the results obtained in other countries which have had considerable experience. Moreover, within recent years in our own country federal and state physical rehabilitation programs have been conducted with considerable success. Retraining for a new occupation, or occupational rehabilitation, may restore earning capacity to persons who are prevented by a chronic disablement from following their ordinary occupation. The retraining programs which are in effect in most states should undoubtedly be available to incapacitated workers insured under the federal social insurance program, and its cost should be met by the insurance fund.

A full program of social insurance against disability would have a threefold purpose: medical and hospital care to prevent and cure chronic disease and sickness; occupational retraining for persons with chronic impairments; cash benefits during periods of sickness and for chronic invalids.

EXISTING GOVERNMENT PROGRAMS
FOR TEMPORARY DISABILITY

By July, 1946, there were three temporary disability insurance laws in the United States covering workers in industry and commerce in Rhode Island and California, and covering railroad workers. About 4 million workers were employed in an average week in jobs covered by these three laws.

The Rhode Island Law

The Rhode Island law is the first of its kind in the United States. It was passed in 1942 and the first benefit payments were made in April, 1943. Under the original provisions, contributions of 1 per cent were required from employees on the first $3000 of annual earnings, but in 1946 the employee rate was increased to 1½ per cent. This contribution did not represent an additional burden on employees, because Rhode Island was collecting 1½ per cent from employees for unemployment insurance, which was reduced to one-half of 1 per cent in 1942 and was discontinued in 1946. The favorable financial status of the unemployment insurance fund made it possible to allocate the employee contributions to a temporary disability insurance fund without impairing the unemployment fund. No employer contribution for disability insurance is required under the present law.

The Rhode Island law in general provides for sickness benefits in the same amount and for the same duration as for unemployment. A one-week waiting period is required after the onset of sickness; hence benefits are payable in the second week of illness. The minimum weekly benefit is $6.75; the maximum, $18. The maximum period in which benefits are paid in any year is 20¼ weeks. Weekly benefits are based upon the highest wages in any quarter of a base year, and the total benefits for any year depend upon the individual's earnings in that year. The smallest total payment possible in a year is $34 (based on earnings of $100 in a year) and the largest is $364.50 (based on wages of $1800 or more).

Some of the important issues involved in the formulation of a temporary disability insurance program and its administration can be illustrated from the Rhode Island experience.

Under the provisions of the original law, the definition of "sickness" was not clear as to whether a worker able to work at a job other than his usual job was entitled to benefits. A Rhode Island court finally ruled that ability to perform any work disqualified a worker from receiving benefits. While such a requirement seems appropriate for long-time disability, it seemed inappropriate in a program providing benefits for only 20 weeks. After recovering from a short-time disability, it is to be expected that a worker will return to his former employer or his usual trade, and that inability to perform his regular or customary work is the more appropriate test as to whether he should receive benefits. The law was amended in this respect in 1946.

The relationship between temporary disability insurance benefits and similar benefits for an industrial injury is an important problem. Under the original law, a worker could receive in full both workmen's compensation and temporary disability insurance benefits. In over 25 per cent of such cases this resulted in the individual's receiving more in total benefits than he normally received in full-time wages while working. Under the law as amended in 1946, if a worker is eligible for workmen's compensation, the combined benefits are limited to 90 per cent of his average weekly wage at his last regular employment. If the total benefits exceed this amount, the excess is subtracted from the disability insurance benefit.

Under the original law, insurance benefits were paid while the individual's employer continued to pay his regular wages. This was later eliminated. The original law did not specifically limit benefits to pregnant women, and in some cases a woman was able to collect up to 40 weeks' benefits if the delivery date happened to be near the end of one year. Under the amended law, benefits for pregnancy are limited to 15 weeks, although they may be extended if unusual complications result from childbirth.

At the end of World War II, many insured persons retired from the labor market. This group mainly included aged persons and housewives. Under the original law, they could collect their insurance benefits during sickness or disability even though they were no longer members of the labor force. The law was therefore amended, to prevent the payment of benefits to anyone who has not worked within six months of any week of sickness, or has not applied for work at the U. S. Employment Service.

The California Law

In 1946, a temporary disability insurance law was passed by the California legislature. Like Rhode Island's law, the California law provides that employee contributions for unemployment insurance shall be used for disability insurance.

One unusual feature of the California law is the provision that if an employer has established a disability plan which meets certain conditions, his employees do not have to contribute to the state plan nor will they be entitled to benefits under it. Employers pay a small additional amount to the state fund for the added administrative expense arising out of their exemption from the voluntary plans.

The exemption or "contracting out" of voluntary plans, permitted under the California law, is a complicated and controversial issue which has arisen repeatedly in all types of social insurance, here and abroad. In general, the weight of expert opinion is against the complete exemption or contracting out of private plans, but favors the encouragement of private plans to supplement to the maximum extent possible the basic social insurance benefits provided by law. The major arguments against complete exemption are that it is inconsistent with the social insurance principle of the broadest possible pooling of the risk, and that exemptions result in a higher cost of benefits for those who do not contract out, and in higher administrative costs and greater administrative difficulties.

The Railroad Law

In 1946 the railroad unemployment insurance law was amended to provide cash benefits to railroad employees during periods of sickness, disability, or maternity. In general the benefits are of the same amount and for the same duration as those paid to an employee while unemployed. In maternity cases, benefits are increased 50 per cent for a two-week period prior to the expected birth of the child and for two weeks afterward, and the maximum duration is limited to 24 weeks instead of the 26 weeks for unemployment benefits. The costs of the temporary disability insurance benefits, estimated at about 1 to 1½ per cent of the pay rolls, are defrayed by the 3 per cent tax on pay rolls paid by employees.

PROSPECTS FOR NEW LAWS

Under the railroad law the employers' contributions for unemployment insurance are used for sickness benefits, whereas under the two state laws the financing of sickness insurance depends entirely upon employee contributions. A 1946 amendment to the Social Security Act permits states which collected employee contributions under unemployment insurance to use these funds for disability insurance. This may accelerate the movement for using employee contributions in whole or in part to finance state disability insurance. The large reserves for unemployment insurance have raised a question in some states as to the possibility of using part of the employer contribution for disability insurance purposes. Thus, if contributions equal to 1½ per cent in a particular state are sufficient to pay unemployment insurance benefits, the state could require the employer to contribute part or all of the cost of temporary disability insurance benefits, and still keep the total cost to him below the original 3 per cent levied for unemployment insurance.

If the federal Social Security Act should be amended to permit either the use of federal funds or a reduction in the employer's unemployment tax for sickness benefit purposes, it is likely that a number of states will adopt disability insurance laws which might not otherwise do so. If federal legislation is not enacted, however, it may be many years before all or substantially all the states enact such laws. The experience with state workmen's compensation laws as contrasted with state unemployment insurance laws is pertinent. With no federal incentive, after thirty-five years there is still one state without a workmen's compensation law, whereas within two years after the passage of federal unemployment insurance legislation, every state had enacted an unemployment insurance law.

Separate Programs for Permanent and Temporary Disability

It is generally conceded that insurance for chronic sickness and permanent disability can be best administered through the existing federal old age insurance program. If insurance for temporary disability is included in the various unemployment insurance programs, as in the three existing plans, a number of administrative problems will arise. For example, if the states enact laws providing sick benefits up to a maximum of 26 weeks, and the federal government enacts a disability insurance law providing benefits after this period, should a person be required to take medical or vocational rehabilitation which might avoid the necessity of paying any federal benefits? If so, should this be required only after the federal government began to pay its benefit, or while the state is paying? Should all cases be transferred immediately from the state to the federal program when it becomes apparent that the disability is permanent? If workers and employers both contribute for permanent disability insurance, as under the present federal old age insurance law, while only the employees or only the employers contribute under a state law, how can the two be dovetailed?

Many problems such as these raise the question as to the desirability of a single unified disability insurance law which would provide for the payment of benefits in case of both temporary and permanent disability. Although the adoption of such a plan seems unlikely in the immediate future, it will undoubtedly be discussed in connection with the improvement and simplification of the entire social security program in this country.

SELECTED REFERENCES

Annual Reports of the Social Security Board, Government Printing Office, Washington.

Buehler, E. C. (ed.), *Free Medical Care,* Debater's Help Book, Noble & Noble, Publishers, Inc., New York, 1935.

Committee on the Costs of Medical Care, *Medical Care for the American People,* University of Chicago Press, Chicago, 1932.

Davis, Michael M., *America Organizes Medicine*, Harper & Brothers, New York, 1941.

Falk, I. S., *Security Against Sickness: A Study of Health Insurance*, Doubleday, Doran & Company, Inc., New York, 1936.

Falk, I. S., Sanders, Barkev, and Federman, David, *Disability Among Gainfully Occupied Persons*, Bureau of Research and Statistics Memorandum No. 61, Social Security Board, Government Printing Office, Washington, 1945.

Kingsbury, John A., *Health in Handcuffs*, Modern Age Books, New York, 1939.

Millis, Harry A., *Sickness and Insurance: A Study of the Sickness Problem and Health Insurance*, University of Chicago Press, Chicago, 1937.

Reed, Louis S., *Health Insurance: The Next Step in Social Security*, Harper & Brothers, New York, 1937.

Stern, Bernhard J., *American Medical Practice*, Commonwealth Fund, New York, 1945.

U. S. Congress, *National Health Act of 1945*. Reports to the Committee of Education and Labor of the Senate Relating to the Bill (S.1606) to Provide for a National Health Program. Senate Committee Prints Nos. 1–5, Government Printing Office, Washington, 1945–1946.

U. S. Congress, *National Health Program Hearings Before the Senate Committee on Education and Labor*, 79th Congress, 2nd Session, Government Printing Office, Washington, 1946.

APPENDIXES

FEDERAL PROTECTIVE LABOR LAWS

APPENDIX I

FEDERAL ANTI-INJUNCTION LAW[1]
(Norris-LaGuardia Act)

(47 Stat. 70)

AN ACT

To amend the Judicial Code and to define and limit the jurisdiction of courts sitting in equity, and for other purposes.

Be it enacted by the Senate and House of Representatives of the United States of America in Congress assembled, That no court of the United States, as herein defined, shall have jurisdiction to issue any restraining order or temporary or permanent injunction in a case involving or growing out of a labor dispute, except in a strict conformity with the provisions of this Act; nor shall any such restraining order or temporary or permanent injunction be issued contrary to the public policy declared in this Act.

SEC. 2. In the interpretation of this Act and in determining the jurisdiction and authority of the courts of the United States as such jurisdiction and authority are herein defined and limited, the public policy of the United States is hereby declared as follows:

Whereas under prevailing economic conditions, developed with the aid of governmental authority for owners of property to organize in the corporate and other forms of ownership association, the individual unorganized worker is commonly helpless to exercise actual liberty of contract and to protect his freedom of labor, and thereby to obtain acceptable terms and conditions of employment, wherefore, though he should be free to decline to associate with his fellows, it is necessary that he have full freedom of association, self-organization, and designation of representatives of his own choosing, to negotiate the terms and conditions of his employment, and that he shall be free from the interference, restraint, or coercion of employers of labor, or their agents, in the designation of such representatives or in self-organization or in other concerted activities for the purpose of collective bargaining or

[1] In effect, 1946.

other mutual aid or protection; therefore, the following definitions of, and limitations upon, the jurisdiction and authority of the courts of the United States are hereby enacted.

SEC. 3. Any undertaking or promise, such as is described in this section, or any other undertaking or promise in conflict with the public policy declared in section 2 of this Act, is hereby declared to be contrary to the public policy of the United States, shall not be enforceable in any court of the United States and shall not afford any basis for the granting of legal or equitable relief by any such court, including specifically the following:

Every undertaking or promise hereafter made, whether written or oral, express or implied, constituting or contained in any contract or agreement of hiring or employment between any individual, firm, company, association, or corporation, and any employee or prospective employee of the same, whereby

(a) Either party to such contract or agreement undertakes or promises not to join, become, or remain a member of any labor organization or of any employer organization; or

(b) Either party to such contract or agreement undertakes or promises that he will withdraw from an employment relation in the event that he joins, becomes, or remains a member of any labor organization or of any employer organization.

SEC. 4. No court of the United States shall have jurisdiction to issue any restraining order or temporary or permanent injunction in any case involving or growing out of any labor dispute to prohibit any person or persons participating or interested in such dispute (as these terms are herein defined) from doing, whether singly or in concert, any of the following acts:

(a) Ceasing or refusing to perform any work or to remain in any relation of employment;

(b) Becoming or remaining a member of any labor organization or of any employer organization, regardless of any such undertaking or promise as is described in section 3 of this Act;

(c) Paying or giving to, or withholding from, any person participating or interested in such labor dispute, any strike or unemployment benefits or insurance, or other moneys or things of value;

(d) By all lawful means aiding any person participating or interested in any labor dispute who is being proceeded against in, or is prosecuting, any action or suit in any court of the United States or of any State;

(e) Giving publicity to the existence of, or the facts involved in, any labor dispute, whether by advertising, speaking, patrolling, or by any other method not involving fraud or violence;

(f) Assembling peaceably to act or to organize to act in promotion of their interests in a labor dispute;

(g) Advising or notifying any person of an intention to do any of the acts heretofore specified;

(h) Agreeing with other persons to do or not to do any of the acts heretofore specified; and

(i) Advising, urging, or otherwise causing or inducing without fraud or violence the acts heretofore specified, regardless of any such undertaking or promise as is described in section 3 of this Act.

SEC. 5. No court of the United States shall have jurisdiction to issue a restraining order or temporary or permanent injunction upon the ground that any of the persons participating or interested in a labor dispute constitute or are engaged in an unlawful combination or conspiracy because of the doing in concert of the acts enumerated in section 4 of this Act.

SEC. 6. No officer or member of any association or organization, and no association or organization participating or interested in a labor dispute, shall be held responsible or liable in any court of the United States for the unlawful acts of individual officers, members, or agents, except upon clear proof of actual participation in, or actual authorization of, such acts, or of ratification of such acts after actual knowledge thereof.

SEC. 7. No court of the United States shall have jurisdiction to issue a temporary or permanent injunction in any case involving or growing out of a labor dispute, as herein defined, except after hearing the testimony of witnesses in open court (with opportunity for cross-examination) in support of the allegations of a complaint made under oath, and testimony in opposition thereto, if offered, and except after findings of fact by the court, to the effect—

(a) That unlawful acts have been threatened and will be committed unless restrained or have been committed and will be continued unless restrained, but no injunction or temporary restraining order shall be issued on account of any threat or unlawful act excepting against the person or persons, association, or organization making the threat or committing the unlawful act or actually authorizing or ratifying the same after actual knowledge thereof;

(b) That substantial and irreparable injury to complainant's property will follow;

(c) That as to each item of relief granted greater injury will be inflicted upon complainant by the denial of relief than will be inflicted upon defendants by the granting of relief;

(d) That complainant has no adequate remedy at law; and

(e) That the public officers charged with the duty to protect complainant's property are unable or unwilling to furnish adequate protection.

Such hearing shall be held after due and personal notice thereof has been given, in such manner as the court shall direct, to all known persons against whom relief is sought, and also to the chief of those public officials of the county and city within which the unlawful acts have been threatened or committed charged with the duty to protect complainant's property: *Provided, however,* That if a complainant shall also allege that, unless a temporary restraining order shall be issued without notice, a substantial and irreparable injury to complainant's property will be unavoidable, such a temporary restraining order may be issued upon testimony under oath, sufficient, if sustained, to justify the court in issuing a temporary injunction upon a hearing after notice. Such a temporary restraining order shall be effective for no longer than five days and shall become void at the expiration of said five days. No temporary restraining order or temporary injunction shall be issued except on condition that complainant shall first file an undertaking with adequate security in an amount to be fixed by the court sufficient to recompense those enjoined for any loss, expense, or damage caused by the improvident or erroneous issuance of such order or injunction, including all reasonable costs (together with a reasonable attorney's fee) and expense of defense against the order or against the granting of any injunctive relief sought in the same proceeding and subsequently denied by the court.

The undertaking herein mentioned shall be understood to signify an agreement entered into by the complainant and the surety upon which a decree may be rendered in the same suit or proceeding against said complainant and surety, upon a hearing to assess damages of which hearing complainant and surety shall have reasonable notice, the said complainant and surety submitting themselves to the jurisdiction of the court for that purpose. But nothing herein contained shall deprive any party having a claim or cause of action under or upon such undertaking from electing to pursue his ordinary remedy by suit at law or in equity.

SEC. 8. No restraining order or injunctive relief shall be granted to any complainant who has failed to comply with any obligation imposed by law which is involved in the labor dispute in question, or who has failed to make every reasonable effort to settle such dispute either by negotiation or with the aid of any available governmental machinery of mediation or voluntary arbitration .

SEC. 9. No restraining order or temporary or permanent injunction shall be granted in a case involving or growing out of a labor dispute, except on the basis of findings of fact made and filed by the court in the record of the case prior to the issuance of such restraining order or injunction; and every restraining order or injunction granted in a case involving or growing out of a labor dispute shall include only a prohibition of such specific act or acts as may be expressly complained of in the bill of complaint or petition filed in such case and as shall be expressly included in said findings of fact made and filed by the court as provided herein.

SEC. 10. Whenever any court of the United States shall issue or deny any temporary injunction in a case involving or growing out of a labor dispute, the court shall, upon the request of any party to the proceedings and on his filing the usual bond for costs, forthwith certify as in ordinary cases the record of the case to the circuit court of appeals for its review. Upon the filing of such record in the circuit court of appeals, the appeal shall be heard and the temporary injunctive order affirmed, modified, or set aside with the greatest possible expedition, giving the proceedings precedence over all other matters except older matters of the same character.

SEC. 11. In all cases arising under this Act in which a person shall be charged with contempt in a court of the United States (as herein defined), the accused shall enjoy the right to a speedy and public trial by an impartial jury of the State and district wherein the contempt shall have been committed: *Provided,* That this right shall not apply to contempts committed in the presence of the court or so near thereto as to interfere directly with the administration of justice or to apply to the misbehavior, misconduct, or disobedience of any officer of the court in respect to the writs, orders, or process of the court.

SEC. 12. The defendant in any proceeding for contempt of court may file with the court a demand for the retirement of the judge sitting in the proceeding, if the contempt arises from an attack upon the character or conduct of such judge and if the attack occurred elsewhere than in the presence of the court or so near thereto as to interfere directly with the administration of justice. Upon the filing of any such demand the judge shall thereupon proceed no further, but another judge shall be designated in the same manner as is provided by law. The demand shall be filed prior to the hearing in the contempt proceeding.

SEC. 13. When used in this Act, and for the purposes of this Act—

(a) A case shall be held to involve or to grow out of a labor dispute when the case involves persons who are engaged in the same industry, trade, craft, or occupation; or have direct or indirect interests therein; or who are employees of the same employer; or who are members of the same or an affiliated organization of employers or employees; whether such dispute is (1) between one or more employers or associations of employers and one or more employees or associations of employees; (2) between one or more employers or associations of employers and one or more employers or associations of employers; or (3) between one or more employees or associations of employees and one or more employees or associations of employees; or when the case involves any conflicting or competing interests in a "labor dispute" (as hereinafter defined) of "persons participating or interested" therein (as hereinafter defined).

(b) A person or association shall be held to be a person participating or interested in a labor dispute if relief is sought against him or it, and if he or it is engaged in the same industry, trade, craft, or occupation in which such dispute occurs, or has a direct or indirect interest therein, or is a member, officer, or agent of any association composed in whole or in part of employers or employees engaged in such industry, trade, craft, or occupation.

(c) The term "labor dispute" includes any controversy concerning terms or conditions of employment, or concerning the association or representation of persons in negotiating, fixing, maintaining, changing, or seeking to arrange terms or conditions of employment, regardless of whether or not the disputants stand in the proximate relation of employer and employee.

(d) The term "court of the United States" means any court of the United States whose jurisdiction has been or may be conferred or defined or limited by Act of Congress, including the courts of the District of Columbia.

SEC. 14. If any provision of this Act or the application thereof to any person or circumstance is held unconstitutional or otherwise invalid, the remaining provisions of the Act and the application of such provisions to other persons or circumstances shall not be affected thereby.

SEC. 15. All Acts and parts of Acts in conflict with the provisions of this Act are hereby repealed

Approved, March 23, 1932.

APPENDIX II

NATIONAL LABOR RELATIONS ACT [1]
(Wagner Act)

(49 Stat. 449)

AN ACT

To diminish the causes of labor disputes burdening or obstructing interstate and foreign commerce, to create a National Labor Relations Board, and for other purposes.

Be it enacted by the Senate and House of Representatives of the United States of America in Congress assembled,

FINDINGS AND POLICY

SEC. 1. The denial by employers of the right of employees to organize and the refusal by employers to accept the procedure of collective bargaining lead to strikes and other forms of industrial strife or unrest, which have the intent or the necessary effect of burdening or obstructing commerce by (a) impairing the efficiency, safey, or operation of the instrumentalities of commerce; (b) occurring in the current of commerce; (c) materially affecting, restraining, or controlling the flow of raw materials or manufactured or processed goods from or into the channels of commerce, or the prices of such materials or goods in commerce; or (d) causing diminution of employment and wages in such volume as substantially to impair or disrupt the market for goods flowing from or into the channels of commerce.

The inequality of bargaining power between employees who do not possess full freedom of association or actual liberty of contract, and employers who are organized in the corporate or other forms of ownership association substantially burdens and affects the flow of commerce, and tends to aggravate recurrent business depressions, by depressing wage rates and the purchasing power of wage earners in industry and by preventing the stabilization of competitive wage rates and working conditions within and between industries.

[1] In effect, 1946.

Experience has proved that protection by law of the right to employees to organize and bargain collectively safeguards commerce from injury, impairment, or interruption, and promotes the flow of commerce by removing certain recognized sources of industrial strife and unrest, by encouraging practices fundamental to the friendly adjustment of industrial disputes arising out of differences as to wages, hours, or other working conditions, and by restoring equality of bargaining power between employers and employees.

It is hereby declared to be the policy of the United States to eliminate the causes of certain substantial obstructions to the free flow of commerce and to mitigate and eliminate these obstructions when they have occurred by encouraging the practice and procedure of collective bargaining and by protecting the exercise by workers of full freedom of association, self-organization, and designation of representatives of their own choosing, for the purpose of negotiating the terms and conditions of their employment or other mutual aid or protection.

DEFINITIONS

Sec. 2. When used in this Act—

(1) The term "person" includes one or more individuals, partnerships, associations, corporations, legal representatives, trustees, trustees in bankruptcy, or receivers.

(2) The term "employer" includes any person acting in the interest of an employer, directly or indirectly, but shall not include the United States, or any State or political subdivision thereof, or any person subject to the Railway Labor Act, as amended from time to time, or any labor organization (other than when acting as an employer), or anyone acting in the capacity of officer or agent of such labor organization.

(3) The term "employee" shall include any employee, and shall not be limited to the employees of a particular employer, unless the Act explicitly states otherwise, and shall include any individual whose work has ceased as a consequence of, or in connection with any current labor dispute or because of any unfair labor practice, and who has not obtained any other regular and substantially equivalent employment, but shall not include any individual employed as an agricultural laborer, or in the domestic service of any family or person at his home, or any individual employed by his parent or spouse.

(4) The term "representatives" includes any individual or labor organization.

(5) The term "labor organization" means any organization of any kind, or any agency or employee representation committee or plan, in which employees participate and which exists for the purpose, in whole

or in part, of dealing with employers concerning grievances, labor disputes, wages, rates of pay, hours of employment, or conditions of work.

(6) The term "commerce" means trade, traffic, commerce, transportation, or communication among the several States, or between the District of Columbia or any Territory of the United States and any State or other Territory, or between any foreign country and any State, Territory, or the District of Columbia, or within the District of Columbia or any Territory, or between points in the same State but through any other State or any Territory or the District of Columbia or any foreign country.

(7) The term "affecting commerce" means in commerce, or burdening or obstructing commerce or the free flow of commerce, or having led or tending to lead to a labor dispute burdening or obstructing commerce or the free flow of commerce.

(8) The term "unfair labor practice" means any unfair labor practice listed in section 8.

(9) The term "labor dispute" includes any controversy concerning terms, tenure, or conditions of employment, or concerning the association or representation of persons in negotiating, fixing, maintaining, changing, or seeking to arrange terms or conditions of employment, regardless of whether the disputants stand in the proximate relation of employer and employee.

(10) The term "National Labor Relation Board" means the National Labor Relations Board created by section 3 of this Act.

(11) The term "old Board" means the National Labor Relations Board established by Executive Order Numbered 6763 of the President on June 29, 1934, pursuant to Public Resolution Numbered 44, approved June 19, 1934 (48 Stat. 1183), and reestablished and continued by Executive Order Numbered 7074 of the President of June 15, 1935, pursuant to Title I of the National Industrial Recovery Act (48 Stat. 195) as amended and continued by Senate Joint Resolution 133 approved June 14, 1935.

NATIONAL LABOR RELATIONS BOARD

SEC. 3. (a) There is hereby created a board, to be known as the "National Labor Relations Board" (hereinafter referred to as the "Board"), which shall be composed of three members, who shall be appointed by the President, by and with the advice and consent of the Senate. One of the original members shall be appointed for a term of one year, one for a term of three years, and one for a term of five years, but their successors shall be appointed for terms of five years each, except that any individual chosen to fill a vacancy shall be appointed only for the unexpired term of the member whom he shall succeed. The President shall designate one member to serve as the chairman of the Board. Any member of the Board may be removed by the President, upon notice and hearing, for neglect of duty or malfeasance in office, but for no other cause.

(b) A vacancy in the Board shall not impair the right of the remaining members to exercise all the powers of the Board, and two members of the Board shall, at all times, constitute a quorum. The Board shall have an official seal which shall be judicially noticed.

(c) The Board shall at the close of each fiscal year make a report in writing to Congress and to the President stating in detail the cases it has heard, the decisions it has rendered, the names, salaries, and duties of all employees and officers in the employ or under the supervision of the Board, and an account of all moneys it has disbursed.

SEC. 4. (a) Each member of the Board shall receive a salary of $10,000 a year, shall be eligible for reappointment, and shall not engage in any other business, vocation, or employment. The Board shall appoint, without regard for the provisions of the civil-service laws but subject to the Classification Act of 1923, as amended, an executive secretary, and such attorneys, examiners, and regional directors, and shall appoint such other employees with regard to existing laws applicable to the employment and compensation of officers and employees of the United States, as it may from time to time find necessary for the proper performance of its duties and as may be from time to time appropriated for by Congress. The Board may establish or utilize such regional, local, or other agencies, and utilize such voluntary and uncompensated services, as may from time to time be needed. Attorneys appointed under this section may, at the direction of the Board, appear for and represent the Board in any case in court. Nothing in this Act shall be construed to authorize the Board to appoint individuals for the purpose of conciliation or mediation (or for statistical work), where such service may be obtained from the Department of Labor.

(b) Upon the appointment of the three original members of the Board and the designation of its chairman, the old Board shall cease to exist. All employees of the old Board shall be transferred to and become employees of the Board with salaries under the Classification Act of 1923, as amended, without acquiring by such transfer a permanent or civil-service status. All records, papers, and property of the old Board shall become records, papers, and property of the Board, and all unexpended funds and appropriations for the use and maintenance of the old Board shall become funds and appropriations available to be expended by the Board in the exercise of the powers, authority, and duties conferred on it by this Act.

(c) All of the expenses of the Board, including all necessary traveling and subsistence expenses outside the District of Columbia incurred by the members or employees of the Board under its orders, shall be allowed and paid on the presentation of itemized vouchers therefor approved by the Board or by any individual it designates for that purpose.

SEC. 5. The principal office of the Board shall be in the District of Columbia, but it may meet and exercise any or all of its powers at any other place. The Board may, by one or more of its members or by such agents or agencies as it may designate, prosecute any inquiry necessary to its functions in any part of the United States. A member who participates in such an inquiry shall not be disqualified from subsequently participating in a decision of the Board in the same case.

SEC. 6. (a) The Board shall have authority from time to time to make, amend, and rescind such rules and regulations as may be necessary to carry out the provisions of this Act. Such rules and regulations shall be effective upon publication in the manner which the Board shall prescribe.

RIGHTS OF EMPLOYEES

SEC. 7. Employees shall have the right to self-organization, to form, join, or assist labor organizations, to bargain collectively through representatives of their own choosing, and to engage in concerted activities, for the purpose of collective bargaining or other mutual aid or protection.

SEC. 8. It shall be an unfair labor practice for an employer—

(1) To interfere with, restrain, or coerce employees in the exercise of the rights guaranteed in section 7.

(2) To dominate or interfere with the formation or administration of any labor organization or contribute financial or other support to it: *Provided,* That subject to rules and regulations made and published by the Board pursuant to section 6 (a), an employer shall not be prohibited from permitting employees to confer with him during working hours without loss of time or pay.

(3) By discrimination in regard to hire or tenure of employment or any term or condition of employment to encourage or discourage membership in any labor organization: *Provided,* That nothing in this Act, or in the National Industrial Recovery Act (U.S.C., Supp. VII, title 15, secs. 701–712), as amended from time to time, or in any code or agreement approved or prescribed thereunder, or in any other statute

of the United States, shall preclude an employer from making an agreement with a labor organization (not established, maintained, or assisted by any action defined in this Act as an unfair labor practice) to require, as a condition of employment, membership therein, if such labor organization is the representative of the employees as provided in section 9 (a), in the appropriate collective bargaining unit covered by such agreement when made.

(4) To discharge or otherwise discriminate against an employee because he has filed charges or given testimony under this Act.

(5) To refuse to bargain collectively with the representatives of his employees, subject to the provisions of section 9 (a).

REPRESENTATIVES AND ELECTIONS

SEC. 9. (a) Representatives designated or selected for the purposes of collective bargaining by the majority of the employees in a unit appropriate for such purposes, shall be the exclusive representatives of all the employees in such unit for the purposes of collective bargaining in respect to rates of pay, wages, hours of employment, or other conditions of employment: *Provided,* That any individual employee or a group of employees shall have the right at any time to present grievances to their employer.

(b) The Board shall decide in each case whether, in order to insure to employees the full benefit of their right to self-organization and to collective bargaining, and otherwise to effectuate the policies of this Act, the unit appropriate for the purposes of collective bargaining shall be the employer unit, craft unit, plant unit, or subdivision thereof.

(c) Whenever a question affecting commerce arises concerning the representation of employees, the Board may investigate such controversy and certify to the parties, in writing, the name or names of the representatives that have been designated or selected. In any such investigation, the Board shall provide for an appropriate hearing upon due notice, either in conjunction with a proceeding under section 10 or otherwise, and may take a secret ballot of employees, or utilize any other suitable method to ascertain such representatives.

(d) Whenever an order of the Board made pursuant to section 10 (c) is based in whole or in part upon facts certified following an investigation pursuant to subsection (c) of this section, and there is a petition for the enforcement or review of such order, such certification and the record of such investigation shall be included in the transcript of the entire record required to be filed under subsections 10 (e) or 10 (f), and thereupon the decree of the court enforcing, modifying, or setting aside in whole or in part the order of the Board shall be made and entered upon the pleadings, testimony, and proceedings set forth in such transcript.

PREVENTION OF UNFAIR LABOR PRACTICES

SEC. 10. (a) The Board is empowered, as hereinafter provided, to prevent any person from engaging in any unfair labor practice (listed in section 8) affecting commerce. This power shall be exclusive, and shall not be affected by any other means of adjustment or prevention that has been or may be established by agreement, code, law, or otherwise.

(b) Whenever it is charged that any person has engaged in or is engaging in any such unfair labor practice, the Board, or any agent or agency designated by the Board for such purposes, shall have power to issue and cause to be served upon such person a complaint stating the charges in that respect, and containing a notice of hearing before the Board or a member thereof, or before a designated agent or agency, at a place therein fixed, not less than five days after the serving of said complaint. Any such complaint may be amended by the member, agent, or agency conducting the hearing or the Board in its discretion at any time prior to the issuance of an order based thereon. The person so complained of shall have the right to file an answer to the original or amended complaint and to appear in person or otherwise and give testimony at the place and time fixed in the complaint. In the discretion of the member, agent, or agency conducting the hearing or the Board, any other person may be allowed to intervene in the said proceeding and to present testimony. In any such proceeding the rules of evidence prevailing in courts of law or equity shall not be controlling.

(c) The testimony taken by such member, agent, or agency or the Board shall be reduced to writing and filed with the Board. Thereafter, in its discretion, the Board upon notice may take further testimony or hear argument. If upon all the testimony taken the Board shall be of the opinion that any person named in the complaint has engaged in or is engaging in any such unfair labor practice, then the Board shall state its findings of fact and shall issue and cause to be served on such person an order requiring such person to cease and desist from such unfair labor practice, and to take such affirmative action, including reinstatement of employees with or without back pay, as will effectuate the policies of this Act. Such order may further require such person to make reports from time to time showing the extent to which it has complied with the order. If upon all the testimony taken the Board shall be of the opinion that no person named in the complaint has engaged in or is engaging in any such unfair labor practice, then the Board shall state its findings of fact and shall issue an order dismissing the said complaint.

(d) Until a transcript of the record in a case shall have been filed in a court, as hereinafter provided, the Board may at any time, upon reasonable notice and in such manner as it shall deem proper, modify or set aside, in whole or in part, any finding or order made or issued by it.

(e) The Board shall have power to petition any circuit court of appeals of the United States (including the Court of Appeals of the District of Columbia), or if all the circuit courts of appeals to which application may be made are in vacation, any district court of the United States (including the Supreme Court of the District of Columbia), within any circuit or district, respectively, wherein the unfair labor practice in question occurred or wherein such person resides or transacts business, for the enforcement of such order and for appropriate temporary relief or restraining order, and shall certify and file in the court a transcript of the entire record in the proceeding, including the pleadings and testimony upon which such order was entered and the findings and order of the Board. Upon such filing, the court shall cause notice thereof to be served upon such person, and thereupon shall have jurisdiction of the proceeding and of the question determined therein, and shall have power to grant such temporary relief or restraining order as it deems just and proper, and to make and enter upon the pleadings, testimony, and proceedings set forth in such transcript a decree enforcing, modifying, and enforcing as so modified, or setting aside in whole or in part the order of the Board. No objection that has not been urged before the Board, its member, agent, or agency, shall be considered by the court, unless the failure or neglect to urge such objection shall be excused because of extraordinary circumstances. The findings of the Board as to the facts, if supported by evidence, shall be conclusive. If either party shall apply to the court for leave to adduce additional evidence and shall show to the satisfaction of the court that such additional evidence is material and that there were reasonable grounds for the failure to adduce such evidence in the hearing before the Board, its member, agent, or agency, the court may order such additional evidence to be taken before the Board, its member, agent, or agency, and to be made a part of the transcript. The Board may modify its findings as to the facts, or make new findings, by reason of additional evidence so taken and filed, and it shall file such modified or new findings, which, if supported by evidence shall be conclusive, and shall file its recommendations, if any, for the modification or setting aside of its original order. The jurisdiction of the court shall be exclusive and its judgment and decree shall be final, except that the same shall be subject to review by the appropriate circuit court of appeals if application was made to the district court as hereinabove provided, and by the Supreme Court of the United States and upon writ of certiorari or certification as provided in section 239 and 240 of the Judicial Code, as amended (U.S.C., title 28, secs. 346 and 347).

(f) Any person aggrieved by a final order of the Board granting or denying in whole or in part the relief sought may obtain a review of such order in any circuit court of appeals of the United States in the circuit wherein the unfair labor practice in question was alleged to have been engaged in or wherein such person resides or transacts business, or in the Court of Appeals of the District of Columbia, by filing in such a court a written petition praying that the order of the Board be modified or set aside. A copy of such petition shall be forthwith served upon the Board, and thereupon the aggrieved party shall file in the court a transcript of the entire record in the proceeding, certified by the Board, including the pleading and testimony upon which the order complained of was entered and the findings and order of the Board. Upon such filing, the court shall proceed in the same manner as in the case of an application by the Board under subsection (e), and shall have the same exclusive jurisdiction to grant to the Board such temporary relief or restraining order as it deems just and proper, and in like manner to make and enter a decree enforcing, modifying, and enforcing as so modified, or setting aside in whole or in part the order of the Board; and the findings of the Board as to the facts, if supported by evidence, shall in like manner be conclusive.

(g) The commencement of proceedings under subsection (e) or (f) of this section shall not, unless specifically ordered by the court, operate as a stay of the Board's order.

(h) When granting appropriate temporary relief or a restraining order, or making and entering a decree enforcing, modifying, and enforcing as so modified or setting aside in whole or in part an order of the Board, as provided in this section, the jurisdiction of courts sitting in equity shall not be limited by the Act entitled "An Act to amend the Judicial Code and to define and limit the jurisdiction of courts sitting in equity, and for other purposes," approved March 23, 1932 (U.S.C., Supp. VII, title 29, secs. 101–115).

(i) Petitions filed under this Act shall be heard expeditiously, and if possible within ten days after they have been docketed.

INVESTIGATORY POWERS

Sec. 11. For the purpose of all hearings and investigations, which, in the opinion of the Board, are necessary and proper for the exercise of the powers vested in it by section 9 and section 10—

(1) The Board, or its duly authorized agents or agencies, shall at all reasonable times have access to, for the purpose of examination, and the right to copy any evidence of any person being investigated or proceeded against that relates to any matter under investigation or in question. Any member of the Board shall have power to issue subpenas requiring the attendance and testimony of witnesses and the production of any evidence that relates to any matter under investigation or in question, before the Board, its member, agent, or agency conducting the hearing or investigation. Any member of the Board, or any agent or agency designated by the Board for such purposes, may administer oaths and affirmations, examine witnesses, and receive evidence. Such attendance of witnesses and the production of such evidence may be required from any place in the United States or any Territory or possession thereof, at any designated place of hearing.

(2) In case of contumacy or refusal to obey a subpena issued to any person, any District Court of the United States or the United States courts of any Territory or possession, or the Supreme Court of the District of Columbia, within the jurisdiction of which the inquiry is carried on or within the jurisdiction of which said person guilty of contumacy or refusal to obey is found or resides or transacts business, upon application by the Board shall have jurisdiction to issue to such person an order requiring such person to appear before the Board, its member, agent, or agency, there to produce evidence if so ordered, or there to give testimony touching the matter under investigation or in question; and any failure to obey such order of the court may be punished by said court as a contempt thereof.

(3) No person shall be excused from attending and testifying or from producing books, records, correspondence, documents, or other evidence in obedience to the subpena of the Board, on the ground that the testimony or evidence required of him may tend to incriminate him or subject him to a penalty or forfeiture; but no individual shall be prosecuted or subjected to any penalty or forfeiture for or on account of any transaction, matter, or thing concerning which he is compelled, after having claimed his privilege against self-incrimination, to testify or produce evidence, except that such individual so testifying shall not be exempt from prosecution and punishment for perjury committed in so testifying.

(4) Complaints, orders, and other process and papers of the Board, its member, agent, or agency, may be served either personally or by registered mail or by telegraph or by leaving a copy thereof at the principal office or place of business of the person required to be served. The verified return by the individual so serving the same setting forth

the manner of such service shall be proof of the same, and the return post office receipt or telegraph receipt therefor when registered and mailed or telegraphed as aforesaid shall be proof of service of the same. Witnesses summoned before the Board, its member, agent, or agency, shall be paid the same fees and mileage that are paid witnesses in the courts of the United States, and witnesses whose depositions are taken and the persons taking the same shall severally be entitled to the same fees as are paid for like services in the courts of the United States.

(5) All process of any court to which application may be made under this Act may be served in the judicial district wherein the defendant or other person required to be served resides or may be found.

(6) The several departments and agencies of the Government, when directed by the President, shall furnish the Board, upon its request, all records, papers, and information in their possession relating to any matter before the Board.

SEC. 12. Any person who shall willfully resist, prevent, impede, or interfere with any member of the Board or any of its agents or agencies in the performance of duties pursuant to this Act shall be punished by a fine of not more than $5,000 or by imprisonment for not more than one year, or both.

LIMITATIONS

SEC. 13. Nothing in this Act shall be construed so as to interfere with or impede or diminish in any way the right to strike.

SEC. 14. Wherever the application of the provisions of section 7 (a) of the National Industrial Recovery Act (U.S.C., Supp. VII, title 15, sec. 707 (a), as amended from time to time, or of section 77 B, paragraphs (l) and (m) of the Act approved June 7, 1934, entitled "An Act to amend an Act entitled 'An Act to establish a uniform system of bankruptcy throughout the United States' approved July 1, 1898, and Acts amendatory thereof and supplementary thereto" (48 Stat. 922, pars. (l) and (m)), as amended from time to time, or of Public Resolution Numbered 44, approved June 19, 1934 (48 Stat. 1183), conflicts with the application of the provisions of this Act, this Act shall prevail: *Provided,* That in any situation where the provisions of this Act cannot be validly enforced, the provisions of such other Acts shall remain in full force and effect.

SEC. 15. If any provision of this Act, or the application of such provision to any person or circumstance, shall be held invalid, the remainder of this Act, or the application of such provision to persons or circumstances other than those as to which it is held invalid, shall not be affected thereby.

Sec. 16. This Act may be cited as the "National Labor Relations Act."

Approved, July 5, 1935.

APPENDIX III

FAIR LABOR STANDARDS ACT [1]
Wage and Hour Act

(52 Stat. 1060)

AN ACT

To provide for the establishment of fair labor standards in employments in and affecting interstate commerce, and for other purposes.

Be it enacted by the Senate and House of Representatives of the United States of America in Congress assembled, That this Act may be cited as the "Fair Labor Standards Act of 1938."

FINDING AND DECLARATION OF POLICY

SEC. 2. (a) The Congress hereby finds that the existence, in industries engaged in commerce or in the production of goods for commerce, of labor conditions detrimental to the maintenance of the minimum standard of living necessary for health, efficiency, and general well-being of workers (1) causes commerce and the channels and instrumentalities of commerce to be used to spread and perpetuate such labor conditions among the workers of the several States; (2) burdens commerce and the free flow of goods in commerce; (3) constitutes an unfair method of competition in commerce; (4) leads to labor disputes burdening and obstructing commerce and the free flow of goods in commerce; and (5) interferes with the orderly and fair marketing of goods in commerce.

(b) It is hereby declared to be the policy of this Act, through the exercise by Congress of its power to regulate commerce among the several States, to correct and as rapidly as practicable to eliminate the conditions above referred to in such industries without substantially curtailing employment or earning power.

DEFINITIONS

SEC. 3. As used in this Act—

(a) "Person" means an individual, partnership, association, corpora-

[1] In effect, 1946.

tion, business trust, legal representative, or any organized group of persons.

(b) "Commerce" means trade, commerce, transportation, transmission, or communication among the several States or from any State to any place outside thereof.

(c) "State" means any State of the United States or the District of Columbia or any Territory or possession of the United States.

(d) "Employer" includes any person acting directly or indirectly in the interest of an employer in relation to an employee but shall not include the United States or any State or political subdivision of a State, or any labor organization (other than when acting as an employer), or anyone acting in the capacity of officer or agent of such labor organization.

(e) "Employee" includes any individual employed by an employer.

(f) "Agriculture" includes farming in all its branches and among other things includes the cultivation and tillage of the soil, dairying, the production, cultivation, growing, and harvesting of any agricultural or horticultural commodities (including commodities defined as agricultural commodities in section 15 (g) of the Agricultural Marketing Act, as amended), the raising of livestock, bees, fur-bearing animals, or poultry, and any practices (including any forestry or lumbering operations) performed by a farmer or on a farm as an incident to or in conjunction with such farming operations, including preparation for market, delivery to storage or to market or to carriers for transportation to market.

(g) "Employ" includes to suffer or permit to work.

(h) "Industry" means a trade, business, industry, or branch thereof, or group of industries, in which individuals are gainfully employed.

(i) "Goods" means goods (including ships and marine equipment), wares, products, commodities, merchandise, or articles or subjects of commerce of any character, or any part or ingredient thereof, but does not include goods after their delivery into the actual physical possession of the ultimate consumer thereof other than a producer, manufacturer, or processor thereof.

(j) "Produced" means produced, manufactured, mined, handled, or in any other manner worked on in any State; and for the purposes of this Act an employee shall be deemed to have been engaged in the production of goods if such employee was employed in producing, manufacturing, mining, handling, transporting, or in any other manner working on such goods, or in any process or occupation necessary to the production thereof, in any State.

(k) "Sale" or "sell" includes any sale, exchange, contract to sell, consignment for sale, shipment for sale, or other disposition.

(l) "Oppressive child labor" means a condition of employment under which (1) any employee under the age of sixteen years is employed by an employer (other than a parent or a person standing in place of a parent employing his own child or a child in his custody under the age of sixteen years in an occupation other than manufacturing or mining) in any occupation, or (2) any employee between the ages of sixteen and eighteen years is employed by an employer in any occupation which the Chief of the Children's Bureau in the Department of Labor shall find and by order declare to be particularly hazardous for the employment of children between such ages or detrimental to their health or well-being; but oppressive child labor shall not be deemed to exist by virtue of the employment in any occupation of any person with respect to whom the employer shall have on file an unexpired certificate issued and held pursuant to regulations of the Chief of the Children's Bureau certifying that such person is above the oppressive child-labor age. The Chief of the Children's Bureau shall provide by regulation or by order that the employment of employees between the ages of fourteen and sixteen years in occupations other than manufacturing and mining shall not be deemed to constitute oppressive child labor if and to the extent that the Chief of the Children's Bureau determines that such employment is confined to periods which will not interfere with their schooling and to conditions which will not interfere with their health and well-being.

(m) "Wage" paid to any employee includes the reasonable cost, as determined by the Administrator, to the employer of furnishing such employee with board, lodging, or other facilities, if such board, lodging, or other facilities are customarily furnished by such employer to his employees.

ADMINISTRATOR

SEC. 4. (a) There is hereby created in the Department of Labor a Wage and Hour Division which shall be under the direction of an Administrator, to be known as the Administrator of the Wage and Hour Division (in this Act referred to as the "Administrator"). The Administrator shall be appointed by the President, by and with the advice and consent of the Senate, and shall receive compensation at the rate of $10,000 a year.

(b) The Administrator may, subject to the civil-service laws, appoint such employees as he deems necessary to carry out his functions and duties under this Act and shall fix their compensation in accordance with the Classification Act of 1923, as amended. The Administrator may establish and utilize such regional, local, or other agencies, and utilize such voluntary and uncompensated services, as may from time to time be needed. Attorneys appointed under this section may appear for and represent the Administrator in any litigation, but all such litigation shall be subject to the direction and control of the Attorney General. In the appointment, selection, classification, and promotion of officers and employees of the Administrator, no political test or qualification shall be permitted or given consideration, but all such appointments and promotions shall be given and made on the basis of merit and efficiency.

(c) The principal office of the Administrator shall be in the District of Columbia, but he or his duly authorized representative may exercise any or all of his powers in any place.

(d) The Administrator shall submit annually in January a report to the Congress covering his activities for the preceding year and including such information, data, and recommendations for further legislation in connection with the matters covered by this Act as he may find advisable.

INDUSTRY COMMITTEES

SEC. 5. (a) The Administrator shall as soon as practicable appoint an industry committee for each industry engaged in commerce or in the production of goods for commerce.

(b) An industry committee shall be appointed by the Administrator without regard to any other provisions of law regarding the appointment and compensation of employees of the United States. It shall include a number of disinterested persons representing the public, one of whom the Administrator shall designate as chairman, a like number of persons representing employees in the industry, and a like number representing employers in the industry. In the appointment of the persons representing each group, the Administrator shall give due regard to the geographical regions in which the industry is carried on.

(c) Two-thirds of the members of an industry committee shall constitute a quorum, and the decision of the committee shall require a vote of not less than a majority of all its members. Members of an industry committee shall receive as compensation for their services a reasonable per diem, which the Administrator shall by rules and regulations prescribe, for each day actually spent in the work of the committee, and shall in addition be reimbursed for their necessary traveling and other expenses. The Administrator shall furnish the committee with adequate legal, stenographic, clerical, and other assistance, and shall by rules and regulations prescribe the procedure to be followed by the committee.

(d) The Administrator shall submit to an industry committee from time to time such data as he may have available on the matters referred to it, and shall cause to be brought before it in connection with such matters any witnesses whom he deems material. An industry committee may summon other witnesses or call upon the Administrator to furnish additional information to aid it in its deliberations.

(e) No industry committee appointed under subsection (a) of this section shall have any power to recommend the minimum rate or rates of wages to be paid under section 6 to any employees in Puerto Rico or in the Virgin Islands. Notwithstanding any other provision of this Act, the Administrator may appoint a special industry committee to recommend the minimum rate or rates of wages to be paid under section 6 to all employees in Puerto Rico or the Virgin Islands, or in Puerto Rico and the Virgin Islands, engaged in commerce or in the production of goods for commerce, or the Administrator may appoint separate industry committees to recommend the minimum rate or rates of wages to be paid under section 6 to employees therein engaged in commerce or in the production of goods for commerce in particular industries. An industry committee appointed under this subsection shall be composed of residents of such island or islands where the employees with respect to whom such committee was appointed are employed and residents of the United States outside of Puerto Rico and the Virgin Islands. In determining the minimum rate or rates of wages to be paid, and in determining classifications, such industry committees and the Administrator shall be subject to the provisions of section 8 and no such committee shall recommend, nor shall the Administrator approve, a minimum wage rate which will give any industry in Puerto Rico or in the Virgin Islands a competitive advantage over any industry in the United States outside of Puerto Rico and the Virgin Islands.

No wage orders issued by the Administrator pursuant to the recommendations of an industry committee made prior to the enactment of this joint resolution pursuant to section 8 of the Fair Labor Standards Act of 1938 shall after such enactment be applicable with respect to any employees engaged in commerce or in the production of goods for commerce in Puerto Rico or the Virgin Islands.[1]

MINIMUM WAGES

SEC. 6. (a) Every employer shall pay to each of his employees who to the proportion or class of employees prescribed by regulation wages at the following rates—

(1) during the first year from the effective date of this section. not less than 25 cents an hour,

---

[1] Amendment provided by Act of June 26, 1940 (Public Res. No. 88, 76th Congress).

(2) during the next six years from such date, not less than 30 cents an hour,

(3) after the expiration of seven years from such date, not less than 40 cents an hour, or the rate (not less than 30 cents an hour) prescribed in the applicable order of the Administrator issued under section 8, whichever is lower, and

(4) at any time after the effective date of this section, not less than the rate (not in excess of 40 cents an hour) prescribed in the applicable order of the Administrator issued under section 8,

(5) if such employee is a home worker in Puerto Rico or the Virgin Islands, not less than the minimum piece rate prescribed by regulation or order; or, if no such minimum piece rate is in effect, any piece rate adopted by such employer which shall yield, to the proportion or class of employees prescribed by regulation or order, not less than the applicable minimum hourly wage rate. Such minimum piece rates or employer piece rates shall be commensurate with, and shall be paid in lieu of, the minimum hourly wage rate applicable under the provisions of this section. The Administrator, or his authorized representative, shall have power to make such regulations or orders as are necessary or appropriate to carry out any of the provisions of this paragraph, including the power without limiting the generality of the foregoing, to define any operation or occupation which is performed by such home work employees in Puerto Rico or the Virgin Islands; to establish minimum piece rates for any operation or occupation so defined; to prescribe the method and procedure for ascertaining and promulgating minimum piece rates; to prescribe standards for employer piece rates, including the proportion or class of employees who shall receive not less than the minimum hourly wage rate; to define the term "home worker"; and to prescribe the conditions under which employers, agents, contractors, and subcontractors shall cause goods to be produced by home workers.[2]

(b) This section shall take effect upon the expiration of one hundred and twenty days from the date of enactment of this Act.

(c) The provisions of paragraphs (1), (2), and (3) of subsection (a) of this section shall be superseded in the case of any employee in Puerto Rico or the Virgin Islands engaged in commerce or in the production of goods for commerce only for so long as and insofar as such employee is covered by a wage order issued by the Administrator pursuant to the recommendations of a special industry committee appointed pursuant to section 5 (e).[2]

---

[2] Amendment provided by Act of June 26, 1940 (Public Res. No. 88, 76th Congress).

SEC. 7. (a) No employer shall, except as otherwise provided in this section, employ any of his employees who is engaged in commerce or in the production of goods for commerce—

(1) for a workweek longer than forty-four hours during the first year from the effective date of this section,

(2) for a workweek longer than forty-two hours during the second year from such date, or

(3) for a workweek longer than forty hours after the expiration of the second year from such date,

unless such employee receives compensation for his employment in excess of the hours above specified at a rate not less than one and one-half times the regular rate at which he is employed.

(b) No employer shall be deemed to have violated subsection (a) by employing any employee for a workweek in excess of that specified in such subsection without paying the compensation for overtime employment prescribed therein if such employee is so employed—

(1) in pursuance of an agreement, made as a result of collective bargaining by representatives of employees certified as bona fide by the National Labor Relations Board, which provides that no employee shall be employed more than one thousand hours during any period of twenty-six consecutive weeks,

(2) on an annual basis in pursuance of an agreement with his employer, made as a result of collective bargaining by representatives of employees certified as bona fide by the National Labor Relations Board, which provides that the employee shall not be employed more than two thousand and eighty hours during any period of fifty-two consecutive weeks,[3] or

(3) for a period or periods of not more than fourteen workweeks in the aggregate in any calendar year in an industry found by the Administrator to be of a seasonal nature,

and if such employee receives compensation for employment in excess of 12 hours in any workday, or for employment in excess of 56 hours in any workweek, as the case may be, at a rate not less than one and one-half times the regular rate at which he is employed.

(c) In the case of an employer engaged in the first processing of milk, whey, skimmed milk, or cream into dairy products, or in the ginning and compressing of cotton, or in the processing of cottonseed, or in the processing of sugar beets, sugar beet molasses, sugarcane, or maple sap, into sugar (but not refined sugar) or into syrup,

---

[3] Amendment provided by Act of October 29, 1941 (Public Law 283, 77th Congress).

the provisions of subsection (a) shall not apply to his employees in any place of employment where he is so engaged; and in the case of an employer engaged in the first processing of, or in canning or packing, perishable or seasonal fresh fruits or vegetables, or in the first processing, within the area of production (as defined by the Administrator), of any agricultural or horticultural commodity during seasonal operations, or in handling, slaughtering, or dressing poultry or livestock, the provisions of subsection (a), during a period or periods of not more than fourteen workweeks in the aggregate in any calendar year, shall not apply to his employees in any place of employment where he is so engaged.

(d) This section shall take effect upon the expiration of one hundred and twenty days from the date of enactment of this Act.

WAGE ORDERS

SEC. 8. (a) With a view to carrying out the policy of this Act by reaching, as rapidly as is economically feasible without substantially curtailing employment, the objective of a universal minimum wage of 40 cents an hour in each industry engaged in commerce or in the production of goods for commerce, the Administrator shall from time to time convene the industry committee for each such industry, and the industry committee shall from time to time recommend the minimum rate or rates of wages to be paid under section 6 by employers engaged in commerce or in the production of goods for commerce in such industry or classifications therein.

(b) Upon the convening of an industry committee, the Administrator shall refer to it the question of the minimum wage rate or rates to be fixed for such industry. The industry committee shall investigate conditions in the industry and the committee, or any authorized subcommittee thereof, may hear such witnesses and receive such evidence as may be necessary or appropriate to enable the committee to perform its duties and functions under this Act. The committee shall recommend to the Administrator the highest minimum wage rates for the industry which it determines, having due regard to economic and competitive conditions, will not substantially curtail employment in the industry.

(c) The industry committee for any industry shall recommend such reasonable classifications within any industry as it determines to be necessary for the purpose of fixing for each classification within such industry the highest minimum wage rate (not in excess of 40 cents an hour) which (1) will not substantially curtail employment in such classification and (2) will not give a competitive advantage to any group in the industry, and shall recommend for each classification in the industry the highest minimum wage rate which the committee determines will not substantially curtail employment in such classification. In determining whether such classifications should be made in any industry, in making such classifications, and in determining the minimum wage rates for such classifications, no classification shall be made, and no minimum wage rate shall be fixed, solely on a regional basis, but the industry committee and the Administrator shall consider among other relevant factors the following:

(1) competitive conditions as affected by transportation, living, and production costs;

(2) the wages established for work of like or comparable character by collective labor agreements negotiated between employers and employees by representatives of their own choosing; and

(3) the wages paid for work of like or comparable character by employers who voluntarily maintain minimum-wage standards in the industry.

No classification shall be made under this section on the basis of age or sex.

(d) The industry committee shall file with the Administrator a report containing its recommendations with respect to the matters referred to it. Upon the filing of such report, the Administrator, after due notice to interested persons, and giving them an opportunity to be heard, shall by order approve and carry into effect the recommendations contained in such report, if he finds that the recommendations are made in accordance with law, are supported by the evidence adduced at the hearing, and, taking into consideration the same factors as are required to be considered by the industry committee, will carry out the purposes of this section; otherwise he shall disapprove such recommendations. If the Administrator disapproves such recommendations, he shall again refer the matter to such committee, or to another industry committee for such industry (which he may appoint for such purpose), for further consideration and recommendations.

(e) No order issued under this section with respect to any industry prior to the expiration of seven years from the effective date of section 6 shall remain in effect after such expiration, and no order shall be issued under this section with respect to any industry on or after such expiration, unless the industry committee by a preponderance of the evidence before it recommends, and the Administrator by a preponderance of the evidence adduced at the hearing finds, that the continued effectiveness or the issuance of the order, as the case may be, is necessary in order to prevent substantial curtailment of employment in the industry.

(f) Orders issued under this section shall define the industries and classifications therein to which they are to apply, and shall contain such terms and conditions as the Administrator finds necessary to carry out the purposes of such orders, to prevent the circumvention or evasion thereof, and to safeguard the minimum wage rates established therein. No such order shall take effect until after due notice is given of the issuance thereof by publication in the Federal Register and by such other means as the Administrator deems reasonably calculated to give to interested persons general notice of such issuance.

(g) Due notice of any hearing provided for in this section shall be given by publication in the Federal Register and by such other means as the Administrator deems reasonably calculated to give general notice to interested persons.

ATTENDANCE OF WITNESSES

SEC. 9. For the purpose of any hearing or investigation provided for in this Act, the provisions of sections 9 and 10 (relating to the attendance of witnesses and the production of books, papers, and documents) of the Federal Trade Commission Act of September 16, 1914, as amended (U.S.C., 1934 edition, title 15, secs. 49 and 50), are hereby made applicable to the jurisdiction, powers, and duties of the Administrator, the Chief of the Children's Bureau, and the industry committees.

COURT REVIEW

SEC. 10. (a) Any person aggrieved by an order of the Administrator issued under section 8 may obtain a review of such order in the circuit court of appeals of the United States for any circuit wherein such person resides or has his principle place of business, or in the United States Court of Appeals for the District of Columbia, by filing in such court, within sixty days after the entry of such order, a written petition praying that the order of the Administrator be modified or set aside in whole or in part. A copy of such petition shall forthwith be served upon the Administrator, and thereupon the Administrator shall certify and file in the court a transcript of the record upon which the order complained of was entered. Upon the filing of such transcript such court shall have exclusive jurisdiction to affirm, modify, or set aside such order in whole or in part, so far as it is applicable to the petitioner. The review by the court shall be limited to questions of law, and findings of fact by the Administrator when supported by substantial evidence shall be conclusive. No objection to the order of the Administrator shall be considered by the court unless such objection shall have been urged before the Administrator or unless there were reasonable grounds for failure so to do. If application is made to the court for leave to adduce additional evidence, and it is shown to the satisfaction of the court that such additional evidence may materially affect the result of the proceeding and that there were reasonable grounds for failure to adduce such evidence in the proceeding before the Administrator, the court may order such additional evidence to be taken before the Administrator and to be adduced upon the hearing in such manner and upon such terms and conditions as to the court may seem proper. The Administrator may modify his findings by reason of the additional evidence so taken, and shall file with the court such modified or new findings which if supported by substantial evidence shall be conclusive, and shall also file his recommendation, if any, for the modification or setting aside of the original order. The judgment and decree of the court shall be final, subject to review by the Supreme Court of the United States upon certiorari or certification as provided in sections 239 and 240 of the Judicial Code, as amended (U.S.C., title 28, secs. 346 and 347).

(b) The commencement of proceedings under subsection (a) shall not, unless specifically ordered by the court, operate as a stay of the Administrator's order. The court shall not grant any stay of the order unless the person complaining of such order shall file in court an undertaking with a surety or sureties satisfactory to the court for the payment to the employees affected by the order, in the event such order is affirmed, of the amount by which the compensation such employees are entitled to receive under the order exceeds the compensation they actually receive while such stay is in effect.

INVESTIGATIONS, INSPECTIONS, AND RECORDS

Sec. 11. (a) The Administrator or his designated representatives may investigate and gather data regarding the wages, hours, and other conditions and practices of employment in any industry subject to this Act, and may enter and inspect such places and such records (and make such transcriptions thereof), question such employees, and investigate such facts, conditions, practices, or matters as he may deem necessary or appropriate to determine whether any person has violated any provision of this Act, or which may aid in the enforcement of the provisions of this Act. Except as provided in section 12 and in subsection (b) of this section, the Administrator shall utilize the bureaus and divisions of the Department of Labor for all the investigations and inspections necessary under this section.

Except as provided in section 12, the Administrator shall bring all actions under section 17 to restrain violations of this Act.

(b) With the consent and cooperation of State agencies charged with the administration of State labor laws, the Administrator and the Chief of the Children's Bureau may, for the purpose of carrying out their respective functions and duties under this Act, utilize the services of State and local agencies and their employees and, notwithstanding any other provision of law, may reimburse such State and local agencies and their employees for services rendered for such purposes.

(c) Every employer subject to any provision of this Act or of any order issued under this Act shall make, keep, and preserve such records of the persons employed by him and of the wages, hours, and other conditions and practices of employment maintained by him, and shall preserve such records for such periods of time, and shall make such reports therefrom to the Administrator as he shall prescribe by regulation or order as necessary or appropriate for the enforcement of the provisions of this Act or the regulations or orders thereunder.

CHILD LABOR PROVISIONS

SEC. 12. (a) After the expiration of one hundred and twenty days from the date of enactment of this Act, no producer, manufacturer, or dealer shall ship or deliver for shipment in commerce any goods produced in an establishment situated in the United States in or about which within thirty days prior to the removal of such goods therefrom any oppressive child labor has been employed: *Provided,* That a prosecution and conviction of a defendant for the shipment or delivery for shipment of any goods under the conditions herein prohibited shall be a bar to any further prosecution against the same defendant for shipments or deliveries for shipment of any such goods before the beginning of said prosecution.

(b) The Chief of the Children's Bureau in the Department of Labor, or any of his authorized representatives, shall make all investigations and inspections under section 11 (a) with respect to the employment of minors, and, subject to the direction and control of the Attorney General, shall bring all actions under section 17 to enjoin any act or practice which is unlawful by reason of the existence of oppressive child labor, and shall administer all other provisions of this Act relating to oppressive child labor.

EXEMPTIONS

SEC. 13. (a) The provisions of sections 6 and 7 shall not apply with respect to (1) any employee employed in a bona fide executive, administrative, professional, or local retailing capacity, or in the capacity of outside salesman (as such terms are defined and delimited by regulations of the Administrator); or (2) any employee engaged in any retail or service establishment the greater part of whose selling or servicing is in intrastate commerce; or (3) any employee employed as a seaman; or (4) any employee of a carrier by air subject to the provisions of title II of the Railway Labor Act; or (5) any employee employed in the catching, taking, harvesting, cultivating, or farming of any kind of fish, shellfish, crustacea, sponges, seaweeds, or other aquatic forms of animal and vegetable life, including the going to and returning from work and including employment in the loading, unloading, or packing of such products for shipment or in propagating, processing, marketing, freezing, canning, curing, storing, or distributing the above products or byproducts thereof; or (6) any employee employed in agriculture; or (7) any employee to the extent that such employee is exempted by regulations or orders of the Administrator issued under section 14; or (8) any employee employed in connection with the publication of any weekly or semiweekly newspaper with a circulation of less than three thousand the major part of which circulation is within the county where printed and published; or (9) any employee of a street, suburban, or interurban electric railway, or local trolley or motor bus carrier, not included in other exemptions contained in this section; or (10) to any individual employed within the area of production (as defined by the Administrator), engaged in handling, packing, storing, ginning, compressing, pasteurizing, drying, preparing in their raw or natural state, or canning of agricultural or horticultural commodities for market, or in making cheese or butter or other dairy products; or (11) any switchboard operator employed in a public telephone exchange which has less than five hundred stations.[4]

(b) The provisions of section 7 shall not apply with respect to (1) any employee with respect to whom the Interstate Commerce Commission has power to establish qualifications and maximum hours of service pursuant to the provisions of section 204 of the Motor Carrier Act, 1935; or (2) any employee of an employer subject to the provisions of Part I of the Interstate Commerce Act.

(c) The provisions of section 12 relating to child labor shall not apply with respect to any employee employed in agriculture while not legally required to attend school, or to any child employed as an actor in motion pictures or theatrical productions.

---

[4] Amendment provided by Act of August 9, 1939 (Public No. 344, 76th Congress. 53 Stat. 1266).

LEARNERS, APPRENTICES, AND HANDICAPPED WORKERS

SEC. 14. The Administrator, to the extent necessary in order to prevent curtailment of opportunities for employment, shall by regulations or by orders provide for (1) the employment of learners, of apprentices, and of messengers employed exclusively in delivering letters and messages, under special certificates issued pursuant to regulations of the Administrator, at such wages lower than the minimum wage applicable under section 6 and subject to such limitations as to time, number, proportion, and length of service as the Administrator shall prescribe, and (2) the employment of individuals whose earning capacity is impaired by age or physical or mental deficiency or injury, under special certificates issued by the Administrator, at such wages lower than the minimum wage applicable under section 6 and for such period as shall be fixed in such certificates.

PROHIBITED ACTS

SEC. 15. (a) After the expiration of one hundred and twenty days from the date of enactment of this Act, it shall be unlawful for any person—

(1) to transport, offer for transportation, ship, deliver, or sell in commerce, or to ship, deliver, or sell with knowledge that shipment or delivery or sale thereof in commerce is intended, any goods in the production of which any employee was employed in violation of section 6 or section 7, or in violation of any regulation or order of the Administrator issued under section 14; except that no provision of this Act shall impose any liability upon any common carrier for the transportation in commerce in the regular course of its business of any goods not produced by such common carrier, and no provision of this Act shall excuse any common carrier from its obligation to accept any goods for transportation;

(2) to violate any of the provisions of section 6 or section 7, or any of the provisions of any regulation or order of the Administrator issued under section 14;

(3) to discharge or in any other manner discriminate against any employee because such employee has filed any complaint or instituted or caused to be instituted any proceeding under or related to this Act, or has testified or is about to testify in any such proceeding, or has served or is about to serve on an industry committee.

(4) to violate any of the provisions of section 12;

(5) to violate any of the provisions of section 11 (c), or to make

any statement, report, or record filed or kept pursuant to the provisions of such section or of any regulation or order thereunder, knowing such statement, report, or record to be false in a material respect.

(b) For the purposes of subsection (a) (1) proof that any employee was employed in any place of employment where goods shipped or sold in commerce were produced, within ninety days prior to the removal of the goods from such place of employment, shall be prima facie evidence that such employee was engaged in the production of such goods.

PENALTIES

SEC. 16. (a) Any person who willfully violates any of the provisions of section 15 shall upon conviction thereof be subject to a fine of not more than $10,000, or to imprisonment for not more than six months, or both. No person shall be imprisoned under this subsection except for an offense committed after the conviction of such person for a prior offense under this subsection.

(b) Any employer who violates the provisions of section 6 or section 7 of this Act shall be liable to the employee or employees affected in the amount of their unpaid minimum wages, or their unpaid overtime compensation, as the case may be, and in an additional equal amount as liquidated damages. Action to recover such liability may be maintained in any court of competent jurisdiction by any one or more employees for and in behalf of himself or themselves and other employees similarly situated, or such employee or employees may designate an agent or representative to maintain such action for and in behalf of all employees similarly situated. The court in such action shall, in addition to any judgment awarded to the plaintiff or plaintiffs, allow a reasonable attorney's fee to be paid by the defendant, and costs of the action.

INJUNCTION PROCEEDINGS

SEC. 17. The district courts of the United States and the United States courts of the Territories and possessions shall have jurisdiction, for cause shown, and subject to the provisions of section 20 (relating to notice to opposite party) of the Act entitled "An Act to supplement existing laws against unlawful restraints and monopolies, and for other purposes," approved October 15, 1914, as amended (U. S. C., 1934 edition, title 28, sec. 381), to restrain violations of section 15.

RELATION TO OTHER LAWS

SEC. 18. No provision of this Act or of any order thereunder shall excuse noncompliance with any Federal or State law or municipal ordinance establishing a minimum wage higher than the minimum wage established under this Act or a maximum workweek lower than the maximum workweek established under this Act, and no provision of this Act relating to the employment of child labor shall justify noncompliance with any Federal or State law or municipal ordinance establishing a higher standard than the standard established under this Act. No provision of this Act shall justify any employer in reducing a wage paid by him which is in excess of the applicable minimum wage under this Act, or justify any employer in increasing hours of employment maintained by him which are shorter than the maximum hours applicable under this Act.

SEPARABILITY OF PROVISIONS

SEC. 19. If any provision of this Act or the application of such provision to any person or circumstance is held invalid, the remainder of the Act and the application of such provision to other persons or circumstances shall not be affected thereby.

Approved, June 25, 1938.

INDEX OF NAMES[1]

[1] Includes names of individual persons and court cases, as well as organizations cited as authors. Other references to organizations are listed in the Index of Subjects.

Index of Names

Millett, John D., 188

Millis, Harry A., 81, 188, 321, 415, 478, 502, 621, 683, 781

Mills, Charles M., 383

Mills, Frederick C., 161

Mitchell, Wesley C., 123, 140

Montgomery, Royal, 188, 321, 415, 478, 502, 621, 683

Morehead v. *People ex rel. Tipaldo,* 391

Moulton, Harold G., 59, 468

Mountain Timber Co. v. *State of Washington,* 738

Muller v. *Oregon,* 449

Mumford, Lewis, 109

Murray, Philip, 350, 553

Myers, C. A., 220

Myers, H. J., 351

Myers, R. J., 131

Myrdal, Gunnar, 26

National Association of Life Underwriters, 673, 706, 736

National Bureau of Economic Research, 26

National Foremen's Institute, 659

National Industrial Conference Board, 140, 219, 287, 363, 374, 382, 383, 425, 429, 443, 487, 659, 673

National Labor Relations Board v. *Fansteel Metallurgical Corp.,* 616

National Planning Association, 683, 706, 736

National Resources Committee, 23, 27, 109, 127, 287

National Resources Planning Board, 736

Necker, Jacques, 247, 248

Nevins, Allan, 214

New York Central Railroad v. *White,* 738

Nickerson, J. W., 332, 345

Norgren, Paul H., 349

Northrup, Herbert R., 519, 542, 569

Northrup, W. B. and J. B., 163

Norton, T. S., 82

Nyman, R. C., 658

Office of Economic Stabilization, 287

Ogden, Gladys, 188

Olsen v. *Nebraska,* 196

Osborn, Frederick, 26

Owen, William V., 658

Parker, Carleton, 58

Parker, Clark M., 83

Parker, Glen L., 59

Parker, James S., 706

Parmalee, Julius H., 59

Parry, D. M., 428

Patterson, S. Howard, 658

Patterson, William F., 219

Peffer, Nathaniel, 219

Pennsylvania Department of Labor and Industry, 756

People v. *Charles Schweinler Press,* 451

Perlman, Selig, 478, 502

Perry, Josephine, 59, 82, 83

Peterson, Florence, 530, 581, 584

Phillips, Wendell, 432

Pierson, Frank C., 553

Pierson, John H. G., 161

Pigou, A. C., 161

Powderly, T. V., 422, 423, 433, 476

Prentice-Hall, 659

Presgrave, Ralph, 351

President's Committee on Cost of Living, 413

Princeton University, 219

Pugh, Grace, 382

Pullman Co. v. *Debs,* 597

Radice v. *New York,* 451

Railroad Retirement Board, 706

Ramond, Albert, 333

Ramser v. *Van Storage,* 618

Raushenbush, Carl, 621

Raushenbush, Paul A., 723

Reed, E. G., 351

Reed, George L., 621

Reed, Louis S., 781

Reitell, Charles, 219

Ribnik v. *McBride,* 196

Ricardo, David, 146, 233, 234, 255

Riches, E. J., 650

Riegel, John W., 109, 321

Ring, Martha D., 765

Ritchie v. *People,* 449

Roberts, Harold S., 82

Robie, E. A., 321

Roosevelt, President Franklin D., 168, 407, 442, 497, 601, 666, 707, 765, 766

Rorem, C. R., 765

INDEX OF SUBJECTS

China, immigration from, 10; quota for, 14

Chinese Exclusion Act, 12, 14

Christian American Association, 611 n.

Chronocyclegraph technique, 332 n.

Civil Aeronautics Board, 458

Civil Employees' Act, 749

Civil service, British, 397 n.

Civil Service Classification Act, 396 n.

Civil Works Administration, 169–170

Civilian Conservation Corps, 170–172

Clayton Act, 591–592

Closed shop, 546, 635–641

Cloth manufacture, see Textile industry

Clothing industry, 77–81; collective bargaining in, 536

Coal mining, 44–49; captive mines, 65; conciliation board in, 563; employment situation in, 45–46; fatalities in, 48, 760–761; improved productivity in, 102, 103; labor agreements in, 534–535; portal-to-portal issue in, 47 n.; safety rules in, 761; sick benefit plan in, 374 n.; strikes in, 489, 583–584, 761; strip mining, 46–47; union organization in, 493; wage rates in, 293, 296 n.; working conditions in, 46–49

Collective agreements, see Labor agreements

Collective Agreement Act of Quebec, 385

Collective bargaining, acceptance of, 482, 500–501, 623; agreements reached by, 544–550; bargaining unit for, 532–540, 603–604; benefit plans through, 374–378; defined, 586; extent of, 551–552; factors influencing, 531–532; impact on wages, 301–305; interpretation of, 498–499; legal protections for, 598–610; legal restrictions on, 587–598; management efficiency and, 623–635; New Deal encouragement of, 601–604; present legal status of, 610–621; process of, 540–544; right to, under N.I.R.A., 491; right to, under National Labor Relations Act, 493, 603–604; state labor relations acts and, 604–607; wage policies and, 305–309; wage rates established

through, 404–405; working hours reduced through, 431, 435–437

College enrollment, 30

Colorado, mass picketing decision, 618; union incorporation law in, 612, 642 n.

Combinations Acts (British), 588 n.

"Comfort" budget, 272, 273

Communist party, 489, 496

Company stores, 48 n., 402

Company unions, 482, 487, 492–493, 600 n., 602

Compensation laws, see Workmen's compensation laws

Conciliation service, 542–543, 563, 565–566; federal, 565–571; state, 571–573

Congress of Industrial Organizations, affiliates, 509; central bodies of, 507–508; formation of, 494–495; functions of, 504; political action and, 495–497; post-war organizational drives of, 499; racial equality in, 519–520; structure of, 505

Connally-Smith War Labor Disputes Act, 496 n., 651 n.

Conspiracy doctrine, 587–590

Constitution, U.S., 1st Amendment, 627 n.; 5th Amendment, 390, 627 n.; 13th Amendment, 615, 627 n.; 14th Amendment, 593; 19th Amendment, 391

Construction industry, 49–51; collective bargaining in, 538; hiring workers for, 193–194

Consumers League, National, 389

Consumers' price indexes, 274–280

Contract, freedom of, 446–448

Contract labor, 11, 12, 78, 195–196, 264–265, 349 n.

Contract work, government, 405–406; hours policy in, 440 n.

Corporations, growth of, 65–66, 71; limited rights of stockholders in, 246 n.; power in bargaining relationship, 249–250; profits of, 356; profits withheld by, 154–155

Costs, labor, relation to total costs, 263–267; living, see Living costs; unit labor, 267–268

Cottage system of production, 228–229

١٨٠١١

1(?9/